Law, Society, and Politics in Early Maryland

 STUDIES IN MARYLAND HISTORY AND CULTURE

Sponsored by the Hall of Records Commission of the Department of General Services, George R. Lewis, Secretary

Series Editor, *Edward C. Papenfuse, State Archivist*

Law, Society, and Politics in Early Maryland

EDITED BY

Aubrey C. Land, Lois Green Carr, and Edward C. Papenfuse

PROCEEDINGS OF THE FIRST CONFERENCE
ON MARYLAND HISTORY, JUNE 14–15, 1974

THE JOHNS HOPKINS UNIVERSITY PRESS
BALTIMORE AND LONDON

The Johns Hopkins University Press, Baltimore, Maryland 21218
The Johns Hopkins Press Ltd., London
Library of Congress Catalog Card Number 76–47374
ISBN 0-8018-1872-9

Library of Congress Cataloging in Publication data will be found on the last printed page of this book.

CONTENTS

Preface   vii

Introduction
  Aubrey C. Land   ix

PART 1: LAW

One. The Maryland Bank Stock Case: British–American Financial
and Political Relations before and after the American Revolution
  Jacob M. Price   3

Two. The Development of the Maryland Orphans' Court, 1654–1715
  Lois Green Carr   41

PART 2: SOCIETY

Three. Maryland's Privy Council, 1637–1715
  David W. Jordan   65

Four. Immigrants and Their Increase: The Process of Population
Growth in Early Colonial Maryland
  Russell R. Menard   88

Five. Servitude and Opportunity in Charles County, Maryland,
1658–1705
  Lorena S. Walsh   111

Six. Maryland and the Chesapeake Economy, 1670–1720
  Gloria L. Main   134

Seven. Economy and Society on Maryland's Eastern Shore, 1689–1733
  Paul G. E. Clemens   153

Eight. The Beginnings of the Afro-American Family in Maryland
  Allan Kulikoff   171

Nine. Landless Husbandmen: Proprietary Tenants in Maryland
in the Late Colonial Period
  Gregory A. Stiverson   197

Ten. Baltimore and the Panic of 1819
  Gary L. Browne   212

Eleven. The Urban Impact on Agricultural Land Use: Farm
Patterns in Prince George's County, Maryland, 1860–1880
  Donald McCauley   228

PART 3: POLITICS

Twelve. The Causes of Electoral Alignments: Some Considerations on How
Partisan Behavior Is Shaped
  David A. Bohmer   251

Thirteen. The Structure of Baltimore's Politics in the
Age of Jefferson, 1795–1812
  Frank A. Cassell   277

Fourteen. The Search for Power: Community Leadership
in the Jacksonian Era
  Whitman H. Ridgway   297

Fifteen. Political Nativism: The Maryland Know-Nothings
as a Case Study
  Jean Baker   318

Bibliography of the Writings of Morris Leon Radoff
  Compiled by Frank F. White, Jr.   333

Index   337

PREFACE

Over the forty years of its existence, the Maryland Hall of Records has been a pioneer in efforts to bring together in one repository the public records of the state and to preserve and make them accessible. In consequence, the Hall of Records has acquired a distinguished reputation among scholars for the richness and importance of its holdings and for the research aids that help the public to use them. As a result, there has been a renaissance of scholarly work in Maryland history that has built upon the numerous studies published between 1880 and 1920 in the monumental series The Johns Hopkins Studies in Historical and Political Science.

In recognition of its role in recent scholarly work on Maryland and in hopes of stimulating even greater interest in its resources, the Hall of Records hosted the first conference on Maryland history in June 1974. The conference had four objectives: to present examples of some of the most distinguished writing on Maryland history derived from Hall of Records sources; to call attention to current research at the Hall of Records; to suggest through the interaction of the participants in the conference what direction historical research may take in the future; and to honor the productive thirty-five year tenure of Morris L. Radoff as archivist of Maryland.

More than eighty historians and other interested people gathered at the first of what is hoped will be biennial conferences on Maryland history. They discussed twenty-five papers—a selection from these comprises the present volume, with one exception. Jacob Price, although unable to attend the conference, has contributed an essay on Maryland's prerevolutionary investment in Bank of England stock, a fitting tribute to Dr. Radoff's innovative calendar of the Bank Stock Papers, which the Hall of Records published in 1947.

The conference papers, revised for publication, cover topics on the legal, social, and political history of Maryland through the post-bellum period, but they concentrate on the colonial and Revolutionary War eras. The essays utilize the rich collections of unpublished court, land, probate, and tax records brought together at the Hall of Records. The prosopographical studies upon which some of the following essays rely would not have been done without the name indexes to major record series at the Hall of Records. Nor would much of the statistical analysis found throughout the essays have been possible in other states where probate, tax, and similar records of a quantifiable nature are scattered, deteriorating, and inaccessible.

All of the essays discuss issues that have implications beyond the study of Maryland history. The sources of population increase, the effects of high mortality and the social and legal inventions it caused, and the timing and consequences of the shift from a predominantly immigrant to a predominantly native-born population are all questions that must be asked about any new society. The essays trace the development of social and economic stratification and analyze in depth the careers of slaves, servants, tenant farmers, and other people at the bottom of the social order. They also connect voting behavior and distribution of political power to social and economic groups in the community. Taken as a whole, the essays ably demonstrate the many ways in which the sources of local history can be employed to address historical questions of more than local importance, and above all, they offer a tantalizing promise of what is yet to come.

We would like to thank the Department of General Services of Maryland, of which the Hall of Records is a part, for its continuing support of the Conferences on Maryland History and of their Proceedings. We would also like to express appreciation to Rhoda Dorsey, president of Goucher College, who devoted hours to helping plan the conference, and to the Jacob and Annita France Foundation, whose grant through the kind offices of The Maryland Historical Society made it possible for us to print the many tables and charts in this volume. All the staff of the Hall of Records did much to make the conference and this book a reality. Two deserve special mention —Dorothy Keith was outstanding in her handling of the arrangements for the conference and the correspondence it necessitated; Frank F. White, Jr., applied his singular editorial talents to many technical problems of editing the essays and checking the bibliography of Dr. Radoff's publications. We are also indebted to the editors of the Johns Hopkins University Press, who have done everything possible to ease the task of transforming a many-authored manuscript into a book. Finally, the authors of this volume wish to acknowledge the criticisms and suggestions that have come from the conference participants. They have proved invaluable in revising the essays for publication.

Aubrey C. Land
Lois Green Carr
Edward C. Papenfuse

INTRODUCTION

Aubrey C. Land

Whether success in this world was a deep desire of Morris Radoff, I do not know, but he achieved it in a way that few men do, and from practicing a calling that at first sight seems unlikely for a man of his training. Furthermore, he enjoyed success during the busy years before his retirement, though he customarily masked any private sentiments thereon under a characteristic muted response to the formal opening gambit, "How do you do?" His reply became a trademark: "Purty good."

His external biography, at least for his formative years, contains little to indicate the direction of his mature professional career. Born Morris Leon Radoff on 10 January 1905 in Houston, Texas, he attended public school in his native city. After graduation he matriculated at the University of Texas, where he completed two and a half years of study toward the baccalaureate. In August 1924 he presented himself for the junior year abroad at the conventional mecca for American students of French, the University of Grenoble. Before Christmas he made his hegira from this provincial center to Paris, specifically to its austere university, older than Philip Augustus and surrounded by the glitter and flesh pots of a world capital. A single piece of memorabilia—a faded photograph—from this Paris of Hemingway, Scott Fitzgerald, and Gertrude Stein shows a youthful Radoff, a matinee idol in appearance, and a very tall, Nordic-looking companion relaxing against a sports car. A photograph cannot capture the more valuable assets: a vocabulary and accent remarkably like the classic French of the late Charles de Gaulle and Italian fluent enough to enable him to later teach it at a major American university. Radoff brought these accomplishments back not to Texas but to a final baccalaureate year at the University of North Carolina, where he received his A.B. in 1926.

The year at Chapel Hill merged into a second, this one in graduate study in romance languages. Understandably, Radoff came under the spell of another recent émigré from the University of Texas, Howard Mumford Jones, just beginning at North Carolina the studies of French culture in America that later brought him the Lawrence Lowell Chair at Harvard and international acclaim as a productive scholar. During his first year of graduate study Radoff completed his thesis, "The Libraries of Etienne

Note: Aubrey C. Land is research professor of history, University of Georgia.

ix

Morris L. Radoff, Archivist and Records Administrator of the State of Maryland, 1939–1975
Photocopy by M. E. Warren of a Portrait by J. B. Thoms, 1973

Pasquier and Claude Fauchet," and received the A.M. degree in 1927. It is the universal fate of masters theses to remain unpublished academic exercises. But exceptional work has a way of surfacing sooner or later, and the heart of Radoff's thesis research did find its way into print shortly as an article under the title, "Claude Fauchet and His Library," in the prestigious *Publications of the Modern Language Association* (1929).

Meanwhile Radoff had made another decision and another move. He had, in the jargon of academics, settled on a career objective: romance languages and literature. To pursue his studies he had matriculated as a doctoral candidate at the Johns Hopkins University in Baltimore. A pioneer among American universities in adopting the German seminar for doctoral training, the Hopkins had from its first years produced Ph.D.'s—among them Woodrow Wilson and Frederick Jackson Turner—whose stellar performances had helped create a unique tradition that confronted entering students. When Morris Radoff took up residence in the autumn of 1929, he could hardly have been overawed by these academic glories. He had behind him the experience of Paris and four years teaching as a junior instructor at North Carolina, one of the South's foremost universities. Nevertheless, the special blend of distinguished faculty, past record, and vibrant student body at the Hopkins made impressions that teased his mind until at last in his sixties he committed them to paper in half a dozen sketches, a delight to those who have seen them in manuscript form.

Radoff's arrival at the Hopkins coincided with the crash that ushered in the Great Depression. He received his Ph.D. three years later in 1932, when the economy reached bottom according to reported statistics. He had completed the required seminars, taught French and Italian as a part-time instructor, and produced his dissertation, "The Characters in Farce and Comedy of the French Renaissance." Somehow, too, he had found time to write three short articles for ranking professional journals and a longer piece, "Censorship among the Learned," for the *American Mercury*. Accordingly, he was qualified by his training, degree status, and publications for a full-time post without even leaving the campus. For the next three years Dr. Radoff held the position of instructor in the department of romance languages at the Hopkins.

Advancement up the academic ladder was not to come. Even more than other private institutions, all of them feeling the pinch of depression, the Hopkins fell on evil days. Among others, Dr. Radoff became a victim of policy changes and financial retrenchment. However, he found refuge against unemployment in one of the most useful of New Deal projects, the Historical Records Survey.

Two years (1937–39) with the Historical Records Survey turned the career of Radoff in a new direction. Under the inconspicuous title, editor, he had major responsibility for organizing and directing an untrained clerical staff (WPA employees) in the work of preparing inventories of historical records within his bailiwick. Simultaneously, he had to acquire expertise in archival science by direct work with the records themselves. Thus, at one and the same time, he served as apprentice and master, teaching himself and directing others. In a sense, he continued in this dual role until his formal retirement from public employment almost four decades later in 1975. But, beyond doubt, the two years with the Historical Records Survey were critical.

The alchemy that transforms scholar into archivist cannot be described easily. Proficiency in the traditional academic discipline requires a critical mind, capable of analysis, of discerning relationships, of formulating hypotheses and putting them to the proof. Archival science calls upon the same intellectual processes. Both archivist and philologist must be sensitive to form and content of documents, adept in *explication du texte.* The observer must take into account these qualities of intellect and previous training in commenting on the transformation process, but when required to produce hard evidence he can only note a by-product: three substantial volumes—inventories of records of Allegany, Garrett, and Washington counties in Western Maryland—compiled and edited by Dr. Radoff and his staff.

The event that confirmed the new direction Dr. Radoff's career had taken occurred in his thirty-fourth year. In 1939 he accepted the post of archivist of Maryland at the Hall of Records in Annapolis. Both the post and the building were relatively new. The Hall of Records, built as a part of the tercentenary of the *Ark* and *Dove*, opened to the public in 1935, shortly after the appointment of Dr. James A. Robertson as first archivist of Maryland. Dr. Radoff's administration of thirty-six years as second archivist, then, virtually coincides with the life of the Hall of Records and its collection. His personal biography is so intertwined with the history of the institution over which he presided that even the most objective annalist can hardly speak of one without mentioning the other.

The task of appraising Dr. Radoff's accomplishments at the Hall of Records properly belongs to a practicing archivist, and in the forthcoming *General Guide to the Holdings of the Maryland Hall of Records* another hand has undertaken to put these accomplishments into perspective. But professional historians may justifiably express their perceptions, in part because they are important constituents of archival institutions, and also because they claim Dr. Radoff—author of several carefully researched books in the specialized field of architectural history—as one of their own. The following paragraphs set forth in rather summary form the perception of one historian, a confessed admirer of both the institution and its presiding archivist for so many years. Neither chronological nor complete in detail, this account perforce refers only in passing to technical matters—accessioning and preserving the records for instance—of considerable importance to professional archivists. If there is a theme in these pages, it might appropriately be formulated in a functional title, "The Making of an Archivist." Whether archivists as a breed come under the heading of scientists or artists may be debated. Certainly the calling demands that creativity and imagination associated with the arts. Beyond doubt the requisite knowledge and skills can be structured and presented as a science. But, until very recently, no university in America offered anything like a comprehensive training program for prospective archivists. Aspirants acquired expertise either by serving an apprenticeship or by teaching themselves on the job after appointment. Dr. Radoff came to the post, Archivist of Maryland, with two years in the rough and tumble of the Historical Records Survey behind him. He turned this experience to account as he developed a program and a philosophy for the Hall of Records. Those who wish to follow the gradual unfolding of this process, step by step, can find abundant data in the series of *Annual Reports of the Archivist of the Hall of Records.** As I read the evidence it tells three concurrent stories: (1) the assembling of a remarkable collection of records, (2) the production of archival tools for using the records, and (3) the development of a philosophy informing the work of the archivist and his staff.

Assembling and preserving records have always been principal responsibilities of archival institutions. During Dr. Radoff's administration the Hall of Records came to enjoy a kind of preeminence among American depositories as a model archives. Professionals from other countries and from other U.S. states frequently came to Annapolis on tours of observation. The archivist—after briefing his guests—conducted distinguished visitors on a tour of the physical plant that began at the back door of the Hall of Records, where incoming archival materials went through the fumigation process. Thereafter, visitors went on to view the work of repair, which included restoration of damaged records and their preparation for binding. The Hall of Records pioneered in laminating fragile and broken manuscripts, that is, the process of encasing the pages in acetate under heat. Behind the beautifully preserved folios available to readers in the public search room lie hours of exacting labor with sophisticated technology. A visit to the two remaining departments, the photographic section and the bindery, wound up the tour of the physical plant. Doubtless visitors took away lively impressions of those processes that transformed incoming records, often battered beyond apparent redemption, into the handsome folios in the search room.

In their preoccupation with the outward and physical, it is entirely possible that transient callers missed the distinctive quality of the collection. No other archives along the Atlantic coast has brought together records of

*Dr. Radoff prepared the Fourth Annual Report for 1933–39 and the following thirty-three.

the central government and local records of all types at a single location. In this respect the collection at the Hall of Records is unique. Students of seventeenth- and eighteenth-century America have in a single building wonderfully complete series of county court proceedings, county land records, and testamentary papers (wills, inventories of estates, and accounts) that offer unparalleled opportunities for reconstructing the social and economic history of early America. Dr. Radoff moved into the Hall of Records, which was virtually empty when he was appointed archivist, supplementary historical records such as parish registers.

This result followed many years of persistent labor by the archivist and his staff—of locating ancient records in basements and attics of county courthouses and of negotiating with jealous local authorities before transferring the materials to Annapolis for safe keeping. Meanwhile Dr. Radoff acquired additional responsibilities that enlarged his functions as archivist and brought records of later periods under rational arrangement. By legislation passed in 1953, Dr. Radoff acquired the additional title, records administrator, and a mandate to supervise a state-wide program designed to insure proper care and handling of records in all state agencies, the destruction of obsolete, nonfunctional materials, and the deposit of essential historical records not needed by agencies in current operations. Thus during his term as archivist and records administrator, activities of the Hall of Records transcended the preservation of the ancient records to include the oversight of contemporary materials with an eye to forestalling loss and preventing gaps that students of earlier periods find so frustrating.

Another step in rationalizing archival control over state records during Dr. Radoff's administration occurred in 1966–67, when the land office became an integral part of the Hall of Records collection. Established in 1680, the land office had maintained two essential series—the warrants and the patents—as well as certain records that pertained to the private revenues of the Lords Baltimore, proprietors of Maryland, namely the rent rolls, debt books, and proprietary leases. After the Revolution ended the whole apparatus of proprietary charges (quit-rents), the sovereign state of Maryland administered land affairs through a constitutional office under a commissioner, who had almost no duties once all the vacant lands had passed by patent into private hands. Constitutional amendment ended the separate land office in 1966 and, in Dr. Radoff's words, united "this handsome collection of records" with the already rich materials in the Hall of Records.

While he developed the archival holdings of the Hall of Records, Dr. Radoff did not neglect the aids to research appropriate to an important collection. Various catalogs, indexes, and calendars in the search room have proved a boon to purposeful scholars and interested antiquarians alike. The calendars deserve special mention because these useful volumes, published by the Hall of Records Commission, extend a kind of access to archival materials beyond the precinct of the original records themselves. Moreover, the calendar as a form is not as well known in America as in Europe. The first volume, *Calendar of Maryland State Papers, No. 1: The Black Books,* appeared in 1943. In succeeding years successive calendars of the Brown Books and the Red Books disclosed to the scholarly community materials for research in the massive miscellany known as the "Rainbow Series" because of its colorful leather binding. Preparation of the calendars—the labor of abstracting and indexing—fell to staff at the Hall of Records under the general supervision of the archivist. Dr. Radoff undertook as a personal enterprise only one, the unorthodox but interesting *Calendar of the Bank Stock Papers,* a successful experiment in "preparing a calendar dealing with one subject but including materials from several sources." His "Summary of the Bank Stock Case," a thirty-three page introductory statement to the calendar proper, remained the only secondary source available until the essay written by Professor Jacob N. Price for this volume. In 1948 Dr. Radoff distilled the knowledge he had acquired from working with this tool into a manual, "A Guide to Practical Calendaring," which appeared serially in *The American Archivist,* volume 10.

This abbreviated account of Morris L. Radoff's activities covers more than three decades during which he had an important organizational role at the Hall of Records. Somewhere in the first decade the novice had become the master. In 1955 the Association of American Archivists recognized his achievements by electing him to their highest office. His presidential address, "What Should Bind Us Together," made an eloquent plea for training archivists of the future, but attentive readers can discern, not so much in explicit words as in the undertones, a philosophy that had guided his handiwork of structuring archival operations and of informing policy at the Hall of Records. Occasionally in conversation with scholars who came to Annapolis for research, he elaborated his doctrine with a twist that harked back to his earlier days at the Hopkins. An archivist and his chief lieutenants—he would say—must not only collect and preserve the records, but they must also be equipped by professional training to offer budding scholars, particularly graduate students, immediate and practical guidance in the research that their masters at a university simply cannot undertake from a distance. In other words, the Hall of Records should be in the full sense an intellectual home away from home. The renaissance in Maryland and Chesapeake studies in the last fifteen years of his administration witnesses the realization of this ambitious goal. With the blessing of their professors, a spate of ambitious students descended on the Hall of Records during these years, creating there an atmosphere of *Freiheitsstudieren.*

It is a fair surmise that Dr. Radoff felt the stimulus of these lively, inquiring minds. He did some of his own best historical work in these years. His personal historical interests had grown out of inquiries into early record keeping and the housing of public records. These studies had resulted in an early volume of text and iconography, *Buildings of the State of Maryland at Annapolis*, published in 1954. Further examination of the local records he was busily assimilating into the Hall of Records collection suggested a major project, *The County Courthouses and Records of Maryland*. Volume one on the courthouses, published in 1960, sorted out the intricate story of the buildings themselves—the first, second, and third structures, as well as their many additions and renovations. For volume two on the records published in 1963, Dr. Radoff had the assistance of Gust Skordas, his assistant archivist for many years, and Phebe Jacobsen, senior archivist, who were responsible for the complete listing of county records. Finally in 1972, Dr. Radoff completed *The State House at Annapolis*, the definitive study of this historic monument that still houses the legislature of Maryland as it did in colonial days.

It seems entirely appropriate that the capstone of Dr. Radoff's career as archivist, historian, and teacher—teacher in a very special way—should have been fitted into place by the generation of younger scholars whose early studies he had fostered. The occasion was a Conference on Maryland History in Honor of Morris L. Radoff, held 14–15 June 1974 at St. John's College, whose campus adjoins the Hall of Records. Twenty-five scholars prepared papers for the formal sessions and the more informal colloquia. The success of this conference, the breadth and distinction of the scholarship displayed, suggested publication of some of the papers in a single-volume collection. The present volume puts in permanent form the results of the first conference on Maryland history as a testamonial to Dr. Radoff. It is pleasant to record the special contribution of two younger scholars, leaders in the recent flowering of Maryland history, to both conference and book: Dr. Lois Green Carr and Dr. Edward C. Papenfuse. Their labors—known only to a few privileged insiders—made possible the selection of papers and smoothed out potential problems in local arrangements to give a festive atmosphere and setting for the array of scholarship at the conference. This volume, then, is quite literally a festival writing, a tribute of scholars to the life work of Morris Leon Radoff.

PART 1

Law

THE MARYLAND BANK STOCK CASE: BRITISH-AMERICAN FINANCIAL AND POLITICAL RELATIONS BEFORE AND AFTER THE AMERICAN REVOLUTION

Jacob M. Price

The Background, 1715–83

A major scholarly contribution of Morris Radoff to the historiography of Maryland was his calendar of the Bank Stock Papers.[1] It is thus appropriate that this volume honoring Dr. Radoff should contain an article on the historical problem revealed by these papers. Maryland's complicated legal and diplomatic efforts in the generation after the peace of 1783 to recover the shares in the Bank of England purchased in the name of the colony before the Revolution reveal much of the changing nature of financial and political relations between the colony-state and Britain both before and after the Revolution.

The learned thirty-four-page introduction to Dr. Radoff's calendar of the Bank Stock Papers is the principal scholarly treatment of the subject thus far published. It is particularly unfortunate, therefore, that this volume has remained relatively unknown to persons working outside of Maryland history and has not been properly used by historians of British–American relations in the generation after 1783.[2] Radoff's calendar and introduction cover the Bank Stock Papers in the Maryland Hall of Records, Annapolis, and related items in the Maryland Historical Society, Baltimore. The present account will be based upon these same documents as well as upon related papers in the United States and England. The most valuable additional source in this country is the papers of Rufus King, heavily utilized by Bradford Perkins.[3] In London, the Foreign Office records in the Public Record Office contain much on the diplomatic side.[4] Substantial documentation on the legal side of the problem can be found in the records of the Court of Chancery and the Treasury Solicitor, also in the PRO.[5] Unfortu-

Note: Jacob Price is professor of history, University of Michigan.

nately, the private papers of Lord Eldon, the lord chancellor, and perhaps the British minister most closely concerned with the case, do not appear to have survived, nor do those of the legal firms involved. Minor additional references can be found in the archives of the Bank of England at Roehampton.

Every person or institution in the Thirteen Colonies that had business in London had to have qualified agents there to handle such business. A number of thoroughly researched and very useful studies have made us familiar with the work of the political agents of the colonial legislatures.[6] Colonial authorities also frequently had occasion for financial representatives in London to pay or to receive funds there. The Maryland colonial government had particular need of a financial agent in London in the eighteenth century. Like Virginia, it levied export duties on tobacco expressed in sterling and needed someone in London to collect the bills of exchange in which those duties were paid; it also needed agents to handle some of its financial relations with Lord Baltimore, as well as arms purchases and the reserve funds set up after 1733 to back Maryland's paper currency. Needless to say, all the larger merchants in London trading to Maryland would have liked to be named the colony's financial representative. Not only would the commissions earned by such a charge add to a firm's income but also the charge itself would give that firm large sums to handle, add to its liquidity, and mark it out in the eyes of both Londoners and Marylanders as a house of financial standing and importance. Even the sketchiest histories of the houses that got such commissions tell us a lot about who was who in the London-Maryland trade between the restoration of the proprietary (1715) and the Revolution.

When, after the accession of George I, the lordship of Maryland was restored to the house of Calvert, it was necessary for the proprietary and the colonial legislature to make certain new financial and administrative arrangements for the colony. One such measure was the act of August 1716 for "ascertaining the Gage & Tare of Tob[acc]o Hhds & . . . for laying Impositions on Tob[acc]o p[er] the Hhd. for the Support of Governm[en]t." Among other things, this act reestablished an export duty of 3d. sterling per hogshead on all tobacco exported from the colony, collected since the 1690s for the purchase of arms. The act provided that this tax, collected in the first instance by the naval officers of the several districts of the colony, was "to be lodged in the hands of such Merch[an]t or Merchants in London as the Upper & Lower Houses of the Assembly shall from time to time direct."[7] The first merchant named under the act was Captain John Hyde, who was already exercising that function, and, in partnership with his son Samuel, was to continue to perform it down to his death in 1732.[8]

It was not strange that this commission should go to the Hydes. John and Samuel Hyde were the greatest merchants in the Maryland trade from the

1690s to the 1740s. They were also the "bankers" to Lord Baltimore in the 1720s and probably earlier. Their correspondents in Maryland (to whom they extended considerable credit) included many of the leading planters and public figures. Challenging their grip on Maryland's London business would be difficult—but not impossible. In 1727–28, the Hydes were under attack in Maryland for selling to the French buyers in London in wholesale lots at low prices tobacco consigned in much smaller lots by numerous planters in the colony. The Hydes got quick cash by such sales, but it was felt that the consigning planters did not get the best price.[9] At a time when this attack was at its height, both houses of the legislature concurred in a resolution ordering that bills of exchange remitted to London on the province's account should henceforth be sent to William Hunt, a rising merchant there.[10] We do not know what proportion of the province's bill remittance business Hunt actually got; the Hydes in practice retained the business relating to the 3d. sterling duty for armaments.[11] Nevertheless, by the 1720s the province's financial business in London had clearly become an important political plum for which rival contenders fought, backed by supporting parties in the Maryland Assembly.

In 1733, the Maryland legislature for the first time authorized the issue of paper money or "bills of credit" (£90,000 worth). To support the credit of this new paper money and to provide for its redemption, the legislature at the same time levied a new tax of 1s. 3d. sterling per hogshead on all tobacco exported. The act further provided "That the Duty . . . so to be collected . . . by the several Naval Officers shall be, with all possible Speed, after Receipts thereof, remitted to Mr. Samuel Hyde, Mr. William Hunt, and Mr. Robert Cruikshank, Merchants in London, or any Two of them, or other Persons, or the Majority of them, who shall be intrusted or appointed Trustees in London. . . ." The sums remitted were to be invested by the trustees in shares or stock of the Bank of England, "to be entered in the Books of the Company [Bank], to be for the Use, and in Trust, for the Province of Maryland." The dividends accruing were to be invested in further shares. The "bills of credit" were to be redeemed in 1748 by bills of exchange drawn upon the London trustees, who, in the meantime, were to receive a two percent commission on sums handled.[12]

There thus came into existence both Maryland's paper money and the Bank stock trust in London that gave it backing. We do not know precisely which elements in Maryland supported Hyde, Hunt, or Cruikshank for a trustee's place, but there was nothing surprising about their being chosen. All three were prominent merchants, chosen by the London–Maryland trade for their committee of management.[13] Samuel Hyde, merchant and some-time East India Company director, of Rood Lane, mentioned earlier as the son and partner of Captain John Hyde, was now his heir and successor. Of Cruikshank we know little except that he was a merchant and sometime

Africa Company director of Poor Jury Lane (now Jewry Street), near
Aldgate (subsequently of Magpie Alley, Fenchurch Street); his name is
Scottish, characteristic of Aberdeenshire and adjacent eastern counties.
William Hunt of Little Tower Street was much better known, though his
origins are obscure. He had been sharing the colony's remittance business
with Hyde since 1727. He was a director of the Royal Exchange Assurance
and stands out as the only Virginia or Maryland merchant of this century to
become a director of the Bank of England. He served on the court of that
company from 1728 till 1763, being also elected deputy governor for 1747–49
and governor, 1749–52. His control of Maryland's Bank stock no doubt
enhanced his electoral importance in the Bank, but his being a Bank director
made him a more than appropriate person to be a trustee. He owned land in
Maryland and may have had family connections there.[14]

These trust arrangements of 1733 persisted until the London tobacco
trade was shaken by several major stoppages in the mid–1740s. (These
appear to have been associated with the wars and with changes in French
buying policy, which redirected business away from London to Glasgow and
other northwestern ports and created cash flow problems for some big
London houses.) Among the merchants that went under ca. 1746 were
Robert Cruikshank and Samuel Hyde. In the emergency, Lord Baltimore
appointed Joseph Adams as substitute for Hyde and Cruikshank so that the
Bank stock trust (now £15,000) could continue operations. (Adams was a
very responsible Quaker merchant, prominent in the trade from the 1720s.)
The legislature confirmed this substitution, and nothing was lost by the
failures. Shortly afterwards, John Hanbury, another Quaker merchant of
London, was added as the third Bank stock trustee.[15] After Samuel Hyde's
failure, the other remittance business of the colony was handled primarily by
Hunt, though a small share went to Joseph Adams during 1747–48 and
thereafter to his son-in-law and executor, Silvanus Grove, a Quaker linen
draper turned merchant, who was to become a figure of great wealth and
reputation in the City.[16]

Grove, however, did not become one of the Bank stock trustees. After
Adam's death in 1748, there were only two—Hunt and Hanbury. When John
Hanbury died in 1758, his place was taken by his cousin and partner, Capel
Hanbury. When Hunt died in 1767, he was succeeded by John's son, Osgood
Hanbury. Though not active in the Bank of England like Hunt, the Quaker
Hanburys were very important figures in the City of London. They were not
only the biggest importers of tobacco in London in the 1750s but also
contractors (with John Tomlinson) for all the government's remittance
business to North America during the Seven Years' War. In addition, the
Hanburys were the personal bankers to the last Lord Baltimore and thus of
considerable political importance in Maryland, particularly in matters of
patronage. This was shown when they were able to get their business and

legal agent in Maryland, Daniel Wolstenholme, appointed to a number of coveted positions in the colony.[17]

The death of Capel Hanbury in 1769 coincided with a periodical renewal of the legal authority for Maryland's paper money. On this occasion, new trustees were not named by Lord Baltimore but were provided for by act of legislature as in 1733. Those so named were Osgood Hanbury, Silvanus Grove, and James Russell.[18] Grove, now an affluent Quaker merchant and perennial director of the London Assurance Company, was Adams's son-in-law and executor and had since Adams's death in 1748 handled part of the colony's financial business in London.[19] James Russell (1708–88) was rather more interesting. The son of a crown attorney (procurator fiscal) for Edinburgh, he had emigrated to Maryland ca. 1730 and a few years later married Ann, sister of Richard Lee (d. 1787), member and subsequently president of the council in Maryland. Russell was for many years a merchant in Prince George's County, Maryland, in correspondence with John Buchanan of London, but in the 1750s moved to London and set up there on his own account. With his Lee and other valuable connections in Maryland and northern Virginia and with a considerable amount of commercial drive, he replaced the Hanburys as the greatest London house in the Maryland (Western Shore) trade and as the biggest importer of tobacco in London. By the 1770s, his principal competition came from his son-in-law and former partner, William Molleson, another eastern Scot. Russell was severely embarrassed by the crash of 1772 but was still trading on a grand scale at the outbreak of the Revolution. He had extensive real estate interests in Maryland, the most important of which was a one-third interest in the Nottingham Iron Works in Baltimore County (worth about £30,000 sterling). His partners there were John Buchanan, his former London correspondent (one third), and the Ewers, West India merchants of London (the remaining third).[20]

The London Bank stock trust thus was not just a technical detail detached from the main stream of public life, but something deeply revelatory of the locus of power in colonial Maryland. Just as very powerful economic needs determined the issue of the paper money and the establishment of the trust funds for its redemption, so very real economic and political influence determined that only London merchants with strong connections or deep roots in the colony could hope to be named trustees for the Bank stock.

This was the situation on the eve of the Revolution. In 1773, the three London trustees held Bank stock with a face value of £27,500, worth £38,500 at the current market price of 140, plus £348:7:6 in cash.[21] By mid-1775, this had risen to £29,000 worth £41,180 at 142,[22] after which events precluded the normal operation of the trust. At first the revolutionary government of Maryland did nothing about the London trust. In no state did the Revolution produce a less radical government than in Maryland. After the excitements and alarms of 1775–76 and the removal of the dependents of the proprietor, Maryland was ruled by substantially the same sort of people who had ruled it before. Although there were sequestrations of real property and liquidation of debts, the new rulers were not unmindful of the sanctity conferred upon even enemy property by eighteenth-century law and custom. The first revolutionary governor was Thomas Johnson, whose own brother, the merchant Joshua Johnson, had remained in London until 1777 to wind up his affairs there.[23] The second revolutionary governor was Thomas Sim Lee, a nephew of Ann Lee, wife of James Russell, one of the London trustees.

At the outbreak of the war, there were three principal issues of paper money (bills of credit) in circulation in Maryland, all expressed in dollars: 1766 ($173,773 authorized), 1769 ($318,000), and 1773 ($480,000). Each was to circulate for twelve years, that of 1766 being due for redemption in 1777. The legislature at first did nothing about the 1777 redemption, but at the end of 1779 (at the same time as it was considering a bill confiscating British property) passed an act calling in the remaining issue of 1766 still outstanding to be exchanged for certificates of indebtedness of the state, or bills of exchange on the London trustees. As the existing trustees might refuse to perform their duties under the new law, the act named a panel of five Americans then in Europe, one of whom was to be selected by Benjamin Franklin, American minister in Paris, as a new and sole trustee.[24] On 4 January 1780, the revolutionary council of Maryland wrote to Franklin informing him of the act and asking him to write the existing London trustees (Hanbury, Grove, and Russell) and ask them "whether they will transact Business, sell out the Stock, [and] accept and pay the Bills drawn in Pursuance of the Act." If the London trustees agreed to accept these orders, the money realized by the sale of the stock was to be placed "in the Hands of some capital Banker in Amsterdam or Paris" upon whom the Maryland authorities could draw. If not, Franklin was to go ahead and appoint the new trustee from the five names sent him, though there could have been very little expectation the old trustees would hand over the stock. The Maryland Council also informed Franklin that a bill had passed the lower house in 1779 for the confiscation of all British property in the state (except mercantile debts), but that the Senate had not concurred "because they deemed a . . . Confiscation of British Property at this Time [NB] improper."[25] The restraint of the Senate was thought to deprive the trustees of any excuse for not paying; it was also a warning to them that their own property in the state was in peril should they refuse to honor the demands on them. When Russell received Franklin's letter of 20 May 1780, he and the other trustees applied to the attorney general (James Wallace) and the solicitor general to be (James Mansfield) for an opinion. The law officers eventually replied (28 August 1780) "that the Trustees could not with safety sell the Stock, or pay the Bills." The trustees accepted the advice and determined not to pay any bills drawn on them.[26] Before being notified of this, Franklin wrote to Governor Lee on 11 August 1780 that he had not yet received a reply from Russell and doubted that one would be forthcoming.[27]

Even before the receipt of Franklin's message, the Maryland legislature passed a new act in 1780 instructing the treasurer of the Western Shore to draw £35,000 sterling worth of bills of exchange on the London trustees and providing, in the event of their refusal to pay, for the seizure of their real property in the state as well as that of Henry Harford, the last proprietor, and the late Lord Baltimore, for the payment of the bills of exchange with normal penalties.[28] Thus authorized, the governor and council on 26 July 1780 drew a bill of exchange for £1500 on the trustees in London payable to Stephen Steward & Son, local merchants. They endorsed it to V. & P. French & Nephew of Bordeaux, who sent it for collection to their London correspondents, French & Hobson. Governor Lee also wrote privately to French's in Bordeaux that his uncle (Russell) faced confiscation should he refuse to honor the bill. Since French & Co. were also the Bordeaux correspondents of James Russell, the message as intended reached the trustees in London promptly. Nevertheless, they refused to pay the bill when presented on 26 September and only then wrote Franklin of the opinions they had received from the law officers.[29]

That winter, the Maryland legislature passed a more general act (1781) confiscating all British property in the state. By article vii of this measure, the iron furnace, forge, and related property belonging to James Russell & Co. in Baltimore County were to be sold to create a special fund "for making good and sinking" the bills of exchange drawn by the treasurer of the Western Shore under the aforementioned act of 1780.[30] Although all British property was confiscated by the 1781 measure, Russell and his heirs always argued that his property had been confiscated specifically because he had followed the instructions of the attorney general and solicitor general. He alone of the three trustees had extensive real estate holdings in Maryland and thus suffered under the act. He estimated the value of his one-third interest in the Nottingham Iron Works in Baltimore County (White Marsh Furnace and Long Caln Forge) at £13,709. After his death in 1788, his widow placed the value of his total losses at £69,729:13:2 sterling (including the value of debts paid into the state treasury in depreciated paper and £11,760 interest).[31] As early as January 1783, James Russell presented a petition to the Lords of the Treasury asking for the Bank stock as compensation, but that board's secretary, George Rose, simply marked it, "proper for the Consideration of Parliament, or of the Ministers in Case a Treaty being entered into with the Province."[32]

There was, of course, no treaty between George III and the province of Maryland. The war was concluded by the preliminary treaty of peace of November 1782, the interim armistice of January 1783, and the final treaty of September 1783 (proclaimed in January 1784). By article v of the preliminary and final treaties, Congress undertook to recommend to the several states the restoration of British property confiscated during the war; article vi prohibited further confiscations or persecution; while article iv unqualifiedly outlawed any legal impediments on either side to the recovery of bona fide prewar debts. Article iv provided some legal support for Maryland's claims to recover the Bank stock, but its impact was weakened by the fact that the several American states in the years following the treaty of peace failed to implement this article and even passed new laws making it more difficult for British creditors to sue in local courts for prewar debts. Virginia was particularly guilty in this respect, but Maryland was not entirely innocent.[33]

Samuel Chase and the Court of Chancery, 1783-97

As soon as news of the preliminary treaty of November 1782 reached Maryland, public figures there began to consider ways of recovering the state's Bank stock.[34] All during the war, the dividends earned by the stock had been reinvested by the trustees so that the £29,000 (face value) of 1775 had become £43,000 by April 1783.[35] In June 1783, even before the signing of the definitive peace treaty, the matter received serious consideration in the Maryland legislature. It was decided to send the lawyer and legislator Samuel Chase to London to recover Maryland's heritage. Chase had been a very active, somewhat demogogic but relatively moderate "patriot" politician before and during the early stages of the Revolution, serving inter alia as a Maryland delegate to the Continental Congress in 1774-78. His enemies had reasons to want him out of the way. His friends sought to reward his public services by granting him an exceptional 4 percent commision on the Bank stock recovered (which should have brought him well over £2000 as the stock was far above par), though others thought that any one of a number of Maryland merchants then in London could have handled the affair for only a 2 or even 1 percent commission. As authorized by an act of assembly, Chase received his commission from the Council on 5 June.[36]

Chase arrived in London on 7 September 1783 just after the final treaty of peace was signed in Paris (3 September). He found affairs rather more complicated than he had perhaps expected. The three trustees were now all old men with long memories and keen senses of grievance. He never did get to see Osgood Hanbury, who was ill in the country and died on 11 January. The amiable Quaker Silvanus Grove, who had conducted his affairs so prudently that he had lost little or nothing through revolutionary confiscations, was quite willing to turn over the trust fund as soon as the other trustees agreed. This left James Russell as the chief but very firm obstacle. His iron works had been sold during the war for the equivalent of £30,000 in prewar Maryland provincial currency, but Russell put their true value at at least £30,000 sterling allowing for the disturbed conditions under which the sales had been made. In addition to £10,000 for his one-third interest there, he estimated that other property of his confiscated during the war was worth £5-6,000 sterling. The rest of his estate was tied up in uncollected prewar debts in Maryland and Virginia, but the collection of these even in Maryland proved very difficult in the 1780s. He turned over his American business to the firm of De Drusina, Ritter, and Clerk, in which his grandsons James de Drusina and James Clerk were partners. James Clerk went out to Maryland in 1783 to collect Russell's debts. His appeal to the Maryland legislature in 1783 for the restoration of Russell's property procured nothing.

Chase, working through Richard Oswald, one of the British peace negotiators and formerly a London merchant, was in touch with the trustees from his arrival in September, but they were reluctant to deal with him until they had concerted a common position. They consulted counsel, including John Lee, attorney general under the Fox-North coalition, and Lloyd Kenyon, attorney general in the early months of the Pitt ministry, as well as the old and new solicitors general, James Mansfield and Richard Pepper Arden. Lee advised turning over the property to Chase, but Mansfield believed that Russell should retain at least the value of his confiscated property. The more anti-American Pittite law officers advised Russell to refuse any transfer until compensated. Grove and Hanbury's executors suggested turning over everything to Chase except £12,000, which would remain in trust until Russell's claims were settled. Russell said in February that he would agree to a transfer provided that he be given £12,000; a few days later, he suggested he would leave the £12,000 in trust provided that he receive the interest. A series of multilateral conferences were held on these points between February and June 1784, but without success. Chase did not have the power to allow anything to Russell, but probably could have agreed to a compromise leaving a portion in trust provided that Maryland did not have to surrender its claim to that portion. At every conference, however, Russell or his solicitor, Hutchinson, or his grandson, de Drusina, created some difficulty that prevented agreement on a compromise.

Chase was in a deep quandary. The simplest thing might have been to reach some private compromise with Russell, but Chase did not feel he had the powers to agree to any arrangement acceptable to Russell. He was reluctant to go to the government, for he realized that the Pitt ministry had other things on its mind during the early months of 1784 and was in no sense sympathetic to American claims. Eventually, on 26 March, Chase did see the foreign secretary, the marquess of Carmarthen, who told him that he could not take cognizance of the matter unless brought to his attention by the American minister (not yet arrived in London). He did, however, assure Chase that he would advise a settlement, sending word through Russell's son-in-law, Molleson, then an auditor of army accounts. (Russell chose not to take his advice.) The third alternative was to have recourse to the court of Chancery (as advised by Carmarthen), but Chase, a lawyer himself, must have foreseen the complications and delays this might entail and hung back. In the end, Russell forced his hand.[37]

Russell appears to have been frightened lest some legal way be found for Grove to transfer the stock to Chase without his concurrence. Alternatively, he was afraid that if he (Russell) died before Grove, the latter as sole surviving trustee could freely transfer the stock to Maryland without any compensation for Russell's estate. To prevent either of these from happening, Russell on 6 February filed a bill in Chancery against the Bank of England, thus beginning a cycle of more than twenty years of suits and countersuits in that court that would have impressed even Dickens. The suit asked that Grove and the Bank be enjoined from making any transfer to Chase, even if Russell should die, and that in the meantime Chase reveal his commission and produce accounts of the sale of Russell's property; the suit further asked that enough of the stock be sold to compensate Russell for the loss of his one-third interest in the iron works and the remainder be held in trust until it could be established what other property Russell had lost in Maryland and whether he would be free to recover his debts there.[38]

On 31 March, Bury Hutchinson, Russell's lawyer, finally notified Chase of the suit and sent him a subpoena to appear in court on 28 April. Chase's first reaction was to refuse to answer in court unless the Bank and Grove also appeared, and unless Russell agreed in advance that "if the Chancellor shall dismiss his Bill, or dissolve the injunction in the whole, or in part, that he will, if in the whole, immediately thereafter transfer all the stock" or, if in part, transfer all except that covered by the court's order. Chase had a series of conferences with Russell, Grove, Hutchinson, and John Maddocks, Russell's counsel, but they could agree on nothing. Maddocks seemed confident of getting from Chancery the sort of order Russell wanted. Chase felt under great pressure. If he left the country, he feared Russell would get his injunction. There was no hope of diplomatic help without an American minister in London. Yet, to go into court opened up the prospect that all sorts of other claimants would appear and the matter be prolonged indefinitely. Through Lord Buchan (David Steuart Erskine, eleventh earl of Buchan), he was introduced to his lordship's brother, Thomas Erskine, a prominent antiministerial lawyer (later famous as defense counsel in the sedition trials of the 1790s and lord chancellor in the Talents' ministry, 1806–7). Erskine advised him to answer Russell's bill, opining that Russell had no case unless he could prove that his property had been confiscated not as that of a British subject but as that of a Bank stock trustee. Chase accepted this advice and governed his conduct accordingly.[39]

A very expensive legal effort took shape. Russell retained three king's counsel, John Maddocks, John Lloyd, and James Mansfield (the last a former solicitor-general). In addition to Erskine, Chase consulted John Stanley, M.P., attorney general of the Leeward Islands, and Richard Pepper Arden, the new attorney general (and a close friend of Pitt). At a conference of counsel on both sides, Chase thought he had worked out a compromise with Maddocks, Russell's chief counsel, by which part of the stock would be transferred to Maryland, but Russell and his solicitor Hutchinson reneged. On the advice of Erskine and Stanley, Chase decided to take the initiative. He refused to answer Russell's bill but simply submitted a demurrer stating that the argument presented did not justify the remedy sought. Before this, however, he filed a bill initiating a suit of his own in Chancery, naming as defendants Russell, Grove, the Bank, the Ewers, and the trustees of the bankrupt John and Gilbert Buchanan (also interested in the ironworks).[40]

Meanwhile, the Ewers had decided to bestir themselves. Before the war Walter Ewer and his nephew John Ewer, West India merchants of 2 Little Love Lane, Aldermanbury, had held a one-third interest in the Nottingham ironworks along with James Russell and John Buchanan. Walter had died in 1779 leaving his residual estate to his nephews John and Walter (II). Walter (II) had died in 1782 leaving his entire estate to John's sons, John the younger and Walter (III). The Ewers had lost substantially by the confiscation of the ironworks but lacked James Russell's negotiating strength, his hold on the Bank stock. Lest their interests be disregarded in any settlement between Russell and Chase, they filed their own bill (6 May 1784) against all concerned (except Chase) alleging that the ironworks had been confiscated only because the Bank stock trustees failed to pay the bills of exchange; that the State of Maryland had settled the bills of exchange out of the proceeds of the sale of the ironworks and hence had no further claim in equity on the Bank stock that was now available to meet their claims as sufferers from the related confiscation.[41]

In early June, the matter finally received a hearing before Lord Thurlow, the lord chancellor. Thurlow ordered—pending a final settlement of the case—that the trustees (Russell, Grove, and Hanbury's executors) transfer Maryland's Bank stock to the custody of the accountant-general of the Court of Chancery, who was to receive the dividends and reinvest them in further Bank stock. Russell was thereby assured that if he died first Grove would not be able unilaterally to transfer the stock to Maryland. Maryland was also assured that if Grove died first, Russell would not be able to keep the stock or the dividends. Nothing else was settled.[42] Stock with a face value of £44,000 and £1,000 in cash was transferred to the accountant-general of the court on 25 June. As stock was then selling at 115 1/2, Maryland's claimed property in the hands of the court was now worth approximately £51,820.

Unable to reach any general or partial settlement with the other parties involved, Chase pushed for a final settlement of Maryland's claims by the Court of Chancery. When the case next came up for hearing before the lord chancellor in mid-July, Chase was represented by the attorney general, Richard Pepper Arden, acting in a private capacity. Arden for Chase moved that the court order its accountant general to retain part of the stock to cover the claims of Russell, the Ewers, and Buchanan's trustees, pending the settlement of those claims, and that the balance (estimated at £17,000 Bank stock at face value, approximately £19,635 at market value) be transferred to Chase for the state of Maryland. Lord Thurlow refused to make such an order, observing that "he must . . . be . . . fully satisfied of the pet[itioner's] Right to the Bank Stock . . . and that as it was stated, that the Stock was held in Trust in Virtue of laws made by the Legislature of the *Colony* of Maryland, and was now claimed on behalf of the *State* of Maryland, he was of Opinion that another Party was necessary, before he could give any Opinion on the Motion." Chase understood that the "Party meant, though not expressed by his Lordship, is the Attorney General of this Kingdom" acting for the crown. In other words, Thurlow brought the government into the question and returned to the point first expressed in the opinion of the law officers in 1780 that there was some question whether the state of Maryland in this case could automatically be taken to be the successor to the property rights of the *ci-devant* colony of Maryland. Lord Chancellor Thurlow was not just a judge but was also a cabinet minister, as he had been in 1780. He was undoubtedly fully aware that in 1784 as in 1780 beyond the legal niceties were questions of public import that might well have to be taken into consideration.

Chase could not have had many illusions about this. His counsel, Stanley, asked the attorney general (who had also been one of Chase's counsel) how he would answer if made a party to the case. Pepper Arden told him he would make the usual answer, claiming for the crown as much of the Bank stock as the lord chancellor might decide belonged to it. This meant that there was a chance at law that all the Bank stock would go to the crown, leaving both Maryland and Russell cut out completely. To prevent this, Chase wrote to the prime minister, William Pitt, explaining the case and basing Maryland's claims strongly on the peace treaty. (He was, of course, impeded by the absence of an American minister in London.) At the same time, he tried to persuade Russell that it was in both their interests to move for an early decision; if Russell would only moderate his claims as the Ewers had done, Chase would undertake to amend his bill to make the attorney general a party (for the crown) and move for a quick decision. When Russell proved adamant, Chase gave up and made plans to return to Maryland in late August 1784.[43]

However, even if Russell had proved more tractable, there was no assurance that the attorney general would, in fact, reply to Chase's bill. (Pitt never replied to Chase's letter.) If the British government regarded Maryland's claims as simply one detail of the broader question of debt claims on both sides, then the attorney general might simply refuse to make any answer to Chase's bill and thus prevent any decision being reached in Chancery until broader diplomatic questions had been settled between the United States and Great Britain. This indeed was to be the scenario for the next twenty years.

Russell's intentions in all this are far from clear. He was now over seventy-five years of age, and showed many of the crotchets and stubbornnesses of the elderly. He refused for example to file a claim with the British government for compensation for his confiscated real estate in Maryland lest such compensation weaken his claim to the Bank stock. Not until ten years after his death in 1788 was his family able to correct this slip and obtain the compensation to which they were entitled.[44]

Before Chase departed from London, he left detailed instructions with his solicitors, William and John Lyon of Gray's Inn. They were to preserve the status quo, leaving the stock in the hands of the accountant general of Chancery; they were not to amend Chase's bill to make the attorney general (for the crown) a party unless Russell agreed to moderate his demands as the Ewers and Buchanan's trustees had done. Chase wanted a further hearing delayed as long as possible so that he could report to the Assembly of Maryland and have a chance to concert new plans agreeable to his Maryland principals.[45]

Chase returned to America empty-handed, his expectations for a large commission lost in the labyrinthine ways of the Court of Chancery and international diplomacy. He tried unsuccessfully to get a further advance from the state of Maryland to cover his legal expenses and had to meet these out of the £500 originally advanced him and his own resources. The legislature did, however, pass an act in January 1785 approving of his actions and declaring the willingness of the state to have its claims decided by the lord chancellor. Chase was given full powers (under the direction of the governor and council) to pursue the state's case in that court and, if necessary, to make the attorney general of Great Britain a party to the suit.[46]

Chase was resourceful, but he could accomplish even less in Annapolis than in London. Sometime in 1785, he had his lawyers in London amend his bill to make the attorney general a party to the suit, but the attorney general failed to reply. Seeing that new initiatives would be needed, Chase obtained from the legislature in March 1786 a new act that requested the "governor and council . . . to receive from the agent . . . any proposals of measures by him to be executed concerning the said stock" and empowering them to authorize the carrying out of any such proposals they deemed for the advantage of the state.[47] Acting under this act, Chase wrote to the council on 7 July informing them that the attorney general had not put in his answer and that it was reliably reported "that the Bank Stock will not be recovered, so long as there is any Impediment thrown in the Way of the recovery of British

Debts by any One of the States." He asked to be given full authority to make any arrangement he thought best, provided only that the state received back £32,000 face value of stock (on which he would get his four percent commission). As the stock accumulating in the hands of the accountant general by then totaled about £49,135 face value, Chase would have had a margin of at least £17,135 with which to bargain with Russell and the Ewers. However, the governor and council declined to accept Chase's proposal. Instead they thought that Congress should be asked to instruct the American minister in London (John Adams) to intercede in the case.[48]

A few months later, Chase thought of an even more ingenious method of reopening the case. In 1774–76, Daniel Dulany had entered into two mortgages totaling £12,121:13:7 to Osgood Hanbury & Co. to cover debts owing to that firm by his late father, Walter Dulany. During the war, the lands covered by the mortgages were seized by the state and sold, without providing for the removal of the liens. Since the peace treaty of 1783 specifically confirmed prewar debts, the buyers of those lands did not have clear title until the mortgages could be removed. A plan was concocted that would serve the interest of the buyers of the Dulany lands as well as that of Chase and Osgood Hanbury's estate. Upon application by the Hanbury interests to Maryland for compensation on the mortgages, a law was passed by the Maryland legislature in January 1787 authorizing Chase, as agent for the Bank stock, to use £11,000 worth of that stock (at face value) to clear the mortgages held by Osgood Hanbury's estate on the former Dulany lands. The same act authorized Chase, with the approval of the governor and council, to make any composition for the Bank stock he deemed prudent.[49] Acting under the authority of this last clause and instructions from the government of Maryland, Chase in June 1787 made a provisional agreement with Russell's grandson, James Clerk (who represented his grand'father's interests in Maryland then), whereby Russell would get £6,000 sterling for his one-third interest in the ironworks and £4525 for his other real estate confiscated in Maryland, provided the owners of the other two-thirds of the ironworks accepted an equivalent offer and the Court of Chancery ordered the balance (over £30,000) paid to Maryland. This arrangement, though allegedly accepted by Russell prior to his death in 1788, was rejected thereafter by his widow.[50] Chase, however, was able to move forward under the other part of the act. On 26 May 1787, he assigned £11,000 (face value) of Maryland's claim on the Bank stock (plus £440 of the same for his own commission) to John Hanbury (Capel Hanbury's son), John Lloyd (Osgood Hanbury's brother-in-law), and David Barclay (Osgood's son-in-law), three Quaker eminences of London, the first two as surviving partners of Osgood Hanbury, the last of as one of his executors.[51]

The transfer of part of Maryland's claim to the Hanbury partners and executors in 1787 opened up an entirely new chapter in the Bank stock litigation, a chapter that was to fill the years 1787–97. In January 1788, the late Osgood Hanbury's partners (John Hanbury and John Lloyd) and executors (David Barclay, John Lloyd and Richard Gurney)[52] filed a bill in Chancery beginning a complicated new suit of *Barclay et al. v. Russell et al.* The defendants in this series of suits were James Russell (and his widow Ann), Silvanus Grove, the Ewers, the trustees of the bankrupt John Buchanan, Henry Harford (late lord proprietor of Maryland), Samuel Chase and His Majesty's attorney general. Barclay et al. asked the court to order the immediate transfer to the Hanbury estate of £11,400 worth of stock from the larger amount held in trust by the accountant general of the Court of Chancery.[53]

Responses were very slow in coming to this bill. Russell had not answered when he died on 1 August 1788, and the court had to be petitioned to make his executrix and widow, Ann Lee, a party to the suit.[54] Delays were also caused by the death of John Ewer the younger in 1788 and his father, John, in 1792.[55] Henry Harford further complicated matters by beginning his own suit against Barclay et al. in 1789, claiming that by the Revolution he had lost an estate in Maryland worth £477,854; of this, the crown commissioners under the compensation act of 1783 had recognized £230,000 but the Treasury had paid him only £70,000. Among the items that the commissioners had refused to recognize was Harford's claim for arrears of quit-rents and manor rents standing due at the time of the sale of his confiscated property. The commissioners claimed that these were still recoverable as ordinary debts under the treaty of 1783, but Harford had been unable to obtain this sort of justice in Maryland. He claimed further compensation out of the Bank stock, basing part of his claim on the argument that as proprietor he was the sole legitimate remnant of the prewar chartered government of Maryland.[56]

The months rolled by and the various parties to the dispute (including the attorney general) filed their answers to the suits of Barclay et al. (the Hanbury interest) and Henry Harford. Little new was revealed by these bills and answers. The stock kept accumulating in value and its face value came to £54,193 in November 1788 and £58,417 in November 1790. Even Ann Russell began to despair of litigation. Although she had rejected the composition Chase had offered in 1787, she departed from her husband's example and in 1789 filed a claim for compensation from the British government for her late husband's real estate confiscated in Maryland. The commissioners found in her favor, but the Treasury declined to pay anything until the Maryland Bank stock case was settled.

Another party to the suits was now, of course, the attorney general. His answers to the bills of Barclay et al. and Harford were most perfunctory. He denied any knowledge of the facts of the case but asked the court to preserve the rights of the crown.[57] However, when the case finally came up for a hearing before Lord Chancellor Thurlow in Hilary term 1791, the attorney general, Sir Archibald Macdonald, "by the authority of the then Secretary of State [for Foreign Affairs, Lord Grenville] . . . waived the rights of the Crown to the Stock claimed by the Plaintiffs [Barclay et al.] in the said Suit but Lord Thurlow did not make any Decree therein."[58] Efforts in 1793 to revive the matter in Chancery—by Chase's attorney, Uriah Forrest, an American merchant in London, among others—led to hearings in February but came to nothing without the further cooperation of the attorney general.[59]

Not till 1797 could the Court of Chancery be stirred to consider the matter more seriously. On 27 June 1797, the entire case (Barclay v. Russell) was heard before the then lord chancellor, Lord Loughborough (who as Alexander Wedderburn had played a conspicuously anti-American role in North's time). Loughborough dismissed the petitioners' (the Hanbury interest) bill, giving his opinion "that the stock was by Law vested in the King [as the property of a defunct corporation], who had a right to dispose thereof in such manner as he should think proper, but upon the benefit of such legal right, the Petitioners [Barclay et al. for the Hanbury interest] . . . had morally and equitably a Claim on the said Bank stock in respect of the said Mortgages made to the said Osgood Hanbury and his partners." (In other words, the Hanbury interest had to depend upon royal charity, not upon any absolute right recognizable by the courts.) Even while making this order, however, Lord Loughborough suspended its operation, leaving the entire matter still inextricably tied up in Chancery.[60]

Thirteen years of litigation had gotten exactly nowhere; by November 1797, the accumulating stock had a face value of £78,742. It was then clear to all that this was a matter that could only be settled at the diplomatic level.

The Diplomatic Phase, 1797–1805

From the very first, there had been reason to doubt whether a diplomatic rather than a litigious approach to the Bank stock problem might not be best for Maryland. Before he left London in 1784, Chase, it will be remembered, wrote to the prime minister, William Pitt, discussing the political dimensions of the case, but did not receive an answer. When John Adams arrived in London in 1785 as the first American resident minister, things did not improve much. Thus, nothing came of the resolution of the Maryland Council in July 1786 that a memorial be sent to the Continental Congress requesting that the American minister in London solicit the aid of the British government in settling Maryland's claims.[61]

With the conclusion of Jay's Treaty of 1794, however, the objective political situation changed. Not only did British-American relations become much more relaxed, if not cordial, but instrumentalities were established for settling controversies still at issue between the two nations. The most important of these instrumentalities were two boards of arbitration commissioners provided for by the treaty. One sat in London, with an American majority, to consider claims of American citizens against the British government (for illegal seizure of ships, for example). The other sat in Philadelphia, with a British majority, to consider claims of British subjects for compensation for bona fide prewar debts from solvent debtors (confirmed by the treaty of 1783) rendered uncollectable by legislation of the United States or of any of the individual states.[62] While the British government was much more conciliatory after Jay's Treaty (its war with France gave it every reason to be tractable on minor matters), it was inevitable that the British ministers would delay any concessions on lesser matters such as the Maryland Bank stock until they found out how the greater matters in the hands of the arbitration commissioners were going.

It took several years before the two commissions were set up and before they started their operations. The one in London worked very well and produced substantial indemnity payments for American claimants; the other in Philadelphia worked less well. The American commissioners refused to accept the judgments of the British majority about what constituted legal impediments to the collection of debts and in the end walked out of the commission. This was a popular step in the eyes of their compatriots but greatly impeded the improvement of British-American relations and the settlement of other issues between the two countries.[63] No one has yet undertaken an historical study of the debt question as an issue in the *domestic* politics of the United States, ca. 1783-1805, and this great topic is far beyond the scope of this paper. However, one must keep in mind that the debt problem was not purely a diplomatic question and that its political sensitivity seriously circumscribed the freedom of negotiation of those representing the new nation.

On the British side, the burden of negotiation over the Bank stock fell primarily on the successive secretaries of state for foreign affairs: Lord Grenville (1791-1801), in the first Pitt government, Lord Hawkesbury in the Addington government (1801-4) and Lord Harrowby in the second Pitt government (1804-5). On the American side, the principal negotiators were the American ministers in London; particularly Thomas Pinckney (1792-96), Rufus King (1796-1803), and James Monroe (1803-7). In addition, one of the United States members of the London commission on American claims was a Marylander, William Pinkney, a political disciple of Samuel Chase. It was inevitable that Pinkney too should be drawn into the negotiations for Maryland.[64]

Even before the Jay Treaty was signed in November 1794, the Maryland authorities wrote Secretary of State Edmund Randolph asking that Jay, who was in London, intercede for Maryland.[65] These documents were forwarded to Jay, but neither he nor Thomas Pinckney did anything for Maryland. Rufus King was to be rather more active. King's instructions, like those to Jay, were to help advance Maryland's interests "not by any formal negotiation but by such occasional instances and good offices as circumstances will permit."

At first, King turned the matter over to William Pinkney, who went through all the papers and had a long discussion with the elder Lyon, one of Chase's solicitors in London. Lyon informed him that no purely legal means could extract a decision from Chancery, that a ruling was ready but was being held up by "Reasons of State," and that Lord Chancellor Loughborough had hinted to him that he would not be averse to a settlement out of court by the various parties concerned.[66] Pinkney could only go back to Rufus King and persuade him to intervene. This King did most delicately in a letter to Grenville in February 1797. Grenville responded in like spirit by referring all the papers on Maryland's claim to the attorney general, solicitor general, and advocate general.[67] The attorney general then, it should be noted, was Sir John Scott, who in 1801 was to become Lord Eldon and lord chancellor. The three law officers delayed until August before giving their opinion that the state of Maryland was the legal successor to the rights of the former colony of Maryland only so far as recognized by the peace treaty of 1783, and that the Bank stock, not being covered by the treaty, had reverted to the crown as the property of a defunct corporation. The crown was free to dispose of it at will and could grant it to the state of Maryland. However, if this were done for reasons of equity, the crown ought also to consider the equitable claims of Mrs. Russell, the Ewers, Henry Harford, the Hanbury estate, and others.[68] This was, of course, consistent with the judgment of Lord Chancellor Loughborough in June, dismissing the Hanbury (Barclay et al.) petition.

Rufus King did not wait for the law officers' report in August but pushed on as best he could. He heard that the Russells had been paid off by the Treasury for their claims and sent this information along to Grenville for the use of the law officers. What actually happened was that in March 1797, Mrs. Ann Russell, despairing of anything coming of the law suits, had appealed once more to the Treasury for the payment of her claim for compensation for her late husband's property confiscated in Maryland. The claim had been allowed in 1790 but not yet paid. The Treasury had referred this to the commissioners handling those claims who decided in April 1798 to pay Mrs. Russell her £10,560 citing Lord Loughborough's ruling of June 1797. Mrs. Russell (who died in 1800) and her son-in-law and advisor, William Molleson, decided not to withdraw their claims in Chancery on grounds that they were still entitled to the difference between the true value of their lost Maryland lands (even Chase had talked of £12,000) and the £10,560 allowed by the government. In a private letter to Grenville's undersecretary, George Hammond, on this matter, Attorney General Scott showed some sympathy to Mrs. Russell, as well as skepticism about King's information.

Rufus King pushed on during 1797 and entered into direct correspondence and conversation with the lord chancellor. For a time, he was most optimistic.[69] His intervention may have influenced Lord Loughborough to render his opinion of June 1797 rejecting the claims of Barclay et al. (and by inference all other claims) in favor of the crown's right to the Bank stock. The implementation of this ruling was, as already pointed out, suspended by Lord Loughborough, who explained privately to King that he had done this so that the king would retain the option, if he so chose from reasons of policy, to refuse the stock and consent to its tranfer to Maryland.[70] King immediately wrote to Grenville (who had been notified by the chancellor) asking for such a transfer, but to no effect.[71]

In this unsatisfactory way negotiations dragged on during the latter part of 1797 and all of 1798, 1799, and 1800. The Maryland legislature commended King's zeal and named him their trustee to receive all or part of the stock, but refused him permission to accept any "if the release . . . of the state's right to any part be insisted on as a condition precedent to the transfer of the residue."[72] Despite these highly restrictive instructions, King kept up his conversations and correspondence with Lord Loughborough and Lord Grenville; he even tried to approach Henry Dundas, secretary of state for war and president of the Board of Control for India, and something of an *éminence grise* in Pitt's government—all to no avail.[73] The delays in the starting of the debt commission at Philadelphia and its utter breakdown in 1799 gve the British government no particular motive for wanting to be generous about Maryland's Bank stock.

The chronology of the Bank stock solicitation merges from 1800 with that of the much bigger debt question. In December 1799, when the commission at Philadelphia operating under the sixth article of the treaty of 1794 ceased its meetings, the United States government proposed to the British "an Explanatory Article for the Regulation of its future Proceedings." In April 1800, the British government replied, turning down the proposed explanatory article, but offering "to accept a Sum of between One and Two millions [sterling] in satisfaction of the Debts contracted before the Peace of 1783, to abolish the American [debt] Commission, and take upon itself the distribution of the Money among the British Creditors." The London commission on American claims would have its operation suspended pending the settlement of British debt claims but would otherwise not be affected.[74]

This British suggestion did not come out of the blue. Since at least 1790, the merchants of London and Glasgow who held most of the prewar debt were organized into local committees to solicit the British government about their uncollected debts in America. The two spokesmen of the London committee who did most of the soliciting or lobbying were John Nutt, a prewar Carolina merchant, and William Molleson, a prewar Maryland merchant and James Russell's son-in-law. The London and Glasgow committees were in constant communication with Lord Grenville during the sitting of the Philadelphia commission and after its breakdown intensified their efforts. From the Glasgow committee in March 1800 came a reminder of an earlier suggestion made by them to Grenville during the negotiations of 1794 for a method of compounding for the sums still outstanding.[75] For the Glaswegians the problem was essentially Virginia. They had some success in federal courts there collecting debts secured by bonds and mortgages but none with book debts or simple notes of hand; nor could they go into federal court for sums under $500. The Glaswegians were thinking of compensation in the vicinity of £2.5 million and suggested that the British government might advance the money if the United States could not pay it all at once.[76]

In August 1800, the United States government refused to accept the British proposal for a lump sum payment to cancel all prewar debts of American citizens to British subjects, but offered instead a more modest "Sum in satisfaction of the Claims of the Creditors upon the American Government [under the treaties of 1783 and 1794]—leaving the Creditors to pursue the recovery of their Debts in the ordinary course of the Judiciary." In response to a further British inquiry, the American government made it clear that it did not want a comparable lump sum from Britain in return for American claims on Britain but wanted the London commission to continue.[77] The next year was spent in tedious negotiations (with the British government fending off the merchants' demands for a harder line) before both sides in August 1801 agreed upon the sum of £600,000 sterling to be paid by the American government to be quit of its immediate obligations to the British creditors under article vi of the treaty of 1794. (The creditors were free to continue suing in America under the ordinary course of law, but in most cases this would prove to be only an illusory right since the ordinary course of law included the statute of limitations.) The political changes of 1800–1801 made this agreement easier to reach. In Britain, the Addington government was more conciliatory, while the election of Jefferson at the end of 1800 convinced the British government that there were insurmountable political obstacles in the United States to recovery of prewar debts. Jefferson himself was one of the larger defaulting debtors in Virginia, the state with more than two-fifths of the upaid debts outstanding. That Jefferson's indebtedness had been publicized by Federalist newspapers during the election campaign could only have exacerbated his feelings on this issue. This goes far to explain the British government's willingness to accept a sum as low as £600,000, perhaps one quarter of the value of the debts still outstanding.[78]

The agreement reached in principle in August 1801 on the amount of compensation to British creditors settled only the most important of the issues left over by the treaty of 1794. During the ensuing months, Rufus King and Lord Hawkesbury continued their negotiations on several other lesser points before concluding what became the British-American convention of 8 January 1802.[79] One of these subordinate issues was, of course, Maryland's Bank stock. Some weeks before Grenville resigned, King had sent him a draft of the proposed new convention including a clause "that the King should release all claim to the Maryland Bank Stock, and that immediate measures should be taken to transfer it to the State." Ever sanguine, King foresaw no difficulty on the Bank stock, provided that agreement could be reached on the larger issue of debt compensation.[80] In March 1801, shortly after Hawkesbury's taking office as Grenville's successor, King sent him a similar draft of the convention, with a comparable clause on the Bank stock.[81] In August, after agreement had been reached on the amount of American compensation for the debts, King sent Undersecretary George Hammond another draft with a similar Bank stock clause; in the margin, King added, "All the late Min[iste]rs concurred in the propriety of this article, and it was firmly expected to have been accomplished a long time."[82] King was inclined to be oversanguine in this matter.

Rufus King also entered into conversations and correspondence with the new lord chancellor, Lord Eldon, who as Attorney General Sir John Scott had been familiar with the Maryland case in the late 1790s. Lord Eldon seemed deceptively agreeable but kept raising minor difficulties.[83] Finally, on 15 October 1801, King had a private conference with Hawkesbury and Eldon at which they worked out most of the clauses of what was to become the convention of January 1802. At the meeting, Eldon told King that Maryland's Bank stock claims could not be included in the convention:

> The Chancellor, adverting to the Maryland Bank Stock, observed that after looking more fully into the question, he felt great difficulty in recommending that it should become the subject of a public Convention or Stipulation between the two countries. The claims of sundry Persons upon that Property, remained still to be decided in the Court of Chancery; and it would be contrary to the usage of this country for the King to enter into any stipulation, affecting or controlling the decisions of his Courts; that if any should be agreed to, it must be with a provisional reserve in favour of these claims; that an assurance from the King's Government that his Majesty's right, subject to such equitable claims as might be established, should be transferred to Maryland, and an Instruction to the Attorney General to bring these claims to a decision would answer all the purposes of a stipulation to the same effect.

On the next day, 16 October, King had a further conference with Hawkesbury alone at which he complained of the unconscionable delays on the Maryland Bank stock and the repeated wavering on the key point of whether or not the Court of Chancery had jurisdiction:

Upwards of sixteen years had elapsed since the State of Maryland had endeavoured to obtain a decision upon her claim to this Stock in the Court of Chancery of this country, to whose Jurisdiction she was willing to submit. Several years after the commencement of a suit for this purpose, the Chancellor discovered, that having no means of enforcing a Decree upon an independent State, he had no jurisdiction to try the merits of the Question before him. The Claim then became the subject of diplomatic representation, and a number of years having been spent in explaining, conferring, and exchanging Notes respecting the claim, it has been recently discovered that it was still depending in the Court of Chancery, and that it would be unusual and indecorous to make a matter of stipulation [that] which was in the possession of the Judiciary.[84]

Although King was greatly peeved by Eldon's tergiversations on the Bank stock, he realized, as he reported to Madison,[85] that he had obtained a significant concession on this: the attorney general would be instructed to bring the matter to a speedy decision; and the crown would yield all its rights in the stock to Maryland, subject only to the equitable claims of the other parties to the suits.

Going back to court was now less hopeless than it had been during the long litigations of 1784–97 because now, with the settlement of the debt issue, there no longer was a "Reason of State" to delay the course of justice. Who, though, were the "sundry Persons" whose "equitable claims" upon the Bank stock Lord Eldon had insisted must be heard in his court? The owners of the ironworks, the Russells, Ewers, and Buchanan's trustees, had been taken care of by the British government. The Hanbury interest was attached to that of Maryland. This left only two other significant claimant interests. One was Henry Harford, late proprietor of Maryland, who was not satisfied with the £70,000 compensation he had received from the British government and had been involved in the Bank stock litigation since 1789. The other was a group of émigrés and speculators in London, Bristol, and elsewhere who still held unredeemed prewar Maryland paper money, which they claimed was pledged against the Bank stock.

There had been three issues of paper money outstanding in Maryland at the start of the war: those of 1766, 1769, and 1773. That of 1766 was clearly based upon the Bank stock; those of 1769 and 1773 were convertible into sterling at redemption but had no clear lien on the Bank stock. All had been called in during the war, but many holders did not surrender them at the time of conversion, either because they had fled the province during the war, or because they did not want to accept in return the new revolutionary paper money of constantly deteriorating value. (When the issue of 1766 was called in, holders were also given the option of taking bills of exchange on the trustees in London, but there was little belief that such bills would be honored and only £1825:12:3 of such bills of exchange were issued on conversion of that issue.)[86] Maryland regarded these hoarded bills of credit as void, but they turned up, by one route or another, in Britain after the war, some in the hands of émigrés (most notably Daniel Dulany), others in the hands of merchants. In 1794, just before the signing of the Jay Treaty, some of the holders sent a memorial to Lord Grenville, asking that their interests be recognized in the negotiations.[87] In 1799, much the same group petitioned Grenville again, asking that, once the Court of Chancery had established the king's right to the Bank stock, their interests should be taken into consideration in discussions with the American minister on the disposal of that stock. On both occasions, the papers were referred to the chancellor, Lord Loughborough, who did not reply.[88] In 1802–3, the memorialists turned to the Privy Council and Treasury, without any greater success. Their holdings then were thought to come to only about £5000, while the face value of the Bank stock and other balances was £107,800 by the end of 1801.[89]

There was great disappointment in Maryland when word was received that the matter of the Bank stock would not be included in the British-American convention of January 1802 and that the whole matter would be sent back to the Court of Chancery. Chase and others pointed out that if the state had not been able to obtain redress when Britain was at war and trying to get redress from the United States for the prewar debts, Maryland could have little hope of justice now that Britain was at peace and the debt question settled. There was little understanding in Maryland of the weight of Lord Eldon's obduracy on this issue, nor did Chase and his friends give very much weight to ministerial assurances to Rufus King that the case would now proceed to an early decision. King was then being talked about as a possible Federalist candidate for the presidency in 1804, and his friends in Maryland were upset because anti-Federalists were spreading stories that he could have obtained more for Maryland from the British government if he had really tried. It was feared that King could never carry the state because of this issue.[90] Maryland's exasperation was ultimately expressed in a joint resolution of both houses of the legislature passed on 31 December 1802 authorizing the president of the United States to intercede for the state.[91]

The Maryland party in London tried to test the sincerity of the government by having the state's allies, Barclay et al. (the Hanbury interest) petition the Court of Chancery for a reopening of the case, which had been in abeyance since Lord Loughborough's suspended decree of June 1797. The petition was put down for a hearing in that court, but nothing was accomplished in the course of 1802.[92] The Hanbury executors tried a petition to the king in October 1802 without any more success.[93]

Rufus King, for his part, by correspondence and conversation sought all through 1802 to remind the foreign secretary, Lord Hawkesbury, of his assurances of a speedy settlement. These efforts had to be suspended during his trip to the continent (August–November 1802). The chancellor for his part remained true to his opinion as attorney general in 1797 that the stock rightly belonged to the king and must be transferred to his majesty before it could be disposed of as policy or equity might dictate; he so informed Lord Hawkesbury in July, but Hawkesbury did no more than refer the matter to the Treasury, where the relevant papers remained gathering dust on the desk of the Treasury solicitor.[94] On 13 November, the Treasury referred the whole matter to the law officers (attorney general and solicitor general) for an opinion on how a decision might be obtained in Chancery.[95] Rufus King, now returned to London, tried to hasten things along a little by writing privately to the prime minister and first lord of the Treasury, Henry Addington, on 7 December, as well as to Hawkesbury on the ninth.[96] This had some effect, for a few days later (15 December) Hawkesbury instructed the attorney general to take the necessary legal steps "for putting the Crown in possession of this property, in order that His Majesty may be enabled to dispose of it in such manner as He may think proper."[97]

Attorney General Spencer Perceval, the future prime minister, deputized the Treasury solicitor, Joseph White, to act for him in this matter. In March 1803, the latter petitioned Chancery asking that the decree of Lord Loughborough of 27 June 1797 (recognizing the king's title to the stock) "may no longer be suspended and that the Register [of Chancery] may be directed to draw up the same in order that any of the Parties dissatisfied therewith may have an opportunity of appealing against such Decree. . . ." After a hearing on 1 April 1803, Eldon dismissed the plaintiffs' petition in the case of *Barclay et al. v. Russell et al.* on the grounds that the old Maryland government was no more, "with liberty for His Majesty's Attorney General to apply to the Court in this Cause and in the Cause of Chase against Russell for a transfer of the said funds standing in the name of the Acc[ountan]t General of the Court in trust . . . and any of the Parties in . . . the said Cause[s] . . . are also to be at liberty to apply to this Court respecting their Claims. . . ."[98] Chase's solicitor, William Lyon, felt that this meant that the stock would be awarded to the crown, for, even without a knowledge of Eldon's privately expressed opinions, he felt that the lord chancellor would agree with his predecessor, Loughborough.[99]

Shortly afterwards, on 20 April, the attorney general moved "that the Accountant General may be directed to transfer the whole of the aforesaid Bank Stock . . . to such person as His Majesty by Warrant under his Royal Sign Manual be pleased to direct or appoint." King now perceived that such a transfer was the only route by which Maryland could get the Bank stock and on the twenty-second instructed Chase's solicitors, Lyon and Collyer, to concur. The motion was, however, opposed by Henry Harford and no order was made upon it. Though Harford filed a new bill against the attorney general and other parties to the suit, approaches were made to Rufus King, during the week 20-27 April, indicating that Harford would be satisfied with only a small part of the stock, perhaps £10,000 (face value). King, however, refused such a settlement, for he did not feel that he had powers from Maryland to make any payment to Harford.[100]

All these delays were particularly embarrassing to Rufus King, who was scheduled to return to the United States at the end of April 1803 and who wanted the stock question settled before he left. Hawkesbury smoothed King's departure by giving him a letter undertaking on behalf of the British government "that in the event of its being decided that the Title of this Stock has accrued, and belongs to His Majesty, His Majesty will cause the same to be transferred to the State of Maryland, together with the Accumulations which shall have accrued from the Re-investment of the Dividends. . . ."[101] King could report this in triumph to Madison and have the good news published in the press in the United States.[102]

King had in 1801 been given powers by the Maryland legislature to receive and transmit the stock.[103] With King departing from England in May and his successor as American minister, James Monroe, not arriving until July, there was also a gap in the management of Maryland's Bank stock affairs.[104] Once more this responsibility was entrusted both by the United States and Maryland to William Pinkney, the Marylander who was an American member of the London claims commission, now almost finished its work. Pinkney was himself planning to return to America in 1804 and naively thought he could finish the Bank stock business by then.[105]

As of 1 May 1803, the ever-accumulating trust fund totaled £187,567:12:0 at current values:

£98,518:2:9 Bank stock at 170	= £167,480:12:0 stg
£15,290:17:9 Bank bonds at par	= £ 15,290:17:9
£ 4,796:2:3 cash in Bank of England	= £ 4,796:7:3[106]

At $4.44 per pound sterling, this was the equivalent of $833,625 in United States currency, a substantial sum for Maryland in those days. Nothing now seemed to stand in the way of the state's getting this save the claims of Henry Harford, their late proprietor. Rufus King did not think that he had authority to satisfy Harford, and Pinkney had no greater delegated powers. On 26 May 1803, Governor John F. Mercer sent him some very vague instructions in a private letter. If Maryland could get the balance immediately, Pinkney was authorized to leave part of the stock (equivalent in value to Russell's old claim) continuing in trust pending the settlement of any outstanding claims: "but if such arrangement cannot be made, the Executive of Maryland conceive themselves authorized in concurrence with the President of the United States and they are disposed to trust to your discretion the power of making this partial but absolute sacrifice, in preference to risking any longer the whole claim."[107] It is not surprising that Pinkney did not interpret these highly qualified words as authorizing him to make a settlement with Harford. Chase, however, had a clear grasp of the promise opened up by Hawkesbury's letter of 25 April, and on 11 July wrote Governor Mercer suggesting that Pinkney be specifically authorized to give up to £10,000 sterling "to any persons" on condition that the balance of the trust fund be paid to Maryland immediately.[108] The Council of Maryland made an order to this effect on 5 August with the added proviso that any such settlement must have the approval of President Jefferson.[109]

Pinkney, like King, was strongly convinced that Maryland's best chance was to concur in the transfer to the crown—rather than proceed by another Chancery procedure (an "Information") towards a definitive settlement of all claims, which might take several years and could be appealed to the House of Lords. However, to get such a transfer expeditiously, it was necessary to obtain the concurrence of Henry Harford, who had blocked the same in April 1803. Harford then had asked for £10,000 in Bank stock (worth perhaps £17,000), while the Maryland Council had since authorized a payment not to exceed £10,000 sterling cash.[110] Nevertheless, Pinkney pushed on with great firmness of purpose, ingenuity and political nerve. He decided to raise Maryland's offer from £10,000 to £11,000 cash, equivalent to £7,746:10 Bank stock at current prices, and persuaded the Hanbury executors (Barclay et al.), whose claim was based on an assignment from Maryland, to contribute £2253:10 in Bank stock from their claim to make up the £10,000 Bank stock demanded by Harford. With that gentleman taken care of, the government caused much less trouble. Pinkney used the assistance of the new American minister, Monroe, to obtain introductions to Lord Hawkesbury and the attorney general, Spencer Perceval, and, after a conference with the latter in November 1803, persuaded him to renew the government's efforts to obtain the transfer of the stock to the crown.[111] Appropriate notice for the attorney general was given on December 14 and this time there were no objections from Harford. On the sixteenth and twenty-first, Lord Eldon considered the matter yet again and ordered that, after deducting legal expenses all around, the balance of the trust be transferred from the accountant general of the Court of Chancery (its custodian since 1784) to a person to be named by the king by his sign manual (personal signature).[112]

Though the resumption of the war against France in May 1803 should have made the British ministers rather anxious to be done with this unending affair, many months were to elapse before the transfer ordered by Lord Eldon in December 1803 could be effected. It took until the end of February 1804 to get the eight sets of legal fees settled. Then the king's mental illness made it impossible to think of asking for his sign manual for several months.[113] Nor were matters hastened by the resignation of Addington and his replacement at the Treasury by William Pitt (10 May). In the new ministry, the earl of Harrowby replaced Hawkesbury at the Foreign Office. Meanwhile, another minor interest reappeared to delay matters a few months more.

The British owners of unredeemed prewar Maryland paper money had never formally entered the Chancery litigation, though they had frequently petitioned the government for compensation out of the Bank stock. They now renewed their applications and reminded the government of their unanswered memorials of 1802 and 1803.[114] The claim was called to the attention of the attorney general and solicitor general, who reported on 28 April 1804 that the paper money holders had "a Claim upon the Justice of the Crown, but which Claim cannot be sustained in any Court in Westm[inste]r Hall or otherwise than by Petition or Memorial." That is, the claim of the paper money holders was moral or political, but not legal.[115] Nevertheless, Lord Hawkesbury's undersecretary, Hammond, in conversations with Pinkney, tried to get Maryland to agree to pay off the paper money holders as part of the final settlement. Pinkney adamantly refused. He realized that the bona fide holdings of the paper money (in the hands of old merchants and émigrés) perhaps came to £8000 but could go much higher if any of the claims of speculators were recognized. Any such settlement was far beyond his authorization. The departure of Lord Hawkesbury from office facilitated things, but first he had to spend several months educating Lord Harrowby about the whole matter. In the end, Harrowby agreed to accept a simple letter from Pinkney assuring him that "justice" would be done by Maryland to the holders of the paper money. (In the end, they got nothing.)[116]

After every conceivable delay and the frequent postponement of Pinkney's departure for Maryland, on 29 July 1804 the king signed the warrant naming Joseph White, solicitor to the Treasury, as the person to whom the stock should be transferred, and who should hold it until otherwise instructed by royal warrant. Next, Pinkney had to get the attorney general to obtain from the Court of Chancery a final order (6 August) for the transfer to White. Its execution required a further warrant from the king, which was not signed until the thirteenth. Pinkney had by then left London to catch his homeward-bound ship between Gravesend and Deal but was summoned back to London because the warrant named only him to receive Maryland's share. He rushed back to London, effected the necessary transfers on the fourteenth and fifteenth and then proceeded posthaste to Falmouth in Cornwall, where the ship had agreed to wait. It cost him £200 for holding up the ship, but he was able to return to America with his family and the satisfaction of two jobs (the claims commission and the Bank stock) well done.[117] It is ironic that a matter under litigation in the Court of Chancery for more than twenty years should have had to be finished in such a breathless rush.

On 14 August 1804, the ledgers of the Bank of England show that stock with a face value of £100,940:0:1 (worth over £160,000 at the current price of ca. 160) was transferred from the accountant general of Chancery (in trust) to Joseph White, Esq., of Lincoln's Inn. The next day (15 August), White transferred £10,000 to Henry Harford of New Cavendish Street, Esq., and the balance of £90,940 to "William Pinkney of Baltimore in America Esq. . . . for the use & benefit of the State of Maryland." That same day, Pinkney transferred stock with a face value of £19,910 to David Barclay & Co. for the interest of the late firm of Osgood Hanbury & Co., and the balance of £71,030 to James Monroe, the American minister, who was to hold the same, pending instructions from Maryland.[118] In addition, the cash balance in the trust (from which the legal expenses had already been deducted) and some miscellaneous bank paper (analagous to modern bonds) in which part of the interest had been invested were also divided between Barclay et al. and Maryland in the same proportions. The Barclay share represented the £11,000 worth of stock (with accumulated dividends) transferred by Maryland to the estate and partners of Osgood Hanbury in 1787 in settlement of the Hanbury's mortgage on the Dulany lands.

An accounting of the Maryland Bank stock trust as of 15 August 1804 would appear to be roughly:[119]

Accumulation

	Face Value		Market Value
Bank Stock	£100,940: 0: 1	at 160	£161,504: 0: 2
Bank 5% annuities (1797)	8,314:16: 1	at par	8,314:16: 1
Bank 5% annuities (navy)	6,976: 1: 8	at par	6,976: 1: 8
Cash	5,865: 7: 5	at par	5,865: 7: 5
Cash spent on legal fees	3,487: 7: 6	—	3,487: 7: 6
Total accumulation	£125,583:12: 9		£186,147:12:10

Disposition

	Face Value		Market Value
To Hanbury Estate	£10,000 Bank stock	at 160	£16,000
To Henry Harford			
Lloyd (Hanbury estate)	£19,910 Bank stock	at 160	£31,856
	1,825 5% ann. (1797)	at par	1,825
	1,531 5% ann. (navy)	at par	1,531
	1,237 cash	—	1,237
	£24,503		£36,449

	Face Value (Con'td.)		Market Value (Con'td.)
Chase's commission	£ 4,037 Bank stock	at 160	£ 6,459: 4: 0
Pinkney's expenses	£ 500 cash	—	£ 500
Legal expenses (Feb.)	£ 3,487: 7: 6		
(Feb.)	210: 0: 0		
	£ 3,697: 7: 6	—	£ 3,697: 7: 6
To Maryland	£ 66,993: 0: 1 Bank stock	at 160	£107,188:16: 2
	6,489:16: 1 5% ann. (1797)	at par	6,489:16: 1
	5,445: 1: 8 5% ann. (navy)	at par	5,445: 1: 8
	3,918: 7: 5 cash	—	3,918: 7: 5
	£ 82,846: 5: 3		£123,042: 1: 4
Total Disbursements	£125,583:12: 9		£186,147:12:10

Many of the items on the above account were only tentatively settled by Pinkney in August 1804. He had allowed Chase's four percent commission only on the Bank stock, leaving the rest of the commission (on the other items received) to be settled when Chase closed his accounts with the state and accounted for both the sums advanced him for expenses and the sums paid in London for legal expenses (his responsibility). Some years later, the settling of these accounts led to a lawsuit between Maryland and Samuel Chase.[120] More generously, Pinkney, who was indebted to Osgood Hanbury's son Sampson for much valuable assistance and advice, tentatively allowed the Hanbury executors (Barclay and Lloyd) their full claim, though he had doubts about part of it. They subsequently refunded a small part to Maryland when the state insisted that the Hanbury estate was entitled to the accumulation on the original £11,000 stock granted only from Chase's conveyance in 1787 and not from the act of legislature.[121]

The energy and acumen of Pinkney's efforts were genuinely appreciated. After the conveyance of August 1804, William Murdock, Chase's financial agent in London, wrote that Maryland would not have gotten a farthing had it not been for Pinkney. He suggested a reward of £4000. Monroe was equally generous in praise. In the event, the legislature awarded Pinkney $12,000 in consideration of his great and successful efforts.[122]

When Pinkney left England in August 1804, the securities and cash belonging to Maryland were left in the hands and name of the American minister in London, James Monroe. The Maryland authorities in April 1805 entrusted responsibility for the sale of the Bank stock and other assets in London and the remittance of the proceeds homeward to Joseph Hopper

Nicholson, a local Republican politician and friend and confidant of Jefferson's secretary of the Treasury, Gallatin.[123] To avoid loss of interest on the funds during the period of remittance, Nicholson, who was very knowledgeable on financial matters, advised the Maryland authorities to sell the stock and other assets in London and convert the proceeds there into American government bonds (even though they were higher in England than America), which could then be remitted. The details of carrying out this plan were entrusted to Monroe and George W. Erving, the United States consul in London and Nicholson's London correspondent.[124]

Monroe and Erving found out that trying to sell more than £100,000 worth of Bank shares quickly on the London stock exchange was likely to depress the market and lead to a loss by the state. Instead, on 8 August 1805, Monroe reached a private and quite favorable agreement with Francis Baring & Co., merchants and bankers of London and financial agents of the United States government. By this arrangement, Barings agreed to buy Maryland's securities at the following rates:

£67,421: 0: 1 face value Bank stock at 176 1/2	£118,998: 1: 3
£ 5,445: 1: 8 face value Bank 5% annuities (navy) at 89 1/2	4,873: 6: 9
£ 6,489:16: 1 face value Bank 5% annuities (1797) at par	6,489:16: 1
Total	£130,361: 4: 1

Barings agreed to pay for these securities in two months (8 October) in any combination of the following:

6% or deferred 6% U.S. stock [bonds] at 95
8% U.S. stock at 104
Bills of exchange with Barings' indorsement, payable in Washington, Baltimore, Philadelphia, or New York at sixty days sight on average (payable upon an average at sixty days after presentation) at the rate of 4s.6d. sterling to the dollar with a one percent premium.[125]

Between 8 and 11 October, in return for the £131,719:19:9 covered by the agreement of 8 August (the £130,361:4:1 shown above plus some cash received from Monroe and the Hanbury executors), Barings delivered to Monroe the following effects:[126]

U.S. 6% stock at 95	£ 5,560: 1: 4
U.S. deferred 6% stock at 95	49,645:18: 8
U.S. 8% stock at 104	14,367:12: 0
Total of U.S. stock [bonds]	69,573:12: 0
Bills of exchange on U.S. at 1% premium	62,146: 6: 9
Grand total	£131,719:18: 9

In addition, Monroe by then had in his custody £8632:17:4 cash representing dividends received during the past year or so. Barings expressed lack of interest in handling this owing to their heavy commitments on the main transaction. In the end, they agreed to furnish bills of exchange for this too, but at a 3 percent premium. The bills delivered on 14 October, like many of the others, were drawn on Robert Gilmor & Sons of Baltimore.[127] That liquidated the last of Maryland's trust fund in London.

The papers now available in the "Bank Stock Papers" in the Hall of Records do not contain a final accounting of the remittance business handled by Nicholson. A partial accounting from Barings contains some obvious errors corrected in a later account. Our own recalculation suggests the following semifinal account of the ultimate disposal of the Bank stock at current values:

To Maryland	£140,352:16: 1
To Hanbury Estate	36,449: 0: 0
To Henry Harford	16,000: 0: 0
To Samuel Chase (unsettled)	6,459: 4: 0
To William Pinkney ($12,000 + £500)	3,200: 0: 0
To legal expenses (London)	3,697: 7: 6
Total	£206,158: 7: 7

In the end, therefore, despite the resolution of the Maryland legislature in 1797 that Rufus King should accept nothing rather than give up Maryland's claim to the whole, the state received a shade under 70 percent of this "million dollar deal." Of course, in 1775 the trust fund had only been worth £41,180. Such are life's lessons and the wonders of compound interest.

Maryland had no immediate plans for the use of funds received and was embarrassed by the large proportion received in cash. Nicholson placed his cash balances temporarily in the Farmers Bank in Baltimore until he could convert them into United States bonds. He completed this work, turned over the bonds to the treasurer of the Western Shore and settled his accounts by 4 December 1806.[128] It would probably take a major research effort in the state accounts to determine exactly how the money received from the Bank stock trust was eventually spent, if the question could be answered at all. We do know that in 1812, $30,000 of Maryland's holdings of 6 percent U.S. bonds were lent to the Potomac Company.[129] In all likelihood, much of the balance eventually ended up in internal improvements of one sort or another. Whether they were profitable or not, that was a not ignoble end to the long history of the state's earlier investments in the stock of the Bank of England.

The long and complicated history of the Bank stock case is essentially the story of the "nationalization" of a local concern. In the colonial period, Maryland's property rights existed within the confines of English law and the protection of English courts. In the immediate postwar years Maryland, through Samuel Chase, sought to reassert some of these rights—those pertaining to the Bank stock—in the accustomed prewar way and came to grief. In the eyes of the British authorities, Maryland was part of the United

States and its claims could be considered only in the context of the general settlement of all British and American claims and counterclaims. Only when Maryland's cause was taken up seriously by the United States representatives in London, and only when British–American relations reached an appropriate conjuncture, could Maryland's claims find their equitable solution—a solution determined by the equity of diplomacy and not that of Chancery.

NOTES

1. Morris L. Radoff, *Calendar of Maryland State Papers, No. 2: The Bank Stock Papers,* Hall of Records Publication No. 5 (Annapolis, 1947), hereafter cited as *Cal.*

2. The principal modern works are Bradford Perkins, *The First Rapprochement: England and the United States 1795–1805* (Philadelphia, 1955); and Charles Ritcheson, *Aftermath of Revolution: British Policy toward the United States 1783–1795* (Dallas, 1969).

3. The most important of these have been published in Charles R. King, ed., *The Life and Correspondence of Rufus King,* 6 vols. (New York, 1894–1900); hereafter cited as *King.* The papers calendared by Radoff are much more complete than those found elsewhere because King and Monroe transferred many of their papers on the Bank stock to William Pinkney, who presented them to the State of Maryland; cf. HR [Hall of Records] Blue Book 2:90 (*Cal.,* no. 203), Pinkney to [Gov. Bowie], 3 Nov. 1804.

4. Particularly in FO [Foreign Office] 5/7, 20, 21, 27, 28, 31, 34, 37, 44.

5. Particularly PRO [Public Record Office] T.S.11/689/2186, ff. 1–52.

6. Including Michael G. Kammen, *A Rope of Sand: The Colonial Agents, British Politics, and the American Revolution* (Ithaca, 1968) and Jack M. Sosin, *Agents and Merchants: British Colonial Policy and the Origins of the American Revolution, 1763–1775* (Lincoln, Nebraska, 1965).

7. William Hand Browne et al., eds., *Archives of Maryland,* 72 vols. (Baltimore, 1883–), 30:627–32; hereafter cited as *Archives.*

8. Ibid., 459, 585; cf. also ibid. 449–50, 455–57, 462, 563, 575–76, 578–81, 584–87, 596–97; ibid., 33:14–15, 100.

9. On the Hydes, see Jacob M. Price, *France and the Chesapeake: A History of the French Tobacco Monopoly, 1674–1791, and of Its Relationship to the British and American Tobacco Trades,* 2 vols. (Ann Arbor, 1973), 1:514–15, 523, 533–534, 536, 586, 651–54, 657, 659, 662, 1007–8, 1016–17, 1058; Charles Albro Barker, *The Background of the Revolution in Maryland* (New Haven, 1940), pp. 74, 84, 88; *Archives* 37:585–86. John Hyde of Poplar, Middlesex (1655–1732), left three sons, Samuel, John, and Herbert, and four daughters, Anna Snelling, Ann Letten, Jane, and Althea. For his will, see PRO Prob. 11/656 (Prerogative Court of Canterbury [hereafter PCC] 11 Price).

10. *Archives* 36:51–52.

11. Ibid., 39:158; 25:514.

12. Ibid., 39:105–6.

13. Barker, *Background of the Revolution,* pp. 73, 88; cf. also *Archives* 38:441.

14. W. Marston Acres, "Directors of the Bank of England," *Notes & Queries* 179 (3 Aug. 1940):83. In 1727, Hunt acquired the Manor House, Woodford, Essex, where he died in 1767. His will (PCC 225 Legard) is in PRO Prob. 11/929; cf. also *Archives* 40:73, 161, 179, 182–83, 390–91, 401; ibid., 28:31, 50, 175–76, 211, 292, 297, 307, 319, 343, 348, 351–52, 354, 391, 408.

15. *Archives* 44:297–300, 355, 358, 694–95; ibid., 46:227–28. Cruikshank appears to have absconded, while Samuel Hyde settled with his creditors in England for 10s. in the £ before his death in 1748; see his will (PCC 178 Strahan) in PRO Prob. 11/762. His brothers John and Herbert continued to be active in London as directors of the London Assurance. The complete (1734–67) set of trustees' accounts in the Scharf Collection, Maryland Historical Society, shows that Cruikshank last signed the accounts in April 1743, and S. Hyde in June 1747. Adams and Hanbury first signed in October 1748.

16. *Archives* 44:652–53; 46:371, 387, 417–19; 52:293, 434, 436; 28:390, 464, 472–73; 31:46, 398, 413–14; 32:49; cf. J. Reaney Kelly, "Portraits by Sir Joshua Reynolds. Return to Tulip Hill," *Maryland Historical Magazine* 62 (1967):64–67.

17. In 1759, friends tried to get a trustee's place for William Anderson, Maryland merchant in London, who was connected to several prominent Eastern Shore families, *Archives* 31:475–76, 479–81, 506–7, 513, 517, 543, 545; 32:220; 55:liii, 24–25, 533–34; 56:xlii, 409, 413, 415; 61:290–91, 348–49; 6:15, 67, 120, 184–85, 240, 401, 423; 9:35, 38–43, 88–89, 128–29, 172, 263, 279, 338–39, 371, 435–38, 515–16, 544; 14:250–52, 255, 399, 407, 416, 482, 488–89; cf. also A. Audrey Locke, *The Hanbury Family,* 2 vols. (London, 1916), vol. 2, ch. 13, and PRO T.1/656/999, ff. 279–87.

18. *Archives* 62:133–44; see also William Kilty, *The Laws of Maryland,* 2 vols. (Annapolis, 1799, 1800), Acts 1769, ch. 14.

19. In 1766 Grove remarried. His second wife, Louise, was the daughter of Edward Hillersden, Hamburg merchant of London; see his will (CC 24 Adderly) in PRO Prob. 11, and *Gentleman's Magazine* 70 (2) (1800):1010; cf. also n. 16.

20. Some correspondence of James Russell has survived at Coutts's Bank, London. For the Russell family, see James Paterson, *Scottish Surnames: Contribution to Genealogy* (Edinburgh, 1866), pp. 55–58. For the Maryland Lees, see Edmund Jennings Lee, *Lee of Virginia* (Philadelphia, 1895), pp. 96–101, 148–61, 304–6. I expect to publish a fully documented paper on James Russell in the *Maryland Historical Magazine* in July 1977.

21. *Archives* 64:54, 103. The trustees' accounts for 1767–73 are in Ms. 2018, Maryland Historical Society.

22. PRO C.12/446/3.

23. On him, cf. Jacob M. Price, "Joshua Johnson in London, 1771–1775," in *Statesmen, Scholars and Merchants: Essays in Eighteenth Century History,* Anne Whiteman et al. (Oxford, 1973), pp. 153–80; and Edward C. Papenfuse, *In Pursuit of Profit: The Annapolis Merchants in the Era of the American Revolution, 1763–1805* (Baltimore, 1975), passim.

24. Kilty, *Laws of Maryland,* Acts 1769, ch. 14; Acts 1773, ch. 26; Acts Nov. 1779, ch. 38.

25. *Archives* 43:50–51.

26. PRO T.1/582/154, ff. 131–32 (memorial of James Russell). Cf. also PRO C.12/2135/32. Franklin's letter of 20 May 1780 is quoted in Russell's answer of 3 June 1784 in PRO C.12/446/3.

27. HR Blue Book 2:43(*Cal.,* no. 1) Franklin to T. S. Lee, 11 Aug. 1780.

28. Kilty, *Laws of Maryland,* Acts June 1780, ch. 24, art. vi, provided that if the trustees paid the bills of exchange or transferred the stock, an equivalent amount of their own property in the state would be exempt from seizure.

29. *Archives* 45:131–33, 142, 144–45; PRO A.O.12/9, f. 16; cf. also n. 26.

30. Kilty, *Laws of Maryland,* Acts Oct. 1780, ch. 45; cf. also chs. 49 and 51. Subsequent legislation clarified procedures for selling the iron works, ibid., Acts May 1781, ch. 33; Nov. 1781, ch. 2; Apr. 1782, ch. 60.

31. PRO A.O.12/9, ff. 10–12 (claim of Ann Russell).

32. PRO T.1/582/154.

33. Cf. Ritcheson, *Aftermath of Revolution,* ch. 4; PRO T.S.11/689/2186, f. 105.

34. HR Blue Book 3:6 (*Cal.,* no. 2).

35. Bank of England Record Office, Roehampton: Bank Stock Ledger 55:840, 1010.

36. Kilty, *Laws of Maryland,* Acts Apr. 1783, ch. 35; HR Blue Book 3:1–4 (*Cal.,* nos. 3–7); cf. *Archives* 48:425–26; and Maryland Historical Society Ms. 1235 for Chase's bond of 13 June 1783. On Chase, subsequently a Supreme Court justice, cf. *Dictionary of American Biography* 4:34–37; David Curtis Skaggs, *Roots of Maryland Democracy, 1753–1776* (Westport, Conn., 1973); and Ronald Hoffman, *A Spirit of Dissension: Economics, Politics, and the Revolution in Maryland* (Baltimore, 1973).

37. HR Blue Book 3:25, 14 (*Cal.,* nos. 9, 12) Chase to Gov. Paca, 23 Feb., 31 Mar./1 Apr. 1784.

38. PRO C.12/2135/32 (*Russell* v. *Bank*), Russell's bill.

39. HR Blue Book 3:14, 23 (*Cal.,* nos. 12, 14) Chase to Gov. Paca, 1, 20 Apr. 1784; cf. also 13 (*Cal.* no. 11) for the subpoena of 28 March.

40. HR Blue Book 3:19 (*Cal.*, no. 15), Chase to Paca, 20 May 1784; PRO C.12/2135/32 (Chase's demurrer, 18 May 1784); C.12/446/3 (*Chase* v. *Russell* et al.: Chase's bill, 28 Apr. 1784).

41. PRO Prob. 11/1059 (PCC 494 Warburton) for W. Ewer's will, 1779; C. 12/1071/18 (*Ewers* v. *Russell* et al.: Ewers' bill, 6 May 1784); C.12/446/3 (*Chase* v. *Russell* et al., Ewer's answer, 17 July 1784); HR Blue Book 3:19 (*Cal.*, no. 15), Chase to Paca, 20 May 1784.

42. HR Blue Book 3:8 (*Cal.*, no. 17), Chase to Paca, 9 June 1784; 2:157 (*Cal.*, no. 18) for writ of execution of court signed by outgoing and new Master of the Rolls, 11 June 1784; cf. also PRO C.12/446/3 for Russell's answer of 3 June to Chase's bill.

43. HR Blue Book 3:9, 5, 16 (*Cal.*, nos. 19, 21, 26), Chase to Paca, 17, 22 July, 14 Aug. 1784; Blue Book 3:18 (*Cal.*, no. 23), Chase to Pitt, 3 Aug. 1784; PRO C.12/2135/32 (Answer of Bank, 26 Aug. 1784). There was a further hearing in Chancery on 28 July in which the lord chancellor allowed Chase's demurrer to Russell's bill, but the case was carried no further.

44. See below, pp. 00.

45. HR Blue Book 3:21 (*Cal.*, no. 24), Chase to W. and J. Lyon, 9 Aug. 1784.

46. Kilty, *Laws of Maryland*, Acts Nov. 1784, ch. 76; Kilty et al., *Laws of Maryland, 7*: Res., 1784, no. 2; HR Blue Book 3:24 (*Cal.*, no. 28), Chase to Paca, 21 Dec. 1784; cf. also Blue Book 2:100, 165 (*Cal.*, nos. 29, 31).

47. Kilty, *Laws of Maryland*, Acts Nov. 1785, ch. 88.

48. HR Blue Book 2:93 (*Cal.*, no. 32), Gov. Smallwood to Chase, 7 July 1786; *Archives* 71:120; Bank Record Office, Bank Stock Ledger 59:L, f. 36.

49. PRO T.S.11/689/2186, f. 2; Kilty, *Laws of Maryland*, Acts Nov. 1786, ch. 50.

50. HR Blue Book 2:29, 35 (*Cal.*, nos. 44, 63). For Chase's authorization to compromise (28 May 1787) and his own instructions to Uriah Forrest in London, see Maryland Historical Society Ms. 1195 (*Cal.*, nos. 36 and 39). Forrest was authorized to go to £22,525:10:2 for a settlement with the Russells, the Ewers and the Buchanans.

51. HR Blue Book 2:137 (*Cal.*, no. 33).

52. These are, of course, the great names of the London Quaker *haute bourgeoisie*. Barclay and Lloyd describe themselves as "bankers of London," Gurney as "banker of Norwich," and John Hanbury as "brewer of London."

53. PRO T.S.11/689/2186, ff. 2–7; C.12/2157/4, membrane 1.

54. PRO C. 12/2153/15 (14 Feb. 1789). For his will (probated 4 Sept. 1788), see PRO Prob. 11/1170 (PCC 455 Calvert).

55. PRO T.S.11/689/2186, ff. 11–21; C.12/1261/7.

56. PRO C.12/2158/1 and T.S.11/689/2186. ff. 53–71 for Harford's bill of 24 July 1789, with attached replies of other parties concerned, 1789–90.

57. See preceding and PRO C.12/2157/4, C.12/2153/15, T.S.11/689/2186, ff. 7–46, and Bank Record Office, Bank Stock Ledger 59:L, f. 46. On the Russell claims, see PRO T.29/62, pp. 122, 226; A.O.12/9, ff. 10–17; A.O.13/92, ff. 421–36; and for the related claims of the Buchanan trustees, see T.1/656/210, ff. 7–10.

58. PRO T.S.11/689/2186, f. 120(5). Chase was optimistic enough about a settlement in 1791 to obtain an act of the Maryland legislature empowering him to appoint trustees in London to receive and sell the Bank stock, Kilty, *Laws of Maryland*, Acts Nov. 1791, ch. 86.

59. HR Blue Book 2:21 (*Cal.*, no. 46); cf. also 2:29, 1, 70 (*Cal.*, nos. 44, 45, 49); PRO T.S.11/689/2186, ff. 123–24.

60. PRO T.S.11/689/2186, ff. 114–15, 120(5).

61. See n. 48 and Maryland Historical Society Ms. 1195 (*Cal.*, no. 37), Gov. Smallwood to J. Adams, 8 June 1787.

62. Cf. n. 2 and Samuel Flagg Bemis, *Jay's Treaty* (New York, 1923). For the work of the commissioners, see John Bassett Moore, ed., *International Adjudications: Modern Series, 6* vols. (New York, 1929–33), esp. vol. 3 (Philadelphia commission), and vol. 4 (London commission).

63. Perkins, *The First Rapprochement*, pp. 116–19.

64. On Pinkney, see *Dictionary of American Biography*, and Henry Wheaton, *Some Account of the Life, Writings, and Speeches of William Pinkney* (New York, 1826).

65. HR Blue Book 2:25, 26 (*Cal.*, nos. 47, 48), T.S. Lee and Council to Randolph, 3 May, John Henry to same, 23 May 1794.

66. HR Blue Book 2:124 (*Cal.*, no. 50).
67. PRO FO 5/20, ff. 113–14 (R. King to Grenville, 10 Feb. 1797, printed in *King* 2:144–45); FO 95/370 (Grenville to law officers, 15 Feb., 28 July, 16 Nov. 1797); cf. also HR Blue Book 2:114, 171, 67, 30 (*Cal.*, nos. 51–54).
68. HR Blue Book 2:2 (*Cal.*, no. 70); PRO FO 83/2204, ff. 186–87.
69. HR Blue Book 2:173A, B, C (*Cal.*, nos. 59–61) R. King to Pickering, 7 July, to Loughborough, 19 June 1797 and enclosure; PRO T.29/70 p. 196 (Treasury minutes, 18 Mar. 1797); T.29/72, p. 369 (Treasury minutes, 7 Apr. 1798); FO 5/20, ff. 131–34, 237–40 (Mrs. Russell's memorial, 15 Feb. 1797, J. Wilmot's report, 30 Mar. 1797); FO 5/21, ff. 171–72 (J. Scott to Hammond, [July 1797]); cf. also HR Blue Book 2:173, 98, 89, 136 (*Cal.*, nos. 55–58). The last indicates that in Dec. 1796, Bank stock was selling at 143, making the £74,401 face value worth £106,393. Mrs. Russell appears to have been paid shortly after 7 Apr. 1798. The chancellor was in touch with Molleson, Mrs. Russell's son-in-law, in February–March 1798 and may have been instrumental in obtaining the payment for Mrs. Russell, PRO FO 5/24, f. 67 (King to [Hammond], 2 Feb. 1798). King was kept in touch with Molleson's intentions through Sampson Hanbury, HR Blue Book 2:12, 5, 4, 4A, 8, 9 (*Cal.*, nos. 73–78). The Ewers' and Buchanans' parallel claims were allowed £8,000 each by the commissioners and apparently paid by 1798. PRO A.O. 12/109, f. 51v; *King* 2:473 (King to Grenville, 1 Dec. 1798); New York Public Library, Mss. Div., Chalmers Papers: Maryland 2:32–35.
70. HR Blue Book 2:173B (*Cal.*, no. 62), R. King to Pickering, 15 July 1797.
71. PRO FO 5/21, ff. 149–50, 161 (King to Grenville, 19, 20 July 1797, printed in *King* 2:202–3); cf. also ff. 155–56 (King to Loughborough, 19 July 1797 and enclosure).
72. Kilty et al., *Laws of Maryland* 7: Res. 1797, nos. 17–21; HR Blue Book 2:23 (*Cal.*, no. 72); *King* 2:281–82. Some speculators in 1797 offered the state £100,000 current money for the Bank stock, then worth about £110,000 sterling or £188,333 current money. HR Blue Book 2:135 (*Cal.*, no. 63). For Chase's correspondence at this time, see HR Blue Book 2:134, 77, 133, 132 (*Cal.*, nos. 65–67, 71). Some in Maryland thought that after 1798 the British government wanted the state to reimburse the crown for the compensation paid to Russell et al; cf. Maryland Historical Society, Vertical File, Chase to J. McHenry, 19 Jan. 1799, Pickering to R. King, 6 Aug. 1799, with Chase's memorandum of 5 Aug. 1799.
73. *King* 2:265–66, 273–74, 323–24, 473, 566; 3:137, 271–74 (King to Pickering, 28 Dec. 1797 [also in HR Blue Book 2:48 and *Cal.*, no. 68 under date, 25 Dec.], 15 Mar., 21 Oct. 1799; to Loughborough, 19 Jan., 1 June 1798; to Grenville, 1 Dec. 1798; to Dundas, 11 July 1800); cf. also HR Blue Book 2:47 (*Cal.*, no 83) Chase to Gov Ogle, 20 Apr. 1799, which shows that by Nov. 1798 the stock had reached £83,148 face value, at 142 worth £118,070 sterling.
74. PRO FO 5/34, ff. 220–21 (retrospective notes sent by King to Addington in his of 3 Nov. 1801); cf. *King* 4:10.
75. PRO FO 5/31, ff. 96–99 (G. Hamilton et al. to Grenville, Glasgow, 29 Mar. 1800); cf. also ff. 41B–42, 53–62, 96–97, 111–34, 141–67; cf. also FO 5/28 ff. 202, 299, 303, 307; FO 5/34 ff. 259–62.
76. PRO FO 5/28, ff. 305–6 (Glasgow memorial, 23 Nov. 1799); FO 5/31, ff. 199–200 (G. Hamilton and R. Findlay to Grenville, 31 May 1800), ff. 207–8 (Grenville to Hamilton and Findlay, 3 June), ff. 214–15, 220–21 (Hamilton et al. to Grenville, 9, 13 June), ff. 234–37 (Molleson to G. Hammond, 3 July, with enclosure), f. 282 (answer of 10 July 1800).
77. PRO FO 5/34, ff. 220–21; cf. also for merchants' input FO 5/31, ff. 190, 192, 194, 196–97, 281, 284–94.
78. *King* 3:335–37, 502–4 (King to Sec. of State, 23 Jan., 24 Aug. 1801); 3: 501–2 (King to Hawkesbury, 20 Aug. 1801=FO 5/34, ff. 209–10); PRO FO 5/31, ff. 332–50, 406, 410–35 (Thomas Macdonald to Grenville, 10 Oct. 1800, with enclosure [important for political background in U.S.], to G. Hammond, 5, 11, Dec. 1800, with enclosure); FO 5/34, ff. 70–72 (King to Hawkesbury, 9 Mar, 1801, with enclosure), f. 94 (newspaper clipping on Jefferson's debts), ff. 138–39 (Macdonald to Hamilton, 4 May 1801), ff. 209–13 (for project).
79. Perkins, *First Rapprochement,* 130, 138–41; *King* 3:520, 527–34, 4:7–8, 10, 17–18, 31–32, 36–37, 44, 47–50, 54–56.
80. *King* 3:376 (King to Sec. of State, 23 Jan. 1801).
81. PRO FO 5/35, ff. 70–72, 79–81 (King to Hawkesbury, 9 Mar. 1801, with enclosures); cf. HR Blue Book 2:49 (*Cal.*, no. 89).

82. PRO FO 5/34, ff. 214–15 (King to Hammond, 22 Aug. 1801); cf. 209–10, to Hawkesbury, 20 Aug. 1801.

83. *King* 3:477–78, 514, 517–18 (to Eldon, 22 June, 10, 24 Sept.), p. 507 (to Sampson Hanbury, 29 Aug. 1801); PRO FO 5/34, ff. 226–27 (R. King to G. Hammond, 3 Sept. 1801); cf. also HR Blue Book 2:16, 17 (*Cal.*, nos. 90, 91).

84. *King* 3:530, 533–34 (King's "Note of conferences . . . ").

85. Ibid., 4:48 (King to Madison, 9 Jan. 1802).

86. HR Blue Book 2:29 (*Cal.*, no. 44), Chase's "Observations."

87. PRO FO 5/7, ff. 422–23 (memorial on behalf of Perry, Hay & Co. of Bristol; Robert Christie, Daniel Dulany, Robert Alexander [former member of Congress], and John Banytine of London; James Christie and Alexander Stenhouse of Fife, Scotland; James Miller and John Mason of Glasgow; and Hugh Dean of Shelburne, Nova Scotia, later of Nassau, Bahamas).

88. PRO FO 5/27, ff. 209–10 (memorial for same, plus Rev. Gilbert Buchanan of Woodmansterne, Surrey [probably son of John Buchanan] and Henry Riddle of Glasgow). The memorialists claimed that the issue of 1769 was also backed by Bank stock; cf. Northampton-shire Record Office, Fitzwilliam–Burke Mss. A. xxvi. 7 for memorandum describing Alexander as the chief manager of the note holders in the 1780s and 1790s.

89. New York Public Library, Mss. Div., Chalmers Papers, Maryland 2:28–46; PRO FO 5/40, ff. 15–17 (memorial of 3 Feb, 1803 to Treasury, enclosing [ff. 18–20] earlier petition to king in council); T.29/80, pp. 412–13. For value of trust, 1 Dec. 1801, see HR Blue Book 2:160 (*Cal.*, no. 93).

90. HR Blue Book 2:76 (*Cal.*, no. 99), R. King to Madison, 9 Jan. 1802; 2:131, 128 (*Cal.*, nos. 100, 111), S. Chase to Gov. Mercer, 13 Feb., 24 Dec. 1802; 3::22 (*Cal.*, no. 101), Mercer to Madison, 16 Feb. 1802; 2:112 (*Cal.*, no. 102), Madison to Mercer, 23 Feb. 1802; 2:130 (*Cal.*, no. 103), Chase to Mercer, 14 Apr. 1802. Cf. also 2:46, 129 (*Cal.*, nos. 92, 104); see esp. *King* 4:182–83 (W. Hindman to King, 21 Nov. 1802), and PRO FO 95/24 (from E. Thornton [No. 53], 28 Dec. 1802).

91. HR Blue Book 2:32 (Cal., no. 117); cf. also 2:123 (*Cal.*, no. 118).

92. PRO T.S.11/689/2186, ff. 112–13.

93. HR Blue Book 2:18, 3 (*Cal.*, nos. 106–112); PRO T.S.11/689/2186, ff. 116–22.

94. PRO FO 5/37, f. 141 (King to Hawkesbury, 30 July 1802); *King* 4:156–58 (to Madison, 10 Aug. 1802), also in HR Blue Book 2:127 (*Cal.*, no. 105); cf. also Blue Book 2:75, 51 (*Cal.*, nos. 107, 108).

95. PRO T.29/79, p. 490.

96. *King* 4:190–91 (to Addington, 7 Dec. 1802); PRO FO 5/37, f. 216 (King to Hawkesbury, 9 Dec. 1802).

97. PRO FO 95/374, p. 39, copies in HR Blue Book 2:116A, 11 (*Cal.*, nos. 109–10).

98. HR Blue Book 2:19, 159, 126 (*Cal.*, nos. 119–120, 139); PRO T.S. 11/689/2186, ff. 123–24 (White's petition), ff. 126–29 (full text of chancellor's order).

99. HR Blue Book 2:167A (*Cal.*, no. 121), W. Lyon to William Murdock (Chase's agent), 14 Apr. 1803.

100. PRO T.S.11/689/2186. ff. 72–80 for attorney–general's information of 20 Apr. 1803; ff. 133–36 for brief of 23 Apr. prepared by the solicitor general, Thomas Manners Sutton; ff. 110–11 for opinion (probably by crown law officers) of ca. 27 Apr. 1803; ff. 96–102 for material relating to Harford's claim; HR Blue Book 2:22, 117, 117a (*Cal.*, nos. 123, 125, 126), King to Lyon and Collyer, 22, 26 Apr. 1803; *King* 4:247–48.

101. PRO FO 5/40, ff. 13, 84, 124–27 (King to Hawkesbury, 1 Feb., 28 Mar., to G. Hammond, 24 Apr., with enclosed draft); FO 95/440 (Hawkesbury to R. King, 25 Apr. 1803); also in HR Blue Book 2:11A, 116 (*Cal.*, nos. 126–27); cf. also *King* 4:215–17.

102. HR Blue Book 2:115 (*Cal.*, no. 129), King to Madison, 1 May 1803, also in *King* 4:247–48.

103. Acts 1801, ch. 103 in HR Blue Book 2:24 (*Cal.*, no. 95).

104. PRO FO 5/40, ff. 173, 208 (King to G. Hammond, Cowes, 20 May, Monroe to Hawkesbury, 20 July 1803).

105. HR Blue Book 2:31, 119, 52, 103 (*Cal.*, nos. 133, 131, 136, 141), Madison to Pinkney, 3 May (2 letters) (also in PRO FO 5/40, ff. 225–26); Madison to Gov. Mercer, 19 May 1803; Pinkney to Mercer, 11 July 1803.

106. HR Blue Book 2:115.

107. HR Blue Book 2:33 (*Cal.*, no. 137).

108. HR Blue Book 2:118, 125 (*Cal.*, nos. 140, 142), Chase to Mercer, Baltimore, 5, 11 July 1803.

109. HR Blue Book 2:108 (*Cal.*, no. 143). Cf. also 2:28A, 28, 35A (*Cal.*, nos. 147, 149, 150).

110. HR Blue Book 2:161, 162, 174 (*Cal.*, nos. 152, 151, 154) Pinkney to Mercer, 20 Sept. (2 letters), 22 Oct. 1803; cf. council order of 5 Aug. 1803 in Maryland Historical Society Ms. 1235.

111. PRO FO 5/40, ff. 221, 239 (Monroe to Hawkesbury, 29 Aug., 7 Sept, 1803); HR Sec. of State, no. 4 (*Cal.*, no. 156), Spencer Perceval to Monroe, 2 Nov. 1803; *King* 4:318–21 (C. Gore to R. King, 1 Nov. 1803); and HR Blue Book 2:90 (*Cal.*, no 164).

112. PRO T.S.11/689/2186, f. 132, contains notice to all parties of 14 Dec., sent by Treasury Solicitor Joseph White, acting for the attorney general, stating motion to be made on the twenty-first; ff. 137–40 contains minute of order to master from chancellor for settling legal expenses (also in HR Blue Book 2:109); ff. 141–52 contains chancellor's order of 21 Dec. On ff. 153–54 is a memorandum of ca. May 1804 indicating that the "Treas[ur]y have agreed to Transfer 10,000 Bank Stock to Mr. Hartford." Legal expenses were paid for Chase (£531:14:9), Barclay et al. (£741:13:2), Henry Harford (£523:13:3), the Ewers (£313:8:1), the Russells and Grove (£553:10:9), Buchanan's trustees (£359:13:2), the attorney general (£397:18:0), and the Bank of England (£65:16:4). Pinkney had to agree to assume all responsibility before Chase's solicitors, Lyon and Collyer, would agree to the transfer; HR Blue Book 2:35, 35B, 36 (*Cal.*, nos. 158, 159, 160); cf. also Blue Book 2:121 (*Cal.*, no. 162).

113. HR Blue Book 2:99 (*Cal.*, no. 164).

114. Cf. n. 89.

115. PRO FO 83/2204, f. 309 (J. Sargent to G. Hammond, 1 May 1804, encl. [ff. 311–12] opinion of 28 Apr.); also in T.S.11/689/2186, ff. 153–54; and FO 5/44. ff. 226–27.

116. HR Blue Book 2:95, 97, 106 (*Cal.*, nos. 202, 181, 199) Pinkney to Madison, 3 Nov., Harrowby to Pinkney, 14 Aug., Pinkney to Harrowby, 17 Aug. 1804; last also in PRO FO 5/44, f. 282. In 1806, Maryland provided for the redemption with interest of the bills of exchange and certificates issued in 1780 in exchange for the 1766 paper money called in. Nothing was done about outstanding paper money or "bills of credit," Kilty et al., *Laws of Maryland* 7: Res., 1806, nos. 8, 9; cf. also New York Public Library, Mss. Div., Chalmers Papers: Maryland, 2:52–59. The money holders were still seeking compensation in 1822.

117. HR Blue Book 2:95, 104 (*Cal.*, nos. 202, 175); PRO FO 5/44, ff. 242–43, 266, 272 (White to Huskisson, 2 Aug., Monroe to Harrowby, 11 Aug., Harrowby to Monroe, 13 Aug. 1804); T.S.11/689/2186, ff. 155–56, 158–61 (petition of White for attorney general, 3 Aug.), ff. 169–76 (Eldon's order of 6 Aug. 1804); cf. also FO 5/44, ff. 186, 224–25 (Monroe to Harrowby, 26 May, Pinkney to same, 2 July 1804); HR Blue Book 2:58, 55, 62 (*Cal.*, nos. 168, 176, 179); HR Sec. of State, no. 11 (*Cal.*, no. 177); cf. also S.M. Hamilton, ed., *The Writings of James Monroe*, 7 vols. (New York, 1898–1903), 4:233–34 (to Madison, 7 Aug. 1804).

118. Bank Record Office, Bank Stock Ledger 64:Q, f. 35; Ledger 67:T, f. 2350; Ledger 66:S, f. 1757.

119. HR Sec. of State, no. 12, Blue Book 2:102, 3:31 (*Cal.*, nos. 178, 193–94).

120. HR Sec. of State, nos. 11, 14 (*Cal.*, nos. 177, 190), Blue Book 2:59, 92, 95, 69, 72, 105, 42, 82, 85, 94, 172 (*Cal.*, nos. 191, 195, 202, 204, 209–10, 318–22).

121. HR Blue Book 2:39, 39A, 79, 95 (*Cal.*, nos. 185, 184, 187, 202); Sec. of State, nos. 11, 15, 21, 28 (*Cal.*, nos. 177, 197, 217, 226).

122. HR Blue Book 2:81, 113, 41, 54 (*Cal.*, nos. 196, 205, 211, 240), W. Murdock to Chase, 16 Aug. 1804; Madison to Pinkney, 16 Nov. 1804; General Assembly joint resolution of 19 Dec. 1804; Monroe to Gov. Bowie, 7 Aug. 1805; cf. also HR Sec. of State, nos. 19, 24, 25 (*Cal.*, nos. 215, 220, 222); Kilty et al., *Laws of Maryland* 7: Res. Nov. 1804, nos. 3–5.

123. HR Sec. of State, nos. 29, 33 (*Cal.*, nos. 223, 234) Gov. Bowie's certificate, 20 Apr. 1805, Gallatin to Monroe, 4 June 1805; cf. also Sec. of State, no. 26 and Blue Book 2:148 (*Cal.*, nos. 224, 221).

124. HR Blue Book 2:96, 146, 158/2 (*Cal.*, nos. 228–29), Nicholson to Gov. Bowie, 29 Apr., to Monroe, 22 May 1805; cf. also 2:66 (*Cal.*, no. 227).

125. HR. Sec. of State, nos. 41, 43, 58, 67, 70 (*Cal.*, nos. 244, 247, 281, 284), A. Baring to Erving, 8 Aug., Erving to A. Baring, 8 Aug., Sir Francis Baring & Co. to Monroe, 15, 29 Aug.

1805; cf. also Sec. of State, nos. 36–40, 46–57, 63–64 (*Cal.*, nos. 237–39, 241–42, 251–60, 263–64, 274–75); Blue Book 2:138/C–F, H, 84 (*Cal.*, nos. 261–62, 265–66, 278, 305).

126. HR Blue Book 2:144B, Sec. of State nos. 75–76 (*Cal.*, nos. 292–94); Francis Baring & Co. to Monroe, 8 Oct. 1805; cf. Blue Book 2:87 (*Cal.*, no 306) for an account by Nicholson.

127. HR Sec. of State nos. 72, 79, 80 (*Cal.*, nos. 287, 296, 299), Barings to Monroe, 3 Sept., Monroe to Barings, 12 Oct., Barings to Monroe, 14 Oct. 1805; cf. also nos. 69, 73, 81 (*Cal.*, nos. 283, 289, 302), and Blue Book 2:153, 153B (*Cal.*, nos. 279, 285).

128. HR Blue Book 2:155, 145, 156, 149, 150, 143, 158–1, 86, 147 (*Cal.*, nos. 308–16), Nicholson to Gov. Bowie, 30 Dec. 1805, 3, 11 Feb., 3 Mar., undated, 23, 26 Oct., 4, 6, Nov.; 2:154 (*Cal.*, no. 317), Resolution of General Assembly, 4 Dec. 1806 (also in Kilty et al., *Laws of Maryland* 7: Res. 1806, nos. 15–16).

129. Kilty et al., *Laws of Maryland* 7: Res. 1812, no. 6; cf. also. Res. 1813, no. 8.

TWO

THE DEVELOPMENT OF THE MARYLAND ORPHANS' COURT, 1654—1715

Lois Green Carr

The orphans' courts of Maryland and Virginia developed during the seventeenth century in response to a critical social need. A man who immigrated to the Chesapeake in the 1600s, regardless of his social class, had a short time to live compared even to Third World inhabitants today. He was unlikely to see any of his children come of age. A child had perhaps one chance in two of spending part of his childhood in the household of a stepfather or other guardian.[1] Legal protections for the persons and property of children were vital matters, especially in a land where settlement was scattered and settlers were predominantly newcomers.

There were two sides to the problem: nurture of the child and protection of his inheritance, if any, from embezzlement or waste. The executor of William Watts's estate, for example, put Watts's sons to hard labor in the fields "equall to any servt or Slave" with "noe manner of cloathes but such Raggs & old Clouts that scarce would cover their nakedness." William Hollis had three stepfathers in four years and only timely intervention by the judge of probate prevented the father's assets from paying the debts of his successors.[2] In a society where men well outnumbered women, young men on their death beds knew their wives would surely remarry. Wills often expressed concern that a stepfather might waste or steal the children's inheritance or treat the children as servants or let them grow up without education to enable them to improve what estate was left them.

Over much of the century, furthermore, there were no networks of kin to whom widows and orphans could turn for assistance. Most adult settlers of the seventeenth-century Chesapeake were immigrants, who had left their families 3,000 miles across an ocean. New family networks could not grow until the children of immigrants reached maturity and began to marry. The process was slow in Maryland, for reasons explained in the paper by Russell

Note: Lois Green Carr is the historian, St. Mary's City Commission, State of Maryland.

Menard. For example, in the 1660s, 84 percent of the testate men and women who died in St. Mary's County, Maryland, and left minor children behind them, mentioned no kin in their wills. For the 1670s the figure was still 62 percent. By the decade 1700 to 1710 the problem was disappearing. Only 24 percent of the testators who left minors mention no kin upon whom their families might rely. But until late in the century the absence of kin made some institutional substitute an urgent matter: hence the orphans' courts.

Similar demographic problems created similar needs and a similar institution in Virginia.[3] Orphan court jurisdiction appeared earlier there and probably influenced early Maryland development; but from the 1660s on, the laws of Maryland were more explicit than those of Virginia in establishing procedures and safeguards against abuses; and preliminary study of Virginia records suggests that from that time Virginia and Maryland practice began to diverge. Unfortunately, until detailed studies of the Virginia orphans' courts become available, comparison with those of Maryland cannot be carried far. This paper will be confined to a discussion of orphans' court jurisdiction in Maryland, with little regard for possible influences from or upon Virginia.

Provisions for care of Maryland orphans and their estates were part of a larger administrative structure for preserving assets of dead men, paying their creditors, and distributing the balance to the heirs. Control of probate was centralized in an office modeled on the English ecclesiastical court of the ordinary, which handled most English probates and administrations in so far as there was personal property to preserve.[4] In Maryland the Prerogative Court, as it came to be called, had a wider jurisdiction than its English counterparts, since it had responsibility for succession to land as well as chattels,[5] and it also had more effective powers of enforcement. As a proprietary rather than an ecclesiastical court, it could imprison for contempt (from 1681), and its bonds for performance could be put in suit in the courts of common law. By contrast, in seventeenth-century England, the common-law courts were refusing jurisdiction over bonds taken in the ecclesiastical courts, thereby rendering these courts powerless.[6]

The development of the Prerogative Office is obscure before 1658, in part because the preceding fourteen years had seen major upheavals in the colony. But from 1658 until his death in 1682, Philip Calvert, the youngest son of the first proprietor, was either chancellor of Maryland or judge of probate or both. He was active in transforming the Prerogative Office into an effective agency for protection of both heirs and creditors.[7] Calvert probably drafted the early legislation that not only guided the development of the Prerogative Court but also established courts and procedures for protection of orphans.

Guardianship Laws

The first law to consider the welfare of orphans passed the Maryland assembly in 1654, before Philip Calvert's time. It required all who controlled orphans' property to file with the county court an inventory of the estate and an account of disbursements from it. The records of Kent County, the only surviving county records for the 1650s, contain a number of such accountings.[8] An act of 1658, passed immediately after Calvert's arrival, provided for yearly oversight by the county justices, who were to send men who refused to account for orphans' assets before the Provincial Court. The higher court was to demand security of these guardians and if necessary put the estate into the hands of more "able and discreet persons."[9] Implied was the right of the county court to appoint the guardians initially if no will specified who was to care for the minor children, as had been law in Virginia since 1643.[10] Later law and practice suggests that the intention was to give authority to the county courts only over orphans of intestates. Any arrangement the deceased parent had made could not be challenged. Maryland court records of the 1660s show that the Maryland justices carried out these duties, but that the Provincial Court exercised concurrent jurisdiction as well as acting on referrals from below.[11] In 1671 a new law centered care and protection of orphans of intestates more firmly in the county courts, with clear powers to appoint and dismiss guardians. From that time the Provincial Court paid little attention to orphans' court matters, except in the county where it sat.[12]

The laws had two objectives: protection of the child's person and preservation of his property. An act of 1663 set requirements for care of the child.[13] Guardians were to maintain and educate orphans according to their income and status. Children whose property provided insufficient income were to be bound as servants, unless someone would support them without requiring repayment in labor. Those bound out were to be taught a trade. No child, whether or not he was bound to service, was to be placed with a guardian of religion different from that of his parents, a provision that in 1715 was modified to allow children whose father was Protestant to be taken from a Catholic mother. These were the guidelines provided by act for placing children or removing them from unsuitable guardians.

Provisions were more elaborate for ensuring that orphans' property was preserved and handed to them intact when they were of age. The act of 1663, followed by those of 1671, 1681, and 1688, laid down the main procedures.[14] Until personal assets had been inventoried and creditors paid, the administrator controlled the estate under supervision of the Prerogative Court, but once this process was finished and the shares of the heirs determined, the final accounts were to be sent to the county courts. The county justices were to "put the person Lands goods & Chattles of the Orphans into the handes of such persons as they shall thinke fitt." These guardians were to give bond to the orphan with two sufficient sureties that they would pay to the orphan or a future guardian the inheritance when it was legally demanded.

These procedures proved insufficient to ensure that if an orphan owned land, his plantation would be properly cared for. The Prerogative Court required an inventory of the moveable property that belonged to an estate, but not of land or its improvements. There was danger that guardians would allow orphans' land to be overplanted or the timber overcut or would let the housing fall into decay. To prevent such waste and to inform the court more fully, the act of 1688 required that the guardian should request a justice of the county court and two indifferent men "of good repute and well skilled in building and Plantation Affairs" to view the land and buildings. The viewers were to determine the condition of the improvements and the amount of land that might be cleared, estimate the costs of proper upkeep, and establish the annual value. They were to prepare a certificate of this information, which was to be put in the county records, where it would be available to show whether or not waste had occurred at any time before the orphan came of age. In the meantime, the justices were supplied with necessary information by which to judge whether the orphan was maintained according to his estate.

The justices were to inquire yearly into the welfare of all orphan children and into the solvency of guardians to those who had property, lest there be no assets to claim if the estate were embezzled or wasted. The acts of 1681 and 1688 increased this investigative capacity of the courts by requiring that a special jury of inquiry be impaneled each June to bring presentments against guardians and masters who mistreated their charges or misused their estates. New securities could be demanded and new guardians could be appointed if the old were found irresponsible or cruel or insolvent. Were waste or embezzlement proved, the guardian had to give bond to reimburse the orphan for the loss; otherwise a new guardian was to be appointed who was to bring an action of waste against his predecessor.

An orphan was considered to be a child whose father had died. His mother could be guardian, but not for the property, unless she could find the sureties required for her bond to pay the child's portion, and she was accountable to the court for the care of the child and his estate. If she had remarried, her new husband had to find such sureties and submit to such supervision; otherwise, the court was supposed to appoint other guardians, at least to care for the property.[15]

During the seventeenth century official jurisdiction over orphans of testators remained with the Prerogative Court, but evidently local supervision was preferable. In 1695 an additional act stated that children of intestate fathers were often better cared for than those of testators. The new law required that the orphan juries inquire into the welfare and estates of all orphans and inform the Prerogative Court of any findings against executors or guardians appointed under wills. In addition, security was to be required from these guardians to pay the orphans' portions. In 1715 the law finally authorized what had evidently already become practice: county court replacement of any guardians proved insolvent or untrustworthy, regardless of how they had been appointed. This change completed development of enacted guardianship law as it stood for the rest of the colonial period.[16]

English precedent for protection of orphans was far from adequate. In England the type of land tenure could determine who would be guardian to a minor heir of a landowner, and feudal notions of guardianship as a privilege of overlordship had slowed development of the idea that guardians had legal responsibility for the welfare of their charges. Guardians to minors whose land was held in socage—the status of all landowners in Maryland—were supposed to account for the estate, but the courts of law had difficulty enforcing these requirements, and nothing required that the profits not used for the children's maintenance be set aside or improved for their benefit. There was, furthermore, little provision in law for appointment or oversight of guardians to infants whose property was not in land. The law courts appointed guardians to act for infants involved in litigation, but otherwise provision was by special custom. In London and a few other English cities, orphans' courts cared for the persons and estates left by freemen of the corporation, whose fortunes were often largely in personalty. In the Province of York, custom gave the power to appoint guardians not otherwise provided for infants with personal property to the ecclesiastical court of the ordinary.[17]

Henry Swinburn's *Treatise of Last Wills and Testaments,* first published in 1590 and still in print in 1728, describes the procedures in guardianship of the ecclesiastical courts of the Province of York.[19] The ordinary of the diocesan court appointed "tutors" for children if their deceased parents had not made arrangements or if a special land tenure had not determined who the guardian must be. These tutors had responsibilities similar to those of Maryland guardians, gave similar bond in the court of the ordinary, and could be removed by the ordinary for being false to their trusts. The grant of these powers to the county courts of Maryland may have been borrowed from this English custom, but the jurisdiction was greater, since guardians appointed by will and the lands, as well as personalty of orphans, were subject to court supervision. Moreover, the machinery for supervision and enforcement, based on statute and operated by secular courts, was undoubtedly more effective.[19]

English justices of the peace had powers parallel to those of Maryland only over indigent orphans. Quarter sessions could order parishes to provide for such children and could bind out those old enough to work. The English justices could also order that any property of such children be put in the hands of the parish overseers of the poor to be used for the children's maintenance.[20] This, at least in theory, the Maryland justices could not do. Any estate belonging to any orphan, no matter how slight, had to be kept intact for him; only the income could be used to help maintain him.

Maryland county courts took seriously their responsibilities towards orphans in so far as their needs were brought to the courts' attention. The justices heard complaints, appointed guardians, and set terms of service in return for maintenance and education if income from the orphan's estate was insufficient. Court records from the 1690s on show the courts keeping track of orphans' plantations, at least if complaints were made, to be sure that timber was preserved and that the soil was not depleted by overplanting. However, except in outlining the steps to be taken in valuing real estate and its improvements, the laws offered little detailed procedural guidance. They authorized juries of inquiry and required that security be given for payment of portions or legacies when legally demanded, but these provisions were not always taken literally, and there was considerable variation from county to county in ways of enforcing agreements and handling complaints. Even the jurisdiction exercised was uncertain, and the relationship of the local courts to the Prerogative Court was not worked out until the eighteenth century was underway.

Appointment of Guardians

The appointment of the guardian was the first step. The laws were aimed primarily at the protection of inheritance, and if the father's estate went through probate, the county courts usually did not act until the commissary general had passed the final accounts of the administrators. Until then responsibility for the personal property, at least, rested with the Prerogative Court. If the mother were alive, the county justices had no need to see that the children were cared for unless the mother could not support them.

Records kept before the 1690s give little indication of any regular procedure by which county justices could learn that an estate was ready for distribution and that portions of the minor children, therefore, needed to be secured. Possibly the court depended on voluntary reporting by administrators. Enforcement may have been weak if no complaints were made. The surviving county records of this early period suggest that if the mother had the minor children in her care, the court made no official appointment of a guardian. Whether in these circumstances the justices at least required that bond be given to secure the orphans' portions is impossible to determine. No such bonds appear in any surviving records before 1690, although the courts regularly ordered that security be taken when they appointed guardians for children who had lost both parents. Despite the requirement of law beginning in 1681, it was not yet practice to record these bonds, perhaps because they were bonds to the orphans instead of to the proprietor. Possibly mothers or stepfathers gave bond. However, court proceedings sampled do not show that courts called in guardians the justices had not appointed to insist that bond be given.[21] It took an order from the Prerogative Court to obtain bond from the stepfather of William Hollis's orphans.[22]

Procedures were tightened under the royal governors of the 1690s.[23] First the commissary began to send copies of final accounts to the county courts. The justices sent subpoenas to the administrators. If the administrator was the mother, she gave bond; if she had remarried, the stepfather acted.[24] Or, if the court appointed other guardians, the administrator would be ordered to turn over the estate to them and they found the required security.[25] A guardian who could not find sureties of estate sufficient to satisfy the court might be removed and the orphan, or at least his property, put in more solvent hands.[26]

Second, the creation in 1692 of the deputy commissary greatly improved communication with the Prerogative Court. The commissary appointed a deputy for each county to probate wills and grant letters of administration. From 1694 this officer could pass accounts for estates in which personal property was valued at £50 sterling or less, provided there were no disputes,[27] and in practice, the commissary usually granted him special commissions to handle larger estates.[28] There is at least one reference in Somerset County to show that its deputy commissary reported to the court what letters of administration he granted,[29] and he may have reported final balances on settlements that fell within his jurisdiction, although the law located this responsibility with the central probate officer. Such reports would have kept the county courts informed to some degree of what orphans needed their protection.

In Kent County, entries for orphan business in the record are fuller than elsewhere and, by the early 1700s prove close cooperation between the court and the deputy commissary, who was then a justice.[30] There, for instance, when John Wells had made up the first account for the estate of Thomas Coursey and requested to be appointed guardian of Thomas's daughter, Jean, the court instructed him to "Give Securytie to the Deputie Commissary for y sd Jean's Estate made up according to the acc Delivered in Court." (Since this was not the final account, the bond was not yet to the orphan.) The deputy was sitting on the bench, and the whole transaction, including the filing of the account and the giving of security, may have been conducted in court. Most probably the deputy commissary dispatched as much of his business as he could in court time in any event. It is also clear that the Kent County Court did not wait for official notification from the commissary general to deliver the personal estates of orphans to their guardians and take security. The deputy commissary informed the court, which acted immediately.[31] However, practice varied. In Prince George's County, although the clerk of court or his deputy was deputy commissary, the court awaited a letter from the commissary general, and despite penalties for delay set in 1704, it could wait for several years.[32]

Maryland law was silent as to who should appoint guardians of orphans whose fathers had left wills but had not specified therein who the guardian would be. This problem had complicated the rescue of William Watts's orphans. Philip Calvert had stated his opinion that English practice allowed him to provide a "tutor" in such cases, but in fact he had left the appointment to the county court.[33] Records of the royal period show that by then local courts did not hesitate to act without prodding from the Prerogative Office. The Kent County court in 1703 appointed John Wells guardian to his stepdaughter, although her father had left a will.[34] In Prince George's County the same year, the court did not actually appoint the stepfather, Henry Acton, guardian to Richard Gambra's orphans, but it supervised a valuation of the real property and took security from Acton for the personal estate when the accounts were finally settled. Since the court had clear authority to investigate Acton's conduct as a guardian, the technical point of whether or not he asked permission of the court to act may not have seemed very pressing.[35]

Landed orphans could need guardians before the father's personal estate was settled, for this process could take a year or longer, while land and housing might deteriorate. The administrator gave bond only to preserve the personal property as inventoried, pay the debts owed by the estate, and return what remained to the heirs. Plantation care was especially urgent if the mother was also dead and none of the children were of age to manage the property. Nevertheless, at first county justices were reluctant to act. Philip Calvert admonished several courts during the 1670s to take both real estate and persons of landed orphans into their care immediately, lest the land lie in waste and the housing run to decay.[36] Even when the courts took action, confusion remained as to the role of the administrator or executor vis-à-vis the guardian. Calvert, for example, in rescuing William Watts's orphans, left their lands in the hands of the executor.[37] Most often, however, the executor or administrator was also the guardian of the children.

Under English law, orphans of intestates who were heirs to land held under socage tenure could choose their guardians at the age of fourteen. Examples of such orphans choosing their guardians are frequent from the beginning in the Maryland county records.[38] The provision allowed children to escape incompatible stepfathers and rescue their estates from incompetent stewardship. The judge of the Prerogative Court in 1684 actually urged

William Hollis and his sister to "looke about them; for their Estate (I doubt) is much Embezzled by soe many stepfathers and an unkareful mother." Hollis chose Justice Miles Gibson of the Baltimore County Court as his guardian, and his mother had to prove that she had not wasted the estates of her children before she and her most recent husband were allowed to give security for the portions of those who were younger.[39]

If the guardian of an orphan had been named by will, the Maryland County courts did not allow a change unless the guardian were proved inadequate. Mareen Duvall, for example, complained to the council when the Anne Arundel County justices would not permit him to choose his guardian in 1696. The court explained that Duvall and his plantation were well cared for and that his father's will required that he live with his stepmother until the age of eighteen.[40] But the commissary himself in 1708 requested the justices of Charles County to remove Anne Courts from the guardian her father had designated. "I know not," he wrote, "Whither M[rst] Anne can fly for Releefe butt to you Worships whose Care and Circumspection in this affaire I beg leave to Ingage that her Education may be Suitable to her fortune."[41] The intention as finally expressed by act in 1715 was to protect the interests of the orphan without violating the will of the testator. Assumed was his intent that the child should be well cared for and his fortune secure.

The common-law rules for guardianship in socage prevented any relative from acting if he might conceivably inherit real property through descent, but there is conflicting evidence about the application of this rule in seventeenth-century Maryland. In 1682, Philip Calvert recommended to the justices of St. Mary's County Court that the mistreated children of William Watts be made wards of their maternal grandfather, "to whom the land can by no possibility descend." On the other hand, six years later, Henry Coursey, chief judge of the Provincial Court, suggested that the rule was not law in Maryland. He had intervened in the affairs of the Cecil County Court to rescue eleven-year-old Sarah Van Heck from marriage to a fortune hunter, and he had returned the child to the custody of her father's sister. Coursey dismissed the argument concerning inheritance in a letter to the council relating the events and alluded to "our law," which allowed any next of kin to be guardians.[42] No Maryland statute covered this rule for guardianship and "our law" must have been judicial precedent. Nearly a century later, in 1774, a handbook of guardianship practice discounted the common-law rule.[43]

The county courts occasionally appointed guardians for minors whose fathers' estates were not administered through the Prerogative Court, thereby escaping its fees. The county justices in these instances sometimes ordered and put on record the court's own inventory of the assets.[44] If a relative or a creditor had objections, he could obtain the right to administer from the judge of probate and the prescribed procedures would then be followed.[45] Usually these estates were small, but many that went through probate were smaller.[46] Probably creditors often prevented the bypassing of the Prerogative Court.

The temptation to avoid probate diminished toward the end of the seventeenth century. The creation of the deputy commissary reduced the burden by eliminating journeys to St. Mary's City, and the law that established the office also reduced the fees for estates of 2,000 pounds of tobacco or less.[47] On occasion, the county courts began to insist that at least an inventory be filed.[48] Nevertheless, guardianship agreements made when children were bound out for their maintenance sometimes still included provisions for payment to the orphan at age the kind and amount of livestock that had belonged to the father, although no estate is otherwise on record.[49]

The laws were primarily concerned with the protection of property, but they also required guardianship appointments for indigent orphan children. Widows requested the court to find homes for children they could not support. Planters petitioned that orphans left in their care be bound to serve until they came of age, promising maintenance in return.[50] Whether indigent orphan children were ever supported without formal court action is impossible to determine with certainty. The laws clearly intended that no child should be without the protection of the court, but proceedings show that justices rarely placed orphans if no one had petitioned on their behalf.[51] On the other hand, it was in the interest of men who expected to benefit from the future labor of a child to obtain a recorded order of court.

A recent study I have made of Prince George's County, Maryland, at the end of the seventeenth century makes it possible to estimate the proportion in that place and time of decedent fathers whose orphans gained the court's attention.[52] Forty-six men whose estates went through probate died in the county over the ten years from 1696 through 1705 and possibly left minor children. Of these forty-six, there are orphan proceedings for the children of twenty-four. The court bound out the children of four, all landless men. The other twenty were landowners. The court took security for the estates of seventeen, in most instances from a mother or a stepfather. In the other three cases, the court investigated trespasses on the orphans' land. The remaining twenty-two of these forty-six men left estates to children, if there were any, who do not appear in the guardianship records. All but one of these men were landowners. Nine may have died childless, and the orphans of two may have been of age. But at least eleven left minors, and four died intestate. The court should have taken security at least for the estates of these. Besides these forty-six men, twenty-three landless men whose estates were not probated left orphans who were bound out to service. Total identified fathers who may have left orphans not of age thus was sixty-nine. From 71 to 84 percent of them left orphans for whom there are guardianship proceedings (see table 2.1).

These figures may be close to the proportion of orphan families in the whole population brought to the notice of the court, but there are some possible holes in the data. Orphaned children not found in the guardianship records are most often identified in wills or other probate records, and estates of some men of property who left minor children may not have gone through probate. However, I have yet to identify a Prince George's County landowner or merchant of this period who died without leaving at least an inventory.[53] Second, stepfathers of poor children whose fathers' estates did not go through probate may not have sought official guardianship of their stepchildren or bound them out to others. But the tally of tenants represented among the sixty-nine possible fathers suggests otherwise. In 1706 about 35 percent of heads of households in the county owned no land, but 49 percent (thirty-four) of these sixty-nine fathers were tenants.[54] That tenants should be more numerous among decedent men with minor children than in the population of heads of households as a whole is not surprising. A study of dead men who left inventories in four Southern Maryland counties, 1658–1705, shows that tenancy was a stage in a man's career; if he had lived long enough to have a child of age he almost always was a landowner.[55] Thus tenants were proportionately somewhat more likely than were landowners to leave minor children behind them. Nevertheless, the high proportion of tenants among identified decedent fathers suggests that no appreciable number of landless orphans went unnoted. The sixty-nine fathers identified should be close to all of the men who died leaving minor children needing care.

TABLE 2.1
Proceedings for Orphans of Men Who Died, 1696–1705, Prince George's County

(A)	Proceedings		No Proceedings		
	Landowners	*Tenants*	*Landowners*	*Tenants*	*Total*
Estate probated	20	4	15	7	46
Estate not probated	0	23	0	0	23
Totals	20	27	15	7	69

(B)	Estates Minors Certain		Estates Minors Uncertain		
	Landowners	*Tenants*	*Landowners*	*Tenants*	*Total*
Security taken	17	0	0	0	17
Children bound	0	27	0	0	27
Other proceedings	3	0	0	0	3
No proceedings	10	1	5	6	22
Totals	30	28	5	6	69

By the end of the seventeenth century, then, the Prince George's County Court was appointing guardians or actively supervising the estates of about three-quarters, and possibly four-fifths, of the orphan families.

Responsibilities of Guardians

The courts not only appointed guardians; they set the terms of guardianship, supposedly within limits set by law. Solvent security had to be given to pay the orphan his portion and rules were laid down for preserving the property; orphans had to be educated according to their estates and, if bound out for a maintenance, were to be taught a trade; and children could not be placed with families of a religion different from that of their parents.[56] These were the main requirements.

In a planting society the requirement that an orphan be taught a trade was not easily put into effect. Indeed, in 1663, the Lower House of Assembly had asked that "the words (Handy Craft, Trade) might be struck out," bringing reply from the Upper House that "to strike out those words . . . was to destroy the very thing Intended . . . which was to breed vp all the indigent youth of this Province to Handy craft Trade and noe other."[57] The Upper House was pushing diversification; the Lower House, profits from tobacco. Not surprisingly, the guardianship agreements found for orphans without property before the 1690s usually omitted any references to training, although they sometimes specified that the ward should have meat, drink, apparel, lodging, and washing "fit for such an apprentice."[58]

By the beginning of the eighteenth century, guardianship agreements began to specify education. The change may have been partly the result of pressure from the royal governor Francis Nicholson, who was active in improving administration during the 1690s. Also reflected may be twenty years of overall stagnation in the tobacco economy, which encouraged diversification.[59] There was great variety in the training that guardians promised, depending in part on the status of the ward. Many children were to be taught to read and most were to learn some skill. In Talbot County little girls were to be taught "the art of housewifery" and not put to work in the ground, a provision that suggests that hard labor in the fields was in fact the fate of many such orphan girls.[60] But often agreements promised nothing but maintenance and some clothing when the children came of age.[61] Such children must have had status similar to that of indentured servants, with one important difference: they could not be sold. If the master did not want to keep the child, he had to bring him to the court, which would find a new home.[62] It was allowable, of course, for guardians to apprentice older boys to another for the purpose of learning a special trade.[63] But most planters themselves taught those under their care what carpentry and other skills were essential to plantation life.

Bonds to perform guardianship agreements—as opposed to bonds to pay orphans their portions—also began to appear in some counties at the turn of the century. By 1700 guardians in Talbot County were apparently routinely required to give such bond, although often no sureties were necessary.[64] But where bond was not given, the record of the agreement was sufficient to enforce compliance or payment of compensation. In Charles County, for example, in 1706, the justices consulted the recorded agreement made eleven years earlier by John Hawkins to teach William Williams to read the Bible; they then ordered Hawkins's administrator to pay William 1,200 pounds of tobacco in place of the education he had not received.[65]

Where there was property, real or personal, to be cared for, the laws made burden of guardianship considerable. On the whole, these were the responsibilities of the guardian in socage as they had been developing in English law.[66] Livestock, servants, and slaves had to be given to the orphan when he came of age in the same number and condition as those put into the hands of the guardians,[67] and the plantation had to be kept in good order without overplanting or overtimbering.[68] The court had the power not only to demand an accounting when it suspected waste, but also to oversee the use of the land. During the 1690s the records show the courts ordering special viewings when waste was complained of and granting or refusing permission to cut timber.[69] The valuation procedures outlined in the law of 1688, however, by which the court was to set advance rules for plantation care, evidently were not put into effect until a supplementary act of 1702 provided penalties for noncompliance.[70] From then on, valuations appear from time to time without any previous complaint of mismanagement, although the number found in some counties is so small as to suggest that many failures to comply with the law went unpunished.[71] As late as 1715, Justice John Bradford of Prince George's County pleaded ignorance of the requirement when reproached for being at least two years late in requesting a valuation for his stepchildren.[72]

Despite the burden, guardianship evidently was not unprofitable, for petitions for custody of children were far more frequent than requests to be allowed to give them up. When there was property to manage, the guardian paid himself an agent's fee, and there was nothing but conscience to stop him from keeping any profits over and above what he spent in maintaining his charge in style proper to his station and income.[73] If the estate were very small, or if there were none, the return to the guardian evidently came from the labor of the child. Court appointed guardians of very young infants who brought with them no livestock or other income-bearing property were paid a sum from the county levy for the first year or two.[74] Presumably this allowance took into account the high death rate of infants, who, if they died, could never make repayment by service. The importance of service of older children appears in petitions of stepparents who requested the court to allow them to keep stepchildren that grandparents wished to take upon the death of the natural parent; the reasons given always recounted the investment already made in maintenance of the children since they were small and the need of the petitioner for their services.[75]

As the laws elaborated the machinery for correction of abuses, great local variety of procedure developed. At first complaints concerning the administration of guardians reached the court in the form of petition, but the acts of 1681 and 1688 specified that an orphan jury was to be impaneled each June and given in charge the laws concerning guardianship and waste. Evidence for the 1680s is scanty, but orphan presentments made at a June court are to be found in the records of several counties.[76] However, there was early uncertainty as to whether the law required that only orphan business come before the June court and whether other sessions could consider orphan matters. In 1674 an act setting court days declared that the June court could take up any business, and in 1692 an act finally stated, in addition, that orphan business was not to be limited to the June court.[77] Charles County records, thereafter, and Prince George's records from the founding of the county (1696) show no signs that the June grand juries were considered different in character from those of other courts, except that orphan presentments were usually made then.[78] Probably references to the appropriate laws were included in the charge to June juries, but there is nothing to suggest that the oath taken differed in any way from those sworn at other courts. In Somerset County, by contrast, by 1700, an orphan jury was especially sworn each June; if other criminal business was pending, another jury was then sworn to handle it.[79] Talbot and Kent counties had the orphan jury resworn to inquire into ordinary matters of law enforcement. What oaths were given and in what form remain unanswered questions.[80]

In the counties where the distinction between orphan and criminal grand juries was preserved, complaints were usually taken to the orphan jury.[81] In those where it was not, direct petition by an orphan or an interested person could also result in a hearing. In Prince George's and Charles counties petitions appear as often as presentments.[82] But whether petition or presentment opened a case, the stages that followed carried a minimum of formality. In rare instances there might be a jury trial.[83] In any case defendants were summoned and heard and witnesses might be sworn. Where the charge was waste, the court might order a viewing. It then made an order, and anyone who defied it was subject to proceedings in contempt.[84] Unfortunately, it is difficult to discover from the record the degree to which the common-law rule that the parties to a dispute are not competent witnesses may have been observed in these cases. Nothing, however, suggests use of written interrogatories of equity proceedings.

The kinds of complaints brought before the courts suggest a wide range of interest in children's welfare and show how the observation of neighbors could protect children from possible abuse. The Kent County grand jury presented Thomas Usher for making sale of orphan Thomas Thorpe, a false allegation as matters turned out. The Somerset jury requested the court to investigate the case of a parentless eight-year-old boy living in great hardship at David Jenkins's home and not likely to be brought up to any trade. John Lewis complained to the Prince George's County justices that he frequently had to feed children in the care of John Bennet. The hearing brought out that Bennet often offered the same care to Lewis's children. The court dismissed the complaint, observing that "where Children are Espeatially where they are Acquainted they will ask for victualls when hungry." St. Mary's County neighbors supported the complaint that William Watts's orphans were "putt to unreasonable Labour supposing them to have been bastard Children much more orphants that had an Estate left them." The children were put in the care of their grandfather. When Ann Courts was denied the education of a gentlewoman, the Charles County Court removed her guardian. And Alexander Magruder was required to give bond to reimburse the orphans of Nicholas Bartram for trees Magruder had accidently cut down upon their land.[85] The county courts investigated all complaints, and while mistreatment of orphans or misuse of their property may have gone unreported, the orphan courts must have offered real protection.

What seems apparent in examining the records is the variety of procedures and independence of action allowed to the county courts in dealing with orphans. Policies differed from county to county in such matters as bonds required for guardianship agreements and procedures to be followed in making complaints.[86] There was, furthermore, little interference by higher courts or by the governor and council. Nothing in the county or Chancery records before 1715 suggests any action by the chancellor or appeals to him from county court decisions on guardianship. After 1671 action in the Provincial Court was uncommon, although it seems to have exercised concurrent jurisdiction at least over orphans old enough to choose their guardians.[87]

The Provincial Court of the royal period handled guardianships only for the county where it sat.[88] Appeals must have been very unusual, for only two have been found. In the 1690s a Somerset County planter challenged a presentment brought against him for waste on the ground that the king could not commence a suit on behalf of an orphan, the Court of Wards and Liveries "being out of doors," but when his case was called he failed to appear. And in April 1703 some Dorchester County Quakers complained that the county court had placed Quaker orphans with non-Quakers; after hearing witnesses and examining the record the higher court ordered that the orphans be placed with families of their religious persuasion.[89] Only one petition to the governor and council seems to have concerned orphan court matters, and while Governor Nicholson required the counties to send him lists of orphans and show how they were "put out," he had no comments on the information he received.[90] Although the commissary general theoretically made the decisions that concerned complaints made to the justices concerning orphans of testators, there is evidence that the county courts acted,[91] and in 1715 the law was changed to reflect what may have been frequent practice.[92] Clearly the personal knowledge of individual people and their circumstances that could be had only by neighbors was considered vital to orphan court procedures, and higher authorities were reluctant to intervene.

By 1715 testamentary and guardianship procedures had taken the form that was to continue for the remainder of the colonial period. The orphans' courts were the social invention of an immigrant society subject to extraordinary mortality and without the social network of kin that could grow only with a native-born population. They continued to prove their usefulness to later generations. Without the orphans' courts, the child whose mother remarried could lose all his property at the hands of an improvident or unscrupulous stepfather before the wheels of the common-law or chancery courts could move to prevent waste or fraud. Without the orphans' courts, an orphaned child could be reduced to the status of a servant to be bought and sold. Without them, he could remain uneducated or untrained to any livelihood but hard labor in the fields. The colonial orphans' court as a "father to us poor Orphans" may not always have prevented abuses, but it must have improved the lot of parentless children of all stations.

NOTES

1. For immigrants, expectation of life at age twenty was about another twenty-two to twenty-three years (Lorena S. Walsh and Russell R. Menard, "Death in the Chesapeake: Two Life Tables for Men in Early Colonial Maryland," *Maryland Historical Magazine* 69 (1974):211–27, hereafter cited as *MHM*). A study of 1,735 people who left inventories in four counties, 1658–1705, shows that 72 percent either had no children or had none of age; only 16 percent are known to have had even one child of age; and 53.6 percent are known to have left only minors. This study, "Social Stratification in Maryland, 1658–1705," undertaken by Lois Green Carr, P. M. G. Harris, and Russell R. Menard and sponsored by the St. Mary's City Commission, has been funded by the National Science Foundation (GS-32272).

Darrett B. and Anita H. Rutman have found that of 239 children born in Middlesex County, Virginia, in the seventeenth century, 49 percent of those who survived to age eighteen had lost their fathers or both parents ("'Now-Wives and Sons-in-Law': Parental Death in a Seventeenth-Century Virginia County," in *Essays on the Seventeenth-Century Chesapeake,* ed. Thad W. Tate and David L. Ammerman [Chapel Hill, forthcoming]).

2. Testamentary Proceedings 12B:238, ms., Hall of Records, Annapolis, Md., hereafter cited as Test. Pro. (All mss. cited are at the Hall of Records unless otherwise specified.) Baltimore County Court Proceedings D, ff. 385–86, ms., hereafter cited as Balt. Ct. Pro.

3. The Rutmans emphasize the contributions of kinship networks as they did begin to grow. For the Virginia orphans' courts, see Evelyn McNeill Thomas, "Orphans Courts in Colonial Virginia" (M.A. thesis, College of William and Mary, 1964).

4. Edith E. MacQueen, "The Commissary in Colonial Maryland," *MHM* 25 (1930):190–206; Elisabeth Hartsook and Gust Skordas, *Land Office and Prerogative Court Records of Colonial Maryland,* Hall of Records Commission Publication No. 4 (Annapolis, 1946), pp. 81–89. The years 1689–92 were an exception. The county courts had jurisdiction over testamentary affairs from Sept. 4, 1689, until late spring of 1692.

For a discussion of the Prerogative Court in the Colony of New York, see Herbert Alan Johnson, "The Prerogative Court of New York, 1686–1776," *American Journal of Legal History* 17(1973): 95–144.

5. William Hand Browne, et al., eds., *Archives of Maryland,* 72 vols. (Baltimore, 1883–), Acts 1691, ch. 27, 2:325–30, hereafter cited as *Archives*; Acts 1681, ch. 2, 7:195–201; Acts 1962, ch. 3, 13:430–37; Acts 1699, ch. 41, 22:533–44; Acts 1704, ch. 20, 26:234–49; Acts 1715, ch. 39; Thomas Bacon, ed., *The Laws of Maryland at Large with Proper Indexes . . .* (Annapolis Md., 1765), hereafter cited as Bacon's Laws.

6. For an administration bond in suit, see Provincial Court Judgments WT no. 3, ff. 449–54, ms., hereafter cited as Prov. Ct. Judg. For powers in contempt, see *Archives* 17:18; Acts 1695, ch. 4, 38:41–43. The provisions of the 1695 act were incorporated in the later acts cited in note 5. English practice is discussed in William Holdsworth, *A History of English Law,* 16 vols. (London, 1903–66) 1:626–29; Ronald A. Marchant, *The Church under the Law: Justice, Administration, and Discipline in the Diocese of York, 1560–1640* (Cambridge, 1969), pp. 109–10.

7. Donnell MacClure Owings, *His Lordship's Patronage, Offices of Profit in Colonial Maryland* (Baltimore, 1953), pp. 122, 125, 130. Philip Calvert's personal notes appear in the margins of many testamentary proceedings.

8. Acts 1654, ch. 44, *Archives* 1:354; 19:92–102.

9. Acts 1658, ch. 8, ibid., 1:374–75.

10. Wesley Frank Craven, *The Southern Colonies in the Seventeenth Century, 1607–1689* (Baton Rouge, La., 1949), p. 272.

11. *Archives* 54:238, 328, 341, 392–93, 400, 713, 41:112, 295, 334–35, 345, 370, 456, 486, 527; 57:i, 199, 236–37, 318, 424–25, 576, 581.

12. For the act, see note 5. From 1671–75, the Provincial Court placed two St. Mary's County orphans and heard a complaint concerning a Kent County guardian it had appointed before the act of 1671. The court sat St. Mary's County, *Archives* 65:90, 95, 178–79, 590–91. Entries in the indexes of succeeding published Provincial Court proceedings (through 1683) under guardians and orphans are few; see also *Archives* 66, 67, 68, 69, and 70.

13. Acts 1663, ch. 16, *Archives* 1:493–95.

14. See act cited in note 5; Acts 1688, ch. 4, *Archives* 13:215–17; Acts 1692, ch. 47, 498–500.

15. For examples, see note 24. In 1695, an act made stepfathers accountable to the Prerogative Court for the administration of their wives, although administration granted before the marriage, see note 6.

16. See notes 5, 6.

17. For discussion of English guardianship, see Holdsworth, *History of English Law* 3:61–66, 512; 6:648–50; Marchant, *The Church under the law,* p. 90. See also Charles Carlton, "Changing Jurisdictions in 16th and 17th Century England: The Relationship Between the Courts of Orphans and Chancery," *American Journal of Legal History* 18 (1974): 124–36.

18. I have used the edition of London, 1640, pp. 167–81; the editions of 1677, pp. 138–49, and 1728, pp. 194–202 contain the same information. Swinburn states that the practice of appointing tutors was based on Roman law.

19. From 1689 until 1715, the crown-controlled Maryland government and the courts of justice were royal rather than proprietary agencies.

20. Sidney and Beatrice Webb, *English Local Government: English Poor Law History: Part I, The Old Poor Law* (London, 1927), pp. 62–65, 149 ff., 196. For actions by English justices concerning orphans, see S.C. Ratcliffe and H.C. Johnson, eds., *Warwick County Records,* 9 vols. (Warwick, Eng., 1935–64), 7:24, 73, 79–80. In the first instance, orphans were settled with their mother and stepfather, and the parish of their birth was ordered to pay a weekly allowance for their maintenance to the parish of their settlement. In the second, orphans abandoned by the mother and refused maintenance by their stepfather were ordered placed as apprentices. In the third, trustees to manage the inheritance of four orphaned children were appointed and made accountable to the overseers of the poor of their parish. The money and goods were to be "employed for the maintenance of the said children."

21. A check of all orphan proceedings in Talbot County, 1675–86, Charles County, 1677, 1685–87, and Somerset County, 1687–89, show no initial appointments of guardians for property if the mother were alive. Talbot County Judgments, 1675–82, ff. 123, 333, 336, 342–43, 444, ms., hereafter cited as Talb. Judg.; ibid., 1682–85, ff. 258, 261–62; Talbot County Land

Records NN no. 6, ff. 86, 87, ms., hereafter cited as Talb. Land Rec.; Charles County Court and Land Records G no. 1, ff. 34, 36, 46, 47, 61, 66, 83, 119, ms., hereafter cited as Ch. Ct. and Land Rec.; ibid., M no. 1, ff. 64, 220, 226; ibid., N no. 1, ff. 163, 266–68; Somerset County Judicial Record 1687–89, ff. 42, 48–49, 60–61, 100, 108, ms., hereafter cited as Som. Jud. Rec.; Test. Pro. 14:89. Some of these proceedings concern landed orphans aged fourteen or over choosing their guardians. I have made no attempt to determine whether or not the mother was alive in these instances. The first bonds to pay portions that I have found recorded are in 1690, Som. Jud. Rec., 1690–92, f. 79.

22. The order of the Prerogative Court is recorded, but not an order of the Baltimore County Court or any bond, Balt. Ct. Pro. D, ff. 385–86. However, it seems likely in the circumstances that security was taken.

23. In 1695, there were complaints in the assembly that accounts were not sent. The following year they appear in the county records; see, for example, Joseph H. Smith and Philip A. Crowl, eds., *Court Records of Prince George's County, Maryland, 1696–1699* (Washington, D.C., 1964), p. 61, hereafter cited as *P G Court Records.*

24. In Prince George's County from 1696 through 1710, the clerk noted eleven bonds given to distribute to orphans their estates when of age. Two were given by mothers, five by stepfathers, Prince George's County Court Record A, f. 59, ms., herafter cited as P G Ct. Rec.; ibid., B, ff. 239–39a, 247a, 250–51; ibid., C. ff. 164a, 219–20; ibid., D, ff. 284, 325a. In the remaining four cases the relationships are unclear, ibid., B, ff. 239, 249, 250, 255, 300.

25. Ibid., ff. 239, 249; see also Talb. Judg. RF no. 11, f. 2.

26. Ch. Ct. and Land Rec. B no. 2, f. 302.

27. Acts 1692, ch. 3, *Archives* 13:436–37; Acts 1694, ch. 27, ibid., 38:22. These provisions were included in the general probate law from 1699 on, see note 5.

28. In Prince George's County, sixty-five accounts passed from 1696 through 1709 are recorded in Prince George's County Accounts IB no. 1, ff. 1–48, ms. This volume was compiled after the American Revolution from the papers filed with the commissary and returned to the countries of origin when the commissary's office was abolished and all probate powers were placed with the county orphans' courts. Only seventeen of the sixty-five accounts were passed by the register of the Prerogative Office in Annapolis. Of the forth-eight passed by the deputy commissary, twenty-six were for estates over £50.

29. Som. Jud. Rec., 1695–96, f. 60.

30. Elias King became deputy commissary in 1692 and was not replaced until 1707—He was a justice from 1701 (Lois Green Carr, "County Government in Maryland, 1689–1709" [Ph.D. diss., Harvard University, 1968], ch. 5, note 108).

31. Kent County Court Proceedings, 1701–5, f. 259, ms., hereafter cited as Kent Ct. Pro.: Wills 11:146, ms.; Inventories and Accounts 21:277, ms., hereafter cited as Inv. and Accts.; ibid., 23:118; ibid., 24:261; ibid., 26:223, 266; ibid., 27:200–201; see also Kent Ct. Pro., 1701–5, ff. 363, 454: Inv. and Accts. 15:127; ibid., 25:171; Kent County Original Accounts, box 1, folder 31, ms.

32. Acts 1704, ch. 20, *Archives* 26:238. From 1696 through 1709, the Prince George's County deputy commissary was Joshua Cecil or Edward Willet, both clerks or deputy clerks, Carr, "County Government in Maryland," appendix 6, table 6, parts 3, 5, 11. Seventeen estates settled between 1701 and 1707 were not reported until August 1707, P G Ct. Rec. C, ff. 152a–54.

33. Test. Pro. 12B:238–54.

34. Kent Ct. Pro., 1701–5, f. 259; Wills 11: 146; Inv. and Accts. 23:18; ibid., 27:200.

35. Richard Gambra died in 1703, but his estate was not finally settled until 1710. Soon after his death, his widow married Henry Acton, Wills 11:387; Prince Goerge's County Administration Bonds, box 1, folder 38, ms.; P G Ct. Rec. B, ff. 239a, 251; ibid., D, f. 284. Long before the estate was settled, Acton arranged for a valuation, which was reported to the county court. The viewers found timber and good land for plantation sufficient until the orphan came of age and declared it so divided that the orphan would suffer no damage.

36. Test. Pro. 8:182, 439; ibid., 10:11.

37. Test. Pro. 12B:238–54.

38. William Blackstone, *A Commentary on the Laws of England in Four Books,* 18th ed. (London, 1922), 1:525, hereafter cited as Blackstone; paging used is that of the first edition as noted in the margins. For examples in Maryland, see *Archives* 41:456; ibid., 57:199, 318; ibid., 54:238, 393, 656; Ch. Ct. and Land Rec. V no. 1, f. 245; P G Ct. Rec. C, f. 134a.

39. Balt. Ct. Pro. D, ff. 385–86.

40. *Archives* 20:404.

41. Ch. Ct. and Land Rec. B no. 2, ff. 525–26.

42. Blackstone 1:524–25; Test. Pro. 12B:238–54; *Archives* 8:32–34.

43. Elie Valette, The Deputy Commissary's Guide within the Province of Maryland (Annapolis, 1774), pp. 144–45.

44. In Kent County in November 1685, William Stanley, orphan, was ordered to live with Edward Plesto until the age of twenty-one, Plesto agreeing to teach him the trade of carpenter and "to take into his possession the plantacon belonging to the sd orpht with all the psonal Estate if any to be found," Kent Ct. Pro. I, f. 126. A similar order issued to Charles Tilden *in re* the orphan Thomas Brown in the following December, ibid., f. 128. In Charles and Somerset counties, inventories, usually only of livestock, were sometimes recorded in these circumstances, Ch. Ct. and Land Rec. G no. 1, ff. 36, 61, 66, 83; Som. Jud. Rec., 1687–89, f. 42.

45. For example, in Somerset County, several relatives of Jenkin Morris petitioned for court order to make them guardians of his children, and Thomas Gordon, one of them, agreed to administer and submitted an inventory. A week later, William Wheatley, another of the group, protested before the judge of the Prerogative Court and obtained administration for himself, Som. Jud. Rec., 1687–89, f. 42; Test. Pro. 14:89.

46. For example, the inventory of the estate of Thomas Warner, deceased, taken for his orphans, came to 1,672 pounds of tobacco in 1677, worth nearly £8 sterling, Ch. Ct. and Land Rec. G no. 1, f. 36. In the four-county region studied in the project described in note 1, six people that year filed inventories that size or smaller.

47. See note 27.

48. In Charles County, for example, the court forced John Loften, who had married the relict of George Scroggin, to file an inventory with the Prerogative Office. In August 1702, after a complaint from the office, the court required him to bring his account to the September court, and in September it ordered the clerk to send it to the commissary general, Ch. Ct. and Land Rec. Y no. 1, ff. 311–12, 369–70; ibid., A no. 2, ff. 87, 108.

49. In 1696 William and Ann Apsley, orphans of Edward, were bound to Michael Miller of Kent County. At the ages of twenty-one and sixteen, respectively, Miller was to give them "Necessary and decent cloathing and deliver them a Yearling Heifer and steere and Two Sowes which were their fathers," Kent Ct. Pro. 1, f. 585. In Prince George's County in 1699 the court acted completely independently of the commissary in settling the estate of the children of Thomas Thickpenny, who had been murdered by Indians in the frontier hundred of New Scotland, PG Ct. Rec. A, f. 464; ibid., B, ff. 15a, 30a. See also ibid., f. 30a for the order that John Green, appointed guardian to Mary Delone, should take into his custody what cattle or other property her father had had. In Somerset County in 1695 the court inventoried and delivered goods of three orphans of James Train to their guardian, Som. Jud. Rec., 1695–96, ff. 104–5. There are no Prerogative Court records for any of these estates.

50. For example, P G Ct. Rec. a, ff. 298, 317; ibid., B, ff. 113a, 289, 352c; ibid., D, f. 74; Kent Ct. Pro. 1, ff. 420, 585, 586.

51. The orphan jury of Somerset once complained of an orphan who needed placement, and the justices of Prince George's County acted for Thickpenny's orphans without prodding, Som. Jud. Rec., 1689–1701, f. 160, note 49 above.

52. The following is based on (1) the study "Social Stratification in Maryland," cited in note 1; and (2) P G Ct. Rec. A, B, C, D, G, H (1696–1720).

53. Carr, "County Government in Maryland," appendix 6, lists all resident Prince George's County landowners in 1706 (based on a carefully corrected rent-roll) and establishes landowning status for all participants in local government, 1696–1709. A later check of all probate and land records has not yet added anyone to the list of landowners over the period or revealed a decedent landowner who left an unprobated estate. A list of merchants compiled from the court proceedings also supplied none who disappeared from the records during the ten years. If a merchant died, he appeared in the probate records. For the purpose of this discussion, craftsmen who were married and had no land are included in the category tenant farmer.

54. Ibid., p. 605.

55. See note 1.

56. These requirements were first explicitly stated in Acts 1663, ch. 16, *Archives* 1:493–95.

57. Ibid., p. 470.

58. See references in note 21, especially Ch. Ct. and Land Rec. N no. 1, ff. 163, 288.

59. For Nicholson and local government, see Carr, "County Government in Maryland," pp. 545–53. For the economy, see Russell R. Menard, P. M. G. Harris, and Lois Green Carr, "Opportunity and Inequality: The Distribution of Wealth on the Lower Western Shore of Maryland, 1638–1705," *MHM* 69 (1974):169–84.

60. Such requirements began to appear in the extant records of all counties by the 1700s. Talb. Land Rec. AB no. 8, f. 194; Ch. Ct. and Land Rec. V no. 1, f. 454; Y no. 1, f. 35; Kent Ct. Pro. 1:498; Som. Jud. Rec., 1701–2, f. 156; P G Ct. Rec. A, f. 355; ibid., C, f. 74. In June 1701 in Talbot Co., twelve orphans were bound at once; bond was given in each case to teach reading and a trade, Talb. Judg., 1700–1, ff. 180–84.

61. Talb. Judg. MTW, f. 103; Ch. Ct. and Land Rec. V no. 1, f. 409; P G Ct. Rec. A, f. 317.

62. For example, in November 1694, Nicholas Hurt of Kent County returned Thomas Andrewe to the court, offering to pay 600 pounds of tobacco to whoever would take him, "he being discomposed in Bodie & therefore unfitt for service." The court ordered William Stanley to take the boy and provide a doctor for him.

63. One such indenture as distinguished from a guardianship record in Prince George's County reads: "Richard Keen with the advice and Consent of his ffriend doe binde himself a Servant to Josiah Willson for ye ffull Space and terme of five whole years to doe Such Service or Services as he shall think fitt to Employ him about Dureing the Said Terme Except Labouring att ax and he and the Said Willson doth binde himselfe to find the said Keen with food Sufficent Meate, washing Lodging & Desscent apparrell dureing the Said Terme and to Use his Endevour to Instruct the Said Keen in writeing and accts & Learne him & bring him up to Buisiness and at ye Expiration of the said terme ye Said Willson is to give him a Suite Desscent apparrell a young horse or mare & Bridle and Saddle," P G Ct. Rec. C, ff. 39–39a.

64. A few guardian bonds for children with estates appear in Somerset County during the revolution of 1689 and after. These combined the provisions required in bonds of administrators not to waste the estate and to pay shares to the orphans when legally required with provisions as guardians to "pform his Care therein," Som. Jud. Rec., 1690–92, f. 79; ibid., 1695–96, ff. 104–5. The first guardian bond I have found in Charles County was given in November 1701, by John Courts of the council, who with one surety promised to pay his orphaned godson 25,000 pounds of tobacco if Courts did not keep the boy at school for two years until he could read, write, and keep accounts through the rule of three; "learne him to know how to gett his living"; clothe and feed him as one of his own; and care for his plantation, Ch. Ct. and Land Rec. Y no. 1, ff. 311–12. In Talbot County in 1699 John King brought an orphan boy, Darby Mecan, to court and asked that the boy be bound. The court so ordered and King gave bond without sureties in £10 that Mecan would be taught to read. Nothing suggests that there was any estate belonging to the orphan. In 1701, twelve such bonds without surety were given, Ch. Ct. and Land Rec., MW no. 1, f. 110; Talb. Judg. 1700–1, ff. 180–84.

65. Ch. Ct. and Land Rec., B no. 2, f. 189.

66. Holdsworth 5:315.

67. In Charles County, for example, an orphan successfully petitioned the court to order a yearling cow paid from the estate of his mistress to reimburse him for one that had died while she was his guardian, Ch. Ct. and Land Rec. A no. 2, f. 133; for references to the laws, see note 5.

68. An excellent example of what was to be avoided in putting an orphan's plantation to use is cited by John Courts of the council in petitioning for guardianship of his godson John Warren. Warren's plantation was let to William Hawton, Jr., who with five servants was clearing and destroying the land "as it is well knowne six hands must doe and abliged to make noe Improvements on it." Courts offered to take the plantation in charge, put no servants of his own on it, plant and care for 100 "Winter Trees" within twelve months, and clear none of the land except for tobacco beds, Ch. Ct. and Land Rec. Y no. 1, ff. 311–12.

69. P G Ct. Rec. A, ff. 19, 165; Ch. Ct. and Land Rec. V no. 1, ff. 353–54, 374–75; Talb. Land Rec. AB no. 8, ff. 442; Talb. Judg., 1698, f. 92. Before 1689 the courts held hearings on presentments and ordered reparations, see Balt. Ct. Pro. D. ff. 151, 165–66.

70. Acts 1702, ch. 2, *Archives* 24:273–75.

71. In Charles County, I found no valuations made, except in connection with proceedings against waste. In Prince George's County there were only three before 1710, and none for the estates of Justices Thomas Hollyday, William Barton, and John Wight, all of whom left minor

children. At least Wight's estate should have been viewed, since he left no will, Carr, "County Government in Maryland," appendix 6, table 8A; P G Ct. Rec. B, ff. 251, 262a, 274a. The two valuations found in Talbot County are very detailed, Talb. Land Rec. RF no. 10, ff. 175, 248; see also Anne Arundel County Judgments TB no. 1, ff. 253–54, ms.

72. By 1713 Bradford had married Joyce Carroll Butler, widow of James Butler, who died about January 1709, see Carr, "County Government in Maryland," appendix 6, tables 8A and 8B.

73. Valette, *Deputy Commissary's Guide,* p. 153, comments on the moral obligation of guardians to account to orphans for the surplus. Acts 1729, ch. 24, similarly stated that "Guardians *ought* to render an Account to their wards, of the Surplus," but set no penalty, Bacon's *Laws,* italics mine. The laws specifically allowed to guardians the profits of slaves after the first year.

74. For example, P G Ct. Rec. A, f. 464; ibid., B, f. 249.

75. Balt. Ct. Pro. F. no. 1, f. 300, 307–8; P G Ct. Rec. D, ff. 219, 276–77, 311–12.

76. Som. Jud. Rec., 1687–89, f. 42; Kent Ct. Pro. 1:176; Talb. Land Rec. NN no. 6, ff. 223–24; Balt. Ct. Pro. D, f. 151.

77. Acts 1674, ch 8, *Archives* 2:398; Acts 1692, ch. 47, *Archives* 13:500.

78. In Charles County orphan juries were empaneled in June 1690, 1691, and 1692 and considered only orphan business. The record was kept in a separate volume, Q no. 1, ff. 8–9, 27–28, 55, along with the other testamentary business of the court undertaken during the revolutionary period, and the regular court proceedings show no grand jury empaneled for June, Ch. Ct. and Land Rec. R no. 1, ff. 2–26, 189–230, 416–20. From 1693 on, the June jury, sworn to inquire into breaches of the peace and penal acts of assembly, made criminal as well as orphan presentments; for example, ibid., S no. 1, ff. 113–14, 279–80; ibid., V no. 1, ff. 1, 210–11, 372–73; ibid., X no. 1, ff. 126–28; ibid., Y no. 1, ff. 13–14, 242–43; ibid., A no 2, ff. 64–65, 210. Orphan presentments occasionally were made at other courts, see ibid., S no. 1, f. 248; ibid., V no. 1, f. 304. In Prince George's County, presentments in orphan matters were brought in June (P G Ct. Rec. A, f. 165; ibid., B, ff. 107, 247a; ibid., C, 150a), but the same jury invariably mixed these with presentments for other offenses.

79. See, for example, Som. Jud. Rec., 1698–1701, ff. 160, 338. In June 1688, however, a June jury had made both orphan and criminal presentments, ibid., 1687–89, f. 42.

80. Talb. Judg. RF no. 11, f. 4; Kent Ct. Pro., 1701–5, ff. 359, 363.

81. Orphan juries were very active in Kent County, and in so far as presentments in Talbot County were recorded, the same statement applies, see, for example, Kent Ct. Pro. 1:425 (3), 513 (1), 587 (3), 747 (1); Talb. Judg., 1692, 1696, 1698, f. 10 (2); Talb. Land Rec. AB no. 8, ff 269 (6), 575 (1); ibid, MW no. 1, f. 99 (2); Talb. Judg., 1703–4, f. 223 (3). I have found no hearings begun by petition in these counties. Except for a few months of 1700, there are no court proceedings—apart from civil judgments—in Cecil County until late in 1708. The orphans' jury of June 1709 was resworn as a grand jury, Cecil County Judgments E, f. 16, ms.

82. In Prince George's County between 1696 and 1703, all complaints (five) were by presentment, P G Ct. Rec. A, f. 165; ibid., B, ff. 106a, 247a, 248. From 1703 through 1709, all complaints (three) were by petition, ibid., 386, 404a; ibid., C, f. 134a. In Charles County between 1694 and 1702, there were three presentments and two petitions, Ch. Ct. and Land Rec. V no. 1, f. 304; ibid., A no. 2, ff. 85–86; ibid., Y no. 1, ff. 16, 311–12. After that time petitions appear more often, e.g., ibid., A no. 2, f. 386 (2).

83. I have found only three instances, Balt. Ct. Pro. G. no. 1, ff. 85, 284; Som. Jud. Rec., 1698–1701, f. 238.

84. For an instance in which the court was forced to use contempt powers, see proceedings in Somerset County as recorded in a transcript to the Provincial Court on appeal, Prov. Ct. Judg. TL no. 1, ff. 84–86. Lawrence Crawford was ordered to prison for refusing to give security for the estate of his wife's orphans.

85. Kent Ct. Pro. 1:747, 765; Som. Jud. Rec., 1698–1701, f. 160; P G Ct. Rec. B, ff. 404a; Test. Pro. 12B:238–54; Ch. Ct. and Land Rec. B no. 2, ff. 525–26; P G Ct. Rec. B, f. 122.

86. Charles County even briefly delegated some of its responsibilities to the parishes, which from 1696 to 1699 had some income from fines authorized by act for bringing up and educating poor orphans. The court in 1696, 1697, and 1698 ordered the vestry of Nanjemy Parish to take several plantations into its possession and care for the orphans to whom they belonged. It also

ordered the parish to care for another child, apparently landless. There are no entries during these years in the court minutes or levy accounts for county support of orphans. Acts 1696, ch. 18, *Archives* 19:428; Ch. Ct. and Land Rec. V no. 1, ff. 53, 240.

87. Prov. Ct. Judg. WC, f. 765; HW no. 3, f. 133.

88. See, for example, ibid., DSC, ff. 55–56; HW no. 3, f. 136; IL, f. 16; TB no. 2, f. 193; PL no. 1, f. 90.

89. Ibid., TL no. 1, ff. 84–86; TL no. 3, f. 125.

90. *Archives* 20:404; 23:315.

91. For example, when Col. Henry Darnall complained that an administrator's security was insufficient, the Prince George's County Court, not the commissary general, took the new security, Wills 11:387; P G Ct. Rec. B,f. 239a; see also ibid., f. 300. In Charles County the court took action to force administrators of estates of testators to turn over to the guardians it had appointed the property belonging to the orphans, Ch. Ct. and Land Rec. Q no. 1, ff. 59–60; S no. 1, ff. 151, 183; Wills 4:140; see also Balt. Ct. Pro. F. no. 1, ff. 416–17, 427; Kent Ct. Pro. 1:745; Wills 2: f. 114.

92. Acts 1715, ch. 39, Bacon's *Laws.*

PART 2

Society

THREE

MARYLAND'S PRIVY COUNCIL, 1637–1715

David W. Jordan

Serving on the governor's council represented the pinnacle of social and political success for residents of the Chesapeake colonies in the seventeenth century. Councillors, according to careful instructions from the crown to its royal governors, should be "men of Estate and Ability and not necessitous people or much in debt and . . . persons well affected to our Government."[1] Cecilius and Charles Calvert, proprietors of Maryland, would have quickly concurred with these criteria for appointment of councillors, for they sought to employ similar standards in their recruitment of assistants. Nevertheless, neither the Lords Baltimore prior to 1689 nor the crown in the subsequent twenty-five years ever found it easy to select and maintain a stable council that was both reflective of these desirable criteria and able to govern effectively. Few individuals in the first century of colonization in Maryland possessed all three of these desirable traits of wealth, ability, and unquestioned loyalty.

The notable scarcity of "men of Estate and Ability" particularly plagued initial proprietary efforts to establish a respected council. It was Cecilius Calvert's formidable task to attract as many such men as possible to his young colony. He often, of necessity, bestowed high offices on wealthy immigrants whose ability and dependability were as yet unproved or on proven colonists who were not exceedingly prosperous. The proprietor encountered frequent disillusionment in such appointments. The political and social turmoil of those early decades, with their recurring civil strife, further complicated Lord Baltimore's search for a strong council. His son Charles Calvert, as governor from 1661 to 1676 and proprietor thereafter, was more successful in fashioning an "ideal" council devoted to the interests that he defined for the government. By defining those interests too narrowly, however, and by relying too exclusively upon fellow Catholics and relatives to ensure loyalty, Calvert alienated many colonists and eventually lost his authority in the revolution of 1689. Maryland then became a royal colony. In the succeeding two decades, the crown drew its councillors from a rapidly

Note: David W. Jordan is associate professor of history, Grinnell College, Iowa.

expanding pool of wealthy and able men, all well affected to the monarchy in principle but not necessarily willing to regard Maryland's interests and the crown's imperial goals as one and the same. This dichotomy became increasingly troublesome for royal governors caught between the crown and council. By 1715, when the colony reverted once more to proprietary control, a newly emergent and largely hereditary elite, jealously protective of local interests, dominated the council and the assembly, which had risen markedly in influence, and shared political power in the provincial government—it was not until these first two decades of the eighteenth century that a wealthy, experienced, and established ruling elite emerged in Maryland, and its loyalty did not go unquestioningly to any outside authority.

Much is known about the institutional development of provincial politics in the seventeenth-century Chesapeake, and particularly about the council that constituted the most powerful ruling body below the governor.[2] Scholars, however, have devoted very little attention to the social composition of this influential executive, judicial, and legislative organ. How did the various governors and proprietors identify the men upon whom they bestowed commissions? Did the council differ significantly in make-up over successive decades? What degree of continuity or stability characterized the tenure of councillors? These questions remain largely unanswered. Some years ago, Bernard Bailyn presented a very stimulating essay on the nature of Virginia's political and social leadership in the seventeenth century.[3] Persuasively challenging the thesis of an early emergence of the noted "First Families of Virginia," Bailyn suggested a three-stage development of the colony's elite before it reached its maturity around the 1670s. Bailyn's provocative thesis, widely read and accepted, has not been systematically tested to any considerable extent in other colonies, nor even documented in great detail for Virginia. Those studies that do focus upon a social profile of the southern elite, and especially the colonial councils, primarily examine the eighteenth century and neglect the earlier and very important evolutionary years.[4]

The council in Maryland affords an excellent opportunity for such a study in the emergence of provincial ruling elites. The records of that colony, so rich for the exciting demographic and social history now being written, will soon provide the most complete model available of any southern colonial society, from indentured servant and slave to the highest provincial officeholder.[5] Ninety-three individuals held either proprietary or royal appointment as councillors between the issuance of the first commission in 1637 and the conclusion of the royal period of Maryland's history in 1715.[6] Examination of the backgrounds and careers of these men both illuminates the study of provincial politics and contributes further to an understanding of the social history of the early Chesapeake world.

Cecilius Calvert, the second Lord Baltimore, issued the first commission for a privy council in Maryland in 1637.[7] Not surprisingly, his initial appointments went to the wealthiest and most reliable men who had accompanied Governor Leonard Calvert to the colony. Thomas Cornwallis and Jerome Hawley, each of prominent English families, had in fact been serving as commissioners or quasi-councillors since 1633. Now they received official recognition as councillors, posts they shared with John Lewger, an old friend and Oxford classmate of the proprietor. Lewger, a Catholic convert, had just migrated to Maryland. In addition to important English connections, each of these men already held or soon owned substantial property in the young colony. Cornwallis acquired over 10,000 acres and built the first mill in Maryland. Hawley, whose relatives had been very active in the colonizing of both Virginia and Barbados, died within a year, leaving one of the largest personal estates in early America. Lewger's educational credentials probably exceeded those of any other colonist in the first decade, and such talents guaranteed profitable patronage positions.[8]

The proprietor had seemingly acquired the services of three able, wealthy, and presumably loyal men to staff the critical council seats. The fate of these first appointees, however, is illustrative of the difficulties Calvert so often encountered in subsequent years. Hawley moved to Virginia in early 1638 to become treasurer of that colony and died just a few months later. Cornwallis increasingly allied with opponents of Governor Calvert, and in September of 1642 he "absolutely refused" to serve any longer as a councillor. Lewger incurred disfavor with acting authorities in 1644, which resulted in his dismissal. After temporary reinstatement later that year, Lewger again lost his commission in 1646. Following the deaths of his wife and his patron Leonard Calvert, Lewger returned permanently to England in 1649.[9] The fourth and fifth councillors, Robert Wintour and Giles Brent, had similarly brief or tempestuous tenures. Wintour died within a year of his appointment. Brent, a source of much dissension in the colony's politics, left the council in early 1649 after six years of intermittent and controversial service.[10]

Seven other men also received commissions during the council's first decade of existence, but by the spring of 1649 only one of the first twelve councillors, Thomas Greene, would still be serving, and he would be dismissed just two years later. Thomas Gerard, omitted from the commission of 1648, would return to the council during the chaotic 1650s and serve until his participation in Fendall's Rebellion in 1660 brought him permanent disbarment from office.[11] A particularly rapid turnover of membership was highly characteristic of the council throughout Cecilius Calvert's proprietorship. Table 3.1, charting longevity of tenure, illustrates that very few men acquired much seniority or experience. Indeed, twelve of the thirty council-

TABLE 3.1
Longevity of Tenure on the Council

Length of Service	Number Appointed 1637–60	Number Appointed 1660–89	Number Appointed 1691–1700	Number Appointed 1700–1715
Two years or less	12 (40%)	6* (21.4%)	2 (11.8%)	4 (20%)
Three to six years	10 (33.3%)	12 (42.9%)	4 (23.5%)	3 (15%)
Seven to ten years	4 (13.3%)	6 (21.4%)	5 (29.4%)	3 (15%)
Eleven to fifteen years	2 (6.7%)	2† (7.1%)	4 (23.5%)	3 (15%)
Sixteen to twenty years	0	2‡ (7.1%)	2§ (11.8%)	2 (10%)
Over twenty years	2¶ (6.7%)	0	0	5 (25%)

*Includes James Neale and Nathaniel Utie, who were reappointed in 1661 and 1674, respectively, after periods of seventeen and fourteen years off the council.
†Thomas Trueman served two separate terms, 1665–76, 1683–85/6.
‡Henry Coursey served two separate terms, 1660–70, 1676–84.
§This includes Thomas Brooke but counts only those years of his first commission, 1691–1708, not the period following his restoration to the council in 1715/16.
¶ Philip Calvert and Baker Brooke began their tenures in 1656 and 1658, respectively.

lors appointed before 1660 (40 percent) sat for less than two full years, while an additional ten (33.3 percent) had tenures of only three to six years. Deaths, departures from the colony, and removals for disloyalty combined to limit stability and continuity on the council.

Abbreviated life expectancy had a profound effect on the entire political system of the colony, creating a continuing vacuum in both local and provincial offices throughout the century and postponing until the 1700s the emergence of any significant number of either long-term or second-generation officeholders. Maryland remained predominantly an immigrant society until after 1700. A first-generation Marylander at age twenty could generally expect at best to live to his early forties, and many councillors, like other colonists, died at a much younger age. These early deaths hampered the evolution of a stable ruling class. Few men lived sufficiently long to establish firmly their own positions in this frontier society, and they rarely had the opportunity to assist their sons' careers.[12] A surprisingly large number of councillors did not even have sons who survived them, and few others had offspring who were of an age to capitalize upon their fathers' success. For example, only six of the fifty-six councillors who sat before 1689 had sons who attained provincial office, and only two of these six received appointment to the council. Another fifteen resident Marylanders served as councillors in the 1690s; six of them died without male heirs, and three others were survived only by very young sons. Only five councillors in the entire seventeenth century had sons who eventually followed their fathers in this high office.[13]

Perhaps the inhospitable climate and rugged conditions of life in Maryland, which brought early death to many settlers, also prompted others, especially among the few more affluent early immigrants, to reconsider their commitment to settle in the New World. While very little is known about the volume and nature of this reverse migration, Calvert was often aware of its consequences. At least eleven, and possibly twelve, of the forty-six men who served as councillors during his proprietorship eventually left the colony.[14]

Wavering allegiance and overt disloyalty constituted the third major obstacle to continuity of membership. In all likelihood, Lord Baltimore could have avoided many of these problems had he been resident in the colony, but he never came to Maryland. His younger brother Leonard commanded reasonable loyalty as governor until his return to England in 1643 resulted in a two-year absence from the colony. Rivalries and dissensions erupted almost immediately, and the suspension of one councillor followed within four months of Leonard's departure.[15] Ingle's rebellion in 1645 enlisted the support of some prominent men, and upon Leonard Calvert's death in 1647, the colony entered a decade of severe turmoil.[16] Not until the arrival of another brother Philip Calvert in 1656 and the proprietor's son Charles Calvert five years later did Lord Baltimore again have strong men in the colony in whom he could place the highest trust. The intervening decade was a period of much strife, which included seizure of the colony by Parliamentary Commissioners Richard Bennett and William Claiborne and the establishment of an alternate government that volleyed for control with Baltimore's provincial officers, some of whom cooperated with the Commonwealth leaders and subsequently lost their proprietary commissions.[17]

The religious struggles within the English-speaking world at this time, and particularly the ascendancy of Puritan forces, magnified Cecilius Calvert's problems of recruiting a viable council. His major appointments in the first decade had gone almost exclusively to Catholics, in keeping with initial proprietary designs for the colony and with the concentration of greater wealth and education among the Catholics in the early population. By the 1640s, however, Protestants comprised a larger and more significant portion of the settlers, and uneasiness over Catholic control of Maryland mounted on both sides of the Atlantic. Circumstances clearly dictated a change in the provincial leadership as well as alterations in governing policies. Calvert initiated a series of non-Catholic appointments in a commission prepared in August of 1648, which went into effect in Maryland the following April. First, he made Protestant William Stone governor of the colony and added three Protestants—John Price, Thomas Hatton, and Robert Vaughan—to the council and dismissed two of the incumbent three Catholic members.[18] At least four, and perhaps five, of the next six commissions, issued between 1649 and 1651, went likewise to Protestants as part of Lord Baltimore's calculated effort to maintain control over his colony in a time of intensified religious strife.[19] Concurrently, Calvert was sponsoring the Act of Religious Toleration to alleviate Protestant fears and yet ensure civil liberties for Catholics.[20]

The quick appointment of so many Protestants was not without its problems. Few such men, already in Maryland, could meet the criteria of wealth, social position, talent, and loyalty that Calvert hoped to maintain. Consequently, he vigorously encouraged promising individuals to migrate to the colony from England, New England, and Virginia. Calvert shrewdly curried the favor of the influential English trading community in his recruitment policies. For example, both Stone and Job Chandler, appointed in 1651, belonged to important London mercantile families.[21] Thomas Hatton, Robert Brooke, and William Mitchell represented other wealthy Protestants enticed to the colony by liberal land grants and council commissions.[22]

Such recruitment indeed brought into office "men of Estate and Ability" and often pleased important men in London, but these appointments carried high risks. Robert Brooke affords a good example. When this newly commissioned councillor departed for Maryland in 1649 with his large family and twenty-eight servants, Cecilius Calvert little suspected that four years later he would be stripping Brooke of all offices for having cooperated too extensively with the parliamentary commissioners who sought to overthrow the proprietor's government.[23] The most infamous of these hazardous appointments, extended to Mitchell in 1650, brought into the council a thoroughly disreputable man who was prosecuted in Maryland for atheism, adultery, murder, and abortion.[24]

Even when successful, this practice of commissioning men either before or very soon after their arrival in the colony had its limitation. These councillors, strangers to the people who were expected to respect and follow them, undoubtedly encountered great difficulty in establishing effective leadership, especially considering the great turnover in council membership. At least fourteen men who served prior to 1660 had received their appointments within a maximum of two years after arrival in Maryland, and probably over half, like Brooke and Mitchell, before they settled in the colony[25] (see table 3.2). With a succession of virtual strangers sitting briefly on the council, with rival Puritan claimants to executive authority from 1652 to 1658, and with a rebellion scarcely two years later, supreme confusion must have attended provincial politics.

Lord Baltimore undoubtedly despaired of ever obtaining a stable council. Temporarily forsaking the recruitment of "men of Estate and Ability," during this unstable period he embarked upon a different strategy and more frequently favored poorer men who had lived in Maryland for some time and had slowly acquired dependable reputation, if not great wealth. John Price, the first such appointment, in 1648, was substantially less affluent than previous councillors, but he had proven his loyalty through many

TABLE 3.2
Length of Residence before Appointment to the Council

Residence in Maryland	Number Appointed 1637–60	Number Appointed 1660–89	Number Appointed 1691–1700	Number Appointed 1700–1715
Two years or less	16 (53.3%)	11* (39.3%)	2† (11.8%)	1† (5%)
Three to five years	4 (13.3%)	0	0	1† (5%)
Six to ten years	5 (16.7%)	6 (21.4%)	1 (5.9%)	1 (5%)
Ten to fifteen years	2 (6.7%)	5 (17.9%)	0	0
Fifteen to thirty years	2 (6.7%)	5‡ (17.9%)	11 (64.7%)	4 (20%)
Over thirty years	0	1 (3.6%)	1 (5.9%)	7 (35%)
Natives	0	0	2 (11.8%)	6 (30%)
Unknown	1 (3.3%)	0	0	0

*Includes James Neale, also counted in the 1637–60 period. Neale returned to Maryland in 1660 after an absence of many years and was reappointed to the council in 1661.

†The four individuals so marked were all royal placemen, who never considered themselves to be permanent residents of Maryland.

‡Includes Nathaniel Utie, also counted in the 1637–60 period. Utie was reappointed in 1674 after 14 years off the council.

valuable services in numerous minor positions over an eight-year period.[26] Calvert repeated the experiment with Robert Vaughan and Robert Clarke, both, probably, former indentured servants. A freeman by 1638, Vaughan had enjoyed gradual upward mobility and had, in particular, assisted in developing more loyal support for the proprietor on troublesome Kent Island in the 1640s. His appointment to the council was a reward for years of satisfactory service and an investment on the part of Calvert.[27] Clarke joined the council in 1653/54 after sixteen years of loyal service in a progression of posts.[28] Price, Vaughan, and Clarke lacked social credentials and the wealth usually held by the councillors, but for a short time at midcentury they contributed desperately needed dependability and stability to the council.

Proprietary reliance on less affluent men distressed Calvert, even as he gratefully benefited from their services. In an age that valued deference and order as the foundations of society and politics, and in a frontier colony that had very little of either, Calvert worried that the settlers would not accord his councillors the proper respect and obedience. He tried to remedy the absence of status and wealth by bestowing on his favored men a profusion of offices and powers that carried wide-ranging influence and conferred extensive rewards. Many of the councillors thereby accumulated much prestige and wealth. In 1666, Calvert even contemplated the councillors "wearing of habbits medales or otherwise" so that "some visible distinction or Distinctions might be drawn."[29]

Charles Calvert, resident governor after 1660, was not content with such artificial devices, nor was he altogether happy with the heterogeneous council that he inherited upon arrival. Former Governor Josias Fendall's ill-fated rebellion had just come to an end. Among its political victims had been Councillors Thomas Gerard, Nathaniel Utie, John Hatch, and Robert Slye, who had extended their support to Fendall and consequently lost their offices. A new commission, issued in 1660, had also omitted Price and Luke Barber, each of but "middling" social origins.[30]

Still, Charles Calvert was not overjoyed with the company of those who remained. Robert Clarke, who died three years later, had clearly exceeded his "proper" station. Edward Lloyd, a Puritan, had obtained his seat in 1658 in another proprietary effort to fashion a coalition council and to defeat the parliamentary party. A merchant with important London ties, Lloyd returned to England in 1668.[31] Baker Brooke, son of the disloyal Robert Brooke, had won appointment from Fendall in 1658 for his "ability and affectionate service" in the assembly that year. Brooke, a very wealthy and astute individual, became a Catholic and later earned Charles Calvert's support and the hand in marriage of Anne Calvert, the governor's cousin; in 1661, however, Brooke was an object of uncertain loyalty. John Bateman, a former haberdasher of London and another councillor closely affiliated with the London mercantile community, had gained preferment from Philip Calvert, the interim governor. Bateman was to die in 1663.[32] Also, the council inherited by Charles Calvert included Philip Calvert and his protege Henry Coursey. These two men were open or covert rivals of the proprietor's son for the next three decades. Charles protested that they contrived to stimulate controversy within the colony, and he specifically charged his uncle with endeavoring to draw the affections of the people from him. Philip Calvert was too valuable a man to dismiss, however, and the young governor later learned to appreciate his uncle's importance. Charles never completely trusted Coursey, whom he later removed from the council.[33]

It was thus a diverse council without coherence that advised the governor as Maryland entered the fourth decade of settlement. Charles Calvert was not content to let the council remain such. Until Calvert's accession to the proprietorship in 1676, his authority was technically subordinate to the wishes of his father, but the son's opinions slowly gained ascendancy. The composition of the council gradually changed in accordance with the governor's preference to favor men of more established wealth and lineage. Charles Calvert also leaned heavily toward appointing fellow Catholics, who began once more to outnumber significantly the Protestants on the council. The ideal councillor, in the governor's estimation, was an individual like Henry Sewall, a wealthy Catholic, who was Charles Calvert's closest friend, or William Talbot and William Calvert, the governor's cousins. These individuals all had wealth, ability, status, and loyalty.[34] Unfortunately for Calvert, there were still too few such men in the colony. While the late 1660s and early 1670s brought into the colony a surprising number of young affluent and talented settlers, often the sons of English gentry or merchants, they were almost exclusively Protestant in religion.[35] Rather than appoint them, Calvert still seemingly preferred to rely occasionally on poorer men like Catholic William Evans, who gained his commission in 1664 after more than two decades of important military service to the proprietary family.[36]

Despite Calvert's efforts, instability, incoherence, and frequent turnovers continued to characterize the council for the fifteen years of his governorship. Nineteen men occupied the councillors' seat, with nine of them serving for four years or less. Reasons other than death now more frequently accounted for these abbreviated terms. Jerome White, William Talbot, and probably Edward Fitzherbert, joined Edward Lloyd in returning to England. Four councillors, in addition to Coursey, were dismissed for a variety of reasons. Charles Calvert complained that other councillors were incapable of governing or too quick to "pretend" service and allegiance when "their actions do not suit accordingly."[37] When his cousin Talbot decided to leave the council and the colony in 1671, Calvert lamented that departure and expressed hope that Talbot would change his mind "for I have little comfort or satisfaction in the society of any of the rest of the council here."[38]

Greater satisfaction soon came to Calvert with the determined implementation of his adamant views on patronage forged over a decade of disillusioning experiences with the council. Starting in 1673, he particularly insisted on a man's unquestioned allegiance and his suitability as an associate, qualities to be demonstrated before appointment. After appointment, Calvert did all he could to bind a councillor's loyalty to himself. For three more years as governor and thereafter as resident proprietor, Calvert experimented whenever possible with means to achieve his goal of a desirable, coherent council. He first successfully encouraged his father to reward Thomas Taylor with an appointment to the council in 1673. Taylor, as speaker of the lower house in 1671, had been instrumental in the assembly's legislating an export duty of two shillings per hogshead of tobacco for support of the proprietary establishment. Moreover, Taylor was an influential Protestant merchant, whose support was well worth currying and whose company was congenial.[39] Calvert had then sponsored Thomas Notley, another wealthy merchant and a relatively recent immigrant from Barbados; the governor contrived successfully to obtain Notley's election, first to the assembly and then to the speaker's chair to replace Taylor.[40] Finally, Calvert had persistently championed the interests of Dr. Jesse Wharton, another former Barbadian, who joined the council in 1672. Calvert especially hoped to encourage other wealthy West Indians of the caliber of Notley and Wharton to move to Maryland. When Calvert returned to England in 1676 for his investiture as the Third Lord Baltimore, he significantly by-passed Philip Calvert, the senior councillor, and made first Wharton and then Notley his choices as deputy governors.[41]

Calvert found that these early experiments worked well, although the deaths of Wharton and Notley soon after their appointments reminded him once again of some frustrating obstacles he could not overcome.[42] He continued to exercise careful selection of promising leaders and then through shrewd use of patronage began to construct a harmonious, loyal council, cleverly cemented by a further pattern of alliances. Through a succession of skillfully arranged marriages, he bound his preferred merchants and great planters to the proprietary family and created a council almost exclusively composed of relatives. He had perhaps been experimenting with this strategy in the wedding that united Baker Brooke and Anne Calvert. A second political marriage had brought the favored Wharton into the fold. After 1676 it became almost essential to be a relative of Lord Baltimore, by blood or marriage, and highly desirable that one also be a Catholic in order to gain admission to the council. With the exception of Thomas Trueman's reinstatement as a councillor in 1683, only one of Charles Calvert's twelve commissions after 1676 went to a man who was neither a Catholic nor in some way a relative. The atypical individual was William Stevens, a Somerset County entrepreneur appointed in 1679. Stevens had been very influential in the settlement and maintenance for the proprietor of the lower Eastern Shore. Only one other appointee, William Joseph, failed to qualify in some way as a relative of the new inner circle. Joseph came to Maryland in 1688 as Calvert's specially designated president of the council, and little is known of his background or possible family connections.[43]

Apart from Trueman, Stevens, and Joseph, Calvert's appointments one by one, brought into the council congenial, proven men of substance, who had previously become related to the proprietor's extended family. Fortunately for these purposes, Calvert had three stepdaughters and a stepson through his own marriage to the widow of his good friend Henry Sewall.[44] Within a few years, Calvert's council had achieved a remarkable homogeneity and semblance of stability, and in marked contrast to Cecilius Calvert's futile efforts, these councillors had clearly achieved a recognizable distinction within the colony. Charles M. Andrews has written that no other advisory body in the English colonies "reached anything like the high level of complete identification on the part of the government with the interests of the proprietary family and the proprietary prerogative."[45]

Complete identification, however, did not extend to the general population, and the growing estrangement between the council and the colony at large soon contributed to the downfall of the proprietary regime. The tightly knit council evoked the protests of men who resented the family concentration of power and feared a government dominated by Catholics in an increasingly Protestant colony. As early as 1676, discontented planters in a "Complaint from Heaven with a huy and crye" were bewailing the new dominance of the council by relatives and "strong Papists . . . with some Protestants for fashion sake."[46] Dissatisfaction grew more widespread by 1683 when even a Catholic, Lawyer Robert Carvile, was complaining of extreme favoritism being shown the family circle. Carvile protested he "was as good a Mann as my Lord, what are the Calverts? My family is as antient as the Calverts."[47]

The frequency of such complaints and new evidence of political unrest, particularly the abortive revolt of 1681, prompted the Lords of Trade to upbraid the proprietor for his flagrant favoritism. Disturbed "that there is partiallity and favour shewed on all occasions towards those of the Popish religion to the discouragement of his Majestie's Protestant subjects," the Lords admonished Lord Baltimore "to show the same if true to be speedily redressed." Calvert hastened to defend himself in 1682 by forwarding a list of the principal officeholders identified further by their religion. He observed in an assertion of vindication that four of the current eight councillors were Protestants, but he failed to indicate that of his six appointments since becoming proprietor, three had gone to Catholic relatives and two others to Protestants who had married his stepdaughters. Baltimore conveniently omitted any reference to the network of family ties existing among the councillors.[48] This response, which temporarily alleviated English concern if not local discontent, had also failed to intimate Calvert's current thinking with reference to future appointments. Within six months, he had expanded the council to nine members, and within another year he had further increased its size to twelve in order to make places for four relatives, three of whom were Catholics. These men then assumed more significant power as Calvert subsequently allowed the council to diminish in number again to eight members to the detriment of Protestant representation. When Calvert departed for England in 1684 to defend his charter and boundaries, he left authority primarily in the hands of a group of deputy governors, who were relatives or fellow Catholics. Within the next three years, Protestants Trueman, Stevens, and William Burgess had died. When Thomas Taylor returned to England in 1688, William Digges remained as the only Protestant on the council, and he was married to the proprietor's stepdaughter.[49]

This interrelated governing body had functioned smoothly for Calvert's purposes as long as he was resident in the colony. In his absence, these men did not operate so effectively, demonstrated weak leadership, and lost the already fragile confidence of both the general populace and English observers. George Talbot, president of the council and cousin of Lord Baltimore, strengthened the opposition in October of 1684 with his murder of Christopher Rousby, a royal customs collector.[50] When the council, lacking instructions from Calvert, failed to proclaim the new monarchs William and Mary in 1689, that hesitancy precipitated a revolution that deprived Lord Baltimore of political control of Maryland.[51]

A rebel group, styled the Protestant Associators, ruled the colony from July 1689 to April 1692, during which time there was no official council. The associators administered the provincial government through an elected convention and a Grand Committee of Twenty, an interim executive body chosen from the convention and consisting of two delegates from each county. There would later be a remarkable carry over from this group to the first royal council and its early replacements.[52]

Whitehall officials carefully solicited recommendations and advice before appointing a new council in 1691. That process of selection reflected the rising importance of the London merchant community and the emerging imperial bureaucracy in determining colonial patronage. The Calverts, especially Cecilius, had always been attuned to the importance of the English traders as many of their council appointments clearly indicate. Now, the role of the colonial merchants became much more forthright. The crown's advisers, for example, directly requested names and recommendations from Micajah Perry, chief spokesman for the Chesapeake tobacco traders. Perry provided assessments of potential nominees on two different occasions. While Whitehall also consulted Lord Baltimore and the recently designated royal governor Lionel Copley, it was the advice of the merchants that proved critical; no one without their approval received actual appointment to the council. In the years thereafter, the merchants maintained an influential voice as did bureaucrats like William Blathwayt, who made it his business to be familiar with Maryland affairs and Maryland men.[53]

One of those new imperial servants was Sir Thomas Lawrence, who became secretary of the colony and senior councillor. He was the only non-Marylander to receive a commission to the first royal council. Nine seats went to men who had actively supported the revolution and had served as leaders in the interim government. Although some English officials apparently expected these ten men to comprise the complete council, two additional appointments went to proprietary adherents James Frisby and Thomas Brooke, probably named in an effort to soothe the complaints of Lord Baltimore over the loss of his government.

The selection of these twelve initial royal councillors constituted a significant departure from proprietary policy. All twelve were Protestants, and with the exception of Presbyterian David Browne, all subscribed to the Anglican faith. No Catholic or Quaker was to sit on the council for the remainder of Maryland's colonial period. Among the new councillors only Thomas Brooke—an Anglican convert—had any close Papist connections; his brothers and other relatives were devout Catholics. Brooke was also the only appointee with any direct familial ties to the former proprietary circle. His uncle and stepfather had been councillors. Otherwise, these men represented a new group in power in the colony. Most had entered Maryland approximately two decades earlier in that important wave of wealthy immigrants with distinguished family ties in England. Only Brooke and John Courts were natives of the colony, the first nonimmigrants to sit in the council, while Frisby had come to Maryland at age twelve with his father.

Although economic prosperity had come quickly to these councillors, most of them had obtained no more than local political prominence, if that, before the revolution had catapulted them into provincial offices. The proprietor's patronage policy and the larger pool of qualified men in the colony accounts for the longer period of political deprivation that these men had experienced in comparison with previous immigrants of "Estate and Ability." Table 3.2 shows that, collectively, they and later royal councillors had been residents of the colony much longer before appointment than their proprietary counterparts. Only two Marylanders named to the council between 1691 and 1715 would receive their commissions in less than fifteen years after arrival and the delay was usually substantially greater.

The new royal council also reflected a more representative geographical balance. Nominations had specified the residence of each man, and the crown consciously avoided the narrow concentration of men from the lower Western Shore that had characterized the proprietary councils. From 1660 to 1689, St. Mary's County had contributed twelve councillors; Calvert, six; Charles, five; Anne Arundel, four; Talbot, two; and Somerset and Cecil, one each. In contrast, eight counties had representation on the new council, and for the next decade careful attention would be given to maintaining this balance and providing as many counties as possible with a seat. Permanent enlargement of the council to twelve members facilitated this policy.

While this council was more diverse and representative, it was also less harmonious. Disputes and factionalism, abetted by Governor Copley's disreputable policies, became quite common. Within nine months of his arrival, Copley had suspended three councillors, and his actions further divided the remaining members. Copley's death in 1693 prompted a struggle for power, and it was not until Francis Nicholson became governor the following year that the royal council acquired any real stability.[54]

It is indicative of Nicholson's strength as governor that during his five-year tenure the council exhibited very little of the acrimonious squabbling of the Copley years, although the membership remained virtually the same. Nicholson had immediately reinstated the ousted councillors, and he also soon swore in Edward Randolph, the crown's surveyor general of customs, to fill one vacancy caused by death. The crown hoped that Randolph's appointment, requested by Nicholson, would assist in the enforcement of the navigation acts.[55]

Nicholson's governorship was an important period in the evolution of the council. His numerous reforms included the elimination of the extensive practice of allowing dual membership in the council and in the provincial court. Nicholson totally separated the two bodies and reduced the number of other offices held by councillors as well. Although the associators had complained of rampant pluralism in officeholding in 1689, they had done nothing to reduce it once they held the offices in question. In nominating men for future vacancies on the council, as in other patronage, Nicholson disregarded the bitter divisions of the revolutionary years in his search for the most qualified individuals. He was careful that all nominees be "free from espousing any Private Parties against his Majestys Royal Authority & Prerogative."[56]

Additional replacements to the council did not come until 1698 in response to the vacancies created by the deaths of three councillors and Lawrence's return to England. The new appointments initially adhered to the geographical balance by county, but that policy soon gave way to a less specific representation by area. Governors had complained in the 1690s and early 1700s of their difficulty in gathering a quorum for business. Nicholson had persuaded the assembly in 1694 to transfer the capitol from St. Mary's City to Annapolis, a more central location, but members from outlying counties still had great distances to travel and were often unable or unwilling to journey to Annapolis except during the regularly scheduled assembly or court days. Ill health particularly plagued some older councillors. To ease the problem, the crown approved the appointment of more men from Anne Arundel and other centrally located counties. By 1703, such counties had acquired a majority of the membership, while St. Mary's County, for example, often was without a councillor. There did continue to be a careful balance between representation for the Eastern and Western Shores.[57]

A significant transition was underway with the eleven new councillors appointed between 1698 and 1704. They comprised an assortment of different backgrounds: former associators nearing the end of their political careers; younger members of established pro-proprietor families who had not themselves been involved in the struggles of the 1680s; and newer figures who had no discernible ties with either faction. These men shared one important characteristic, distinguished and active service as burgesses in the general assembly. Only one appointee during these years was without such legislative service: Thomas Lawrence, Jr., succeeded his father as secretary but actually died before he ever took his oath of office. Otherwise, the assembly had become a valuable crucible for identifying men of ability and for training future councillors. Men gained helpful experience in working with individuals from other areas of the colony and in addressing the major problems and issues of provincial government. No longer were councillors likely to be total strangers even to the leading colonists. Counting service in the Associators' Convention, thirty of thirty-three resident Marylanders named to the council after 1689 had previously sat in the assembly, while considerably less than half of the proprietary councillors had prior legislative experience.[58]

Increasingly, the crown was to select men of much greater wealth. No resident Marylander commissioned to the council under the royal government is known to have left an estate of less than one thousand acres of land

and under £1,000. Most had real or personal property much in excess of these totals and ranked conspicuously among the top 2 percent of the population in the select company of those men whom Aubrey Land has called the "great planters." These individuals actively engaged in commerce and other speculative ventures. Such new councillors as John Hammond, William Holland, Richard Smith, Thomas Tasker, Edward Lloyd, Francis Jenkins, and Thomas Ennalls, for example, were all involved in trans-Atlantic commerce and, as a rule, owned their own vessels.[59] While the vast majority of the councillors throughout the seventeenth century had acquired wealth exceeding the average colonist, appointments of poorer men had been fairly common. Now, even Marylanders of "middling" wealth had virtually no realistic access to council membership, and the differentials in wealth between councillors and other settlers became quite extreme.[60]

Nicholson and his successor, Nathaniel Blakiston, received good-spirited cooperation from their councils, but John Seymour, who followed them as governor in 1704, encountered much dissension and antagonism. This was partly a consequence of Seymour's personality, but in larger measure it signaled the emergence in the council and concurrently in the assembly of a more confident native interest.[61] Seymour's response to this entrenched resistance was reminiscent of Charles Calvert's policies. He became determined that, whenever feasible, his appointments would go to carefully chosen men so dependent on him that they would be unlikely to oppose his policies. Seymour pursued this goal through two tactics—the appointment of relatives, as Calvert had done, and the promotion of new men not currently a part of the emerging political elite.[62] For example, Seymour commissioned two in-laws, John Contee and Philip Lynes, before the crown had actually approved the nominations or dispatched official papers.[63] The appointment of Thomas Greenfield represented the second approach. Nearing sixty years of age, Greenfield had been a prominent figure in local politics and in the assembly for two decades, but preferment for provincial office had always been denied him by the families of Councillors Thomas Brooke and John Addison, who constituted a rival and more powerful clique in Prince George's County. An angry Seymour obtained both the dismissal of Brooke and the appointment of Greenfield in 1707.[64]

Seymour's other major nominations and appointments promoted men without established constituencies or connections with dominant cliques. Seth Biggs, commissioned in 1707, was one of the two Maryland men appointed after 1691 without prior legislative experience. The governor's nominees for future council vacancies submitted in 1707 and 1708 included five other men who had not served as burgesses.[65]

The governor lived but a year after initiating his extensive and futile efforts to remold the council. By 1709, three of his four actual appointees —Contee, Lynes, and Biggs—were also dead, and the dreams of a more accommodating council perished with them. The other membership continued to acquire a coherence and personality likely to displease English officials and any future governor.

In the closing years of the royal period, the council achieved a permanent stability and distinctiveness unknown in its chaotic earlier history. Significantly, for the five years 1709–14, the council, under its senior member as president, ruled in the absence of a royal governor as the solitary executive organ of the colony. This exercise of administrative authority by totally local rulers was highly symbolic. Not only did these men exhibit a more local orientation on matters of patronage and economic and defense policies, but also for the first time a majority of the councillors were indeed native Marylanders.[66] These men represented a new generation and a new spirit in the colony, now over eighty years of age and populated increasingly by people without a firsthand acquaintance with England. Time had largely dimmed the memories of partisanship in the revolution of 1689, and colonists were becoming more suspicious of outsiders than of each other.[67] Future factionalism and divisions were more likely to arise between a native or country party and those individuals who would strongly espouse the "outside" interests of crown or proprietor.

The council also now represented something much more specific than just a native interest. The select membership constituted a core of powerful, well-established and interrelated families, and their presence marked the final successful emergence of a recognizable, hereditary provincial elite. It was not so narrow an oligarchy or network of family connections as had dominated Charles Calvert's council for slightly over a decade in the 1670s and 1680s. Instead, several different families had acquired predominance in their respective counties and had solidified their positions through intermarriage with similarly influential families. The status of these extended kinship groups was now sufficient to command relatively certain appointment or election to important offices for younger members as they came of age. The "first families of Maryland," who would preside over the colony's affairs through the late eighteenth century, established their positions of leadership here in the initial fifteen years of that century.

Two families especially exemplify this new phenomenon, the Lloyds of Talbot County and the Addisons of Prince George's County, and they represent two different avenues to prominence. Two of Edward Lloyd's grandfathers had been councillors under the proprietary regime, but his father's early death and the revolution interrupted the family's political power. Young Lloyd entered politics under the administration of Nicholson, who actively recruited such talent from former proprietary adherents. Rapid advancement followed for Lloyd, who reached the council in 1701 at age thirty-two and served as its president after 1709. A younger brother Philemon joined the council in 1710, followed in rather quick succession in the ensuing years by brothers-in-law Richard Tilghman and Matthew Tilghman Ward, and brother James Lloyd. Each of these men had served a prior apprenticeship on the county bench and in the assembly, and each gained preferment at a much younger age than had been customary in previous decades.[68] Thomas Addison's rise was even more dramatic and by-passed the usual intermediate offices. Capitalizing on his father's elevation to provincial prominence and to the council through participation in the revolution of 1689, Addison almost automatically received a commission shortly after his father's death; at the time he was only twenty-nine and had not been a burgess. Soon, Addison too would observe familiar faces about the council table. Thomas Brooke, married to Addison's half-sister, would rejoin the council in 1715/16, and Brooke's son-in-law Philip Lee, Addison's brother-in-law Benjamin Tasker, and then Addison's own son-in-law James Bowles would all sit in that comfortably related company by the early 1720s.[69]

The Lloyd and Addison interests were only the two most spectacular examples of what was occurring to varying lesser degrees elsewhere in the colony. This authority was possible for a variety of reasons. The individuals were very wealthy, by and large very able, and tested through an effective system for identifying men of talent and dependability. Charles Sydnor has engagingly described a similar system for the neighboring colony of Virginia.[70] Perhaps equally important, however, these men now enjoyed significantly longer tenures in office, which enabled them to secure their own positions, assist their younger relatives and allies, and contribute an important degree of stability to the colony.[71] Furthermore, they identified themselves with the local interests of the majority of the freeholders, an identification sometimes reached voluntarily and sometimes pressed upon them by an assertive lower house of the assembly now demanding and obtaining an equal voice in the provincial government.

These developments were disturbingly apparent to Robert Quarry, the one outsider who sat on the council during these years. Quarry, whose fascinating career projected him into the politics of numerous colonies, had succeeded Edward Randolph as customs collector and royal watchdog in the New World, and he had inherited Randolph's seat on the Maryland council. Much alarmed by his colleagues' willingness to subordinate royal interests to more local concerns and appalled by legislation the council was willing to approve in 1709, Quarry severely chastized these men and "beg'd them again to consider the Queen's Instructions and their oaths." When they sought to justify their actions with references to pressures from the lower house, Quarry reminded them that he thought "the end of Her Majesty's appointing me one of her Council for that Province was that I might to the utmost of my Power defend her Prerogatives and just Rights" and not surrender them to whatever pressures might exist. Quarry's concern was so great that he strongly advised the Lords of Trade that in the future it would be wisest not to give the councils power to pass acts after the death of governors—"the generallity of the Councills being Gentlemen of the Country are wholly in the interest of the Assembly and as ready to lessen the Prerogative in all things as they [the assembly] are and therefore it requires care in the choice of them and those that are steady to the Queen's interest ought to be Supported and Encouraged. I could mention many wrong Stepps that have been taken by some governors in their recommending persons to your Honorable board fitt to be of the Council." Quarry also urged that a royal governor be sent out immediately.[72]

President Lloyd and the other councillors, whose espousal of royal prerogatives had noticeably diminished, fully recognized the difficulty of resolving serious problems of trade and defense to the crown's satisfaction. They found themselves repeatedly caught in a dilemma. They had sworn oaths to uphold Her Majesty's interests in Maryland, as they would soon subscribe a similar oath to Charles Calvert, the fifth Lord Baltimore. Complete adherence to these oaths, however, would often place the councillors in direct opposition to their own perceptions, the wishes of most colonists, and most pointedly to the will of the lower house. The burgesses obstinately balked at rubber-stamping executive programs, and in November of 1712 a bold lower house had threatened the council if it did not come into line on legislative matters.[73]

With this discomforting tension between oath and conviction or self-interest, there occurs the first evidence that some men were unwilling to become councillors and place themselves in such trying circumstances. They preferred instead to retain seats in the assembly and remain unbeholden to the governor or a power outside the colony. Seymour had reported in 1707 that some men whom he wished to nominate "refuse to act having straight lac'd consciences."[74] Men who did accept commissions now insisted upon more remuneration and benefits to counterbalance the additional pressures and burdens of office. Governors soon found it expedient to bestow additional patronage on the men whom they desired in the council if they were to retain support for controversial measures, and even this "encouragement" did not always guarantee that support. Meanwhile, widespread pluralism in officeholding became more manifest than it had been since Francis Nicholson's reforms in the mid-1690s.[75]

The council had much matured as an institution since 1637. In its growth under proprietor and crown, the council had finally acquired the much sought-after continuity, stability, and distinction of membership, but, ironically, in the process of achieving those goals it had also lost much of its independence and power to the lower house of the assembly. In 1715, however, the two bodies were not yet so far apart. Councillors had spent apprenticeships in the lower house, and their younger brothers, sons or other relatives and friends were still among its members. Maryland now had many more "men of Estate and Ability" than there were positions to fill in the council or even the assembly. Those men who reached the council remained an especially select group at the apex of what could at last be termed a recognizable, established, provincial aristocracy. The particular problems that they now encountered as native councillors, frequently caught between their dutifully sworn oaths of loyalty and their own considerations of what was best for them and for the colony, were but the newest manifestation of the continuing dilemma of councils and councillors in Maryland's transition from a colonial settlement to a self-governing society.

NOTES

1. William Hand Browne et al., eds., *Archives of Maryland*, 72 vols. (Baltimore, 1883–), 8:272, hereafter cited as *Archives*; see also ibid., 24:218.

2. Standard sources include Charles M. Andrews, *The Colonial Period of American History*, 4 vols. (New Haven, 1934–38); Wesley Frank Craven, *The Southern Colonies in the Seventeenth Century, 1607–1689* (Baton Rouge, 1949); Richard L. Morton, *Colonial Virginia*, 2 vols. (Chapel Hill, 1960), vol. 1; and Newton D. Mereness, *Maryland as a Proprietary Province* (New York, 1901). Mereness, pp. 174–77, provides a succinct discussion of the council's powers and responsibilities.

3. Bernard Bailyn, "Politics and Social Structure in Virginia," in *Seventeenth-Century America: Essays in Colonial History*, ed. James Morton Smith (Chapel Hill, 1959), pp. 90–115.

4. Eugene Sirmans, "The South Carolina Royal Council, 1720–1763," *William and Mary Quarterly*, 3d ser. 18 (1961):373–392, hereafter cited as *WMQ*; William S. Price, Jr., "'Men of Good Estates': Wealth among North Carolina's Royal Councillors," *The North Carolina Historical Review* 49 (1972):72–82; and Jackson Turner Main, *The Upper House of Revolutionary America* (Madison, 1967). A promising start has been made by James La Verne Anderson, "The Governors' Councils of Colonial America, a Study of Pennsylvania and Virginia, 1660–1776" (Ph.D. diss., University of Virginia, 1967).

5. Other essays in this volume are excellent examples of such work. See also the special issue of the *Maryland Historical Magazine* 69 (1974) devoted to the St. Mary's City Commission's ambitious study of colonial Maryland (hereafter cited as *MHM*); Aubrey C. Land's two pioneering articles, "Economic Base and Social Structure: The Northern Chesapeake in the Eighteenth Century," *Journal of Economic History* 25 (1965):639–54, and "Economic Behavior in a Planting Society: The Eighteenth Century Chesapeake," *Journal of Southern History* 33 (1967):469–85; Russell R. Menard, "From Servant to Freeholder: Status Mobility and Property Accumulation in Seventeenth-Century Maryland," *WMQ*, 3d ser. 30 (1973):37–64; Lois Green Carr and David William Jordan, *Maryland's Revolution of Government, 1689–1692* (Ithaca, 1974).

6. The author has compiled biographies of the fifty-six proprietary councillors and the thirty-seven royal appointees. These career studies provide the basis for the prosopographical analysis of the council. Russell R. Menard has very kindly shared his invaluable biographical files on men prominent in Maryland politics before 1689.

This study includes all those individuals officially issued commissions by the proprietor and the crown or their designated representatives, although some appointees died before ever swearing their oaths. The men who served under the parliamentary commissioners, 1652–58, and the chief executives of the colony do not appear in this study, except where they also served before or after under proprietary commission as councillors.

7. *Archives* 3:49–55.

8. Sebastian F. Streeter, *Papers Relating to the Early History of Maryland*, Maryland Historical Society Fund Publication No. 9 (Baltimore, 1876), pp. 104–275 provides a full discussion of these three men.

9. Ibid., 29, 122, 179–85, 264–75, *Archives* 4:125. Cornwallis served again briefly as a councillor in 1657 and later returned to England.

10. *Archives* 1:2, 27; 3:70–71, 85, 86, 114, 130; 4:85–89, 128, 164, 337, 444.

11. Ibid., 3:103, 114–16, 131, 138–39, 157–60. Greene was discharged from all offices in 1650 for misbehavior; ibid., 313–23. On Gerard, see Edwin W. Beitzell, "Thomas Gerard and His Sons-in-Law," *MHM* 46 (1951):189–206.

12. Lorena S. Walsh and Russell R. Menard, "Death in the Chesapeake: Two Life Tables for Men in Early Colonial Maryland," *MHM* 69 (1974):211–27; Russell R. Menard, "The Growth of Population in Early Colonial Maryland, 1631–1712" (ms. report, St. Mary's City Commission, April 1972, on file at the Hall of Records, Annapolis, Md); Arthur E. Karinen, "Maryland Population: 1631–1730: Numerical and Distributional Aspects," *MHM* 54 (1959):365–407. The same dependence on immigration to sustain the population was also true of Virginia. See Wesley Frank Craven, *White, Red, and Black: The Seventeenth-Century Virginian* (Charlottesville, 1971).

13. No significant number of second-generation officeholders appeared until the last years of the royal period. Preliminary findings of the St. Mary's City Commission's study of inventory and other probate records in the seventeenth century indicate that at least 70 per cent and perhaps as many as 80 to 85 percent of male decedents succumbed either without sons or with sons not of age. I am grateful to Lois Green Carr, P. M. G. Harris, and Russell R. Menard for sharing this material.

14. Jerome Hawley, John Langford, James Neale, Edward Lloyd, William Talbot, Jerome White, and Thomas Taylor left while still holding commissions as councillors. Neale returned seventeen years later and served again briefly. Thomas Cornwallis, John Lewger, Giles Brent, and Thomas Gerard departed after completing their service in the office. The other probable immigrant was Edward Fitzherbert.

15. *Archives* 3:151.

16. For discussions of these troubled years, see particularly Bernard C. Steiner, *Maryland during the English Civil Wars,* 2 vols. (Baltimore, 1906–07) and *Maryland under the Commonwealth: A Chronicle of the Years 1649–1658* (Baltimore, 1911).

17. The first two parliamentary commissions, both issued in 1652, included some of the current proprietary councillors, but by 1654 most of the latter had declined to serve further under any orders but from Lord Baltimore. Three of the twenty-seven known Puritan commissioners—Edward Lloyd, Robert Slye, and John Hatch—later served on the council, although Slye and Hatch received appointment from Governor Fendall, not Calvert, during the rebellion in 1660, *Archives* 3:352; 53:76. Councillor Robert Brooke lost his seat for cooperating too extensively with the Puritan government, and William Stone was reduced from governor to Councillor, ibid., 308; 1:323–24.

18. *Archives* 3:201–13. The commission omitted Giles Brent and Thomas Gerard, continued Thomas Greene, and added Catholic John Pile.

19. The known Protestants were Robert Brooke, William Mitchell, Edward Gibbons, and Job Chandler. William Eltonhead was probably a Protestant. The sole Catholic, Gerard, who was reappointed in 1650/51, had many Protestant connections and was not raising his own children as Catholics, Beitzell, "Thomas Gerard and His Sons-in-Laws."

20. Craven, *Southern Colonies*, pp. 233–36; *Archives* 1:244–47.

21. Harry Wright Newman, *The Stones of Poynton Manor* (privately printed, 1937); *Archives* 3:271–72, 275–76.

22. Christopher Johnston, "The Hatton and Johnson Families," *WMQ*, 1st ser. 23:113; Patents 3:415–18, ms., Hall of Records, Annapolis; *Archives* 10:44, 49, 50. All mss. cited are at the Hall of Records unless otherwise indicated.

23. Steiner, *Maryland under the Commonwealth,* pp. 37–38, 53, 76; *Archives* 3:237–40, 240–41, 271–72, 275–76, 308; Christopher Johnston, "The Brooke Family," *MHM* 1 (1906):66–73.

24. Steiner, *Maryland under the Commonwealth,* pp. 38–42.

25. This total includes Hawley and Cornwallis, since their appointments as commissioners or quasi-councillors came immediately upon their arrival.

26. Price had been a burgess in several assemblies, a militia officer, and mustermaster general. *Archives* 1:1, 28–31; 3:215–16; 4:312. He probably owned about 300 acres of land at the time of appointment to the council.

27. Menard, "From Servant to Freeholder," 44–45. Vaughan probably owned only 500 acres or less when appointed. He left a small personal estate and 2,100 acres when he died in 1668.

28. *Archives* 3:63, 300, 338, 340; Donnell MacClure Owings, *His Lordship's Patronage, Offices of Profit in Colonial Maryland* (Baltimore, 1953), pp. 85, 135, 171. Clarke's personal estate at death in 1664 was a relatively small £70. 12s. 4d, but he did leave between 1,000 to 2,000 acres, probably acquired largely after his appointment.

29. *Archives* 15:16.

30. Barber lived until 1674, but he apparently held no other office. Price, a planter, died in the early months of 1661, *Archives* 3:323–24, 394.

31. Ibid., 257, 352; ibid., 54:xxiii–iv; and Christopher Johnston, "The Lloyd Family," *MHM* 7 (1912):420–23.

32. On Brooke, *Archives* 3:342, and Johnston, "Brooke Family," 69–70; for Bateman, *Archives* 49:291, 3:394, 487; Wills 1, f. 192, ms.

33. *Calvert Papers, Number One*. Maryland Historical Society Fund Publication No. 28 (Baltimore, 1889) pp. 240–41, 251, 283.

34. Sewall had immigrated with Calvert in 1661 and immediately became secretary and judge of Probate, as well as a councillor. His grandfather had been mayor of Coventry, Christopher Johnston, "The Sewall Family," *MHM* 4 (1909):240–45; Owings, *His Lordship's Patronage*, p. 125. Talbot eventually succeeded to a baronetcy in 1671, *Archives* 5:87. William Calvert was the son of Leonard Calvert and became secretary and attorney general, John Bailey Calvert Nicklin, "The Calvert Family," *MHM* 16 (1921):190–91.

35. Menard, "Growth of Population in Early Colonial Maryland"; Carr and Jordan, *Maryland's Revolution of Government*, pp. 65–71.

36. Evans had been in Maryland eighteen years. He had served as a soldier under Leonard Calvert during Ingle's Rebellion and was condemned to death for opposing the Puritans in 1655. The execution was not carried out, and Evans later became a burgess and a sheriff. He was mustermaster general from 1660/61 until his death, Steiner, *Maryland under the Commonwealth*, pp. 99–100; *Archives* 1:380, 396; 3:481; 4:358–59; 41:62; 51:281–85.

37. *Calvert Papers Number One*, pp. 248, 241, 280.

38. Ibid., 276.

39. *Archives* 2:239; 15:23; 5:141, 309; Patents 17:15. Baltimore received the 2s. duty in return for his agreement to accept tobacco at the rate of 2d. per pound in payment for quit-rents.

40. *Calvert Papers Number One*, pp. 264–65, 288; *Archives* 49:131. Notley had served previously in the assembly, but Calvert apparently had to maneuver to assure Notley's reelection in 1671 by establishing new seats in the assembly for St. Mary's City.

41. *Calvert Papers Number One*, pp. 260–61, 284, 298; *Archives*, 5:141; 15:109–11, 132–35.

42. Wharton died in 1676 and Notley just three years later; Sewall had served only four years before his death in 1665.

43. Carr and Jordan, *Maryland's Revolution of Government*, pp. 37–45.

44. Ibid.; see also, Andrews, *Colonial Period*, vol. 2, pp. 376–78.

45. Andrews, p. 328.

46. *Archives* 5:137.

47. Ibid., 17:181–84, the quote appears on p. 184. Carvile was a prominent lawyer and a burgess, ibid., 2:345, 474; 7:5, 112, 219, 261, 335.

48. W. Noel Sainsbury et al., eds., *Calendar of State Papers, Colonial Series, America and West Indies*, 44 vols. (London, 1860–), *1681–1685*, nos. 184, 260, 275, hereafter cited as *Cal. State Papers Col.*; *Archives* 5:300–301 (quote), 309–10, 348–50.

49. Calvert filled two non-Protestant vacancies with Catholics Clement Hill and William Joseph in 1685 and 1688, respectively. He expressed considerable anger over the remaining councillors' continued kindnesses to Protestant Henry Coursey following his dismissal, *Archives* 17:252–53; 8:15,66.

50. Ibid., 17:298–99, 302–3.

51. The revolution and its causes are treated most fully in Carr and Jordan, *Maryland's Revolution of Government*.

52. *Archives* 13:231–47; 8:99–301, especially 199.

53. Carr and Jordan, *Maryland's Revolution of Government*, pp. 162–73 details the selection process and the analysis that follows.

54. The three suspended were Thomas Lawrence, Henry Jowles and James Frisby; David W. Jordan, "The Royal Period of Colonial Maryland, 1689–1715" (Ph.D. diss., Princeton University, 1966), pp. 106–130, presents the most comprehensive account of Copley's tenure.

55. *Archives* 8:129; 20:107, 115, 128, 132, 155–56. Randolph replaced Nehemiah Blakiston. Nicholson felt it important to have non-Marylanders on the council to counter any possible "self interest" of the resident members, see Nicholson's Memorial, 5 March 1693/94, CO5/713/III, no. 106, Public Record Office Photostats, Library of Congress; Nicholson to Board of Trade, 1 July 1699, *Cal. State Papers, Col., 1699, no. 579.*

56. *Archives* 23:418–19 (quote). See ibid., 8:104, 215, 219 on earlier complaints by the associators and compare council membership with provincial court commissions from 1691 to 1694, ibid, 242–45, 306–7; Provincial Court Judgments, DSC, ff. 38–40, 323–25, ms.; ibid., TL no. 1, f.1; *Archives* 20:137; Nicholson to Board of Trade, 27 March 1697, CO5/714/I and *Cal. State Papers, Col. 1697–1698,* no. 756 list the nominees. Jordan, "Royal Period," pp. 132–200, discusses Nicholson's tenure as governor. For his similar policies in other colonies, see Stephen Saunders Webb, "The Strange Career of Francis Nicholson," *WMQ* 3d ser. 23 (1966):513–48, and Sirmans, "South Carolina Royal Council," pp. 382–83.

57. Nicholson's first four replacements to the council came from the same counties as the deceased members. For complaints on lack of quorums, see *Archives* 25: 109, 112, 189, 243, 265; "Unpublished Provincial Records," *MHM* 16 (1921); 359–60.

58. The only resident councillors without the legislative experience after 1689 were Thomas Brooke, Seth Biggs, and Thomas Addison. On the latter two, see discussion, n. 65 and n. 69.

59. Land's research, summarized in the two essays cited in note 5, has suggested important demarcations in wealth among colonial Marylanders; see also Robert G. Schonfeld and Spencer Wilson, "The Value of Personal Estates in Maryland, 1700–1710," *MHM* 58 (1963):333–43. On the mercantile activities of the councillors, compare, for example, the names of appointees with the owners of ships built in Maryland, 1692 to 1697, *Archives* 25:595–601.

60. The incidence of exceedingly great wealth increased during these decades. For example, only seven (21.8 percent) of the resident councillors sitting between 1660 and 1689 owned both over 5,000 acres and personalty worth over £2,000, while at least 16 (48.5 percent) and probably as many as 20 (60.6 percent) of those sitting between 1691 and 1715 had such extraordinary wealth with the majority of them sitting after 1700.

61. Jordan, "Royal Period," pp. 208–65, 305–8 detail Seymour's problems as governor. During one of his many disputes with the assembly, Seymour obstinately stated, "I am an English Protestant Gentleman and can never equivocate," *Archives* 26:46.

62. Seymour lamented his problems in finding suitable men for appointment in a letter to the Board of Trade, 10 March 1708/09, CO5/716/IV no. 69. Speaking of court appointments, he despairingly wrote that most of the justices were also burgesses who "allmost believe themselves independent of the Queen's Governor, and were I to change them for others, there is so little Choice the remedye might be worse than the disease." Nevertheless, Seymour did attempt a complete reform of judicial commissions.

63. Contee, a merchant, had come to Maryland by 1699. He first married the widow of Councillor John Courts, and his second wife was Mary Townley, Seymour's cousin. The governor then made Contee a quorum justice, militia colonel, naval officer, commissary general, and finally councillor, Charles County Court and Land Records, X no. 1, f. 140; B no. 2, f. 94; C no. 2. ff. 217–19; Owings, *His Lordship's Patronage,* pp. 130, 161; *Archives* 25:74, 240. Lynes, as late as 1699, when he applied to be sheriff, had been characterized by the council as a "person well Affected to the Government but in no wise qualifyed . . . having much abused his Creditt and the people of the County much averse thereto." After his marriage to Seymour's sister, preferment followed, *Archives* 17:440; 22:311 (quote); 27:498; 60:521; 65:24–28; Provincial Court Judgments, TL no. 3, ff. 258–59. Seymour's three letters to the Board of Trade, 10 June 1707, 23 June 1708, and 7 Sept. 1708, *Cal. State Papers, Col., 1706–1708,* no. 955 and CO5/716/III nos. 54 and 56, document the appointments.

64. Undoubtedly at Addison's suggestions, earlier governors had nominated his business partner William Hutchinson and his brother-in-law William Hatton for any future vacancy from Prince George's County, *Archives* 24:218 and Nicholson to Board of Trade, 27 March 1697, CO5/714/I. Greenfield was also a close friend of Lynes, see Wills 12B:151–54, ms. Greenfield also was sworn in before official arrival of his commission. Seymour sought

Brooke's dismissal because of the latter's close Catholic connections and his infrequent attendance, prompted at least in part by the governor's hostility. Brooke was restored to the council in 1715/16, Seymour to Board of Trade, 10 June 1707, CO5/716/II, no. 29; *Archives* 25:245, 327.

65. Biggs was a merchant in Anne Arundel county. For Seymour's two lists of nominees, see *Cal. State Papers, Col., 1706–1708,* no. 957i and CO5/716/III no. 54.

66. Jordan, "Royal Period," pp. 260–65 discusses these years. Six councillors were natives; three others had been born in Virginia.

67. As early as 1694, the assembly had passed an "Act for the Incouragement of Learning and Advancement of the Natives of this Province," which required a three-year residence in Maryland before qualifying for offices of trust or profit unless under direct commission from the crown. The act also sought to prevent absentee officeholders, *Archives* 19:100–101; 26:429–30; Jordan, "Royal Period," pp. 226–28. After 1691, only two men, excluding the four royal placemen who became councillors, acquired their commissions in less than seventeen years after arrival in Maryland.

68. Johnston, "Lloyd Family," 424–26; Christopher Johnston, "The Tilghman Family," *MHM* 1 (1906) 280–82; *Archives* 33:297; 25:395; Wills 15:80–83.

69. Jordan, "Royal Period," pp. 215–18; *Archives* 25:327; 34: 121, 485; 35:195.

70. Charles S. Sydnor, *Gentlemen Freeholders: Political Practices in Washington's Virginia* (Chapel Hill, 1952).

71. The average tenure of councillors sitting between 1660 and 1689 was just over seven years, with only six men serving over ten years. The average rose slightly to nine years for men appointed between the revolution and 1700. The twenty individuals appointed 1700–1715 served an average of thirteen years, while the council of eleven men sitting in 1715 would have an average tenure of nineteen and one-half years.

72. Quarry to [David Pulteney, Lord of Trade], 2 Dec. 1709, CO323/7 no.1.

73. Lloyd to Board of Trade, 7 May 1711 and 20 Nov. 1712, CO5/717/II no. 41 and CO5/717/III no. 52; *Archives* 29:188–89; Jordan, "Royal Period," pp. 264–65, 304–15.

74. *Archives* 25:265.

75. *Cal. State Papers, Col., 1697–1698,* no. 716. In 1729, Benedict Leonard Calvert explained to the proprietor that "Such men as ought to be Chosen are not Easily got, and few men Care for an Empty Honour attended with trouble without some recompense." *Calvert Papers Number Two,* Maryland Historical Society Fund Publication No. 34 (Baltimore, 1814). p. 80. In 1715, three of the four provincial court justices were once again councillors, as just one example of the recurring pluralism in officeholding. For the council in the years after the royal period, see Charles Albro Barker, *The Background of the Revolution in Maryland* (New Haven, 1940), especially 122–26, and Thomas O'Brien Hanley, "His Excellency's Council: Maryland, 1715–1720," *American Catholic Historical Society* 74 (1963):137–150.

FOUR

IMMIGRANTS AND THEIR INCREASE: THE PROCESS OF POPULATION GROWTH IN EARLY COLONIAL MARYLAND

Russell R. Menard

. . . nor hath it at any time bin inquired into, whence it comes to pass, that, that colony . . . is not better Inhabited, considering what vast Numbers of Servants & others, have yearly bin transported thither.—Edward Randolph on Virginia, 1696

Materials for estimating the total population of the Chesapeake colonies during the seventeenth century are sparse. Contemporary counts of inhabitants survive for only a few years in Virginia and for only one in Maryland. Reports of the number of taxable persons (roughly, black adults and white males of working age) are more often available, but it is impossible to know precisely what part of the whole they formed. Nevertheless, by combining this evidence with information on local population change, immigration, the age and sex characteristics of the inhabitants, and the changing state of the economy, it is possible to construct a rough description of growth. Figure 4.1 summarizes the results of such a process. A mere handful of settlers at Jamestown in 1607 grew to about 11,000 colonists by 1640, 35,000 by 1660, and just over 60,000 in 1680. In 1700, roughly 100,000 people lived along the tobacco coast.[1]

Despite this rapid growth, Edward Randolph was unimpressed. In 1696 he remarked on how few people lived in Virginia. Why, Randolph asked, had so many immigrants over the course of the seventeenth century produced so small a population at century's end? Randolph, who thought land engrossment by the gentry lay behind Virginia's failure to grow more rapidly, suggested that the Board of Trade investigate and impose appropriate reforms. The board, busy with practical questions of trade and empire, ignored the suggestion. Despite the obvious importance of the issue,

Note: Russell R. Menard is assistant professor of history, University of Minnesota. He would like to thank Lorena S. Walsh for sharing evidence and insight into the sources of population growth in the early colonial Chesapeake region.

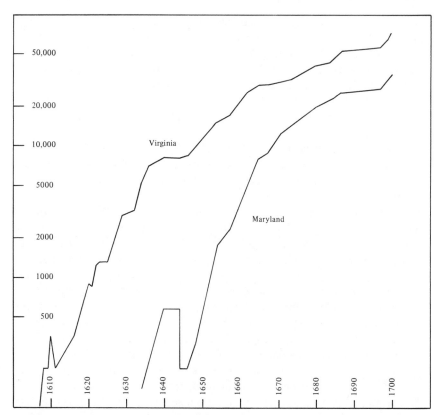

FIGURE 4.1. Population Growth in Virginia and Maryland, 1607–1700

historians have given it scarcely more attention than did the Board of Trade.[2]

Wesley Frank Craven is an exception. In a recent essay, Craven argued that the population of Virginia in 1700 was at most only equal to the total number of immigrants in the seventeenth century.[3] Is Craven correct? Did continuous waves of new settlers obscure a failure to achieve reproductive increase in the seventeenth century? If so, why? When and why did natural population growth begin? This essay, using evidence drawn principally from Maryland sources, addresses these questions. Only the European immigrant experience is considered. Africans, who had a broadly similar demographic history, have been discussed elsewhere.[4]

Although Craven's argument is persuasive, his evidence is inadequate. His principal source is the record of headright grants kept by the clerks of Virginia land office. His conclusion rests on a comparison of the total number of grants before 1700 with estimates of total population in 1700. However, as Craven notes, the record of headrights is not a fully reliable guide to immigration. The system was plagued by abuses that could lead to a substantial overestimate of the volume of immigration. At the same time, Craven assumed that nearly all immigrants appeared in the headrights without attempting a test.[5] Before a count of headrights can be used to measure the volume of immigration, an adjustment for omissions and duplications is necessary.

Maryland's land records, as Craven recognized, have some advantages over Virginia's as a measure of immigration. There is no evidence that the abuses that plagued the Virginia headright system were a serious problem in Maryland. More important, it is possible to determine the approximate relationship between the number of headrights and total immigration.

The Early Settlers of Maryland, an index to land warrants from 1634 to the abolition of the headright system in 1681, contains about 25,000 names.[6] With a few exceptions, the entires are claims to headrights. A check of the first 2,000 entries indicates that 6 percent are second, third, and fourth listings of persons who had already appeared. However, as anyone who attempts biographical work soon discovers, the index is not a comprehensive list of immigrants, and the omissions far outnumber those who appear more than once. Therefore, eliminating the multiple listings (roughly 1,500 of the 25,000 entries) establishes a lower bound figure for total immigration: at least 23,500 people immigrated to Maryland between 1634 and 1681.

By comparing the names in the *Early Settlers* index to independently generated lists of immigrants, it is possible to estimate the number of omissions. The record of servants brought into the county courts to have their service period determined provides a useful check. Of 872 servants, 545 (62.5 percent) brought into Charles and Talbot county courts from 1662 to 1680 appeared in the index, indicating a multiple of 1.6 for converting headrights to total immigrants.[7] Since it is probable that free immigrants were more likely to register than servants, the total of just under 38,000 produced by this multiple is a reasonable upper bound. The mean of the upper and lower bound figures, just under 31,000, can serve as a "best estimate" of total immigration to Maryland from 1634 to 1681. This figure finds support in a comparison of a list of all adult male residents of Kent Island in 1652 with the *Early Settlers* index, which produced a multiple of 1.3 for converting the 23,500 headrights into total immigration.[8] Checks against lists of immigrant landowners, an obviously biased source for this purpose, produced lower multiples.[9]

Between 23,500 and 38,000 Europeans migrated to Maryland from 1634 to 1681. While this range is large, the figures are useful. In particular, they point to an important fact about Maryland's demographic history and provide powerful support for Craven's argument: during much of the seventeenth century, Maryland's population was not self-sustaining. In 1681, there were about 19,000 whites in the province, more than 5,000 fewer than the minimum estimate of total European immigration for the years since 1634.[10]

The wills left by men who died in Maryland support this conclusion. A comparison of the number of sons mentioned by male testators with the number of male testators provides a rough guide to the rate at which men replaced themselves in the population. The procedure was to count in an annual series all wills written by male residents of Maryland between 1635 and 1720 that appear in Baldwin's *Maryland Calendar of Wills*.[11] All sons mentioned in those wills were also counted. The replacement rate is the ratio of sons mentioned in a year to wills written in that year. Men whose wills did not specify the number or sex of their children were excluded. However, if a testator mentioned no children it was assumed that he had none when he made his will. Excluded wills were less than 2 percent of the total. The date used was the date the will was written, the date of the latest codicil, or, for wills otherwise undated, the date of probate. In order to make patterns more apparent, a rate based on a three-year-moving-average of wills and sons appears in figure 4.2.

While the construction of replacement rates is a simple task, translation of the results into a measure of natural increase is more complex. In the first place, the measure overstates the rate of reproduction. Testators were older, wealthier, more often married, and more likely to have children than the decedent population as a whole. Furthermore, naming a son in a will did not guarantee that he would live long enough to take his father's place in the adult male population. Because of these biases, replacement rates cannot be translated directly into a rate of net natural increase per generation. A replacement rate of one does not mean that the population maintained its size by reproductive increase from one generation to the next. In fact, a replacement rate of one is strong evidence of a net natural decline. Growth probably required a rate of at least one and one-quarter and perhaps one and one-half.

The problem of interpretation is aggravated because replacement rates are based on an event that occurred after the event we are trying to measure. The date of a replacement rate is determined by an adult's death, not a child's birth, yet it is the latter that is critical in locating changes over time with precision. Demographers who have used measures resembling this one have assumed that the rate described births occurring sixteen years (half a generation) earlier.[12] However, the short life expectancies and late age at marriage for immigrant males (discussed below) suggest that sixteen years is much too long an interval between a man's death and the birth of his middle son—six to eight years seems closer to the mark. Native Marylanders married earlier and lived longer than their immigrant fathers, and sixteen

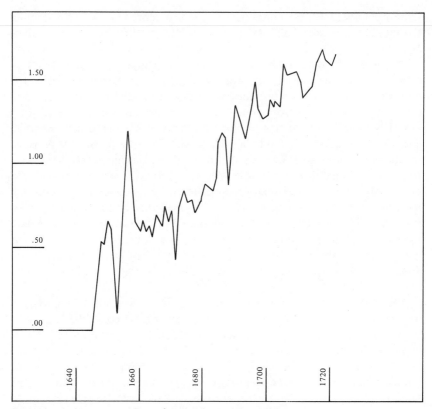

FIGURE 4.2. Replacement Rates for Maryland Males, 1634–1720

years is perhaps a more accurate estimate of the interval for those born in the province. Thus, as long as the adult decedent population was almost entirely immigrant, certainly the case well into the 1680s, replacement rates should be interpreted as describing births that occurred six to eight years earlier. As the proportion of natives among adult decedents increased, the interval lengthened, perhaps approaching sixteen years by the end of the period covered by figure 4.2.[13]

Despite these problems, the measure is useful. It certainly indicates that Maryland's population did not grow by natural means during most of the seventeenth century. Five factors—emigration, mortality, marriage, fertility, and the sex ratio among immigrants—need to be examined in accounting for the colony's failure to grow by reproductive increase.

Emigration was of little importance. There are occasional references to colonists who returned to England, but they are few and largely confined to merchants and gentry.[14] Certainly the number who returned was not large enough to have a major impact on population growth. Migration to other colonies, particularly to Virginia, was more frequent, but this too was numerically insignificant. In the seventeenth century, migration from Virginia to Maryland was by far the more common pattern.[15] It was not until the mid-1690s, when a prolonged depression in the tobacco trade and the attractions of Pennsylvania, the Jerseys, and the Carolinas led many ex-servants to leave the Chesapeake, that emigration had an important impact on Maryland's population.[16]

Mortality, on the other hand, proved critical. A mortality of extraordinary dimensions plagued Maryland's inhabitants during the seventeenth century. All immigrants seem to have been afflicted by a "seasoning," and the mortality among new arrivals must have been frightening. Unfortunately, a method of measuring deaths during seasoning has yet to be discovered.[17] Nor is it possible to measure directly mortality for immigrant women or for infants and children born in the province. Measures of life expectancy for adult male immigrants who survived their seasoning are available, however; they can serve as a rough guide to mortality levels for the entire population.

Survival of the seasoning period was no guarantee of a long life in Maryland. A recent study of mortality, based upon a coupling of ages listed in depositions with probate records, concluded that men who immigrated to the colony in the middle decades of the seventeenth century and survived to age twenty-two could expect to live only an additional twenty to twenty-four years. Or, to state the results differently, 17 percent of all immigrant males who reached age twenty-two died before reaching age thirty, 41 percent before age forty, and 70 percent before age fifty.[18]

Whether men outlived women in the seventeenth-century Chesapeake is still an open question; the evidence so far assembled is contradictory. The absence of adequate death registers forced the use of indirect methods in the initial efforts to measure relative mortality by sex. Two such methods suggested that women enjoyed greater longevity than men. The first used probate records to gain insight into relative mortality by sex among slaves. All slaves appearing in inventories taken in Calvert, Charles, Prince George's, and St. Mary's counties, Maryland, between 1658 and 1710 were classified by age and sex. In the age category sixteen to fifty years, men outnumbered women by one and one-half to one, a reflection of the sex distribution of immigrants, while among slaves over fifty years old there were nearly twice as many women as men. This pattern may reflect the importation of old slave women, but a more likely explanation is that females lived longer.[19] The second indirect method examined marriages. The study surveyed 411 seventeenth-century marriages among whites in Charles County and concluded that wives survived husbands by a margin of about two to one. A study of marriages in Somerset County, Maryland, produced similar results.[20] Since brides were usually younger than grooms, the method exaggerates the relative longevity of females. Nevertheless, this seemed firm evidence that women outlived men.

However, life tables developed by Darrett and Anita Rutman for men and women born in Middlesex County, Virginia, during the seventeenth century contradict this conclusion. Based on a massive prosopography and a rigorous definition of the population at risk, the Rutmans discovered that native-born men who married and reached age 20 could expect between 24 and 30 additional years of life, while their female counterparts could expect to live only 15 to 25 more years. The Rutmans' preferred estimate allows men who reached age 20 an additional 28.8 years and women only 19.8 years. Although there is a slight overlap in the range of their estimates, this is firm evidence that men outlived women. Higher female mortality, the Rutmans suggest, was due principally to the hazards of childbirth in a society plagued by malaria.[21]

Can this conflict be resolved? The Middlesex life tables are clearly the stronger evidence, and one could simply dismiss the indirect methods as unreliable. Indeed, using a hypothetical group of marriages, the Rutmans have demonstrated that it is mathematically possible for the same persons to generate both the Middlesex life tables and the marriage survival rates of Somerset and Charles. However, mathematical possibility is not actual experience; one could feel more comfortable with the Rutmans' demonstration were not the differences between men and women in the Middlesex life tables so large. And, the evidence of higher mortality for men among slaves remains unchallenged.

Perhaps the differences between the results produced by the two types of measures are real, reflecting differences in the populations covered. The Middlesex life tables describe only the experience of the native born, while the indirect measures include both immigrants and creoles. Sex differentiated work roles may have left immigrant males more susceptible to the rigors of seasoning, while immigrant women, because of their relatively late age at marriage (discussed below), escaped exposure to the hazards of childbirth during much of their reproductive lives. The sex roles of creoles probably did not differ from those of immigrants, but native-born men were not subject to seasoning, and creole women, because they married early, were exposed to the hazards of childbirth for a larger proportion of their lives than were immigrants. In short, it is possible that among immigrants, women lived as long or longer than men, while among natives men outlived women.

Further analysis of the indirect measures provides some support for this hypothesis. In Somerset County marriages in which both partners were immigrants, wives survived their husbands in nearly 70 percent of the cases; when both partners were natives wives survived only 55 percent of the time. In the Western Shore slave population, the surplus of women among those aged fifty and above disappeared in the second decade of the eighteenth century, roughly when one would expect native-born blacks to first appear in significant numbers in that age category.[22]

While the question of relative mortality by sex remains open, and caution is required in making inferences about the longevity and health of women and children from the experience of men, the evidence will support some general conclusions of importance to an investigation of reproductive increase. First, immigrant females led short lives, and death prematurely ended the childbearing careers of many. Second, so short an expectation of life for adults suggests high rates of infant and childhood mortality; rough estimates indicate that from 40 to 55 percent of the children born in Maryland in the seventeenth century died before reaching age twenty.[23] Third, such a low expectation of life implies high rates of morbidity and chronic ill health that may have limited the fertility of immigrant women.[24] Finally, despite all the difficulties of measurement, it is clear that mortality among immigrants was high enough to limit severely the rate of reproductive population growth.

High rates of morbidity and mortality contributed to Maryland's failure to grow by natural increase, but they were not the sole cause. The preponderance of males among immigrants also placed severe restrictions on growth by reproduction. Table 4.1 presents sex ratios—expressed as the number of men per hundred women—for immigrants to Maryland and Virginia in the seventeenth century. The proportion of women was very low in the 1630s, improved markedly about midcentury, and continued to increase, although at a much slower rate, for the remainder of the century. During the period of heaviest immigration to Maryland, from the late 1640s to the late 1670s, men outnumbered women by two and one-half or three to one among new arrivals, while earlier in the century men were relatively more numerous.[25]

The shortage of women prevented many men from marrying and forced others to delay marriage until relatively late in their lives. Over 20 percent of the men who left inventories on Maryland's lower Western Shore between 1658 and 1705 were unmarried at death; a similar proportion of bachelors appears among men who died in Somerset between 1665 and 1700. Earlier in the century the proportion was even higher: more than 60 percent of the men who left wills in Maryland between 1635 and 1650 died unmarried.[26] Age at first marriage for immigrants is difficult to discover, but limited evidence suggests a mean of about thirty years for men who migrated to the Chesapeake region during the seventeenth century.[27]

Although the sex ratio placed severe limits on the opportunities for men to form families, its importance must not be overdrawn. Marriage patterns mitigated the full impact of the shortage of women. First, given the rapid growth of population, the differences between the ages of brides and grooms increased men's chances to marry beyond what would have been possible

TABLE 4.1
Sex Ratios for Adult Immigrants to the Chesapeake

	Sex Ratio (Number of Men per 100 Women)
London immigrants, 1634–35[1] (N = 1907)	603.7
Maryland headright sample, 1634–45[2] (N = 20)	*
Maryland headright sample, 1646–57[2] (N = 99)	312.5
Virginia headright sample, 1648–66[3] (N = 4272)	341.8
Bristol immigrants, 1654–86[1] (N = 5065)	308.1
Servants in Maryland inventories, 1658–79[4] (N = 584)	320.1
Maryland headright sample, 1658–81[2] (N = 625)	257.1
Servants in Maryland inventories, 1680–1705[4] (N = 960)	295.1
London immigrants, 1682–87[5] (N = 856)	242.4
Virginia headrights, 1695–99[6] (N = 1094)	296.4
Liverpool immigrants, 1697–1707[7] (N = 1394)	245.0

Sources:
1. Herbert Moller, "Sex Composition and Correlated Culture Patterns of Colonial America" *WMQ*, 3d ser., 2 (1945):117–18.
2. Russell R. Menard, "Society and Economy in Early Colonial Maryland" (Ph.D. diss., University of Iowa, 1975), ch. 5.
3. Wesley Frank Craven, *White, Red, and Black: The Seventeenth-Century Virginian* (Charlottesville, 1971), p. 27.
4. Servants appraised in inventories filed in Calvert, Charles, St. Mary's, and Prince George's counties.
5. C. D. P. Nicholson, *Some Early Emigrants to America* (Baltimore, 1965); Michael Ghirelli, *A List of Emigrants from England to America, 1682–1690* (Baltimore, 1968); London indentures, 1682–83, ms., Folger Shakespeare Library, Washington, D.C.
6. Edmund S. Morgan, "Slavery and Freedom: The American Paradox," *Journal of American History* 59 (1972):27.
7. Elizabeth French, *List of Emigrants to America from Liverpool, 1697–1707* (Baltimore, 1969).
*20 adults in sample, all were men

had the sex ratio been the only consideration.[28] Second, differences by sex in the propensity to remarry affected opportunities for men to find wives. Since many Maryland marriages were dissolved by death while the surviving spouse was still young, and since widows remarried more often than widowers, a larger proportion of the men were able to marry than the sex ratio alone would indicate.[29] Third, wives survived marriages more often than husbands and thus were more often available for remarriage.[30] As a result of these mitigating circumstances, most men who reached age forty in Maryland were able to marry at least once in their lives despite the shortage of women.[31]

One would expect the Chesapeake sex ratio to have encouraged youthful marriages among women, thereby increasing the number of children they would bear in their lifetimes.[32] However, most single females immigrating to Maryland and Virginia in the seventeenth century were indentured servants in their early twenties.[33] Although a few were purchased by men in the market for a wife,[34] and many others had illegitimate children,[35] the majority remained childless for four or five years while completing their terms. Most immigrant women who were single when they arrived did not marry until their middle twenties.[36] Those who migrated with husbands, if they followed English practice, were also in their mid-twenties when they first married.[37] The sexual imbalance of the immigrant group restricted natural increase by excluding many men from the procreative process, but it did not produce a compensating lower age at marriage for women that would have extended their reproductive lives. Relatively few women came to the tobacco coast, and many who did come did not begin families until they were well advanced in their childbearing years.

High rates of mortality and morbidity, late marriages, and a shortage of women—any one of them acting alone could place severe restrictions on the natural increase of population. It is not possible to assess the relative impact of these several factors on the rate of reproductive growth, or even to single out one as critical. But—and this is perhaps the more important point—they reinforced each other, worked together rather than at cross purpose. Had expectation of life been longer, the proportion of women higher, or age at marriage lower, the Chesapeake colonies might have overcome the remaining obstacles to natural increase. However, with all acting to depress the reproductive growth rate, demographic failure along the tobacco coast was inevitable. Until at least one of these variables changed dramatically, Maryland and Virginia would prove incapable of sustained growth without the benefit of continued immigration.

When did Maryland's population first achieve reproductive increase? Dating this "demographic transition" is a matter of interest. It might be argued that when the population began to grow independently of immigration the colony had successfully completed the transition from a frontier settlement to a provincial society. Precision is not yet possible, but there is evidence to support a tentative date for the beginning of reproductive population growth. Census returns indicate that the colony had achieved reproductive increase by the first decade of the eighteenth century. The number of whites increased from 30,614 in 1704 to 35,794 in 1710, a growth rate of more than 2.5 percent per year. This growth occurred, moreover, during a period of low immigration. Indeed, there is evidence of heavy emigration from Maryland in these years, as the relative decline in the number of white males described by table 4.2 suggests.[38] Children were the most rapidly growing part of the population, suggesting a birth boom in the early eighteenth century.

The replacement rates in figure 4.2 are helpful in locating the beginnings of natural population increase. The rate was fairly stable in the 1600s and 1670s, and its level in those decades, fluctuating between .5 and .75 sons per male testator, makes it clear that the population was not growing by natural means. The rate began to rise rapidly about 1680, permanently passed 1 in the mid-1680s, and continued to grow, reaching 1.5 sons per testator by the early eighteenth century. Since replacement rates refer to births that occurred before the date of the will, these data suggest that further inquiry should concentrate on the 1680s and 1690s.

Why did the Maryland population achieve reproductive increase near the turn of the century? The factors principally responsible for the failure to grow by natural means—high mortality, sexual imbalance, and a late age at marriage—were characteristics of immigrants. As might be expected, the beginnings of natural increase were associated with a decline in immigration and the emergence of a native-born majority in the province. Native adults married earlier and lived longer than their immigrant parents, and, of course, the sex ratio among those born in Maryland was approximately equal.

Natives probably became a majority among white adults during the decades around 1700, although the exact date varied by region. The tobacco trade stagnated from the 1680s to about 1715—prices were low, production stable, and the economy depressed. As a consequence, relatively few Europeans migrated to the Chesapeake during these years. Only in the brief booms of the mid-1680s and at the turn of the century did the colony receive a substantial number of new settlers. In addition, many of the young men who had come to Maryland as servants completed their terms, found themselves free men in a depressed economy promising few opportunities,

TABLE 4.2
Maryland Population, 1704-1710

Year	Total Whites	White Male Taxables	White Women	White Children
1704	30,614	11,212	7,163	12,239
1710	35,794	11,340	8,548	15,906
Percentage of increase	16.9%	1.1%	19.3%	30.0%

Source: William Hand Browne et al., eds., *Archives of Maryland*, 72 vols. (Baltimore, 1883–), 25:256, 258–59.
Note: Figures have been adjusted to correct apparent errors according to procedures described in Russell R. Menard, "Economy and Society in Early Colonial Maryland," (Ph.D. diss., University of Iowa, 1975), ch. 8.

and left the colony in search of better prospects elsewhere.[39] A declining rate of immigration and the emigration of ex-servants led to a reduction of the proportion of immigrants in the population and a gradual improvement of the sex ratio. At the same time, the children of colonists who had immigrated earlier in the century were coming of age and having children of their own. Some time between 1680 and 1710, persons born in the province became a majority of Maryland's population.[40]

Improvements in the sex ratio doubtless played a role in the beginnings of natural increase, but their importance should not be overemphasized. As late as 1704, men outnumbered women in Maryland by more than three to two. While the proportion of males had been swollen by the boom in immigration around 1700, evidence of the marital status of decedents demonstrates that throughout the late 1680s and early 1690s, a period of low immigration and high emigration, the sex ratio remained sufficiently unequal to prohibit marriage for a substantial proportion of the eligible men. Natural increase began while the province still suffered a shortage of women.[41]

A decline in mortality among the native born also contributed to the beginnings of natural population growth. As Philip Curtin has pointed out, immigration almost invariably results in higher rates of morbidity and mortality for the migrant. Disease environments exhibit a wide range of local variation throughout the world; immunities acquired in one place often offer little protection in another. "Childhood disease environment," Curtin writes, "is the crucial factor in determining the immunities of a given adult population. Not only will the weakest members of the society be removed, leaving a more resistant population of survivors; childhood and infancy are also a period of life when many infections are relatively benign." As a rule, Curtin suggests, the native born are healthier and live longer than their immigrant parents.[42] Studies of longevity for males born in the Chesapeake colonies in the seventeenth century confirm Curtin's suggestion: the life tables so far completed indicate that native-born men who reached age twenty were, on average, in their late forties or early fifties at death; immigrants, on the other hand, were usually in their early forties.[43] Doubtless this improved life expectancy increased the natural growth rate.

However, the precise impact of improvements in longevity on the rate of reproductive increase is difficult to gauge. First of all, the evidence on male life expectancy is rough and will not support too close a comparison. Second, no direct measure of the relative mortality of native and immigrant women is available, and inferring changes in female longevity from the experience of males may be unjustified. It is possible that the gains in longevity achieved by native-born men did not extend to women. Third, there were regional variations in the life expectancy of Chesapeake natives—the advantage of creoles over immigrants who survived their seasoning ranged from slight (two or three years) to substantial (eight to ten years).[44] Probably, the most that can be said at this stage of knowledge is that greater longevity among creoles led to some gain in the rate of natural increase. However, even in Somerset County, where the improvement was greatest, the death rate remained high enough to constitute a serious impediment to reproductive growth.

Although more evidence would be welcome, differences in age at marriage between immigrants and natives are more firmly documented and easier to assess than changes in mortality. Table 4.3 summarizes the available information on age at first marriage in Maryland and Virginia during the seventeeth and early eighteenth centuries. Natives, both male and female, were much younger at first marriage than their immigrant parents and than brides and grooms in either old or New England. The decline for females is particularly sharp and critical for understanding the sources of change in the natural growth rate. If immigrant females were usually in their mid-twenties when they married, the decline for women was roughly five to ten years.

TABLE 4.3
Age at First Marriage in the Chesapeake Colonies

	Males	Females
Immigrants in Chesapeake gentry study, born by 1700[1]	30.2 (N = 16)	
Immigrants to the Eastern Shore, born 1610–58[2]	29.2 (N = 32)	24.7 (N = 11)
Immigrants to Charles Co., Md., born 1610–59[3]	30.3 (N = 60)	25.0 (N = 20)
Natives in Charles Co., Md., born 1640–79[3]	24.1 (N = 40)	17.8 (N = 15)
Natives in Somerset Co., Md., born 1648–69[2]	23.1 (N = 30)	16.5 (N = 44)
Natives in Somerset Co., Md., born 1670–1711[2]	22.8 (N = 25)	17.0 (N = 32)
Natives in Somerset Co., Md., born 1700–40[4]	24.1 (N = 25)	19.0 (N = 13)
Natives in Middlesex Co., Va., born by 1710[5]	24.7 (N = 184)	20.6 (N = 203)
Natives in lower Western Shore of Md., born 1680–99[6]	23.1 (N = 48)	18.2 (N = 29)
Natives in lower Western Shore of Md., born 1700–19[6]	23.7 (N = 72)	18.5 (N = 72)
Natives in lower Western Shore of Md., born 1720–49[6]	25.9 (N = 100)	21.4 (N = 64)

Sources:

1. A study of gentry families from genealogies now being conducted by the author.
2. Russell R. Menard, "The Demography of Somerset County, Maryland: A Preliminary Report" (paper presented at the Conference on Early American Social History, Stony Brook, N.Y., June 1975).
3. Lorena S. Walsh, "Charles County, Maryland, 1658–1705: A Study of Chesapeake Social and Political Structure" (Ph.D. diss., Michigan State University, in progress), ch. 2.
4. Michael J. Kelly, "Family Reconstitution of Stepney Parish, Somerset County, Maryland" (M.A. thesis, University of Maryland, 1971), pp. 18–25.
5. Darrett B. and Anita H. Rutman, "'Now-Wives and Sons-in-Law': Parental Death in a Seventeenth-Century Virginia County," in *Essays on the Seventeenth-Century Chesapeake*, ed. Thad W. Tate and David L. Ammerman (Chapel Hill, forthcoming).
6. Allan Kulikoff, "Tobacco and Slaves: Population, Economy, and Society in Eighteenth-Century Prince George's County, Maryland" (Ph.D. diss., Brandeis University, 1976), ch. 3.

Why such youthful marriages? Early parental death is one possible answer.[45] As a result of short life expectancies and late marriages, few immigrants lived to see their children reach adulthood. When children reached their legal majority, they often found themselves free to marry and set up households without parental permission. In Somerset County, Maryland, however, early paternal death seems to have had little impact on age at marriage. Grooms who were orphaned before they reached the mean age at first marriage were not younger than grooms whose fathers were still alive. Brides who were orphaned before the mean age at marriage were actually slightly older than those with living fathers, perhaps reflecting a community sense that parental approval was necessary for marriages in which the bride had not yet reached age sixteen.[46]

The sex ratio seems the obvious explanation for youthful marriages among women. Females born in Maryland and Virginia in the seventeenth century matured in a society with a large surplus of marriageable males. Doubtless they were pressured to marry as soon as they were able to bear children. In the eighteenth century, as the sex ratio moved toward equality, the age at marriage for women in the Chesapeake colonies gradually increased.

However, the sex ratio cannot account for the relative youth of native-born grooms. Indeed, one would expect it to work in the opposite direction, pushing the age at first marriage higher than the English or colonial norm. Perhaps native men, who were, on average, more firmly established in the community and who had easier access to wealth than immigrants, had advantages in competing for the hands of prospective brides sufficient to override the effects of the shortage of women.

Were there significant differences in the fertility of native-born and immigrant women in the Chesapeake colonies? Reliable measures of fertility have yet to be developed. The only age-specific rates currently available—for native-born women who married in Somerset County between 1655 and 1695—are low by colonial standards, suggesting that a substantial number of children who were stillborn or who died in infancy were not entered in the birth register. The alternative explanation, that women successfully controlled their fertility throughout marriage, seems unlikely. Despite this defect, it is possible (assuming no difference in the registration habits of immigrants and natives) to develop measures of relative fertility. Two such measures, one based on the number of births per woman-year of marriage before the wife reached age forty-five, the other on birth intervals, indicate that at least in Somerset County the fertility rates of immigrant and native-born women were nearly identical.[47] Nevertheless, native-born women usually had more children than their immigrant mothers, principally because they were younger at first marriage.[48] At the age-specific rates discovered in

Somerset County, a woman who married at age sixteen and lived to forty-five would bear just over 9 children; one who married at twenty-five would have fewer than 6. Completed family size for creole women in Somerset County was 9.4 children, while for immigrants it was only 6.1. The average number of children in all Somerset families in which the wife was native born was 6.0, enough for rapid natural increase. Families in which the wife was an immigrant had an average of only 3.9 children. Given the prevailing rates of infant and childhood mortality, this was, at best, barely sufficient to prevent a natural decline.[49]

A summary of the argument may prove helpful. Several characteristics of the immigrant population limited its ability to reproduce. Immigrants suffered high rates of morbidity and mortality and a severe shortage of women. Those women who did migrate, furthermore, usually did not marry until relatively late in their lives. Consequently, European immigrants to the Chesapeake colonies failed to reproduce themselves fully. They did have some children, however, who transformed the region's demography. Native-born males, at least, lived longer than their immigrant fathers, although creole women may not have shared the gains in longevity achieved by their brothers. Moreover, the sex ratio among those born along the tobacco coast was roughly equal. Most important, native-born women married at much younger ages than their immigrant mothers. Creole women had enough children to reverse the direction of reproductive population change despite apparently stable age-specific fertility, a still unbalanced sex ratio, and a persistent high mortality.[50]

The demographic contrasts between the Chesapeake colonies and New England are striking. Judged in terms of natural increase, the Puritan settlements were a demographic success, Virginia and Maryland failures. The populations of the two regions were of roughly equal size in 1700, yet New England had been colonized by only a few more than 20,000 settlers, while seven or eight times that number had migrated to the Chesapeake.[51] As Craven has noted, this was partly a matter of timing: Chesapeake immigrants arrived throughout the century, while the great majority of New England colonists came during the 1630s and thus had a longer time to reproduce.[52] Since the New England settlers were not followed by continuous waves of immigrants, a creole majority emerged more quickly there than in the Chesapeake. In 1700, when natives were just beginning to dominate politics in Maryland and Virginia, government in New England was firmly in the hands of a third-generation leadership.[53]

More important than the timing of the migration were differences in the people who moved to the two regions. Migration to the Chesapeake was principally a matter of meeting the tobacco economy's voracious labor demands. Merchants recruited most heavily among those whose labor would bring the highest price. As a consequence, the typical white immigrant was an indentured servant, usually a young man in his late teens or early twenties. Most colonists arrived alone rather than with their families, and the ships deposited relatively few women and even fewer children and older settlers along the tobacco coast.[54] New Englanders sailed to other winds. Although the motives of many were doubtless mixed and complex, religious conviction was clearly a primary force: persecution and despair over the moral decay of their society pushed them out of England; the myth of a saving remnant and the hope of building a city upon a hill pulled them toward the New World. "God," a decendant of these early settlers explained, "sifted a whole nation that he might bring choice Grain over into this Wilderness."[55] Migration to New England was more often an affair of families than of individuals, and the age distribution of immigrants approximated that of a settled population. Most important, New England's first settlers included a much larger proportion of women than appeared among immigrants to the Chesapeake colonies.[56]

Not only were the immigrants different, the disease environments they encountered and created in the New World contrasted sharply. Again, the advantage went to the northern settlements. Native-born residents of rural New England who reached age twenty could expect to live fifteen to twenty years longer than their Chesapeake counterparts. Urban New Englanders were less favored, but they still enjoyed substantially longer lives than inhabitants of the tobacco coast. Rates of infant and childhood mortality were also much lower in New England. While between 40 and 55 percent of the children born in Maryland during the seventeenth century died before age twenty, nearly eight of ten children born in Andover, Ipswich, and Plymouth, Massachusetts lived to adulthood.[57] Low rates of mortality and a more equal sex ratio ensured that New England's natural growth rate would far exceed that of the Chesapeake colonies.

Despite these differences, there may have been some similarities in the demographic history of the two regions. New England's sex ratio was less imbalanced than the Chesapeake's, but men did outnumber women by roughly three to two among immigrants.[58] Seasoning was less severe in New England, but there were some years of heavy mortality in the 1630s.[59] Unlike most women who went to Virginia and Maryland, females who moved to New England were usually married when they arrived and did not have to wait several years before beginning families. However, some were servants, and the married women were often well advanced in their childbearing-years when they moved to the New World.[60] As a result, although there is no evidence that New England experienced a negative growth rate, there was a period of fairly slow natural growth in several towns that lasted into the middle 1650s.[61] The growth rate accelerated in the late 1650s as native-born women, who were very young at first marriage by English standards, came of age and had children of their own.[62] We still know too little to argue with conviction that the population history of the northern settlements paralleled that of the Chesapeake colonies in some broad respects, but at least there is evidence to suggest that a systematic inquiry into demographic differences between immigrants and their increase might reward students of early New England.

It is becoming convention for historians of colonial populations to conclude essays with a plea for further research. In an effort of this character, when so many of the propositions are speculative and rest on assumptions not yet thoroughly tested, when so much of the evidence is more suggestive than definitive and is derived by unorthodox procedures, such a conclusion is especially appropriate. In particular, the discussion lacks precision. When did the Chesapeake population begin to grow naturally? Was the change sudden and dramatic, or gradual and little noticed? Were there significant regional variations? How can they best be explained? Can the relative impact on population change of mortality, fertility, the sex ratio, and nuptuality be measured more precisely? The effects of the peculiar demography of the Chesapeake colonies also need study. How did the slow development of natural increase affect opportunity, political stability, capital accumulation, the demand for labor, and family life?[63]

Answers to such questions will not come easily. Historians used to the conveniently assembled detail of a parish register may be tempted to abandon the task, convinced that there is simply not enough evidence. In the absence of traditional data, sources only infrequently used by demographers may prove invaluable. Estate inventories, for example, contain a wealth of detail on the sex and age structure of the slave population, while the rate at which probate records were filed provides a rough guide to fluctuations in mortality. Massive career study projects linking all surviving records for a region into a biographical file, such as those of Darrett and Anita Rutman and of the St. Mary's City Commission, are providing valuable information on a wide range of issues. The vital registers that do survive, although seldom adequate for extensive reconstitution, can yield useful bits and pieces of data as well as clues to the timing of vital events. The usefulness of such registers can be enhanced by a prosopographical method coupling evidence from the registers with data from other sources, especially, although not exclusively, probate materials. Nor should the labors of genealogists be ignored. Historians may conclude that there is insufficient evidence for a full demographic history of the tobacco coast. Nevertheless, Edward Randolph's question deserves our attention. Whether or not an answer is found, close study of population problems and their relation to economic development and social change promises a deepened understanding of Chesapeake society.

That answer, if the hypothesis advanced here stands the test of further research, may prove of more than merely local interest. Preliminary investigation suggests that new settlements often experienced a period of negative, or at least relatively low, reproductive increase followed by a higher rate of natural growth once native-born adults became a substantial proportion of the population. The initial growth rate and the interval between first settlement and the beginnings of more rapid natural increase varied widely from region to region, apparently depending on mortality rates, the age structure and sex ratio among immigrants, and whether the initial settlers were followed by continuing waves of immigration that tended to delay the emergence of a creole majority. However, the basic demographic mechanisms—a gradual balancing of the sex ratio, declining rates of morbidity and mortality, and the lower age at marriage of native-born women—may have been nearly universal. The hypothesis may apply, furthermore, not only to new settlements but also to immigrants to urban environments who, because of racial or cultural prejudice or a strong sense of their own ethnic identity, remained isolated from their neighbors. Investigation of the demographic characteristics of immigrants and their increase may yield insight into an experience shared by people as diverse as the Europeans and Africans who settled the New World, New Englanders who moved to the American West, Chinese in San Francisco, and the descendants of slaves who trekked toward the promise of an industrialized north.

NOTES

1. A full defense of these estimates along with a description of the procedures used in their construction will be presented elsewhere. A preliminary discussion of the evidence and its difficulties appears in Russell R. Menard, "Economy and Society in Early Colonial Maryland" (Ph.D. diss., University of Iowa, 1975); idem, "The Growth of Population in Early Colonial Maryland, 1631–1712" (ms. report, St. Mary's City Commission, April 1972, on file at the Hall of Records, Annapolis, Md.). The following works proved especially helpful in constructing the estimates: Arthur E. Karinen, "Numerical and Distributional Aspects of Maryland Population, 1631–1840" (Ph.D. diss., University of Maryland, 1958); idem, "Maryland Population: 1631–1730: Numerical and Distributional Aspects," *Maryland Historical Magazine*, 54 (1959):365–407; Evarts B. Greene and Virginia D. Harrington, *American Population before the Federal Census of 1790* (New York, 1932); U.S. Bureau of the Census, *Historical Statistics of the United States, Colonial Times to 1957* (Washington, D.C., 1960), series Z 1–19; Edmund S. Morgan, "Headrights and Head Counts: A Review Article," *Virginia Magazine of History and Biography* 80 (1972):361–71.

2. Randolph to the Committee for Trade and Plantations, Aug. 31, 1696, in Robert N. Tappan and Alfred T. S. Goodrick, eds., *Edward Randolph: Including His Letters and Official Papers . . . 1676–1703*, 7 vols. (Boston, 1898–1909), 7:487. See also Henry Hartwell's comment that in 1697, Virginia was "very ill Peopled," in Hartwell to William Popple, 14 Sept., 1697, C.O. 5/1359, 94, Public Record Office (Colonial Virginia Records Project microfilm, Colonial Williamsburg Research Library, reel M-228), hereafter cited as Col. Va. Rec. Proj., microfilm, C.W.

3. Wesley Frank Craven, *White, Red, and Black: The Seventeenth-Century Virginia* (Charlottesville, 1971), pp. 25–28. See also Irene W. D. Hecht, "The Virginia Muster of 1624/5 as a Source for Demographic History," *William and Mary Quarterly,* 3d ser. 30 (1973): 65–92; Wyndham B. Blanton, *Medicine in Virginia in the Seventeenth Century* (Richmond, 1930), pp. 32–34; idem, "Epidemics, Real and Imaginary, and Other Factors Influencing Seventeenth-Century Virginia's Population," *Bulletin of the History of Medicine* 31 (1957):454–62; Thomas J. Wertenbaker, *The Planters of Colonial Virginia* (Princeton, 1922), pp. 98–99, 142; Edmund S. Morgan, *American Slavery-American Freedom: The Ordeal of Colonial Virginia* (New York, 1975), pp. 158–63.

4. Russell R. Menard, "The Maryland Slave Population, 1658 to 1730: A Demographic Profile of Blacks in Four Counties," *William and Mary Quarterly,* 3d ser, 32 (1975):29–54.

5. On the adequacy of headrights as a measure of immigration, see Morgan, "Headrights and Head Counts," and Russell R. Menard, "Immigration to the Chesapeake Colonies in the Seventeenth Century: A Review Essay," *Maryland Historical Magazine* 68 (1973): 323–29.

6. Gust Skordas, ed., *The Early Settlers of Maryland* (Baltimore, 1968). The records on which the list is based are described in Elisabeth Hartsook and Gust Skordas, *Land Office and Prerogative Court Records of Colonial Maryland,* Hall of Records Commission Publication No. 4 (Annapolis, 1946). The Maryland Land Office did not grant headrights for slaves; therefore, with a very few exceptions, the *Early Settlers* index includes only European immigrants.

7. The names of servants come from the county court records for Charles and Talbot counties at the Hall of Records, Annapolis, Md. Those prior to 1676 are printed in William Hand Browne *et al.*, eds., *Archives of Maryland,* 72 vols. (Baltimore, 1883–), vols 53, 54, and 60, hereafter cited as *Archives.*

8. The list is in *Archives* 54:4–5.

9. Lists of landowners in Charles and St. Mary's counties in 1659 and Somerset County in 1671 were checked against the *Early Settlers* index, producing a multiple of 1.1. The names of Charles and St. Mary's landowners appear in Rent Roll O, Ms., Hall of Records, Annapolis. The list of Somerset landowners was assembled from patents, deeds, and wills, see Menard, "Economy and Society in Early Colonial Maryland," pp. 241–44.

10. I have estimated the total population of Maryland in 1681 at about 20,000, of whom roughly 4 to 5 percent were black. See note 1, above. Lord Culpeper estimated that blacks made up about 4 percent of Virginia's population in 1681, C.O. 1/47, 270 (Col. Va. Rec. Proj., microfilm, C.W., M-327).

11. Jane Baldwin, ed. and comp., *The Maryland Calendar of Wills,* 8 vols. (Baltimore, 1928).

12. On the use of replacement rates, see T. H. Hollingsworth, *Historical Demography* (Ithaca, 1969), pp. 375–88; Josiah C. Russell, *British Medieval Population* (Albuquerque, 1948); Sylvia L. Thrupp, "The Problem of Replacement Rates in Late Medieval English Population," *Economic History Review,* 2d ser. 18 (1965):101–19; Carville V. Earle, "The Evolution of a Tidewater Settlement System: All Hallow's Parish, Maryland, 1650–1783" (Ph.D. diss., University of Chicago, 1973), p. 57.

13. Preliminary biographical studies now being conducted by the staff of the St. Mary's City Commission indicate that natives became a majority of the adult decedent population on the lower Western Shore of Maryland in the first two decades of the eighteenth century.

14. See for examples, Bernard Bailyn, "Politics and Social Structure in Virginia," in *Seventeenth-Century America: Essays in Colonial History,* James Morton Smith (Chapel Hill, 1959), pp. 93–94; Menard, "Economy and Society in Early Colonial Maryland," pp. 70–71, 136–37.

15. For evidence of migration from Virginia to Maryland during the seventeenth century, see Menard, "Economy and Society in Early Colonial Maryland," pp. 213–24.

16. The emigration during the 1690s is documented in ibid., 398–99.

17. For an effort to estimate the proportion of indentured servants who fell victim to seasoning, see article by Lorena S. Walsh, "Servitude and Opportunity in Charles County," in this volume. The rate of mortality among new arrivals, certainly frightful in the early years of settlement, apparently declined in the middle decades of the seventeenth century. Wertenbaker, *Planters of Colonial Virginia,* pp. 39–40; Edmund S. Morgan, "Slavery and Freedom: The

American Paradox," *Journal of American History* 59 (1972):18–20; Morgan, *American Slavery-American Freedom*, pp. 180–84; Blanton, *Medicine in Virginia*, pp. 37–41. According to Gov. William Berkeley, writing in 1671, "there is not often unseasoned hands (as we term them) that die now, whereas heretofore not one of five escaped the first year," William Waller Hening, *The Statutes at Large: Being a Collection of all the Laws of Virginia . . . ,* 9 vols. (New York, 1823), 2:515; see also Berkeley's comments in *A Discourse and View* (London, 1663), pp. 2–3.

18. Lorena S. Walsh and Russell R. Menard, "Death in the Chesapeake: Two Life Tables for Men in Early Colonial Maryland," *Maryland Historical Magazine* 69 (1964):214–17. A study of mortality among men who immigrated to the lower Eastern Shore of Maryland and Virginia reports nearly identical findings.—Russell R. Menard, "The Demography of Somerset County, Maryland: A Preliminary Report" (paper presented at the Conference on Early American Social History, Stony Brook, N.Y., June 1975), pp. 12–13.

19. Menard, "Maryland Slave Population," p. 33.

20. Walsh and Menard, "Death in the Chesapeake," p. 219; Menard, "Demography of Somerset County," p. 16.

21. Darrett B. and Anita H. Rutman, "'Now-Wives and Sons-in-Law'; Parental Death in a Seventeenth-Century Virginia County," in *Essays on the Seventeenth-Century Chesapeake,* ed. Thad W. Tate and David L. Ammerman (Chapel Hill, forthcoming); Rutman and Rutman, "Of Agues and Fevers: Malaria in the Early Chesapeake," *William and Mary Quarterly,* in press. Life tables for persons born in the last half of the seventeenth-century in Somerset County also indicate that men outlived women, although the male advantage appears to have been smaller than in Middlesex. However, the Somerset measure of female mortality is weak and should be used cautiously. Menard, "Demography of Somerset County," pp. 16–17.

22. Menard, "Maryland Slave Population," pp. 32, 43; idem, "Demography of Somerset County," p. 18, see also Morgan, *American Slavery-American Freedom,* p. 162.

23. Walsh and Menard, "Death in the Chesapeake," pp. 219–22: Menard, "Demography of Somerset County," p.15.

24. In particular this is likely if, as is suspected, malaria approached pandemic proportions in the Chesapeake colonies, since that disease is associated with chronic ill health and a high incidence of spontaneous abortion, see Rutman and Rutman, "Of Agues and Fevers."

25. The increasing proportion of women may have been part of a larger change in the immigrant group. Early in the seventeenth-century, Chesapeake planters were able to meet their labor needs with the most desirable type of servant—young men from families of middling status. Later in the century, demographic and economic change in England combined with growing colonial demand to produce a labor shortage in Maryland and Virginia. Planters and merchants responded by recruiting more heavily among alternative sources of labor, a response that led to a gradual increase in the number of women, Irishmen, convicts, lower-class Englishmen, and Africans brought to the Chesapeake. This argument is elaborated in Menard, "Economy and Society in Early Colonial Maryland," pp. 336–56.

26. Figures from the St. Mary's City Commission Inventory Project, "Social Stratification in Maryland, 1658–1705" (National Science Foundation Grant GS-32272), under the direction of Lois Green Carr, P.M.G. Harris, and Russell R. Menard; Baldwin, *Maryland Calendar of Wills,* vol. 1, and Menard, "Demography of Somerset County," p. 20.

27. See table 4.3. An indirect calculation of mean age at marriage for immigrant males based on the men whose age and marital status at death were known and who left inventories on the lower Western Shore of Maryland between 1658 and 1705 yielded 28.7 years, St. Mary's City Commission, "Social Stratification in Maryland," For the method used see J. Hajnal, "Age at Marriage and Proportions Marrying," *Population Studies,* 7 (1953):111–36.

28. For a demonstration see J. Hajnal, "European Marriage Patterns in Perspective," in *Population in History: Essays in Historical Demography,* ed. *D.V. Glass and D. E. C. Eversley* (London, 1965), p. 129.

29. Kevin P. Kelly, "Economic and Social Development of Seventeenth-Century Surry County, Virginia" (Ph.D. diss., University of Washington, 1972), p. 84. Lorena S. Walsh, "'Till Death Do Us Part': Marriage and Family in Maryland in the Seventeenth Century," in *Seventeenth-Century Chesapeake,* ed. Tate and Ammerman.

30. See note 20 above.

31. All but one of the 102 men aged forty or more whose age and marital status at death were known and who left inventories on the lower Western Shore between 1658 and 1705 were married or widowed at death, St. Mary's City Commission, "Social Stratification in Maryland,"

32. Daniel Scott Smith, "The Demographic History of Colonial New England," *Journal of Economic History,* 32 (1972):176–77; Roger Thompson, *Women in Stuart England and America: A Comparative Study* (London, 1974), pp. 23–24.

33. In a sample drawn from Maryland headright entries, only 2 of 806 immigrants were free, unmarried, adult women, Menard, "Economy and Society in Early Colonial Maryland," p. 197. The mean age of 112 female servants who left London for the Chesapeake between 1683 and 1685 was 21.4 years, C. D. P. Nicholson, *Some Early Emigrants to America* (Baltimore, 1965). The mean age of 192 female servants who left Liverpool for the Chesapeake between 1699 and 1707 was 22.5 years, Elizabeth French, *List of Emigrants to America from Liverpool, 1697–1707* (Baltimore, 1969). The mean age of 257 women who left London for the Chesapeake in 1635 and who did not appear to be the wives or daughters of male immigrants was 22.2 years, John Camden Hotten, ed., *The Original Lists of Persons of Quality . . . and Others Who Went from Great Britain to the American Plantations, 1600–1700* (London, 1874), pp. 35–154.

34. See Mildred Campbell, "Social Origins of Some Early Americans," in *Seventeenth-Century America,* ed. Smith, pp. 73–74: Thompson *Women in Stuart England and America,* pp. 36, 40–41.

35. Illegitimate births accounted for betweeen 6 and 12 percent of all births recorded in Somerset County during the seventeenth century, Menard, "Demography of Somerset County," pp. 22–23. This is clearly a high rate of illegitimacy, see Peter Laslett and Karla Oosterveen, "Long-Term Trends in Bastardy in England," *Population Studies* 27 (1973):255–86. High rates of illegitimacy in the Chesapeake have also turned up in unpublished research of Lorena Walsh in Charles County, Gwenda Morgan in Richmond County, Elizabeth Friedberg in Accomac County, and Lois Carr in lower Norfolk County. Bridal pregnancy was also common among immigrant women, Menard, "Demography of Somerset County," pp. 23–24.

36. See table 4.3. Craven argues for a late age of marriage among immigrant women in *White, Red, and Black,* p. 27.

37. On age at marriage in England see Peter Laslett, *The World We Have Lost: England before the Industrial Age,* 2d ed. (New York, 1965), pp. 82–83; Hajnal, "European Marriage Patterns in Perspective," pp. 101–43; E. A. Wrigley, "Family Limitation in Pre-Industrial England," *Economic History Review,* 2d ser. 19 (1966):86.

38. Menard, "Economy and Society in Early Colonial Maryland," pp. 417–20.

39. Ibid.

40. Support for this dating is found in the appearance of large numbers of natives in positions of political power in both Maryland and Virginia around the turn of the century, see David W. Jordan, "The Royal Period of Colonial Maryland, 1689–1715" (Ph.D. diss., Princeton University, 1966), pp. 201–65; Lois Green Carr, "County Government in Maryland, 1689–1709" (Ph.D. diss., Harvard University, 1968), pp. 676–91; John C. Rainbolt, "The Alteration in the Relationship between Leadership and Constituents in Virginia, 1660 to 1720," *William and Mary Quarterly,* 3d ser. 27 (1970):411–34; Martin Quitt, "The Virginia House of Burgesses, 1660–1706: The Social, Educational, and Economic Bases of Political Power" (Ph.D. diss., Washington University, 1970).

41. The sex ratio for 1704 is from *Archives* 25:256. For the proportion of men who died unmarried see Walsh, "'Till Death Us Do Part.'"

42. Philip D. Curtin, "Epidemiology and the Slave Trade," *Political Science Quarterly* 83 (1968):196–97.

43. Walsh and Menard, "Death in the Chesapeake," p. 218; Rutman and Rutman, "'Now Wives and Sons-in-Law'"; Menard, "Demography of Somerset County," pp. 11–15.

44. See note 43, above.

45. On the relation between early parental death and age at marriage see G. Ohlin, "Mortality, Marriage, and Growth in Pre-Industrial Populations," *Population Studies* 14 (1961):190–97, and Daniel Scott Smith, "Parental Power and Marriage Patterns: An Analysis of Historical Trends in Hingham, Massachusetts," *Journal of Marriage and the Family* 35 (1973):422–23.

46. Menard, "Demography of Somerset County," pp.21–22.

47. Ibid., pp.22–24.

48. Marriages among natives lasted longer and were less frequently interrupted by death while the wife was still in her childbearing-years than marriages among immigrants, which would tend to increase the number of children born to creole women, Walsh, "'Till Death Us Do Part'"; Menard, "Demography of Somerset County," p. 22.

49. Menard, "Demography of Somerset County," pp. 22–24.

50. For evidence of contemporary recognition of the importance of youthful marriages for the rapid growth of population in the Chesapeake colonies, see Gov. William Gooch to the Board of Trade, 23 July, 1730, C.O. 5/1322, f. 72 (Col. Va. Rec. Proj., microfilm, C.W., M–241). See also Gooch's statement of 1749 to the Board of Trade in C.O. 5/1327, 81 (ibid., M–243).

51. For New England's population in 1700 see Robert Paul Thomas and Terry L. Anderson, "White Population, Labor Force and Extensive Growth of the New England Economy in the Seventeenth Century," *Journal of Economic History* 33 (1973):636, 655. The accepted figure for migration to New England is the 21,200 reported by Edward Johnson, see J. Franklin Jameson, ed.., *Johnson's Wonder-Working Providence, 1628–1651* (New York, 1910), p. 58.

52. Craven, *White, Red, and Black*, p. 26.

53. David W. Jordan, "Political Stability and the Emergence of a Native Elite in Maryland," in *Seventeenth-Century Chesapeake*, ed. Tate and Ammerman.

54. Craven, *White, Red, and Black* pp. 1–37; Menard, "Economy and Society in Early Colonial Maryland," pp. 73–75, 153–73, 213–24.

55. William Stoughton, *New-Englands True Interest . . .* (Boston, 1670), p. 19.

56. Recent studies of migration to New England include: Carl Bridenbaugh, *Vexed and Troubled Englishmen, 1590–1642* (new York, 1968), pp. 434–73; T. H. Breen and Stephen Foster, "Moving to the New World: The Character of Early Massachusetts Immigration," *William and Mary Quarterly*, 3d ser. 30 (1973):189–222; John T. Horton, "Two Bishops and the Holy Brood: A Fresh Look at a Familiar Fact," *New England Quarterly* 40 (1967):339–63; Norman C. P. Tyack, "Migration from East Anglia to New England before 1660" (Ph.D. diss., University of London, 1951). The contrasts between New England and Chesapeake immigrants are readily apparent in the passenger lists printed in Hotten, *Original Lists of Persons of Quality,* and in Charles Edward Banks, *The Planters of the Commonwealth: A Study of the Emigrants and Emigration in Colonial Times . . . 1620–1640* (Boston, 1930).

57. Recent studies of adult mortality in New England are surveyed in Maris A. Vinovskis, "Mortality Rates and Trends in Massachusetts before 1860," *Journal of Economic History* 32(1972):184–213. For infant and childhood mortality see Philip J. Greven, Jr., *Four Generations: Population, Land, and Family in Colonial Andover, Massachusetts* (Ithaca, 1970), p. 189; John Demos, *A Little Commonwealth: Family Life in Plymouth Colony* (New York, 1970), p. 192; Susan L. Norton, "Population Growth in Colonial America: A Study of Ipswich, Massachusetts," *Population Studies* 25 (1971):442–43.

58. Herbert Moller, "Sex Composition and Correlated Culture Patterns of Colonial America," *William and Mary Quarterly*, 3d ser. 2 (1945):114–17. Breen and Foster, "Moving to the New World," p. 194, argue that the preponderance of males reported by Moller "is largely the product of his reliance on Banks (rather than Hotten) and his classification of a large portion of the women as of undetermined sex because of their apparently 'unfeminine' names." However, Moller failed to classify only 93 of 3,172 immigrants by sex, while a sampling of the lists in Hotten yielded sex ratios among adults of between 150 and 200.

59. Jameson, ed., *Johnson's Wonder-Working Providence*, pp. 66, 254–56; James K. Hosmer, ed., *Winthrop's Journal, "History of New England," 1630–1649*, 2 vols. (New York, 1908), 1:58, 283–84; William T. Davis, ed., *Bradford's History of Plymouth Plantation, 1606–1646* (New York, 1908), pp. 107–8.

60. See the immigrant lists cited in note 56 above.

61. P. M. G. Harris, "The Social Origins of American Leaders: The Demographic Foundations," *Perspectives in American History* 3 (1969):314; Kenneth A. Lockridge, "The Population of Dedham, Massachusetts, 1636–1736," *Economic History Review*, 2d ser. 19 (1966):321, 327–28; Norton, "Population Growth in Colonial America," pp. 435, 437–38.

62. On age at marriage in New England see Greven, *Four Generations,* pp. 34, 119, 121; Demos, *Little Commonwealth,* p. 193; Lockridge, "Population of Dedham," p. 330; Norton, "Population Growth in Colonial America," p. 445; Smith, "Demographic History of Colonial New England," p. 177; Robert L. Goodman, "Newbury, Massachusetts, 1635-1685: The Social Foundations of Harmony and Conflict" (Ph.D. diss., Michigan State University, 1974), pp. 189-90; Linda A. Bissell, "Family, Friends, and Neighbors: Social Interaction in Seventeenth-Century Windsor, Connecticut" (Ph.D. diss., Brandeis University, 1973), p. 45.

63. The works cited above by Carr, Jordan, Menard, Walsh, and the Rutmans are beginning the exploration of the social consequences of Chesapeake demographic patterns.

FIVE

SERVITUDE AND OPPORTUNITY IN CHARLES COUNTY, MARYLAND, 1658-1705

Lorena S. Walsh

Studies of seventeenth-century Chesapeake society turn repeatedly to two central questions—What sort of people immigrated and what opportunities for economic advancement and social assimilation did they find in the New World? The backgrounds and fortunes of white servants are of key importance, because at least three-quarters of the settlers reached this region under some form of short-term labor contract. Analyses of lists of indentured servants leaving England for the colonies have produced some general conclusions about the character of part of the immigrant group.[1] Evaluations of the nature and extent of economic and social opportunity in the region have resulted in somewhat less consensus.[2] Firm generalizations require studies of people who immigrated to particular areas and of the economic and social opportunities they encountered. This paper seeks to answer these questions for Charles, a Southern Maryland tidewater county, from its founding in 1658 through the year 1705.

Backgrounds of Immigrants

Who were the immigrants? Men and women from every part of England came to Charles County as servants. The origins of only a few are recorded, but these suggest a wide variety of sources of immigration. Servants left from all of the three major ports of embarkation—London, Bristol, and Liverpool—and listed such diverse counties of origin as Yorkshire, Middlesex, Wiltshire, and Derbyshire. Nevertheless, the majority of English immigrants must have come from the southeast, with the West Country a distant second.[3] Ireland supplied the next largest group of servants. Much smaller numbers came from Scotland, Barbados, Holland, and Portugal.

About three times as many men servants came into Charles County as women. Men were more in demand for field labor and were probably more actively recruited than women. Doubtless, men also were more likely than

Note: Lorena S. Walsh is a research associate, St. Mary's City Commission, State of Maryland.

women to leave the country to seek their fortunes. The resulting sexual imbalance meant that many of the men would not be able to marry, while every woman who chose to marry could.

The motives that led these Europeans to try their luck in the Chesapeake are seldom revealed. Those of a few can be inferred. Some of the older immigrants listed such occupants as wool comber, carder, and spinner, indicating that the decline of the cloth trade was one circumstance that contributed to immigration to the Chesapeake. Among women, many—even most—may have left home in order to improve their chances of marrying. Female servants arriving in Charles County were consistently older than males. On immigrant lists kept in Liverpool, 1699–1707, 40 percent of the women were twenty-two years of age or older. Given that the mean age at marriage for women in England then ranged from the mid-twenties to nearly thirty,[4] many women apparently stayed at home long enough to test their chances for an early, advantageous marriage. When it became clear that this was not to occur, perhaps they then decided to try their luck in the colonies.

The analysis of the background of Charles County servants is based on the career histories of 1,387 individuals, identified as servants, who were brought into Charles County between 1658 and 1705. The list was compiled from the names of servants without indentures whose ages were recorded in the county court records, from claims for headrights, from lists of servants in inventories, from court cases in which servants participated, from bills of sale, and from vital records.[5] Because the servants' names come primarily from court judgments, the list describes most completely the characteristics of those who had no indentures and thus served according to the custom of the country. Servants without indentures were younger, served longer terms, and possessed fewer skills than those with indentures. Hence, this study deals especially with the lowest levels of white immigrants. Tests suggest that these 1,387 individuals represent from two-thirds to three-quarters of the estimated total servant population across the whole period.[6]

To produce a comprehensive profile of Charles County servants, the data found in the county records must be supplemented, and where appropriate, modified by information about the unrecorded groups. Consideration must be given to how many and what kinds of servants failed to appear in the records. If approximately three-quarters of the names of the total servant population were recorded, then in the forty-eight-year span covered by this study, about 450 persons served in the county without their names appearing. Servants not found in the records may have been purchased and their ages recorded outside the county; they may have had indentures; or they may have been twenty-two or older when they arrived. The second two reasons very likely account for most.

It is important to determine what proportions of the servants had indentures, because there were doubtless systematic differences between those who had them and those who served instead according to the custom of the country. In Charles County nearly half of the servants, at least, were in the second category. Eight hundred and four of the 1,387 servants were specifically identified as serving without indentures. Only 97 were recorded as having indentures, and status of the remaining 486 was not given.[7]

Length of service was one difference that distinguished the two types of servants. Servants with indentures usually served for 4 years, occasionally for 5, and in a few instances for a maximum of 6 years. The terms of those who depended on the custom of the country varied with their ages and the state of the law. In Maryland, prior to 1666, servants aged 22 years and above were to serve 5 years; those aged 18 to 22, 6 years; those aged 15 to 18, 7 years; and servants under 15 years, to age 22. The law required that a master bring his servants before a court to have their ages judged within 6 months after their arrival in the province if he wished to claim more than 5 years' service.[8] From 1658 to 1681 the servants whose ages were judged in Charles County served a mean term of 6.8 years and a median of 6.0 years. From 1682 to 1705 the mean term of service was 6.9 years but the median had risen to 7.0. This increase is a reflection of changes in the ages at which these servants immigrated. The mean age of men servants whose ages were judged dropped from 16.47 in the period 1658–81 to 15.82 in 1682–1705. A similar decline occurred in the mean age of women, 18.19 to 17.44.

Age at immigration provides another difference between the two groups, and this may in itself indicate that there were additional variations in background. Information about age for indentured servants leaving for the Chesapeake can be obtained from lists of indentured immigrants to all the English colonies from the ports of London for 1683–85, and of Liverpool for 1699–1707. The mean age of indentured males leaving London for Maryland and Virginia between 1683 and 1685 was 22.08 years and that of women 21.48. By 1699–1707 the mean age of men leaving Liverpool was lower, 19.48, while the mean age of women had not changed.[9] Thus, although the ages of servants who arrived with indentures also declined, Charles County servants who had indentures would in most instances have been older than those who had come to Maryland without a written contract.

Evidence from the immigrant lists and fragmentary information about indentured servants in the county records suggest that there may have been other differences between the two groups. It seems likely that a higher proportion of indentured servants possessed a skill.[10] In addition, some of the indentured Charles County servants were couples who had married before immigrating. No examples of unindentured married couples appeared.

The combined data from the Charles County records and the immigrant lists suggests that while the age of entering servants declined in the second half of the seventeenth century, the shift was not so dramatic as it would appear from reliance on lists of indentured servants alone[11] (see figure 5.1). The county records show that substantial numbers of servants in the ten

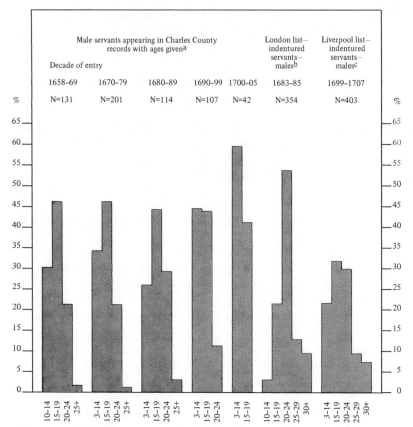

FIGURE 5.1. Ages of Male Indentured and Unindentured Servants, 1658–1707
    Sources: [a] Walsh file of Charles County servants. [b] C. D. P. Nicholson, *Some Early Emigrants to America* (Baltimore, 1965); and the Folger Shakespeare Library ms. v.b.16. [c] Elizabeth French, *List of Emigrants to America from Liverpool* (Baltimore, 1969)

to fourteen and fifteen to nineteen age categories immigrated throughout the century, but the data from the London and Liverpool lists suggest that prior to the 1960s servants in these young age groups frequently did not obtain written indentures in England. By 1699, apparently all servants in the lower age categories who left Liverpool were being indentured. Thus, the contrast in the proportions of younger boys found on the London lists of the 1680s and the Liverpool lists of the early eighteenth century may be in part due to a change of practice in the issuing of indentures as well as to a real decline in the age of immigrants.[12] Similarly, the virtually complete disappearance from the Charles County records after 1698 of servants arriving at age twenty or above is a reflection of the fact that apparently almost all persons in this age category were often then obtaining indentures in England, as well as a reflection of an absolute decline in the numbers of older persons immigrating.[13]

Thus the composition of the Charles County servant population during the second half of the seventeenth century did not dramatically change. The mean age at which servants immigrated declined by about one year because increased numbers immigrated between ages ten and fourteen, and fewer persons left between ages twenty to twenty-four. In addition, a growing number of Irish immigrants did increase the proportion of non-English servants. However, elements of continuity appear to outweigh indications of change. One must look primarily to forces outside the servant class itself to explain the changing prospects that these immigrants faced over the course of the last half of the century.

Careers of Charles County Servants

The story of the fortunes of servants in Charles County must begin with the admission that little can be said about the careers of large numbers. The most striking result of an attempt to trace the lives of the 1,387 recorded servants is that most of them simply disappeared without further mention. In addition, many of those who did reappear briefly in the records could not be found as free men after the expiration of their terms. Women proved impossible to trace. Most probably changed their names by marriage shortly after being freed, and, in the absence of marriage records, the careers of a significant number could not be followed.

How can we account for the disappearance of two-thirds or more of the servants who entered Charles County? The noncomprehensive character of the records is a possible explanation. Men might have remained in the county but lived obscure lives, neither owning land, registering livestock marks, witnessing documents, holding minor offices, or serving on juries, nor suing or being sued in the county court. In the absence of tax lists, this possibility cannot be entirely dismissed. However, it clearly cannot account for the disappearance of most ex-servants. The names of slightly more than 2,400 free adult male residents appear in the records for the years 1658 through 1705. Since on a census taken in 1704 the number of free adult males in the county was less than 700, it seems most unlikely that unrecorded obscurity can account for the subsequent careers of any large numbers of former servants.

Instead, a combination of death and emigration must explain the fates of most of the Charles County servants who disappeared. There is evidence that the rates of both processes were substantial; the problem is to determine the parameters of each. With the evidence currently available, it is possible only to suggest what the broadest limits of the two factors must have been.

Early death was the fate of many immigrants to the Chesapeake, both bound and free. A man arriving in Maryland at age twenty-two could expect to live only an additional twenty-three years. Not included in this measure are the hazards of "seasoning." During their first year in the Chesapeake most newcomers experienced illnesses of varying severity as they adjusted to the new climate, diet, and disease environment. Contemporary accounts suggest that many newcomers in fact succumbed "in their seasoning." Unfortunately there are no data from which to determine the proportion of immigrants who died shortly after arrival.[14]

Many other former servants left Southern Maryland at the expiration of their terms. During the depression in tobacco prices of the early and mid-1690s, both Governor Nicholson and the Assembly complained that "young English Natives and Servants when they are free, leave these Colonies, and goe either Southward [to the Carolinas] or Northward [for the Jerseys or Pennsylvania]."[15] A brief interlude of higher tobacco prices may have stemmed out-migration between 1698 and 1702, but emigration (and complaints about it) resumed when prices entered a new period of decline in 1703. Data from censuses sent to England in 1704 and 1710 make clear that most of the emigrants were single men. The number of white male taxables on the lower western shore decreased 11 percent between 1704 and 1710, while the number of white women increased by 6 percent, and the population grew by 7 percent.[16]

Table 5.1 illustrates the effects of various possible seasoning rates and the resulting rates of emigration. The experience of the Charles County servants who disappeared from the records lies somewhere within the limits outlined here. It was assumed that the maximum rate of seasoning would not have been greater than the 43 percent mortality experienced by slaves imported into Barbados in 1740s.[17] There is some evidence that 40 percent is not an unreasonable upper limit for seasoning deaths in Maryland. Russell Menard studied two groups of servants who arrived in Maryland within the first twenty years after settlement. Because both the settled areas and the population were small, problems of name correlation were few, and he could search the records of all Maryland counties and adjacent Virginia counties for the reappearance of these individuals. His studies can be used to calculate a maximum bound for mortality, because they provide some control over the other variable—emigration. The results suggest that deaths during seasoning could have been as high as 35 to 40 percent.[18]

It is also assumed here that the minimum rate of seasoning was 10 percent. Over a three-year period, 5 percent of acclimated male immigrants in the twenty-two to twenty-nine age category could be expected to die. Since contemporaries considered seasoning an extraordinarily hazardous time, the death rate of recent arrivals must have been noticeably higher than that of longer-settled immigrants. Nearly all servants were under age thirty, and thus a doubling of the proportion of those already "seasoned" who might die in their twenties seems a reasonable lower bound.

Given an upper limit on seasoning deaths of 40 percent, and a lower limit of 10 percent, it follows that rates of emigration could have varied between

TABLE 5.1
*Impact of Several Seasoning Rates on Survival and Emigration of
1,040 Male Charles County Servants*[a]

Seasoning Rate (Percentage)	Percentage of Initial Number Surviving Servitude	Percentage of Survivors Remaining in County	Percentage of Survivors Emigrating Immediately
43[b]	53[c]	42	58
40	56	40	60
35	61	37	63
30	65	35	65
25	70	33	67
20	75	31	69
15	79	29	71
10	84	28	72

Sources:
a. Walsh file of Charles County servants.
b. J. Harry Bennett, Jr., "The Problem of Slave Labor Supply at Codrington," *Journal of Negro History* 36 (1951):406–41. Bennett's seasoning rate is for the first three years after immigration. The rest of the table is calculated on the same assumption.
c. Life table for Chesapeake immigrants in Lorena S. Walsh and Russell R. Menard, "Death in the Chesapeake: Two Life Tables for Men in Early Colonial Maryland," *Maryland Historical Magazine* 69 (1974):211–27.

Method: The table assumes that the 1,040 males who are recorded as entering the county as servants immigrated to Maryland at age 17 and were age 23 when freed after a term of service of 7 years. The following example illustrates how the table was calculated. At a seasoning rate of 43%, 447 of the 1,040 men would die during the first 3 years of service. According to the life table for immigrants cited above, an additional 39 would die during the remaining 4 years. Thus 554 men or 53% of the initial group would live to the end of their terms. The 216 freedmen known to have remained in the county were increased by 3% to compensate for men who may have also stayed but did not appear in the records. Thus 233 or 42% of the survivors would then have remained and the 321 men (58% of the survivors) left unaccounted for must have emigrated immediately.

34 and 61 percent of the men who entered Charles County as servants. Is it probable that up to 60 percent of the servants who entered service left the area upon being freed? Studies of servant groups in two other counties have produced even higher proportions of quick disappearance from county records. Although failure to reappear in a record is not in itself proof of out-migration, these similar results show that the Charles County phenomenon was not unique. The apparent disappearance of the majority of ex-servants from several older Maryland counties beginning in the 1690s, when coupled with other evidence of significant amounts of out-migration certainly suggests that large-scale emigration of portions of the population, at least by then, was taking place.[19]

What was the fate of those former servants who did survive their terms of service and who did remain, at least for a while, in Charles County? What opportunities did they find as free men in the society in which they had formerly served?

Two hundred and sixteen Charles County servants have been identified as freedmen. The majority never became landowners while in the county but worked other men's farms as sharecroppers or tenants, or made their livings as itinerant laborers or craftsmen. Forty-three percent (93) married; most of the remainder never established their own households, but instead continued as residents in other men's houses. Economic status could be determined for 167 of the 216. Of these, 97 or 58.1 percent were laborers or, at most, tenant farmers. About one-third acquired land, but most of these (32 or 19.2 percent of the 167) remained small planters, who supplied their households with little beyond real necessities. Such men owned about 200 acres of land and usually commanded only their own and their family's labor. A smaller number of former servants (28 or 16.8 percent of the 167) ended up better off than the average planter. These ex-servants owned between 250 and 600 acres of land; they could count a few comforts among their personal possessions; and occasionally they owned some bound labor. Only 5 ever achieved substantial wealth. These men acquired 1,300 acres or more, consistently owned labor, and at death had personal estates of at least £200.

Sixty-four of these 167 freedmen left the county, most within one to nine years after being freed. Nearly all these were unmarried and 54 left as landless laborers. However, the majority of those who remained had greater success. Of those who died in Charles County during the years covered in this study (1658–1705), over half (28 or 53.8 percent) had acquired some land, and 15, or 29 percent, had accumulated enough wealth to bring them above the level of the small planter. Those who had been free at least ten years had done nearly as well, if their landholdings on the rent roll of 1705 are a measure. Not many ex-servants became rich, but those who persisted achieved integration into the local economy, and the majority of them improved their position. However, these opportunities would not have been available had not large numbers of freedmen departed the county either immediately after serving their terms or after a short trial of their local chances.

Changes in Status of Servants

Who owned servants and what were the relationships between servants and masters?

The opportunity to own a servant changed over time with the fortunes of the tobacco economy. Tobacco was the cash crop of the Chesapeake and it was highly labor intensive. Until the mid-1660s the expanding Chesapeake economy offered a man without large capital opportunity to acquire servant labor that could increase his tobacco production and in good years, at least, his profits. During these early years, the purchase of white servants could advance the fortunes of small and middling planters, who had usually once been servants themselves. A slow-down followed, which ended about 1680 in stagnation that lasted about thirty years. Credit constrictions that accompanied these changes limited the ability of poorer planters to purchase servants. At the same time the supply of servants in proportion to the number of households in need of labor was steadily decreasing. Improving economic conditions in England kept more Englishmen at home, and brighter opportunities in the newer settlements of Pennsylvania and the Carolinas attracted many of those who did immigrate. As the labor shortage in the Chesapeake grew and credit remained tight, ownership of servant labor became more and more concentrated among already well-to-do families (see table 5.2). Thus servants were increasingly likely to be the property of wealthy men, and less likely, once freed, to acquire servants themselves.[20]

The social distance between small or middling planters and their servants was probably not great. In households where there were but one or two laborers, master and servant often worked together in the fields, servants

TABLE 5.2
Proportions of Laborers and Labor Owners by Total Estate Value, 1662–1705

TEV Category*	Number of Households	Number of Labor Owners	Number of Servants	Number of Slaves	Percentage of Labor†
£0–49					
1662–1670	13	3	4	—	5
1671–1680	29	8	8	—	7
1681–1690	27	3	3	—	2
1691–1700	77	10	12	—	5
1701–1705	24	3	3	—	2
£50–89					
1662–1670	6	4	5	1	8
1671–1680	˙5	8	8	1	8
1681–1690	.9	11	15	5	10
1691–1700	11	5	7	—	3
1701–1705	5	2	5	—	3
£90–199					
1662–1670	11	9	36	—	48
1671–1680	18	16	44	5	42
1681–1690	14	11	20	9	15
1691–1700	21	17	26	20	18
1701–1705	12	9	15	6	11
£200+					
1662–1670	6	6	14	15	39
1671–1680	9	9	31	21	44
1681–1690	11	11	63	77	73
1691–1700	15	15	47	150	75
1701–1705	11	10	49	108	84

*TEV (Total Estate Value) is the amount of personal moveable assets at death.
†Percentage of labor is the proportion of all servants and slaves owned in a given ten-year period that were held by each of the four wealth groups.

slept and ate in the master's house and were probably treated much like members of the family. Freed servants of small planters could anticipate achieving similar economic status, and those who did—about two-fifths of those studied did this well or better—then served on juries and held minor offices, sometimes in company with their former masters.[21]

John Wathen's biography illustrates such successes. Wathen was a servant of Hugh Thomas, himself a former laborer who became a middling planter. In 1671 Wathen built for Thomas's neighbor, Nicholas Grosse, a fifteen-by-ten foot house, a bedstead, and forms for 500 pounds of tobacco. Once freed, Wathen continued to work at his trades of carpenter and wheelwright. He married, and fathered five sons and three daughters. By 1702 he had saved enough to acquire 200 acres, which he named "Wathen's Adventure," and several lots and houses in the town of Newport. He had purchased another 200 acres by 1705. In 1697 and 1698 Wathen served on four juries and acted as an overseer of highways. He died in 1705, having accumulated personal property worth £147.[22] There was little in John Wathen's career that distinguished it from his master's. Thomas also married, accumulated 750 acres, and had served on five juries and as an overseer by the time of his death in the mid-eighties.[23]

Christopher Breams apparently became a friend as well as a tenant of his master's eldest son. Breams began as a servant to Richard Pinner, also a former servant who had risen to the station of a middling planter. Freed in 1666, by 1669 Breams had patented 200 acres adjacent to a tract that the elder Pinner had bequeathed to his sons Richard and William. Breams sold the land within four years, however, and was probably thereafter a tenant of Richard Pinner the younger. In 1685 Pinner divided his estate between his wife and daughters and Breams, willing Breams "one heyfer of two year old and my old Gunn and all my wearing cloathes both linnen and wollen . . . and to have a lease of the house that he lives in for his life raising half stock of Hoggs and liveing upon itt hieselfe." Breams died in 1689 having never married. He had acquired little in the way of material assets, yet, in contrast to the elder and the younger Pinners, who never participated in local government, Breams served on eight juries between 1678 and 1685.[24]

Relations between servants and masters higher up on the social scale were more distant. In addition to the gap created by the greater disparity in rank and material surroundings, there was also much less opportunity for intimate contact. Many of the servants of larger planters lived and worked in groups on outlying plantations or, if residing on the home plantation, were usually housed in separate quarters detached from the main house. Larger planters often did not directly supervise their servant's labors but, instead, employed overseers to perform this task.[25] These conditions may have resulted in more deferential and perhaps harsher relationships between servant and master than occurred in small planter households. In addition, highly placed masters often retained former servants in menial positions as laborers, sharecroppers, overseers, or tenants on their often extensive landholdings, extending credit (at terms highly favorable to themselves, one supposes) to buy supplies or to pay taxes. Often freed servants chose wives from among their former master's maidservants. Given such circumstances, servants could not so easily aspire to achieve their master's status. On the other hand, such servants might benefit from the assistance wealthy masters could offer, especially in the form of credit or opportunity to lease land.

Some examples will illustrate the experience of men who served wealthy or powerful masters. James Lynes was a servant of a former county justice, Philip Lynes, when it was reported in 1696 that he had run away for 34 days. The court ordered him to serve the additional 340 days that Maryland law prescribed as the punishment for this offense. In 1697 James complained that he had neither clothing nor bed, and the court ordered that Philip Lynes either provide them or free him. Finally freed in 1698, James protested that Philip refused to pay him his freedom dues or wages owed for the extra 6 months that Philip had held him in servitude. Sympathetic to his plight, the court admitted him to sue Lynes in forma pauperis and assigned him a lawyer. After winning his suit, James remained in the county as a laborer. In 1702 when he was sharecropping at Justice Henry Hardy's, he purchased the remaining time of Elinor Dayler, a servant of Hardy's, and married her. James died within a few months after his marriage, never acquiring land nor participating in government. At death he owned his share of the crop of corn and tobacco, six cows, some beans and corn, a jacket, a pail, and three hoes. He was indebted to Philip Lynes for a gown and petticoat purchased for his wife and to Hardy for accommodations, for corn and wheat advanced to him, and for his levy, which Hardy had paid. After his death his bride was forced to petition the court to prevent her former master from reclaiming her as a servant.[26]

Lawrence Hoskins arrived in 1669 at age seventeen. He was purchased by Justice John Bowls, and by Bowls' will in 1675 transferred to Bowls' nephew and heir, James Tyer, for the remainder of his term. After being freed, Hoskins, an illiterate, continued to room in Tyer's house and plied the trade of a cooper. Tyer, like his uncle, became a justice. Hoskins died in 1687 at age thirty-five, never having played a role in local government. Having also never married, he left his possessions, consisting mostly of livestock and tobacco received for his work, to Tyer's wife and son. Even after serving out his term, Lawrence Hoskins's world continued to revolve around that of his ex-master's.[27]

Lancelot Wilkinson was more successful than Lynes or Hoskins. He arrived in 1672 at eighteen years of age and served Justice Humphrey Warren until 1679. He then became a tenant of Warren's, and in 1681 married Margaret Moulton, widow of another of Warren's tenants. He was eventually able to buy 200 acres of his own, and he served on two juries in 1688. Wilkinson had embarked on his career as an underling of his former master but had been able later to progress to the status of independent freeholder.[28]

Samuel Luckett's career was exceptional. He rose from the status of servant of one justice to that of son-in-law of another, and although he never held an office of power, he did become wealthier than some of the county rulers. Luckett was born about 1650 in Kent and appeared as a servant in Charles County in 1675 in the inventory of James Wheeler with two and a half years to serve. Wheeler, also an ex-servant, had enjoyed the favor of a deputy governor and had become a justice and large landowner. Luckett first sat on a jury in 1682. Sometime between 1683 and 1685 he married Elizabeth, one of the two daughters of Thomas Hussey, a justice and owner of over 2,000 acres. Luckett probably acquired by his marriage a minimum of 1,000 acres and was soon able to purchase other land. Although illiterate, he was constable in 1687 and an overseer of highways in 1692. Due partly, in all likelihood, to the fact that he ran the ordinary, which also served as the court house, Luckett sat on a total of fifty-five juries. When he died in 1705, Luckett had amassed landholdings of 2,510 acres, which he divided among his four sons. He possessed an eight room "home house" with adjoining kitchen, milk house, and salt house, two other quarters, an ordinary, seven slaves, and six servants, together valued at over £1,000. Unlike the great majority of the servants belonging to local rulers, Luckett had been able to bridge the gap between himself and his master's associates.[29]

At any period of Charles County history the experiences of a Lawrence Hoskins or of a James Lynes were probably more common than those of a John Wathen or a Christopher Bream, but table 5.2 shows that the chances that a servant would serve a small or middling planter decreased steadily after 1680. Other changes also helped to establish greater social distance between servants and masters. As labor shortages grew, wealthy planters purchased slaves, and working beside slaves instead of other Englishmen doubtless degraded the poor man's labor. In addition, by the turn of the century, many planters were men who had been born in the colony. Soon the majority of masters would no longer share with their servants the common experience of immigration, and even fewer servant owners would themselves have known some kind of servitude. The differing life experiences of the creole and immigrant may have served to further differentiate and separate master and servant.

Economic and Political Opportunities for Ex-Servants

The state of the economy, combined with demographic forces, had great effect on the degree to which the local community was able to find a place for freed servants.

When Charles County was established in 1658, the tobacco economy was generally prosperous and the population was small. Almost one out of four of its adult male settlers—who totaled about 100—had formerly served in adjacent St. Mary's and Calvert counties, and many of them prospered in the new region. Three-fifths of the former servants who had settled in the county by 1664 became landowners; moreover, those who did acquire land usually built up substantial holdings. The mean acreage accumulated by this earliest group of ex-servants at the peak of their careers was slightly more than 1,000 acres. In addition, at least half of the group became labor owners.

With the acquistion of wealth came offices of power. Thirteen former servants who emigrated from other counties to Charles became county rulers. Eleven of them served as justices; four were named in the first commission for the bench. Five of these ex-servants served as sheriff, and four were elected burgesses. One, John Hatch, was appointed to the Council. These men had distinguished themselves from their fellows through enterprise, perhaps by displaying qualities of leadership, and also through the sheer good luck of outliving many of their companions. They were not a group that possessed many special advantages. They included James Lindsay, an Irishman, who found "great difficultie to deliuer himself in ow English tounge," and John Cage and Randall Hanson, who were both illiterate. Thirty-one other emigrant ex-servants held minor county offices, and fifty-six men who did not occupy any offices served on juries. These men were in a position to grasp the opportunities that came with the opening of a new area and to fill needed positions of leadership at a time when there were few men who possessed the qualities of wealth, status, and education later expected of local rulers.[30]

Charles County did not long remain an area of special opportunity for servants. Table 5.3 summarizes across the seventeenth century the experiences of the 167 Charles County servants whose later careers could be followed. Clearly those who had arrived earliest had the greatest success. Among those freed after 1674, the percentages owning land or bound labor declined sharply, and only a handful from this group rose above small planter status. Table 5.4 shows that the experience of ex-servants who had served elsewhere followed a similar pattern, although the decline for those who appeared as freedmen after 1674 was somewhat less severe. Men without capital trying to establish themselves in southern Maryland were suffering from a slowing and then stagnating economy.[31]

Political participation, and hence having some say in how one was governed or even exercising some measure of power over others, was also dependent upon early arrival in the county. Only those who came earliest achieved major office. As shown in tables 5.3 and 5.4, the participation of most former servants was limited to jury service, and even this opportunity declined sharply for those freed after the mid-1680s. Here demographic as well as economic conditions were at work. Not only were poor men less likely to acquire property sufficient to entitle them to serve but also as more

TABLE 5.3
Economic Status and Political Participation of Former Charles County Servants

Period First Appears as Freedman	Number	Economic Status at Death or Last Appearance before 1706				Political Participation	
		% Laborer/ Tenant	% Small Planter	% Middling or Large Planter	% Labor Owner	% With Either Jury Service or County Office	% In Any Capacity above Juror
1658–1664	13	54	8	38	38	31	8
1665–1669	19	37	37	26	27	58	21
1670–1674	22	27	27	45	41	59	18
1675–1679	27	63	15	22	30	48	15
1680–1684	36	69	19	11	17	44	11
1685–1689	17	77	24	—	12	29	6
1690–1694	18	72	11	17	11	28	—
1695–1699	8	88	13	—	11	13	—
1700–1705	7	100	—	—	13	14	—

Note: N = 167
Source: See text.

TABLE 5.4
Economic Status and Political Participation of Former Servants Emigrating to Charles County

Period First Appears as Freedman	Number	Economic Status at Death or Last Appearance before 1706				Political Participation	
		% Laborer/ Tenant	% Small Planter	% Middling or Large Planter	% Labor Owner	% With Jury Service or County Office	% In Any Capacity above Juror
1648–1654	9	—	11	88	78	78	56
1655–1659	25	20	8	72	44	72	44
1660–1664	19	53	—	47	42	63	42
1665–1669	22	45	18	36	9	64	18
1670–1674	26	50	8	42	31	42	15
1675–1679	24	63	8	29	25	58	13
1680–1684	25	80	—	20	16	44	12
1685–1689	16	56	13	31	19	56	31
1690–1694	10	70	20	10	10	20	10
1695–1699	5	80	—	20	—	20	—
1700–1705	9	67	—	33	11	22	11

Source: See text.
Note: N = 190. Date of first appearance as freedman is less precise in this table than in table 5.3. The figure in this table is based on first appearance in the county records, as precise information about the terms of servants freed in other counties is unavailable.

English merchants and gentry came into the county, and as the sons of the earlier settlers came of age, the pool of wealthy and socially prominent men increased. Consequently standards for eligibility rose. In the 1660s a servant could obtain his freedom in the morning and sit on a jury in the afternoon; by 1700 he was unlikely to serve (if he did so at all) for some time after he had established a household and acquired land.[32]

When the economic achievements of ex-servants are compared with the landholdings and personal wealth of all county residents, it becomes even clearer that opportunities for men beginning without capital were indeed limited in Southern Maryland probably as early as the mid-1660s.[33] Examination of the 1659 and 1705 rent rolls reveals the extent of initial opportunity and its subsequent decline.[34] In 1659, 115 persons, about 90 of them residents, held land in Charles County. Of these, 24, or 26.7 percent were former servants, most of whom had recently moved from adjacent St. Mary's County. The mean acreage of all landowners was 546 acres, while the mean holding of former servants was 366 acres. Many of the ex-servants had just recently acquired the first of what would later become many tracts, yet they already held 13.4 percent of the land in the second year of the county's history. Forty-six years later, in 1705, 340 persons, about 293 of them residents, held land in the county. Only 1 of the ex-servants who had appeared on the 1659 rent roll was still alive. Ex-servant landholders numbered only 27, or 7.9 percent of the whole and owned only 8.1 percent of the land, although one of them, Philip Lynes, was the biggest landholder in the county. The mean acreage of all landowners was 468. That of ex-servants (here excluding Lynes) was 245 acres. The disparities were growing.

The former servants from other counties who owned land in Charles County in 1659 had had only to move from a neighboring county in order to become landowners. This was not true for the freed servants who at a later period moved away from Charles County. Only four or five identified former Charles County servants held land in adjacent Prince George's County in 1706, and they had acquired their tracts by 1691 or earlier.[35] Nor did the freed servants move into St. Mary's County. Fewer than five former Charles County servants could be identified as St. Mary's County residents, and none of them held land on the 1705 rent roll. Similarly, none held land on the Calvert County rent roll of the same period.[36]

A look at the personal assets of ex-servants as shown in probate inventories also demonstrates the relationship between early arrival in the county and economic success. Inventories have survived for seventy-seven men identified as former servants, including thirty-one of the fifty-two freedmen known to have served and died in Charles County between 1658 and 1705. Not surprisingly, they usually died with less personal property than appears overall in the estates of county residents: mean and median personal wealth for all county residents over the period was £116 and £46 respectively,[37] whereas for former county servants it was £88 and £29. However, servants who were freedmen by 1664 did much better than those who came later. Most of these earliest freedmen had emigrated to Charles after serving in other counties. The mean and median values of their personal estates were £141 and £112. Estates of later arrivals had a mean value of £70 and a median value of £32.[38]

Among servants freed after 1664, the personal estates of those who had served in the county show an interesting difference from the estates of those who had served elsewhere. The mean value of the personal estates of the first group was higher than that of the second, £80 as opposed to £54, although the medians were £32 as opposed to £34. A possible explanation lies in the fact that the two groups invested differently. Tables 5.3 and 5.4 show that the men who had come from elsewhere had higher rates of landownership, apparently choosing to put more in this resource and less in labor, livestock, and consumption goods. The men who had served in Charles County had lower rates of landownership. They frequently continued to rent, often from former masters, rather than purchase their own land, and instead invested more in their personal estates.

To summarize, as the tobacco economy slowed down and as population increased in the settled regions, opportunities for men beginning without capital decreased. The best land was taken up, and labor, a necessity if a man was to rise above the level of "rude sufficiency," became increasingly scarcer and more expensive. Men who had immigrated as servants found that the initial advantages possessed by native-born sons and free immigrants with capital was one that was more and more difficult for them to overcome. A decrease in chances for political participation paralleled the decline in economic opportunity.

The chances for integration of ex-servants into the community diminished in other ways. Social integration of former master and former servant was easiest in the period when population was small and the need for labor great. In the early years of the county, furthermore, servants often worked for masters who had themselves once been servants, and sometimes for ex-servants not very long freed. By the end of the century, native-born masters—men who had not known servitude—were becoming numerous, and masters were more likely than earlier to have wealth and status to which their servants could not aspire. Such men more easily established and maintained deferential relationships with those who served them or who had formerly served them.

Most of the immigrants who served in Charles County did not remain there long. A number died "in their seasoning," and many others who survived left the county as soon as their terms expired. The low level of persistence indicates that many of those who chose to immigrate to Maryland as servants were not integrated into the region in which they served their time. As the area's population increased, out-migration was not simply a matter of moving to the next county. By the 1680s many freed servants found it necessary to leave the tobacco coast entirely. This is not to argue that colonists without capital did not find opportunities to improve their lots in other regions. It is clear, however, that many more men immigrated to southern Maryland to satisfy that region's labor needs than could be absorbed into the local economy and body politic.

Appendixes

1. Total Servant Population

When studying any group of individuals, it is essential to determine what portion of the whole population the group represents and whether or not its characteristics differ from those of omitted groups. The problem of differences between the detected and omitted groups is dealt with in the text and Appendix 2. What follows is an attempt to define the size of Charles County's total servant population and the relation of the group studied to the whole.

Determining the actual number of servants in the county is extremely difficult because there are no extant tax lists for the period. The only helpful census figures for Charles County are for the year 1704, and these do not separate servants from nonhouseholding freemen.

TABLE A.1
1704 Census

Population	Masters of Households	Free Men and Servant Men	Free Women and Servant Women	Free Children	Servant Children	Slaves
2,989	408	390	485	931	197	578

Source: Archives 25:256

However, the number of slaves is given. Consequently the number of servants can be estimated by using the ratios of servants to slaves found in period inventories. This produces a servant population in 1704 of 364 (578 × .63).

TABLE A.2
Servants and Slaves in Charles County Inventories, 1701–5

Year	Servants	Slaves
1701	6	16
1702	19	23
1703	20	29
1704	4	—
1705	23	46
Total	72	114

Ratio 72/114 = .63

Source: Charles County Inventories, 1701–1705; St. Mary's City Commission Inventory Project, "Social Stratification in Maryland, 1658–1705" (National Science Foundation Grant GS-32272).

The next step is to find what proportion of the 364 appeared in the records and thus in this study. To the number who first appeared in 1704 was added those who first appeared over the preceding six years (seven years was the mean term of service). The result was 290, or 80 percent of the total servant population estimated from the census.

Attempts to derive estimates of the servant population for other years were abandoned. One cannot derive the numbers of servants directly from taxable figures because of inadequate information about the composition of the white population. This is particularly true because of the disproportionate influence of a small number of slaves on the number of taxables, and the absence of information about the numbers and ages of the slaves in the population. Attempts to reconstruct the servant population for other years by multiplying the number of servants per household derived from inventories by an estimate of the number of households yielded too wide a range of results to be useful.

2. Proportions of Servants with and without Indentures

	Number	Percentage
Hypothetical total number of servants entering Charles County, 1658–1705	1,850	100.0
Number whose names were recorded	1,387	75.0[a]
Number identified as serving without indentures	804	43.5
Number identified as having written indentures	97	5.2
Number whose status was undetermined, assumed to have indentures	486	26.3
Number whose names were not recorded, assumed to have written indentures	463	25.0
Number without written indentures	804	43.5
Number assumed to have written indentures	1,046	56.5[b]

Notes:
[a]If a range of recorded names of 66.6% to 80.0% is assumed, then the range of unrecorded individuals is 696 to 347.

[b]56.5% probably overstates somewhat the proportion of servants who had indentures. The "undetermined" category very likely includes individuals who were purchased and their ages recorded outside the county, unindentured servants who entered at age 22 or above, and unindentured servants under that age whose masters had neglected to bring before the court for judgment of age.

3. Possible Seasoning Rates of Two Groups of Maryland Servants

The two tables that follow show how the upper bound of Maryland seasoning deaths was calculated using Menard's studies. They were calculated according to the method described in table 5.1 of the text.

TABLE A.3
Servants Arriving before 1643 (N=275)

Seasoning Rate (Percentage)	Number of Seasoning Deaths	Number of Normal Deaths	Number Surviving, Recorded	Number Surviving, Unrecorded
40	109	5	161	0
35	96	6	161	12
30	83	6	161	25

Method: This table was calculated according to the method described in Table 5.1 of the text with two exceptions: the term of service was assumed to be five years, and men were assumed to have immigrated at age 19 and to have been age 23 when freed. These assumptions reflect the differing terms of service and ages of the earlier immigrants.

Sources: Figures are from Russell R. Menard, "From Servant to Freeholder," *William and Mary Quarterly*, 3d ser. 30 (1973):37–64.

TABLE A.4
Servants Arriving 1648–52 (N=137)

Seasoning Rate (Percentage)	Number of Seasoning Deaths	Number of Normal Deaths	Number Surviving, Recorded	Number Surviving, Unrecorded
40	55	3	72	7
35	48	3	72	14
30	41	3	72	21

Source: Figures come from Russell R. Menard, "Economy and Society in Early Colonial Maryland" (Ph.D. diss., University of Iowa, 1975), ch. 5.

Note: See table A.3 above for method.

Thirty-five percent seems a reasonable seasoning rate for the first group and thirty-five or even forty percent for the second. Thirty percent clearly seems to represent the minimum rate of seasoning. It is unlikely that in this period more men survived but did not appear in the records.

NOTES

1. See especially Mildred Campbell, "Social Origin of Some Early Americans," in *Seventeenth-Century America: Essays in Colonial History,* ed. James Morton Smith, (Chapel Hill, 1959), pp. 63–89. A recent evaluation of the literature on the composition of immigrant servants is found in Wesley Frank Craven, *White, Red, and Black: The Seventeenth-Century Virginian* (Charlottesville, 1971), pp. 3–9.

2. See Thomas J. Wertenbaker, *The Planters of Colonial Virginia* (Princeton, 1922); Richard B. Morris, *Government and Labor in Early America* (New York, 1946); Abbot Emerson Smith, *Colonists in Bondage: White Servitude and Convict Labor in America, 1607–1776* (Chapel Hill, 1947); Edmund S. Morgan, "Slavery and Freedom: The American Paradox," *Journal of American History* 59 (1972):5–29; Russell R. Menard, "From Servant to Freeholder: Status Mobility and Property Accumulation in Seventeenth-Century Maryland," *William and Mary Quarterly*, 3d ser. 30(1973):37–64; idem, "The Transformation of the Chesapeake Labor System, 1680–1710," (paper presented at the annual meeting of the Southern Historical Association, Nov. 1972, on file at the Hall of Records, Annapolis, Md.); Lois Green

Carr and Russell R. Menard, "Servants and Freedmen in Early Colonial Maryland," in *Essays on the Seventeenth-Century Chesapeake,* ed. Thad W. Tate and David L. Ammerman (Chapel Hill, forthcoming).

3. Craven, *White, Red, and Black,* pp. 1–2; Carr and Menard, "Servants and Freedmen."

4. P. E. Razzell, "Population Change in Eighteenth-Century England, a Reinterpretation," *Economic History Review,* 2d ser. 18 (1965):315, cites mean age at marriage as 23.76 years for 7,242 women in Yorkshire, 1662–1714 and 24.6 years for 280 women of Wilts., Berks., Hants., and Dorset, 1615–21. Peter Laslett, *The World We Have Lost: England before the Industrial Age,* 2d ed. (New York, 1971), pp. 84–86, shows a mean age of 23.58 years for 1,007 women in the Diocese of Canterbury, 1619–90. E.A. Wrigley, "Family Limitation in Pre-Industrial England," *Economic History Review,* 2d ser. 19(1966); 86–88 shows mean ages at marriage in Colyton, Devon, for 259 women ranging from 26.15 years to 30.0 years, 1600–1699. For the Liverpool list see Elizabeth French, *List of Emigrants to America from Liverpool, 1697–1707* (Baltimore, 1969).

5. Age judgments, court cases, bills of sale, and vital records are found in Charles County Court and Land Records, ms., hereafter cited as Ch. Ct. and Land Rec. Headrights are entered in the Patent series, mss.; the names of persons for whom headrights were claimed and their dates of entry are compiled in Gust Skordas, ed., *The Early Settlers of Maryland* (Baltimore, 1968). This source should be used with some caution because the dates listed are not always the year of entry; some dates refer to the time at which the headright was claimed and not to the time that the person for whom the right was claimed entered the colony. Inventories are found in Inventories and Accounts, libers 1 through 26, mss., hereafter cited as Inv. and Accts. Unless otherwise indicated, all mss. are in the Hall of Records, Annapolis.

6. See appendix, 1.

7. See appendix, 2.

8. The Acts settling the length of servants' terms are in William Hand Browne et al., eds., *Archives of Maryland,* 72 vols. (Baltimore, 1883–) 1:409–10; 2:147–48; hereafter cited as *Archives.*

9. See Menard, "Transformation of the Chesapeake Labor System." The lists of immigrants are found in C. D. P. Nicholson, *Some Early Emigrants to America* (Baltimore, 1965); Michael Ghirelli, *A List of Emigrants from England to America, 1682–1692* (Baltimore, 1968); and French, *List of Emigrants to America from Liverpool.* Folger Shakespeare Library ms. v.b. 16 (Washington, D.C.) consists of 66 additional indentures that were originally part of the London records. Some of the servants on the London list in fact served their terms in Charles County. See Folger ms. v.b. 16 (15); Ghirelli, *List of Emigrants from England to America,* p. 25; and Ch. Ct. and Land Rec. N No. 1, ff. 104, 308; M No. 1, f. 91; R No. 1, f. 462; S No. 1, f. 243.

10. Many of those men whose occupations were noted on indentures recorded in London listed skills; tanners, knitters, joiners, sawyers, weavers, tailors, and house carpenters were frequently mentioned as well as laborers and husbandmen. Most of the Charles County servants known to have been skilled were either recorded as having indentures or were among those whose status was undetermined and who thus may have been indentured. Many fewer servants who served according to the custom of the country appeared in the records as having a skill that they might have acquired prior to emigration.

11. It is clear in the case of Bristol, at least, that not all the servants who sailed from that port during the period covered by the registry had indentures. Ship captains sailing from Bristol claimed headrights in Maryland for many servants whose names do not appear on the Bristol register, as well as claiming rights for passengers whose names were registered, unpublished research of Russell R. Menard.

12. For example, if the percentages in the various age categories from the London list for 1683–85 are combined with the percentages derived from the Charles County records for 1680–89, the results are fairly close to those found in the Liverpool list, the shift from the 20 to 24 to the 10 to 14 age category expected.

Age group	10–14	15–19	20–24	25–29	30+
London list	2.8%	21.5%	53.7%	12.7%	9.3%
London list + Charles County records	14.2	32.7	41.4	7.7	4.7
Liverpool list	21.1	31.8	30.0	9.7	7.4

13. The argument that a marked decline in the age of servants leaving England indicates in itself a lowering of the social origins of immigrants becomes less convincing as the magnitude of the decline is decreased. Although more young Englishmen of lower status may in fact have emigrated, further evidence, such as proof of a decline in literacy in the various age categories is needed to sustain the argument, see Menard, "Transformation of the Chesapeake Labor System."

14. Lorena S. Walsh and Russell R. Menard, "Death in the Chesapeake: Two Life Tables for Men in Early Colonial Maryland," *Maryland Historical Magazine* 69 (1974):211–27.

15. Nicholson to Board of Trade, 27 March, 1697, *Archives* 33:87–88. For other evidence of emigration from Maryland in the mid-1690s see ibid., 19:225–26, 237, 238, 250, 258, 539–40; ibid., 2:279, 328–29; ibid., 23:84, and other sources cited in Russell R. Menard, "Economy and Society in Early Colonial Maryland" (Ph.D. diss., University of Iowa, 1975), ch. 8.

16. For the relationship between tobacco prices, emigration, and population, see Menard, "The Growth of Population in Early Colonial Maryland, 1631–1712" (ms. report, St. Mary's City Commission, April 1972, on file at the Hall of Records Annapolis, Md.).

17. J. Harry Bennett, Jr., "The Problem of Slave Labor Supply at Codrington," *Journal of Negro History* 36(1951):406–41. Bennett's figures were selected because they were based on precise data. Bennett notes that, "West Indian writers of the slavery period varied in placing the loss of new Negroes at from one-third to one-half of the number imported." The West Indian death rate represents the most extreme seasoning losses known to have occurred in British North America.

18. Menard, "From Servant to Freeholder," and "Economy and Society in Early Colonial Maryland," ch. 5., see also appendix 3, table A.3.

19. Menard found that only 10% of 95 servants brought into Somerset County between 1699 and 1701 could later be found in Maryland. Four or five appeared on a Somerset County tax list for 1724 as heads of households, and 1 other lived in the household of another. Only 9 or 10 left evidence of ever establishing households in Maryland, and only 3 acquired land. Similarly, only 5 to 8 of 116 servants brought into Prince George's County between 1696 and 1706 appeared on a nearly complete list of heads of households for 1719, Menard, "Economy and Society in Early Colonial Maryland," ch. 8.

20. Ibid., ch. 7, and St. Mary's City Commission Inventory Project, "Social Stratification in Maryland, 1658–1705," National Science Foundation Grant under the direction of Lois Green Carr. P. M. G. Harris, and Russell R. Menard (GS32272).

21. See Campbell, "Social Origins of Some Early Americans," and Menard, "Economy and Society in Early Colonial Maryland," ch. 5.

22. Ch. Ct. and Land Rec. E no. 1, ff. 50–51; V no. 1, ff. 254, 414; A no. 2, f. 268; Rent Roll 8:333, ms.; Wills 3:453, 698, mss.; Inv. and Accts. 26: 139, 182.

23. Ch. Ct. and Land Rec. B no. 1, ff. 205–6; E no. 1, f. 99; L no. 1, ff. 53–54; Rent Roll 8:327–28.

24. Ch. Ct. and Land Rec. C no. 1, f. 131; E no. 1, f. 73; M no. 1, ff. 165–66; Rent Roll 8:347, 350; Patents 12:542; Wills 4:147.

25. For examples of outlying quarters see Inv. and Accts. 7C:98; 15:318; 17:6,11; 19:127; 31:6; 33A:71; Wills 3:576, 718. For quarters detached from the main house, see Gary Wheeler Stone, "St. John's: Archaeological Questions and Answers," *Maryland Historical Magazine* 69 (1974):146–68, and *Archives* 70:86–89.

26. Ch. Ct. and Land Rec. V no. 1, ff. 89, 165, 455; A no. 2, f. 43; Inv. and Accts. 21:286; 22:20.

27. Ch. Ct. and Land Rec. D no. 1, f. 62; Wills 4:259; Inv. and Accts. 9:353; 10:97, 163; 12:21, 22, 67.

28. Ch. Ct. and Land Rec. E no. 1, f. 52; I no. 1, f. 108; Rent Roll 8:307.

29. Ch. Ct. and Land Rec. L no. 1, f. 3; N no. 1, f. 165; R no. 1, f. 462; V no. 1, ff. 107, 193; A no. 2, ff. 302–3; Q no. 1, f. 11; Rent Roll 8:318–20, 323, 328, 331–32, 351, 353–55, 357, 360; Wills 3:576, 649; Inv. and Accts. 1:394; 25:256; 27:12, 92, 234; Harry Wright Newman, *The Lucketts of Port Tobacco* (Washington, D.C. 1938), pp. 7–8, 73.

30. For documentation see Lorena S. Walsh, "Charles County, Maryland, 1658–1705: A Study of Chesapeake Social and Political Structure" (Ph.D. diss., to be submitted to Michigan State University), ch. 6. For confirmation of the opportunities available in this period, see

Menard, "From Servant to Freeholder." Menard studied the careers of 275 men who entered Maryland before the end of 1642, some of whom appear in this study.

31. For Maryland tobacco prices see Russell R. Menard, "Farm Prices of Maryland Tobacco, 1659–1710," *Maryland Historical Magazine* 68 (1973):80–85, and idem, "A Note on Chesapeake Tobacco Prices, 1618–1660," *Virginia Magazine of History and Biography,* in press. For a similar description of declining opportunity for servants who arrived after 1660 in Virginia, see Wertenbaker, *Planters of Colonial Virginia.* Freedmen in southeastern Pennsylvania apparently found a similar situation there by the end of the next century, see James T. Lemon, *The Best Poor Man's Country:* A Geographical Study of Early Southeastern Pennsylvania (Baltimore, 1972), pp. 84–96.

32. See Walsh, "Charles County, 1658–1705," ch. 6; and Menard, "From Servant to Freeholder." For similar developments in Virginia see Bernard Bailyn, "Politics and Social Structure in Virginia," in *Seventeenth-Century America,* ed. Smith, pp. 90–115. The results of this study do not support T. H. Breen's argument that a rise in tobacco prices during the 1680s eliminated a "'giddy multitude'" of poor whites and servants (who had before this time constituted a threat to peace in the Chesapeake) by increasing their access to land and eliminating "grinding poverty." Rather, tobacco prices and resulting economic opportunity moved in the opposite direction. Nor is there any evidence for his assertion that post–1680 immigrants were of higher social rank than their predecessors, "A Changing Labor Force and Race Relations in Virginia, 1660–1710," *Journal of Social History* 7 (1973):3–25.

33. That a change in equality of wealth distribution occurred, at least by 1670, is supported by results of the St. Mary's City Commission Inventory Project, "Social Stratification in Maryland." Between 1640 and 1660 the mean value of personal estates fell and the median rose, indicating that wealth became more equitably distributed in that period. From 1660 to the early 1680s the mean increased substantially, while the median leveled out by 1670, and perhaps earlier. Thus, inequality increased. From the 1680s through 1705 the mean and median remained stable, and further shifts in wealth distribution did not occur, see Russell R. Menard, P. M. G. Harris, and Lois Green Carr, "Opportunity and Inequality: The Distribution of Wealth on the Lower Western Shore of Maryland, 1638–1705," *Maryland Historical Magazine* 69 (1974):169–84.

34. Rent Rolls 0 and 8.

35. For lists of all landowners and biographies of officeholders in Prince George's County between 1696 and 1709, see Lois Green Carr, "County Government in Maryland, 1689–1709" (Ph.D. diss., Harvard University, 1968), appendix 6. It might be supposed that there were former Charles County servants among the nonofficeholding, nonlandholding residents of Prince George's County, a group not so extensively covered in the above study. However, it appears that most former servants moved further away than an adjacent county. A complete name index appears in the published Prince George's County records; Joseph H. Smith and Philip A. Crowl, eds., *Court Records of Prince George's County, Maryland, 1696–1699* (Washington, D.C. 1964). These early Prince George's County records share the advantage of the early records of Charles County in that the names of most of the male residents appear in them. A search of the index revealed no additional men whom I could identify as former Charles County servants other than those land and/or officeholders or craftsmen who also appeared in Carr's study.

36. Rent Rolls 3, 4, and 8. The St. Mary's City Commission is currently assembling biographical files of all seventeenth century St. Mary's County residents who appear in period records.

37. St. Mary's City Commission, "Social Stratification in Maryland,"

38. This disparity in total estate value appears to be influenced more by time of entry than it does by length of economic career. There were twenty-four inventories for the pre-1665 emigrant freedmen and twenty-two for the post-1665 group. Men in the earlier group whose economic careers lasted 13 years or less (7) were less wealthy than their longer-lived companions (17). The mean value of their estates was £96, below the mean value of those who lived longer—£159. In the later group, the mean value of the estates of the men whose economic careers lasted 19 years or longer (6) was only £59, less than the mean value of the estates of the shorter-lived members of the earlier group, and only £5 more than the mean value of £54 of the estates of those who died younger (16).

SIX

MARYLAND AND THE CHESAPEAKE ECONOMY, 1670–1720

Gloria L. Main

One need only match up the population figures of Virginia and Maryland in *Historical Statistics* to its series on English tobacco imports during the colonial period to encounter a little-known paradox in American history, the rise of slavery in the Chesapeake during a half-century of slow growth and then stagnation in the total output of its major crop.[1] Between the years 1670 and 1730, the population of Virginia and Maryland quadrupled in size, but the annual average export of tobacco from these two colonies never rose above 40 million pounds until the end of that period, even though peaks as high as 37 million were attained decades earlier (figure 6.1). During these very same years, slavery came to engross a large portion of the labor force. Blacks made up only 5 percent of the population in 1670, more than half a century after Virginia's adoption of its staple, but their proportion doubled between 1680 and 1690 and continued to rise until by 1710 one-fourth of the

TABLE 6.1
Population Growth and Tobacco Production in the Chesapeake, 1670–1760

Year	Total Population Va. and Md. (in thousands)	Percentage Negro	Tobacco Exports per Capita
1670	48.5	6.6	350?
1680	61.5	7.5	350?
1690	77.0	14.9	370?
1700	88.2	22.3	400
1710	121.0	25.7	230
1720	153.9	25.4	210
1730	205.1	23.0	186
1740	296.5	28.3	158
1750	372.1	38.9	138
1760	502.0	37.8	94

Source: U.S. Bureau of the Census, *Historical Statistics of the United States, Colonial Times to 1957* (Washington, D.C., 1960), series Z 1–19, pp. 756–57 and series A 223–37, pp. 765–66.

Note: Ms. Main resides in Setauket, New York. The author wishes to thank the editors for their assistance and encouragement.

134

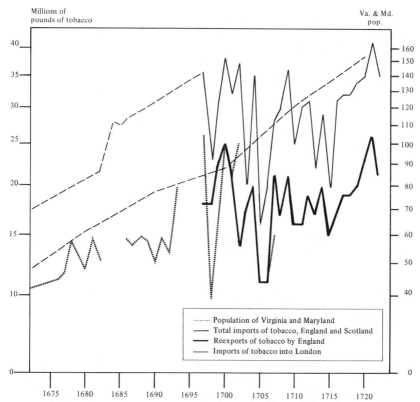

FIGURE 6.1. The Chesapeake Economy: Tobacco and Population, 1672-1722
Sources: U.S. Bureau of the Census, *Historical Statistics of the United States, Colonial Times to 1957* (Washington, D.C., 1960), series Z 1-19, pp. 756-57 and series A 223-37, pp. 765-66.

colonies' people were black (table 6.1). This essay attempts to explain that seeming paradox and in so doing will outline some major changes in Maryland's economy during a crucial half-century of her history.

Slavery and tobacco waxed and waned together later in the eighteenth century in a manner that foreshadowed the future course of the "cotton South," following the pattern already established in the sugar islands of the West Indies. Production of all of the great semitropical staples of the New World rested on slave labor: rice and coffee as well as sugar and cotton. Slaves, of course, were used in other ways and cultivated other crops, but these were ancillary activities, supplemental and incidental to the major purpose that propelled the African slave trade: supplying laborers to raise the crops whose European demand overcame the costs of transoceanic supply.

Although there had always been a few blacks among those hoeing tobacco in the New World, the relationship between slavery and tobacco was not as strong as that between slavery and the other great staple crops. White farmers tended the "smokers' weed" from early in the seventeenth century and continue to do so to the present day. In the English islands of the Caribbean, tobacco raised mainly by white labor furnished the principal source of income until the Dutch taught the planters how to produce sugar and sold them the workers with which to do it.[2] The problem posed by the present paper is to discover why the plantation system based on black slavery grew up at all among the tobacco growers of the Chesapeake and why it did so at a time when the population as a whole was reducing its commitment to the same staple crop that later fostered slavery's fullest flowering there.

The initial task is to measure that commitment to tobacco. Maryland will furnish the preponderance of sources, although one must not assume too blithely that Virginia's experience paralleled precisely that of her sister colony.

Because of the great increase in the numbers of children and blacks in her population during the Chesapeake's transition from an immigrant, male-dominated society to one more stable and native-born, output per member of the labor force provides a better measure of productivity during these years than does output per capita.[3] The labor force comprises that portion of a population engaged in income-generating activity, and this paper will follow the colonists' own definition of such a person, which they settled upon for tax collection purposes—white males above the age of fifteen and blacks of both sexes above that age. The use of "taxables" as equivalent to the total number in the labor force permits official enumerations to serve here as a basis for estimating output per worker.[4]

Table 6.2, based on lists of taxables and census data from both Chesa-peake colonies combines estimates of the size of the labor force with published data on the annual imports of tobacco into England from 1672 to 1720.[5] Due to the use of linear interpolation for the purpose of estimating the numbers of taxables in the years lacking such information, the exports column can provide only a rough guide to tobacco production per hand during these years. However, certain valid points do emerge from examina-tion of the table. Production per taxable peaked in 1688 and in the years 1697–1704, contracting thereafter, particularly so through the years up to 1716, and reviving slightly in the final years of the series. The upturn did not close the gap to the level attained in former years, about 1,000 pounds per worker. The year 1700 witnessed the peak output, over 37 million pounds produced by a labor force fully a third smaller than what it was in 1720.

The contents of table 6.2 confirm our previous impression that a decline in tobacco production per member of the labor force had, indeed, taken place, which resulted in the stagnation of total output of tobacco exports

TABLE 6.2
Tobacco Imported by England and the Number of Taxables in the
Chesapeake Colonies, 1672–1720

Year	Tobacco (thousands of pounds)	Maryland[a] Taxables	Virginia[a] Tithables	Estimated Total	Tobacco per Taxable
1671		5,631			
1672	17,559				
1673				(19,831)	0.885
1674			14,200		
1675		6,610			
1682	21,399	(8,379)	17,000	25,379	0.843
1688	28,386	(9,894)	(18,100)	27,994	1.014
1690		10,400			
1696		10,381	19,566	29,947	
1697	35,329	11,029	20,000	31,029	1.139
1698	22,738	(11,677)	20,253	31,930	0.712
1699	30,641	(12,325)	21,606	33,931	0.903
1700	37,166	12,973	24,291	37,264	0.997
1701	31,754	(13,416)	(24,695)	38,111	0.833
1702	36,749	(13,858)	25,099	38,957	0.943
1703	19,451	(14,301)	26,771	41,072	0.474
1704	34,665	14,743	26,928	41,671	0.832
1705	15,573	(15,109)	27,053	42,162	0.369
1706	19,379	(15,475)	(28,035)	43,510	0.445
1707	27,684	15,840	(29,017)	44,857	0.617
1708	28,716	(16,039)	30,000	46,039	0.624
1709	34,467	(16,238)	(30,257)	46,495	0.741
1710	23,351	(16,437)	(30,513)	46,950	0.497
1711	28,100	16,637[b]	(30,770)	47,407	0.593
1712	30,502	(17,037)	(31,026)	48,063	0.635
1713	21,573	(17,437)	(31,282)	48,719	0.443
1714	29,248	(17,837)	31,540	49,377	0.592
1715	17,783	18,238[bc]	(32,316)	50,554	0.352
1716	28,305	(18,677)	(33,092)	51,769	0.547
1717	29,450	(19,125)	(33,868)	52,993	0.556
1718	31,740	(19,584)	(34,645)	54,229	0.585
1719	33,503	(20,054)	(35,421)	55,475	0.604
1720	34,138	(20,535)	(36,197)	56,732	0.602

Sources: Tobacco imports, U.S. Bureau of the Census, *Historical Statistics of the United States, Colonial Times to 1957* (Washington, D.C., 1960), series Z 238–40, 223–37, pp. 765, 766; Maryland Taxables and Virginia Tithables 1671–1708, Russell R. Menard, "Economy and Society in Early Colonial Maryland," (Ph.D. diss., University of Iowa, 1975), p. 456; Maryland Taxables and Virginia Tithables 1709–22, Evarts B. Greene and Virginia D. Harrington, *American Population before the Federal Census of 1790* (1932; reprint ed., Gloucester, Mass., 1966), pp. 123–24, 127–29, 149–51.

a. Numbers in parentheses estimated by linear interpolation.

b. Assumes that 0.667 "Negroes" were taxable.

c. Assumes that white taxables form the same proportion of the population as they did in 1711.

from the Chesapeake, a process that did not reverse itself until the later 1730s. The decline in tobacco production per hand did not follow a smooth downward path, however, but reversed direction in 1697 and again in 1716. The reason for these interruptions of the trend becomes clear when one

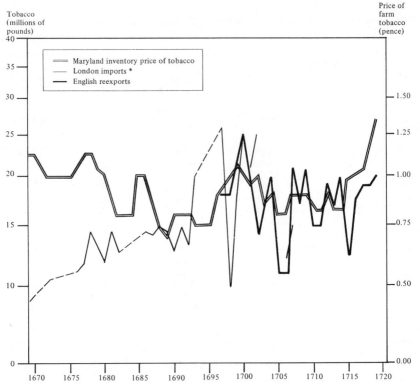

FIGURE 6.2. London Imports of Tobacco, English Reexports, and Maryland Inventory Prices of Farm Tobacco, 1669–1719 (Prices in pence per pound, sterling)

Sources: Import and export figures, U.S. Bureau of the Census, *Historical Statistics of the United States*, pp. 765–66; *series not continually available. Tobacco prices to 1710, Russell R. Menard, "Farm Prices of Maryland Tobacco, 1659–1710," *Maryland Historical Magazine* 68 (1973): 80–85. Prices after 1710 were collected by the author from the inventories of six counties: Inventories and Accounts, vols. 31–39; Inventories, vols. 1–3.

examines a newly available series on domestic tobacco prices.[6] Figure 6.2 projects this series against one depicting annual exports from the Chesapeake during the years 1699 through 1719. The expansion, contraction, and subsequent expansion of tobacco production followed a pattern closely similar to that of the annual average price of crop tobacco in Maryland's probate court records.

The long-term stagnation in total output is clearly associated with the low levels of the domestic price of tobacco that prevailed over much of the period, but the continuing downtrend in output per worker results from more complex causes. The supply of labor and its racial make-up played an important, if not crucial, role in the declining significance of tobacco in the Chesapeake economy. A first step toward assessing that role is determination of the size of the black population over time, but such data are unavailable for Maryland until 1704, the year of the first census.[7] Unfortunately, the county summaries of that year harbor some misleading numbers with regard to "Negroes" among their population, because some appear to have counted only black taxables, while others included children.[8] The summaries of the census in 1710 and in 1712 appear to be free of this kind of error.

Reliable figures on the numbers of blacks and their proportion of the total population do not exist before these early censuses, but inventories of probated estates provide useful information on the relative numbers of servants and slaves, plus data on their ages, sex, and physical condition.[9] Those used here originated in six counties of Maryland during the years 1674 through 1719: Anne Arundel, Baltimore, Calvert, Charles, Kent, and Somerset.[10] Collectively these counties contained over half the colony's population and reflect all of the attributes of the colony's economy, situated as they are on both sides of the bay, north as well as south.

As a general rule, inventories enumerate the personal chattels of their deceased owner and evaluate them in the local currency. The numbers of nonwhite servants and slaves that appear in these lists of property appear to reflect actual changes in their proportion in the living population, particularly in the years before the emergence of a significant population of free blacks. By calculating the average number of slaves per inventory each year, one can chart the progress of slavery in the Chesapeake. Figure 6.3 does this for the six county sample and compares these annual averages with those for indentured servants, most of whom were white.

The lines in figure 6.3 make clear that servants outnumbered slaves three to one before 1680, but the expansion in the black population closed the gap during the following decade. The average number of servants per inventory declined sharply between 1689 and 1696, years of severely depressed tobacco prices, after which it recovered and kept pace with the numbers of slaves until 1705. Subsequently, again in response to poor tobacco prices, servants faded almost entirely from the scene until a sharp upturn in tobacco prices in the final years of the period once again attracted a renewed supply, though in numbers far below those of former years. This period of decline corresponds to one of decisive growth for the slave population of colonial Maryland.

The timing of sharp changes in the relative numbers of servants reflects the influence of the current or expected price of tobacco on the demand for labor in the early Chesapeake, but the upward trend in the numbers of slaves stands out as one that was relatively independent of short-run prices. Indeed, the rate of increase for inventoried slaves rose most sharply well after the commencement in 1703 of the prolonged period of low tobacco prices. For light on the subject, one must turn to the supply side of the picture.

A fact long familiar to historians is the decline in English emigration to the New World, which began around 1660. The close of the Elizabethan era

Mean number
per inventory

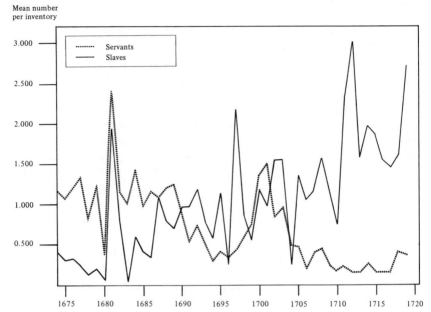

FIGURE 6.3. Average number* of Servants and Slaves in Maryland Inventories, Six Counties, 1674–1719.

*Unweighted

Sources: Inventories of six counties in Inventories and Accounts, 39 volumes; Inventories, vols. 1–3; Accounts, vols. 1–4; miscellaneous will books, country records, and testamentary proceedings. All are in the Hall of Records, Annapolis.

saw rapid population growth, economic depression, the extension of poverty, and the dawn of a new technology. Similar conditions elsewhere in Europe accompanied similar responses from a threatened human population: prolonged religious and civil strife. Although the Restoration did not entirely resolve the conflict in England, economic conditions gradually improved at the same time that population growth slackened to diminish unemployment.[11] English subjects became less interested in gambling their chances in the distant colonies, which exacerbated the perennial labor shortage abroad. The price that planters received for their staple, however, placed a ceiling on their ability to pay for the labor they so earnestly desired.

Due to this secular shortfall in the supply of English servants to the Chesapeake, particularly those of prime age and sex, the demand for slaves there was bound to grow at a faster long-term rate than did the resident white population. Upturns in the price of tobacco, then, brought requests for more laborers than the supply of white servants could satisfy, and ultimately, at the end of the seventeenth century, popped the cork on the African slave trade. That pent-up demand did not entirely spend itself for more than a decade after the delivery of the first cargo direct from Africa, despite the eventual downturn in tobacco prices.[12]

The cycle of tobacco prices determined the level of production, but the continuing growth of the resident population during a prolonged period of stagnation in tobacco exports suggests that a growing part of the population either raised no tobacco at all or governed their planting according to its price. The continuing demand for slaves, moreover, testifies to the fact that another part of the population found investment in servile labor satisfactorily profitable. The adjustments of Maryland's economy during the crucial half-century of this study brought permanent and profound changes in the social and political structure of this Chesapeake colony.

When the domestic price of tobacco fell well below a penny per pound, the more mobile segments of the population, made up chiefly of freed servants, fled the province. They did this in the early 1690s and again between 1704 and 1710.[13] Among those who stayed, a geographical redistribution placed a growing proportion of the population in areas outside prime tobacco lands. Analysis of the composition of assets listed in the inventories of estates reveals that regional specialization in Maryland's economy had already emerged by the end of the seventeenth century. Tables 6.3 and 6.4 summarize the findings for the six counties included in the present study. Of these, Anne Arundel, Calvert, and Charles raised most of the tobacco and claimed most of the servants and slaves. Only Charles, however, devoted itself so narrowly to cultivation of the staple crop. Fewer than a tenth of Charles County inventories mentioned wheat or plows, and three-quarters of these appeared after 1710, when tobacco prices showed no sign of recovering. Kent and Somerset on the Eastern Shore devoted more of their resources to wheat growing than did the other counties, while they also produced the majority of the craftsmen. Most of the mercantile activity, on the other hand, concentrated in Anne Arundel and Calvert.

TABLE 6.3
Economic Activities of the Counties, 1674–1719 (percentage)

	Value Farm Crops	Raising Wheat	Artisans	Commerce
Anne Arundel	25.5	14.3	11.2	15.0
Calvert	24.6	13.1	7.6	11.8
Charles	11.0	8.3	8.7	5.3
Baltimore	17.3	13.7	14.0	3.9
Kent	15.9	26.5	17.0	7.1
Somerset	6.7	26.0	19.3	5.4
	100.0			

Source: Inventories and Accounts, vols. 1–27; Inventories, vols. 1–3; Accounts, vols. 1–9; Testamentary Proceedings, various counties; Wills 3, Hall of Records, Annapolis, Md.

TABLE 6.4
Distribution of Servants and Slaves among the Counties (percentage)

County	Servants	Slaves	All	Inventories
Anne Arundel	25.8	31.3	29.4	20.5
Calvert	26.8	29.6	28.6	19.9
Charles	20.2	17.9	18.7	17.4
Baltimore	10.6	6.9	8.2	12.7
Kent	7.8	5.7	6.4	11.9
Somerset	8.7	8.6	8.6	17.6
Total	99.9	100.0	99.9	100.0

Source: Inventories and Accounts, Hall of Records, Annapolis, Md.

Uneven rates of growth among the counties redistributed the population into areas with different resources, bringing about the reduction in tobacco exports per capita observed at the aggregate level. As Table 6.5 indicates, the three counties that relied least on tobacco, Baltimore, Kent, and Somerset, housed only 31 percent of the total taxable population of the six counties in 1675, but by 1712, 55 percent of adult white males were living there.

Changes within each county also worked in the same direction. Both Anne Arundel and Calvert shifted resources into wheat growing between 1687–96 and 1697–1701, and again, more substantially after 1706. Even Charles County residents participated in the trend towards alternative crops.

Handicrafts also increased among the colonists, who previously had been almost entirely dependent on English manufactures, but such endeavors spread at different rates among the counties: Kent and Somerset relatively early, Calvert, Charles, and Baltimore relatively late. Rather than expanding home manufactures, Anne Arundel turned towards commerce, particularly after becoming the provincial capital. By the close of the period, 20 percent

TABLE 6.5
Distribution of Taxables and White Males Aged Sixteen and Above by County, 1675–1712 (percentage)

	Anne Arundel	Calvert	Baltimore	Kent	Somerset	Charles
1675	20.8	27.9	8.2	7.7	15.4	20.0
1694	23.4	27.1	7.1	7.0	21.9	13.6
1695	23.1	27.1	7.5	7.1	22.0	13.2
1696	26.1	17.4	8.3	8.6	23.1	16.5
1700	24.8	17.1	10.4	9.5	23.0	15.4
1704	21.6	16.4	10.6	11.6	25.6	14.1
1710	16.2	11.3	11.7	15.6	29.9	15.2
1712	16.8	11.0	13.4	14.2	27.6	17.0

Sources: Taxables, Menard, "Economy and Society," pp. 457–59: White Males Aged Sixteen and Above, *Archives* 25:255–59.

of Anne Arundel inventories show evidence of mercantile activity compared to just 6 percent in the years before 1697.

While a limited withdrawal of land and manpower from tobacco culture took place in every county during the long depression in tobacco prices following 1702, geographical redistribution of the population accounts for much of the reduction in per capita exports as it reduced the relative numbers of planters able to produce tobacco at a profit when its domestic price fell below a penny per pound.

Not too surprisingly, the geographical pattern for the black population proceeded in a manner directly contrary to that of the white population. Despite the shrinking proportion of whites, Anne Arundel and Calvert exerted a growing monopoly over the labor supply of the six counties. As table 6.4 showed, these two counties listed 53 percent of the servants and 61 percent of the slaves. The timing of their acquisitions underlines the importance of the years after 1702–6. Table 6.6 dramatizes this fact by showing that before 1706 estates from Anne Arundel and Calvert owned half of all the six counties. Thereafter, their proportion rose to two-thirds.

Only a minority of planters, even in Anne Arundel and Calvert counties, ever purchased servile labor, no matter what the price of tobacco. The proportion of estates without either slaves or servants rose from roughly three-fifths of all estates from the six counties in the years before 1690 to about two-thirds during the period 1691 to 1704. Thereafter, about three-quarters of inventoried estates listed neither form of labor. The prices of slaves, roughly three times that of servants of equivalent physical condition, placed them well beyond the reach of the majority even in times of good prices, but the depression in the tobacco market served to concentrate both kinds of labor into estates with large holdings. English servants in such estates probably served in supervisory positions over the newly enslaved Africans.

TABLE 6.6
Distribution of Servile Labor Force among the Counties (percentage)

	Anne Arundel	Calvert	Charles	Baltimore	Kent	Somerset
1674–1680	30.1	34.8	14.2	8.7	8.2	4.0
1681–1686	19.3	30.3	33.8	2.3	6.7	7.6
1687–1696	27.2	28.2	14.0	13.2	4.2	13.2
1697–1701	28.5	22.7	26.2	7.1	7.1	8.4
1702–1706	30.4	18.7	25.9	12.8	5.1	7.2
1707–1711	25.5	39.1	10.8	4.5	11.3	8.7
1712–1716	36.9	27.3	14.2	4.0	7.6	9.8
1717–1719	33.4	30.1	15.0	12.3	1.8	7.4

Source: Inventories and Accounts, Hall of Records, Annapolis, Md.

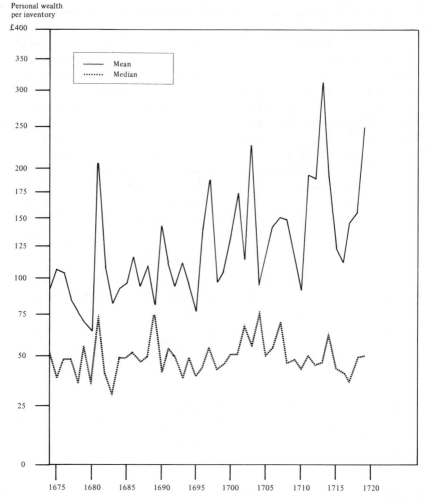

Personal wealth
per inventory

FIGURE 6.4. Net Personal Wealth, Six Counties of Maryland, 1674–1719 (Pounds sterling)
  Sources: As for Figure 6.3.

The growth of slavery rested on the emergence of the large plantation. The percentage of estates with ten or more slaves increased slowly but fairly steadily throughout the years under study, but their share of the total number of slaves listed in the inventories jumped from 42 percent in 1697–1706 to 55 percent in 1707–11, jumped again to 61 percent in 1712–16, reaching 67 percent in the final years, 1717–19. A simple count of the estates from 1711 and after yielded a figure of 45 out of a total of 831 that owned ten or more slaves, a rate of appearance in the inventories two-and-a-half times

Smoothed mean personal
wealth per inventory

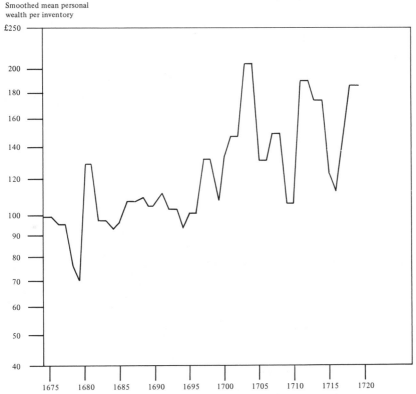

FIGURE 6.5. Smoothed Mean, Net Personal Wealth, Six Counties of Maryland, 1674–1719 (Pounds sterling)

    Sources: As for Figure 6.3.

greater than that prevailing in earlier years. Thirty-five of those 45 great estates came from Anne Arundel and Calvert counties.

    Perhaps the real paradox encountered in the Maryland inventories lies not in the regional specialization of economic activity that replaced white workers with black, but in the discovery that the class that purchased the new laborers grew rapidly richer during the prolonged downturn in the cycle of tobacco prices. The upper strata of estates acquired increasing wealth of all kinds along with its slaves. Figure 6.4 shows the widening gap between the median and mean inventory wealth of the six counties, figure 6.5 clarifies the course of the mean over time through a smoothing procedure, and figure 6.6 shows the average wealth of the richest estates compared to the others in eight consecutive periods. The deep depression in tobacco prices that marked the years 1687 to 1696 dampened the growth of wealth among the

Mean personal wealth of various strata of inventories

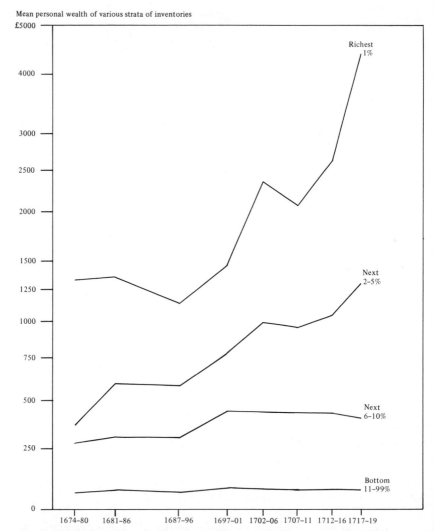

FIGURE 6.6. Mean Net Personal Wealth, Ranked Percentiles of Estates, Six Counties of Maryland, 1674–1719 (Pounds sterling)
   Sources: As for Figure 6.3.

top estates, but the decline after 1702 scarcely interrupted the long-term process, and from 1711 on, the wealth of the richest 5 percent really ballooned.[14]

The two major slaveholding counties, not surprisingly, enjoyed the highest averages of inventory wealth. Table 6.7 shows the mean inventory wealth, exclusive of debts receivable, of each county in eight time periods.

TABLE 6.7
Personal Wealth per Inventory[a] by County
(£ current money)

	Anne Arundel	Calvert	Charles	Baltimore	Kent	Somerset
1674–1680	96.3	124.6	71.4	64.1	61.3	107.9
1681–1686	105.1	126.1	120.5	60.0	98.9	198.8
1687–1696	119.4	127.1	80.7	106.5	97.6	68.6
1697–1701	159.9	137.2	124.7	85.2	120.7	139.5
1702–1706	202.4	155.1	192.4	88.8	118.9	91.0
1707–1711	196.4	237.1	111.1	109.8	105.1	100.7
1712–1716	279.5	174.7	106.3	97.7	150.3	100.0
1717–1719	337.8	315.8	97.0	179.8	123.2	62.8
Average	187.1	174.7	113.0	99.0	109.5	108.7

Source: Inventories and Accounts, Hall of Records.
[a]Excludes debts receivable.

Analysis of the table uncovers a strong trend in mean wealth away from Charles, Kent and Somerset to the other counties, commencing with the period 1707–1711. The final three years exhibited the greatest total variation of any time period in the table, due probably to the population effects of the rise in tobacco prices, since these years produced an enormous increase in the numbers of relatively poor estates from Charles and Somerset Counties (those whose values fell below £40).[15]

The relative changes in mean personal wealth among the six counties reveal a regional redistribution of probate wealth in which Anne Arundel County was the greatest gainer and Charles and Somerset Counties the principal losers. The redistribution of the slave labor force during the same years followed a similar pattern, while the flow of free white labor was in the reverse direction. Wealth and slaves centered in a handful of estates in two counties.

What accounted for the prosperity of a few? Any erosion of farm income suffered by the top level of Maryland estates during the years of the depression in the tobacco market appears to have been well absorbed by a reorganization of their agricultural activities. They operated multiple farm units, diversified their crops, and clothed their laborers in home-manufactured cloth and shoes. Their growing stocks of cattle, swine, and horses undoubtedly found markets in coastal New England, in Pennsylvania due to the flood of new immigrants, and in the sugar plantations of the West Indies.

Merely maintaining previous levels of farm income by reallocating resources could not, however, have sufficed to finance the development of the great plantation enterprises that distinguish the post-1710 years in Maryland. Although little is known about the business careers of those making up this small group of planter elite, the lists of assets compiled at the end of their lives do furnish some interesting clues to their major sources of income. One inventory item in particular is very suggestive. That which distinguishes the top 10 percent of estates and the top slaveholders who formed a part of that class is the proportion of their total assets in shipping and imported goods, particularly the latter. Virtually every inventory of the top slaveholders in Anne Arundel and Calvert Counties in the last nine years of this study owned stocks of "new goods," some of them hundreds of pounds' worth. The composition of estate assets among these men, and of the richest 10 percent generally, differs markedly from that of poorer men. Table 6.8 compares the proportion of net personal wealth invested in labor, livestock, and nonfarm income-producing assets, such as craft tools, stocks of goods for sale, shipping, and so forth, of the top slaveholders of Anne Arundel and Calvert Counties in the years after 1710 and all the estates grouped into percentage groups ranked by wealth from the years 1695 to 1719. One may note that labor made up 35 percent of their net personal wealth, livestock formed 22 percent, and goods associated with commerce over 11 percent. When we add in the value of tools and miscellaneous farm and home products, about three-quarters of the value of these estates consisted of income-producing assets.

The capital-intensive character of the richest estates and their distinctive investment in stocks of imported goods suggests that prior success in trade may have financed their acquisition of slaves either by direct purchase from English suppliers or through the liquidation of loans, mortgages, and mercantile debts owed to them. While tobacco prices were good, income from commission sales, storekeeping, and moneylending quite obviously

TABLE 6.8
Composition of Personal Wealth in Maryland Inventories[a]
Six Counties, 1695–1719 (percentage of personal wealth

Classes of Owners	Labor	Livestock	Commerce[b]
Top slaveholders[c]	35.6	21.8	8.9
Top ten percent	34.0	19.8	11.4
Second ten percent[d]	27.0	29.2	4.3
Next thirty percent[d]	12.9	40.2	3.4
Lower thirty percent[e]	4.3	50.9	1.2
Bottom twenty percent	0.0	38.7	1.1

Source: Inventories and Accounts, Hall of Records.
[a]Excludes debts receivable.
[b]Consists of ships, cargoes, new goods only for top slaveholders. For all others, also includes raw materials and domestic manufacturers.
[c]Anne Arundel and Calvert Counties, 1711–19.
[d]Percentiles ranked by personal wealth 51–80.
[e]Percentiles ranked by personal wealth 21–50.

benefited those who engaged in such activities, but the years that witnessed the increase in the numbers and wealth of the top level of estates followed a seven-year period of low tobacco prices. Years of general prosperity in the Chesapeake may have laid the groundwork of the few great fortunes in early Maryland history but probably cannot account entirely for their sudden blossoming.

Mercantile enterprise of another sort, one unrelated to the tobacco market, may have provided the necessary propellant. Although Queen Anne's War, which lasted from 1702 to 1713, at first brought losses in shipping and cut off communication between the colonies and the mother country, it later proved a great boon to the colonial economy in the form of the Royal Navy. By clearing the waters of privateers and pirates, British war ships reduced the risks, and freight charges, which had so long encumbered colonial commerce. A still more immediate source of gain, however, lay in English expenditures in the New World for military purposes.

The British war fleets that patroled the waters off the Atlantic coast required periodic provisioning of their crews. The government ultimately spent over £192,000 sterling for this purpose on ships stationed off Virginia during the years 1708 to 1711.[16] Paying for these by written drafts on governmental agencies at home, ships' captains contracted for supplies with local merchants. Since these drafts were promises to pay only, and not negotiable instruments readily transferred or sold, the merchants who accepted them had to await payment while government officials conducted critical reviews of the procedures, costs, and exchange rates behind each draft.[17] Opportunity to exploit the needs of the Royal Navy, therefore, restricted itself to those with the ability to command the supplies and to wait months or years for their pay. The risks were high, but these contracts proved highly lucrative to northern merchants, including Robert Livingston of New York and the brothers Faneuil of Boston.[18] There is no reason why men of the Chesapeake, using capital accumulated in the years of good tobacco prices, could not have done as well.

Summary and Conclusion

The history of the Chesapeake economy during the years of transition from its seventeenth-century pattern was a matter of many small changes producing, in the end, two major ones: the extension of slavery through the purchase of blacks direct from Africa, commencing in 1697, and the rise of large-scale plantation agriculture more than a decade later. Initially, the broadening of slave ownership took place side by side with the old system using white indentured servants. The one did not drive out, but gradually superseded the other. As tobacco prices weakened, the freed servants left the province and few were purchased to replace them. Black slaves, however, could not leave and new cargoes continued to arrive. The years of the depression in the tobacco market redistributed the growing population of slaves into fewer estates and from some counties to others. Blacks did replace whites, but in a limited area and for a limited few.

Maryland in 1720 still supported a relatively simple agriculture society, whose members, on the whole, were poor and undistinguished. The winds of change were stirring, however, as wheat and sheep crept over the landscape and as white sails on the Chesapeake promised a bright commercial future. Still brighter stars in the social firmament signaled the great new wealth of a native-born elite in the process of replacing their immigrant ancestors. More distinctively, too they were assembling a permanent work force made up of new immigrants—laborers of a baser status. At the top and at the bottom, Maryland's social structure exhibited far greater contrasts than those which had characterized the colony in the seventeenth century. The complex interplay of tobacco prices and labor supply in an international setting beset by wars and market reversals promoted a type of farm organization virtually unknown in Maryland before, one which ultimately created a monolithic stereotype for an entire region, the myth and mystique of the "plantation South."

NOTES

1. U.S. Bureau of the Census, *Historical Statistics of the United States, Colonial Times to 1957* (Washington, D.C., 1960), series Z 1–19, p. 756 and series A 223–37, pp. 765–66.

2. Carl and Roberta Bridenbaugh, *No Peace beyond the Line: The English in the Caribbean 1624–1690* (New York, 1972), p. 83; Richard S. Dunn, *Sugar and Slaves: The Rise of the Planter Class in the English West Indies, 1624–1713* (Chapel Hill, 1972), pp. 60–62, 65–66, 230–31, 314; Richard S. Sheridan, *Sugar and Slavery: An Economic History of the British West Indies, 1623–1775* (Baltimore, 1974), p. 129.

3. Wesley Frank Craven, *White, Red, and Black: The Seventeenth-Century Virginian* (Charlottesville, 1971), pp. 16–17; Russell R. Menard, "The Growth of Population in Early Colonial Maryland, 1631–1712," (ms. report, St. Mary's City Commission, April 1972, on file at the Hall of Records, Annapolis, Md.), idem, "Immigration to the Chesapeake Colonies in the Seventeenth Century: A Review Essay," *Maryland Historical Magazine* 68 (1973):323–29; idem, "Economy and Society in Early Colonial Maryland" (Ph.D. diss., University of Iowa, 1975), pp. 285–314.

4. The precise role of women as income earners in the hoe culture of the early Chesapeake must await further research. Suffice it to remark here that their presence in the labor force may have increased proportionately with the increase in their numbers and the real decline in tobacco production per worker would then have accelerated as the sex ratio in the population gradually righted itself.

5. Menard, "Economy and Society in Early Colonial Maryland," p. 456; Margaret S. Morriss, *Colonial Trade of Maryland, 1689–1715* (Baltimore, 1904), pp. 34–35; William Hand Browne et al. eds., *Archives of Maryland,* 72 vols. (Baltimore, 1883–)25:255–59; same census data are also in Evarts B. Greene and Virginia D. Harrington, *American Population before the Federal Census of 1790* (1932; Gloucester, Mass., 1966), pp. 123–24, 127–29.

6. Russell R. Menard, "Farm Prices of Maryland Tobacco, 1659–1710," *Maryland Historical Magazine* 68 (1973):80–85. Prices after 1710 are from the inventories of six counties, collected by the writer.

7. Greene and Harrington, *American Population,* p. 129.

8. Menard, "Growth of Population in Early Colonial Maryland."

9. Because they draw from so restricted a sector of society, probate records harbor biases that require caution in their use and interpretation. See Gloria L. Main, "On the Correction of Biases in Colonial Probate Records," *Historical Methods Newsletter* 8 (1974):10–28 for a discussion of the problem and for some methods of overcoming them. Maryland records of the years of the demographic transition are particularly difficult to interpret due to the rapidly changing make-up of the living population and the shift in the mortality structure associated with the replacement of an immigrant society by one native born. The numbers of taxables and the census counts of adult white men suggest that out-migrations of these during the middle 1690s and again after 1704 would tend to remove potential probate types from the population subject to probate. Such emigration did take place according to a letter of Gov. Francis Nicholson to the Board of Trade, *Archives* 23:87–88 and numerous other sources cited in Menard, "Growth of Population in Early Colonial Maryland," note 44. The extent of such emigration is conjectural, but analysis of inventoried decedents identified as single, married with children under age, and married with at least one adult among living offspring shows that the married men among them increased substantially in proportion during the years 1705 to 1716. These men appear at all levels of wealth, but a true bias exists against the very poorest. Age bias, however, affects the behavior of the median value far more than the mean and cannot account for the changes in the upper end of the distribution of Maryland's inventoried estates discussed below. For a careful attempt to correct for such bias in these before 1705, see Russell R. Menard, P.M.G. Harris, and Lois Green Carr, "Opportunity and Inequality: The Distribution of Wealth on the Lower Western Shore of Maryland, 1638–1705," *Maryland Historical Magazine* 69 (1974):176–78.

10. Important boundary changes took place in 1696 and 1706 that account for Calvert's loss of taxable population in the first year and the oscillation in Kent County wealth levels. About a fourth of the inventories encountered gave no clue to their county of origin. In the interest of efficiency, these were noted only as to year and inventory value. They are not included in the set of inventories serving the present work, a fact that imparts an upward bias to the mean and median, particularly so in the seventeenth-century data, when such inventories were most common. The mean of these averaged only half that of the six-county set, a level reduced by the fact that additional inventories and accounts pertaining to those individuals were ignored. Because there is no reason to believe that these inventories did not derive from all over Maryland, the bias introduced by their exclusion is somewhat modified. Since the six counties averaged about half the population of Maryland, let us assume that half of the excluded estates originated with them and proceed to estimate the effects of their exclusion on the mean of the merged estates: their presence in the merged set lowered the mean by five to seven per cent in various time periods, the greatest such effect occurred in the years 1699–1702 when the mean declined by 9 percent. After 1712, their fewer numbers altered the mean by 2 percent. For the period prior to that year, the unidentified estates would have raised the size share of the richest 10 percent by a few percentage points at most.

11. The outlines of English economic development in the seventeenth century are still far from clear, and this statement rests on mere scraps of evidence. Carl Bridenbaugh vividly describes the unrest and turmoil in England during the years of colonial settlement in *Vexed and Troubled Englishmen,* 1590–1642 (New York, 1968). The demographic changes are still under study but, in any case, do not contradict evidence of economic revival: F. P. Braudel and F. Spooner, "Prices in Europe from 1450 to 1750," *The Cambridge Economic History of Europe* 4:374–486; E. L. Jones, "Agriculture and Economic Growth in England, 1660–1750," *Journal of Economic History* 25 (1965):1–18; Ralph Davis, *England Overseas Trade 1500–1700* (London, 1973), chaps. 3 through 6. Statistical series with which to chart short-term fluctuations in the economy are as yet unavailable.

12. In Virginia the shipments continued until 1709 but did not recommence in significant numbers until a decade after. U.S. Bureau of the Census, *Historical Statistics,* series Z 294–97, p. 769.

13. Menard, "Growth of Population in Early Colonial Maryland," note 44.

14. Prices of slaves, tobacco, and imported goods rose after 1716, introducing thereby an upward bias in the values of estates listing these commodities. Official proclamation money defined Maryland's exchange with England at 133.3 to 100.0, but current money after 1709

deviated from sterling by much less than that in the inventories. The maximum increase in the inventory values of the most standardized type of slaves, prime field hands, was roughly 40 percent, and much of this increase was attributable to a rise in world prices rather than to the revaluation of Maryland's currency. The growth in the wealth of the top 5 percent of estates greatly exceeded such increases in the price level.

15. The technique of analysis underlying this paragraph is based on the work of R. A. Fisher, *Statistical Methods for Research Workers* (London, 1925; 13th ed., 1958). On the use of analysis of variance, see Gloria L. Main, "Personal Wealth in Colonial America: Explorations in the Use of Probate Records from Maryland and Massachusetts, 1650–1720" (Ph.D. diss., Columbia University, 1972), pp. 91–103. The boundary years selected for use in the above tables attempt to capture the turning points of the cycle of tobacco prices. Shifting the boundary years to end in 5 or 0, a more familiar but quite arbitrary procedure, muddies the picture that emerges through analysis of variance but does not alter the interpretation.

16. Curtis P. Nettles, *The Money Supply of the American Colonies before 1720* (1934; New York, 1964), p. 195.

17. Ibid., pp. 187–88.

18. Ibid., pp. 188, 192.

SEVEN

ECONOMY AND SOCIETY ON MARYLAND'S EASTERN SHORE, 1689–1733

Paul G. E. Clemens

Along the northeastern shore of the Chesapeake Bay, relatively isolated from the chief arteries of mid-seventeenth century trade, stretched several hundred thousand acres of tidal marshes, poorly drained lowlands, and rich, fertile soil. Immigration to this region began in the 1660s. The first farmers, artisans, and merchants to arrive in Talbot County, that region of the Eastern Shore between the Chester and Great Choptank Rivers, found food scarce, consumption goods that they had previously bought in England expensive, and the supply of servants inadequate, making the clearing of land difficult. But in less than a decade, farms began producing enough tobacco to attract English shipping. The establishment of regular trade assured Talbot planters the flow of capital and labor that they required to profit from the tobacco market. By the outbreak of the Anglo-French war in 1689, the nucleus of a landed planter class had emerged.[1] Over the next forty years these settler families attempted to maintain their mastery of the environment and their exploitation of the market, while newer immigrants fought an uphill battle to secure a foothold in the region. The nature of this struggle and its social consequences are the subject of this essay.

The state of the tobacco market dominated economic life. The price of tobacco had fallen steadily since the 1620s, but neither the secular price decline nor frequent short, sharp drops in the market value of the crop kept planters from obtaining ample remuneration for their labor. The fall in tobacco prices allowed English and continental European consumption to spread as colonial production increased. In the 1680s, however, the secular decline in the price of tobacco bottomed out, and until the mid-1730s, the market fluctuated at about a penny per pound of oronoco leaf.[2]

Diversified agricultural production and trade provided alternatives to complete reliance on the tobacco staple. Patterns of diversification and intercolonial trade appeared in the rural economy of the Eastern Shore as

Note: Paul G. E. Clemens is assistant professor of history, Rutgers University. The author wishes to thank Lois Green Carr, Roberta L. Clemens, and Rudolf M. Bell for comments.

early as the 1690s; such activity clearly occurred as much because of prosperous market conditions as because of declining returns to the tobacco staple, and diversification and trade provided substantial sources of income for many of the richer planter-entrepreneurs. Until the end of the 1689–1733 period, however, only a very small number of families were drawn into this new economic world.

Consequently, between the outbreak of war in 1689 and the depression of the early 1730s, most Eastern Shore tobacco planters had to adjust to a squeeze between cost and return. As table 7.1 indicates, the farmers' difficulties were greatest between 1689 and 1713, when almost continuous war between England and France precluded opportunities to expand the continental European market; but even after the end of Queen Anne's War in 1713, economic recovery did not bring a return to the prosperity of the mid-seventeenth century. To be sure, land and labor costs rose after 1688 relative to tobacco prices, partly because planting was profitable, and investments in land and labor continued to produce adequate returns. But this squeeze altered Eastern Shore society, affected the new settler more than

TABLE 7.1
Tobacco Prices and Production Costs in Talbot County, Maryland, 1670–1733

	Indexes				
			(C)		
	(A)	(B)	Production	(D)	(E)
	Labor	Land	Costs	Tobacco	Cost/Price
Years	Costs*	Costs†	(A+B/2)	Prices‡	(100xC/D)
1670–1679	77	55	66	130	51
1680–1688	87	60	74	100	74
1689–1696	86	98	92	85	108
1697–1701	94	101	98	123	80
1702–1713	100	100	100	100	100
1714–1719	108	98	103	127	81
1720–1724	115	120	118	125	94
1725–1729	113	105	109	128	85
1730–1733	110	129	120	121	99

Sources: Inventories and Accounts, 1670–1718; Inventories, 1718–33; Talbot County Land Records.

Note: The periodization reflects the movement of tobacco prices. If only data from Talbot inventories were used, the years 1714–19 would not be as good, and the years 1720–29 would be somewhat better.

*Computed from Maryland rather than Talbot County data compiled by Russell Menard for the St. Mary's City Commission. His index uses servants from 1670 to 1673, and slaves from 1710 to 1733. The base, used in the above table, 1703–13, corresponds to slave prices of £28.5 and servant prices of £11.8.

†Base, 1702–13, of 100 equals 65 pounds of tobacco per acre. Prices were left in tobacco because of the difficulty of converting the value of low grades of tobacco, with which land was purchased, to sterling.

‡Base, 1702–13, of 100 equals .81 pence per pound of tobacco. Prices for 1670–79 from Maryland inventories; prices for 1680–1733 from Talbot inventories.

the established family, hurt the poor more than the rich, and limited options for some while creating them for others. Within this context, for the period 1689–1733, three questions will be explored: First, what conditions had to be fulfilled by those seeking upward economic mobility? Second, did mobility remain possible throughout this period? Third, did changes in economic opportunity alter Talbot County's social structure?

Mobility: The Structure of Opportunity

Talbot County was a market-oriented agricultural economy in which planters measured their success by the accumulation of land and labor. The process of upward economic mobility is best viewed as a series of steps: forming a household, renting land, purchasing a plantation, and eventually obtaining servants and slaves. Common laborers, freed servants, share-croppers, and poor immigrants began the process of upward mobility by leasing a farm and furnishing a household. If a man became a tenant, he could then attempt to become a landowner, while the landed planter's station in society could be enhanced through the acquisition of a servile work force. Each settler had the greatest opportunity during upswings in the short-term economic cycles, when tobacco prices were high, credit ample, and labor available. Success depended on good harvests, and many men supplemented their farm income by engaging in either artisan or mercantile enterprise.

For the lowest stratum of society, mobility began with forming a household and renting land. The poor had to put subsistence first; they worried over corn and pork, cotton shirts and jackets, and a suitable lodging in a planter's home. Inevitably, freed servants, poor immigrants, and the sons of small farmers were dependent upon men who could advance them the goods and produce they needed for subsistence, often paying for the advance of food, clothing, and tools by entering into sharecropping and labor agreements. The goal of these sharecroppers and laborers was to obtain a lease, which would give them land, a home, and a measure of economic independence. Talbot County inventories contain numerous examples of the paltry belongings of both dependent laborers and tenants, each with a bed, some blankets, a chair, several iron pots, a sheep or two, a few pigs, occasionally a cow, and some dunghill fowl.[3]

Men needed little capital to form a household. Provisions, clothing, and agricultural and kitchen implements required a credit advance of £5 to £10 sterling.[4] The cost of renting land, however, is more difficult to determine. Data on rents come from two sources. The first is a series of twenty-nine Talbot and Queen Anne's leases recorded between 1721 and 1750. The shortest of these leases ran for three years, the longest for two lives, the mean length being eleven years. The highest rent was 1,500 pounds of tobacco annually, and the average and median were 600 pounds. The longer the lease ran, the higher the annual rent. None of the leases specified acreages because, although a tenant held an entire plantation, usually consisting of fifty to one hundred acres, under the terms of the lease he could clear and plant each year only what he needed for a new tobacco crop (generally one to three acres). The second source of rent records is a collection of seventy-three documents listing the annual rent a guardian owed a minor whose property he was managing. These evaluations of annual returns from plantations were not really rents, but they suggest that few estates were leased for under 150 pounds of tobacco yearly. One survey from 1716 lists the tenants on a large plantation belonging to the children of Richard Bishop. When the survey was first taken in June, the rents ran from 100 to 400 pounds of tobacco; someone, obviously unsatisfied with these returns, interceded for the children, a new guardian was appointed, and the rents were raised to between 200 and 600 pounds.[5]

Most tenants paid rents of between 500 and 600 pounds of tobacco, about £2 annually for a fifty-acre farm. Rent, then, brought the tenant's cost of forming a household to £7 to £12. No clues exist that would indicate how many men reached this level and persisted, but table 7.2 suggests the types of economic conditions tenants faced. Adding annual clothing and household costs as well as taxes to rent and initial expenses shows that unmarried tenants spent £5 to £7 per year and married tenants without children £6 to £8; income on these farms ranged from £4 when a single tenant planted 1,000

TABLE 7.2
Annual Expenses and Returns on a Talbot County Tenant Farm in the Early Eighteenth Century (£ Sterling)

| | Tenant Farmer | | Tenant and Wife | |
	Best	Worst	Best	Worst
Initial costs*	1.0	2.0	1.0	2.0
Rent†	2.0	2.5	2.0	2.5
Expenses‡	2.0	2.0	3.5	3.5
Total	5.0	6.5	6.5	8.0
Production§	9.0	4.0	16.5	6.0
Net	4.0	−2.5	10.0	−2.0

Sources: See text and Paul G. E. Clemens, "The Operation of a Chesapeake Tobacco Plantation in the Early Eighteenth Century," *Agricultural History*, in press, especially tables 2 and 4. Production estimates taken from inventory crop reports.

*Costs are equivalent to initial household expenses of £5 and £10 paid over six years at six percent interest.

†Rent of 500 to 600 pounds of tobacco. All tobacco figures used in calculations converted to sterling at a penny per pound and rounded to nearest half £ sterling.

‡Expenses include head taxes of 150 pounds of tobacco on the male tenant and 350 pounds of clothing and incidentals per person.

§Production estimates for a single tenant range from 1,000 to 2,100 pounds per year. For husband and wife the range is 1,500 to 4,000 pounds.

pounds of tobacco to almost £17 when husband and wife harvested 4,000 pounds. The table supports the argument that those who became tenant-householders rather than remaining common laborers often were married, for husband and wife together had a far better chance of breaking even, although children, because they initially consumed more than they produced, did not aid the struggling family immediately.[6] Other householders probably supplemented their incomes using their skills as artisans; wage rates were high when work was available, and roughly one out of every seven white males could serve as a carpenter, cooper, blacksmith, or tanner.[7]

Household formation became possible for such men when credit expanded. This tied the fate of the poor directly to short-term fluctuations in the Anglo-Chesapeake economy. When tobacco prices rose, trade accelerated. Merchants then extended credit to the wealthier planters, who in turn could underwrite the creation of new tenancies. The laborer who became a tenant had only to accumulate a small surplus to weather bad years, find a credit source, and accept the risk, both psychological and economic, that independent status entailed. In this process, the recently freed servants probably fared worse than other poor people. Most servants arrived during booms, when demand for labor was high, but did not obtain their freedom until after tobacco prices had fallen and credit contracted. Consequently, they had to begin farming as laborers and sharecroppers at a time when economic conditions were unfavorable, and many left the county before the next upswing in prices and expansion of credit.[8]

Tenant-householders remained on the margin of self-sufficiency. William Holte's career, for example, parallels that of numerous poor in Talbot. Holte probably arrived during the 1697–1701 immigration boom; after living a decade in the region, he owned a blanket, two iron pots, some old lumber or furniture, a file, two cows with calves, and two small hogs, or £4 in property. Shortly before his death in 1709, he planted enough tobacco to yield a crop of 1,750 pounds, which his administrator sold for £5. This small sum had to cover rent, taxes, clothing, and repayment of loans, leaving what would be barely enough to purchase a cow. Actually, Holte had borrowed steadily and died in debt.[9]

The purchase of land was a symbolic step, for landowners gained a degree of independence, a level of status, and an ability to provide for their children that tenants did not have. But poor men trying to become landowners faced major difficulties. Although they began their landowning careers when tobacco prices were high, most of them had bought on credit and experienced six or seven years during which payments made it virtually impossible to accumulate much surplus. Several bad crops, excessive purchases of household goods, and gifts to sons and daughters who reached their majority all might extend the time during which the planter could not save enough for further investment. Moreover, these small proprietors may have cultivated depleted soil. Theoretically, since a planter's crop consumed at most three acres in four years, and since twenty years of fallow would revive the soil, a fifty-acre tract could be used indefinitely by a single proprietor. Extensive leasing near the bay, however, may have resulted in overworked soil. Often the new farmer had the choice of buying relatively fertile soil away from the bay or an exhausted tract near a river mouth.[10] Rising land prices, furthermore, made the acquisition of a plantation increasingly difficult. The cost of a fifty-acre tract in Talbot County rose from £8 in 1683 to £14 in 1694, and then to roughly £16 by the late 1720s, or two to three times the cost of beginning a tenancy.[11] Land prices rose because Talbot planters had cleared land and erected homes on most of the bayside. The fertile necks of land between the Chesapeake and the county's rivers provided the readiest access to the market. The population was denser here, most tobacco was produced here, and most buying and selling of land occurred here. Consequently, as long as returns on agricultural investment remained satisfactory, land prices for this region of the bayside rose. Edward Lloyd's patent, Hier Dier Lloyd, for example, increased in value from 30 pounds of tobacco per acre in 1663 to 80 pounds by 1700, and eventually to 150 pounds by midcentury, while throughout the eighteenth century the tract remained one of the most heavily farmed patents in Talbot County.[12]

For a landowner, continued upward mobility was contingent upon acquisition of laborers. Investments in servants and slaves probably yielded a lower rate of return after the 1680s, as table 7.1 suggests, but servile laborers still proved profitable when carefully managed. If, in the 1690s and after, production costs rose relative to tobacco prices, this circumstance had little effect on the demand for labor. Planters had few other ways to utilize their capital. Trade could bring 10 percent returns but involved risk and a large initial investment; land offered an alternative, but it acquired most of its value through the application of labor.[13]

The market for servants differed from that for slaves, particularly after the 1680s, when the supply of immigrant white labor decreased, both in absolute terms and relative to the growing population of farmers who might employ field hands.[14] Moreover, between the 1680s and the 1730s, Talbot County tobacco planters had increasing difficulty negotiating favorable terms for white field hands and frequently received only four years of labor from a servant. Consequently, planters had to profit quickly. Aware of the risk involved in purchasing a servant's labor when staple prices dropped, most farmers did not do so; demand consequently declined, generally more than supply, and the cost of a servant fell sharply in Talbot County. The drop in prices was most notable in the 1690s and in the late 1720s and early 1730s. During more favorable periods, such as after Queen Anne's War, demand probably increased more than supply. At any rate, servant prices rose appreciably. Only during the 1697–1701 boom did an unusually large supply of servants force Talbot prices down.[15]

Slave prices, on the other hand, were more stable, as the social and economic utility of a slave could be expected to outlast the recession during which he or she was purchased. The preference for slaves during a recession was most apparent during the late 1720s and early 1730s, when the ratio of slave to servant prices rose, first from an average of 2.7:1 to 3.2:1 by 1730, and then to 4.2:1 by 1733.[16] Eventually slaves came to dominate the bound labor force of Talbot County, but until the 1720s, servants held their own in the economy. What kept them an integral part of the social structure was their profitability during upswings in the price cycle, their low cost—roughly 35 percent that of a slave—and the general scarcity of labor; this scarcity, in turn, placed limits on the economic mobility of Talbot landowners.

The servant trade between England and the Eastern Shore had little formal organization. Before the 1680s, great urban centers such as London and Bristol drew sufficient numbers of laborers and craftsmen from their rural hinterlands to supply the Chesapeake with an agricultural work force. But in the last quarter of the seventeenth century, with a diminished supply of servants from southern English ports and the development of demand for settlers in Pennsylvania and Carolina, the Chesapeake servant trade became more sporadic, and merchants increasingly recruited their human cargoes from the rural poor of Ireland and northwest England. While major London contractors continued to supply many regions of Virginia, less populated, more isolated areas such as the Eastern Shore had to depend on small shipments from Whitehaven, Liverpool, and secondary London firms. From 1718, the full opening of the convict trade added to the flow of servants, but Eastern Shore planters could only count on small shipments of prisoners from Bideford.[17] After the 1680s, Talbot planters received a large supply of servants only when tobacco prices peaked: between 1697 and 1701 they purchased over six hundred white laborers; between 1715 and 1718, they bought roughly four hundred. The bulk of these servants were men, and thus were ideally suited to their assigned task: to increase production in order to exploit the short-term price rise. But with a landowning population of over six hundred planters, this number of servants could not supply most of the farmers continuously with the labor they needed to accumulate wealth.[18]

The Chesapeake slave trade offered another, but also irregular, source of labor. English slavers obviously preferred the shorter voyages, higher prices, and return cargoes associated with the South Carolina and West India markets. In the 1720s, for example, the Caribbean sugar planters received almost twelve times as many blacks as the Chesapeake tobacco growers, and South Carolina rice cultivators obtained roughly twice as many. The farmer on Maryland's Eastern Shore thus had little prospect of acquiring regular, direct shipments from the major firms in the Atlantic trade; instead, planters bought slaves in Virginia, made occasional purchases when New England vessels returned to the Chesapeake from Barbados, and eventually sent their own vessels to the West Indies.[19]

The planter thus faced, first, the problem of judging the state of the tobacco economy and deciding whether to buy servants or slaves; second, the problem of obtaining an adequate supply of labor; and third, the problem of cost. At approximately £11 for a male servant and £27 for a male slave, the price of bound labor ranged from high to prohibitive for the nonlanded.[20] A male slave, for example, cost more than the expense of forming a household and purchasing a fifty-acre farm; indeed, the price exceeded the average value of the personal estate of a sharecropper or laborer. With credit, however, landowners could afford labor; with luck and careful management, they could gain 6 or 7 percent returns from their field hands; and with time they could improve their status and accumulate wealth.

Everyone—laborer, tenant, landowner—had to surmount a specific economic barrier to improve his status. It took £7 to £12 to form a household and lease a plantation, £14 to £16 to buy land, and £11 to £27 to purchase a servant or slave. Using wealth estimates from the early 1730s, these costs constituted respectively 28 to 48 percent of the average inventoried estate value of sharecroppers and laborers (£25), 23 to 27 percent of the estate value of tenants (£60), and 9 to 23 percent of the inventoried wealth of landowners without slaves (£120).[21] Clearly, those who moved up in society had accumulated more than average, a factor that probably was most critical in the case of the poor. Most aspirants acquired the added capital through marriage, a small inheritance, or their skill as craftsmen. The acquisition of wealth improved their credit rating, facilitating their ability to exploit short-term upswings in tobacco prices.

The Development of Society

The secular decline in immigration and trends in tobacco prices affected the social mobility of all groups. In the seventeenth century, Talbot's population was composed chiefly of male immigrants; when the pace of immigration slowed, native-born families became the basic unit of social and economic organization. The families of landowners, in particular, by their redistribution of wealth through control of marriage and inheritance, acquired an increasingly important role in Talbot County. During the short 1697–1701 boom these families did not yet control the process of mobility, but by the time of the next upswing of the tobacco price cycle in 1713, economic opportunity in Talbot had become a function of joining or belonging to a landed family.

The sex ratio and age pattern of Talbot's seventeenth-century population suggest that before 1700 families had a limited impact on social mobility. In the land patent records between 1660 and 1680, headright claims were made for two-and-one-half times more men than women. The same imbalance can be found in the lists of servants entering Talbot throughout the seventeenth century, in the inventory records of servants, as illustrated in table 7.3, in the wills, which show the deaths of numerous landowners without wives or children, and in the records of immigrants who left Liverpool for Maryland and Virginia in the 1680s and 1690s.[22] This sex ratio had two consequences: first, it meant that maybe one out of two freed male servants could marry. If freed female servants married into landed families, then the chances of a freed male forming a household with the assistance of a wife were less. Second, even landowners remained unmarried and childless because of the sex ratio. The majority of these people had arrived between 1662 and 1689 and made most of their purchases in the 1670s. Many members of this generation died in the 1690s, some without children, the rest with children who did not reach maturity until the early eighteenth century. Consequently, during the 1690s, most new landowners were either free immigrants or former servants. The number of new landowners who established themselves

TABLE 7.3
Servant and Slave Population in Talbot County during the 1680s

	Listed in Inventories	Estimates for the County*
Landed planters	58	400†
Servants		
Male	56	390
Female	28	190
Children	27	190
Total	111	770
Slaves		
Male	17	120
Female	6	40
Children	4	30
Total	27	190

Sources: Inventories and Accounts, Talbot Land Conveyances, Wills, Hall of Records, Annapolis, Md. Talbot Rent Roll of 1706/7, Lloyd Collection, Maryland Historical Society, Baltimore.

*These estimates were made by multiplying the figures in column one by the ratio of landowners to landowners in the inventories (400/58) and rounding off to the nearest ten. Inventories overrepresent the wealthy and thus the estimates may be too high. On the other hand, these estimates do not include the few servants held by nonlanded, free whites. Moreover, column one does not include Philemon Lloyd's estate. Lloyd had 35 slaves.

†Exact figure, to the nearest ten, for 1680.

in Talbot decreased from twenty six per year during the 1680s to seventeen per year during the 1690s, but enough of these new arrivals took the place of childless, first generation settlers to increase the male, landed population from over four hundred in the 1680s to a little under six hundred before King William's War ended in 1697.[23] The stagnation of the tobacco economy made the acquisition of land more difficult but did not end all mobility.

The decline in immigration, however, eventually altered the structure of opportunity. The number of free whites, servants, and slaves entering Talbot fell from over one hundred per year in the 1680s to thirty to forty per year in the 1720s.[24] The sharpest drops occurred during King William's War and Queen Anne's War. During both wars, the county lost taxable population, partly because some settlers moved to adjoining, less-developed counties, and partly because the death rate was high, but chiefly because immigration during these periods was slow.[25]

Once immigration slackened and daughters of the first settlers reached marriageable age, the population became increasingly native born, with important social consequences. Several indicators reveal the process. During the 1660s and 1670s, when most Eastern Shore inhabitants were immigrants, there were 2.5 men for each woman. As the number of native-born adults increased, this ratio dropped to 1.6 men for each woman by 1704, 1.3 by 1710, and 1.2 by 1712. At the same time, the number of children and average family size increased substantially. Wills also reveal the change in population. In each decade after 1700, the number of male heirs in every Eastern Shore county outnumbered the number of male testators.[26]

The growth of a native-born population gave established families a greater role in the economy. The boom of 1697–1701, which momentarily reversed the trend in immigration, was probably the last to offer opportunities to newcomers. The boom facilitated the acquisition of servants, the purchase of land, and probably the formation of households. The influx of servants allowed 70 percent of the landowners to obtain a man, woman, or child to help with field work. The number of new landowners increased, bringing the total in Talbot to approximately six hundred seventy.[27] The expansion of credit should also have helped the lowest stratum begin farming tenancies, but documentation does not exist that would prove whether it did.

The recession that began in 1703 froze the process of upward social mobility. Supply of and demand for servants dropped; tobacco prices fell, credit contracted, and the number of new purchasers of land during Queen Anne's War fell 50 percent below the 1697–1701 level of eighteen per year. Commercial and agricultural capital became increasingly concentrated in the hands of established landed families. When recovery began in 1713, economic prosperity failed for the first time to increase the rate at which new landowners began their careers; moreover, those who did become landowners came almost exclusively from native-born families.[28]

Three patterns of mobility should be noted for the period following Queen Anne's War. First, the slave-owning families proved the chief beneficiaries of the economic upswing of 1713. While the number of slaves entering Talbot increased, trade continued to be organized around small annual consignments, and this circumstance made it easier for the richest planters to purchase all the new slaves. Only the arrival of large shiploads of African laborers would have forced slavers to risk extending credit to small landowners, and since Talbot did not receive such large shipments, few landowners became new slaveowners despite the growth of the black population.[29]

Second, the sons of landowners were no longer assured a secure place in the social stucture. When economic conditions deteriorated again in the late 1720s, sons were often unable to begin independent farming. They either left or became tenants and overseers, pushing even lower or out members of the lower strata.[30]

Third, the booms of 1697 and 1713 triggered a migration of the poor. Settlers moved to the back country of Talbot County, then north into Queen Ann's County, a new county established in 1706 as a result of migration from Talbot during the economic upswing. Eventually, they pushed east into Kent County's rich hinterland. Land sales in these regions climbed sharply during the second and third decades of the eighteenth century, and by about 1740, the population density of the eastern half of the Eastern Shore counties had reached the same level as that of the bayside. While determining the exact sources of this population movment is difficult, a significant number of settlers in other Eastern Shore counties had come from Talbot rather than directly from England. Geographical mobility increasingly became the means by which the lower classes of an older region, such as Talbot, improved their social-economic position.[31]

Society and Economy

Between 1689 and the depression of the early 1730s, the composition, size, wealth, and relationship of the social classes on the Eastern Shore changed remarkably. In the 1680s, Talbot's agricultural economy had been farmed by 1,350 taxable inhabitants. The taxable population included free adult males, adult male servants, and adult male and female slaves. The number of taxable servants and slaves (550) can be projected from the inventories, as has been done in table 7.3; to these taxables must be added 400 landowners, who can be positively identified from deeds, wills, and a rent roll as residing in Talbot in 1680. The remaining taxables were nonlanded, free white adults. The number of free white women and children probably was between 700 and 1,000, based on the predominance of males among immigrants. To recapitulate: 400 landowners, 200 slaves, 750 servants, 400 nonlanded freemen, and 1,000 free white women and children lived in Talbot during the third decade of the county's initial, rapid development.[32] By the 1730s, although Talbot had lost 80,000 acres to Kent and Queen Anne's, the county had 600 landowners, over 800 nonlanded freemen, an equal number of adult slaves, and roughly 4,000 white women and children. Within this population, the lines of wealth and status had become far more clearly delineated.[33]

Talbot in 1733 was dominated by a small number of merchant-planters. Their lavish, two-story brick manor houses, which conspicuously differentiated them from their contempor ries, were furnished in luxury and flanked by innumerable smaller buildings that transformed the plantations into small communities. Their landed estates were between 1,000 and 20,000 acres, of which they leased a sizeable portion, leaving much in pasture or woodland, and farming the remainder by dividing it into small, self-contained slave-labor plantations. They employed between twelve and forty field hands, who could plant and harvest annually tobacco, wheat, and corn crops worth over £100, and with their economic and social standing, the merchant-planters assured themselves patronage positions in the provincial government, seats on Maryland's Council, election to the Assembly, and membership in the Anglican vestry.[34]

The merchant-planters of the 1730s had few counterparts in Talbot during the 1680s. Many merchant-planters could trace their families back to the pre-1689 settlers, but since that time, especially in the prosperous years following Queen Anne's War, these men had entered West Indian trade, begun law careers, diversified agricultural production, and established partnerships with English tobacco firms. Their careers were distinguished by a variety and scale of economic undertakings seldom attempted in Talbot during the seventeenth century. In 1733, as table 7.4 indicates, fifteen landowners could be classified as wealthy merchant-planters; in the 1680s, only one resident of Talbot fitted such a description. In 1733, the wealthiest member of this stratum held over £20,000; in the 1680s, only one man had had over £2,000. Moreover, by the 1730s, the links among family, wealth, political power, and social status were tighter and far more secure than they had been in the 1680s.[35]

As table 7.4 demonstrates, one-fourth of the other landowners were slaveowners. Many of them were sons of merchant-planters. They generally held estates of 300 to 1,000 acres and also leased a sizeable portion of their land to tenants. Their homes were large and well furnished, and the status they had acquired assured them appointments in county government and election to the Maryland Assembly. If merchant-planters are excluded from the calculation, then the average inventoried wealth of the other slaveowners had increased from £300 in 1680 to £410 by 1730. Marriage and inheritance practices helped keep this wealth concentrated within a small circle of families.[36]

TABLE 7.4
The Structure of the Taxable Work Force in Talbot County in 1733

		Percentage of	
Class of Taxables	Number	Total	Free Males
Merchant-planters (with slaves and land)	15	1	1
Other slaveowners (with land)*	155	7	11
Other landowners†	460	20	31
Tenants	150	6	10
Sharecroppers and laborers‡	690	29	47
Male servants	130	6	—
Male and female slaves	750	32	—
Total	2,350	101	100

Sources: Talbot County Tax List of 1733, Maryland Historical Society, Baltimore; Talbot Debt Book of 1733; Inventories, 1727–37; Hall of Records, Annapolis, Md.

Note: Taxables included all free males sixteen years of age or older, all male servants sixteen or older, and all male and female slaves sixteen or older.

    *Included several nonlanded, middling merchants.

    †Included undetermined number of craftsmen and merchants whose chief occupation was not farming.

    ‡Men without households, included sons of landowners.

The control of the economy by the merchant-planters and other slave-owners tightened enormously between the 1680s and 1730s. More slave-owners lived in Talbot at the end of this period than at the beginning, but throughout they remained a minority of the landed population. According to the inventories, the ratio of landowners to slaveowners went from 5:1 in 1680 to 4:1 by 1700 and was still 4:1 in 1730. The first ratios are probably low; nonetheless, the distribution of labor in Talbot remained inequitable. At the same time, the slave population increased from 200 in 1680 to 460 in 1706, and to 1,300 by 1733. Over this period, the ratio of taxables to slaves fell from 7:1 to 2:1. The planter elite thus gained even greater command over agricultural production in Talbot.[37]

Below the slaveholders in the social hierarchy came the nonslaveholding planters. They were far less wealthy than slaveowners, as table 7.5 demonstrates. They lived in crude twenty-by-twenty-feet clapboard homes, partitioned into two rooms, with the occasional luxury of a brick chimney; and, while virtually excluded from political office, they served on juries, voted, and carried out less pleasant responsibilities such as road building and militia duty. Unlike the non-slaveholding planters of the 1680s, many of these planters now engaged in diversified economic activity, not only selling grain and cattle but also practicing a craft. The number of landowners who were artisans had been greatest between 1689 and 1713, when the market for tobacco was poorest, but even after Queen Anne's War, landowners continued to engage in trades. The landowners of the 1730s were slightly wealthier than those in the 1680s; they had little more opportunity to

TABLE 7.5
The Distribution of Wealth in Talbot County in 1733

Percentile Group of the Free Male Population	Percentage of Wealth	Status of Most of Group	Average Wealth of Members of Groups in £ Sterling
1st (poorest 10%)	0.5		
2d	0.8		
3rd	1.4	Laborers and sharecroppers†	25‡
4th	2.7		
5th	4.0		
6th	5.2	Tenants	60‡
7th	6.4		
8th	9.7	Landowners	120‡
9th	14.3		
10th (richest 10%)	54.9	Landed slaveowners	660‡

Source: Inventories, 1730–35, Hall of Records, Annapolis, Md.

*Inventoried wealth for the period 1730–35 deflated 10% to convert prices of items in the inventories to their 1680–88 level.

†Includes sons of landowners. See table 7.3 for additional data on social structure. Excluding these sons from the table could increase the percentage of wealth held by the poorer strata of society (bottom 50%) from 9 to as much as 13%.

‡Wealth estimates include cattle, slaves, servants, clothing, household goods, crops, debts owed the planter by English merchants, merchandise, and shares in vessels but not land. The value of land would add an average of £64 to the estate of each landowner; this would increase the share of the landowners from 85% (percentile groups 7 through 10) to 88%. Inventories overrepresent the rich and landed. Data in table 7.4 were used to adjust for this.

improve their status; and their children had more difficulty becoming landed planters.[38]

In the bottom stratum of free society were the laborers, sharecroppers, and tenants. Table 7.4 indicates that the laborers and sharecroppers, constituted 50 percent of the free male population. The 150 tenants accounted for another 10 percent. Since tobacco prices were low in the early 1730s, household formation was difficult, and consequently 10 percent is a lower bound for the percentage of tenants in the free male population between 1689 and 1733. In 1704, after the 1697–1701 boom, 15 percent of the free male population were tenants—an upper bound for the period.[39] Overall, between 1689 and 1733, the number of laborers, sharecroppers, and tenants increased from 400 to 740 men, constituting in 1730 a slightly larger percentage of the free population than they had fifty years earlier (an increase from 50 percent to 57 percent). Many of these people, of course, may have been poor only because they were young and still dependents of landowners. In any case, this bottom stratum held only 15 percent of the personal property in Talbot County; and average wealth had fallen from £38 to £31 since 1680.[40] By 1730, geographical movement presented the only opportunity for advancement by those in society's lowest stratum.

Landowners, as well as tenants, laborers, and sharecroppers, faced somewhat more difficult circumstances by the 1730s. A society that had been relatively open, economically mobile, male, immigrant, and tied to the staple in 1680 gave way to one which was more closed, geographically mobile, family-dominated, native-born, and economically diversified. Only the slaveowners and their children were able both to remain in Talbot and to prosper. For them, a gradual improvement in trade connections lowered the cost of consumption goods, provided a limited supply of African laborers, facilitated the marketing of corn and wheat, as well as tobacco, and allowed the accumulation of European merchandise.[41]

But as the social process solidified in one part of the Chesapeake, development was always beginning in another area more recently penetrated by the Anglo-Chesapeake market economy. Agricultural diversification and geographic mobility affected the Eastern Shore planter advantageously and provided hope to the men and women of the early 1730s that the decline of opportunity in the older Chester-Great Choptank region might not prove as lasting or as unbearable as it must have seemed at that time.

NOTES

1. Food prices from Talbot inventories in the Inventories and Accounts, 1660–1718, mss., Hall of Records, Annapolis, Md. All manuscripts and archival material mentioned hereafter are located at the Hall of Records unless otherwise indicated. For a fuller discussion of Talbot's settlement see Paul G. E. Clemens, "The Settlement and Growth of Maryland's Eastern Shore during the English Restoration," *The Maryland Historian* 5 (1974):63–78.

For general background on the Chesapeake, the reader should consult Aubrey C. Land, "Economic Base and Social Structure: The Northern Chesapeake in the Eighteenth Century," *Journal of Economic History* 25 (1965):639–54; L. C. Gray, "The Market Surplus Problems of Colonial Tobacco," *Agricultural History,* 2 (1928):1–34; Jacob M. Price, *France and the Chesapeake: A History of the French Tobacco Monopoly, 1674–1791, and of its Relationship to the British and American Tobacco Trades,* 2 vols. (Ann Arbor, 1973), 1:509–617; Lois Green Carr, "County Government in Maryland, 1689–1709" (Ph.D. diss., Harvard University, 1968), especially the chapter on Prince George's County; Russell R. Menard, "Economy and Society in Early Colonial Maryland" (Ph.D. diss., University of Iowa, 1975).

2. For tobacco prices see Russell R. Menard, "A Note on Chesapeake Tobacco Prices, 1618–1660, "*Virginia Magazine of History and Biography,* forthcoming. All other tobacco prices taken from the Talbot inventories in the Inventories and Accounts, 1660–1718.

3. The careers of individual members of the poorest stratum of society can be traced only with great difficulty. Consequently, this section of the essay is speculative and depends on analysis of aggregate data. Data come from a study of all Talbot inventories, wills, and land records from the period 1660–1750, and from the construction and analysis of price series and immigration statistics. Quantitative data are collected in Paul G. E. Clemens, "From Tobacco to Grain, Economic Development on Maryland's Eastern Shore, 1660–1750" (Ph.D. diss., University of Wisconsin, 1974), pp. 163–74.

4. Household costs from Talbot inventories in the Inventories and Accounts.

5. The lease and estate evaluations are in the Talbot and Queen Anne's Land Records, mss.

6. See table 7.2. Most new landowners married before obtaining land; this suggests that marriage was also a significant step in maintaining a tenancy. Marriage connections are generally given on land deeds in the Talbot County Land Records.

7. Data on the skills of the poor are in the Talbot Court Records, mss. Plantiffs and occasionally defendants listed their occupations. The figure of one out of seven males with artisan skills comes from land deeds and court records.

8. This paragraph is based on a study of immigration, population growth, and the movement of tobacco prices (see note 2 above). On credit, see John Hemphill, "Virginia and the English Commercial System, 1689–1733: Studies in the Development and Fluctuations of a Colonial Economy under Imperial Control" (Ph.D. diss., Princeton University, 1964), pp. 98–148. For a discussion of seventeenth-century conditions, see Russell R. Menard, "From Servant to Freeholder: Status Mobility and Property Accumulation in Seventeenth-Century Maryland," *William and Mary Quarterly,* 3d ser., 30 (1973):37–64; Lorena S. Walsh, "Servitude and Opportunity in Charles County, Maryland, 1658–1705," in this volume; and Lois Green Carr and Russell R. Menard "Servants and Freedmen in Early Colonial Maryland," in *Essays on the Seventeenth-Century Chesapeake,* ed. Thad W. Tate and David L. Ammerman (Chapel Hill, forthcoming).

9. Inventories and Accounts 32B: 13–14, 37–38.

10. The names and occupations of over 1,600 men who purchased land between 1662 and 1750 are given in the Talbot Land Records. From these data it was possible to determine the number of people who bought land for the first time in a given year, the occupation of most purchasers, and whether or not the purchaser came from a landed family. The data was arranged chronologically to fit the periodization utilized in table 7.1. This data will hereafter be cited as "Chronological List of Names and Occupations of Land Purchasers." It was also possible to determine the number of purchases made each year and to correlate these figures with the movement of tobacco prices (see note 2 above). The length of mortgages is seldom given in land conveyances, but many appear to have run over ten years. The discussion of soil exhaustion is speculative, but based on known population densities of the bayside region in the 1680s, 1704, 1722, and 1733, and on contemporary and modern calculations of the effects of the tobacco crop on soil fertility.

11. Data on land prices were analyzed in several ways. Separate series of prices were constructed for sterling and tobacco purchases. Prices were also determined for acreage ranges of 1–99, 200–299, and 1–1,000 acres. By examining price changes for tracts of different sizes and locations, judgments can be made about some factors affecting cost. Prices include the cost of plantation houses and improvements. The best descriptions of the Chesapeake land system are found in Michael Lee Nicholls, "Origins of the Virginia Southside, 1703–1753: A Social and Economic Study" (Ph.D diss., William and Mary College, 1972), and Carville V. Earle, *The Evolution of a Tidewater Settlement System: All Hallow's Parish, Maryland, 1650–1783,* University of Chicago Department of Geography Research Paper, no. 170 (Chicago, 1975). See also Russell R. Menard, "Immigration to the Chesapeake Colonies in the Seventeenth Century: A Review Essay," *Maryland Historical Magazine* 68 (1973):323–29.

12. Talbot Land Records.

13. In working through questions of the relationship of servants to slaves in the Chesapeake, the author has been aided by Russell Menard, "The Transformation of the Chesapeake Labor System, 1680–1710" (paper presented at the annual meeting of the Southern Historical Association, Nov., 1972, on file at the Hall of Records, Annapolis, Md. Menard will publish an expanded version of this paper shortly.

14. This analysis of supply and demand is based on price movements for servants, slaves, and tobacco. All prices are from the Talbot inventories in the Inventories and Accounts, 1660–1718, and the Inventories, 1718–1776, mss. Slave prices are based on evaluations of slaves between the ages of eighteen and thirty-five. Servant prices are based on evaluations of servants with four or more years to serve; see Clemens, "From Tobacco to Grain," pp. 163–74.

15. Ibid.

16. Ibid. John Hemphill has suggested that the Chesapeake labor market must be viewed as part of a larger Anglo-American marketing structure; his work on this topic as yet remains unpublished. One can estimate that the natural growth of the slave population began in the 1720s by comparing age profiles for the population constructed for ten-year intervals and based on data in the Talbot inventories in the Inventories. The best data on the number of slaves

brought to Talbot County come from the Hollyday Account Book, Hollyday Papers, mss., Maryland Historical Society, Baltimore (hereafter M.H.S.).

17. On the servant trade see Abbot Emerson Smith, *Colonists in Bondage: White Servitude and Convict Labor in America, 1607–1776* (Chapel Hill, 1947). The Talbot County Court Records contain the names of unindentured servants brought to the region; some evaluation of the pace of immigration can be obtained from the number of names in the records. Immigration estimates can also be made from changes in yearly population totals. Until the mid-1720s, taxable population totals are given in the Talbot County Court Records, generally at the conclusion of the November court session. Other data on immigration come from the Oxford Naval Office Records, mss., Hall of Records and M.H.S., but they contain reports only for the 1730s. The Hollyday Account Books, M.H.S. report a tax on slaves, Irish servants, and convicts brought to Maryland in the 1720s and 1730s. Finally, all the convicts brought to Queen Anne's County had their names recorded in the Queen Anne's Land Records.

18. The estimates of the number of servants that arrived are based on changes in the taxable population of Talbot County, on the number of unindentured servants brought before the Talbot county court, and on estimates of the total servant population in 1700 and 1718 made from the inventories of Talbot landowners; Talbot Court Records, and Talbot inventories in the Inventories and Accounts. The composition of the immigrant population was determined from these same sources. In 1706 there were 530 adult male landowners in Talbot and 670 separate owners of land, in 1718 there were 600 landowners in the county; Talbot Rent Roll of 1706/7, Lloyd Papers, mss. M.H.S. and Talbot Land Records.

19. Ibid. Comparative slave figures can be found in W. Noel Sainsbury et al., eds., *Calendar of State Papers, Colonial Series, America and West Indies*, 44 vols. (London, 1860–), for the period 1726–35. There is some information on the Maryland slave trade around 1700 in the Maryland Naval Office Records, mss., Public Record Office, London (photocopies, Library of Congress). The activities of Talbot merchants in the slave trade can be traced in the Oxford Naval Office Records, Hall of Records and M.H.S., and in the various West Indian Naval Office Records for the 1720s and 1730s (on microfilm at the University of Virginia Library).

20. Prices from Talbot inventories.

21. See table 7.5.

22. Talbot wills from the record series Wills have been used to calculate the rate at which male children replaced deceased male planters in the population, see T.H. Hollingsworth, *Historical Demography* (Ithaca, 1969). The sex ratio of the immigrant population can be determined by the sex ratio of servants in Talbot inventories and by checking the names in the Maryland Land Patents, mss. Russell Menard has studied lists of Liverpool immigrants to Maryland and Virginia and shared his findings with the author. For a fuller discussion of demographic conditions in the Chesapeake, see Lorena S. Walsh and Russell R. Menard, "Death in the Chesapeake: Two Life Tables for Men in Early Colonial Maryland," *Maryland Historical Magazine* 69(1974):211–27.

23. Data on land purchases from "Chronological List of Names and Occupations of Land Purchasers." Statements about consequences of the sex ratio draw on a study of Talbot wills and land conveyances. It would be possible to improve the argument by introducing data on life expectancy, age of marriage, and rate of remarriage by men and women, but research on these subjects is not yet complete. Lois Green Carr has suggested that frequent remarriage by females may have altered the patterns discussed in this paper.

24. See notes 17 and 18 above. The 1680 estimate of 100 immigrants annually is based on changes in the taxable population. Another estimate of average annual immigration can be made by dividing the servant population (750) by the average length of service (7 years). For the servant population see table 7.4. The average length of service was determined from Talbot inventories and the periods of service assigned unindentured servants by the Talbot County court (listed in the Talbot Court Records, generally near the beginning of each session record). The estimates for immigration during the 1720s come from a tax recorded in the Hollyday Account Book, M.H.S., on Irish servants, slaves, and convicts.

25. Taxable population figures given in the November session records of the Talbot Court Records.

26. See note 22 above, and William Hand Browne et al., eds., *Archives of Maryland*, 72 vols. (Baltimore, 1883–), 25:256. Hereafter cited as *Archives*.

27. Talbot Rent Roll of 1706/7, ms., M.H.S., and Talbot Land Records.

28. Talbot Land Records and "Chronological List of Names and Occupations of Land Purchasers."

29. Talbot Tax Lists of 1722, mss., M.H.S., and Wills.

30. Talbot Tax List of 1733, ms., M.H.S., Wills, and Talbot Land Records

31. Some idea of the movement of people out of Talbot can be obtained by comparing the rate of immigration to Talbot with the county's population growth. Migration can also be measured indirectly by noting population growth and immigration statistics for adjoining counties. Population statistics are from county court records. Land sales are from Queen Anne's Land Records. Prices taken from these records indicate that land cost about one-half as much in the back country as along the Talbot bayside. Population density based on taxable population figures in the county court records and the Talbot, Queen Anne's, and Kent Levy Lists of 1722, mss., M.H.S.

32. See tables 7.3, 7.4, and 7.5 for data and sources used in the following discussion. The estate evaluations in the Queen Anne's Land Records provided most of the information on the dwellings and plantations of Eastern Shore farmers. Lists of officeholders and those who served on juries were taken from the Talbot Court Records. For a fuller discussion of the 1680s, see Clemens, "Settlement and Growth."

33. For the 1730 figures see table 7.4. The estimate of the number of white women and children was made by multiplying the taxable population by three and subtracting from this figure the number of free adult males, servants, and slaves. The loss of land can be calculated by comparing the Talbot Rent Roll of 1706/7, ms., M.H.S., with the Talbot Debt Book of 1733, ms.

34. See note 32 above. Queen Anne's and Kent Debt Books were also checked to determine the landholdings of Talbot merchant-planters. Richard Bennett had 35,000 acres; no other merchant-planter had over 20,000 acres.

35. See note 32 above.

36. Ibid.

37. Ibid. and *Archives* 25:257.

38. See note 32 above. Data on crafts from "Chronological List of Names and Occupations of Land Purchasers" and Talbot Land Records.

39. The 1704 figure was calculated as follows: the census of 1704 indicates that there were 712 male householders in that year, of which 532 were male landowners, leaving 180 tenant-householders. The total free male population consisted of the 1,534 men listed as fit to bear arms minus the number of male servants. From the inventories the author has estimated that there were 320 male servants in Talbot. Thus 15 percent (180/1,530–320) of the free male population were tenants. Some of the 532 male landowners were nonresidents, but the number has yet to be determined. If there were 30 nonresidents landowners, however, this would increase the number of tenants to 210, or to 18 percent of the free male population.

40. Ibid. For the £38 figure, see Clemens, "Settlement and Growth," pp. 74. The £31 figure is the average of the wealth of sharecroppers, laborers (£25), and tenants (£60), adjusted for the numerical representation of these groups in the free population, see tables 7.4 and 7.5. The adjustment assumes that all free males over sixteen who were not householders were share-croppers and laborers. In neither the 1680s nor the 1730s was this actually the case because many of these men were children of landed planters. Work on this question remains to be done, but the author's impression is that the figure of £31 is too low, and that average wealth of the poor may have changed little over the period 1680–1730.

41. Food prices fell sharply between 1680 and 1730. European imports seemed to fall in price. The only reliable price series is for pewter, but pewter constituted only 5 percent in value of the imports to Chesapeake planters. Prices taken from the Inventories and Accounts and the Inventories.

EIGHT

THE BEGINNINGS OF THE AFRO-AMERICAN FAMILY IN MARYLAND

Allan Kulikoff

Sometime in 1728, Harry, a recently imported African, escaped from his master in southern Prince George's County, Maryland, and joined a small black community among the Indians beyond the area of white settlement. The following year, Harry returned to Prince George's to urge his former shipmates, the only "kinfolk" he had, to return there with him. Over forty years later, another Harry, who belonged to John Jenkins of Prince George's, ran away. The Annapolis newspaper reported that "he has been seen about the Negro Quarters in *Patuxent,* but is supposed to have removed among his Acquaintants on Potomack; he is also well acquainted with the Negroes at Clement Wheeler's Quarter on Zekiah, and a Negro Wench of Mr. Wall's named Rachael; a few miles from that Quarter is his Aunt, and he may possibly be harboured thereabouts."[1]

These two incidents, separated by two generations, are suggestive. African Harry ran away *from* slavery to the frontier; Afro-American Harry ran *to* his friends and kinfolk spread over a wide territory. The Afro-American runaway could call on many others to hide him, but the African had few friends and seemingly, no wife. These contrasts raise many questions. How did Afro-Americans organize their families in the Chesapeake colonies during the eighteenth century? Who lived in slave households? How many Afro-American fathers lived with their wives and children? What was the impact of arbitrary sale and transfer of slaves upon family life? How did an Afro-American's household and family relationships change through the life cycle?

Note: Allan Kulikoff is a fellow of the Institute of Early American History and Culture and assistant professor of history at the College of William and Mary. He would like to thank Ira Berlin, Lois Green Carr, John P. Demos, David H. Fischer, Rhys Isaac, Aubrey C. Land, Elizabeth Pleck, and the staff of the Institute of Early American History and Culture for their perceptive comments on earlier versions of this paper and, especially, Russell R. Menard for his many useful suggestions and Herbert G. Gutman for his valuable critique. Research for this essay was supported by Brandeis University through a Rose and Irving Crown fellowship and research grant and by the National Science Foundation (GS35781).

This paper attempts to answer these questions.[2] While literary documents by or about slaves before 1800, such as runaway narratives, WPA freed-slave interviews, black autobiographies, or detailed travel accounts are very infrequently available to historians of colonial slave family life, they can gather age and family data from probate inventories, personal information from runaway advertisements, and depositions in court cases. These sources, together with several diaries and account books, kept by whites, provide a great deal of material about African and Afro-American family life in the Chesapeake region.

Almost all the blacks who lived in Maryland and Virginia before 1780 were slaves. Because his status precluded him from enjoying a legally secure family life, a slave's household often excluded important family members. Households, domestic groups, and families must therefore be clearly distinguished. A household, as used here, is a coresidence group that includes all who shared a "proximity of sleeping arrangements," or lived under the same roof. Domestic groups include kin and nonkin, living in the same or separate households, who share cooking, eating, childrearing, working, and other daily activities. Families are composed of people related by blood or marriage. Several distinctions are useful in defining the members of families. The immediate family include husband and wife or parents and children. Near kin include the immediate family and all other kin, such as adult brothers and sisters or cousins who share the same house or domestic tasks with the immediate family. Other kinfolk who do not function as family members on a regular basis are considered to be distant kin.[3]

The process of family formation can perhaps best be understood as an adaptive process. My ideas about this process owe much to a provocative essay by Sidney Mintz and Richard Price on Afro-American culture. Blacks learned to modify their environment, learned from each other how to retain family ties under very adverse conditions, and structured their expectations about family activities around what they knew the master would permit. If white masters determined the outward bounds of family activities, it was Africans, and especially their descendants, who gave meaning to the relationships between parents and children, among siblings, and with more distant kinfolk. As a result, black family structure on the eve of the Revolution differed from both African and white family systems.[4]

Africans who were forced to come to the Chesapeake region in the late seventeenth and early eighteenth centuries struggled to create viable families and households, but often failed. They suffered a great loss when they were herded into slave ships. Their family and friends, who had given meaning to their lives and structured their place in society, were left behind and they found themselves among strangers. They could never recreate their families and certainly not devise a West African kinship system in the Chesapeake. The differences between African communities were too great. Some Africans lived in clans and lineages, others did not; some traced their descent from women but others traced descent from men; mothers, fathers, and other kin played somewhat different roles in each community; initiation ceremonies and puberty rites, forbidden marriages, marriage customs, and household structures all varied from place to place.[5]

Though African immigrants did not bring a unified West African culture with them to the Chesapeake colonies, they did share important beliefs about the nature of kinship. Africans could modify these beliefs in America to legitimate the families they eventually formed. They saw kinship as the principal way of ordering relationships between individuals. Each person in the tribe was related to most others in the community. The male was father, son, and uncle; the female was mother, daughter, and aunt to many others. Because their kinship system was so extensive, Africans included kinfolk outside the immediate family in their daily activities. For example, adult brothers or sisters of the father or mother played an important role in childrearing and domestic activities in many African societies.[6]

Secondly, but far less certainly, African immigrants may have adapted some practices associated with polygyny, a common African marital custom. A few men on the Eastern Shore of Maryland in the 1740s, and perhaps others scattered elsewhere, lived with several women. However, far too few African women (in relation to the number of men) immigrated to make polygynous marriages common. Nevertheless, the close psychological relationship between mothers and children, and the great social distance between a husband and his various wives and children found in African polygynous societies might have been repeated in the Chesapeake colonies. In any event, African slave mothers played a more important role than fathers in teaching children about Africa and about how to get along in the slave system. Both African custom, and the physical separation of immigrant men and women played a role in this development.[7]

Africans faced a demographic environment hostile to most forms of family life. If African men were to start families, they had to find wives, and that task was difficult. Most blacks lived on small farms of less than 11 slaves; and the small black population was spread thinly over a vast territory. Roads were rudimentary. Even where concentrations of larger plantations were located, African men did not automatically find wives. Sex ratios in southern Maryland rose from 125 to 130 (men per 100 women) in the mid-seventeenth century to about 150 in the 1710s and 1720s, and to around 180 in the 1730s. In Surry County, Virginia, the slave sex ratio was about 145 in the 1670s and 1680s, but over 200 in the 1690s and 1700s. Wealthy slaveowners did not provide most of their African men with wives; the larger the plantation, the higher the sex ratio tended to be.[8]

Africans had competition for the available black women. By the 1690s, some black women were natives, and they may have preferred Afro-

American men. White men were also competitors. Indeed, during the seventeenth and early eighteenth centuries, white adult sex ratios were as high (or higher) than black adult sex ratios. At any period whites possessed a monopoly of power and some of them probably took slave women as their common-law wives. African men competed for the remaining black women, and probably some died before they could find a wife. In 1739 African men planned an uprising in Prince George's County partly because they could not find wives.[9]

Foreign-born male slaves in Maryland and Virginia probably lived in a succession of different kinds of households. Newly imported Africans had no blood kin in the Chesapeake. Since sex ratios were high, most of these men probably lived with other, unrelated men. African men may have substituted friends for kin. Newly enslaved Africans made friends with their nearest shipmates during the middle passage, and after their arrival in Maryland, some of them lived near these men. New Negroes could live with other recent African immigrants because migration from Africa occurred in short spurts from the 1670s to the late 1730s. The high sex ratios of large plantations indicate that wealthy men bought many of these Africans. Even if his shipmates lived miles away, the new immigrant could share the experiences of others who had recently endured the middle passage.[10]

Despite the difficulties, the majority of Africans who survived for a few years eventually found a wife. In societies with high sex ratios, women tend to marry young, but men have to postpone marriage. This increases the opportunity of older men to marry by reducing the sexual imbalance. (That is, there are as many younger women as older men.) By the 1690s, large numbers of Afro-American women entered their midteens and married Afro-American and African men.[11] Because the plantations were small, and individual farm sex ratios likely to be uneven, the wives and children of married African men very often lived on other plantations. These men still lived mainly with other unrelated men, but at least they had begun to develop kin ties.[12] A few African men lived with their wives and children, and some limited evidence suggests that the longer an African lived in the Chesapeake, the more likely he was to live with his immediate family.[13]

Unlike most African men, African women commonly lived with their children. Some African women may have been so alienated that they refused to have children, but the rest bore and raised several offspring, protected by the master's reluctance to separate very young children from their mothers. Since the children were reared by their mothers, and eventually joined them in the tobacco fields, these households were domestic groups, although incomplete as families.[14]

A greater proportion of African women than African men lived with both spouses and children. These opportunities usually arose on large plantations. There was such a surplus of men on large plantations that African women who lived on them could choose husbands from several African or Afro-American men. The sex ratio on large plantations in Prince George's during the 1730s, a period of heavy immigration, was 249. This shortage of women prevented most recently arrived African men from finding a wife on the plantation. For them the opportunity to live with a wife and children was rare. More Africans probably lived with their immediate families in the 1740s; immigration declined, large planters bought more African women, and the sex ratio on big plantations fell to 142.[15]

Because African spouses were usually separated, African mothers reared their Afro-American children with little help from their husbands. Even when the father was present, the extended kin so important in the lives of African children was missing. Mothers probably taught them the broad values they brought from Africa and related the family's history in Africa and the Chesapeake. When the children began working in the fields, they learned from their mothers how to survive a day's work and how to get along with master and overseer.

Each group of Africans repeated the experiences of previous immigrants. Eventually, more and more Afro-American children matured and began families of their own. The first large generation of Afro-Americans in Maryland probably came of age in the 1690s; by the 1720s, when the second large generation had matured, the black population finally began increasing naturally.[16]

The changing composition of the black population combined with other changes to restructure Afro-American households and families. Alterations in the adult sex ratio, the size of plantations, and black population density provided black people with opportunities to enjoy a more satisfying family life. The way masters transferred slaves from place to place limited the size and composition of black households, but Afro-American family members separated by masters managed to establish complex kinship networks over many plantations. Afro-Americans used these opportunities to create a kind of family life that differed from African and Anglo-American practices.

Demographic changes led to more complex households and families. As the number of adult Africans in the population decreased, the sex ratio in Maryland declined to between 100 and 110 by the 1750s. This decline gave most men an opportunity to marry by about age 30. The number of slaves who lived on plantations with more than 20 blacks increased; the density of the black population in tidewater Maryland and Virginia rose; the proportion of blacks in the total population of Prince George's County, in nearby areas of Maryland, and throughout tidewater Virginia rose to half or more by the end of the century; and many new roads were built. The number of friends and kinfolk whom typical Afro-Americans saw every day or visited with regularity increased, while their contact with whites declined because large areas of the Chesapeake became nearly black counties.[17]

How frequently masters transfered their Afro-American slaves, and where they sent them, affected black household composition. Surviving documents do not allow a systematic analysis of this point, but several conclusions seem clear. First, planters kept women and their small children together but did not keep husbands and teenage children with their immediate family. Slaveowner after slaveowner bequeathed women, and their "increase" to sons or daughters. However, children of slaveowners tended to live near their parents; thus, even when members of slave families were so separated, they remained in the same neighborhood.[18] Secondly, Afro-Americans who lived on small farms were transferred more frequently than those on large plantations. At their deaths small slaveowners typically willed a slave or two to their widows and to each child. They also frequently mortgaged or sold slaves to gain capital. If a slaveowner died with many unpaid debts, his slaves had to be sold.[19] Finally, relatively few blacks were forced to move long distances. Far more blacks were affected by migrations of slaves from the Chesapeake region to the new Southwest in the nineteenth century than by long-distance movement in the region before the Revolution.[20] These points should not be misunderstood. Most Afro-Americans who lived in Maryland or Virginia during the eighteenth century experienced separations from members of their immediate families sometime in their lives. Most, however, were able to visit these family members occasionally.

These changes led to a new social reality for most slaves born in the 1750s, 1760s, and 1770s. If unrelated people and their progeny stay in a limited geographic area for several generations, the descendants of the original settlers must develop kin ties with many other people who live nearby. Once the proportion of adult Africans declined, this process began. African women married and had children; the children matured and married. If most of them remained near their first homes, each was bound to have siblings, children, spouses, uncles, aunts, and cousins living in the neighborhood. How these various kinspeople were organized into households, families, and domestic groups depended not only upon the whims of masters but also upon the meaning placed on kinship by the slaves themselves.

The process of household and family formation and dissolution was begun by each immigrant woman who lived long enough to have children. The story of Ann Joice, a black woman who was born in Barbados, taken to England as a servant, and then falsely sold into slavery in Maryland in the 1670s, may have been similar to that of other immigrant women once she became a slave. The Darnall family of Prince George's owned Ann Joice. She had seven children with several white men in the 1670s and 1680s; all remained slaves the rest of their lives. Three of her children stayed on the Darnall home plantation until their deaths. One was sold as a child to a planter who lived a few miles away; another was eventually sold to William Digges, who lived about five miles from the Darnall farm. Both the spatial spread and the local concentration of kinfolk continued in the next generation. Peter Harbard, born between 1715 and 1720, was the son of Francis Harbard, who was Ann Joice's child. Peter grew up on the Darnall farm, but in 1737 he was sold to George Gordon, who lived across the road from Darnall. As a child, Peter lived with or very near his grandmother Ann Joice, his father, and several paternal uncles and aunts. He probably knew his seven cousins (father's sister's children), children of his aunt Susan Harbard, who lived on William Digges's plantation. Other kinfolk lived in Annapolis but were too far away to visit easily.[21]

As Afro-American slaves were born and died, and as masters sold or bequeathed their slaves, black households were formed and reformed, broken and created. Several detailed examples can illustrate this process. For example, Daphne, the daughter of Nan, was born about 1736 on a large plantation in Prince George's owned by Robert Tyler, Sr. Until she was two, she lived with her mother, two brothers, and two sisters. In 1738, Tyler died and left his slaves to his wife, children, and grandchildren. All lived on or near Tyler's farms. Three of Daphne's siblings were bequeathed to grand-daughter Ruth Tyler, who later married Mordecai Jacob, her grandfather's next-door neighbor. Daphne continued to live on the Tyler plantation. From 1736 to 1787, she had six different masters, but she still lived where she was born. Daphne lived with her mother until her mother died, and with her ten children until 1779. Children were eventually born to Daphne's daughters; these infants lived with their mothers and near their maternal grandmother. When Robert Tyler III, Robert senior's grandson and Daphne's fifth master, died in 1779, his will divided Daphne's children and grandchildren between his son and daughter. Daphne was thus separated from younger children, born between 1760 and 1772. They were given to Millicent Beanes, Robert III's daughter, who lived several miles away. Daphne continued to live on the same plantation as her four older children and several grandchildren. An intricate extended family of grandmother, sons, daughters, grandchildren, aunts, uncles, nieces, nephews, and cousins resided in several households on the Tyler plantation in 1778, and other more remote kinfolk could be found on the neighboring Jacob farm.[22]

Family separations might be more frequent on smaller plantations. Rachael was born in the late 1730s and bore ten children between 1758 and 1784. As a child she lived on the plantation of Alexander Magruder, a large slaveowner in Prince George's; before 1746, Alexander gave her to his son Hezekiah, who lived on an adjoining plantation. Hezekiah never owned more than ten slaves, and when he died in 1769, he owned only two—including one willed to his wife by her brother. Between 1755 and 1757, he mortgaged nine slaves, including Rachael, to two merchants. In 1757, Samuel Roundall (who lived about five miles from the Magruders) seized Rachael and six other slaves mortgaged to him. This and subsequent transfers can be seen

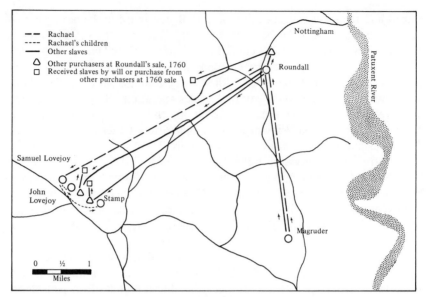

FIGURE 8.1. Sale and Later Transfer of Hezekiah Magruder's Slaves, 1755–1780

on figure 8.1. In 1760 Roundall sold Rachael and her eldest daughter to Samuel Lovejoy, who lived about nine miles from Roundall. At the same time, four other former Magruder slaves were sold: two to planters in Lovejoy's neighborhood, one to a Roundall neighbor, and one to a planter living at least fifteen miles away in Charles County. Rachael's separation from friends and family members continued. In 1761, her eldest child was sold at age three to George Stamp, a neighbor of Lovejoy. By the time Samuel Lovejoy died in 1762, she had two other children. She and her youngest child went to live with John Lovejoy, Samuel's nephew and near-neighbor, but her second child, about age two, stayed with Lovejoy's widow. Her third child was sold at age six, but Rachael and her next seven children lived with John Lovejoy until at least 1787.[23]

These three examples suggest how Afro-American households and families developed in the eighteenth century. Husbands and wives and parents and children were frequently separated by the master's transfers of family members. At the same time, as generation followed generation, households, or adjacent huts, became increasingly complex, and sometimes included grandparents, uncles, aunts, or cousins, as well as the immediate family. Since other kin lived on nearby or distant plantations, geographically concentrated (and dispersed) kinship networks that connected numbers of quarters emerged during the pre-Revolutionary era.

How typical were the experiences suggested by the examples? How were families organized into households and domestic groups on large and small

TABLE 8.1
Afro-American Household Structures on Three Large Plantations
in Prince George's and Anne Arundel Counties, Maryland, 1759–1775

| Household Type | Percentage in Household Type | | | | Percentage of Total in Household Types |
	Males 15+	Females 15+	Children 0–9	Children 10–14	
Husband-wife-children	40	43	55	44	47
Mother-children	2	17	22	10	14
Mother-children-other kin	4	14	8	13	9
Siblings	7	4	6	12	7
Husband-wife-children-other kin	2	2	2	2	2
Father-children	5	0	3	5	3
Husband-wife	2	2	0	0	1
Three generation	1	2	2	3	2
Unknown or mixed	36	16	3	12	15
Total percentage	99	100	101	101	100
Number people	142	129	178	77	526

Sources: PG Inventories, GS No. 1, f. 73 (1759; James Wardrop's, 32 slaves); and GS No. 2, ff. 334–36 (1775; Addison's 3 plantations, 109 slaves) and Charles Carroll Account Book, Maryland Historical Society (rest of slaves). The three-generation households include grandparents and grandchildren, but not the generation in between. The unknown or mixed category includes all those apparently living away from all kinfolk, but perhaps living near them. Some of the slaves in this category probably belong in the others, but the sources (especially the Addison and Wardrop documents) do not permit location of them.

quarters? Data from three large planters' inventories taken in 1759, 1773–74, and 1775, and from a Prince George's census of 1776 permit a test of the hypotheses concerning changes in household structure, differences between large and small units, and the spread of kinfolk across space. Table 8.1 details household structure on large quarters of over twenty and table 8.2 shows the kinds of households on small farms. About half of all slaves probably lived on each plantation type.[24] This evidence provides a good test, because by the 1770s most Afro-Americans could trace a Chesapeake genealogy back to immigrant grandparents or great-grandparents.[25]

Kinfolk (immediate families and near kin) on large plantations were organized into three kinds of residence groups. Most of the slaves of some quarters were interrelated by blood or marriage. Domestic groups included kinfolk who lived on opposite sides of duplex slave huts and who shared a common yard and eating and cooking arrangements. Finally, most households included members of an immediate family.

The kinship structure of large plantations is illustrated by a household inventory taken in 1773–74 of 385 slaves owned by Charles Carroll of Carrollton on thirteen different quarters in Anne Arundel County. Because Carroll insisted that the inventory be "taken in Familys with their Ages," the document permits a detailed reconstruction of kinship networks.[26] Though the complexity and size of kinship groups on Carroll's quarters were

TABLE 8.2
Afro-American Household Structures on Small Plantations (1-8 Slaves),
Prince George's County, Maryland, 1776

| Household Type | Percentage in Household Type | | | | Percentage of Total in Household Types |
	Males 15+	Females 15+	Children 0-9	Children 10-14	
Husband-wife-children	17	18	22	10	18
Mother-children	2	35	56	29	32
Father-children	2	*	4	1	2
Siblings	7	5	6	17	8
Mixed	72	42	12	43	41
Total percentage	100	100	100	100	101
Number of people	275	276	325	162	1038

Source: 1776 Census. The household types were assumed from black age structures on individual farms. Children and mothers were matched if a woman in the household could have been a mother to children in the same household. (E.g., a woman 25 years old was assumed to be the mother of children aged 4, 2, and 1 years on the same plantation). Men and women were linked as husband and wife if a man and woman in the same household were close in age (e.g., a man of 35 linked with a woman of 25). Children and young adults (to c. 25) were assumed to be siblings if no parents were in the household, and the ages of the children were close. (Children aged 8, 10, 13 were linked as siblings when no adult in household could be their parent.) A man was assumed to be father to children who lived on the same farm if no other person who could be a parent was present (man aged 35 was father to children aged 12, 10, 8 when no woman was present in household to be wife). The mixed category included all others who could not be placed: these could include kinfolk like older siblings, or brothers or parents to women with children in the same household, or they could be unrelated. If more than one type was found on a farm, it was counted as two households despite the probability that the people lived in the same hut. The statistics must be treated as educated guesses. Since slave mothers and their children were usually kept together in slave sales and in wills of masters, it is fairly certain that all the children in the first two categories lived with their mothers. The other linkages must include many errors.
* = less than ½%.

probably greater than on other large plantations, the general pattern could easily have been repeated elsewhere.[27]

The ten men and three women who headed each list were probably leaders of their quarters. Five of the quarters were named for these individuals.[28] They tended to be old slaves who had been with the Carroll family for many years. While the mean age of all adults was 37 years, the mean age of the leaders was 49, and six of the thirteen were over 55.[29] The leader often lived with many kinfolk; he or she was closely related to about 36 to 38 percent of all the other slaves on the quarter. For example, Fanny, 69 years of age, was surrounded by at least forty near kinfolk on the main plantation at Doohoregan, and Mayara James, 65 years of age, lived with 23 relatives on his quarter.[30]

The two slaves genealogies presented in figures 8.2 and 8.3 provide detailed examples of the kinds of kinship networks that could develop on quarters after several generations of relative geographic stability. Because most slave

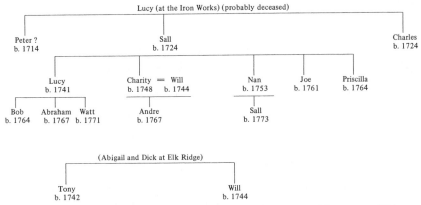

FIGURE 8.2. Kinship Ties Among Charles Carroll's Slaves at Annapolis Quarter, 1774

Source: Charles Carroll Account Book, Maryland Historical Society.

Note: Will, son of Abigail and Dick and Charity's husband, appears twice. Peter may not be Lucy's son, but it seems probable. Mark (b. 1758) and Jem (b. 1754) apparently were not related to others on the quarter, but had relatives elsewhere on Carroll's plantations.

quarters had between fifteen and thirty slaves, the network included just two or three households. The kin group shown in figure 8.2 may have been typical. Thirteen of the seventeen slaves who lived at Annapolis Quarter in 1774 were descendants of Iron Works Lucy. Ten were children and grandchildren of Sall. One of Sall's sons-in-law and his brother also lived there. Peter and Charles, other descendants of Lucy, lived on the quarter but had families elsewhere.

Nearly half the slaves who resided on Riggs Quarter, Carroll's main plantation, were kinfolk (63/130). A network of this size could develop only on the home plantation of the largest Chesapeake planters.[31] Each of the members of the group was either a direct descendant or an affine (inlaw) of old Fanny. She was surrounded on her quarter by five children, nineteen grandchildren, nine great-grandchildren, four children-in-law, and three grandchildren's spouses. The network grew through the marriage of Fanny's children and grandchildren to children of other residents of the quarter. For example, Cooper Joe, his wife, and thirteen children and grandchildren were closely related to Fanny's family. By the early 1750s Cooper Joe had married Nanny of Kate, and about 1761 Fanny's son Bob married Frances Mitchell of Kate. Joe and Nanny's children were first cousins of the children of Bob and Frances, and thereby more remotely connected to all the rest of Fanny's descendants. The alliance of the two families was cemented in 1772, when Dinah, the daughter of Kate of Fanny married Joe, the son of Cooper Joe.[32]

The intraquarter kinship network was also a work group. Fanny's and Lucy's adult and teenage kinfolk worked together in the fields. Masters separated their slaves by sex, age, and strength, and determined what each

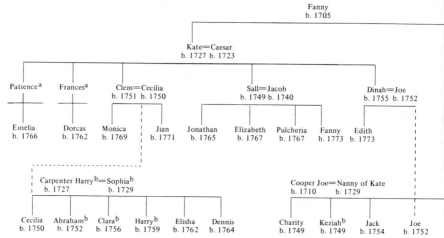

FIGURE 8.3. Fanny and Some of Her Kinfolk on Doohoregan Manor, 1773

[a]Those without a birthdate not resident on any Carroll farm. [b]Did not live at Rigg's Quarter (Fanny's Quarter). [c]This family lived at the sawmill at the main quarter of Doohoregan Manor. Frances Mitchell was a sister of Nanny, who was the wife of Cooper Joe.

Source: Charles Carroll Account Book, Maryland Historical Society.

would do, but blacks judged each other in part by the reciprocal kinship obligation that bound them together. Afro-Americans worked at their own pace and frequently thwarted their master's desires for increased productivity. Part of this conflict can be explained by the Afro-American's preindustrial work discipline, but part may have been due to the desires of kinfolk to help and protect each other from the master's lash, the humid climate, and the malarial environment.[33]

Landon Carter's lament upon the death of his trusted old slave Jack Lubbar suggests the dimensions of kinship solidarity in the fields. Lubbar had been a foreman over many groups of slaves. In his old age, he worked at the Fork quarter "with 5 hands and myself; in which service he so gratefully discharged his duty as to make me by his care alone larger crops of Corn, tobacco and Pease twice over than ever I have had made by anyone. . . ." Other blacks did not share Lubbar's desire to produce a large crop for Carter. "At this plantation," Carter writes, "he continued till his age almost deprived him of eyesight which made him desire to be removed because those under him, mostly his great grandchildren, by the baseness of their Parents abused him much." Lubbar's grandchildren and great-grandchildren, who worked together, were related in intricate ways: parents and children, maternal and paternal cousins, uncles and aunts, and brothers and sisters. They united against Lubbar to slow the work pace and conserve their energy.[34]

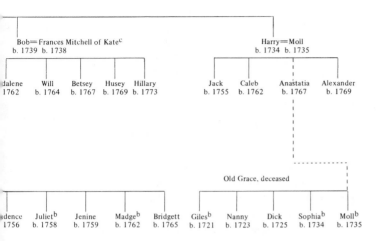

Bob=Frances Mitchell of Kate[c]
b. 1739 b. 1738

Harry=Moll
b. 1734 b. 1735

dalene Will Betsey Husey Hillary
1762   b. 1764 b. 1767 b. 1769 b. 1773

Jack Caleb Anastatia Alexander
b. 1755 b. 1762 b. 1767 b. 1769

Old Grace, deceased

dence Juliet[b] Jenine Madge[b] Bridgett Giles[b] Nanny Dick Sophia[b] Moll[b]
1756 b. 1758 b. 1759 b. 1762 b. 1765 b. 1721 b. 1723 b. 1725 b. 1734 b. 1735

When Afro-Americans came home each night from the fields, they broke into smaller domestic groups. Their habitat set the scene for social intercourse. On large plantations "a Negro quarter is a Number of Huts or Hovels, built at some distance from the Mansion House; where the Negroes reside with their wives and Families, and cultivate at vacant times the little spots allow'd them."[35] Four early-nineteenth-century slave houses still standing in Southern Maryland suggest that slave families living on the same quarter were very close. Each house included two rooms of about sixteen-by-sixteen feet, separated by a thin wall. In three of the homes, the two huts shared the same roof but had separate doorways. Two had separate fireplaces, the residents of one duplex shared a fireplace, and one quarter (which was over a kitchen) did not have a fireplace.[36] Neither family had much privacy, and communication between them must have been commonplace. No activity could occur on one side of the hut without those on the other knowing about it. And the two halves of the hut shared a common yard, where residents could talk, eat, or celebrate.

On the quarters the smallest local residence unit to contain kinfolk was the household. Household members were not isolated from other kinfolk; they worked with their relatives in the fields, associated with neighbors in the common yard, and cooked meals or slept near those who lived on the other side of their duplex. Nevertheless, kinfolk who lived in the same household were spatially closer when at home than any other group of kin. Who lived in typical households on slave quarters? How many husbands lived with their wives and children? How many children were separated from their parents? Did kin other than the immediate family live in many households?

Nearly half of all the Afro-Americans who lived on the three large plantations described in table 8.1 resided in households that included both parents and at least some of their children. Over half of the young children on all three plantations lived with both parents, but a far higher proportion of adults and children 10 to 14 years of age lived in two-parent households on the Carroll quarters than on the three Addison farms and Wardrop's plantation in Prince George's. While 49 percent of the women, 51 percent of the men, and 52 percent of children between ages 10 and 14 on Carroll's farms lived in two-parent households, only 28 percent of the women, 24 percent of the men, and 30 percent of those 10 to 14 year olds could be found in two-parent homes on the other farms. Almost all the other children lived with one parent, usually the mother; but over a quarter of those 10 to 14 years of age lived with siblings or with apparently unrelated people.

The differences between Carroll and the other two large slaveowners is striking. Carroll, unlike all but a few other Chesapeake gentlemen, was able to provide his people with spouses from his own plantations and chose to keep adolescent children with their parents. Over six-tenths of the men (62 percent) and 28 percent of the women on Addison's and Wardrop's plantations lived with siblings, were unmarried, or lived away from spouses and children. On Carroll's quarters only 27 percent of the men and 12 percent of the women were similarly separated from wives and children.

Many blacks on these three large farms lived with or near kin other than their parents or children. About 7 percent were in the household of a brother or sister, and over a tenth (13 percent) of parents and children shared their homes with another kinsperson. There were several types of these extended households: seven included parent(s), children, and sibling(s) of the mother; two included grandmother living with her children and grandchildren; in one household grandparents took care of two young grandchildren; and in one hut, an adult brother and sister lived with her children and one grandchild.

Far less can be learned about families on small plantations. On these farms, the slave quarter could be in an outbuilding or in a small hut.[37] All the slaves, whether kin or not, lived together, cooked together, reared children together, and slept in the same hut. Table 8.2 very roughly suggests the differences in household composition of large plantations and small farms. Only 18 percent of the blacks on small units lived in two-parent households. About a third resided in mother-child households, and that included over half the young children and three-tenths of those 10 to 14 years of age. Nearly three-quarters of the men and two-fifths of the women—some unmarried—lived with neither spouse nor children. Over two-fifths of the youths 10 to 14 years of age lived away from parents and siblings.

By the 1750s, a peculiar Afro-American life cycle had developed. Afro-Americans lived in a succession of different kinds of households. Children under 10 years almost always lived with their mothers, and over half on large plantations lived with both parents. Between 10 and 14 years of age, large numbers of children left their parents' home. Some stayed with siblings and their families, others were sold, the rest lived with other kin or unrelated people. Women married in their late teens, had children, and established households with their own children. Over four-tenths of the women on large plantations and a fifth on small farms lived with husbands as well as children. The same proportion of men as women lived with spouses and children, but because children of separated spouses usually lived with their mothers, large numbers of men, even on big plantations, lived with other men.

These life cycle changes can perhaps best be approached through a study of the critical events in the lives of Afro-Americans. Those events probably included the following: infancy, leaving the matricentral cell, beginning to work in the tobacco fields, leaving home, courtship and marriage, childrearing, and old age.[38]

For the first few months of life, a newborn infant stayed in the matricentral cell, that is, received his identity and subsistence from his mother.[39] A mother would take her new infant to the fields with her "and lay it uncovered on the ground . . . while she hoed her corn-row down and up. She would then suckle it a few minutes, and return to her labor, leaving the child in the same exposure." Eventually, the child left its mother's lap and explored the world of the hut and quarter. In the evenings, he ate with his family and learned to love his parents, siblings, and other kinfolk. During the day the young child lived in an age segregated world. While parents, other adults, and older siblings worked, children were "left, during a great portion of the day, on the ground at the doors of their huts, to their own struggles and efforts."[40] They played with age-mates or were left at home with other children and perhaps an aged grandparent. Siblings or age-mates commonly lived together or in nearby houses. On the Potomac side of Prince George's County in 1776, 86 percent of those 0 to 4 years of age, and 82 percent of those 5 to 9 years of age lived on plantations with at least one other child near their own age. Many children lived in little communities of five or more children their own age. Children 5 to 9 years old, too young to work full time, may have cared for younger siblings; in Prince George's in 1776, 83 percent of all children 0 to 4 years of age lived on a plantation with at least one child 5 to 9 years of age.[41]

Black children began to work in the tobacco fields between 7 and 10 years of age. For the first time they joined fully in the daytime activities of adults.[42] Those still living at home labored beside parents, brothers and sisters, cousins, uncles, aunts and other kinfolk. Most were trained to be field hands by white masters or overseers and by their parents. Though these young hands were forced to work for the master, they quickly learned from their kinfolk to work at the pace that black adults set and to practice the skills necessary to "put massa on."

At about the same age, some privileged boys began to learn a craft from whites or (on the larger plantations) from their skilled kinfolk. Charles Carroll's plantations provide an example of how skills were passed from one generation of Afro Americans to another. Six of the eighteen (33 percent) artisans on his plantations under 25 years of age in 1773 probably learned their trade from fathers and another four (22 percent) from other kinfolk skilled in that occupation. For example, Joe, 21, and Jack, 19, were both coopers and both sons of Cooper Joe, 63. Joe also learned to be a wheelwright, and in turn probably helped train his brothers-in-law, Elisha, 11, and Dennis, 9, as wheelwrights.[43]

Beginning to work coincided with the departure of many children from their parents, siblings, and friends. The ages of slaves in single slave households in Prince George's in 1776 (table 8.3) suggest that children were typically forced to leave home between 7 and 15 years of age, and this included many between 7 and 10. Young blacks were most frequently forced from large plantations to smaller farms.[44] The parents' authority was eliminated, and the child left the only community he had known. Tension and unhappiness often resulted. For example, Hagar, age 14, ran from her master in Baltimore in 1766. "She is supposed to be harbor'd in some Negro Quarter," he claimed, "as her Father and Mother Encourages her in Elopements, under a Pretense she is ill used at home."[45]

TABLE 8.3
Age of Slaves in One-Slave Households, 1776

Age Group	Slaves in One-Slave Households		Number in Age Group	Percentage of Age Group in One-Slave Households
	Number	*Percentage*		
0–4	1	1	657	*
5–9	15	19	526	3
10–14	21	27	473	4
15–19	12	15	329	4
20–29	10	13	533	2
30–39	7	9	353	2
40+	12	15	431	3
Totals	78	99	3,302	2

Source: Prince George's County Census of 1776. All but two of the fifteen slaves in the 5-9 category were ages 7, 8, or 9. Eight of the slaves in the 15–19 category were age 15.
* = less than ½.

Courtship and marriage were highly significant *rites de passage* for many Afro-American men and women. The process began earlier for women: while men probably married in their mid- to late twenties, women usually married in their late teens.[46] Men initiated the courtship. They typically searched for wives, visiting numbers of neighboring plantations, and often found a wife near home, though not on the same quarter. Some evidence for this custom, suggestive but hardly conclusive, can be seen in the sex and age of runaways. Only 9 percent (22/233) of all Southern Maryland runaways, 1745–79, were women. Few men (in terms of the total population) ran away in their late teens, but the numbers rose in the early twenties when the search for wives began, and crested between twenty-five and thirty-four when most men married and began families. Courtship on occasion ended in a marriage ceremony, sometimes performed by a Roman Catholic or Anglican clergyman, sometimes celebrated by the slaves themselves.[47] (See table 8.4.)

Marriage was more important for women than men. After the relationship was consummated, the woman probably stayed with her family (parents and siblings) until a child was born, unless she could form a household with her husband.[48] Once she had a child, she moved from her parents' home into her own hut. Though almost all women were field laborers, their role as wives and mothers gave them a few privileges. Masters sometimes treated

TABLE 8.4
Ages of Runaway Men, 1770–1779, Southern Maryland

Age Group	Number in Group	Percentage in Group	Percentage, 1776 Census	Percentage in in Group/ Percentage in 1776
15–19	4	6	19	.30
20–24	22	31	19	1.65
25–29	22	31	15	2.01
30–34	17	24	11	2.13
35–39	3	4	8	.50
40–49	4	6	13	.43
50+	0	0	15	.00
Totals	72	102	100	1.00

Source: All runaway slave ads published in the *Maryland Gazette*, 1745–79, the *Maryland Journal*, 1773–79, and *Dunlap's Maryland Gazette*, 1775–79, from Prince George's, Charles, Calvert, Frederick (south of Monocacy River), and Anne Arundel (south of Severn River, excluding Annapolis) counties, and any slave born in or traveling to those areas. Each slave runaway equals a single observation, but when the same slave ran away twice during the same time period, he was counted only once. The fourth column is from Prince George's County Census, 1776, and is included to provide a rough test of the likelihood that slaves of particular ages will run away. The index in the last column is a more precise measure of the same thing: an index of 2.01 means that about twice as many slaves in that age group ran away as one would expect from the age structures in 1776.

pregnant women—and their children after birth—with greater than usual solicitude. For example, Richard Corbin, a Virginia planter, insisted in 1759 that his steward be "Kind and Indulgent to pregnant women, and not force them then with Child upon any service or hardship that will be injurious to them." Children were "to be well looked after."[49]

There was less change in the life of most new husbands. Many continued to live with other adult men. Able to visit his family only at night or on holidays, the nonresident husband could play only a small role in childrearing. If husband and wife lived together, however, they established a household. The resident father helped raise his children, taught them skills, and tried to protect them from the master. Landon Carter reacted violently when Manuel tried to help his daughter. "Manuel's Sarah, who pretended to be sick a week ago, and because I found nothing ailed her and would not let her lie up she ran away above a week and was catched the night before last and locked up; but somebody broke open the door for her. It could be none but her father Manuel, and he I had whipped."[50]

On large plantations, mothers could call upon a wide variety of kin to help them raise their children: husbands, siblings, cousins, and uncles or aunts might be living in nearby huts. Peter Harbard learned from his grandmother, father, and paternal uncles how his grandmother's indentures were burned by Henry Darnall and how she was forced into bondage. He "frequently heard his grandmother Ann Joice say that if she had her just right that she ought to be free and all her children. He hath also heard his Uncles David Jones, John Wood, Thomas Crane, and also his father Francis Harbard declare as much." Peter's desire for freedom, learned from his kinfolk, never left him. In 1748, he ran away twice toward Philadelphia and freedom. He was recaptured, but later purchased his freedom.[51]

As Afro-Americans grew older, illness and lack of stamina cut into their productivity, and their kinfolk or masters were forced to provide for them. On rare occasions, masters granted special privileges to favored slaves. When Thomas Clark died in 1766, he gave his son Charles "my faithful old Negro man Jack whom I desire may be used tenderly in his old age." Charles Ball's grandfather lived as an old man by himself away from the other slaves he disliked. Similarly, John Wood, Peter Harbard's uncle, was given his own cabin in his old age.[52]

Many old slaves progressed through several stages of downward mobility. Artisans and other skilled workers became common field hands. While 10 percent of men between 40 and 59 years of age were craftsmen, only 3 percent of men above 60 years of age held similar positions.[53] Mulatto Ned, owned by Gabriel Parker of Calvert County, was a carpenter and cooper most of his life, but he had lost that job by 1750 when he was 65. Abraham's status at Snowden's Iron Works in Anne Arundel County changed from master founder to laborer when he could not work full time. As slaves became feeble, some masters refused to maintain them adequately, or sold them to unwary buyers. An act passed by the Maryland Assembly in 1752 complained that "sundry Persons in this Province have set disabled and superannuated Slaves free who have either perished through want or otherwise become a Burthen to others." The legislators uncovered a problem: in 1755, 20 percent of all the free Negroes in Maryland (153/895) were "past labour or cripples," while only 2 percent (637/29,141) of white men were in this category. To remedy the abuse, the assembly forbade manumission of slaves by will, and insisted that masters feed and clothe their old and ill slaves. If slaveholders failed to comply, they could be fined £4 for each offense.[54]

As Afro-American slaves moved from plantation to plantation through the life cycle, they left behind many friends and kinfolk, and established relationships with slaves on other plantations. And when young blacks married off their quarter, they gained kinfolk on other plantations. Both of these patterns can be illustrated from the Carroll plantations. Sam and Sue, who lived on Sam's quarter at Doohoregan Manor, had seven children between 1729 and 1751. In 1774, six of them were spread over four different quarters at Doohoregan: one son lived with his father (his mother had died); a daughter lived with her family in a hut near her father's; a son and daughter lived at Frost's; one son headed Moses' quarter; and a son lived at Riggs. Figure 8.3 shows how marriages increased the size and geographic spread of Fanny's relations. A third of the slaves (85/255) who lived away from Riggs Quarter (the main plantation) were kin to Fanny or her descendants. Two of Kate's children married into Fanny's family; Kate and one son lived at Frost's and another son lived at Jacob's. Cecilia, the daughter of Carpenter Harry and Sophia married one of Fanny's grandchildren. Harry and Sophia lived with three of their children at Frost's, and two of their sons lived at Riggs, where they were learning to be wheelwrights with kinsperson Joe, son of Cooper Joe.[55]

Since husbands and wives, fathers and children, and friends and kinfolk were often physically separated, they had to devise ways of maintaining their close ties. At night and on Sundays and holidays, fathers and other kinfolk visited those family members who lived on other plantations. Fathers had regular visiting rights. Landon Carter's Guy, for instance, visited his wife (who live on another quarter) every Monday evening.[56] Kinfolk, friends, and neighbors gathered in the yard around the slave cabins and talked, danced, sang, told stories, and drank rum through many an evening and special days on larger plantations.[57] These visits symbolized the solidarity of slave families and permitted kinfolk to renew their friendships, but did not allow nonresident fathers to participate in the daily rearing of their children.

The forced separation of Afro-American kinfolk by masters was not entirely destructive. Slave society was characterized by hundreds of interconnected and interlocking kinship and friendship networks that stretched from plantation to plantation and from county to county. A slave who wanted to run away would find kinfolk, friends of kinfolk, or kinfolk of friends along his route who willingly would harbor him for a while.[58] As Afro-American kinship and friendship networks grew ever larger, the proportion of runaways who were harbored for significant periods of time on slave quarters seemed to have increased in both Maryland and Virginia.[59]

There were three different reasons for slaves to use this underground. Some blacks, like Harry—who left his master in 1779, stayed in the neighborhood for a few weeks and then took off for Philadelphia—used their friends, and kinfolk's hospitality to reach freedom.[60] Others wanted to visit. About 27 percent of all runaways from Southern Maryland mentioned in newspaper advertisements from 1745 to 1779 (and 54 percent of all those whose destinations were described by masters) ran away to visit. For example, Page traveled back and forth between Piscataway and South River in 1749, a distance of about forty miles, and was not caught. He must have received help at many quarters along his route. And in 1756, Kate, 30 years old, ran away from her master, who lived near Georgetown on the Potomac. She went to South River about thirty miles distant, where she had formerly lived. Friends

TABLE 8.5
Profile of Runaways Who Visited Other Slaves, 1745–1779, Southern Maryland

| Years | Motive of Runaway Slave | | | Number of Runaways | Number of Visitors/ Number of Runaways |
	To Visit Spouse	To Visit Other Kinfolk	To Visit Friends		
1745–54	2	2	4	30	.267
1755–59	3	0	4	25	.280
1760–64	0	0	1	29	.035
1765–69	1	1	3	23	.217
1770–74	7	3	11	57	.368
1775–79	7	3	11	69	.304
Totals	20	9	34	233	—
% All Runaways	9	4	15	27	
% All Visitors	32	14	54	100	

Source: See table 8.4. Each slave runaway equals a single observation, but when the same slave ran away twice during the same time period, he was counted only once. The "to visit spouse" column includes husbands and wives who ran off together; the "to visit friends" column includes all slaves who visited friends, were harbored on slave quarters, or who returned to the neighborhood of a former home. (The listing of former homes is insufficient; the master must have asserted that the slave went there.) The categories are exclusive and should be read from left to right: an ad that mentions both visiting a spouse and visiting a friend is placed in the "to visit spouse" column. There were 203 ads in total. New Negroes were counted; 15 slaves could be identified as new Negroes, and if excluded from the table, the pattern would not change.

concealed her there. Her master feared that since "she had been a great Rambler, and is well known in *Calvert* and *Anne Arundel* Counties, besides other parts of the Country," Kate would "indulge herself a little in visiting her old Acquaintances," but spend most of her time with her husband at West River.[61]

Indeed, 20 of 233 Maryland runaways (9 percent) left masters to join their spouses. Sue and her child Jem, 18 months old, went from Allen's Freshes to Port Tobacco, Charles County, a distance of about ten miles, "to go and see her husband." Sam, age 30, lived about thirty miles from his wife in Bryantown, Charles County, when he visited her in 1755. Will had to go over a hundred miles, from Charles to Frederick County, to visit his wife, because her master had taken her from Will's neighborhood to a distant quarter.[62]

This essay has pointed to the basic cultural and demographic cleavage between African and Afro-American families. African immigrants, like free and servant immigrants from Britain, remembered their native land but had to adjust to the new conditions of the Chesapeake. As free Africans they had lived among many kinfolk; in the Chesapeake, kin ties were established with difficulty. Because most immigrants were young adult males and because plantations were small, two-parent households were rare. Mothers, by default became the major black influence upon Afro-American children.

After immigration from Africa slowed, the sex ratio declined, and plantation sizes increased. As generation followed generation, Afro-Americans in Maryland and Virginia created an extensive kinship system. More households, especially on large plantations, included two parents and their children. Although most households did not include kinfolk other than the immediate family, other relations lived in adjacent huts. Mothers and children worked in the tobacco fields with kinfolk, ate and celebrated with many relations, and invited kin who lived elsewhere to share in the festivities. Afro-Americans forcibly separated from relatives managed to maintain contact with them. And finally, slave resistance—whether expressed in the fields or by running away—was fostered and encouraged by kinfolk.

This article has attempted to portray African and Afro-American family life among slaves in the eighteenth-century Chesapeake. It is based upon all the available evidence and upon speculations from that evidence. Many important questions about black family life in the colonial period remain to be answered. In the first place, we need to know more about household and family structure. Could the same structures be found in other parts of the region? In South Carolina? In the northern and middle colonies? Was the pattern of change described here repeated in other areas? Secondly, we must go beyond this essay and describe in greater detail the nature of the Afro-American developmental cycle and the emotional content of relationships among kinfolk in various places at different times. When this work is completed, a clearer picture of changes in slave family life from the 1670s to the 1850s, and of regional differences in black family structure, ought to emerge.

NOTES

1. Prince George's County Court Record O, f. 414, ms., Hall of Records, Annapolis, Md., hereafter cited as PG Ct. Rec.; *Maryland Gazette* (Annapolis), 12 March 1772. All manuscripts, unless otherwise noted, can be found at the Hall of Records.

2. Pioneering essays by Russell Menard, "The Maryland Slave Population, 1658-1730: A Demographic Profile of Blacks in Four Counties," *William and Mary Quarterly,* 3d ser. 32 (1975):29-54, and Peter Wood, *Black Majority: Negroes in Colonial South Carolina through the Stono Rebellion* (New York, 1974), ch. 5, suggest some characteristics of colonial black families. Much more is known about slave families in the nineteenth century. Herbert G. Gutman, *The Black Family in Slavery and Freedom, 1750-1925* (New York, 1976) is the standard reference. Other studies include Eugene D. Genovese, *Roll, Jordan, Roll: The World the Slaves Made* (New York, 1974), pp. 443-524; E. Frank Frazier, "The Negro Slave Family," *Journal of Negro History* 15 (1930):198-266; John Blassingame, *The Slave Community: Plantation Life in the Ante-Bellum South* (New York, 1972), ch. 3; George P. Rawick, *From Sundown to Sunup: The Making of the Black Community* (New York, 1972), ch. 5.

3. There are no standard definitions of household, domestic group, and family. I have borrowed my definitions of household and domestic group from Donald R. Bender, "A Refinement of the Concept of Household: Families, Co-residence, and Domestic Functions," *American Antropologist* 69 (1967):493-504, quote on p. 498. The use of "immediate family," "near kin," and "distant kin" were suggested to me by Herbert Gutman, and would be rejected by Bender.

4. Sidney W. Mintz and Richard Price, "The Study of Afro-American Culture History: Some Suggestions" (working paper presented to the Schouler Lecture Symposium, Creole Societies in the Americas and Africa, John Hopkins University, April 1973) cited with the permission of Mr. Mintz. This paper will be published in fall, 1976 by Ishi Publications, Philadelphia, as *An Anthropological Approach to the Afro-American Past: A Caribbean Perspective,* Occasional Papers in Social Change. A more systematic application of these hypotheses to the colonial Chesapeake will be found in Allan Kulikoff, "Tobacco and Slaves: Population, Economy, and Society in Eighteenth-Century Prince George's County, Maryland" (Ph.D. diss., Brandeis University, 1976), ch. 6.

5. It is difficult to be more precise because most data on African kinship systems comes from twentieth-century anthropological works. The following works suggest variations in African kinship patterns: A. R. Radcliffe-Brown, "Introduction" to *African Systems of Kinship and Marriage,* ed. Radcliffe-Brown and Daryll Ford (London, 1950), pp. 1-85; Meyer Fortes, "Kinship and Marriage among the Ashanti," ibid., pp. 252-84; Jack Goody, *Comparative Studies in Kinship* (Stanford, 1969), ch. 3; Robert Bain, *Bangwa Kinship and Marriage* (Cambridge, England, 1972); William J. Goode, *World Revolutions and Family Patterns* (New York, 1963), pp. 167-200.

6. Mintz and Price, "Afro-American Culture History," pp. 56-78 but esp. pp. 61-62; John S. Mbiti, *African Religions and Philosophy* (New York, 1969), pp. 104-9.

7. Goode, *World Revolutions,* pp. 167-68, 196; Mbiti, *African Religions,* pp. 142-45. Women in polygynous societies also nursed infants for three to four years and abstained from intercourse during part of that period. If this pattern was repeated in the Chesapeake, it was partially responsible for the low gross birth rate among blacks in seventeenth-century Maryland; see Kulikoff, "Tobacco and Slaves," ch. 4; Menard, "Maryland Slave Population," p. 41; Mbiti, *African Religions,* p. 111. For polygyny on the Eastern Shore, see "Eighteenth-Century Maryland as Portrayed in the 'Itinerant Observations' of Edward Kimber," *Maryland Historical Magazine* 51 (1956):327.

8. For Maryland, see Kulikoff, "Tobacco and Slaves," ch. 4, table 4–3; Menard, "Maryland Slave Population," p. 32, for sex ratios; Kulikoff, "Tobacco and Slaves," ch. 6, for density. For Virginia, see Robert A. Wheeler, "Mobility of Laborers in Surry County, Virginia, 1674–1703;; (paper presented at the Stony Brook, N.Y. Conference on Early Social History, June 1975), p. 6.

9. For the uprising of 1739 and some evidence concerning the competition of whites and Afro-Americans for African and Afro-American women, see Kulikoff, "Tobacco and Slaves," ch. 6.

10. Mintz and Price, "Afro-American Culture History," pp. 35–37, 61–62; Kulikoff, "Tobacco and Slaves," ch. 4, tables 4–2 and 4–3; PG Inventories, 1730–69, mss. Large plantations were those with ten or more adult slaves.

11. Menard, "Maryland Slave Population," pp. 42–47; Kulikoff, "Tobacco and Slaves," ch. 4, table 4–1 shows mean age at conception of first child of slave women born 1710–39 to be about 17.6.

12. These statements are based upon PG Wills, mss., for the 1730s and 1740s.

13. See the inventory of the plantation of Daniel Carroll of Duddington found in the Charles Carroll of Annapolis Account Book, ms 220, Maryland Historical Society, Baltimore (the inventory was never probated). The inventory was taken in 1735, a time of high slave imports, but Carroll sold rather than bought slaves. There were only two men between 15 and 29 years of age (but twelve women) on his plantations, and seven above 60; two of the four men in their 40s, two of the three in their 50s, and six of seven in their 60s or older lived with wives and children.

14. White common-law husbands found open cohabitation with black women socially undesirable. When William Hardie of Prince George's accused Daniel Carroll of Upper Marlborough, a wealthy merchant of the same county, of buggery and of keeping mulattoes, since "he . . . could use them as he pleased," Carroll sued him for slander, finding both charges equally harmful; see Clinton Ashley Ellefson, "The County Courts and the Provincial Courts of Maryland, 1733–1764" (Ph.D. diss., University of Maryland, 1963), pp. 544–46.

15. PG Inventories, 1730–44.

16. Menard, "Maryland Slave Population," pp. 42–46; Kulikoff, "Tobacco and Slaves," ch. 4.

17. These points are fully developed in Kulikoff, "Tobacco and Slaves," ch. 6.

18. These statements are based upon PG Wills, 1730–69 and court cases discussed below.

19. PG Wills, 1730–69; mortgages in PG Land Records, libers T, Y, and PP, mss. Estate sales were sometimes advertised in the *Maryland Gazette*. Slaves could not be sold from an estate until all other moveable property had been used to pay debts. Elie Valette, *The Deputy Commissary's Guide within the Province of Maryland* (Annapolis, 1774), pp. 91, 134–35.

20. Eighteen-century migrations of slaves are discussed in Kulikoff, "Tobacco and Slaves," ch. 4, and slave migrations in the nineteenth century are analyzed in idem, "Black Society and the Economics of Slavery," *Maryland Historical Magazine* 70 (1975):208–10.

21. Court of Appeals of the Western Shore, BW no. 10(1800–1801), ff. 456–83, but esp. ff. 459–60, mss.

22. Chancery Papers no. 5241 (1788) mss.; PG Wills 1:280–5; PG Original Wills, box 7, folder 66, and box 13, folder 51, mss.; PG Inventories DD no. 1, ff. 22–24; DD no. 2, ff. 379–86; GS no. 1 ff. 246–48; and ST no. 1, ff. 96–100.

23. Chancery Records 16:298–304, ms.; PG Land Record PP (second part) 4; NN, f. 407; PG Original Wills, box 7, folder 3, and box 9, folder 52; PG Inventories DD no. 1, ff. 438–41, and GS no. 2, ff. 111–12.

24. About 40 percent of Prince George's slaves lived on large units from 1750 to 1779 (estimate based upon probate inventories), and 52 percent of the slaves in that county lived on big units in 1790 (federal census); see Kulikoff, "Tobacco and Slaves," table 6–1 for references.

25. Large in-migrations of Africans to the Chesapeake region occurred in the 1670s and 1690s (see Kulikoff, "Tobacco and Slaves," ch. 4, and references there). The great-grandmother of a man born in 1755 could have immigrated from Africa as a young woman in the 1690s.

26. "A List of Negroes on Dooheregan Manor taken in Familys with their Ages Dec[r] 1 1773," and other lists of slaves at Popular Island, Annapolis Quarter, and Annapolis taken in February and July 1774, Carroll Account Book. There were ten quarters on the 10,500 acres of Doohoregan. I am greatly endebted to Edward Papenfuse for calling this list to my attention.

27. Only a handful of people in the Chesapeake colonies owned as many slaves as Carroll. He could therefore afford to keep most of his slave families together, an option not open even to the very large slaveowner with several children and 100 slaves. Nevertheless, two-thirds of Carroll's slaves lived on units with less than 40 people, and 57 percent of them on quarters with less than 30. Only the 130 slaves who lived at Riggs (the main plantation at Doohoregan) developed more extensive kinship networks on a single quarter than was possible for slaves who lived on other large Chesapeake quarters of 15 to 30 slaves.

28. See Menard, "Maryland Slave Population, pp. 35–36 for seventeenth-century examples of quarters named for slave residents.

29. There were 139 married adults (all ages) and single people 21 years and over in the group. While 46 percent of the leaders were over 55, only 11 percent (15/138) of all adults were over 55. The oldest member of a quarter kin group did not necessarily head the list. For example, Carpenter Harry, 46, headed Frost's Quarter even though his mother, Battle Creek Nanny, 78, was also living there.

30. The statistics are means: 36 percent of all slaves counted together, 38 percent with each quarter counted separately (sum of means). The number of people related to leaders on each quarter was as follows:

Quarter	Leader	Age (years)	No. of Kin Ties	No. on Quarter (excluding leader)
Riggs	Fanny	69	40	129
Sukey's	Sukey	69	9	21
Moses'	Moses	41	7	18*
Jacob's	Jacob	34	2	21*
Mayara James	Mayara James	65	23	27
Folly	Nacy	45	7	19*
Sam's	Sam	57	6	21
Frost's	Carpenter Henry	46	8	36
Sten's	Judith¹	21	7	22
Capt. Field's	Phil	34	3	7*
House Servants at Annapolis	Johnny	30	4	12
Annapolis	Peter	60	13	16
Popular Island	James	73	3	25*

Note: The first ten quarters listed were all on Doohoregan. Because affines were unknown (except for Riggs, where they were eliminated for the sake of comparison), the figures are minimums.

*Only known relations were immediate family.

†Daughter of Long Grace, 47, on that quarter, who had lost the use of her feet.

31. Only a maximum of 6 percent of all the slaves in Prince George's, Anne Arundel, Charles, and St. Mary's Counties, Md., in 1790, lived on units of more than 100. (The 6 percent is a maximum number because the census taker sometimes put slaves from several of the same master's quarters in the same entry.) *Heads of Families at the First Census of the United States Taken in the Year 1790; Maryland* (Washington, 1907), pp. 9–16, 47–55, 92–98, 104–9.

32. Joe married his mother's sister's husband's mother's grandchild.

33. See Kulikoff, "Tobacco and Slaves," ch. 7.

34. Jack Greene, ed., *The Dairy of Landon Carter of Sabine Hall, 1752–1778* (Charlottesville, 1965), p. 840 (27 July 1775).

35. Kimber, "Itinerant Observations," p. 327. See Kulikoff, "Tobacco and Slaves," ch. 6, for a fuller description of slave quarters.

36. Three of the structures are in St. Mary's; the other once stood in Prince George's. I am indebted to Cary Carson, coordinator of research, St. Mary's City Commission, for sharing the data on St. Mary's with me, and to Margaret Cook (a local historian, who lives in Oxon Hill,

Md.) for her descriptions and slides of the Prince George's hut. These ideas will be expanded elsewhere.

37. On a small plantation a slave quarter located in a kitchen is described in Provincial Court Judgments, EI no. 4, ff. 110–12, ms.

38. For a similar perspective on the succession of households and on life cycles, see Lutz Berkner, "The Stem Family and the Developmental Cycle of the Peasant Household: An Eighteenth-Century Austrian Example," *American Historical Review* 77 (1972):398–418.

39. For the matricentral cell, see Meyer Fortes, "Introduction," to *The Developmental Cycle in Domestic Groups*, ed. Jack Goody, Cambridge Papers in Social Anthropology, no. 1 (Cambridge, 1958), pp. 1–14, but esp. p. 9, and Sidney W. Mintz, "A Final Note," *Social and Economic Studies* 10 (1961):528–535, but esp. pp. 532–33.

40. Samuel Stanhope Smith, *An Essay on the Causes of the Variety of Complexion and Figure in the Human Species* (Philadelphia, 1787), p. 35; ibid., ed. Winthrop D. Jordan (Cambridge, Mass., 1965 [reprint of 1810 ed.]), pp. 61–62, 156–57.

41. Prince George's County Census, 1776, found in Gaius Marcus Brumbaugh, ed., *Maryland Records, Colonial Revolutionary, County, and Church*, 2 vols. Lancaster, Pa., 1915–28), 1–88. Since most of the county's large plantations (located on the Patuxent side of the county) are not on the census, the figures overestimate the proportion of children without playmates. The distribution of children on plantations is as follows:

No. of Children on Plantations	Percentage of Children in Age Groups		
	0-4 years	*5-9 years*	*0-14 years*
1	14	18	8
2-4	45	51	33
5-9	22	19	29
10+	19	11	31
Total Percent	100	99	101
Number	657	526	1,183

42. Kulikoff, "Tobacco and Slaves," ch. 7.

43. Carroll Account Book. Elisha and Dennis were sons of Carpenter Harry and Sophia. Joe married Dinah of Kate and Ceasar; her brother married Cecilia of Harry and Sophia. Elishia and Dennis were therefore Joe's wife's brother's wife's brothers.

44. See table 8.3. Only the children of slaveowners or those who had just bought their first slave were likely to have only one slave, so this data is a useful indicator of the age children were first sold. The transfers from large to small plantations can be seen in the fact that 12 percent of all slaves 10 to 14 years of age on large plantations, but 43 percent on small farms, lived away from parents and kinfolk (see tables 8.1 and 8.2).

45. *Maryland Gazette*, 1 Oct. 1766.

46. Kulikoff, "Tobacco and Slaves," table 4–1, shows that the median age at first conception for slave women born 1710-59 was 17 years. Age at marriage cannot be determined with precision but can be approximated from the age differences of husbands and wives. On the Carroll, Addison, and Wardrop plantations, 47 husbands were 6.8 years (mean) older than their wives, Carroll Account Book; PG Inventories GS no. 1, f. 73; GS no. 2, ff. 334–36.

47. Thomas Hughes, *History of the Society of Jesus in North America Colonial and Federal*, 4 vols. (London, 1910–17), *Text, 1645-1773*, 2:560–61; William Stevens Perry, ed., *Historical Collections Relating to the American Colonial Church*, 4 vols. (Davenport, Iowa, 1870), 4:306–7; Thomas Bacon, *Four Sermons upon the Great and Indispensible Duty of All Christian Masters and Mistresses to Bring Up Their Negro Slaves in the Knowledge and Fear of God* (London, 1750), pp. v, vii.

48. Sixty percent of all marriages of slave women, 1740–59 birth cohorts, took place between 16 and 19 years of age (marriages defined as age at first conception), Kulikoff, "Tobacco and Slaves," table 4–1. Substantial numbers of these teenage girls should have been pregnant with their first children between ages 16 and 19. If they were living with husbands, then their households would include only a husband and wife. On the three large plantations analyzed in table 8.1, there were only three husband-wife households, and the women in them were 19, 27, and 56 years old. There is evidence that five of the sixteen women, 16 to 19 years old, were married—three who had children lived with sisters; one lived with her husband; one was

separated from her husband but had no children; and the other lived with her husband and children. Ten of the other eleven lived with their parents.

49. For female occupations, see Kulikoff, "Tobacco and Slaves," ch. 7; quote from William Kauffman Scarborough, *The Overseer: Plantation Management in the Old South* (Baton Rouge, 1966), pp. 183–84.

50. Greene, *Diary of Landon Carter,* p. 777 (22 Sept. 1773).

51. Court of Appeals of the Western Shore, BW no. 10 (1800–1801), ff. 459–60; *Maryland Gazette,* 2 Nov. 1748.

52. PG Original Wills, box 10, folder 35; Charles Ball, *Fifty Years in Chains* (1836; New York, 1970), pp. 21–22; Court of Appeals of the Western Shore, BW no. 10, f. 549 (1802). These were the only examples I found in all the wills and court records I examined.

53. Kulikoff, "Tobacco and Slaves," table 7–6. Ages were collected from PG Inventories, 1730–69.

54. Snowden Account Book, Private Accounts, ms.; Inventories 43:320, ms.; Chancery Records, 7:2–12, 25–34, 50–52; William Hand Browne, et al., eds. *Archives of Maryland,* 72 vols. (Baltimore, 1883–), 50:76–78; *Gentleman's Magazine* 34 (1764):261. For two examples of ill slaves sold from master to master, see *Maryland Journal,* 28 Sept. 1778, and Chancery Records 16:469–78 (1789).

55. Carroll Account Book.

56. Greene, *Diary of Landon Carter,* pp. 329, 348, 648, 845, 1109–10; *Maryland Gazette,* 11 July 1771.

57. See references cited in Kulikoff, "Tobacco and Slaves," ch. 6, note 44.

58. My work on slavery owes much to the pioneering book of Gerald Mullin, *Flight and Rebellion: Slave Resistance in Eighteenth-Century Virginia* (New York, 1972), but my perspective on runaways differs from the ones he presents in chapters 3 and 4 of his book. Mullin has, I believe, missed the significance of kin networks in helping most runaways.

59. See table 8.5; Kulikoff, "Tobacco and Slaves," table 6–4; Mullin, *Flight and Rebellion,* p. 129, shows that the proportion of visitors (as defined in table 8.5) increased from 29% before 1775 to 38% of all runaways whose destinations can be determined from 1776 to 1800. The major problem with this data and Mullin's is the large number of unknowns (52% in Maryland and 40% in Virginia).

60. *Maryland Gazette,* 6 July 1779. Other examples of slaves using the underground to escape slavery are found in ibid., 28 April 1757, and 11 July 1771.

61. Ibid., 4 Oct. 1749; 11 Nov. 1756; for other extensive visiting networks, see ibid., 11 Aug. 1751; 12 March 1772; 30 Jan. and 22 May 1777.

62. Ibid., 9 March 1758; 6 Feb. 1755, and 12 Aug. 1773; table 8.7. John Woolman claimed that husbands and wives were often separated, *The Journal of John Woolman* (Corinth ed., New York, 1961), p. 59.

NINE

LANDLESS HUSBANDMEN: PROPRIETARY TENANTS IN MARYLAND IN THE LATE COLONIAL PERIOD

Gregory A. Stiverson

By the end of the colonial period, the majority of heads of households in Maryland did not own land. Because the economy of the colony was overwhelmingly dependent upon agriculture, most nonlandowners supported their families by renting farms. In spite of their numerical importance, little is known about tenants in the province because they appear infreqently in the public and private records available to the historian—leases were often only oral agreements, the papers of private landlords are incomplete or have disappeared, and few tenants left personal papers that shed light on their life experiences.[1]

But one rich source of information relating to eighteenth-century Maryland tenants does exist—the proprietary manor papers. Maryland was the property of the successive Lords Baltimore, and as proprietors of the province they could dispose of land in the colony as they saw fit. Although the proprietors granted most land as freeholds, reserving only an annual quit rent for themselves, a decision was made in the last third of the seventeenth century to set aside land in each county for the proprietor's personal use. These tracts were called proprietary manors. They were not manors in the feudal sense, but simply land on which freeholds could not be surveyed unless the proprietor gave special permission.

Although favorites were occasionally allowed to establish freeholds on the manors, the proprietor concluded at an early date that dividing the manors into leaseholds would be the best means of achieving the "valuable augmentation of riches" he desired.[2] Toward that end, the successive Lords Baltimore continued to order new manors erected as the area of settlement in the colony expanded. By the mid-1760s, Frederick, the sixth and last

Note: Gregory A. Stiverson is the assistant state archivist, Hall of Records Commission, Department of General Services, Annapolis, Maryland.

Lord Baltimore, owned twenty-three manors encompassing approximately 190,000 acres in the province.[3]

With so much vacant land in the colony, the proprietors could not have expected to rent much land in the seventeenth century. In establishing the proprietary manors, the Calverts had committed themselves and their heirs to a form of land speculation in which they would benefit from the rise in land values as the population of the colony increased. Toward the end of the seventeenth century the price of tobacco fell precipitously, and this, combined with a rise in the population of the colony, made it increasingly difficult for the poor to accumulate the capital necessary to acquire a freehold. Consequently, the demand for leaseholds rose, and the proprietor was able to begin leasing his manors in the early years of the eighteenth century.[4] By 1733, the manors in the oldest settled counties on the lower Western Shore were already well tenanted, and there were a few proprietary leaseholders on the Eastern Shore; the manors on the frontier in the north and northwest sections of the province, however, were still vacant.[5] Thirty years later—in the mid-1760s—nearly all the land on every proprietary manor had been leased.[6]

The majority of the proprietary leases were issued between 1733 and 1755. During this period, one hundred acres of manor land could be rented for 10 shillings sterling per annum. Leases were valid for three lives, meaning that they expired only when the last of three named persons had died. In exchange for the low rent and long tenure, leaseholders were required to make specific improvements on their tenements, including building a dwelling house twenty feet wide by thirty feet long and planting an orchard of 100 fruit trees. Proprietary lease terms were, nevertheless, far more advantageous to the leasee than leases on private estates, where rents were as much as thirteen times higher and the tenure shorter and less secure.[7]

Because of administrative inefficiencies, the manors never became a major source of proprietary income, and in 1765, Frederick, sixth Lord Baltimore, decided to sell them all.[8] This decision made it necessary to resurvey each manor and to make lists of all the tenants and the condition of their leaseholds. These proprietary manor papers, supplemented by information from the public records, enable the historian to construct a picture of what life was like for tenants in Maryland in the late colonial period.

Two of the proprietary manors offer contrasts that can assist such an enterprise: Zachiah Manor on the lower Western Shore and Monocacy Manor in the northwest section of the colony. The two manors differed in their dates of settlement, in the quality of their natural resources, in the kinds of crops that were grown on them, and in the ethnic composition of their tenant populations. A study of these manors permits exploration of factors that might have been important in affecting the life experiences of tenants.

Zachiah Manor was surveyed in 1667, one of the earlier tracts set aside for the Calverts. The manor was located in Charles County to the west of Zachiah Swamp on a tributary of the Wicomico River. Although Zachiah Manor contained nearly 10,000 acres when it was resurveyed in 1767, three large patented tracts had been laid out early in the eighteenth century that reduced the land available for leasing to 5,407 acres. Tenants held leases on the manor as early as 1714, and by 1767, nearly 4,000 acres was in the possession of twenty-nine leaseholders. Individual holdings ranged from 12 to 619½ acres, with the median being 92¾ acres.[9]

Monocacy Manor, situated in Frederick County on the east side of the Monocacy River, was surveyed in 1724, over fifty years after Zachiah Manor. Even at that date Monocacy Manor was on the extreme northwest frontier of the province, and the first leases for tenements on the manor were not issued until 1741. Although three of the four leases granted in 1741 were to persons of English extraction, Germans quickly dominated the manor population. The manor contained 9,231 acres in 1768, nearly 7,500 acres of which was leased by fifty-five tenants. Individual holdings ranged from 7½ to 380¾ acres; the median was 115¾ acres.[10]

Inferior natural resources characterized Zachiah Manor. When the manor was examined in 1767, the soil on most tenements was found to be poor or swampy. Slightly more than a fifth of the tenanted tracts (20.3 percent) were described as worn out from cultivation. Furthermore, sixteen of the forty-seven leaseholds had either no water or an inadequate supply, and thirty-three tracts had too little wood to support the tenement.[11]

The natural resources on Monocacy Manor were far superior to those on Zachiah. When the manor was resurveyed in 1768, the soil on most tracts was described as being good or very good. Much of the manor was still covered with virgin timber, and only two leaseholds had an insufficient amount of wood to support the tenement. Water was the only natural resource that was deficient on the manor, but less than half the leaseholds were affected.[12]

Population stability was high on both manors. About five out of six tenants in the mid-1760s were either original leaseholders of their tracts or direct descendants of the original leaseholders. The length of time tenants had been on the manors varied. One Zachiah tenement that had been leased as early as 1714 was in the possession of the same family in 1767, and many other tenements that were first leased in the 1720s and 1730s were still held by the original leaseholder or his heirs. Although Monocacy Manor was settled much later than Zachiah, when it was resurveyed in 1768, several tenants had held their leaseholders for twenty or more years. The stability of residency on the two manors resulted in a proliferation of kinship groups. The twenty-nine tenants on Zachiah Manor represented twenty-one family names, and the fifty-five tenants on Monocacy Manor represented just thirty-five families. The marriage of daughters to other tenants, although impossible to trace completely, undoubtedly occurred frequently, further linking the families on the manors.[11]

Although tenancy on Zachiah and Monocacy manors were similar in that tenements on both averaged about 100 acres and the tenant populations on each demonstrated considerable continuity over time, the economic condition of residents on the two manors differed markedly. Probate records provide economic data on many people who lived in colonial Maryland, but the poor are underrepresented in them.[14] Therefore, if most tenants were at the lower end of the economic spectrum, as their nonlandowning status would imply, few would have left the estate papers necessary for a detailed analysis of the personal property they owned at the time of their deaths. At best, the absence of tenants in the probate records can be interpreted as negative confirmation of poverty. The few tenant estates that are found must be interpreted with extreme caution, always bearing in mind that they probably reflect the property owned by the wealthier tenants on the manor.

The probate records suggest, negatively, that most residents on Zachiah Manor were very poor because most tenants do not appear in them, and positively, because the majority of those who do were demonstrably poor. Just twenty-five of the forty-five people who at one time or another leased land on Zachiah Manor were found in the probate records, and only fourteen were resident tenants.[15] Of these fourteen, three had estates that were settled with negative balances (in the red), five others had estates valued at less than £50, one was valued between £50 and £99, and two were rated at between £100 and £199. Thus, over half of the resident tenants on Zachiah Manor who appear in the probate records had estates valued at under £50 and over three-fourths were valued at under £200. Furthermore, there is nothing to suggest that the vast majority of the resident tenants who cannot be found in the probate records were even as well off as those who do appear.[16]

The inventories of eight of the fourteen resident Zachiah Manor tenants contained no slaves or servants, a condition that must also have characterized most tenants not found in the probate records. Consequently, although Charles County was a tobacco-staple area where slaves provided much of the labor, most Zachiah tenants could not afford them and were dependent on their own family for labor. Families on the manor were large, however, if the six that can be reconstructed are at all representative. The six families averaged 7.7 children living at the time of the father's death. Sons and daughters were undoubtedly put to work in the fields at an early age, but tenants with large families to support, nevertheless, would have had to devote much of their available labor to the cultivation of crops for home consumption. The tenants on Zachiah Manor were not entirely self-sufficient—they bought some store goods each year and paid for them with tobacco cash crops—but they did attempt to produce all of the food for their families and animals, and these crops could be grown only at the expense of the acreage and labor devoted to cash crops. The inventories suggest that the average tenant was rarely able to produce more tobacco than was required to pay for necessary store purchases.[17]

As on Zachiah Manor, the majority of Monocacy tenants were not found in the probate records. Of the seventy-nine tenants who at one time or another leased land on the manor, thirty appear in the probate records, twenty-one of whom resided on the manor at the time of their deaths. Of the twenty-one estates, which date from 1753 to 1792, only one was settled with a negative balance, but seven others were valued at under £100, and all but three were valued at less than £300. One resident tenant owned three slaves, but the others were dependent upon their own families for labor. Fourteen families can be reconstructed—they had an average of seven children living at the time of the father's death, only a fraction smaller than the average family on Zachiah Manor.

Although small estates dominated on both manors, a qualitative difference is discernible in the kinds of goods owned by Monocacy tenants. As soon as a Zachiah tenant was able, he purchased a slave. This may have been a wise investment in a tobacco-staple region, but it did little, at least immediately, to improve the living conditions of the tenant and his family. Monocacy tenants preferred to invest in livestock, farm tools, and buildings on their tenements, the kind of expenditures that improved the quality of life and made their land more productive. Furthermore, although most Monocacy tenants had small personal estates, a larger number of them had assets that placed them above the the poorer classes of free whites. Only a fifth (21.4 percent) of the Zachiah tenants had personal property valued between £100 and £299, whereas a third of the Monocacy estates fell within that range. Thus, although most tenants on both manors were far from being well-to-do, Monocacy leaseholders were somewhat better off and had a better chance of leaving something to be divided among their children when they died.

Because of the underrepresentation of the poor, the probate records are of limited utility for studying tenants. They show that the preponderance of tenants for whom probate records were filed had small to moderate sized estates, but they reveal nothing about the majority of the manor residents who do not appear in them. But the probate records can be supplemented by the lists of improvements on the tenements that were compiled in the 1760s following the proprietor's order to sell the manors. From the description of improvements, an idea of the physical setting in which the tenants lived can be attained, and the number, size, and quality of the buildings on the leaseholds provide an alternative means of assessing the economic condition of the tenants.

The single improvement necessary to make a tenement habitable was a dwelling house. There were twenty-eight dwellings on Zachiah Manor in 1767, and dimensions were given for twenty. The largest house was 16 feet by 32 feet; the smallest only 12 feet square. The average dwelling contained 278.2 square feet and measured 14.6 feet wide by 19.0 feet long.[18] No dwelling was as large as the 20-by-30 foot structure (600 square feet) required in the tenants' leases, and the average house was less than half that size.[19]

Detailed descriptions of dwellings on Zachiah Manor were not given, but, based on information for similar houses in Southern Maryland, some conjectures concerning the appearance and construction of tenant dwellings on the manor can be made.[20] Most of the houses were simple framed structures of one and one-half stories. The smaller dwellings contained only one room, and only the largest houses had more than two rooms on the ground floor. Some of the houses probably had nothing but dirt floors, but others may have had plank flooring covering at least half of the main floor. Windows may have been shuttered rather than glazed. Finally, the single fireplace probably had a wooden chimney rather than one constructed of stone or brick; wooden chimneys were hazardous, but the fact that they could be built cheaply from readily available materials would have been the overriding consideration for poor tenants.

The most important factor concerning housing on Zachiah Manor—what it was like to live in such an environment—is not revealed in any contemporary source. Many, perhaps most, of the houses must have been little better than hovels. Their small size coupled with large families must have taxed tempers as well as sanitary conditions to the limit. Privacy within the house, if desired, would have been difficult to achieve.[21] Furthermore, the physical appearance of the tenant's house was a result of his poverty and was a constant reminder to him of his economic condition. How this environment affected tenants and their children is almost beyond imagining. Recognizing the situation, however, renders the pejorative statements made by upper-class critics of common planters seem less like aristocratic snobbery and more like a commentary on the mental and motivational impairment that could result from abject poverty.[22]

The other improvements on Zachiah Manor were few in number and poor in quality. Tobacco barns were an exception because they were essential for curing tobacco, the tenants' primary cash crop. There were nearly as many tobacco barns as residences on the manor, and dimensions were given for twelve. The most frequently occurring size was 22 by 32 feet, and the average, with slightly more than 636 square feet, was more than twice the size of the average dwelling on the manor.[23]

Planters in Southern Maryland frequently built kitchens separate from their dwellings. Few tenants on Zachiah Manor enjoyed this convenience, however, as only eight of the twenty-eight houses had detached kitchens. Among other improvements on the manor were six corn houses, the small number suggesting that most tenants stored their maize in tobacco barns, temporary cribs, or in the lofts of their dwellings. The low rate of slaveholding by manor tenants is reflected in the presence of only one slave quarter. Not a single barn or stable was found, indicating that the manor tenants followed the common but deleterious practice of providing no shelter for their animals. Three small tub mills, three dairies, and five outbuildings of unspecified use completed the complement of buildings. The only other improvement was orchards. The proprietary requirement that 100 trees be planted on each leasehold was exceeded by many manor tenants, although half of the manor lots had no fruit trees on them. Orchards ranged in size from 30 to 500 trees; the average contained over 190 (190.7). Apples dominated with over 3,000 trees, followed by peaches with over 1,200, and one orchard contained 6 cherry trees. The fruit from these orchards, either fresh or preserved, would have been an important supplement to the tenants' diet, but most of the product was undoubtedly processed into cider or brandy.[24]

The following picture emerges of tenancy on Zachiah Manor in the late colonial period. Most tenants had been on the manor for years; many had inherited their father's leasehold and had brothers, sisters, and other relations on the manor. But familiar surroundings and nearby friends and family could not entirely compensate for the lack of economic opportunity. Zachiah tenants may have been better off than their neighbors who paid much higher rents to private landlords, but the soil on the manor was poor and crop yields were low. Large families necessitated that much of the tenant's labor be devoted to the production of crops for home consumption, and the few acres that could be planted in cash crops barely covered necessary expenditures. Most tenants could not acquire the surplus capital needed to make improvements on their tenement, let alone to invest in land or labor. Cramped and crude dwellings constantly reminded tenants and their children that they were poor, and discouragement must have taken its toll on motivation and initiative. Frequent drafts of homemade cider and brandy may have provided temporary relief, but the fact of poverty was a reality that few could escape.

William Eddis, that "intelligent observer of the colonial [Maryland] scene," visited Frederick County early in 1771. Impressed by the settlements along the Monocacy River, Eddis attributed their prosperous look to the "disciplined . . . habits of industry, sobriety, frugality, and patience" of the Germans who had immigrated there.[25] Whether Eddis journeyed to Monocacy Manor on this trip is not known, but in spite of the small value of tenants' inventories, the number and quality of improvements on the manor indicate that Eddis's description could probably be applied to most tenants on the manor. The soil was productive, and the tenants were diligent husbandmen; as a result, residents on Monocacy Manor led more comfortable lives than tenants on Zachiah Manor.

There were sixty-four dwellings on Monocacy when the manor was examined in 1768, ranging in size from a 12-foot square structure to one that measured 22 feet wide by 48 feet long. The average house was 19.4 feet wide and 28.2 feet long and contained 558.2 square feet. The average dwelling on the manor still was not as large as the 600-square-foot building required in the tenants' leases, but it was more than twice the size of the average house on Zachiah Manor.[26]

The larger size of houses was in itself an important factor in making the quality of life on Monocacy Manor superior to that on Zachiah. Most Monocacy houses had sufficient floor space so that the ground floor could be divided into three rooms. Although only one dwelling on the manor was described as being two stories high, even the loft in the average Monocacy house would have been much more spacious than those on Zachiah Manor.[27] As a result, Monocacy tenants could better segregate activities within the house; they had more room for working, sleeping, and storage; and they had better opportunity to achieve some privacy in their homes.

Dwellings on Monocacy Manor were built of logs. Most were of simple construction, but they must have been more durable and provided better protection than the crude framed structures on Zachiah.[28] Chimneys, for example, were far superior on Monocacy houses. Of the thirty-six chimneys that are described, twenty-six were built of stone, nine of brick, and one of a combination of stone and brick. The other houses on the manor may have had wooden chimneys similar to those that appear to have characterized Zachiah dwellings, but at least a majority had chimneys of a more permanent and less hazardous construction.[29]

The larger size of the houses and the cooler climate of Frederick County minimized the necessity for separate kitchens on Monocacy Manor. Nevertheless, probably because of culturally inherited preferences, three tenants with English surnames had built detached kitchens on their tenements. The kitchens averaged 15.3 feet wide by 18.7 feet long, and although their construction is not described, they were undoubtedly built of logs in the same way as the dwellings on those tenements.[30]

Monocacy tenants grew little or no tobacco, which accounts for the presence of only one tobacco house on the manor. The care tenants bestowed on their crops and animals, however, is demonstrated by the number and size of their barns. The forty-nine barns on the manor tenements ranged in size from a lowly 17-by-20 foot structure to one that was 30 feet wide and 90 feet long. The average barn contained over 1,000 square feet, and many may have had more than one story. Although most dwellings on the manor were roofed with shingles, thatching was common on other buildings. Of the thirty-nine barns for which roofing is specified, nineteen were shingled and twenty were thatched. Thatching was not reserved for the humbler structures; the largest barn on the manor had a thatched roof.[31]

Eighteen stables provided additional shelter for animals on the tenements. Log side walls and thatched roofs again predominated. The average stable contained 277.2 square feet, exactly one square foot smaller than the average dwelling on Zachiah Manor. Other improvements on the manor included three blacksmith's shops, two weaver's shops, a "Dutch Church," and fifty-two outbuildings of unspecified use. Slightly more than 60 percent of the tenements had orchards, ranging from 8 to 360 trees; the mean size was 97.4 trees.[32]

What the probate records suggest, the description of manor improvements confirm: tenants on Monocacy Manor were relatively better off than tenants on Zachiah Manor. Tenants on both manors were dependent on agriculture as their major means of support, hence the higher standard of living Monocacy residents enjoyed must have been due to their ability to produce larger surpluses from their crops.

Three major factors appear to account for the fact that Monocacy tenants lived in better houses, had more improvements on their tenements, and left larger estates when they died than did tenants on Zachiah Manor. The first is the difference in ethnic composition of the tenant populations. Eddis's comments concerning the industry and frugality of the Germans in the Monocacy Valley is supported by numerous other eighteenth-century observers. Germans were particularly well suited to settle in the back country because they customarily practiced mixed farming instead of staple production, they usually did not need or want slaves, and they were willing to work hard for many years for little more than subsistence. They also had building skills particularly well adapted to life on the frontier. They knew how to build large, durable log houses, they could construct buildings and chimneys out of stone, and they could utilize local plant materials for thatching. The tenants on Zachiah Manor, on the other hand, lived in a region where one crop dominated the economy and where every neighborhood had a conspicuous example of a person who enjoyed great wealth and owned a large number of slaves. The differences in environment undoubtedly affected the way tenants on the two manors spent their money and time and what goals they set for themselves. But cultural factors were also important. As one historian has stated, English colonists "set their eyes on profits, with the comforts and social position these would bring," while Germans "dreamed of . . . bigger and better barns."[33] Some Englishmen had always lived on Monocacy Manor, and there is little discernable difference between them and the Germans in the type of improvements on their tenements or in the agricultural practices they followed. But this fact does not discount the superior abilities of the Germans. Rather, it indicates that the English, when removed from their traditional environment, would adopt the more economical and productive practices of their neighbors.[34]

A second and even more important reason why Monocacy tenants were able to produce larger surpluses from their crops was the quality of natural resources on the manor. In contrast to the deforested and depleted tracts on Zachiah Manor, Monocacy tenements were heavily timbered and had very rich soil. These natural resources, combined with an industrious tenantry, were undoubtedly important in accounting for the larger and more remunerative crops grown on the manor.

Finally, the fact that Monocacy tenants planted crops that required less labor to produce may have been the most important factor accounting for their greater prosperity. The labor available to tenants on both manors was essentially equal, since few tenants on either manor owned slaves or servants and families averaged about the same size. In spite of limited labor and poor natural resources, tenants on Zachiah Manor relied on two of the most labor-intensive crops possible: tobacco for sale and maize for home consumption. Tobacco required almost constant attention during the entire year, and corn had to be cultivated frequently during the growing season. Since Zachiah tenants could not afford to purchase or hire year-round laborers, the acreage they could plant was strictly limited by the number of field hands they could generate from within their own families.[35]

In contrast, the principal cash crop grown on Monocacy Manor was wheat, with rye grown as an important consumable. The ground had to be prepared before sowing both crops, but once that was accomplished it was neither necessary nor possible to cultivate the fields. Harvesting required two or three weeks of hard labor, but thereafter the grain could be either trod out quickly with horses or stored away to be threshed at a more convenient time. Because no labor was necessary during the growing season, the number of acres Monocacy wheat producers could plant was only limited by the number of workers available for the short period of harvest. If one or more additional laborers could be hired to assist in harvesting, or if neighbors could agree to help each other, the acreage planted could be increased well beyond what the family alone could manage.[36]

Just how much more profitable wheat was as a cash crop than tobacco depended on the number of workers in the tenant's family, the annual price of each commodity, and for wheat growers the availability of seasonal laborers. Tobacco prices fluctuated widely during the late-colonial period, but few tenants could have produced more than a hogshead a year, from which they would rarely have received more than £10 currency.[37] Because of the labor-conserving feature of wheat, most tenants could plant at least fifteen acres in the crop. Using a colony-wide average of between six and eight bushels per acre, fifteen acres would have produced about a hundred bushels of wheat.[38] In the 1760s, wheat usually sold for between 4 and 5 shillings currancy per bushel. At the lower price, a tenant would have made £20 from the sale of one hundred bushels. But Monocacy tenants undoubtedly produced larger crops than were usual elsewhere in the colony. One contemporary, noting that the manor contained "some of the most productive land" in the province, stated that some tenements yielded as much as twenty or twenty-five bushels of wheat per acre.[39] Consequently, the relative prosperity of Monocacy tenants compared to persons on Zachiah Manor was due to their concentration on labor-saving crops, and because those crops were planted on exceptionally fertile soil. The quality of life on Monocacy Manor was superior because the tenants invested their surpluses in the kinds of improvements that were conducive to that end.

In spite of better profit potential of wheat for persons who could not afford slaves or servants, Zachiah tenants remained dependent on tobacco as their principal cash crop. What a tenant could grow was determined by the trade and credit network of the area in which he lived. With large planters specializing in tobacco and local storekeepers demanding payment in the commodity, tenants had little recourse but to plant it also. Furthermore, farmers are traditionally conservative about altering their agricultural practices, and tenants who lacked surplus labor and risk capital could hardly have been expected to initiate innovations in the regional crop base.[40]

But if the prospects for economic success were so remote, why did so many Zachiah tenants remain on the manor instead of moving in search of greater opportunity? One reason is that the low rents and secure tenures of proprietary leases were more favorable than terms that could be gotten from most private landlords. Consequently, many tenants stayed on the manor and developed strong local attachments. Furthermore, even if they did occupy a position near the bottom of white society, tenants were socially superior to the large class of slaves and servants. Finally, by staying on the manor, a tenant could at least be assured of providing food for his family, something of which a man with little or no capital could not be certain even if be traveled to the frontier in search of cheap land.

In summary, tenants on Zachiah and Monocacy manors illustrate a range of life experiences possible for nonlandowners in Maryland in the late-colonial period. Although most tenants were poor, those who were industrious, cultivated wheat, and enjoyed the benefits of superior natural resources were able to provide a reasonably comfortable life for themselves and their families. But Monocacy Manor was exceptional in many respects. Zachiah tenants were able to produce only a bare subsistence, and what was true for them must have been typical for many small freeholders. Tenants on private land, who paid higher rents, must have had even greater difficulties. We do not know what percentage of the householders in Maryland in the mid-1760s were tenants, but there were probably nearly as many as when the 1783 state assessment was compiled. At that date, nonlandowners in Charles County comprised 53 percent of the households, and an additional 11 percent owned less than 100 acres of land. Few of these people could have been much better off than Zachiah tenants in the mid-1760s. The situation was similar in other parts of the province as well. By 1783, over 55 percent of the households in Talbot County on the Eastern Shore owned no land, nor did nearly half of those in Harford County at the head of Chesapeake Bay.[41] With limited opportunities for employment outside of agriculture, tenancy was one of the few viable alternatives for nonlandowners. Consequently, by the end of the colonial period, two large groups had developed in Maryland: those who owned land, and tenants who had little chance of ever doing so.

After the War for Independence, urban expansion and greater opportunities for migration gradually relieved the population pressure that had caused the growth of tenancy in Maryland.[42] Moving to the West or to the city may have offered tenants more of a perceived than an actual avenue for economic mobility, but many nonetheless left their leaseholds in the years following the war. As a result, tenancy in Maryland in the last decade of the colonial period represents the apex of its development rather than the foundation of a permanent and hereditary agrarian class.

NOTES

1. The statement concerning the number of nonlandowners in Maryland is based on an analysis of the 1783 State Assessment returns for Harford, Caroline, Charles, Calvert, Somerset, and Talbot counties. The assessment lists are in the Scharf Collection, Maryland Historical Society (hereafter cited as MHS). David Curtis Skaggs found a much higher percentage of nonlandowners in the colony than is indicated by the 1783 assessment. His study of colonial-Maryland society indicates that by 1756 freeholders comprised less than 50 percent of the free adult males in three of his four test counties (Baltimore, Prince George's, Queen Anne's, and Talbot), and by 1771, nonlandowners accounted for between 65.8 and 72.7 percent of the adults in those counties (*Roots of Maryland Democracy, 1753–1776* [Westport, Conn., 1973], pp. 40–41). Skaggs relied on the county Debt Books, which may underrecord the actual number of landowners. The important point, however, is that both Skaggs's work and the data from the 1783 assessment indicate that numerically, nonlandowners comprised the single largest group of householders in the province in the last half of the eighteenth century. Since there were few opportunities for employment outside agriculture, most of the nonlandowners must have been either tenants or laborers on other men's land.

2. Cecilius Calvert to Benjamin Tasker, 9 July 1752, *Calvert Papers, Number Two,* Maryland Historical Society Fund Publication No. 34 (Baltimore, 1894), pp. 148–49.

3. "A State of the Sales of His Lordships Mannours," signed by Horatio Sharpe and Daniel Dulany, n.d. [ca. April 1768], Executive Papers, portfolio 3, folder 19, mss., Hall of Records. (Unless otherwise noted, all documents cited are at the Hall of Records, Annapolis, Md.).

4. For the increase in the population of colonial Maryland, see *U.S. Bureau of the Census, Historical Statistics of the United States, Colonial Times to 1957* (Washington, D.C., 1960), series Z 13, p. 756. For the trend in land prices in the seventeenth century, see V. J. Wyckoff, "Land Prices in Seventeenth-Century Maryland," *American Economic Review* 28 (1938):82–88. The effect of the growing scarcity of vacant land on the demand for leaseholds is discussed by Clarence P. Gould in *The Land System in Maryland, 1720-1765,* Johns Hopkins Studies in Historical and Political Science 31 (Baltimore, 1913), pp. 67–81. The impact of the decline in tobacco prices is discussed by Russell R. Menard in "From Servant to Freeholder: Status Mobility and Property Accumulation in Seventeenth-Century Maryland," *William and Mary Quarterly,* 3d ser. 30 (1973):57–64.

5. The list of tenants on the manors is in the proprietary accounts for the year 1733, Calvert Papers, no. 914, MHS.

6. Manuscript lists of tenants on the manors in 1767–68 are in the Scharf Collection, box 12, MHS. The lists are printed in Gaius Marcus Brumbaugh, ed., *Maryland Records, Colonial, Revolutionary, County and Church,* 2 vols. (1915-28; reprint ed., Baltimore, 1967), 2:4–73. Brumbaugh made some errors in transcription, but for convenience further citation to those documents will refer to the printed source.

7. Proprietary Leases A–C; for examples of private leases, see Charles Carroll of Annapolis Account Book, 1754-84; Robert Darnall Ledger, 1787-1821; Hollyday Account Book, 1760-75; Edward Lloyd Memorandum Book, 1768-72, Lloyd Papers, box 4, all of which mss. are at the MHS.

8. Lord Baltimore initially ordered the sale of only five manors that he mistakenly believed were untenanted. He later expanded the commission to include all manors and reserved land in the colony; see Baltimore to Sharpe, 16 Jan. 1765, William Hand Browne et al., eds., *Archives of Maryland,* 72 vols. (Baltimore, 1883–), 14:189–93; ibid., 23 Feb. 1766; ibid., 32:134–40.

9. The manor contained only 6,000 acres when first surveyed in 1667. For relevant surveys and plats, see Patents 10:488, ms.; Executive Papers, portfolio 3, folder 19; Plats, division 4, no. 34, ms. For tenants on the manor, see Brumbaugh, *Maryland Records* 2:29–33.

10. Monocacy Manor was surveyed for 10,000 acres, see Patents IL no. B:198; Prince George's County Unpatented Certificates of Survey no. 1491–A, ms.; for tenants on the manor, see Brumbaugh, *Maryland Records* 2:51–60; the Claim of Henry Harford, ms., Audit Office 12/79 (hereafter cited as A.O. 12/79), Public Record Office, London, England.

11. A.O. 12/79, ff. 139/40.

12. Ibid., ff. 142–43.

13. Brumbaugh, *Maryland Records* 2:51–60; A.O. 12/79, ff. 142–43.

14. The underrepresentation of the poor in colonial Maryland probate records varied over time and from one county to another. In general, poor whites were more likely to have their estates inventoried in the seventeenth and early eighteenth century than they were at the end of the colonial period. The conclusion that the poor were substantially underrepresented in the probate records filed after the mid-eighteenth century is based on my own work with Talbot County inventories and an unpublished report prepared by Lois Green Carr of the St. Mary's City Commission. For general comments on the failure of some people, especially the poorer members of the community living outside population centers, to register vital statistics, see James H. Cassedy, *Demography in Early America: Beginnings of the Statistical Mind, 1600-1800* (Cambridge, Mass., 1969), pp. 36–37.

15. The probate records ranged in date from 1768 to 1794.

16. Estate size is defined as the total value of the inventory in current money, less the value of manor land if included, plus any additional inventories and assets added in the accounts of the estate. The inventory consisted of an itemized list of all personal property owned by the deceased. It was made by two court-appointed citizens, usually with the assistance of a relative and one or more creditors of the estate. The account was a report submitted by the executor or administrator to the county court listing the value of the inventory, all money received from debts due the estate, and all other income generated by the estate, as for example, the value of crops harvested. Because of the small number of tenants found in the probate records, no attempt has been made to weight the inventory values according to the age of the decedent or the date of death.

17. For a discussion of the economic problems faced by the small tobacco grower in late-colonial Maryland, see Edward C. Papenfuse, Jr., "Planter Behavior and Economic Opportunity in a Staple Economy," *Agricultural History* 46 (1972):297–311.

18. The dimensions of the average house were derived from the mean length and width of all houses on the manor. The dimensions given do not include the attached sheds that were recorded as being present on two dwellings.

19. Proprietary Leases A–C.

20. Excellent comparative evidence regarding tenant housing in Southern Maryland can be found in "Valuation of the Estate of Elizabeth Plater, orphan of Col. George Plater," St. Mary's County Valuations and Indentures, 1780–1808, ff. 159–60, and "Valuation of the orphan of Justinian Lewellin, viewed 10 May 1788," ibid., ff. 22–23; cf. Thomas Jefferson, *Notes of the State of Virginia,* ed. William Peden (Chapel Hill, 1955), p. 152; John Ferdinand Dalziel Smyth, *A Tour in the United States of America, 2 vols.* (1784; facsimile reprint, New York, 1968), 1:49.

21. John Demos discusses the relationship between large families, small dwellings, and personal tensions, although even in the early decades of settlement Plymouth houses were often larger than the average house on Zachiah Manor; see, *A Little Commonwealth: Family Life in Plymouth Colony* (1970; reprint. ed., Oxford University Press paperback, 1971), pp. 24–35, 46–51. The question of privacy and its relationship to dwelling size and construction is discussed by David H. Flaherty in *Privacy in Colonial New England* (Charlottesville, Va., 1972), pp. 33–59.

22. See for example, Fred Shelley, ed., "The Journal of Ebenezer Hazard in Virginia, 1777," *Virginia Magazine of History and Biography* 62 (1954):414 (hereafter cited as *VMHB*); Marquis de Chastellux, *Travels in North America in the Years 1780, 1781, and 1782 by the Marquis de Chastellux,* trans. and ed. Howard C. Rice, Jr., 2 vols. (Chapel Hill, 1963), 2:438; John Beale Bordley, *Essay and Notes on Husbandry and Rural Affairs,* 2d ed. (Philadelphia, 1801), pp. 182–83.

23. A.O. 12/79, ff. 139/40.

24. Ibid. A tub mill was the simplest form of grist mill utilizing a water wheel as the power source. The capacity of tub mills was small, so they usually served only one family or a few families in a neighborhood, see David D. Plater, "Grain Milling in Colonial Virginia: A Social and Economic History" (M.A. thesis, Tulane University, 1969), pp. 60–62.

25. Aubrey C. Land ed., *Letters from America* (Cambridge, Mass., 1969), p. 51.

26. A.O. 12/79, f. 142.

27. A two-story log tavern was located on the Lancaster Road on Lot 63 of the manor, see ibid.

28. Jefferson wrote: "The poorest people build huts of logs, laid horizontally in pens, stopping the interstices with mud. These are warmer in winter, and cooler in summer, than the most expensive construction of scantling and plank" (*Notes on Virginia,* p. 152). For information on log houses, see Harold R. Shurtleff, *The Log Cabin Myth: A Study of the Early Dwellings of the English Colonists in North America* (Cambridge, Mass., 1939); C. A. Weslager, *The Log Cabin in America: From Pioneer Days to the Present* (New Brunswick, N.J., 1969), esp. pp. 68–258; and Henry Glassie, *Pattern in the Material Folk Culture of the Eastern United States* (Philadelphia, 1968), pp. 36–55, 65–69, 79–83.

29. A.O. 12/79, f. 142.

30. Ibid.

31. Ibid. For a discussion of barn construction, see Glassie, *Folk Culture,* pp. 55, 92–93.

32. A.O. 12/79, f. 142.

33. Richard H. Shryock, "British versus German Tradition in Colonial Agriculture," *Mississippi Valley Historical Review* 26 (1939):46.

34. See for example, William Strickland, *Observations on the Agriculture of the United States of America* (1801; printed in facsimile in William Strickland's *Journal of a Tour in the United States of America, 1794–1795,* ed. J. E. Strickland [New York, 1971]), pp. 43–44. Other comments praising Germans for superior husbandry practices and frugality are discussed in James T. Lemon, *The Best Poor Man's Country: A Geographical Study of Early Southeastern Pennsylvania* (Baltimore, 1972), pp. xiv–xv, 235–36, n. 39. Lemon argues that cultural factors were less important than the social setting in determining how immigrants of any ethnic group responded to the challenges of the environment. He correctly observes that there were lazy

Germans in America, and that good husbandry was not confined to persons of that nationality, ibid., pp. xiv–xv, 17–18, 177, 183. Nevertheless, the fact that tenants on Monocacy Manor differed from Zachiah tenants in their willingness to spend capital and considerable labor in providing commodious structures for their families, crops, and animals, and that they preferred to invest in these instead of in slaves, silverware, carriages, and other items of display, suggests that the dominance of Germans on the manor did exercise an influence in altering the spending priorities typical of other inhabitants of Maryland.

35. According to William Tatham, "he who would have a good crop of tobacco, or of maize, must not be sparing of his labour, but must keep the ground constantly stirring during the whole growth of the crop" (G. Melvin Herndon, *William Tatham and the Culture of Tobacco. Including a Facsimile Reprint of an Historical and Practical Essay on the Culture and Commerce of Tobacco by William Tatham* [Coral Gables, Fl., 1969], pp. 17–18). For a good discussion of the labor involved in the production of tobacco, see Herbert S. Klein, "The Slave Economics of Cuba and Virginia: A Comparison," in *American Negro Slavery, a Modern Reader*, ed. Allen Weinstein and Frank Otto Gatell (New York, 1968), pp. 123–34; see also, Bordley, *Essay and Notes*, pp. 184–85.

36. Bordley, *Essay and Notes*, pp. 39, 245, 247, 269, 542.

37. Papenfuse, "Planter Behavior," pp. 303–5.

38. Among the more important sources of information on crop yields are Bordley, *Essay and Notes;* idem, *A Summary View of the Courses of Crops, in the Husbandry of England and Maryland* (Philadelphia, 1784); R. O. Bausman and J. A. Munroe, eds., "James Tilton's Notes on the Agriculture of Delaware in 1788," *Agricultural History* 20 (1946):183–84; [John Mitchell], *The Present State of Great Britain and North America* (1767; reprint ed., New York, 1970), p. 140; George Washington, "Estimate of the Cost of Mrs. Franch's Land . . ." [1790?], in *The Writings of George Washington from the Original Manuscript Sources, 1745–1799*, ed. John C. Fitzpatrick, 39 vols. (Washington, D.C., 1931–44), 31:188–89; Gertrude R. D. Richards, ed., "Dr. Stuart's Report to President Washington on Agricultural Conditions in Northern Virginia," *VMHB* 61 (1953):287; A. G. Bradley, ed., *The Journal of Nicholas Cresswell, 1774–1777*, 2d ed. (New York, 1928), p. 25. Cf. Lemon, *Best Poor Man's Country*, p. 154; Harry Roy Merrens, *Colonial North Carolina in the Eighteenth Century* (Chapel Hill, 1964), p. 234 n.

39. J[ohn] A[nstey], "Maryland. Upon the Subject of Confiscation," 20 April, 1787, Loyalist Claims, Series I, Reports from State Governments, 1787, Audit Office 12/94, Public Record Office, London, England, f. 114 (available on microfilm, Research Department, Colonial Williamsburg Foundation).

40. I elaborate on this theme in "Early American Farming: A Comment," *Agricultural History* 50 (1976):37–44; "'Gentlemen of Industry, Skill, and Application': Plantation Management in Eighteenth-Century Virginia" (unpublished report, Research Department, Colonial Williamsburgh Foundation, 1975), pp. 89–116; "Poverty in a Land of Plenty: Proprietary Tenants in Eighteenth-Century Maryland" (unpublished manuscript), ch. 4.

41. See note 1.

42. The reason tenancy had become a self-perpetuating institution in Maryland by the end of the colonial period, while the problem was not nearly so severe in the neighboring provinces of Pennsylvania and Virginia, is explained by the tenants' hesitancy to leave a familiar area and the financial difficulty of embarking on a long geographical move, compounded by the engrossment of fertile western lands by speculators and by the lack of a substantial frontier area in the colony. For the engrossment of western lands, see Aubrey C. Land, *The Dulanys of Maryland: A Biographical Study of Daniel Dulany, the Elder (1685–1753) and Daniel Dulany, the Younger (1722–1797)*, Studies in Maryland History No. 3 (Baltimore, 1955), pp. 170–84, and Charles Albro Barker, *The Background of the Revolution in Maryland* (1940; reprint ed., Archon Books, 1967), pp. 23–24. The lack of a frontier area to relieve population pressures within Maryland is graphically presented in the map, "Rural Population 1780," in Lester J. Cappon, Barbara Bartz Petchenik, and John Hamilton Long, eds., *Atlas of Early American History: The Revolutionary Era, 1760–1790* (Princeton, N.J., 1976), p. 64.

TEN

BALTIMORE AND THE PANIC OF 1819

Gary L. Browne

The panic of 1819 and the depression that followed transformed Baltimore's society and economy. New men with new patterns of behavior rose to power because their behavior conformed to the new realities, and the result made Baltimore very different by 1830 from what it had been in 1815. Naturally, those who could adapted the economic transformation to their own ends. Specifically, Baltimore's commercial elite used the financial revolution of the 1820s to gain control of their own marketing system. The nature of the transformation and the the way that the merchants used it is the subject of this study.[1]

The panic was not uniform everywhere but was a phenomenon composed of various causes and circumstances. There were two panics in Baltimore, one local and only indirectly related to the other, nationwide crisis. Both panics were complex, inescapable as they unfolded, and their combined effect upon the city cannot be overstated. They made changes irreversible that had begun with the aftermath of the War of 1812. The tremendous growth Baltimore had experienced during the previous three generations stopped, and after 1815 the city declined both absolutely and relative to other major American seaports. Though her merchant leaders did what they could to return to their prewar "golden age," nothing they did changed their postwar situation.[2]

Alterations in Baltimore's business and economic environment at the end of the war helped bring about the panic and its long-term consequences. These changes, which began in February 1815, occurred both in the domestic market economy—Baltimore's back country trade of Pennsylvania, Maryland, and Virginia—and in the international market economy. Both markets had shaped the character of Baltimore as a commercial or exchange market rather than a self-sufficient industrial center. The community was a depot for the two trades, and disruption in one produced repercussions in the other.

Note: Gary L. Browne is assistant professor of history, University of Maryland Baltimore County.

The first disturbances appeared in the domestic market. News of the end of the war caught westerners in the hinterland with high commodity prices and an expanded currency system based on country bank notes. Within one month, commodity prices plummeted, and most Baltimore merchants refused to accept the bank notes of western or country banks because of the notoriously small amounts of specie available for redeeming them. By October, every Baltimore bank was refusing to accept country bank notes, although several produce dealers, who were most dependent upon the trade, continued to accept them. Eventually, in November 1818, Baltimore's merchants jointly declared that they could no longer accept such nonnegotiable paper because it was not acceptable for their own debts at the banks.[3]

Dislocations in Baltimore's international trade first appeared in 1816, when two things became evident. One was that more goods were received from Britain than could be sold. This problem stemmed mainly from the traditional organization of Anglo-Baltimore trade. Baltimore merchants were merely seaport links in the chain of international credit that stretched from the back country American farmer to the British manufacturer or merchant. British manufacturers and merchants had long used the Baltimore market as a dumping ground in the sense that they determined what qualities and quantities of goods were sent there. They read the Baltimore market from 1815 to 1819 as (1) starved for industrial goods because of the war just ended, and (2) threatened by crudely made American goods that must be driven from the marketplace. Consequently, British goods inundated the Baltimore market and drove prices very low.[4]

Two things then happened. Prices were driven down to levels where the usually cheap and coarser American-made goods were no longer cheaper, and this democratized the selling structure of Baltimore's market. Traditionally, a small group of merchants had handled both the importing of goods and the auction sales. British shippers had consigned or sold their goods to specific merchants in Baltimore with whom they had had long-established relationships, and the legislature had designated two of the importers as licensed auctioneers. However, after 1815, British exporters were sending more goods than their traditional customers had ordered or even wanted. This situation invited almost any Baltimorean with connections and perhaps a little capital to set up as an importing merchant, although not always in the traditional way. The difficulties developing in the domestic marketing system led more and more importers to avoid purchasing British goods on their own account and begin advertising themselves as "commission merchants," meaning that they merely held the goods on consignment until sold. These changes also put pressure on the auction system, for the quantity of imported goods drove prices down so far that the auction system became the most practical selling method. But an expanded number of merchants without auctioneers licenses resented the legal monopoly on this form of selling, and there began a decade of controversy that finally ended in the destruction of the eighteenth-century auction system.[5]

These changes did not in themselves produce the panic or promote the depression that followed, but a second and more serious development in Baltimore's marketing methods did. The disappearing negotiability of country bank notes made it difficult for the Baltimore merchant importing from Britain to sell his goods in the hinterland without extending credit for long terms. As conditions deteriorated after 1816, more and more merchants sold to country buyers on credit for produce rather than for country bank notes. Baltimore merchants customarily purchased their goods from a British supplier on a nine-month credit and sold to a country buyer on a twelve-month credit. But with rising inventories and declining prices after 1815, and country bank notes neither negotiable in specie at the bank of issue nor acceptable in Baltimore banks, more and more merchants extended their sales credits from twelve to eighteen and then to twenty-four months. By 1819, many merchants were caught in the cash-flow problem of having no collections receivable to pay their own bills for several months. When this occurred, they had little choice but to "suspend" or fail. They and their British suppliers thus bore the brunt of the breakdown of the financial mechanism within the United States.[6]

The closing of Baltimore's traditional overseas markets intensified the financial problem. In 1815 several West European countries reverted to their pre-1793 mercantilist policies, which prevented Baltimoreans from trading with their colonies. Inasmuch as that trade had flourished during the wars from 1793 to 1812, this reversion in 1815 drastically circumscribed Baltimore's economic environment. The community not only lost the means of paying for an increasing volume of imported goods, but actually faced a declining export base.[7]

Specifically, Baltimore's merchants found themselves unable to export produce to the West Indies, the sources of the city's prosperity in foreign trade for four generations. Baltimore had exported foodstuffs, lumber, and naval supplies to the West Indies, where they were exchanged for cocoa, coffee, and sugars that were returned to Baltimore for reexportation in Europe. This vee-shaped pattern of trade underpinned the growth of Baltimore from the 1740s to 1783, and then from 1793 to 1812, as the town grew from a tiny cluster of houses into the third largest seaport in America. Now it was ended.

We are not disposed to risk our funds in shipments to any place whilst profits are small, and the losses probably very great. [wrote William and Richard H. Douglass in December 1816] We trust, however the time is not distant when an *old-fashioned commerce* [SIC] will come into play, and make the trade at last to the W Indies as interesting & profitable as it used to be.[8]

Throughout the 1820s, Baltimoreans consistently supported the efforts of the federal government to reopen the West Indies trade through commercial reciprocity agreements. But the British would not treat evenly with the Americans, partly because they were trying to make their West Indies colonies a re-export center for the American cotton trade, and partly because they were trying to undercut their American shipping rivals who had flourished during the wars of the French Revolution. Because of these circumstances in the historical trade pattern of the community, the Panic of 1819 contributed to a long depression in Baltimore's maritime economy.

In Baltimore, the panic itself began with a local banking crisis. Banking in Baltimore began in 1790, when some merchants, in response to their need for additional credit, organized the Bank of Maryland. Adapted from Philadelphia's model, the Bank of North America, founded in 1781,[9] the Maryland bank was launched as a form of mercantile credit: short-term, renewable loans called discounts, made only to businessmen. And then came the wars of the French Revolution that expanded opportunities even beyond the expectations and financial means of Baltimore's already prosperous merchants. Banks proliferated—the Bank of Baltimore appeared in 1795, the Union Bank of Maryland in 1804, the Mechanics' Bank in 1807, the Commercial & Farmers' Bank in 1810, the Farmers' & Merchants' Bank in 1810, the Franklin Bank in 1810, the Marine Bank in 1810, and the City Bank in 1813. A branch of the first Bank of the United States also operated in Baltimore from 1792 until 1811. Their names suggest how these early banks served as credit institutions for specific occupations: for mechanics, that is, manufacturers, the Mechanics' and Franklin banks; for importing merchants, the Union and the Farmers' & Merchants' banks; for dealers in western produce, the Commercial & Farmers' bank; for coastal traders, the Marine bank; and for Jeffersonian Republicans, the Union bank. One can also see that four banks replaced the branch of the first Bank of the United States in 1811. None of these were banks of deposit in our modern sense; they were lending institutions only; and where deposits were referred to, they were really loans credited to (or "deposited" in) the accounts of borrowers.[10]

The proliferation of banks as credit institutions contributed to the monetization of credit, of course, but therein lay one source of later banking problems. Bank notes made merchants' business relationships more impersonal than did the older forms of money, such as bills of credit or bills of exchange. With these older forms of money, the merchants' property and personality stood directly behind their notes, but with bank notes only the bank's property stood behind them. A bank was dependent upon the personal reputation of its officers and members of its board of directors. Its property was usually negligible: office supplies, a little specie, and possibly the building and the lot on which it stood. Banks were legal fictions; and bank notes were really evidences of debt rather than legal tender required by law to be convertible into specie. Banks merely represented the financial aspect of a merchant's activity, and though they could legally function as a financial equal to a merchant, they were clearly devices without a merchant's personality. To use Adam Smith's distinction, bank notes were measures of value but were not wealth in themselves.[11] In 1819, after the prosperity that obscured this knowledge had vanished, Baltimoreans were forced to redefine this social basis of money.

In 1815, Baltimore's nine banks had a paid-in capital of $6,503,685. Their specie holdings cannot be ascertained, but contemporaries remarked that in comparison with either Philadelphia or New York, Baltimore had very little. From 1815 to 1819 most of it came from the South American trade, not because the trade was large—it was not—but because specie was the only commodity that the South American revolutionaries had to trade. When specie arrived in Baltimore, however, New York and Philadelphia banks quickly drained off most of it by drafts on Baltimore banks, because New York and Philadelphia represented more inclusive trading markets, and their banks usually carried balances against those in Baltimore. Baltimore banks thus reflected the community's postwar shrinkage of exports and the consequent inability of bankers to advance credit to importing merchants, who were gradually being drawn into the cash-flow predicament.[12]

Table 10.1 presents the fullest picture available of the Baltimore banks from 1817 through 1830. The calculations of their circulation and deposits are in percentages and reflect the changes from one year to the next. The enormous decrease of 62 percent in the note circulation from 1817 through 1823 alone testifies to the severity of the financial collapse; but even for the fourteen-year period as a whole, bank note circulation declined over 52 percent. Simultaneously, bank deposits, that is, loans already credited to accounts, fell off by over 40 percent from 1817 through 1823, and 35 percent for the entire period. Less money and less credit were two sides of the same coin; together, they reflected the general depression in Baltimore's maritime economy resulting from the new environment after the war.

Social as well as economic circumstances were responsible for this devastating reduction of banking facilities; a scandal involving breaches of faith and trust among bankers themselves contributed to the onset of the Panic of 1819 and the ensuing depression. The scandal centered upon the branch Bank of the United States, whose president and directors were among the leading merchants of the city—and, indeed, of the United States. Because this scandal triggered the Panic of 1819 in Baltimore, contemporaries confused the behavior of local bankers with the changing objective conditions in which they lived. Contemporaries were right, however, in focusing attention upon the actions of these men; their behavior, though not

TABLE 10.1
Circulation and Deposits in Baltimore Banks, 1817-1830

| | | | Percentage Changes from One Year to Another | |
| | | | Circulation Increase (Decrease) | Deposits Increase (Decrease) |
Year	Circulation	Deposits		
1817	$2,727,230	$2,108,560		
1818	1,742,780	1,697,290	(36)	(20)
1819	1,662,320	1,248,470	(5)	(26)
1820	1,229,540	1,226,690	(26)	(2)
1821	1,020,080	1,382,850	(17)	13
1822	1,214,030	1,533,440	19	11
1823	1,031,750	1,261,330	(15)	(18)
1824	1,113,750	1,441,160	8	14
1825	1,537,610	1,581,850	38	10
1826	1,519,190	1,528,220	(1)	(3)
1827	1,347,690	1,629,620	(11)	7
1828	1,272,190	1,724,160	(6)	6
1829	1,422,970	1,633,010	12	(5)
1830	1,299,760	1,349,770	(9)	(17)

Source: Alfred Cookman Bryan, *History of State Banking in Maryland* (Baltimore, 1899), p. 137.

criminal, grossly violated traditional business practices and precipitated social changes as potent as those stemming from Baltimore's altered environment.

When the Panic of 1819 broke on May 20, 21, and 22, contemporaries referred to the men involved as a "Club" of speculators. At the inception of the second Bank of the United States during the winter of 1816–17, the "Club" had originated among men eager to speculate in the bank's stock and to dominate the institution if possible. James A. Buchanan, partner and first cousin of Samuel Smith in one of the largest mercantile firms in the United States, probably directed the "Club's" operations. Buchanan, whose political faction dominated Baltimore politics, was well connected and enjoyed a national reputation among seaport merchants and politicians. John Jacob Astor had nominated him for the presidency of the new national bank; and such was Buchanan's prestige that, even after that honor fell to William Jones, the Baltimorean occasionally offered Jones suggestions about bank policies. Given his national connections, his standing in Baltimore, and his reputation for financial sagacity, it was hardly surprising that Buchanan was chosen president of the Baltimore branch of the national bank.[13]

The cashier of the branch was James William McCulloh [not McCulloch, as it usually appears in print] of *McCulloch vs. Maryland* fame. Born in Philadelphia and educated in the Baltimore counting-house of George

Williams, McCulloh was only twenty-seven years old in 1819. His later career as banker, lawyer, Speaker of the House of Delegates in the Maryland legislature, land speculator in association with Duff Green, and finally, first comptroller in the United States Treasury Department, testifies at least to his energy and attention to opportunity. He, too, wrote President Jones long letters suggesting national bank policies, usually in vein similar to Buchanan's. Joining Buchanan and McCulloh were a clique of Massachusetts-bred brothers and their Rhode Island cousin: George, Amos A., and Cumberland Dugan Williams, and cousin Nathaniel Williams, who participated in the stock speculations from the very beginning, along with two other merchants, Lemuel Taylor and Dennis A. Smith (no relation to Samuel). At first, these officers and directors of the branch bank merely used their existing stockholdings as security to finance additional stock purchases, but soon they were using the branch's credit without any such security. "Club" members then used the bank's credit and money as their own to finance their private and individual mercantile operations. During 1817 the accounts of the branch were increasingly confused by this blending of private with public enterprise. Beginning in the summer of 1818, the price of the bank's stock declined because of the generally collapsing financial and marketing systems and because of rumors about these bank stock speculators.

Apart from its internal difficulties, the national bank was enmeshed in the deteriorating postwar economic situation; and this, together with the behavior of President Jones, who was also speculating in his bank's stock, turned businessmen against the management of the bank. More than Jones's rumored stock speculations was involved, however; his business ability was also questioned. For example, his handling of the major postwar financial problem, the resumption of specie payments, created much dissatisfaction and some financial loss. Specifically, the resumption of specie payments by Baltimore banks on 20 February 1817, when the national bank began operations, grew to crisis proportions within five months because the national bank and its branches now joined New York and Philadelphia banks in drafting specie from Baltimore banks. This move forced the Baltimore institutions to restrict their credit and thus reduce their note circulation. In August 1817, the banks went so far as to refuse to discount the business paper of the auctioneers, who were doing the heaviest importing business in the city, and in September, the Baltimore branch of the national bank stopped issuing drafts to eastern banks (especially those in New York) that were drafting specie from Baltimore. Such financial instability in the operations of the national bank raised questions about its management, doubts partially expressed in the declining price of the bank's stock.

At this point, the "Club" of speculators might have been able to weather the declining price of the bank stock if either external conditions or the management of the bank had improved. Neither did. In October 1818, a committee of the House of Representatives, chaired by the recently elected John Canfield Spencer of upstate New York, began an investigation of the bank's management. When Jones's stock speculations stood revealed, he resigned in January 1819, and Langdon Cheves of South Carolina was elected to replace him. Cheves immediately turned his attention to the Baltimore branch, and the members of the "Club" faced an investigation from February through May.

To begin with, President Cheves authorized the parent bank in Philadelphia to draft specie from the Baltimore branch. This forced the branch to demand that the balances due it from the other Baltimore banks be paid in specie. The ensuing "run" on the other banks was compounded when the community learned about what was happening, and everyone who could do so presented his bank notes to the banks of issue and demanded specie. Furthermore, because banks, as a vestiage of eighteenth-century private society, were not subject to legal regulations governing holdings of specie and note circulation, and because it was painfully obvious that there were far more bank notes in circulation than there was specie in the bank vaults, the bank notes rapidly depreciated in value during February. On 24 February 1819, the Maryland legislature tried to halt the depreciation by enacting a law prohibiting bank officers from trading notes of any Maryland bank for less than their denominational values and forbidding money brokers to present notes to the banks of issue and demanding specie. Such legal remedies failed, and the drain of specie, together with its contraction of circulation, continued.

Coming on top of the lengthened periods of credit in the western trade, this new credit and monetary crisis broke many merchants who could no longer acquire bank loans on their accounts receivable to pay their own debts. In consequence Baltimore's commercial structure collapsed in a chain reaction. Failures among merchants began in March, increased in April, and rose to a crescendo in May. In this last month, the financial collapse reached the banks themselves. The newest banking house, the City Bank, failed and the Union Bank of Maryland almost failed because their cashiers, James Sterett and Ralph Higgenbotham, respectively, had embezzled their bank's funds in order to speculate in the stock of the national bank for their personal accounts.[14]

But the worst event in May was the collapse of the "Club" of speculators connected with the Baltimore branch of the Bank of the United States. After months of investigation President Cheves' administration dismissed McCulloh from the cashiership and appointed John White in his place. At the time, McCulloh's accounts were about $150,000 in arrears. Unlike McCulloh, James A. Buchanan, the president of the branch, could not be dismissed because he had been elected by the directors of the branch, not by the parent bank. He remained in office until 26 May when pressure from several directors forced him to resign. His successor, John Donnell, and John White, the new cashier, discovered the following day that their first teller, John L. La Reintrie, had pilfered approximately $50,000 since his appointment in December 1816.[15]

These bank defalcations severely jolted the community. The loss of currency and bank credit was in itself considerable. It totaled according to estimate over $806,548 for the three banks, but in actuality it added up to an unknown figure. A second and more serious jolt was the blow to the social economy of banking. The defaulters were members of some of Baltimore's old and powerful families, who made up the city's mercantile-landed gentry elite. Their failure of character was neither a personal, private matter nor a matter of their mere incompetence; it was a matter of public or social concern, because it undermined one of the corner-stones of eighteenth-century society—the faith and trust in the elite as exemplifying the best in society. The fraudulent conduct involved in these bank failures called into consciousness the need for more adequate social controls to prevent such behavior in the future. But changing Baltimore's banking practices involved changing their social moorings; and therein lay one source of the transformation of eighteenth-century society during the 1820s.

After the banking crisis had brought about several prominent mercantile failures in May, the second panic—originating in the larger network of Baltimore's national and international relationships—struck the city in June. The two panics blended into one during the summer of 1819 to produce a community-wide crisis. Mercantile failures continued regularly from May through August and sporadically through September, October, and November. Though the failures occurred in clusters, the collapse was general because the credit and financial network was socially interdependent. A merchant, caught in his cash-flow predicament and faced with the bank's curtailment of circulation and credit, was forced to "suspend" —meaning that he gave public notice, not that he was bankrupt, but that he was stopping business transactions in hopes that his collections would catch up to his debt payments. If and when they did, he would engage in business again. But when he failed, or "suspended," merchants to whom he was indebted could no longer count upon payments from him, and they found themselves in the same cash-flow predicament as the first merchant. Of course, many of these failures resulted from mercantile failures in other cities and countries, as well as from uncollected western debts; and in this sense, the panic was universal. Although part of the origins of the panic in Baltimore may have been very different from its origins in other major American seaports, the course of the panic was the same for all.[16]

Baltimore society turned a corner, as it were, after the Panic of 1819: the 1820s marked a different era from the one before. Fundamental economic relationships changed in both the domestic and international contexts that enabled Baltimoreans to shed their market vassalage to Great Britain and to become economically independent for the first time. True, the post-panic depression was merely one of a number of general conditions present during the twenties—others included domestic problems within all the West European societies, a general reversion to the ideals of their pre-French Revolution "golden ages," and the reestablishment of mercantilist policies —but the financial revolution in the United States, coupled with Britain's preoccupation with its own troubles, were the proximate causes of Baltimore's and American's, new independence.

The financial revolution in the United States began a new, more sophisticated stage in the economy of banking, a stage that would eventually dominate American banking theory and practice during the nineteenth century. Increasing numbers of Baltimore merchants and bankers agreed with their British counterparts that money could no longer be mere credit, that it must represent a more permanent and stable value than the words of men. They read and accepted the ideas of David Ricardo's *Proposals for an Economic and Secure Currency* (1816), Dr. Justus Erick Bollmann's *A Letter to Thomas Brand, Esq., M. P. for the County of Hertford, on the Practicability and Propriety of a Resumption of Specie payments* (1819), and William Huskisson's *The Question Concerning the Depreciation of our Currency Stated and Examined* (1810), all of which favored a specie-based currency system. Money changed meaning and became more than the measure of value: it became wealth itself.[17]

The idea of a specie-based currency acquired great popularity during the depressed twenties because it suggested permanence and stability; and, accordingly, banking practices underwent certain changes for the same reason. One change was that banks began to require property—personal and real—as collateral security for loans. Baltimoreans had not required such collateral before November 1819. Lenders had granted credit on the basis of the borrower's personal note together with one or sometimes two cosigners, called "endorsers". If a bank debtor wished to extend his loan, or to enlarge it, he had to add other endorsers. This kind of credit policy reflected the personal and social basis of business activities; it also explains why the failures of 1819 were so devastating. They were moral and social failures, and the tearing of the social fabric necessitated its repair by changing the social underpinning of banking in the name of adjusting the financial mechanism itself. Changing the social system of trust from men to property paralled the shift from credit to specie-based money, and both reflected the depersonalization—and democratization—of society during the 1820s.[18]

Changes also occurred in the administrative procedures of banking. The failure and near failures of the three banks in 1819 stemmed from the fact that bank cashiers were in positions to abuse their office. Because they handled the day-to-day business of their banks, they knew more about the condition of their banks at any one time than did the bank presidents or directors. In fact, cashiers had all too easily blended the routine affairs of their office with the policy decisions. After 1819, the boards of directors became the powerful, policy makers of banking administration, and committees of the directors fulfilled particular functions. The roles of both the cashier and the president were restricted to implementing the policies established by the board. Such a change democratized banking by broadening administrative decisions.[19]

But the broadest change characterizing the financial revolution of the 1820s was the work of the second Bank of the United States. The BUS standardized domestic exchange markets through its branch offices by providing a national currency system for country merchants to use on their buying trips to the seaports. The country merchant could now exchange his country bank notes for BUS notes, at par value, in one of the western branches, or else open a credit there, and bring either the BUS notes or a draft with him to the Atlantic seaport. Since his country notes were not discounted, he lost no money in the exchange; he now had ready currency with which to purchase his goods; and he was no longer restricted to buying from seaport merchants, who would advance him credit by accepting either country bank notes at a huge discount or western produce at the merchant's price. With ready currency in hand the country buyer was free to shop for the lowest price. The result threatened a change in the national marketing structure as the seaport merchants lost their power to dominate the country buyer.[20]

Once prices and not credit became the focus of bargaining, seaport sellers had little choice but to reduce profit margins and try to expand sales. Baltimore's importers attempted to do this in three ways. First they continued the attack, begun before the panic, on the legal monopoly of auctioneering and, in 1827, finally succeeded in expanding the number of auctioneers from two to twenty. Second, they adopted an English merchandising device—the "commercial traveler"—into the American economy as the "drummer." A traveling representative of an importing merchant firm, the drummer had become a fixture in the domestic marketing process by the end of the 1820s. His function was to undercut the sales methods of auctioneers—cash sales at high volume and low prices—by selling direct to country merchants in their own markets so that they would not have to visit the seaport selling markets. Third, the importers began sending business partners to Great Britain to act as purchasing agents, or appointing native Britons as buyers. Like their country merchant customers, the Baltimore merchants now could shop for goods because they did not sell the goods on long-term credit and were less dependent on credit themselves. Such buying innovations cut the importer's cost in the trans-Atlantic trade. These savings were passed on to the country merchants, thus enabling the importers to compete with auctioneers in selling to the country buyers.[21]

These last measures did more than enable Baltimore importers to sell at competitive prices. By employing buyers in England who could shop for bargains, the Baltimore merchant achieved independence from his supplier. The British merchant no longer determined the kind and amount of the goods his Baltimore customer could sell. For the first time in the peacetime history of the city, the merchants began to control their imports.

As their controls became firmer in the trans-Atlantic trade, the importers turned to the domestic market and especially the operations of the BUS. They were hostile to the BUS for its disruption of both the traditional "commercial interest" and the national marketing system. The merchants were determined to recapture control of the domestic market and restore the old ways, and the traveling drummer was a long step in this direction. The "Bank War" of the early 1830s, which destroyed the BUS, was the culmination of their efforts. Epitomizing the cultural conservatism of Jacksonian politics, the merchants overrode the socially progressive functions of the BUS.

All told, during the 1820s Baltimore's commercial leaders proved creative and resourceful in putting the changes that had disrupted their earlier marketing system to work for their own benefit. But this story of how a powerful social interest responded to changes that threatened it should not obscure the irony. The merchants achieved their autonomy at the very time that their city's maritime economy went into a long and severe decline. Their banding together in 1827 to create the Baltimore & Ohio Railroad Company as a means of enlarging their markets is evidence that they understood their predicament perfectly well. But the railroad—as a symbol for all internal improvements—introduced something more than a quantitatively larger domestic market. It introduced the qualitative changes in Baltimore's social and economic organization that we have come to associate with the later nineteenth century. In this way, Baltimore's merchants contributed to the historical changes that eventually undermined their society and economy.

NOTES

1. Three studies treat the general impact of the Picnic of 1819 upon American society as a whole: Samuel Rezneck, "The Depression of 1819–1822, A Social History," *American Historical Review* 32 (1933):28–47; William W. Folz, "The Financial Crisis of 1819: A Study in Post-War Economic Readjustment" (Ph.D. diss., University of Illinois, 1935); and Murray N. Rothbard, *The Panic of 1819, Reactions and Policies* (New York, 1962). Other studies that focus upon particular localities are Dorothy Baker, Dorsey, "The Panic of 1819 in Missouri," *Missouri Historical Review* 29 (1935):79–91; Thomas H. Greer, "Economic and Social Effects of the Depression of 1819 in the Old Northwest," *Indiana Magazine of History* 44 (1948):227–43; and Joseph H. Parks, "Felix Grundy and the Depression of 1819 in Tennessee," *Publications of the East Tennessee Historical Society* 10, no. 10 (1938):19–43. But also see George Dangerfield, *The Era of Good Feelings* (New York, 1952), pp. 175–96; idem, *The*

Awakening of American Nationalism, 1815–1828 (New York, 1965), ch. 3; Douglass C. North, *The Economic Growth of the United States, 1790–1860* (New York, 1966), pp. 182–88; Malcolm J. Rohrbough, *The Land Office Business: The Settlement and Administration of American Public Lands, 1789–1837* (New York, 1968), ch. 7; Walter Buckingham Smith, *Economic Aspects of the Second Bank of the United States* (Cambridge, Mass., 1953), pp. 26–28, 40–41, 75–78, 99–133; George Rogers Taylor, *The Transportation Revolution, 1815–1860* (New York, 1951), pp. 334–38; and Frederick Jackson Turner, *The Rise of the West, 1819–1829* (New York, 1962), ch. 9.

2. Summary paragraphs such as this one are drawn from the fuller description of post war Baltimore in Gary Lawson Browne, "Baltimore in the Nation, 1789–1861: A Social Economy in Industrial Revolution" (Ph.D. diss., Wayne State University, 1973), pp. 120–206.

3. Thomas and Samuel Hollingsworth to Levi Hollingsworth, 20 Feb., 16 and 18 March, 9, 20, 23, and 26 Oct., 26 Nov. 1815, 6 March, 22 July, 5 Sept. 1816, 2 Jan., 3, 13, and 18 Feb., 27 March, 4 July, 2 and 10 Sept., 31 Oct., 5 Nov. 1817, 30 Oct., 23 Nov., 14 Dec. 1818, Hollingsworth Papers, mss., Historical Society of Pennsylvania; R. Crane to James Cox, 27 April, 1815, Alexander Lanier to James Cox, 26 Oct. 1817, Corner Collection, mss., Maryland Historical Society; Matthew Smith to James Potts, 12 Jan. 1816, to John Wyld, 27 Nov. 1818, Tyson Papers, mss., Maryland Historical Society; William and Richard H. Douglass to R. Richardson, 6 Jan. 1817, Douglas Letterbook, ms., Maryland Historical Society; James Robinson to Benjamin Clap, 11 Oct. 1817, Clap Family Papers, mss., Burton Historical Society; Alex. Brown & Sons to William Gihon & Son, 15 Dec. 1818, Brown Letterbooks, mss., Library of Congress; Thomas Bond to Major James Thomas, 21 May 1817, Thomas Family Papers, mss., Maryland Hall of Records; *Federal Gazette & Baltimore Daily Advertiser,* 15 Oct. 1815, 6 June, 10 and 12 Sept., 18 Dec. 1816, 5 and 7 Aug. 1817, 27 Nov. 1818; *Niles' Weekly Register,* no. 15, 12 Dec. 1818, p. 283; Baltimore *Patriot,* 13 Oct. 1818.

4. Isaac and Thomas Edmondson to Mayson, Grave & Co., 5 Nov. 1816, to John Roberts, 6 Nov. 1816, to John and Jacob Wakefield, 8 Nov. 1816, to Richard Blackstock & Co., 8 Nov. 1816, 30 Sept. 1817, 12 Oct. 1818, to James Schofield, 12 Nov. 1816, 27 Sept. 1817, to John W. Adams & Co., 14 Nov. 1816, 17 May 1817, 23 March 1818, to John Horsburgh, 15 Nov. 1816, 10 June 1817, Edmondson Letterbook, ms., Maryland Historical Society; Matthew Smith to James Potts, 4 and 26 Sept. 1815, 18 April 1816, 26 Feb., 26 Nov. 1818, to John Wyld, 17 Oct., 28 Nov., 15 Dec. 1815, 20 July, 8 Oct., 16 Nov. 1816, 28 Feb. 1818, to William Redhead & Co., 18 April 1816, Tyson Papers; William and Richard H. Douglass to Staniforth & Blunt, 10 Sept., 1 Nov., 2 Dec. 1816, 28 April, 14 June, 18 July 1817, to W. & A. Maxwell, 7 Sept., 31 Oct. 1816, Douglass letterbook; Thomas and Samuel Hollingsworth to Levi Hollingsworth, 6 and 18 March 1815, 6 March 1816, 2 Jan., 10 May 1817, Hollingsworth Papers. An excellent editorial about the nature of the social economy being a "chain of Credit that needs to be reaffirmed" is in the *Morning Chronicle & Baltimore Advertiser* for 15 Dec. 1820.

5. Licensing of auctioneers was the prerogative of the state until 1797 when Baltimore was incorporated and the city assumed that power. By a City Ordinance of 27 April 1797, the number of auctioneers (two) was continued as under the state's former authority. Both auctioneers enjoyed a virtual monopoly over auction sales in the sense that fines were prescribed for others who sold goods at auctions. Their monopoly continued until 1827, when the state reasserted its prerogative over the licensing of auctioneers, expanded their number from two to twenty, and retained the receipts dereived from such licensing and fees. *Laws of Maryland,* 1781, ch. 11; 1784, ch. 61; 1785, ch. 77; 1790, ch. 12; 1827, ch. 111; *City Ordinances,* 27 April 1797, 20 Feb. 1801.

6. In addition to the sources cited in note 5, see William Morris to Alexander Fridge, 14 March 1815, George Morris to Fridge & Morris, 14, 17, 22, 23, 24, 26, 28, 30, and 31 July, 6, 10, and 12 Aug. 1819, Bond Family Papers, mss., Maryland Historical Society; William Cooke to William E. Williams, 14 and 22 May, 7 and 13 June 1816, 11 June 1817, Otho Holland Williams Papers, mss., Maryland Historical Society; Charles F. Mayer to Mayer & Brantz, 17 and 26 May, 5 and 13 June, 14 and 20 Aug. 1818, Brantz Mayer Papers, mss., Maryland Historical Society; Hall Harrison to Hugh Thompson, 5 July 1816, David Stewart to Samuel Thompson, 3, 15, and 23 May 1816, Hugh Thompson Papers, mss., Maryland Historical Society; Donald Chester to John Myers, 20 Sept., 4 Oct., 11 Aug. 1817, 29 Aug., 3 Dec. 1818, to Frederick Myers, 15 April 1819, John Hastings to John Myers, 17 and 23 June, 1 July, 1 and 23 Sept. 1819, Myers Family Papers, mss., Norfolk Museum of Arts and Sciences.

7. Browne, "Baltimore in the Nation," pp. 120–65.

8. William and Richard H. Douglass to R. H. Windsor, 4 Dec. 1816, Douglass Letterbook.

9. George Salmon to George Moore, 15 March 1784, Woolsey & Salmon Letterbook, 1774–84, ms., Library of Congress.

10. A list of the banks in Baltimore in 1817 can be found in *Niles' Weekly Register*, no. 13, 27 Dec. 1817, p. 281. The list includes such information as their dates of incorporation, their capitalization, the amounts of capital paid in, and the names of their presidents and cashiers. Additional information about the early banks in Baltimore is scarce and must be pulled together from several sources. Individual charters were printed in the newspapers, especially the *Baltimore American & Daily Commercial Advertiser* after 1800. The only study of the general subject is Alfred Cookman Bryan, *History of State Banking in Maryland* (Baltimore, 1899). My understanding of the social economy of late eighteenth and early nineteenth-century banking is derived from a wide reading in primary sources, and from Bray Hammond, *Banks and Politics in America from the Revolution to the Civil War* (Princeton, N.J., 1957), pp. 40–226; Thomas Payne Govan, *Nicholas Biddle: Nationalist and Public Banker, 1786–1844* (Chicago, 1959): and Fritz Redlich, *The Molding of American Banking; Men and Ideas: Part I: 1781–1840* (New York, 1947).

11. Adam Smith, *An Inquiry into the Nature and Causes of the Wealth of Nations* (New York, 1937), p. 398.

12. *Federal Gazette & Baltimore Daily Advertiser,* 6 March, 6, 7, 9, and 10 Sept., 12 Dec. 1816, 3, 6, 12, and 26 Feb., 26 April, 28 May, 16 July 1817; *Baltimore Patriot,* 15 and 16 Oct., 5 Dec. 1818; *Niles' Weekly Register,* no. 15, 12 Dec. 1818, p. 285; Robert & John Oliver to John & Thomas H. Perkins, 29 Aug. 1815, Letterbook, 1809–1817, Oliver Record Books, mss., Maryland Historical Society; William and Richard H. Douglass to John Cullen, 1 Oct. 1816, to S. & J. C. Hollingsworth, 19 Dec. 1816, Douglass Letterbook; Matthew Smith to James Potts, 29 Dec. 1815, 12 Jan., 18 April 1816, to William Redhead & Co., 18 April 1816, to John Wyld, 12 Dec. 1816, Tyson Papers; Thomas and Samuel Hollingsworth to Levi Hollingsworth, 9 and 26 Oct., 10 Nov. 1815, 22 July, 5 and 26 Sept. 1816, 13, 18 and 22 Feb., 4 July, 2 and 10 Sept. 1817, 30 Oct., 23 Nov., 14 Dec. 1818, Hollingsworth Papers; Henry Didier to John D'Arcy, 7 and 27 March, 5 May 1815, Didier Collection, mss., Maryland Historical Society. Baltimore's banking capital actually paid in was almost 80 percent of that for the entire state of Maryland (calculated from the table of Maryland banks in *Niles' Weekly Register,* no. 13, 27 Dec. 1817; p. 281).

13. I have pieced together the following story of the Baltimore branch of the Bank of the United States from these sources: the Jonathan Meredith Papers, mss. in both the Library of Congress and the Duke University Library; the Langdon Cheves Papers, mss., South Carolina Historical Society; Records of the Baltimore Branch of the Second Bank of the United States, mss., Library of Congress; the Samuel Smith Papers, mss., in the Maryland Historical Society, the Library of Congress, and the University of Virginia Library; John White Papers, mss., in the Maryland Historical Society and the Duke University Library; Nicholas Biddle Papers, mss., Library of Congress; Uselma C. Smith Papers, mss., Historical Society of Pennsylvania; Hollingsworth Papers; Biddle Family Papers, mss., Library of Congress; Etting Papers, mss., Historical Society of Pennsylvania; Brown Letterbooks, Lyde Goodwin's Diary, mss., Maryland Historical Society; Gratz Collection, mss., Historical Society of Pennsylvania; William H. Crawford Papers, mss., in the Library of Congress and the Duke University Library; Ralph C. H. Catterall, *The Second Bank of the United States* (Chicago, 1960), pp. 39–53, 64–69, 78; Govan, *Nicholas Biddle,* pp. 57–58; Hammond, *Banks and Politics,* pp. 260–62; W. B. Smith, *Economic Aspects,* pp. 99–116.

14. Thomas and Samuel Hollingsworth to Levi Hollingsworth, 14 Jan., 13 and 27 Feb., 27 March, 2, 8, 10, and 12 April, 20 May 1819, Hollingsworth Papers; Langdon Cheves to John White, 18, 22, 26, and 27 May, 9, 12, 16, 23, and 28 June, 19 and 24 July, 3 and 5 Aug., 17 Oct. 1819, John White to Langdon Cheves, 20 and 23 May, 28 June, 3, 12, 18, 21, 22, and 26 July, 9 and 13 Aug., 15, 20, and 29 Sept., 4, 6, 8, and 14 Oct. 1819. R. L. Colt to John White, 4 Aug. 1819, Richard B. Magruder to John White, 7 Sept. 1819, John White Papers; Thomas and Isaac Edmondson to Richard Blackstock & Co., 17 April 1819, to Rathbone, Hodgson & Co., 20 April 1819, Edmondson Letterbook; Alex. Brown & Sons to William Gihon, 3 and 30 April, to John Cumming, 6 April, to Robert Dickey, 6 and 26 April, to James Carruthers, 22 April 1819, Brown Letterbooks; *Baltimore Patriot,* 7 and 18 June 1819.

15. James Robinson to Benjamin Clap, 26 May, 1, 9, 16, and 23 June, 12 July 1819, Clap Family Papers; Ann C. Smith to Francis Blackwell, 5 June 1819, Brantz Mayer Papers; Henry Thompson Diary, entries for 28, 29 May 1819, Hugh Thompson Papers; John McHenry to his uncle, John McHenry, 23 May, 23 June 1819, Anna Boyd to John McHenry, 12 and 26 July, 2 and 23 Aug. 1819, McHenry Papers, mss., Maryland Historical Society. On 6 August, 1819, Anna Boyd wrote to her brother, John McHenry:

> I think John, one of the most provoking parts of the business is, that these destroyers of widows, and Orphans, affect to Consider themselves as persecuted men. McCulloh for example struts about in all the pride & gaiety belonging to an honest heart, and unspotted name boasting as it were; that he is stript of his feathers, that they were determined to bring him down & have succeeded.

Also see John Hastings to John Myers, 17 and 23 June, 1 July, 1 and 23 Sept. 1819, Myers Family Papers; Langdon Cheves to John White, 18 May 1819, White's reply to Cheves, 20 May 1819, John White Papers; John White to Langdon Cheves, 27 May 1819, Langdon Cheves Papers.

16. By June, about fifty of the most prominent merchants had failed because of the collapse of the "Club" of stock speculators. Though shocking because of their numbers and the enormity of their losses, these failures were mild in comparison with those that followed during June and July, when perhaps one hundred more merchants failed because of the banks' refusal to abandon their demand for specie payments. The best running commentary about these failures can be found in the Brown Letterbooks: Alex. Brown & Sons to William Cumming, 20 May, to Adger & Black, 21 May, to James Carruthers, 25 May, to William Gihon & Son, 29 May, 1 June, to William & John Cumming, 31 May, to McLanahan & Bogart, 2 June, to Dunlop & Orgain, 4 June, to William Gihon & Son, 18 June, to Neilson & Neale, 3 July, and to Robert Dickey, 7 July 1819, Brown Letterbooks. Alexander Brown was one of Baltimore's new men of the 1820's; see Gary L. Browne, "Business Innovation and Social Change: The Career of Alexander Brown after the War of 1812," *Maryland Historical Magazine* 69 (1974):243–55.

17. For evidence that Baltimore's capitalists were reading and circulating these writings of Ricardo, Bollman, and Huskisson, see George Hoffman to Langdon Cheves, 11 July 1819, Langdon Cheves Papers. Hezekiah Niles' first endorsement of a specie-based currency can be found in *Niles' Weekly Register*, no. 13, 11 Oct. 1817, p. 97.

18. The change from endorsement to collateral mortgages as loan security can be followed in the Records of the Baltimore Branch of the Second Bank of the United States, the Jonathan Meredith Papers, Library of Congress (Meredith was the first prominent specialist in business law in Baltimore and was the attorney for the branch bank there); the John White Papers, Maryland Historical Society; and to a lesser extent in the Langdon Cheves Papers.

19. The Records of the Baltimore Branch of the Second Bank of the United States, the John White Papers, the Brown Letterbooks, and the Hollingsworth Papers all bear out this interpretation. So also does an analysis of the next banking crisis in Baltimore in 1834, a crisis that contemporaries believed was caused by the bank presidents' usurpation of powers that properly belonged to the boards of directors.

20. Catterall, *Second Bank,* pp. 38–113, Govan, *Nicholas Biddle,* pp. 60–11; Hammond, *Banks and Politics,* ch. 11; Redlich, *Molding of American Banking,* pp. 43–66, 96–162. The Brown Letterbooks and the Riggs Family Papers, mss., in the Library of Congress illustrate the business operations described above, as do the Garrett Family Papers, mss., Library of Congress; the Matthew Smith Letterbook, ms., Tyson Papers; the Riggs & Gaither Letterbook, ms., the Oliver Record Books, and the Jacob Hall Pleasants Papers, mss., all in the Maryland Historical Society.

21. Lewis Atherton, "Itinerant Merchandising in the Antebellum South," *Bulletin of the Business Historical Society* 19 (1945): 35–59, and idem, "Predecessors of the Commercial Drummer in the Old South," *Bulletin of the Business Historical Society* 21 (1947): 17–24; Lee M. Friedman, "The Drummer in Early American Merchandise Distribution," *Bulletin of the Business Historical Society* 21 (1947):39–42; and Stanley C. Hollander, "Nineteenth-Century Anti-Drummer Legislation in the United States," *Business History Review* 38 (1964):479–500. The Baltimoreans who were sent out to England as buyers were young men in their twenties: Richard Bell for John Gibson & Co.; William B. Bend for Hoffman, Bend & Co.; Thomas G.

Edmondson for Joseph Todhunter & Co.; Donald McIlvain for Campbell & McIlvain; Edward S. Norris for William Norris & Son; and George Peabody, who would have the most spectacular career of them all, for Riggs, Peabody & Co.

ELEVEN

THE URBAN IMPACT ON AGRICULTURAL LAND USE: FARM PATTERNS IN PRINCE GEORGE'S COUNTY, MARYLAND 1860–1880

Donald McCauley

Farming in Prince George's County, Maryland, diverged increasingly from the general pattern of southern agriculture in the period after the Civil War. Yet just before the war, this county, located on the Potomac River across from Mount Vernon, had resembled the plantation counties of the lower South. In 1860 the system of large-scale staple crop production with slave labor was as entrenched within Prince George's County as in the Black Belt areas further South. While slavery was declining in Western Maryland, the county's planters had continued to expand their slave labor forces during the 1850s. Large plantations also had been noticeable. The 1860 federal census listed two farms of over 1,000 acres and sixty-one of more than 500 acres in the county. Some farmers had turned to market gardening and dairying in the 1850s, but tobacco had continued to dominate the county's agriculture. In 1859, the county's tobacco crop had been the largest in the United States.[1]

The Civil War had essentially the same impact on the agricultural economy of Prince George's County as on the plantation counties of the lower South. The county suffered similar population and capital losses during the war and experienced a comparable labor disorganization during the transition from a slave to a free labor system. With the disruption of the plantation system after 1860, the same weakened state of agriculture that characterized the lower South was evident in the county. In 1870 the values of livestock, farm machinery, and farm lands in the former Confederate states were 45 to 50 percent below their 1860 levels. Comparable declines of 49 to

Note: Donald McCauley is working as a research analyst at the Federal Energy Administration while completing graduate work at the University of Maryland. The author acknowledges the assistance of Lois Carr, David Grimsted, and Edward Muller.

52 percent in these important agricultural variables were reported in Prince George's County.[2]

Prince George's County, however, reestablished a balanced farm economy in the 1870s that diverged in important respects from the characteristics of farming in the post-bellum South. This article argues that the strength of the county's new agricultural system was closely related to economic advantages of urban centers. A low level of urbanization and deflated capital markets retarded agricultural recovery in the South. Under the system of sharecropping, with the local merchant extending credit, the crop-lien system fostered concentration on the production of staple crops for cash in the South. Therefore, the region's agriculture showed declining rates of self-sufficiency in foodstuffs. Baltimore and Washington, however, furnished Prince George's County with financial and commodity markets for an efficient reorganization in agriculture. The availability of farm credit contributed to a system of mortgaged farms during the period of land division after 1860. The necessity for sharecropping and crop-lien arrangements therefore was lessened. Consequently, fewer farmers depended on staple-crop agriculture and tobacco declined in importance. The county's farmers responded to the market demands of Baltimore and Washington and developed a balanced agricultural system of diversified production.

While Maryland did not secede, Prince George's County felt the economic and social impact of the Civil War. Confederate raids, currency depreciation, and contraction in credit retarded the entire state's business growth during the early stages of the war. Increased federal expenditures for war supplies fostered a resurgence of commercial growth by the end of the war, but market restrictions and control of the state's transportation system by Union troops interfered with normal agricultural marketing. The pro-Southern sentiment of some residents brought additional troops to the county. Isolated "disloyal citizens," including Clement Hill, a past president of the Prince George's County Agricultural Society, had their property confiscated and sold for aiding the Confederate cause. Further restrictions on economic activities continued beyond 1865. A garrison of federal troops was stationed in Southern Maryland. While the garrison remained, any person not taking an unconditional oath of allegiance to the United States government was prohibited from engaging in "any occupation, trade, or profession" in the area.[3]

The disorganization of the slave-labor system created additional problems for the county's farmers. Slave fugitives escaping on the Potomac River or into the bordering District of Columbia had been an increasing threat to the institution of slavery in the county during the 1850s.[4] The number of slave escapes increased during the war.[5] John Bayne, a local planter, wrote to President Lincoln in 1862 that the losses of slaves were so great along the

Potomac River that many fields were left untilled. He pleaded that something be done to protect county slaveholders before the "agricultural interests [were] utterly prostrated."[6] The enlistment of blacks as federal troops further depleted the county's labor supply.[7]

The state constitution of 1864 emancipated the remaining slaves within Maryland, and residents of Prince George's County had to make social and labor adjustments similar to those in the lower South.[8] Reports from the Freedmen's Bureau established in Southern Maryland indicate that the county's response to the end of slavery was not distinct from the well-known Southern pattern. The white residents complained of the insubordination of their former slaves and, late in 1865, reported the common fear of a Christmas rebellion of the freedmen. Looking back toward slavery, illegal servitude was continued in late 1864 and early 1865 under the guise of apprenticeship. The intercession of the Freedmen's Bureau halted this practice, but the freedmen continued to report violations of their civil rights. The thirty-nine lashes and six-month jail sentence that Robert Carroll of Upper Marlborough received for defending himself against a white man offers a vivid portrayal of continuing ante-bellum social attitudes and practices. The transformation in the labor system was equally difficult. The free negroes registered repeated complaints to the bureau of their difficulties in obtaining work contracts and collecting wages for farm labor.[9]

The high migration rate among the black population continued after emancipation. By 1870 the black population of 9,780 was only 72 percent the size of the combined slave and free negro population in 1860. With Baltimore and Washington close and accessible, the county's free negroes were quite likely joining the steady migration to the largest and fastest growing centers of black population in the United States.[10]

James Higgins, a professor at the Maryland Agricultural College (now the University of Maryland) located north of Washington, recognized the significance of this population decline and sought to remedy the situation by attracting immigrant settlers. In 1867, Higgins wrote a classic example of "booster" literature. Addressing himself to prospective settlers, he praised the healthy climate, the cultural advantages, and economic opportunities of Maryland. Higgins noted that the general disturbances of the war and the disruption of the agricultural labor force would "render necessary the change of ownership in a large portion of the land." The greatest part of the pamphlet was devoted to Southern Maryland, where "the abstraction and derangement of labor was greatest" because of slave emancipation and subsequent population losses. Immigrants were told that they could "find here the cheapest and best inducements . . . for the largest portion of land will be offered for sale."[11] By 1870, however, the immigrant population had only increased by 130 within Prince George's County, and the county's total population of 21,000 was nearly 10 percent below the 1860 census level.[12]

The scarcity of labor fostered the same forms of land division and declining farm size that characterized the post-bellum South. Within similar counties of the Virginia-Carolina tobacco belt, the number of farms doubled between 1860 and 1880.[13] During the same twenty-year period, the total number of farms in Prince George's County increased by 58 percent, and the farms under 100 acres increased by 71 percent. As Table 11.1 indicates, the county's average farm of 159 acres in 1880 was within the range of reduced size common to the tobacco belt and other regions of the lower South.

Land division and labor scarcity in the South after 1860 were accompanied by a rapid rise in farm tenancy. In 1880, 38 percent of all southern farms were tenant operated. The corresponding tenancy rate in the tobacco belt was 36 percent. With the largest tobacco-producing counties the proportion of tenant operators to all farmers in 1880 ranged as high as 44 percent.[14]

Tenancy emerged in Prince George's County, but its incidence was lower and its pattern distinct from the lower South. Table 11.2 lists the distribution of farms by size and tenure in 1880. About the same percentage of farms were rented in the county and in the South; the distinction was between sharecropping and ownership. The percentage of operators owning farms in the county was above the average for Maryland and 10 percent higher than in the South. Croppers operated over one-fourth of the southern farms as compared to 16 percent in Prince George's County. An even greater contrast occurred between the types of sharecropping. While 71 percent of the southern sharecroppers operated farms of under 50 acres, 72 percent of the county croppers operated farms of over 100 acres. The average sharecropped farm in the county was about 223 acres as compared to the 70-acre average size in the South. Sharecroppers were not only relatively fewer in number in

TABLE 11.1
Average Farm Size in Southern Regions and Prince George's County, 1860–1880

	Average Farm Size (in Acres)		
	South	*Tobacco Belt Counties (Range)*	*Prince George's County*
1860	327	92–346	263
1870	226	75–208	243
1880	157	115–204	159

Sources: Roger L. Ransom and Richard Sutch, "Debt Peonage as a Cause of Economic Stagnation in the Deep South Following the Civil War," *Southern Economic History Project, Working Paper No. 9* (Berkley, 1970), table 8, p. 19. Tobacco-belt counties are the three Virginia and nine North Carolina counties in the core of the bright-tobacco region, see Nannie May Tilley, *The Bright Tobacco Industry, 1860–1929* (Chapel Hill, 1948), p. 90. U.S. Bureau of the Census, *Agriculture of the United States in 1860,* (Washington, D.C., 1864), pp. 203, 210, 218; ibid., *The Statistics of Wealth and Industry . . . Ninth Census,* pp. 354, 359, 364; ibid., *Report on the Productions of Agriculture . . . Tenth Census,* (Washington, D.C. 1865), p. 119.

TABLE 11.2
Distribution of Farms by Size and Tenure of Farm Operator, 1880

Size and	Prince George's Co.		South		Maryland	
Tenure Class	N	%	N	%	N	%
Under 50 acres						
Owners	340	76.23	140,489	29.65	9,491	78.10
Renters	63	14.13	101,751	21.48	1,529	12.58
Sharecroppers	43	9.64	231,509	48.87	1,132	9.32
Total	446	100.00	473,749	100.00	12,152	100.00
50–99 acres						
Owners	200	72.74	173,325	70.63	5,571	71.73
Renters	40	14.55	24,089	9.82	726	9.35
Sharecroppers	35	12.73	47,967	19.55	1,471	18.94
Total	275	100.00	245,381	100.00	7,768	100.00
100–499 acres						
Owners	603	68.15	400,338	62.57	12,384	62.57
Renters	102	11.53	25,383	7.83	1,549	7.83
Sharecroppers	180	20.34	44,008	29.60	5,859	29.60
Total	885	100.00	469,729	100.00	19,792	100.00
Over 500 acres						
Owners	60	72.29	56,690	89.43	532	66.09
Renters	6	7.23	3,160	4.99	74	9.19
Sharecroppers	17	20.48	3,540	5.58	199	24.72
Total	83	100.00	63,390	100.00	805	100.00
All Sizes						
Owners	1,203	71.23	770,842	61.56	27,978	69.05
Renters	211	12.49	154,383	12.33	3,878	9.57
Sharecroppers	275	16.28	327,024	26.11	8,661	21.38
Total	1,689	100.00	1,252,249	100.00	40,517	100.00

Sources: Roger Ransom and Richard Sutch, "Debt Peonage as a Cause of Economic Stagnation in the Deep South," table 10, p. 22; U.S. Bureau of the Census, Report on the Productions of Agriculture as Reported at the Tenth Census (Washington, D.C., 1885), pp. 60–61.

TABLE 11.3
Farm Mortgages in Selected Regions, 1890

Region	Number of Farms	Number of Farm Mortgages	Number of Mortgages per 100 Farms
Prince George's County	1,805	1,215	67.3
Maryland	40,798	21,139	51.8
South	1,524,948	348,073	22.8
United States	4,564,641	2,303,061	50.5

Sources: U.S. Bureau of the Census, Report on Real Estate Mortgages in the United States at the Eleventh Census: 1890, vol. 12 (Washington, D.C., 1895), p. 482; ibid., Report on Farms and Homes: Proprietorship and Indebtedness in the United States at the Eleventh Census: 1890, vol. 13 (Washington, D.C., 1896), p. 301; ibid., Abstract of the Eleventh Census: 1890 (Washington, D.C., 1896), pp. 93–96, 216.

Prince George's County; they were also in an apparently stronger economic position.

Recent research has added further evidence to the traditional argument that the lack of credit was a major reason for the prevalence of sharecropping in the post-bellum South.[15] The South's financial system collapsed during the Civil War and it had not recovered by 1880. The region's percentage of the nation's banks declined from 15 percent in 1860 to under 10 percent by 1870. The average capital stock per bank also fell continually below the national average. As a result, the merchant replaced the banker and the crop lien prevailed over the mortgage in the South's post-bellum farm economy.[16]

The availability of credit during the period of land division gave farmers within Prince George's County viable alternatives to sharecropping. Baltimore, the commercial center of Maryland, was within twenty miles of the county. In 1880 Baltimore had twenty-five banks, which equaled the entire number of banks in Louisiana and surpassed by eleven the number of banks in Arkansas. Maryland also had fourteen savings institutions with over $24 million worth of deposits; the entire lower South had only five savings banks with less than $1.5 million in deposits. In addition, the county's largest town of Laurel supported two building and savings institutions.[17]

Because of available credit, the mortgage rather than the crop lien became the typical mechanism for the change in farm ownership that James Higgins forecast for the county. Mortgage data was not collected for the 1860 to 1880 period, but the 1890 census report reflects the magnitude of the county's divergence from the Southern pattern in farm credit. Table 11.3 lists the computations of the number of mortgages for every 100 farms. There were less than 23 mortgages per 100 farms in the lower South, and within the tobacco belt the ratio was as low as 15. The morgage rate of 67 in Prince George's County was nearly triple the Southern level and significantly above the national average.

Farm production figures offer evidence that the lower percentage of farmers locked into crop liens in the county allowed for a more efficient market response within the new agricultural system. Table 11.4, which lists the per capita values of key agricultural variables in 1870 and 1880 as a percentage of their 1860 levels, offers specific indicators of the slow recovery of post-bellum southern agriculture. During the 1860s, the Confederate states' agricultural inputs of land and livestock had declined to a level of 82 percent or less of their 1860 level, and declines in output were even more severe. Depressed conditions were not restricted to the Civil War decade. By 1880, inputs had recovered to 85 percent or less of their 1860 levels, and crop outputs remained at least 25 percent below their prewar production figures.

TABLE 11.4
Inputs and Outputs in Southern and Prince George's County Agriculture,
1870 and 1880 as Percentage of 1860 Levels

	South			Prince George's County		
Farm Variables per Capita	1860	1870	1880	1860	1870	1880
Inputs						
Total land in farms	100	77	70	100	79	84
Improved land in farms	100	82	85	100	76	79
Number of horses	100	78	82	100	80	105
Number of mules and asses	100	72	85	100	42	41
Crops						
Wheat	100	70	75	100	37	46
Corn	100	62	69	100	82	83
Potatoes	100	43	50	100	243	261
Tobacco	100	52	67	100	30	43
Cotton	100	51	72	—	—	—
Livestock						
Number of swine	100	57	61	100	61	61
Number of milch cows	100	73	74	100	71	88
Number of cattle	100	76	73	100	71	52

Sources: Southern estimates in Richard Easterlin, "Regional Income Trends, 1840–1880," in *American Economic History*, ed. Seymour Harris (New York, 1961), p. 528. County agricultural statistics compiled from U.S. Bureau of the Census, *Agriculture of the United States in 1860* (Washington, D.C., 1864), pp. 72–73; ibid., *The Statistics of the Wealth and Industry of the United States*, vol. 3 (Washington, D.C., 1872), pp. 172–73; ibid., *Report on the Productions of Agriculture*, vol. 3 (Washington, D.C. 1883), pp. 119, 192, 282–85. County population statistics compiled from U.S. Bureau of the Census, *Compendium of the Tenth Census*, pt. 1 (Washington, D.C., 1885), p. 354.

The same general pattern of reduced inventories and yields prevailed in the county in 1870. Yet several key differences emerged during the following decade. The recovery of staple-crop production in the county was significantly lower than that of the South. While the Southern tobacco crop in 1880 was 67 percent of the area's 1860 crop, production in Prince George's County was still under one-half of its 1860 level. On the other hand, the county reported higher rates of recovery in diversified categories of corn production and milch cow inventories, as well as a near trebling of the per capita potato production.

The county's diversified agricultural pattern differed markedly from that of the lower tobacco belt. There, agricultural reformers complained repeatedly that the undue emphasis on the cash crop was a detriment to agricultural recovery. The lure of high profits and the "lock-in" effect of the crop lien, however, led to steady increases in tobacco production within the old planter counties, as well as expansion of the crop into newer Piedmont counties.[18] There was a simultaneous reduction in the acreage devoted to wheat and corn and a general decline in self-sufficiency. At the height of tobacco production in this belt, the money spent for imported food and feed in several counties reportedly exceeded the proceeds from the entire tobacco crop.[19]

Estimates of reduced per capita gain surpluses within the South after 1860 offer more affirmative evidence of the region's general decline in self-sufficiency. With surplus grain production prior to 1860, the ante-bellum South was largely self-sufficient in foodstuffs.[20] Roger Ransom and Richard Sutch, using similar methods to analyze the post-bellum South, concluded that by 1880 "even in regions with relatively high average (grain) surpluses, there were substantial numbers of farms which could not have been self-sufficient." Of the farms with under twenty-four acres in cultivation, between 25 and 53 percent lacked enough grain to meet even their seed and livestock requirements. As many as 45 percent of the farms in some areas with fifty to ninety-nine tilled acres could not meet their minimum food consumption needs with their grain production.[21]

. To calculate the level of self-sufficiency in Prince George's County, similar estimates of residual grain surpluses were constructed on a county-wide basis for 1860, 1870, and 1880. The county's total grain output was converted into corn-equivalent units. Seed and livestock feed requirements were then subtracted. The remaining figure is the residual expressed in corn-equivalent units. A further subtraction of minimal human consumption needs of the county's population yielded a rough estimate of the excess grain surplus.[22]

Table 11.5 lists the county's estimated grain surpluses. While the grain residual declined after 1860, the per capita residual of about twenty-two for the entire population suggests a relatively high degree of self-sufficiency within the agricultural system.[23] Estimates of average per capita residuals among only the owners of fifty acres or more, for instance, ranged as low as twenty-four in some areas of the lower South.[24] Rather than declining in self-sufficiency, the county actually maintained an excess grain surplus throughout the post-bellum period.

TABLE 11.5
Total Grain Surplus in Prince George's County after Allowing for Seed and Livestock Feed Requirements in Bushels of Corn Equivalents, 1860–1880

	Total Grain Residual in Bushels of Corn Equivalents	*Per Capita Grain Residual*	*Grain Surplus after Adjusting for Home Consumption*
1860	733,466	31.4	500,196
1870	460,992	21.8	249,612
1880	565,512	21.5	301,002

Source: See Table 11.4.

The county's relative high standing in foodstuff production reflected an efficient mix of diversified commodities (see table 11.6). In addition to the rising potato crops noted above, dairying and truck farming made notable advances between 1860 and 1880. The significant increases in the production of perishable dairy products and bulky horticultural produce suggest the extent of the farmers' possible response to proximate market demands.

The low level of urbanization and poorly developed transportation networks were closely connected to the shortage of credit within Southern agriculture.[25] Farmers within Prince George's County, however, had the advantages of both markets and transportation routes within the expansive hinterland of Baltimore and Washington. As figure 11.1 shows, Washington provided the closest urban market. All points were within twenty miles of the Capitol and sixty miles of Baltimore. During the ante-bellum period, only the northern districts along the Washington Branch Railroad were affected by these markets, as the "neck-breaking, vehicle destroying condition" of local bridges and the "notorious" roads limited travel and freightage from other areas.[26] By 1880, however, the railroad system had expanded considerably the thresholds for economic utilization of the Baltimore and Washington markets. James Higgins's claim that all areas of Prince George's County were within ten miles of a railroad was an exaggeration typical of the prevailing "boosterism" in 1867; by 1880 it was a reality for over three-fourths of the county. Higgins clearly recognized the market potential of the area when he noted that "we have at the very threshold of this section very large, populous and growing cities; all ready . . . consumers of its various agricultural products."[27]

The absence of data on actual farm commodity flows makes it difficult to gauge the exact impact of proximate urban markets on the county's

TABLE 11.6
Production of Foodstuffs in Prince George's County, 1860–1880

	1860		1870		1880	
Agricultural Products	Total	Per Capita	Total	Per Capita	Total	Per Capita
Corn, bushels	699,144	30.00	518,131	24.51	656,888	24.83
Wheat, bushels	312,796	13.42	79,181	3.75	129,946	4.91
Potatoes, bushels	30,936	1.33	68,278	3.23	91,698	3.47
Butter, pounds	78,629	3.37	69,658	3.30	126,358	4.78
Milk, gallons sold	n.a.	n.a.	21,090	1.00	147,192	5.56
Market garden and orchard produce, value in 1860 $'s	$35,853	$1.54	$45,794	$2.17	$188,701	$6.87

Source: See table 11.4.
Note: N.a. means data not available.

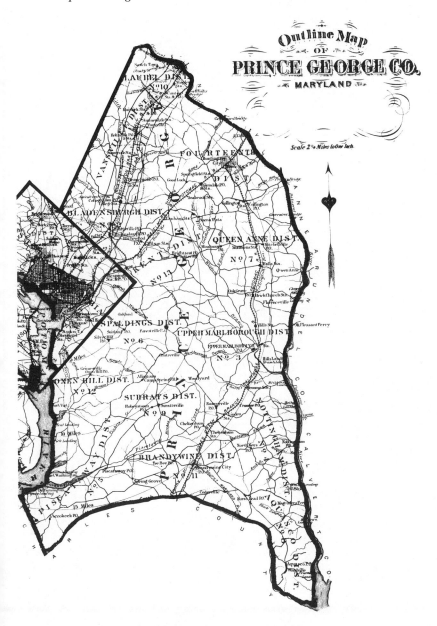

FIGURE 11.1 Outline Map of the County and Washington, D.C., 1878

Source: G. M. Hopkins, *Atlas of Fifteen Miles Around Washington, Including the County of Prince George, Maryland* (Philadelphia: F. Bourquin, 1878). Republished by the Prince George's County Historical Society in 1975; map used with the Society's permission.

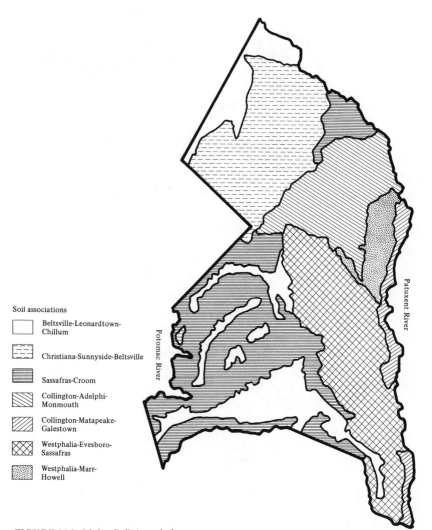

FIGURE 11.2. Major Soil Associations
   Source: Adapted from *Soil Survey of Prince George's County, Maryland*, U.S. Department
of Agriculture, Soil Conservation Service, in Cooperation with Maryland Agricultural Experiment Station (Washington, D.C.: Government Printing Office, 1967).

agriculture. Diversification may have been as much a function of local
demand as available external markets. An analysis of changing agricultural
production zones within the county, however, suggests that an efficient
response to external markets as well as to internal soil variations prevailed in
the county.

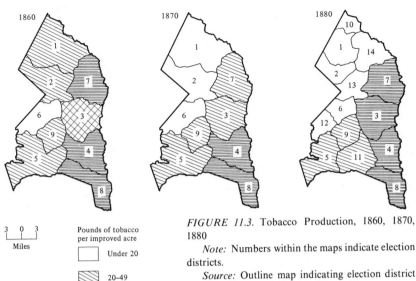

FIGURE 11.3. Tobacco Production, 1860, 1870, 1880

Note: Numbers within the maps indicate election districts.

Source: Outline map indicating election district boundaries for 1860, 1870, and 1880 was developed on a 3-mile scale map of the County from the following sources: G. M. Hopkins, *Atlas of Fifteen Miles Around Washington, Including the County of Prince George, Maryland* (Philadelphia: F. Bourquin, 1878). S. J. Martenet, *Martenet's Map of Maryland*, atlas ed. (Baltimore: Simon J. Martenet, 1866). Idem., *Martenet's Map of Prince George's County, Maryland* (Philadelphia: T. S. Wagner, 1861). Idem., H. F. Walling, and O. W. Gray, *New Topographical Atlas of Maryland and the District of Columbia* (Baltimore: Stedman, Brown, Lyon, 1873).

Before comparing the actual crop patterns in the county with any hypothetical zones of expected land use, variations in soil capability must be considered. Figure 11.2 shows the patchwork of soils in present-day Prince George's County. While erosion has altered the capability of some of these soils during the last century, the mapped pattern offers a rough indication of variation present during the nineteenth century.

Indices of relative crop productivity for soil types reflect three major crop regions within the county. The zone of highest productivity is on the eastern side of the county along the Patuxent River. Yields of quality tobacco are significantly higher on the Westphalia soil associations than elsewhere in the county and only slightly less so on the Collington-Adelphi-Monmouth soils. With the minor exception of soybeans, the highest productivity of all crops grown in the county are obtained on the Westphalia and Collington soil

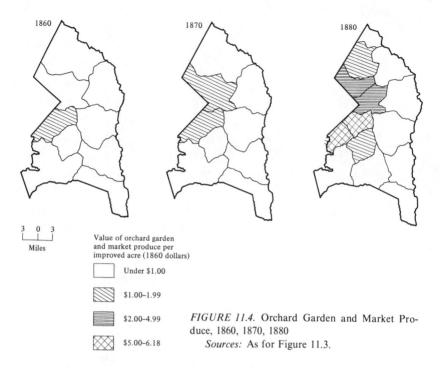

Value of orchard garden
and market produce per
improved acre (1860 dollars)

☐ Under $1.00

▨ $1.00–1.99

▤ $2.00–4.99

▩ $5.00–6.18

FIGURE 11.4. Orchard Garden and Market Produce, 1860, 1870, 1880
        Sources: As for Figure 11.3.

3   0   3
Miles

associations. The Sassafras-Croom association interlaced with Beltsville soils defines a second zone in the southwest of the county. These soils are best suited to general farming but are capable of producing favorable yields of lower quality tobacco. The third zone characterized by the Christiana association in the northern corner of the county is a soil area ill-suited for tobacco but capable of supporting general farming.[28]

An analysis of changing tobacco production zones offers a clear indication of the fundamental shift in the county's agricultural system that occurred between 1860 and 1880. As shown on figure 11.3, the high per acre yields of tobacco production throughout the county in 1860 reflect the major role of staple crops in the ante-bellum agricultural system.[29] The center of tobacco production was in the fertile areas along the Patuxent River. This area around the county seat of Upper Marlborough was dominated by plantations of increasing size and expanding slave-labor forces during the 1850s.[30] The less fertile soil regions characterized by smaller farms in the northern corner of the county, however, also had relatively high acreages in tobacco in 1860. On the eve of the Civil War, tobacco rather than market diversification dominated the entire county's agriculture.

A less extensive system of tobacco production prevailed in the county after 1860. Tobacco farming had virtually ceased in the northernmost corner

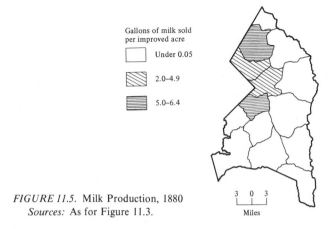

Gallons of milk sold
per improved acre

Under 0.05

2.0–4.9

5.0–6.4

FIGURE 11.5. Milk Production, 1880
Sources: As for Figure 11.3.

3 0 3

Miles

of the county by 1880.[31] Production continued at a level below 1860 yields in all areas of the county, but concentrated increasingly along the Patuxent River. This was an understandable market response. The high yields of quality tobacco on the fertile soils of the area made production of the dark-leaf variety of tobacco grown in Maryland especially profitable here. With tobacco auctions in Upper Marlborough, and the Baltimore and Potomac Railroad providing transportation to Baltimore, the close proximity of urban markets was not an essential consideration to the tobacco farmer. Tobacco production no longer dominated the county's agriculture after 1860; it continued as a specialized crop geared to soil capability.

The entrenchment of the tobacco producing areas within Prince George's County differed from the general pattern of expanding zones of bright-leaf production within the Virginia-North Carolina tobacco belt. Bright-leaf tobacco thrives on sterile soils that are often ill-suited for general agriculture. The development of bright-leaf varieties after 1865 was seen as a panacea for formerly impoverished areas. Tobacco therefore expanded into areas of the Piedmont plateau that had not specialized in dark-leaf tobacco production prior to the Civil War. The new bright-leaf varieties did bring short-term economic growth to some counties, but the general pattern of overproduction and declining diversification followed in the long run.[32] Dark-leaf tobacco, which requires fertile soil for favorable yields, offered no special inducement for expansion in Prince George's County after 1860.

Market gardening and orchard produce for urban markets were the most noticeable areas of expansion in the county's new agricultural system. The value of this produce increased from $35,853 in 1860 to $188,701 in 1880 (in constant 1860 dollars).[33] As figure 11.4 indicates, this production increase followed the Washington market quite closely. Truck farms, however, also

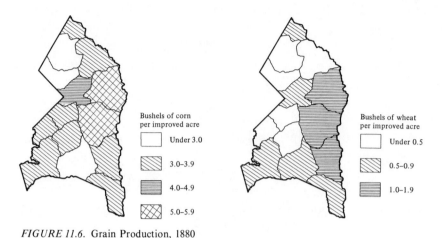

FIGURE 11.6. Grain Production, 1880
Sources: As for Figure 11.3.

expanded into the former tobacco areas in the northern corner of the county along the Baltimore-Washington transportation routes.

Milk production emerged in the same specialized zone of agriculture developing in the northern corner of the county. Prior to the Civil War, a few large planters like Horace Capron and Charles B. Calvert had already developed significant dairy farms to serve Baltimore and Washington.[34] Dairying developed slowly after 1860, but by 1880 the same heightened activity that characterized truck farming was evident. As figure 11.5 indicates, dairy farms concentrated close to the truck farms north of Washington. Butter production expanded along with the dairy industry in the areas north and east of Washington. Since butter is a less perishable product, it was less dependent than milk on close-by markets. A smaller center of butter production, for instance, emerged in the isolated eighth district in the southeastern corner of the county.[35]

The emergence of dairying and horticulture altered grain production zones within the county. In 1860 district six east of Washington had the largest production of wheat per improved acre in the county. By 1880, production had declined to less than one-fourth the 1860 level as truck gardening displaced small grain crops. Corn production, often for home consumption, remained widely dispersed throughout the county. As figure 11.6 indicates, the 1880 level of corn production was also lowest in the areas bordering the Washington market. By 1880, the center of extensive grain production had gravitated to the county's tobacco belt, along the Patuxent River.

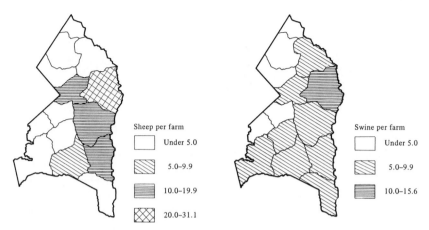

FIGURE 11.7. Livestock Production, 1880
Sources: As for Figure 11.3.

Changes in livestock inventories followed a similar pattern after 1860. Swine inventories remained 40 percent behind their 1860 per capita level in 1880.[36] This reduction in stock was evident throughout the county but most apparent near Washington (see figure 11.7). Sheep grazing similarly gravitated away from Washington toward the outlying lands.

The agricultural zones that emerged in Prince George's County between 1860 and 1880 suggest an efficient mix in an area influenced by accessible urban markets. While former highly valued lands along the Patuxent River declined in value after 1860, land near Washington either remained stable or increased in value. In 1880, as figure 11.8 shows, land values were highest in the newly diversified agricultural zone of horticulture and dairying. With intensive agricultural activities concentrating on the most valuable land near Washington, the more extensive farm activities established thresholds in outlying areas. Wheat as well as corn production gravitated to the middle region along the Patuxent River, and sheep grazing established two major centers of wool production. Tobacco assumed an understandable zone of concentration geared to soil fertility.

While the evidence is admittedly tentative and exact relationships have not been shown, the connection between nearby urban markets and agricultural recovery in Prince George's County seems clear.[37] Washington and Baltimore furnished important financial and commodity markets to the county's farmers. With credit available for mortgages, the necessity for sharecropping was lessened. The low incidence of farmers locked into crop liens allowed for an efficient response to market demands of growing cities.

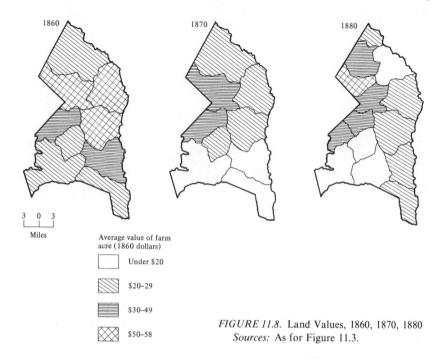

FIGURE 11.8. Land Values, 1860, 1870, 1880
Sources: As for Figure 11.3.

Diversification was therefore possible, and self-sufficiency was maintained. While a low level of urbanization and deflated capital markets retarded agricultural recovery in the South after the Civil War, Prince Georgian farmers developed a balanced agricultural system of diversified production.

NOTES

1. See Donald McCauley, "The Limits of Change in the Tobacco South: An Economic and Social Analysis of Prince George's County, Maryland, 1840–1860" (M.A. thesis, University of Maryland, 1973), for a survey of the county's ante-bellum development.

2. Regional estimates from Eugene M. Lerner, "Southern Output and Agricultural Income, 1860–1880," in *The Economic Impact of the Civil War,* ed. Ralph Andreano, (Cambridge, 1967), pp. 109–11, and Stanley Engerman, "Some Economic Factors in Southern Backwardness in the Nineteenth Century," in *Essays in Regional Economics,* John F. Kain and John R. Meyer, eds. (Cambridge, 1971), pp. 300–306. Unless noted otherwise, the South is defined as the eleven former Confederate States for the purposes of this article. County statistics were computed from U.S. Bureau of the Census, *Agriculture of the United States in 1860* (Washington, D.C. 1864), pp. 72–73; ibid., *The Statistics of Wealth and Industry of the United States . . . from the Original Returns of the Ninth Census,* vol. 3 (Washington, D.C. 1872), pp. 172–73; ibid., *Report on the Productions of Agriculture as Returned at the Tenth Census,* vol. 3 (Washington, D.C. 1883), p. 119. County values for 1870 and 1880 were deflated to 1860 prices with wholesale price index for Maryland in Roger Hale, *Prices Paid for Maryland Farm Products, 1851–1927,* University of Maryland Agricultural Experiment Station Bulletin No. 321 (September 1930), p. 183.

3. Richard Duncan, "The Social and Economic Impact of the Civil War in Maryland" (Ph.D. diss., Ohio State University, 1963), passim; Vivian Wiser, "The Movement for Agricultural Reform in Maryland, 1785-1865" (Ph.D. diss., University of Maryland 1963), pp. 497-501; J. Thomas Scharf, *History of Maryland,* 3 vols. (1879; Hatboro, Pa, 1967), 3:553-56, 642, 656-57.

4. Thomas Turner, the editor of the county paper, noted that "it is our great misfortune as a slaveholding community that we are brought into juxtaposition with the District of Colombia." He advocated forcible measures to control slave runaways. *The Planters Advocate* (Upper Marlboro), 20 May 1857.

5. In the summer of 1863, the sheriff of Prince George's County requested permission from the governor to call out a posse comitatus to deal with the increasing number of runaway slaves. Duncan, "Impact of the Civil War in Maryland," p. 211.

6. Jno. H. Bayne to President Lincoln, Prince George's County, 17 March 1862, John H. Bayne Papers, mss., Maryland Historical Society.

7. In October 1863, Thomas Clagett, Jr., and seven colleagues from the county seat of Upper Marlboro protested to Reverdy Johnson that federal recruiting troops were "harassing us, plundering us, (and) abducting our negroes," quoted in Charles Wagandt, *The Mighty Revolution: Negro Emancipation in Maryland, 1862-1864* (Baltimore, 1964), p. 118.

8. Wagandt's *The Mighty Revolution* provides a full study, especially on the political issues of emancipation. For additional details, see John Crowl, "Emancipation in Maryland" (M.A. thesis, University of Maryland, 1961), and Duncan, "Impact of the Civil War in Maryland," pp. 207-27.

9. Crowl, "Emancipation in Maryland," pp. 70-77.

10. The black populations of Washington and Baltimore increased by 203 percent and 42 percent respectively during the 1860s, U.S. Bureau of the Census, *Compendium of the Tenth Census,* pt. 1, (Washington, D.C., 1885), pp. 340, 354.

11. James Higgins, *A Succinct Exposition of the Industrial Resources and Agricultural Advantages of the State of Maryland,* Maryland Senate Document U., 1867 (n.p., n.d.), pp. 6-9, 18, passim.

12. U.S. Bureau of the Census, *Compendium of the Tenth Census,* pp. 354, 425.

13. For purposes of statistical comparison in this article, the tobacco belt is defined as the three south central Virginia counties and nine North Carolina counties that formed the core of the flue-cured bright tobacco belt following the Civil War. The number of farms within this area increased from 12,688 in 1860 to 25,404 by 1880, U.S. Bureau of the Census, *Agriculture in 1860,* pp. 210, 218. Nannie May Tilley, *The Bright Tobacco Industry, 1860-1929* (Chapel Hill, 1948), pp. 12, 90, passim. Three of these counties, Halifax and Pittsylvania in Virginia and Granville in North Carolina, also ranked among the top ten dark-leaf-producing counties in the United States in 1860. See Joseph C. Robert, *The Tobacco Kingdom, Plantation, Market, and Factory in Virginia and North Carolina, 1800-1860* (Durham, 1938) for a discussion on the ante-bellum dark-leaf industry.

14. Roger L. Ransom and Richard Sutch, "Debt Peonage as a Cause of Economic Stagnation in the Deep South Following the Civil War," *Southern Economic History Project,* Working Paper No. 9 (Berkley, 1970), p. 15; Tilley, *The Bright Tobacco Industry,* pp. 93-103.

15. C. Vann Woodward presents the traditional interpretation in *Origins of the New South, 1877-1913* (Baton Rouge, 1951), pp. 175-86.

16. Roger L. Ransom and Richard Sutch, "Debt Peonage in the Cotton South after the Civil War," *The Journal of Economic History* 32 (1972):642-54. A more detailed discussion is provided in their working paper, "Debt Peonage as a Cause of Economic Stagnation in the Deep South."

17. State of Maryland, *Report of the State Tax Commissioner of Maryland to the General Assembly as Its Regular Session, January 1882* (Annapolis, 1882); Ransom and Sutch, "Debt Peonage as a Cause of Economic Stagnation," pp. 26, 39.

18. See note 13 for definition of tobacco belt. Pittsylvania County registered the largest increase with its 1880 production 174 percent of its 1860 base level. The production level for the entire region in 1880 was 13.3 percent above the 1860 base, U.S. Bureau of the Census, *Agriculture in 1860,* pp. 105, 109, 155, 159; ibid., *Compendium of the Tenth Census,* pp. 800-803, 823-27.

19. Tilley, *The Bright Tobacco Industry,* pp. 103–12, 123–54.

20. Robert Gallman, "Self-Sufficiency in the Cotton Economy of the Antebellum South," *Agricultural History* 44 (1970):5–24.

21. Ransom and Sutch, "Debt Peonage in the Cotton South," pp. 656–65.

22. The ratios for conversion into corn-equivalent units were: corn, 1.000; wheat, 1.104; barley, 0.866; buckwheat, 0.866; oats, 0.433; rye, 1.050; peas, 0.946; beans, 0.946; Irish potatoes, 0.220; sweet potatoes, 0.362. The deductions from the available stock for seed were: corn, 2 percent; wheat, rye, and barley, 9 percent; oats and buckwheat, 7 percent; peas and beans, 8 percent; Irish and sweet potatoes, 3 percent. The deductions for livestock feed requirements were the lower-bound estimates (expressed in bushels of corn) of: horses, 23.3; mules, 15.5; oxen, 23.3; milch cows, 5.0; other cattle, 1.0; sheep, 0.25; and swine, 6.0. The minimum per capita human consumption requirement was assumed to be ten bushels; ibid., pp. 660–61, 663. Since the interest of this study was in comparing the county with the post-bellum South, Ransom and Sutch's lower-bound estimates of feed requirements rather than Gallman's higher estimates were used, Gallman, "Self-Sufficiency in the Cotton Economy," pp. 10–11.

23. One should not infer from these aggregate grain surpluses that all farmers were self-sufficient. It is quite possible that the degree of self-sufficiency was related closely to farm size in the county as in the lower South.

24. Ransom and Sutch, "Debt Peonage as a Cause of Economic Stagnation," p. 61.

25. In 1880, less than 10 percent of the population in the lower South lived in towns of 2,500 or more. Ransom and Sutch, "Debt Peonage in the Cotton South," pp. 646–48; Woodward, *Origins of the New South,* pp. 107–41, 175–85.

26. McCauley, "Limits of Change in the Tobacco South," pp. 105–9.

27. Higgins, *Industrial Resources and Agricultural Advantages of Maryland,* pp. 22–25, 52–55.

28. U.S. Department of Agriculture, Soil Conservation Service, in Cooperation with Maryland Agricultural Experiment Station, *Soil Survey of Prince George's County, Maryland* (Washington, 1967), pp. 5–9, 142–49.

29. The agricultural production maps were prepared from population data in U.S. Bureau of the Census, *Compendium of the Tenth Census,* p. 354 and individual farm statistics compiled from the manuscript census returns, U.S. Bureau of the Census, *Products of Agriculture,* 1860, 1870, 1880, in the Maryland State Library, Annapolis.

30. In 1860, the average farm size was 433 acres in this third election district, and the slave population outnumbered the whites by three to one, see McCauley, *"Limits of Change in the Tobacco South,"* pp. 22–26, 129–50, for a further discussion of the county's ante-bellum agricultural developments.

31. Only 6,200 pounds of tobacco were listed in the 1880 census agricultural schedules for districts 10, 1 and 2. The combined crop production for districts 10, 1, 2, 13, and 14 in 1880 was about 500,000 pounds as compared to 1,500,000 pounds for districts 1 and 2 in 1860, U.S. Bureau of the Census, *Products of Agriculture,* 1860, 1880.

32. Tilley, *The Bright Tobacco Industry,* pp. 11–18, 108–12, 123–54.

33. See table 11.6.

34. McCauley, "Limits of Change in the Tobacco South," pp. 136–37.

35. District 8 produced 11,800 pounds of butter in 1880 as compared to the production of 21,500 pounds in district 1 north of Washington, U.S. Bureau of the Census, *Products of Agriculture,* 1880.

36. See table 11.6.

37. The land utilization theory of Johann Heinreich von Thünen offers some theoretical support to the connection between the county's farm patterns and proximate urban markets. The Von Thünen theory argues that in an area with one central city, land values will follow a distance-decay function from that city, and crops yielding the highest rent per acre will gravitate toward the city. Agriculture in Prince George's County fits this general pattern after 1860. Michael Chisholm, *Rural Settlement and Land Use, an Essay in Location* (London, 1968), offers a clear introduction of the von Thünen model; William C. Found, *A Theoretical Approach to Rural Land-Use Patterns* (New York, 1971), presents a more theoretical analysis within the context of current microeconomic theory. Recent research reflects the applicability of Von Thünen to various geographic scales of analysis. Richard Peet analyzes the expansion

of wheat into the Midwest within the framework of a dynamic Von Thünen model in "Von Thünen Theory and the Dynamics of Agricultural Expansion," *Explorations in Economic History* 8 (1970):181–201. Examples of local area analysis are Michael P. Conzen, *Frontier Farming in an Urban Shadow: The Influence of Madison's Proximity on the Agricultural Development of Blooming Grove, Wisconsin* (Madison, Wis., 1971), pp. 74–96, and James T. Lemon, *The Best Poor Man's Country: A Geographical Study of Early Southeastern Pennsylvania* (Baltimore, 1972), pp. 184–217. Research of this type is needed at both the local and regional level to explore the relationship between the cities that did exist in the New South and the relative rate of agricultural recovery.

PART 3

Politics

THE CAUSES OF ELECTORAL ALIGNMENTS: SOME CONSIDERATIONS ON HOW PARTISAN BEHAVIOR IS SHAPED

David A. Bohmer

Introduction

In the United States, a nation that has generally been free of bitter, prolonged, class struggles, and that has seen few uprisings or rebellions, the political arena has often provided the most direct incorporation of major divisions or conflicts.[1] Political parties, although not necessarily the torchbearers of internal struggles, have frequently represented or reflected the major competing interests in the nation. Historians, therefore, have given special consideration to electoral alignments because of what they may reveal about American society in general.

Given this purpose, historians have emphasized the personal attributes of voters—religion, economic status, occupation, ethnic background, and age—as the determinants of electoral alignments. These shape the way in which a person views the world around him and hence the way in which he perceives and relates to the political parties and casts his ballot on election day. To determine the personal attribute that at any given time most relates to voter alignments is to suggest a fundamental area of difference or conflict in American society during that period.[2]

Other characteristics, however, may vitally affect electoral behavior. The population composition of a given area—as described by aggregating the attributes of its individuals—in conjunction with that area's past history, may structure or shape the pattern of an alignment. Ethnic concentrations, wealth distributions, religious affiliations, occupational differences, and the interrelations of such attributes over time can vary substantially from one locality to the next. Thus, the kinds of voter alignments that occur in one area may not be possible in another. Within any particular population, furthermore, the most

Note: David A. Bohmer, a former research associate, St. Mary's City Commission, lives in Charlottesville, Virginia.

immediate environment of a voter, that is, his social contacts, could have a major effect in shaping his partisanship, regardless of his personal attributes. While Irish in general might heavily favor a particular political party, an Irishman residing in an area dominated by another ethnic group might be inclined to deviate. Finally, personal attributes in combination could shape alignment patterns by exerting either reinforcing or conflicting influences upon the individual voter. If, for example, Catholics strongly favor one party while rich merchants support the other, then wealthy Catholic merchants might feel torn in their loyalties and display less cohesiveness. At least these three variables—an area's population composition and history, the immediate social contacts of individual voters, and their reinforcing or conflicting personal attributes—should be considered in an analysis of how partisan behavior is shaped.[3]

These three characteristics are unquestionably interrelated. Individual attributes, when aggregated for a specific neighborhood or church congregation, constitute a person's immediate social environment. The combination of such environments in politically distinct units like a city or county constitutes the overall population composition of that unit. Even with this interaction, each of the three characteristics could exert an independent effect upon behavior. A neighborhood, town, or congregation may encourage a particular behavioral mold apart from the personal attributes of each of the residents or members. The composition of the overall population of a county might affect the direction and extent to which immediate environment would influence voting. None of the three characteristics is independent of the other two, but this interrelatedness does not offset the possibility that each could exert a distinctive influence upon partisan behavior.

Although the study of a small area over a short time cannot fully determine the impact of these three variables, it can indicate the possible influence of each upon behavior, particularly if the electoral data is detailed. This paper undertakes to analyze the voting patterns of two Maryland counties, Frederick and Kent, in eight elections between 1796 and 1802. The time and place are suitable for several reasons; Kent and Frederick poll books survive for these elections that reveal both how and if each voter cast his ballot from one election to the next;[4] furthermore, in Maryland by the late 1790s a two-party system had come into being, and Kent and Frederick counties were evenly divided between the Federalist and Republican parties. Most eligible residents between 1796 and 1802 participated in these elections, and over 75 percent of the voters consistently supported the same political party.[5] These behavioral characteristics compare favorably with those of subsequent party systems in the United States. Thus Frederick and Kent counties in the late 1790s should provide evidence with which to assess whether variables besides personal attributes shaped the way voters aligned themselves with the two parties.

The Data

Of the reasons for choosing to analyze early national Maryland, the availability of individual voting data is by far the most important. The presence of a two-party system, coupled with widespread participation and consistent party voting on the part of the electorate, assures some comparability with later time periods. But it is the presence of the poll books that allows intensive testing of the effect on voter behavior of population composition, social contacts, and personal attributes in combination.[6]

Poll lists have survived in both Frederick and Kent counties for eight elections held between 1796 and 1802, the year in which viva voce voting was abolished in Maryland. These elections were held for the four offices that were popularly chosen in the state during the period: presidential electors, congressmen, state senate electors, and delegates to the General Assembly. Voters selected one presidential elector by district, one congressman by district, and two senate electors and four delegates, all by county. Seven of the eight poll books cover the same elections in both counties: the 1800 presidential election, the 1798 and 1801 congressional elections, the 1801 election for senate electors, and the elections in 1800, 1801, and 1802 for the House of Delegates. The eighth election in Frederick was for president in 1796; in Kent, a special election for one delegate in 1801.[7] Both parties contested at least six of the eight elections in each county. For most purposes, then, the data base is parallel for Kent and Frederick.

Extensive processing of the eight poll lists and other records was necessary. Individuals had to be matched from poll list to poll list. Only then could a full record of a person's voting pattern over time be determined. The procedures and assumptions applied in the linkage process are too detailed to be discussed here, but over 85 percent of all individuals included in the poll lists could be linked without introducing possible biases into the final analysis.[8] At the same time, the names on the poll lists were linked to information in supplementary records, such as assessment books, censuses, and church records, which provided knowledge of personal attributes. These additional records introduced shortcomings of their own into the analysis, but none of these appeared to be severe enough to threaten the findings seriously.[9] It should be possible to utilize the final data set with reasonable confidence that the information it contains is accurate.

Other problems also had to be resolved. Most notably, it was necessary to define precisely what constitutes a supporter of the Federalist and Republican parties. There was ample opportunity for a person to vacillate between the parties. Fortunately, few voters did so. In Kent over 60 percent and in Frederick over 80 percent of those who voted two or more times always supported the same party. When minor ticket-splitting (casting one of the four ballots in House of Delegate elections for a candidate of the opposition party) was tolerated in the definition of a stable voter, even more persons were consistent in their behavior. Over 75 percent of the electorate in Kent and 85 percent in Frederick could then be classified as regular party supporters.[10] In the discussion that follows, this second category—stable party voting over time with minor deviation in a House of Delegates election—defines the population of party voters. Those persons who behaved in any other fashion, a minority of the electorate in both counties, are treated as "independent" voters.[11]

Population Composition, Local History, and Partisan Alignments

The first hypothesis to be tested asserts that the population composition and past history of a given area help structure the pattern of voter alignments. This would in some ways appear to be a tautological assertion. Since, in general, electoral differences are reflections of differences within a society, the population make-up of that society would be expected to shape voter alignments. While this point has not been questioned at the macro level, its importance at the micro level has been implicitly ignored or refuted in many historical studies. Studies based upon particular regions, states, or counties have frequently implied a generality to alignment patterns without considering possible peculiarities in the population or history of the area being examined.[12] Yet if population composition and local history do influence electoral divisions, then alignment patterns in a given area may merely reflect that area's demographic and historic peculiarities, rather than a more general pattern. For this reason, it is useful to examine whether population characteristics and historical differences do affect electoral behavior.

The two counties to be studied, Frederick and Kent, present major contrasts in their histories prior to 1800. Kent, established in 1642, was the second county created in the Maryland colony. Initially encompassing the entire eastern shore of the Chesapeake within Maryland's boundaries, Kent gradually diminished in size over the next sixty-five years as thousands of immigrants settled the area and new counties were established. By 1706, Kent was confined to its modern boundaries, lying in the northern part of the Eastern Shore. Like most of the tidewater Chesapeake, the area was heavily committed to a tobacco economy almost from the outset of its settlement. Tobacco remained the staple crop for over three generations, a long-enough period to see the planters of Kent make the commitment to slave labor that occured throughout the region during the late seventeenth and early eighteenth centuries. By the 1760s, when Kent and the rest of the Eastern Shore had passed out of tobacco and into less labor-intensive staples, primarily wheat, the institution of slavery was firmly entrenched.

Well before that time, the county had been fully settled. Most of the immigrant population had arrived before the early 1700s, and by that time a majority of the residents were probably born in the county.

With the area settled and the economy well established, there was little opportunity for newcomers in the eighteenth century. Immigrants in this period either never came to Kent or left shortly after they arrived. Both the economy and the established population suggest a basic homogeneity to the area, as did the presence of a colony-sanctioned religion, the Anglican Church. Unlike St. Mary's, Calvert, and Charles counties, where there were large numbers of Catholics, or Somerset and Worcester, where there were many Presbyterians, the vast majority of Kent's churched population was Anglican. Only in the decade before the American Revolution did another religion, the Methodists, compete with and threaten the Anglican establishment in the county.[13]

Frederick County, by contrast, was much more recently settled and far more diverse economically and socially. Located in Western Maryland, where the Piedmont meets the Appalachians, the area remained an unsettled frontier for close to a hundred years after the colony was founded. Immigrants had passed southward through the area prior to the 1730s, but actual settlement did not begin until speculators, especially Daniel Dulany the elder, offered land and capital on credit in a fashion that enticed people to stay. In another decade there was enough population in the area to necessitate the creation of Frederick as a separate county, and by the eve of the Revolution the original Frederick was carved into three counties, including Montgomery to the southeast and Washington to the west. Dulany's initial speculation was in part intended to connect the town of Baltimore with developing or potential grain-producing areas inland. Partially for this reason and partially because of its inland location, wheat rather than tobacco became the county's staple crop. Slaveholding, as a result, never became as widespread as it was in the tidewater. Some persons who came to Frederick from coastal counties brought slaves with them, but most farmers were not dependent upon bound labor. The major immigration to the area, in fact, was from Germans moving south out of Pennsylvania, none of whom owned slaves when they arrived.

The early presence of large numbers of Germans in Frederick, many of whom were recent arrivals to the colonies, in combination with the native Marylanders who moved into the area, brought an ethnic diversity to the county that was uncharacteristic of the tidewater. The Germans also brought their own religions, particularly Lutheran and Evangelical Reformed, and these churches additionally provided a place of worship for non-Anglican Marylanders, who often had no church to attend in the areas from which they had come. Although the Anglican Church was established in the county, its impact was far less pervasive there than it was in Kent, due in large part to this early religious diversity. In total, the history of Frederick in the eighteenth century was marked by far greater diversity than had been the case in Kent.[14]

The distinctive histories of the two counties clearly differentiate them along the lines of wealth distribution, ethnicity, and religion in the early national period. Wealth, of course, was distributed unequally in both counties. Large numbers of white adult males owned neither land nor slaves, whereas a few possessed hundreds of acres of land and large slave labor forces to work it. Nevertheless, the different economic histories of the two counties resulted in a notable difference. While both economies were based upon wheat by the 1790s, Kent was far more dependent upon slave labor to raise it. About half of the county's households owned slaves and over 15 percent owned ten or more. In Frederick, less than 20 percent of the households owned slaves and fewer than 3 percent possessed more than ten. The counties differed even more substantially in the ethnic compositions of their populations. Almost all of Kent's residents could trace their ancestry directly to England, and almost all of the 10 percent who could not were from English-speaking Scotland and Ireland. By contrast, approximately half of Frederick's population was German in background. The relative ethnic heterogeneity of Frederick was further reflected in the greater number of persons naturalized in the county during the 1790s. Numerous religions were also represented in Frederick from the outset. Among the Germans there were congregations of Lutherans, Reformed, and Moravians, while the native Marylanders who settled the area included Catholics, Presbyterians, Quakers, and Methodists, as well as Anglicans. Beyond the small drain from taxes they paid to support the established church, a majority of Frederick County residents felt no effect from the Anglican Church. In Kent, on the other hand, the establishment had been a pervasive one. A few residents were Quakers, and there may have been some Catholics and Presbyterians, but for much of the eighteenth century the vast majority who attended church were Anglican. By the end of the century, Methodism had gained a foothold in the county and may have rivaled the Anglicans in numbers. But even with this development, the religious, ethnic, and economic compositions of the two counties still differed markedly in the 1790s.[15]

The discussion of the populations and histories of Frederick and Kent has emphasized three components—wealth, ethnicity, and religion—all selected because of the impact they have been found to have upon voter alignments. Electoral divisions could occur in other fashions, of course, perhaps along the lines of rural-urban or occupational differences. While such distinctions are possible, they have generally played a secondary role in the United States as compared to divisions along the lines of economic class, ethnic background, or religious affiliation.[16] For this reason, the examination of how population composition and past history of an area may shape alignment patterns will focus exclusively upon these three characteristics.

Using these three components, it is possible to test whether demographic and historic differences contributed significantly to differences in patterns of electoral alignment that may have occurred in Frederick and Kent. If electoral divisions followed economic lines, then both counties could exhibit similar voting patterns. If either ethnic or religious influences affected support for the two political parties, then considerable differences could appear. The ethnic heterogeneity of Frederick provided an alternative way for voters to divide between the Federalists and Republicans. Given the ethnic homogeneity of Kent, no such alignment could have developed there and supported a competitive two-party system. Religious differences in the two counties might have further encouraged variation in alignment patterns. The challenge to the Anglican establishment from one specific denomination in Kent could have increased the possibility of an electoral division along established versus dissenting lines. The fact that a variety of denominations competed with the Anglican Church from the outset in Frederick may have permitted a more general division along religious lines, perhaps in the pietistic-liturgical fashion suggested by other voter studies,[17] or the variety found may have canceled out religion-caused differences. In any case, the observed differences in the populations and histories of the two counties could have structured a variety of electoral alignments, even along only three distinctions.

In assessing the influences of wealth, ethnicity, and religion upon party voting, the variables will be considered separately, beginning with the impact of economic differences. Of the three, this is the one that would most readily produce similar voting patterns. If the patterns were similar, then wealthier persons in both Kent and Frederick should have supported one party, while poorer individuals should have supported the other.

A number of indices could be utilized in measuring the relationship between wealth and party voting. Perhaps the best procedure would be to include all of a person's assets—land, household goods, and investments—thus comparing his total net worth to all other persons in the population. Unfortunately, such detailed information is available for only a small minority of individuals. Another approach might be to focus strictly upon landed wealth. Both counties were predominantly agricultural and land was one of the most important capital commodities.[18] However, information on real property holdings during the period covered by the elections is easily available only in Frederick County.[19] The only readily available indicator of wealth that encompasses most of the voting population of both counties is slaveholding. Because of data limitations, slaveholding must serve as a surrogate of relative wealth.

There is some merit in using slaveholding as a measure of wealth, beyond its availability. In the first place, Maryland was a slave state and many individuals owned slaves. While the number of slaveholding households varied from area to area within the state, as shown by the differences between Frederick and Kent, there were sizeable numbers of slaveowners in both counties. Secondly, a slave was a major capital investment. Next to land, a slave was the most expensive item that an individual was likely to acquire. While a particular slave's value was largely dependent upon his age and health, it is plausible to suppose that quantitatively the possession of slaves reflected differences in overall wealth and surely reflected relative potential for acquiring it. Finally, there is good evidence that slaveownership was directly related to other forms of wealth in both counties. Individuals with greater amounts of personal property or large holdings of land were more likely to own larger numbers of slaves.[20] This relationship is by no means absolute, in part because the sources—tax lists and estate inventories—catch men at varying stages in their careers, but it is strong enough to allow use of slaveholding as an indicator, given the limitations of other wealth surrogates.

Using slaveholding as the surrogate, a relationship between wealth and party voting does appear in both counties, despite notable distinctions between the two areas. Table 12.1 presents the voting patterns for five categories of slaveownership.[21] Voters are classified as Federalist, Republican, or "Independent" on the basis of the flexible definition of stability discussed earlier. The percentage of those voting Federalist in each category when the independent voters are excluded is also presented. In both counties, there was a tendency for slaveholders, especially those with large slaveholdings, to favor the Federalist party and a lesser tendency for those persons not owning slaves to favor the Republicans.[22] The relationship was most pronounced in Frederick, where Federalist strength increased as the slaveholding category increased. Nevertheless, slaveholders in all categories were strongly Federalist, while nonslaveholders tended to be Republican. In Kent, the pattern was different. There were no dramatic partisan distinctions between those persons owning zero, one, two to four, or five to nine slaves, as all four groups displayed a slight Republican tendency. Only those in the largest slaveholding category revealed much of a tendency in the opposite direction, and they were far less Federalist than their Frederick counterparts. Nevertheless, differences in wealth did appear to have some impact upon partisan voting in both counties and the pattern was consistent: Large slaveholders favored the Federalist party, persons without slaves were inclined to favor the Republicans.[23]

Even though the pattern of alignment was consistent in the two counties, the lack of any dramatic polarization along the lines of wealth, particularly in Kent, suggests the presence of other influences upon partisan voting. Ethnic differences offer such a possibility, and these can be tested in Frederick County. The diversity of the population in that area, particularly

TABLE 12.1
Slaveholding Categories and Party Voting

Number of Slaves Owned	% of Straight Party Voters Voting Federalist	% Federalist	% Republican	% Independent	Total Number
Frederick County					
None	43	34	46	20	1,968
1	61	52	33	15	197
2–4	65	54	29	17	219
5–9	77	68	20	12	125
10 and Over	91	79	8	13	92
All Slaveholders	71	60	25	15	633
Totals	50	40	41	19	2,601
Kent County					
None	48	31	34	35	220
1	39	32	47	21	81
2–4	49	35	37	28	142
5–9	47	40	46	14	137
10 and Over	63	56	32	12	126
All Slaveholders	51	41	40	19	486
Totals	50	38	38	24	706

Note: In this and subsequent tables in which demographic attributes are related to partisan voting, the totals are not equivalent to the total number of voters in either county. Some voters were excluded, of course, because they did not exhibit partisan tendencies. Either they did not vote in more than one or two elections or they did not consistently support the candidates of one or the other party. Still other voters could not be classified as to their religion, their ethnic background, their place of residence, or their possession of slaves. The lack of demographic information on all partisan voters decreased even further the number of voters whose behavior could be analyzed in this and subsequent tables.

Of all voters who exhibited partisan tendencies, 69 percent in Frederick and 68 percent in Kent could be classified positively as slaveholders or nonslaveholders. The ethnic background could be determined for 62 percent of the Frederick and 75 percent of the Kent partisans. Religious affiliations could be determined for a far smaller subset, for only 35 percent of the Frederick and 28 percent of the Kent partisans. When any of these variables were combined with each other or with place of residence for multivariate comparisons, the subset of partisans included was even smaller. Thus, none of the demographic analyses encompasses 100 percent of all partisans in either county.

In spite of the fact that all of the demographic analysis is based upon subsets of the total partisan group, there is reason to believe that these subsets represent an adequate cross section of the total. Essentially, in both counties the partisan voters were evenly divided, approximately 50 percent supporting the Federalists and 50 percent supporting the Republicans. In each of the demographic variables, whether it be religion, place of residence, slaveholding, ethnicity, or a combination of these categories, the same 50-50 breakdown occurred. Had that breakdown been 60-40, or even 55-45, for all those identified within a demographic variable, then the representativeness of that subset would have been questionable at best. As it is, the partisan behavioral similarities between those who could and could not be classified in each demographic category indicates that the subsets in this and subsequent tables can be treated as rough cross sections of the entire partisan population under examination.

the sharp contrasts between persons of German and English background, might readily affect partisanship.[24] Consequently, an electoral polarization along ethnic lines in Frederick would strengthen the argument that voter alignments are, in part, affected by the ethnic composition of a given population. Conversely, the lack of any ethnic impact upon voting in Frederick might suggest that a more general alignment pattern was occurring, regardless of population differences.

Although a person's ethnicity can be determined without reliance upon a surrogate measure, indirect procedures are nevertheless necessary. No source provides information on ethnicity for a large segment of the population in this study. Individuals were therefore classified into ethnic groups on the basis of their surnames.[25] This method has some obvious drawbacks. It does not distinguish between generations. Germans who were immigrants or who were third-generation Marylanders by the late 1790s are both classified as German, even though the latter may have been fully integrated into the predominantly English society. Similarly, entire dependence upon the paternal surname fails to distinguish between persons whose families had married within the same ethnic group and persons whose families had married into other groups. Thus, some individuals classified into a specific group may, in fact, have been of mixed ethnic stock.[26] Finally, because of the ways in which county clerks interpreted the spelling of surnames, some persons could not be classified.[27] Nevertheless, despite the crudeness of the ethnic categories, they offer a rough means for distinguishing voters.[28] It should be possible to assess the impact of Frederick's ethnic heterogeneity upon electoral divisions.

Polarization along ethnic lines in Frederick was considerably more pronounced than it was among categories of slaveholders. Table 12.2 presents the partisan patterns of the four largest ethnic groups in the county. For comparative purposes, the voting patterns are also tabulated for the corresponding groups in Kent. When only regular party voters are considered, over three-fourths of those persons of English background supported the Federalist party in Frederick. Likewise, the other two ethnic groups of British background, the Scotch and Irish, were heavily Federalist. Germans, on the other hand, were strongly Republican. Close to two-thirds of the regular party voters of German background were in the Republican fold. In Kent, by contrast, there was almost no polarization along ethnic lines. Since the county was evenly split in the aggregate between the two parties, those of English background also divided their votes evenly, as did the small number of persons of Scottish background. Only the few Irish voters showed any proclivity to favor one of the parties (Republicans), and their behavior was not as cohesive as that of the four major groups in Frederick. Such ethnic differences as did exist in Kent did not have much bearing upon the overall pattern of alignment there. Thus the evidence supports the proposition that

TABLE 12.2
Ethnicity and Party Voting

Ethnic Group	% of Straight Party Voters Voting Federalist	% Federalist	% Republican	% Independent	Total Number
Frederick County				(62% Identified)	
English	75	63	20	17	894
Scotch	82	72	16	12	75
Irish	71	60	24	16	57
German	34	28	53	19	1,305
Totals	53	43	39	18	2,331
Kent County				(75% Identified)	
English	51	40	38	22	717
Scotch	50	36	36	28	25
Irish	37	21	36	42	33
German	0	0	75	25	4
Totals	51	39	38	23	779

where there is ethnic diversity—a product of historical circumstance—it can help to structure partisan divisions. Where there is none, other influences dominate.

One such influence upon voter alignments could be patterns of religious affiliation. Both Kent and Frederick exhibited some religious diversity, but there were important differences. The long-term predominance of Anglican establishment in Kent, coupled with the recent appearance of the Methodists as a major dissenting group, suggest that any extrapolation of religious differences into politics would be likely to follow an established-dissenting pattern. While such a pattern could also have developed in Frederick, its religious history made this more unlikely. Anglicanism had never been firmly entrenched in Frederick; a variety of denominations had been present from the county's formation. If religious affiliation independent of ethnicity exerted an influence upon voting in Frederick, it would be more likely to follow the lines of a pietistic-liturgical division. The different histories of the two counties, then, could create different relationships between religion and partisan voting.

Unfortunately, a full examination of this proposition is not possible, since information for religious affiliation is weaker than that for either wealth or ethnicity. Only 33 percent of the voting population in Frederick and 28 percent in Kent could be positively associated with a specific denomination. These small percentages suggest a greater amount of bias in the data, and hence more caution is required in interpreting the findings.[29] Furthermore, Methodists in Kent cannot be identified. Any Kent Methodist records kept during the late eighteenth century have long since disappeared.[30] Good records on membership have survived for the Episcopal churches and the

Quaker meeting in Kent,[31] making it possible to identify voters of these two denominations, but the remaining voters cannot be considered Methodists. The unidentified group also includes Episcopalians and Quakers unmentioned in the surviving records, along with persons who were not affiliated with any church.

Even with these shortcomings, some work can be done with the available information. In Frederick, religious affiliation of enough people could be determined to permit some behavioral comparisons between eight different denominations. At the same time, the unidentified population in Kent can at least be contrasted with the known Anglicans and Quakers. If the voting patterns differ sharply, inferences about Methodist behavior in the county are possible. Thus, there is the potential to make some general observations on patterns in the two counties.

The voting patterns of the various denominations are presented in table 12.3. In both counties, the denominations are listed along a general continuum from liturgical to pietistic (Catholic to Quaker in Frederick, Episcopal to Quaker in Kent), the ordering provided by the studies of Kleppner and Jensen.[32] Otherwise, the table follows the format of the two that precede it.

The behavior of the various religious groups indicates some important differences between the two counties. In Kent, a difference in voting appears

Table 12.3
Religion and Party Voting

Denomination	% of Straight Party Voters Voting Federalist	% Federalist	% Republican	% Independent	Total Number
Frederick County					(33% Identified)
Catholic	83	66	14	20	65
Episcopalian	86	74	12	14	65
Lutheran	32	26	55	19	320
Luth.-Reformed	35	31	56	13	198
Evangelical Reformed	41	33	47	20	369
Presbyterian	86	79	12	9	89
Methodist	68	58	27	15	33
Quaker	72	52	21	27	44
Unidentified	49	41	42	17	2,516
Religious Totals	48	40	43	17	1,235
Kent County					(28% Identified)
Episcopalian	59	50	34	16	250
Unidentified	45	33	41	26	748
Quaker	61	53	33	14	36
Totals	49	38	39	23	1,034

to follow the suggested established-dissenting division. The unidentified group, although mixed, leaned toward Republicanism, Anglicans toward Federalism.[33] However, there was not a full-fledged pietistic-liturgical division, since Quakers divided similarly to the Episcopalians. In Frederick neither pattern appeared. Catholics and Anglicans, along with Presbyterians, Methodists, and Quakers, were all heavily Federalist. Essentially, a third pattern prevailed. The three primarily German denominations[34] were strongly Republican, while all of the basically British religions were predominantly Federalist. Religion in Frederick appeared to affect voter alignments only inasmuch as it symbolized ethnic differences in the county. Denominational affiliation appears to have been reflected in partisan voting in Kent, but not in Frederick.[35]

Thus, demographic and historical differences evidently had some effect upon the voting patterns of the two counties. Although wealth seemed to be related to party voting in both, ethnicity was relevant only in Frederick, religion only in Kent. Furthermore, these two variables appeared to have more impact upon voting than did wealth. The idea is plausible that demographic and historical differences can produce various patterns of alignment within the same party system.

Immediate Social Contacts and Behavioral Patterns

The immediate social contacts of an individual voter might also produce variations in electoral behavior. A person's neighbors, the company he keeps at the local tavern, the religious congregation that he is part of, the voluntary associations that he belongs to, all provide experiences that could help shape or reinforce political attitudes and party attachments. Such contacts might shape a person's electoral behavior regardless of his relative wealth or ethnic background.

In most situations, this immediate environment supplements political proclivities that individuals have already acquired. Much of a person's political socialization derives from more primary associations, in particular his family. His parents' concerns, interests, and discussions stimulate and develop his political awareness or unawareness in childhood and the way in which he, subsequently, identifies with the various parties. Nevertheless, this initial orientation is frequently supplemented (although it can be contradicted) by a person's most direct secondary contacts.[36]

These social contacts may have been especially important in the period under examination. The first party system in Maryland was still new in the late 1790s, and this fact may have given secondary associations as important or more important a role than family experience for many persons in the development of their political attachments. In addition, the openness of the voting process strengthened the impact of a person's social contacts. An individual's neighbors, friends, or fellow church members had no difficulty in finding out how he voted. Consequently, voters may have felt greater pressure to behave like their associates than they would have if the ballot had been secret.[37] The newness of parties and the viva voce voting process may have given secondary environment exceptional importance during this period in shaping political attachments.

These associations, then, might be expected to have an effect upon electoral alignments, independent of wealth, ethnicity, and religion. A man's neighbors may have been as important as his ownership of slaves in shaping his political allegiances. Where he lived may have been as relevant as his German origins. Or, the specific church that he attended may have been as important as the fact that he was Lutheran.

One way to test the impact of social contacts is to specify an immediate environmental context for individual voters in the two counties. Information about a voter's residence among slaveholders, Germans, or Methodists can be used to assess whether this immediate environment altered his "expected" behavior, given only his personal attributes. For example, a German residing in a heavily German area might be more inclined to vote Republican, while a German living among persons of English background might be less inclined to do so. Election districts (three in Kent, seven in Frederick) offer a possible breakdown of voters that might be related to such environmental differences, provided these districts differed considerably in their demographic characteristics.[38]

Table 12.4 indicates considerable demographic variation among the seven election districts in Frederick County, but comparatively little among the three districts in Kent. Ethnic concentrations varied substantially across the seven Frederick districts. Only 33 percent of the Buckeystown district population was of German background, compared to 77 percent of the residents in Westminstertown district. There were minor differences between the three units in Kent, but in all cases persons of English background constituted around 90 percent of the population. Similarly, the concentration of slaveholders in particular areas varied to a greater degree in Frederick. Approximately 30 percent of the Buckeystown households owned slaves, compared to only 10 percent of the households in Westminstertown. In Kent, where slavery was generally more widespread, all three districts were rather evenly divided between slaveholding and non-slaveholding households. Such distinctions indicate that voters within Frederick County were exposed to markedly different environments and contacts, whereas the experience of Kent voters was relatively homogeneous, regardless of where they resided.[39]

Considering the population characteristics of the seven election districts in Frederick, there appear to be three basic types of environments—English-slaveholding, German-nonslaveholding, and an essentially "mixed" environment. All of these distinctions are, of course, relative. There were large

TABLE 12.4
*Slaveholding and Ethnic Estimates for Frederick and
Kent Election Districts*

Election District	% English	% German (Minorities in Kent)	% Slaveholders
Frederick County			
Buckeystown	63	33	30
Fredericktown	26	70	23
Middletown	27	69	17
Emmitsburgh	36	58	16
Taneytown	42	52	13
Westminstertown	20	77	10
Libertytown	56	40	21
Totals	40	54	19
Kent County			
Wilmer's	96	4	55
Chestertown	92	8	49
Georgetown	87	13	44
Totals	92	8	49

numbers of Germans in all seven districts, and persons without slaves were a majority of the householders in all seven. Nevertheless, the variations were substantial enough to permit these three rough typologies. Buckeystown and Libertytown districts best characterize the English-slaveholding environment. These were the only two areas in the county where those of English background constituted a majority of the population and were two of the three districts where the percentage of slaveholders was greater than that of the overall county. Middletown and Westminstertown districts, on the other hand, best represent the opposite environment. The German population here was a distinct majority and slaveholding concentrations were lower than in the county as a whole. Fredericktown district had a similar concentration of Germans, but the percentage of slaveholders in the area was more comparable to Buckeystown and Libertytown. Emmitsburgh fell between the contrasting units in both slaveholding and ethnic concentrations. These last two units, then, constitute what could be termed a "mixed" environment, where the population characteristics either conflict or approximate the county as a whole.[40]

If these three distinct types of immediate social environment in Frederick did influence partisan behavior, then persons living in English-slaveholding areas should have shown a greater tendency toward Federalism, persons living in German-nonslaveholding areas a greater tendency toward Republicanism, and persons living in "mixed" areas a tendency to behave similarly to the original subgroup (that is, the way Germans or slaveholders divided in the county as a whole). Table 12.5 tests this proposition by comparing the partisan preferences of slaveholders, nonslaveholders, Germans, and English

TABLE 12.5
Slaveholding, Ethnicity, and Party Voting in Frederick,
Controlling for Type of Environment

Type of Environment	Nonslaveholders		Slaveholders		Totals 44%	
	% Federalist	N	% Federalist	N	% Federalist	N
English Slaveholding	71	696	87	272	75	968
Mixed	33	602	68	197	42	799
German Nonslaveholding	21	675	35	125	23	800
Totals	42	1,973	70	594	49	2,567
	Germans		*English*		*Totals 31%*	
English Slaveholding	64	266	87	397	77	663
Mixed	31	423	64	207	42	630
German Non-slaveholding	17	425	45	127	23	552
Totals	33	1,114	73	731	49	1,845

Note: Independent voters excluded.

in the three types of environments and in the county overall. The evidence indicates that contrasting social contacts had a pronounced influence on partisan behavior. While nonslaveholders overall voted 42 percent Federalist, those residing in German-nonslaveholding areas voted only 21 percent Federalist, whereas 71 percent of those residing in English-slaveholding areas supported the Federalist party. Slaveholders in the "mixed" districts more closely approximated the partisan behavior of the county as a whole. The same pattern was evident in the other three categories. Persons residing in English-slaveholding districts were more inclined to vote Federalist than would have been expected from their personal attributes alone; persons in German-nonslaveholding districts were more inclined to vote Republican, and persons in the "mixed" districts behaved the way one would expect on the basis of their personal attributes alone. Controlling for this immediate environment did not remove the partisan impact of any personal attribute. In all three environments slaveholders were more likely to vote Federalist than nonslaveholders, and English were more likely to vote Federalist than Germans. Essentially, a person's social contacts appeared to reinforce or moderate the partisan inclinations stemming from his other attributes, exerting an independent effect upon the way he cast his ballots.

Another way to examine the effect of a person's social contacts (outside his family) is to consider the behavior of voters in specific towns or religious congregations. Small towns and churches both provided direct secondary contacts for those who resided in or belonged to them. If such contacts exerted a strong independent influence, then residents in a small town or members of a small church should have favored one of the two political parties overwhelmingly.

In most of the observed cases in Frederick County, this pattern was very clear. Table 12.6 shows the ranges of political cohesion found for twenty-six towns and religious congregations in Frederick. (The cohesion value represents the percentage of persons in a given group voting for the party favored by that group and always falls between 50 and 100 percent.) Almost all of the towns and churches considered had cohesion rates greater than 60 percent and in seventeen of the twenty-six cases over 75 percent of the individuals favored the same party.[41] In five cases, 100 percent supported the same party.

Although the available information is far from complete (it was not possible in Kent County to construct useful surrogates of social contacts), and the observations are limited to one county over a short span of time, the evidence suggests that the voter's immediate environment had bearing upon the way he behaved. In Frederick County, where a person resided made a tremendous difference in the way he voted, regardless of whether he was German, English, slaveholder, or nonslaveholder. Among groups in which there was likely to be continuous personal contact, political cohesion was marked. All told, the evidence suggests that an individual's day-to-day experiences, his immediate surroundings and contacts, had an important bearing upon the way he affiliated with the political parties, regardless of his own personal attributes.[42]

Personal Attributes and Social Contacts as Reinforcing or Conflicting Forces

The various factors that can influence and shape partisan behavior do not always have the same effect. A person raised in a family that identified strongly with one party might later in life belong to a religious group identified with another. The variety of such conflicting experiences is potentially endless. Perhaps as important as the fact that they exist is the way in which particular individuals respond to them. Some persons may reject their upbringing and choose to vote with their new associates when the two are in conflict. Others may become disenchanted or confused and refrain from identifying with either party. Still others may ignore or filter

TABLE 12.6
Cohesion Ratings for Towns and Religious Groups in Frederick County

Category	100%	90–99%	75–89%	60–75%	Under 60%	Total
Number of Towns	4	0	1	3	1	9
Number of Church Groups	1	4	8	2	2	17
Totals	5	4	9	5	3	26

out the influences they experience in later life and continue to vote as their families have done.[43] Not all persons, of course, would have to experience such conflict. Family background, personal status, and social contacts might all reinforce each other. Personal experiences vary and their variations influence the overall pattern of electoral alignments.

With the data that have been presented in previous sections, it is possible to define the partisan direction that any specific personal attribute would have. In both counties, a person who owned slaves (in Kent a person who owned ten or more) would be inclined toward Federalism, while the remaining population would tend to vote in the opposite direction. In Frederick, persons of English background and persons residing in areas with higher concentrations of English and slaveholders would be more inclined toward Federalism, while those of German background and those living in areas with higher concentrations of Germans and a smaller percentage of slaveowners would be more inclined toward the Republican party. In Kent, members of the Anglican Church would be more likely to vote Federalist than nonmembers, Quakers excepted.

When these attributes are combined, they would either reinforce or modify the partisan inclination of any one of them. A Frederick resident who owned slaves, was of English background, and lived in a heavily English, slaveholding district would experience three positive influences to vote for the Federalist party. A Kent resident who owned slaves but did not belong to the Anglican church might experience some conflict in his partisan choice. If personal attributes in combination act as either reinforcing or conflicting forces, then voters who experienced no conflict should exhibit the greatest cohesiveness in their behavior, while those who experienced some conflict should behave in a more random fashion, dividing their votes more evenly between the two parties.

This proposition is examined in Table 12.7, which presents data for both Frederick and Kent counties. In Frederick, three attributes—wealth, ethnicity, and place of residence—could be identified as partisan forces while only

TABLE 12.7
Partisan Behavior When Attributes Reinforce and Conflict

Partisan Direction of Personal Attributes in Combination	Frederick County			Kent County		
	% Federalist	% Republican	Number	% Federalist	% Republican	Number
3 Federalist	93	7	166	—	—	—
2 Federalist	80	20	80	67	33	76
2 Federalist, 1 Republican	75	25	338	—	—	—
1 Federalist, 1 Republican	53	47	196	53	47	160
1 Federalist, 2 Republican	52	48	330	—	—	—
2 Republican	27	73	354	44	56	372
3 Republican	15	85	379	—	—	—

two—wealth and religion—could be so classified in Kent. In some cases, only two attributes were applicable to Frederick residents. Some persons resided in election districts that were not heavily German and nonslaveholding, or heavily English and slaveholding. Indeed, two of Frederick's districts, Emmitsburgh and Fredericktown, were considered to exert a neutral influence upon the partisan inclinations of their residents. In Kent, of course, only two attributes were used throughout.

The data confirm the expectation that personal attributes in combination produce cohesive behavior when reinforcing and random partisan patterns when in conflict. Cohesive behavior was strongest for those persons whose attributes supplemented each other, whether the direction was toward the Federalist or toward the Republican party. Such cohesiveness diminished when only two attributes were reinforcing, but partisan behavior in these groups was still stronger than among those persons who experienced any kind of conflict. When one of the attributes conflicted with the other(s), the individual was as likely to support one party as the other. The only exception was that group for whom two attributes were pro-Federalist and one was pro-Republican. Three-fourths of such persons were Federalist supporters, but even this group was less cohesive than those who experienced no conflict. The overall pattern was less pronounced in Kent than in Frederick, perhaps partly because there was one less attribute to work with. Nevertheless, even in Kent, the pattern was consistent. Cohesive behavior was strongest among persons with attributes that reinforced and virtually nonexistent (or at least less pronounced) for individuals who experienced conflict of any sort.

In summary, personal attributes and social contacts, taken in combination, also structured the overall pattern of electoral alignment in Frederick and Kent counties. When personal attributes and social environment were reinforcing, voter alignment was clear and could be firmly associated with any characteristic, be it wealth, ethnicity, or place of residence. Where such influences conflicted, cohesive partisan voting was always less pronounced and usually nonexistent. In such cases, the effects of any particular influence were noticeably modified or disappeared.

Conclusion

These specific findings in Kent and Frederick counties do not extend to other places or times in the history of the United States. The newness of political parties in the late 1790s and early 1800s, the peculiar process of viva voce voting, and the specific ecological characteristics of the two counties all militate against such claims. The fact that party organization was in its formative stages may have given secondary associations a greater role in electoral behavior than would occur in later party systems. The public nature of an oral vote may have put pressure on men to agree with their neighbors. The specific histories of the two counties and the composition of their populations doubtless affected voting behavior in ways that would not be found in other areas with different populations and histories.

Nevertheless, the findings of this paper suggest that no one characteristic, such as wealth or religion, by itself explains voting alignments. The population composition and history of a given area appear important in determining which of a variety of factors produce voter polarization. An individual's social contacts can temper or intensify his expected proclivity to support a particular party. And his own attributes in combination or combined with his social contacts either modify or reinforce his partisan tendencies.

Studies of American partisan behavior, then, should emphasize the interaction of such variables and deemphasize the importance of any single one. There have been some trends in this direction recently. The interest in multivariate analysis has brought an implied acknowledgment that no single factor explains electoral behavior. Even there, however, the effort has often focused upon ferreting out the single variable that most "explains" partisan voting. This study of two Maryland counties during the early national period suggests that any variable depends upon a combination of others and is thus likely to vary in importance across place and time. Full understanding of the causes of political alignments requires careful analysis of how the social characteristics of a voter interact in a social context to influence the way he casts his ballot.

NOTES

1. This is not to argue that the United States has been a "society without classes," or that the nation has never been divided on fundamental matters. It does appear, however, that the United States has not experienced a pervasive, continuing, internal division related to fundamental economic and social matters; see Daniel J. Boorstin, *The Genius of American Politics* (Chicago, 1953); Richard Hofstadter, *The American Political Tradition* (New York, 1948), esp. pp. v–xi, 3–44; Louis Hartz, *The Liberal Tradition in America* (New York, 1955), esp. pp. 3–32, 67–87; Lee Benson, *The Concept of Jacksonian Democracy: New York as a Test Case* (Princeton, 1961), pp. 27–328; and Samuel P. Huntington, *Political Order in Changing Societies* (New Haven, 1968), pp. 93–139.

2. Thus there has been an ongoing debate in the profession over whether economic class or ethnocultural distinctions form the basis of electoral divisions in the United States. Charles A. Beard, in *Economic Origins of Jeffersonian Democracy* (New York, 1915), especially pp. 165–247, was one of the first to espouse the class thesis. Later scholars, including Manning Dauer, *The Adams' Federalists* (Baltimore, 1953), pp. 1–34, Frank Otto Gatell, "Money and Party in Jacksonian America: A Quantitative Look at New York City's Men of Quality," *Political Science Quarterly* 82 (1967):235–52, and Arthur Schlesinger, Jr., *The Age of Jackson* (Boston, 1945), pp. 18–30, 250–306, have continued to stress this class theme. More recent studies, such as Benson, *Concept of Jacksonian Democracy*, 165–207, Robert Swierenga, "Ethnocultural Political Analysis: A New Approach to American Ethnic Studies," *Journal of American Studies* 5 (1971):59–79, Richard Jensen, *The Winning of the Midwest: Social and Political Conflict, 1888–1896 (Chicago, 1971), pp. 58–68, Paul Kleppner, The Cross of Culture:*

A Social Analysis of Midwestern Politics, 1850–1900 (New York, 1970), pp. 65–95, and Ronald P. Formisano, *The Birth of Mass Political Parties: Michigan, 1821–1861* (Princeton, 1971), pp. 102–92, have emphasized the importance of ethnic and religious affiliations and played down the impact of social class upon partisan behavior. (Actually, the ethnocultural literature is far more extensive than the above citations would suggest. For a recent bibliography, see Richard L. McCormick, "Ethno-Cultural Interpretations of Nineteenth-Century American Voting Behavior," *Political Science Quarterly* 89 (1974):351–77. While the major debate has focused around these three variables—wealth, ethnicity, and religion—a few scholars have suggested other specific causes of electoral divisions. Some, including John A. Munroe, *Federalist Delaware, 1775–1815* (New Brunswick, 1954), p. 239, have suggested a rural-urban distinction, while others, such as Richard Jensen, "The Religious and Occupational Roots of Party Identification: Illinois and Indiana in the 1870s," *Civil War History* 16 (1970):325–43, have suggested that occupational groupings may have affected electoral alignments. In almost all of these cases, the stress has been upon a single variable as the primary cause of electoral divisions.

3. The influence of such characteristics upon electoral behavior has been suggested by Erik Allardt in "Aggregate Analysis: The Problem of Its Informative Value," Tapani Valkonen, "Individual and Structural Effects in Ecological Research," Edwin K. Scheuch, "Social Context and Individual Behavior," and David R. Segal and Marshall W. Meyer, "The Social Context of Political Partisanship," all in *Quantitative Ecological Analysis in the Social Sciences*, ed. Mattei Dogan and Stein Rokkan (Cambridge, 1969), pp. 41–51, 53–68, 91–131, 133–55, 217–32; Alan S. Meyer, "The Independent Voter," William N. McPhee and Robert B. Smith, "A Model for Analyzing Voting Systems," and Philip H. Ennis, "The Contextual Dimension in Voting," all in *Public Opinion and Congressional Elections*, ed. William N. McPhee and William A. Glaser (New York, 1962), pp. 65–77, 123–54, 180–211; and Bernard R. Berelson, Paul F. Lazarsfeld, and William N. McPhee, *Voting: A Study of Opinion Formation in a Presidential Campaign* (Chicago, 1954), pp. 129–132, 318–320.

4. Maryland voted viva voce in all elections until the secret ballot was adopted in time for the 1803 congressional election. Before 1803, both the name of the voter and the way he cast his ballot(s) were recorded on tally sheets (poll books). Most of the surviving lists for Maryland, including those for Frederick and Kent, are in the Hall of Records, Annapolis, Md.

5. There has been considerable debate on whether and when political parties developed during the late eighteenth century. Jackson Turner Main, *Political Parties before the Constitution* (Chapel Hill, 1973), has argued on the one hand that parties were well established in the 1780s; on the other hand, Ronald P. Formisano, "Deferential Participant Politics: The Early Republic's Political Culture, 1789–1840," *The American Political Science Review* 68 (1974):473–87, has questioned whether a viable party system ever existed during this early national period. Based upon a rigorous and frequently used definition of party, David A. Bohmer, "The Maryland Electorate and the Concept of a Party System in the Early National Period," in *The History of American Electoral Behavior*, ed. Joel H. Silbey, Allan G. Bogue, and William H. Flanigan, Mathematical Social Science Board Series (Princeton, forthcoming), has determined that a party system in Maryland began to develop only in the mid-1790s but continued to operate for the next twenty years. Bohmer also found that most voters participated in elections and continued to support the same party throughout the period.

6. Most particularly, the availability of poll books permits circumvention of the problems posed by inferring individual behavior from aggregate characteristics. Statistical techniques have been developed since W. S. Robinson first posed the problem in his classic article, "Ecological Correlations and the Behavior of Individuals," *American Sociological Review* 15 (1950):351–57, but the availability of individual-level data, either in the form of surveys or poll books, remains the most thorough way to specify and study the interaction of personal attributes and ecological environment in shaping behavior.

7. One of the four elected delegates in Kent died shortly after his victory. A special election was held two months after the first election to choose a successor.

8. Actually, the potential bias of the final data set is far less than 15 percent and more likely in the realm of 5 percent. For a full discussion of the linkage procedure that was used and the assumptions that were involved in creating the data file used in this analysis, see David A. Bohmer, "Voting Behavior during the First American Party System: Maryland 1796–1816" (Ph.D. diss., University of Michigan, 1974), pp. 311–20.

9. The federal census returns used, for 1790, 1800, and 1810, are located in the National Archives, Washington, D.C. Assessment lists and church records for the two counties are located in the Maryland Historical Society in Baltimore and the Hall of Records, Annapolis. For a full discussion of the sources used and the possible shortcomings that they introduce see Bohmer, "Voting Behavior," pp. 294-310.

10. Bohmer, "Maryland Electorate."

11. Even with this definition of what constitutes a partisan voter, a decision must be made about what segment of the electorate to focus upon in the analysis. All persons who cast a ballot in the eight elections examined could be included, but this would encompass persons who only voted once or twice, perhaps too few times to establish a pattern of partisan behavior. As an alternative, the voting population could be limited to those who voted in at least three of the eight elections. While this subset would eliminate those whose voting patterns were not established, it could decrease the population being analyzed to such a degree, especially in the multivariate comparisons, that it would not be possible to draw any conclusions. Fortunately, these potential difficulties are alleviated by the fact that both populations behaved in a similar partisan fashion. In both the entire electorate and those who voted in at least three elections there were similar percentages of Federalists, Republicans, and independents. To satisfy both objectives, then, to focus upon a group whose partisan behavior was established and to include enough voters so that meaningful conclusions can be drawn from the multivariate analysis, the bivariate comparisons will deal with those persons who voted in three or more elections, while the multivariate analysis will encompass all persons who cast a ballot in any of the eight elections.

12. To substantiate this point, one need only survey the literature that deals with the various party systems in the United States. Numerous monographs have focused upon the development of and competition between political parties in a single state, and many of these works have touched upon the question of what kinds of people supported these parties. Other studies have dealt more directly with the subject of electoral alignments, examining who the Federalists were in Massachusetts, who voted Republican in New York, who supported the Democrats in Alabama, or who made up the Whig vote in Pittsburgh. Some of these studies focus upon a larger region, such as four or five midwestern states or two or three states in the Northeast. None of these works explicitly states that their findings are applicable to the rest of the United States, but neither do most of them explicitly state that their findings are confined to the area of analysis. It is this lack of qualification or caution about the results that frequently implies a broader generality than the area that is focused upon.

13. For background on Kent County and the Eastern Shore in the seventeenth and eighteenth centuries see George A. Hanson, *Old Kent: The Eastern Shore of Maryland* (Baltimore, 1876); Charles B. Clark, ed., *The Eastern Shore of Maryland and Virginia*, vol. 1 (New York, 1950); and Frederic Emory, *Queen Anne's County, Maryland: Its Early History and Development* (Baltimore, 1950). A recent study by Paul G. E. Clemens, "From Tobacco to Grain, Economic Development on Maryland's Eastern Shore, 1660-1750" (Ph.D. diss., University of Wisconsin, 1974), has examined the transition from tobacco to wheat in Talbot County. The work of St. Mary's City Commission, in particular that of Lois Green Carr and Russell Menard, has been useful to this historical sketch. Their studies of economic and demographic developments in the Maryland colony have helped to provide a general framework in which to place Kent County in this period; see, for example, Russell R. Menard, "Economy and Society in Early Colonial Maryland" (Ph.D. diss., University of Iowa, 1975); idem, "The Growth of Population in Early Colonial Maryland, 1631-1712" (ms. report, St. Mary's City Commission, April 1972, on file at the Hall of Records, Annapolis, Md.); and idem, P. M. G. Harris, and Lois Green Carr, "Opportunity and Inequality: The Distribution of Wealth on the Lower Western Shore of Maryland, 1638-1705," *Maryland Historical Magazine* 69 (1974), 169-84.

14. For background on Frederick County see Dieter Cunz, *The Maryland Germans: A History* (Princeton, 1948); J. Thomas Scharf, *History of Western Maryland*, 2 vols. (1882; Baltimore, 1968), vol. 1; and Thomas John Chew Williams, *History of Frederick County, Maryland*, vol. 1 (Baltimore, 1967). Dulany's part in the settlement of Frederick is discussed in Aubrey C. Land, *The Dulanys of Maryland: A Biographical Study of Daniel Dulany, the Elder (1685-1753) and Daniel Dulany, the Younger (1722-1797)*, Studies in Maryland History No. 3

(Baltimore, 1955), pp. 175–84. The research of Elizabeth A. Kessel, "Germans on the Frontier: A Social History of Frederick County 1730–1800" (Ph.D. diss. in progress, Rice University), has also been of use to this historical sketch of Frederick. I am indebted to Lois Carr for pointing out many aspects of the Anglican establishment in both Kent and Frederick.

15. Slaveholding patterns in Frederick and Kent were calculated from the federal census returns of 1800. The ethnic compositions of the two units were calculated by a more indirect procedure based upon the frequency of types of surnames in the 1800 census. See Bohmer, "Voting Behavior," pp. 113 and 272, for a discussion of how these estimates were obtained. The number of naturalizations in the two counties was obtained from the county court minute books, located in the Hall of Records. Approximately three-hundred persons were naturalized in Frederick between 1789 and 1800 compared to only six persons in Kent. It is virtually impossible to calculate the percentage breakdown of various religious denominations in the two counties due to the lack of such information in the Federal censuses of this period and to the incompleteness of the church records themselves. An examination of the church records, however, leaves little question of the greater diversity of religious groups in Frederick County throughout the eighteenth century.

16. See, for example, Berelson et al., *Voting*, p. 54: Robert R. Alford, *Party and Society: The Anglo-American Democracies* (Chicago, 1963), pp. 37–39; Seymour Martin Lipset and Stein Rokkan, "Cleavage Structures, Party Systems, and Voter Alignments: An Introduction," in *Party Systems and Voter Alignments: Cross-National Perspectives*, ed. Seymour Martin Lipset and Stein Rokkan (New York, 1967), p. 12; and Benson, *Concept of Jacksonian Democracy*, pp. 270–78.

17. Two studies in particular have stressed this pietistic vs. liturgical (ritualistic) dimension to electoral alignments; see Kleppner, *Cross of Culture*, pp. 65–95, and Jensen, *Winning of the Midwest*, pp. 58–68.

18. John Kenneth Galbraith, *The New Industrial State* (Boston, 1967), pp. 62–65, has an excellent summary of the primary role played by land in a preindustrial economy.

19. The only assessment list available during this period in Kent County is for the year 1783. While this list was coded and linked to the final data set, the period it represents is too far removed from the period in which persons voted for this data to be used in the analysis.

20. Bohmer, "Voting Behavior," p. 138, found a Pearson's *r* correlation above .5 between the number of slaves and the value of land owned across all individuals in Frederick County. This is a particularly high relationship given the large number of individuals included in the data set.

21. Individual slaveholding data was obtained from the 1800 manuscript census. The categories selected here are, admittedly, rather arbitrary. They were chosen primarily because they coincide with the breakdowns given in the 1790 census. These categories do fulfill two useful purposes. First, they provide a sensitive measure of slaveholding increments at the lower level (0, 1, 2–4). Second, they insure that enough individuals fall into each group to permit overall comparisons. Thus, the 1790 categories of 10–19, 20–49, and 50 and over have been combined, since too few people in both Frederick and Kent owned twenty or more slaves.

22. There was a tendency for nonslaveholders to behave in a less partisan fashion. A greater percentage of this group in both counties split their vote over time than did the voters in any of the slaveholding categories. This tendency was most pronounced in Kent, where over one-third of those without slaves divided their loyalties. An explanation for the more independent behavior of this group would shed additional light on the subject of electoral behavior during the early national period. Since the focus of this study is upon partisan rather than independent behavior, such an examination lies outside the scope of this essay.

23. In Frederick, where there was information on the ownership of land in the period covered by the elections (1798 assessment), there was a similar relationship between wealth and partisan behavior. Only 44 percent of all persons with small amounts of land, worth less than 100 pounds, supported the Federalist party. As the landowning category increased, so did the strength of Federalist support. In the wealthiest category, those persons owning land worth over 1,000 pounds, 82 percent of the voters were Federalists.

24. Cunz, *Maryland Germans*, pp. 73–78, 92, 114–18, 158. Kessel's work on Frederick County has indicated sharp contrasts in life styles, especially in the early years of the county's history. Some of these differences had probably diminished after nearly three generations of

settlement, but an analysis of probate inventories between 1800 and 1807 by Bohmer, "Voting Behavior," pp. 106–10, suggests that there were still considerable differences in life styles between the Germans and English at the turn of the century.

25. The method used is the same as that followed by The American Council of Learned Societies in "Report of Committee on Linguistic and National Stocks in the Population of the United States," *Annual Report of the American Historical Association 1931* (Washington, D.C., 1932). Only those surnames that could be positively connected to just one ethnic group were classified.

26. Kessel's research, however, suggests that marriages between English and Germans were uncommon throughout the eighteenth century.

27. Common English names like Baker, Miller, and Smith could not be classified because they sometimes represented Anglicizations of the German surnames Becker, Mueller, and Schmidt.

28. There is indirect evidence that the ethnic classifications are fairly good ones. First, the fact that German and English groups had such distinctive patterns of behavior (table 12.2) suggests that the criterion used here did differentiate the population. Second, since those who could not be classified divided almost evenly between the two parties, there does not appear to have been any systematic bias introduced as a result of their exclusion. They appear to have represented a cross section of the county's population.

29. Information on religious affiliation for voters in both Frederick and Kent was obtained primarily through church records. In Frederick, this was supplemented by information on place of burial provided by Jacob Mehrling Holdcraft, *Names in Stone: 75,000 Cemetery Inscriptions from Frederick County, Maryland*, 2 vols. (Ann Arbor, 1966). For a discussion of the shortcomings of the data on religious affiliation, see Bohmer, "Voting Behavior," pp. 301–5.

30. The lack of Methodist records in this period is largely due to the itinerant behavior of the ministry. Most Methodist ministers traveled from place to place preaching. Since they were also responsible for keeping the vital statistics, the records of a single or of several congregations traveled with them on the circuit. This transitory state of the records enhanced the chances of their being lost, first because they had to be carted around from place to place, and second, because they frequently disappeared when the minister died. I am indebted to Phebe Jacobsen, archivist in charge of church records, Maryland Hall of Records, for this information on the early Methodist Church in Maryland.

31. The surviving records include those of the three largest Anglican churches, Chester Parish, Shrewsbury Parish, and St. Paul's Parish, along with the one Quaker meeting in the county, the Cecil Monthly Meeting. Originals or copies of the records used are in the Hall of Records.

32. For the specific listings and explanations of why these denominations have been ranked in this particular fashion along the pietistic-liturgical dimension, see Kleppner, *Cross of Culture*, pp. 71–83, and Jensen, *Winning of Midwest*, pp. 60–64. For a shorter and more focused discussion of this continuum, see Jensen, "Party Identification," 336–38.

33. In all likelihood, the data difficulties with religion bias the distinctions observed in partisan behavior in the direction of revealing no differences in the electoral realm. First, the non-Episcopal category probably includes some individuals who belonged to, or at least attended, the Episcopal churches. Second, unless it is plausible to believe that unchurched individuals should have behaved in a cohesive fashion (and the evidence for Frederick County, where those who could not be classified split evenly between the two parties, suggests that there is no reason to adhere to that proposition), it is likely that the non-Episcopal category actually blurs behavioral distinctions between members of the Methodist and Anglican faiths. The fact that distinctions were revealed in spite of these weaknesses indicates that religious differences did influence the electoral alignment that occurred in Kent County.

34. These included Lutherans, Evangelical Reformed, and the two denominations combined. In areas of Frederick where there were not enough persons to sponsor a Lutheran or Reformed minister, the two congregations joined together to form one church. Not all who attended these churches (or either of the two for that matter) were German. English non-Anglicans often did not have a church of their own faith in the area and thus attended the German churches because they most closely approximated their own denominations. Nonetheless, the vast majority of individuals who married and had their children baptized in the Lutheran and Reformed churches were Germans.

35. It is possible that this tenuous relationship between religion and partisan behavior is a spurious one. As was the case in Frederick, where religious distinctions were actually a product of ethnic differences, the distinctions observed in Kent may be caused by the impact of another variable. In particular, it may be that most of the county's slaveholders with large slaveholdings were Anglicans, thus revealing a pro-Federalist inclination among that religious group that disappears when slaveholding is controlled. In fact, a disproportionate number of slaveowners with large holdings were members of the Anglican churches, but even when slaveholding was held constant, Episcopalians were more likely to vote Federalist than were those voters who were not associated with any church. This relationship persisted across all slaveholding and nonslaveholding categories. When ethnicity was held constant in Frederick, religious distinctions disappeared, but a similar control in Kent failed to diminish the differences observed in table 12.3.

36. For discussions of the impact of immediate secondary associations in the modern electorate, see Angus Campbell, Philip E. Converse, Warren E. Miller, and Donald E. Stokes, *The American Voter*, abr. (New York, 1964), pp. 168–71; Avery Leiserson, *Parties and Politics: An Institutional and Behavioral Approach* (New York, 1958), p. 153; Berelson et al., *Voting*, pp. 57–74, 126; Herbert McClosky and Harold E. Dahlgren, "Primary Group Influence on Party Loyalty," in *Politics and Social Life*, ed. Nelson W. Polsby, Robert A. Dentler, and Paul A. Smith (Boston, 1963), pp. 256–57; Volkonen, "Ecological Research," pp. 60–61; Scheuch, "Social Context," p. 142; Segal and Meyer, "Context of Partisanship," pp. 217–32; Ennis, "Contextual Dimension," pp. 184–85; William H. Flanigan, *Political Behavior of the American Electorate* (Boston, 1968), pp. 57–61; and Robert E. Lane, *Political Life: Why and How People Get Involved in Politics* (New York, 1959), pp. 264–5.

37. The influence of the viva voce voting process upon partisan behavior has been suggested by Philip E. Converse, "Change in the American Electorate," in *The Human Meaning of Social Change*, ed. Angus Campbell and Philip E. Converse (New York, 1972), pp. 283–89, Charles S. Sydnor, *American Revolutionaries in the Making* (New York, 1966), pp. 26–33, and Staughton Lynd, "Who Should Rule at Home? Dutchess County, New York, in the American Revolution," in *Class Conflict, Slavery and the United States Constitution*, ed. Staughton Lynd (New York, 1967), pp. 38–40.

38. A more focused approach would be to determine the specific location of each individual voter, thus identifying his most direct neighborhood contacts. Such an attempt would be possible in both counties by doing a tract map based upon the assessment lists and land records. Although possible and potentially productive, such a project would require as much, if not more, time than was required to collect and process the poll book and supplementary data presented here. For that reason, it was decided that a person's election district of residence would provide a rough approximation of his most immediate social environment.

39. It is possible that Methodists in Kent were especially concentrated in one or two of the three election districts, but the evidence is too limited to examine that possibility. Since the Anglicans in Kent appeared in roughly equal percentages of the total voting population in each of the three districts, however, this possibility would seem to be a remote one.

40. Taneytown district could also be included in this "mixed" category. The concentration of English in Taneytown was the third highest in the county, falling below only Buckeystown and Libertytown. At the same time, the percentage of slaveholding households was the second lowest of the county's seven districts. The area, however, appeared to produce a partisan momentum that was unrelated to either of these population characteristics. As a whole, the Taneytown district voted 83 percent Federalist, giving that party the strongest support it received from any of the seven districts. Furthermore, this overwhelming support persisted regardless of personal attribute. Nonslaveholders, slaveowners, Germans, and English all favored the Federalist party by over a 4 to 1 margin. In essence, there were no marked differences in the partisan behavior of these four groupings, a phenomenon that did not occur in any other part of the county. The deviant behavior of the Taneytown residents could make an interesting case study of how local context can shape behavior in very atypical fashions. Since the district differs so drastically in its partisan patterns from the six remaining areas of Frederick, however, it will be excluded from subsequent analysis.

41. Only those towns and churches in which at least 11 residents or members voted in three or more elections were included in this examination. The range was from 11 voters in the Emmitsburgh Presbyterian Church to 325 voters in the Fredericktown Evangelical Reformed

Church. Only two or three groups, however, had more than 100 voters. Even though most of the groups are small, the cohesion displayed by the voters within them was considerable. Only 3 of the 26 groups (less than 12 percent) did not reveal a pronounced partisan preference (over 60 percent for one of the two parties). It is possible that this cohesiveness of small towns and religious congregations actually reflects the ethnic homogeneity of such units and therefore is an artifact of ethnic voting patterns in Frederick and does not represent an independent influence upon alignments. Without question, almost all members of the small Lutheran and Reformed churches were German, and several small towns were populated mainly by one ethnic group. Nevertheless, the evidence suggests that most of these smaller groups did exert an influence upon partisan behavior that was independent of ethnicity. First, "minority" members of these units—English attending German churches or Germans residing in a predominantly English town—were likely to behave in the same fashion as the unit as a whole rather than in the county-wide pattern of their ethnic group. Second, most of the cohesion rates for towns and congregations surpass the rates for either of Frederick's two major ethnic groups. With independent voters excluded, the county-wide cohesion rates for German and English voters were 66 and 75 percent respectively (table 12.2). While these figures reveal considerable partisan cohesion along ethnic lines, the cohesion rate for 18 of the 26 towns and congregations examined was greater than that for the county-wide English population.

42. A recent study of partisan behavior in the 1964 general election in Great Britain by C. Neal Tate, "Individual and Contextual Variables in British Voting Behavior: An Exploratory Note," *The American Political Science Review* 68 (1974):1656–62, has questioned whether an individual's environment (his immediate social contacts) has any impact in shaping his preferences. Using a multiple regression program—A.I.D.—developed by the Institute for Social Research, Ann Arbor, Michigan, Tate concluded that personal attributes alone explained most of the observed partisan behavior. No such statistical measure has been used here to assess the relative impact of personal attributes and social contacts, since the purpose of this essay has been to suggest additional influences and to show how they could have an impact upon behavior. The evidence presented here does suggest that such influences were operative in the two areas studied and could have some impact in other areas and time periods as well. A study of New Haven, Connecticut, by Raymond E. Wolfinger, "The Development and Persistence of Ethnic Voting," *The American Political Science Review* 59 (1965):896–908, further suggests that such influences are operative in the modern electorate. While Italians in the United States as a whole have been decidedly Democratic, New Haven Italians have been and remain decidely Republican, due in large part to the community's population composition and history.

43. There has been much discussion in the political science literature on how voters behave when they experience some form of cross pressure, see for example, Flanigan, *Political Behavior*, pp. 67–71; Berelson et al., *Voting*, pp. 129–32, 320; Angus Campbell, Gerald Gurin, and Warren E. Miller, *The Voter Decides* (Evanston, 1954), pp. 86–87, 157–64; and Meyer, "Independent Voter," p. 75.

THIRTEEN

THE STRUCTURE OF BALTIMORE'S POLITICS IN THE AGE OF JEFFERSON, 1795–1812

Frank A. Cassell

Studies of urban political development in the early national period are appropriate at this time because they represent a natural extension of research during the last twenty years into the development of political parties at the state level.[1] Analyses of the political party system as it evolved in urban settings will hopefully enrich historical understanding of the first critical decades of the new American republic. As at present, American cities a hundred and seventy-five years ago were centers of economic and cultural activity. Most early cities were places of racial, ethnic, and social diversity, and they suffered from the tensions that resulted from such heterogeneity. No city was free of crime and poverty. With their concentrated wealth and population, early American cities were quite different from the sparsely settled rural and agrarian areas that lay nearby. Their political experience, therefore, was distinctive.[2]

Of the half dozen cities in America around the turn of the eighteenth century, Baltimore affords an interesting opportunity to examine the struggle for power between Federalists and Republicans in an urban milieu. Although not the most populous American city, Baltimore was the newest. Unlike its sister cities, Baltimore did not reach maturity during the colonial era. Rather, its politics and institutions were shaped to a large extent by forces current in the age of Jefferson; democracy, nationalism, and the new economic opportunities presented by the West, and by an international trade freed of colonial restraints. It was in the context of these new forces that the citizens of Baltimore grappled with problems that have a modern ring. How could the city be governed so as to satisfy the aspirations of its diverse and often contentious population? By what means could the city's interests be effectively promoted before state and federal officials? Baltimore's solution to these questions was to work through the political party system that emerged in the middle and late 1790s.

Note: Frank A. Cassell is assistant chancellor and associate professor of history, University of Wisconsin, Milwaukee.

The origins of Baltimore's political parties in the early national period derive in part from the city's history. Created in 1729 by act of the Maryland legislature, Baltimore remained a small village for many years. Despite its favorable location on Chesapeake Bay, its abundant water sources, and its fine harbor, Baltimore by 1750 could claim but a few hundred residents. The Seven Years War marked an important turning point for the city. Already a major exporter of wheat and flour to Ireland and Scotland, Baltimore found that the war created new markets in the sugar islands of the West Indies. As a result of its growing prosperity, Baltimore attracted large numbers of immigrants from both Europe and other parts of the colonies. New industries sprang up, such as milling, iron making, brewing, and rope making. The War for Independence did little to impede the city's development. Baltimore, one of the few American cities unoccupied by the British, became a center for privateering, smuggling, and military storage and repair facilities. Baltimore's merchants made immense profits fulfilling government contracts for arms, clothing, and food needed for American troops.[3] Following the Revolution, Baltimore's economic expansion continued unabated. In 1790, over 13,500 citizens were counted in the first census. By 1800, the population had ballooned to nearly 32,000, making Baltimore the third largest city in America. A decade later the census revealed that 46,555 people lived within the city limits, an increase of over 240 percent in the twenty-year span.[4]

This growth had far-reaching implications for Maryland politics. With its economy based on commerce and manufacturing, its population a mixture of Irish, German, French, and English, its society new, raw, and constantly in flux, Baltimore stood in clear opposition to the older rural society centered in Southern Maryland and the Eastern Shore that had traditionally ruled the state. A struggle for power between these two societies was perhaps inevitable, for their interests and outlooks were fundamentally at variance. Representation in the assembly, location of the new national capital, the terms of a charter for the city, voting and office-holding qualifications, and the city's effort to have more banks incorporated were but a few of the issues that divided the state. It is not surprising, therefore, that as the Tilghman's, the Howards, the Carrolls, and the other influential families that composed the plantation interest drifted into the Federalist party in the 1790s, there was a natural predisposition in Baltimore to embrace Republicanism.[5]

But local political squabbles do not entirely explain the triumph of the Republican party in Baltimore. In other cities the Federalist party had been adopted by entrenched mercantile elites, who had long occupied positions of social and political superiority. No such group existed in Baltimore. The very newness of the city, the middle-class origins of even the wealthiest merchants, and the opportunity for social and economic advancement available in the boom-town atmosphere prevailing up to the War of 1812 arrested the evolution of a self-conscious aristocracy. Unlike their comrades in New York, Philadelphia, or Boston, Republicans in Baltimore did not have to struggle against an organized group of wealthy men fighting to maintain control.[6] Indeed, the Republicans found widespread support and leadership among the ranks of rich merchants, manufacturers, and bank directors.

In addition, certain aspects of Jeffersonian philosophy and policy appealed to important groups within the city. Republicans were more sympathetic to immigrants than were Federalists, and Baltimore's population was heavily spiced with recently arrived European settlers. The Alien and Sedition Acts were passionately hated in Baltimore, and the reaction against these laws contributed to the crushing defeat of the Federalists in the fall elections of 1798.[7] Republicans were also generally well disposed toward France and its revolution, and, at the same time, distrustful of England. Many in Baltimore shared this attitude. French-Americans naturally favored their former homeland, while the Irish historically disliked the British. Ethnic hostilities were reinforced by other factors. Some could not forget the passions aroused against England during the Revolution. Others remembered fondly the period when the French army had camped near the city in 1782. Baltimoreans had made friends with the French troops, and the city's merchants profited from selling them supplies. Finally, there were economic reasons behind Baltimore's anti-British feelings. Much of the city's trade traditionally had been with the West Indies. With the beginning of war with France in the 1790s, Great Britain seized a number of Baltimore ships attempting to trade with these islands. Neither the merchants nor the craftsmen, laborers, and manufacturers who depended on a healthy commerce had any reason to support England or her policies. On the contrary, Baltimore's citizens had strong motives to give their votes to those who promised an end to what they saw as British tyranny.[8]

Between 1795 and 1812, Baltimore's political history passed through three distinct stages. The first, from 1795 to 1801, witnessed the rapid growth of a vigorous two-party system within the city. For the next six years, however, the Republican party enjoyed almost unchallenged political supremacy. In the final five-year period, 1807 to 1812, national crises provoked a modest resurgence of Federalist activity and a corresponding development of a more reliable party machine by the Republicans, who were able to strengthen their hold on the city's politics.

Although the Hamiltonian financial schemes and the French Revolution were closely watched in Baltimore, it was not until 1795 that party development began in earnest.[9] The issue was the Jay Treaty. Among Baltimore's merchants there was no consensus as to whether the treaty would benefit or harm the city's commerce. The city's middle classes, however, generally expressed dissatisfaction with the agreement. Many objected on patriotic grounds, while others saw the treaty as anti-French. Taking their lead from Philadelphia, anti-treaty forces in Baltimore circulated petitions asking the president to reject the agreement. Then in July 1795 a large public meeting passed a series of resolutions condemning Jay's Treaty. Despite such protests President Washington and the Senate approved the treaty, and attention shifted to the House of Representatives, which would be called upon to vote appropriations to carry some provisions of the agreement into effect.[10] Preliminary votes in the House alerted administration supporters that the appropriations bill would face stiff opposition. They took steps, therefore, to pressure antitreaty congressmen into changing their position.

Samuel Smith, Baltimore's representative and a leading merchant, received the personal attention of Secretary of War James McHenry. McHenry, himself a Baltimorean, instigated a movement in the city to threaten Smith with defeat in the fall elections should he vote against the treaty appropriations. The origins of Baltimore's Federalist party are to be found in a letter from McHenry to Federalist merchant Robert Oliver written in April 1796. In that letter the secretary warned of the consequences if the treaty should be frustrated. McHenry suggested an extensive plan of political organization. Observing speed and secrecy, Baltimore Federalists were to organize a large protreaty meeting at which an "instruction" to Smith would be approved. The instruction, a draft of which was included in McHenry's letter, demanded that Smith respect the wishes of his constituents and cast his vote for the appropriations. Copies were to be circulated throughout the city for signatures and then mailed to Smith.[11]

McHenry's scheme was largely implemented by Oliver and other Federalist merchants in Baltimore. Within a week over six hundred signatures had been obtained. To keep up the pressure the Federalists organized a committee of correspondence that frequently wrote Smith demanding that he obey the instruction.[12] The aggressiveness of the Federalists caught the antitreaty forces in the city off balance. Under the leadership of the Mechanical Society, the city's oldest volunteer fire company, another public meeting was held that approved resolutions praising those congressmen who had expressed reservations about the treaty. Antiappropriation petitions were also circulated. Yet these efforts were not nearly as successful as those of the Federalists. Lacking any real direction or organization, the antitreaty faction failed to counteract the impact of the instruction.[13] Although Smith probably would have voted for the Jay Treaty appropriations anyway, despite his personal reservations, the instruction made it difficult for him to do otherwise. On 1 May the bill passed by three votes as Smith joined with the Federalists.[14]

The year 1796 was the high tide of Federalism in Baltimore. The limited goal of securing Smith's vote for the appropriations had been achieved. But Federalist leaders failed to translate their ad hoc efforts into permanent party machinery. They remained a small group of merchants and lawyers who relied heavily on McHenry and the national administration for direction and patronage. Moreover, the appropriations battle had created a potentially powerful opposition party. The birth of this party can be traced to an exchange of letters between Congressman Smith and William Jessop, a leader of the Mechanical Society. At the height of the appropriations controversy, Jessop had written Smith to convey the Society's support. Smith, among the richest men in the city, replied that "I am not a little gratified by the approbation of a society, at once so numerous and respectable; a society who have always been the supporters of order and good government."[15] The political marriage of Smith with the small businessmen and skilled craftsmen who made up the membership of the Mechanical Society drew sneers from Federalists, one of whom wrote to McHenry that it "may be politic for ought I know for him to count on numbers since he has so openly relinquished all claim to support from orderly and 'responsible' citizens." But the union could not be so easily dismissed. It was soon to become the basis of a political coalition that ruled the city for many years to come.[16]

In the fall elections of 1798 the Federalists suffered a severe defeat. Following McHenry's lead, they determined to oust Samuel Smith from his congressional seat for reasons that were not hard to discover. Since 1796 Smith had moved clearly into the national Republican party. His vote against the Sedition Act, his well-known pro-French attitude, and his friendship with Thomas Jefferson made him a prime target for the Federalists.[17] McHenry's hand-picked candidate to oppose Smith was a young lawyer named James Winchester. To manage his campaign, Winchester selected Maryland's most famous veteran of the Revolution, former United States Senator John Eager Howard. Since both sides lacked formal organization, the contest was carried on in public meetings, parades, and newspaper columns. After several months of witnessing unprincipled scurrility and mob violence, the citizens of Baltimore—those who possessed the necessary property to vote and, apparently, many who did not—went to the polls and reelected Smith by a margin of 800 votes out of the 4,600 ballots cast.[18]

The congressional election of 1798 marked the beginning of a swift decline in the political fortunes of Baltimore's Federalists. By contrast, the city's Republicans faced the future with considerable optimism. These new attitudes found full expression in the presidential election of 1800. For his part, McHenry declined to organize support for the Federalist presidential electoral candidate, confiding to a friend that he was motivated "not from any indifference to the good old cause, but from a kind of conviction that our labor would be lost."[19] McHenry's lethargy deprived the Baltimore Federalists of effective leadership. Little campaigning occurred, and there is some evidence that the Federalists were divided over the merits of Samuel Chase, their candidate for presidential elector.[20] The Republicans, in contrast, vigorously prosecuted the campaign for their candidate, Gabriel Duvall. In mid-November 1800 the election was held, and Duvall easily defeated Chase, outpolling him by over a thousand votes in the city.[21]

The ease with which the Federalists had been defeated surprised even many Republicans. The *American and Daily Advertiser,* a staunch Jeffersonian supporter, reflected on the amazing turn of events even as it trumpeted news of Republican election victories. Noting that the Federalist candidate for elector attracted only about one-sixth as many votes as were cast for Winchester in the hotly contested congressional election of 1798, the editor asked "Whence comes such a mighty declension of federal votes? The effect is visible," he continued, "the cause must lay somewhere."[22]

Republican ascendancy in Baltimore can in part by explained by the composition of the city's population and economy, the historical urban-rural division in the state, and the comparative ineffectiveness of Baltimore's Federalists as political organizers. In addition, however, some attention must be paid to the skill with which the Republicans maintained the political coalition of wealthy merchants and manufacturers with middle-class businessmen and craftsmen that Samuel Smith had initiated in 1796. That such a coalition existed is apparent from a survey of Republican party leaders. A study of newspapers, correspondence, and government records reveals that approximately three hundred men constituted the political leadership of the Baltimore Republican party in the years 1795 to 1812. These were the men who held office, ran the party machinery, led the political societies, and edited the party newspapers. While merchants constituted the largest contingent among the Republican leadership, there were also manufacturers, store owners, grocers, stonecutters, carpenters, brewers, innkeepers, tailors, auctioneers, and editors who played active roles. In contrast, the Federalist leadership, which included slightly more than two hundred individuals, was composed almost entirely of merchants, lawyers, bank officials, and a few newspaper editors.

Building this coalition and then holding it together through the turbulent years of the late 1790s required a substantial effort on the part of the Republicans, who labored under significant handicaps. Until 1799 there was no Republican party newspaper in the city, while state and federal patronage appointments in these years were entirely in the hands of the Federalists. Another problem was the almost total absence of formal party institutions. Not until after Jefferson's election as president did Baltimore's Republicans develop a committee system to direct party activities. Given these difficulties, the Republicans were forced to work through existing local groups and organizations in their struggle for political dominance. In the climactic struggles of 1798 and 1800, Republicans relied on a faction surrounding

Congressman Samuel Smith, the city militia, and a large number of private societies.

Smith's adoption of Republicanism had provided the party with several assets. He brought, first of all, money, which he generously contributed to party operations. Secondly, Smith brought with him into the party a cadre of rich merchants and bankers, many of them his relatives, who were personally loyal to him. For example, James A. Buchanan, John Hollins, William Patterson, and Robert Smith were all relatives and business associates of Samuel Smith, as well as major figures in the developing Republican party.[23] Thirdly, Smith contributed his influence among Baltimore's middle and lower classes. This influence resulted not only from his material and political success but also from his activities as a soldier. Smith was a hero of the Revolution, having been decorated by Congress for bravery while serving with Washington's army. After his retirement from the Continental Army in 1779, he had received an appointment as commander of the Baltimore militia. Later promoted to brigadier general, he had led his men against the whiskey rebels in 1794. Within a year he had been commissioned a major general and given command of the third division of Maryland's militia, which included men drawn from Baltimore and Maryland's Western Shore counties.[24] Because of Smith's involvement in Baltimore's politics, first as a delegate to the assembly and later as a congressman, it was natural that he would use his position in the militia to further his political ambitions as well as those of the Republican party.

The political influence of the Baltimore militia was dependent on the international situation. In periods of relative calm with no immediate threats of war, the militia virtually ceased to exist as an organization. Only when tensions were high and passions inflamed did volunteer companies appear in great numbers. Such conditions existed between 1798 and 1801 as relations with France deteriorated to the point that an undeclared naval war raged between the two nations. During the crucial congressional campaign of 1798, military fervor in Baltimore was at its highest pitch. The pro-French sympathies of the city evaporated as several thousand men rushed to form companies, purchase uniforms, and acquire weapons in order to defend their city against a possible French attack. Each company was allowed to choose its own name, adopt by-laws, levy fines on its membership, and elect its own officers, although captains and lieutenants technically received their commissions from the governor. Regimental, battalion, brigade, and divisional officers were directly appointed by the governor and his council. These officials, however, relied heavily on nominations from the appropriate commanding officers.

In 1798 most officers of field rank in Baltimore had received their commissions prior to the political party contests of the 1790s. As party development intensified, many generals, colonels, and majors followed their divisional commander, Samuel Smith, into the Republican party. Among those that did not were John Swan, the brigadier general directly in charge of the Baltimore militia, and John O'Donnell, a lieutenant colonel commanding the city's Sixth Regiment of militia. A few Federalists could also be found among the officers of the militia companies, but, taken as a whole, the militia structure was thoroughly dominated by the Republicans. The militia parade on 4 July 1800 illustrated the situation. Of the twenty companies that marched, sixteen were commanded by Republicans. Eleven other volunteer companies failed to assemble on this occasion, but their commanding officers were all supporters of Jefferson. A Republican newspaper did not exaggerate when it claimed that "nine-tenths of all the citizens of Baltimore, who have armed themselves . . . possess republican principles."[25]

The political leanings of the Baltimore militia were apparent from the names the volunteer companies adopted. Such appellations as the Republican Company, the Sans Cullottes, and the Democratic Greens were not uncommon.[26] But the militia were far more than passive supporters of the Baltimore Republican party. In the congressional election of 1798, for example, militia units publicly campaigned for Samuel Smith. On at least one occasion several companies marched through the city to Smith's house and gave him a boisterous salute. In return he provided them with great quantities of whiskey and rum. Federalists deplored the episode, accusing Smith of buying votes, and denounced military participation in the election. In response ten militia captains published a letter defending Smith and the actions of the militia.[27]

One critical function of the politicized militia system was to bring the affluent merchants and manufacturers of the city into partnership with the numerous skilled craftsmen and artisans who largely composed the middle class. Although there was a preponderance of rich men in the upper echelons of the command structure, men of less exalted stature were able to achieve high rank. It was not uncommon to find carpenters, butchers, or grocers serving as captains and majors. A few, including a watchmaker and a cabinetmaker, even reached the rank of lieutenant colonel and commanded regiments. Not great wealth, but party loyalty and some military aptitude seem to have been the chief criteria for advancement. Thus the militia provided a structure in which Republicans representing different groups in the city's society regularly associated in a manner that encouraged unity and harmony, and that was mutually advantageous. In short, the militia was exactly what one Federalist accused it of being: a "political engine."[28]

While the militia constituted a reliable and important organizational component of the Republican party, other groups also contributed to its success. The volunteer fire brigades, like the militia companies, attracted Baltimore's small-businessmen and skilled laborers as well as a sprinkling of the more affluent. Essentially private clubs with uniforms, constitutions, and membership rules, the fire companies had considerable political potential. Republican politicians flocked to join companies with such names as Franklin, Liberty, Mechanical, and Republican. Eventually they controlled the majority of leadership positions.[29]

The Republican party also received support from ethnic organizations such as the Hibernian Society and the German Republican Society. On the other side, Federalists dominated the Scottish St. Andrews Society and the English St. George Society. The influence of these latter groups, however, was far less than their Republican counterparts. Republicans also were more active than Federalists in forming private political clubs. In the late 1790s there were no Federalist equivalents to the Republican Society or Tammany.[30] In sum, the Republican party that capured control of Baltimore between 1798 and 1800 was remarkably informal in structure. Nonetheless, it was sufficiently effective to overcome the Federalists, who were fatally burdened by popular mistrust and organizational incompetence.

On 4 March 1801, Thomas Jefferson was sworn in as president of the United States, and the Baltimore Republicans joyously celebrated the event. And, indeed, they had good reason to exhibit high spirits. Within Baltimore they controlled the city's congressional seat as well as both seats in the Maryland House of Delegates.[31] The Federalists had been thoroughly defeated and demoralized. Nationally, Jefferson was president, the crisis with France had ended, and general peace was returning to Europe. Economic and political prospects had never looked better.

Yet the Republican party was entering a troubled period; the first indication of difficulty came on 4 July 1801. The Fourth of July was a traditionally important holiday for Republicans that signaled the beginning of the fall election campaigns. Since 1798 the party had mounted massive parades on the Fourth with the militia as the central attraction. In 1801, however, only a few militia units turned out, a fact that caused both dismay and embarrassment to Republicans. They hoped the hot weather was responsible, but, as time would show, Baltimore would not see another military parade until 1807. With no threat of war after 1801, the volunteer soldiers lost interest and the militia companies simply disappeared.[32]

The sudden disintegration of the militia structure was a blow to the Republicans; it deprived them of an important segment of their campaign organization. It was not that Republican hegemony in Baltimore was threatened, for the Federalists could offer no serious challenge. Rather, the problem was how to maintain party unity. Without the militia, a national crisis, an obnoxious national government, or strong Federalist competition in the city, the Republicans found it increasingly difficult to hold their coalition together. The failure of the Republicans to establish more formal party institutions in the late 1790s now assumed great significance. The struggle for power between Federalists and Republicans had been replaced by a situation where individuals and groups competed for preferment within the dominant Republican party. Since no mechanisms existed to mediate among these internal factions, the Republican party began to lose all coherence.

The stresses affecting the Baltimore Republicans were most apparent in the party's annual dilemma of selecting candidates for the city's two seats in the House of Delegates. In 1801 the party newspaper, the *American and Commercial Advertiser,* endorsed two Republican candidates, and they were elected without opposition. Within a few years, however, order and discipline collapsed. In 1804 three Republicans declared for the two seats, and the numbers of candidates increased in subsequent years until, in 1807, nine Republicans opposed each other.[33]

The 1804 election underlined the Republican party's organizational vulnerability. Andrew Ellicott, a Federalist, was elected to the House of Delegates together with John Stephen, a Republican. Ellicott's triumph embarrassed the Republicans, for it was clear that their own disunity explained the outcome of the election. The three Republican candidates had divided the party vote and allowed Ellicott to win. Yet the full explanation for the election result was even more disturbing. Ellicott, despite his well-known Federalism, attracted many Republican votes. His strategy had been shrewdly conceived. He did not run as a Federalist, and there was no discernible Federalist campaign on his behalf. Instead, he exploited a bitter argument within Baltimore over whether the city charter should be amended to make it more democratic. The issue had badly divided the Republicans; Ellicott capitalized on the situation by holding the support of the city's Federalists and attracting enough dissident Republican votes to win.[34] "His success," noted the *American,* "can alone be attributed to violent prejudices and powerful interests of a local nature . . . ." The editor denied that Ellicott's election signaled a decline in Republican strength. As evidence he could cite the fact that Federalist Robert Goodloe Harper, who ran for the congressional seat in Baltimore, fared poorly against the winning Republican, who polled over eighteen hundred votes.[35]

The Ellicott affair was not an isolated example of the Republican party's institutional weakness. Each election in the 1801–7 period found more Republicans contesting for every elective office. Inevitably these angry disputes began to threaten the coalition of merchants and mechanics that was the Republican party. By 1805 a clearly defined mechanic faction had emerged in Baltimore. Composed of small retail businessmen, skilled craftsmen, and manufacturers, the mechanic interest had both economic and political dimensions. The mechanics believed that they were being discriminated against by the wealthy merchants who dominated the city's banks and controlled the flow of credit. In 1806 the mechanics exercised their political muscle and obtained a charter from the Maryland legislature for the

Mechanics Bank. The articles of incorporation were specific in stating that a majority of the bank's directors must be mechanics.[36] At least some Republican merchants opposed creation of the Mechanics Bank, probably fearing competition with their own institutions. More disturbing to these merchants was the news that Robert Goodloe Harper, a leading Federalist, had drafted the charter of the Mechanics Bank. It was immediately assumed that Harper was seeking support among the mechanics for another of his congressional campaigns. If such was Harper's hope, it proved empty; few mechanics voted for him and he was again defeated.[37]

The establishment of the Mechanics Bank came amidst a major effort by the mechanics to secure a larger voice in the politics of the city. Shortly before the 1805 election for representatives to the House of Delegates, an important letter appeared in the pages of the *American* signed by "Another Mechanic." The author declared that it was "well known that the mechanic interest has always been able to elect whom they please, and consequently [was] sought for by those who wished to be exalted to places of honor, and sometimes offices of profit." While admitting that this power had always been used on behalf of Republicans, "Another Mechanic" attacked the Republican merchants who denied mechanics access to bank credit. He concluded with the suggestion that the mechanics should use their political leverage "to place ourselves on an equal footing with the merchant and trader. . . ." "Another Mechanic" touched a responsive chord, and Baltimore's mechanics soon acted on his ideas. They determined that their candidate for the House of Delegates would be Robert Steuart. Although Steuart did not win in 1805, he drained off enough Republican votes to allow that clever Federalist, Andrew Ellicott, to win reelection.[38]

Steuart seemed an unlikely character to lead a major political movement. Born in Falkirk, Scotland, Steuart and his brother had come to America as indentured servants in 1768. Steuart had fought on the American side during the Revolution and then settled in Baltimore as a successful stonecutter. His emergence as an important political figure touched off a hot political quarrel within the Republican party. A few days after the 1805 election, Steuart published a note thanking his supporters. His defeat, he said, was entirely due to the lateness of his entry into the contest. He claimed that "had the Mechanics of Baltimore determined on him, or any other Mechanic, but a few days sooner than they did, they would have been fully able to have carried for their candidate in opposition to *any* other interest that may exist in the city." Steuart's publication drew an immediate response from a Republican who blamed him for allowing Ellicott's election. He also condemned Steuart for calling "on the Mechanics of Baltimore to set up a separate interest from their fellow-citizens. . . ."[39] Steuart, however, could not be dismissed so easily. He won election to the House of Delegates in 1807 and 1808. In 1809 and 1810 he was defeated, but only by the slimmest of margins and by another mechanic who was more acceptable to the Republican merchants.

The Steuart phenomenon and the Ellicott embarrassment plainly showed that despite outward appearances of health, the Baltimore Republican party between 1801 and 1807 was dangerously drifting. The obvious remedy was a more solid and efficient party organization, one capable of settling intra-party disputes, nominating candidates, and effectively mounting campaigns. By 1804 the need for greater institutionalization was already so apparent that William Pechin, editor of the *American*, launched an effort to create Republican caucuses in each of the city's eight wards. His plan called for the Republicans to meet in their respective wards and name conferees to a general ward committee. The general ward committee would then agree upon Republican candidates for Congress and the House of Delegates. For awhile the plan appeared to be successful. The ward caucuses were held and conferees elected. Additionally, all but one of the ward caucuses nominated candidates for both houses of the city council. In late September, shortly before the election, the general ward committee met and unanimously agreed on its choices for office.[40] On 2 October 1804, the *American* printed the election results, which revealed that Pechin's plan had badly misfired. Of the general ward committee nominations, the candidates for Congress had succeeded. However, they had not faced significant opposition. But in the critical House of Delegates race, only one of the two official candidates was elected; the other winner was the Federalist Ellicott. Equally disturbing, over half of those nominated by the ward caucuses for seats on the city council were defeated. The Pechin plan failed for a number of reasons. The idea was both ambitious and complex and had come forward so late in the campaign that implementation was difficult. Ward caucuses attracted only light attendance, and, as a consequence, candidates who did not receive official endorsement had no reason to respect the caucus nominations. Moreover, Federalists discredited the ward caucuses to an extent by pointing out their undemocratic implications, a charge that Pechin had difficulty refuting.[41]

The disaster of 1804 so depressed Republicans that the caucus system did not operate in the 1805 elections. The problems of disunity among the Republicans, however, had become worse, not better. On the eve of election day in 1805, Pechin flogged those Republicans who put *"local* interests and *personal likes and dislikes"* ahead of political principles. He contended that "from these baneful sources flow the divisions which exist among us, as to our choice of men." Until individuals subordinated personal ambition to the larger welfare of the party "it will be impossible to cultivate a union of efforts, in favor of the democratic-republicans." Pechin's conclusion aptly stated the situation. "With *system,*" he claimed, "republicans in this city could always carry their men; but whilst they continue to disregard such means as would insure it, we must submit to the hazard of defeat, which we impose on ourselves, by our want of concert."[42] In 1806 the party once more attempted to bring some order to the nominating process. As in 1804, ward caucuses met and named delegates to a general ward committee that in turn nominated two candidates for the House of Delegates. Once more the system failed, as neither of the officially endorsed candidates won. While those elected were Republicans, the party had again demonstrated its organizational ineptness. The process of internal disintegration had not been halted.[43]

The problem of the Baltimore Republicans in the years 1801 to 1807 mirrored the difficulties of the party throughout the United States; by 1807 the Republican party nationally had been rocked by schisms in New York and Pennsylvania. In 1806 that talented but erratic Virginian, John Randolph of Roanoke, had broken with Jefferson and now led a congressional faction in opposition to many of the president's policies. The question of Jefferson's successor was also being widely discussed, and a number of potential candidates were maneuvering for position. Increasingly, however, American politics were being affected by events in Europe. The renewal of war between France and Great Britain created important national issues such as impressment and the restriction of American trade by the decrees of both combatants. An effort to settle outstanding disputes with the British by treaty was unsuccessful in 1806. Then, in June 1807, the British frigate *Leopard* attacked the American warship *Chesapeake*. After the *Chesapeake* struck her colors, British officers boarded the battered vessel and removed four sailors alleged to be deserters from the British navy. Once more, as in 1798, the United States was plunged into a crisis that was bound to affect its internal politics.

Even before news of the *Chesapeake* affair reached Baltimore, the city's politics had been undergoing change. Undoubtedly stimulated by the disarray of the Republicans, as well as the worsening foreign situation, Baltimore's Federalists had become more visible and active. In the spring of 1807, a new Federalist paper, the *Federal Republican*, appeared in Baltimore. Edited by Alexander Contee Hanson, the *Federal Republican* specialized in vituperation but was nonetheless an effective proponent of the Federalist party. Hanson soon involved himself in a controversy with Republican editors over the Burr treason case. Aaron Burr, Jefferson's first vice president, had been arrested in early 1807, along with others, for alleged treasonable activities. Supposedly, he had conspired to organize a separatist movement in the western portions of the United States. During the subsequent legal proceedings, Burr and his codefendants were represented by two prominent Baltimore lawyers, Luther Martin and Robert Goodloe Harper, both leading Federalists. The Burr case was therefore of intense local interest in Baltimore and a major issue between the two political parties. Republicans insisted on Burr's guilt out of loyalty to Jefferson and because of

Martin and Harper's involvement in the case. The Federalists supported Burr, hoping that an acquittal would embarrass the president. News that Burr had been indicted by a grand jury in Richmond arrived in Baltimore the same day that the *Chesapeake* story appeared in the city's papers.[44]

For awhile at least, the *Chesapeake* incident virtually eliminated party competition in Baltimore. The sheer magnitude of the insult, as well as the very real danger of war, brought the citizens together as perhaps at no previous time. On 29 June a mammoth town meeting elected Republican Samuel Smith, now a United States senator, as chairman, and discussed what measures Baltimore should take. A committee, chosen to draft resolutions, included such well-known Republican merchants as Alexander McKim, Thomas McElderry, and James Calhoun. Two Federalists, Mark Pringle and Samuel Sterret, were also members. The resolutions adopted by this bipartisan committee and accepted by the town meeting were belligerent in tone. The president was urged to "enforce satisfaction for the outrage so daring and injurious to the honor and dignity of our country." The citizens of Baltimore pledged their "lives and fortunes" in support of any policy, including war, that Jefferson chose to adopt. In the meantime, all intercourse with British naval vessels would be halted. A committee was then named to carry these resolutions to Annapolis, Washington, and nearby communities.[45] A few days later, on the Fourth of July, the celebrations were far larger than in the past few years. The toasts were patriotic in their rhetoric, with emphasis on national unity. At one celebration Federalists and Republicans joined together in honoring the nation's birthday. This interlude of party harmony proved all too brief. As time passed and Jefferson failed to declare war, the Federalists reevaluated their position and soon returned to their traditional pro-British stance.[46]

The *Chesapeake* affair helped the Republicans in several ways. Under the new conditions of national emergency, dissent within the party was muffled though not entirely silenced. Additionally, the crisis provoked an immediate rebirth of the militia organization that had been so useful to the Republicans in the 1798–1801 period. For six years there had been no militia structure at all in Baltimore. But within days of the attack on the *Chesapeake*, hundreds of men came forward to join volunteer companies. By early August one regimental officer, a Republican, could report to the governor that "there never was perhaps so great a military spirit displayed in any city as there is in Baltimore at this time."[47]

As in 1798, the overwhelming majority of individuals and units associated with the Baltimore Brigade were Republican in sentiment. Active Republican politicians commanded all four of the city's regiments, and the brigadier general commanding the Baltimore Brigade was John Stricker, among the most prominent Republican leaders in the city. Stricker's commander was Major General Samuel Smith. Republican control of the militia was further reinforced by the fact that the governor of Maryland and the members of the governor's council were all Republicans who strictly relied on the recommendations of the Baltimoreans in issuing officers' commissions. Typical was a letter from one of Samuel Smith's officers to the governor urging the promotion of a well-known Baltimore Republican to the rank of lieutenant colonel. It read in part: "Capt. Biay's character as a patriot and Republican stands unrivaled in Baltimore. His attachment to the present administration, and unwearied exertions in promoting the democratic cause must be too well known to your Honour to need any commendations." The appointment was quickly made.[48]

Federalists did not entirely abandon the militia. Robert Goodloe Harper, for example, tried to form a number of Federalist companies. One of the few cavalry companies in the brigade was commanded by Federalist Samuel Hollingsworth.[49] Generally, however, Federalist officers faced intense pressure to resign. Stricker's predecessor as brigadier general of the Baltimore Brigade had been John Swan, a wealthy Federalist merchant. He was forced out less than three months after the *Chesapeake* affair. William Belton, a Federalist commanding a battalion in the Twenty Seventh Regiment, resigned even earlier, noting that his position was "not agreeable to a part of my fellow citizens."[50] Some Federalists attracted the particular attention of the Republican militia. During the Fourth of July celebrations in 1808, a young Federalist attorney who was also adjutant of the Thirty Ninth Regiment was overheard offering a toast: "Damnation to all Democrats." Word quickly spread, and the volunteer companies refused to muster until the offender had resigned. About the same time Federalist editor Alexander Contee Hanson also felt the wrath of the Republican militia. Hanson, a lieutenant in the militia, was actually courtmartialed for printing an anti-Republican article in his newspaper. Eventually he was acquitted, but only because of a legal technicality. The Federalists certainly never questioned the fact that the Baltimore militia was a Republican bastion.[51]

Following the brief respite from party warfare in 1807 that occurred as a result of the *Chesapeake* incident, the Federalists resumed their efforts to construct a party organization in Baltimore. Central to the Federalists' plans was the Washington Benevolent Society. The Society was a national organization whose local branches masked their political nature behind a facade of operating free schools for poor children. The Washington Benevolent Society of Baltimore was in operation by late 1807, but its operations attracted little attention until 1810.[52] On 4 July 1810, the society held a joint celebration with Robert Goodloe Harper's militia company. By 1811 Washington Benevolent societies existed in every Maryland county and seem to have closely controlled the nomination of candidates in an important election that year. The Washington Benevolent Society branch in Baltimore, under the leadership of James McHenry, Charles Ridgely of

Hampton, John Eager Howard, Robert Goodloe Harper, and Alexander Contee Hanson, provided pamphlets and, perhaps, money to the other county organizations. On at least one occasion in 1811, the Washington Benevolent Society of Baltimore hosted a meeting of delegates from Maryland to plot election strategy. Despite this activity, the Federalists were again defeated in 1811 both in Baltimore and in Maryland generally.[53] The Washington Benevolent Society concept constituted an interesting experiment in party organization. Its strength was in its centralization of decision making. Its weaknesses lay in its secretiveness, its inability to win significant support among the middle classes, and its pro-British bias. It simply had no appeal to the masses in Baltimore. In at least one way the Washington Benevolent Society actually damaged the Federalists; it provided a convenient target for Republican editors. Portraying the society as a secret conspiracy against democracy, the Republican papers warned that only a maximum effort could avert defeat at the polls.[54]

The *Chesapeake* affair and the revival of Federalist opposition also spurred the Republicans to new organizational efforts. In late 1807 a new newspaper, the *Whig*, began publication under the editorship of Baptiste Irvine. Irvine was fully the equal of Alexander Contee Hanson in name-calling and character assassination. But he was also an effective political leader who used his newspaper as a tool to direct the activities of the Republican party. The Republicans particularly needed Irvine's talents in the elections of 1808. For the first time Federalist candidates were entered in nearly every race from city councilman to congressman. Moreover, the elections came in the midst of Jefferson's embargo, which had severely hurt Baltimore's economy. If the Republicans remained divided as they had been for the past few years, the Federalists could reasonably hope to win at least some offices in the city.

The challenge Irvine confronted was not new: to unite the Republicans behind a common slate of candidates. To do this, he carried on consultations with Republican leaders and then published a list of candidates his newspaper endorsed. For two months prior to the election, Irvine periodically printed his slate and filled the columns of his paper with letters urging Republican unity. In late September the ward caucuses met and, in the main, approved Irvine's endorsements. The results of the 1808 election were a tribute to Irvine's ability as a political organizer. Not a single Federalist won elective office. Of equal importance, the official Republican candidates, those named by Irvine and the ward caucuses, also triumphed over other Republican challengers who had nominated themselves. In the House of Delegates contest, for example, the two endorsed candidates received well over three thousand votes, while their nearest competitor could boast of less than eight hundred votes. A similar pattern was apparent in other contests.[55] Having conquered themselves as well as the Federalists, the Baltimore

Republicans staged a massive celebration. Over seven thousand Baltimoreans participated in a huge parade that included a fully rigged miniature schooner carrying many of the successful Republican candidates. "Never was an election conducted with more perfect order," Irvine exulted, "nor a triumph enjoyed with more good humor and moderation . . . worthy of the men of seventy-six, worthy of their latest posterity, worthy of demigods."[56]

In the elections of 1809 and 1810, Irvine's system of endorsing candidates was again employed successfully. During those two campaigns only Robert Steuart dared to challenge the official party candidates for the House of Delegates, and he was defeated on both occasions. Still, Steuart and the mechanic interest represented a dangerous element of instability within the party. To strengthen the authority of the party's nominations, Irvine in 1811 supported a return to the general ward committee idea that had been so unsuccessful in 1804 and 1806. This time the plan worked; the two nominees were elected without challenge from other Republican candidates. There were, however, problems. The general ward committee delayed for too long in determining its choices and thereby reduced the time available for campaigning. Moreover, the two candidates were not popular with many Republicans. As a result many did not vote, and one Federalist candidate came uncomfortably close to election.[57] Nonetheless, the Republicans between 1807 and 1812 had made marked progress towards correcting the organizational deficiencies that had bedeviled the party in earlier years. In spite of a vigorous Federalist challenge and the discontent of the Steuart supporters, the Republicans had managed to maintain control of Baltimore's politics.

Baltimore's party history in the first years of the Republic evolved out of the complex relationships between local, state, and national politics. Issues of national importance had stimulated the development of the city's parties in the late 1790s and encouraged organizational innovation after 1807. In the absence of national crisis, as in the years between 1801 and 1807, party unity was very difficult to maintain. The Federalists in that period had little visibility, while the dominant Republicans were buffeted by personal and factional dissensions they seemed incapable of mastering. The Federalist party fared poorly in Baltimore because of its antiimmigrant and pro-British policies, its antidemocratic prejudice, and its inability to construct a strong local organization. The Republicans triumphed because they built a broad-based coalition of the city's middle classes and merchants, actively defended the city's interest before state and national governments, and generally appealed to the democratic aspirations of Baltimore's citizens. Additionally, the Republicans enjoyed better leadership than the Federalists and exhibited greater skill in political organizing. The ward caucuses, the general ward committees, and the party newspapers were important aspects of the Republican party structure. But of equal if not greater significance to the Republicans were the militia, the fire companies, and the ethnic and political societies. It was by working through these groups that the Republicans reached the city's middle classes and won their support. Baltimore's Republicans, in short, were better politicians than their adversaries.

NOTES

1. See for example, Alfred F. Young, *The Democratic Republicans of New York: The Origins, 1763-1797* (Chapel Hill, 1967); Paul Goodman, *The Democratic-Republicans of Massachusetts: Politics in a Young Republic* (Cambridge, 1964); Harry Ammon, "The Formation of the Republican Party in Virginia, 1789-1796," *Journal of Southern History* 19 (1953): 283-310; Carl Prince, *New Jersey's Jeffersonian Republicans: The Genesis of an Early American Party, 1789-1817* (Chapel Hill, 1964); John A. Munroe, *Federalist Delaware, 1775-1815* (New Brunswick, 1954); Harry Marling Tinkcom, *The Republicans and Federalists in Pennsylvania, 1790-1801: A Study in National Stimulus and Local Response* (Harrisburg, 1950); Sanford W. Higginbotham, *The Keystone in the Democratic Arch: Pennsylvania Politics, 1800-1816* (Harrisburg, 1952); L. Marx Renzulli, *Maryland: The Federalist Years* (Rutherford, N.J., 1972).

2. Young, *Democratic Republicans of New York*, pp. 392-413, 468-95; William Bruce Wheeler, "Urban Politics in Nature's Republic: The Development of Political Parties in the Seaport Cities in the Federalist Era" (Ph.D. diss., University of Virginia, 1967).

There is a considerable body of literature dealing with the questions of what constitutes a political party and whether political parties existed in the 1790-1815 period. For example, William Nisbet Chambers, in *Political Parties in a New Nation: The American Experiment 1776-1809* (New York, 1963), argues that parties did operate in the early national period. He contends that political parties exist if six "critical functions" are performed in a "continuous, co-ordinated, and visible" manner. The six functions are: nominating, electing, shaping opinion, mediating among groups, managing government, and supplying connections between branches of government. Additionally, he asserts parties are distinguishable from factions because of the "range, density, and stability" of their public support, and because they possess "a distinguishable set of perspectives, or ideology, with emotional overtones" (see pp. 45-48). Frank J. Sorauf in "Political Parties and Political Analysis," in *The American Party Systems: Stages of Political Development*, ed. William Nisbet Chambers and Walter Dean Burnham (New York, 1967), pp. 33-55, asserts that three elements define what a party is and justify the use of the term: first, the "organization proper," which refers to party officials, activists, and members who are the "purposeful, organized, initiating vanguard;" second, the "party in office," which includes party members in office and the paraphernalia of caucuses and floor leaders; and third, the "Party in the Electorate" or those who identify with the party but are less involved with party activities. Using Sorauf's definitions, Ronald P. Formisano suggested that there were no real parties in the early national period (see Formisano, "Deferential-Participant Politics: The Early Republic's Political Culture, 1789-1840," *The American Political Science Review* 68:[1974] 473-87). All of these analyses are mainly concerned with political parties at the national or state level. Insofar as Baltimore in the early national period is concerned, application of the definitions of either Chambers or Sorauf would seem to indicate that a rough form of a party system did exist, although the two parties were loosely structured and often performed party functions in an imperfect and inconsistent manner.

3. Stuart Weems Bruchey, *Robert Oliver, Merchant of Baltimore, 1783-1819* (Baltimore, 1956), pp. 29-35; Hamilton Owens, *Baltimore on the Chesapeake* (Garden City, New York, 1941), pp. 23-86.

4. Owens, *Baltimore*, pp. 126-49; J. Thomas Scharf, *The Chronicles of Baltimore* (Baltimore, 1874), p. 304.

5. Wheeler, "Urban Politics in Nature's Republic," pp. 147-54; L. Marx Renzulli, "Maryland Federalism" (Ph.D. diss., University of Virginia, 1962), pp. 202-74. For a concise analysis of Maryland politics in these years see W. Wayne Smith, "Politics and Democracy in Maryland,

1800–1854," in *Maryland: A History, 1632–1974*, ed. Richard Walsh and William Lloyd Fox, (Baltimore, 1974), pp. 239–56.

6. Wheeler, "Urban Politics in Nature's Republic," pp. 147–48.

7. Scharf, *Chronicles of Baltimore*, pp. 40, 51–56, 209, 303; Bruchey, *Robert Oliver*, p. 108; Raphael Semmes, *Baltimore As Seen by Visitors, 1783–1860* (Baltimore, 1953), p. 17.

8. Wheeler, "Urban Politics in Nature's Republic," p. 160; Matthew Page Andrews, *History of Maryland: Province and State* (New York, 1929), pp. 406–7; John C. Miller, *The Federalist Era, 1789–1801* (New York, 1960), pp. 140–41; Renzulli, "Maryland Federalism," p. 213.

9. Scharf, *Chronicles of Baltimore*, p. 267; Eugene P. Link, *Democratic-Republican Societies, 1790–1800* (New York, 1942), p. 181.

10. *Federal Intelligencer & Baltimore Daily Advertiser*, 1, 25, and 28 July 1795; Miller, *The Federalist Era*, pp. 168–71.

11. James McHenry to Robert Oliver, 12 April 1796, McHenry Papers, mss., Library of Congress.

12. *Federal Gazette & Baltimore Daily Advertiser*, 22, 28, and 30 April, and 5 May 1796.

13. Ibid., 23 April and 4 May 1796; U.S., Congress, *Debates and Proceedings in the Congress of the United States*, 42 vols. (Washington, D.C., 1834–56), 4th Cong., 1st sess., 1849, vol. 1, p. 1171; hereafter cited as *Annals of Congress*.

14. *Annals of Congress*, pp. 1153, 1155–56, 1280; Rufus King to Alexander Hamilton, 20 April, 1796, Hamilton Papers, mss., Library of Congress.

15. *Federal Gazette & Baltimore Daily Advertiser*, 23 and 24 April 1796.

16. James Winchester to James McHenry, 1 May 1796, McHenry Papers.

17. Frank A. Cassell, *Merchant Congressman in the Young Republic: Samuel Smith of Maryland, 1752–1839* (Madison, 1971), pp. 82–83.

18. Ibid., pp. 83–89; *Federal Gazette & Baltimore Daily Advertiser*, 5 Oct. 1798. The property qualification was defined as the possession of either a fifty-acre freehold or real property valued at £30 (current money). Approximately 50% of the eligible voters in Baltimore City voted in 1798 compared with 14% in the presidential election of 1796 and 40% in the presidential election of 1800; see J. R. Pole, "Suffrage and Representation in Maryland from 1776 to 1810: A Statistical Note and Some Reflections," in *Voters, Parties, and Elections*, ed. Joel H. Silbey and Samuel T. McSweeney (Lexington, Mass., 1972), p. 66.

19. James McHenry to Oliver Wolcott, 9 Nov. 1800, in *Memoirs of the Administrations of Washington and John Adams. Edited from the Papers of Oliver Wolcott*, ed. George Gibbs, 2 vols. (New York, 1846), vol. 2, p. 445.

20. *The American and Daily Advertiser*, 29 Oct. 1800.

21. Ibid., 18 Nov. 1800.

22. Ibid., 15 Nov. 1800.

23. Cassell, *Merchant Congressman*, pp. 69–72.

24. Ibid. pp. 58–59; William Kilty, *The Laws of Maryland*, 2 vols., 1799, 1800 (Annapolis, 1810), pp. 448–51.

25. *The American and Daily Advertiser*, 3 May 1800; Militia Appointment Books, mss., Hall of Records, Annapolis, Md., passim (all mss. cited are at the Hall of Records unless otherwise specified); *Federal Gazette & Baltimore Daily Advertiser*, 6 July 1796, 5 Oct. 1798.

26. *The American and Daily Advertiser*, 1 and 7 July 1800.

27. *Federal Gazette & Baltimore Daily Advertiser*, 7 and 16 Aug. 1798.

28. Ibid., 7 Aug. 1798.

29. The manuscript records of the Mechanical and Union fire companies are located in the Maryland Historical Society. Scattered information on other companies can be found in the Baltimore city archives, which are kept in City Hall, Baltimore, Md. A sketchy history of the Mechanical Society can be found in George W. McCreary, *The Ancient and Honorable Mechanical Company of Baltimore* (Baltimore, 1901). Complete lists of the memberships of the various fire companies were periodically published in Baltimore's newspapers.

30. Wheeler, "Urban Politics in Nature's Republic," p. 170; *American and Commerical Advertiser*, 7 March 1801.

31. *American and Commercial Advertiser*, 23 Feb., 5 and 16 March 1801.

32. Ibid., 6 July 1801, and 8 July 1805.

33. Ibid., 6 Oct. 1801; 2 Oct. 1804; 6 Oct. 1807.

34. Ibid., 26 Oct. 1804.

35. Ibid., 2 Oct. 1804.

36. Ibid., 3 June 1806.

37. Ibid., 7 Oct. 1806; Samuel Smith to Wilson Carey Nicholas, 24 May 1806, Samuel Smith Papers, mss., Library of Congress.

38. *American and Commerical Advertiser,* 5 and 8 Oct. 1805.

39. Ibid., 6, 10, and 12 Oct. 1805.

40. Ibid., 13, 25, and 29 Sept. 1804.

41. Ibid., 2 and 25 Oct. 1804.

42. Ibid., 7 Oct. 1805.

43. Ibid., 6 and 7 Oct. 1806.

44. Ibid., 27 June 1807.

45. Ibid., 30 June 1807.

46. Ibid., 9 July 1807.

47. James Mosher to Governor Robert Wright, 4 Aug. 1807, Adjutant General's Papers, mss.

48. Tobias Stansbury to Governor Wright, 30 Dec. 1808, ibid.

49. *American and Commercial Daily Advertiser,* 28 July 1807.

50. Ibid., 11 Sept and 27 July 1807; see also William Lowry to Ninian Pinkney, 30 July 1807, Adjutant General's Papers.

51. *The Whig,* Baltimore, 23 and 26 Aug. 1808; Record of the Trial of Lieutenant Alexander Contee Hanson, 13 Feb. 1809, Adjutant General's Papers.

52. *The Whig,* 19 Nov. 1807 and 23 Feb. 1811; see also David Hackett Fischer, *The Revolution of American Conservatism* (New York, 1965), pp. 110–28.

53. *The Whig,* 6 July 1810, 3 March, 7 and 10 Aug. 1811; Robert Goldsborough to James McHenry et al., 1 June 1811, McHenry Papers; Alexander Contee Hanson to ——, 11 May 1811, McHenry Papers, mss., Maryland Historical Society.

54. See, for example, *The Whig,* 7 and 19 Aug. 1811.

55. Ibid., 18, 22, and 27 Aug., and 5 Oct. 1808.

56. Ibid., 5 Oct. 1808.

57. Ibid., 11, 12, 17, 23, and 24 Sept. and 8 Oct. 1811.

FOURTEEN

THE SEARCH FOR POWER: COMMUNITY LEADERSHIP IN THE JACKSONIAN ERA

Whitman H. Ridgway

Historians commonly perceive the Jacksonian Era as the pinnacle of the American quest for political democracy between 1790 and 1860. They have concluded that the continued expansion of the franchise, the growth of the second party system, and the integration of new leaders into the political culture were manifestations of a growing egalitarianism. This transformation to mass participatory democracy eclipsed the restrictive oligarchical system of the early national period. By the eve of the Civil War, the political system was characterized by the rule of the people by the right of their numbers. The exclusive elite that had ruled earlier as a perquisite of its wealth and societal position was allegedly displaced.

Recent histories of Maryland generally reaffirm the interpretation that an oligarchy governed in the eighteenth and nineteenth centuries, and that its power gradually eroded as the people were enfranchised and claimed the right to govern themselves.[1] Nevertheless, some of the assumptions that underlie this view have not always been recognized, much less tested. No systematic study has yet been made of the distribution of power over the period between the Revolution and the Civil War. Many political historians emphasize the rise and fall of party systems or the vicissitudes of personal or party strife but rarely deal directly with the underlying question, "Who governs?" In order to perceive change, scholars need to determine who held power; in order to identify who held power, they must define and study it systematically. Unless we understand how an elite is identified and how it ruled, or exactly how a new group displaced it, and how the new group ruled in turn, it is impossible to generalize about changes in the distribution of power over time. To cope with

Note: Whitman H. Ridgway is assistant professor of history, University of Maryland. The author wishes to acknowledge the financial assistance given by the Research Board of the Computer Science Center and the Graduate School General Research Board of the University of Maryland, College Park.

this problem, we need to reconceptualize the basic questions and research strategies of political history.

This paper centers on the distribution of power at the community level in Maryland during the 1820s and the 1830s. These were the years when the major impulse of massive change was purportedly taking place. The study is an attempt to grapple with the complexities of identifying various elites and assessing their place in the larger society, especially as their political roles changed over time. It offers an opportunity to test the validity of common assumptions about Jacksonian democracy.

"Who Governs?"

The best method of identifying who governs in any community is to determine who makes the important decisions. Assembling and ranking community leaders requires a systematic method for identifying significant community decisions and assessing the participation of individuals in making them. Historical monographs provide many insights that illuminate facets of power and its uses, but they contain few systematic procedures for identifying community leaders. The literature on modern community power, however, is a plentiful source for systematic and innovative analysis.

Community power literature presents a divided opinion as to the best way to identify people who held power.[2] Essentially there are three competing approaches: the positional, the reputational, and the decisional. The positional approach, favored intuitively by historians, assumes that power is exerted by those in public office. One need only identify those individuals who hold the positions of public trust to locate the ruling elite. The reputational approach identifies leaders by asking community informants, "Who gets things done around here?" Those who use this method stress the need to locate persons who might exercise power covertly, rather than accept the notion that officeholders, in fact, make the important community decisions. The decisional method stipulates an explicit relationship between decisions and power. Only by studying decision making directly can community leaders be identified. Confronted by this methodological debate among students of community power, the historian faces the operational problem of selecting the method most appropriate to his data base, which differs from that available to social scientists who are studying contemporary society.

A modified decisional approach is the most satisfactory method available to the historian for identifying community leaders. The positional method, with its tantalizingly simple procedure of studying those holding office, is predicated on the unwarranted assumption that power and office-holding are synonymous. Officeholders may be shown to exercise power, but a research design should be structured to test that assertion rather than to affirm it as an antecedent condition. On the other hand, the procedures of reputational studies—the interrogation of persons knowledgeable about community decision making—are all but impossible to replicate in the imperfect data bank of the past. Few diarists or correspondents are reliable informants. It may be asked, furthermore, whether reputation for power conforms to the actual functioning of community decision making. The decisional method is preferable to either of the other approaches because it treats power as an active phenomenon that may be located by analyzing important community decisions.

While the decisional method is the most appropriate, it must be modified for use in a historical context. The first problem was to identify important decisions. Using as criteria the number of persons affected, the amount of money actually or potentially expended, the change in the use or probable redirection of community resources, the specific issues appropriate for intensive analysis that emerged were political nominations, internal improvements, and political reform. A more complex problem then arose as to how to differentiate levels of participation in the decisional process in these issues. Leadership roles were scored and the leaders ranked. These rankings determined the decisional elite used in subsequent analysis.

Once identified, the decisional elite should be contrasted to strategic elites to understand the distribution of power in a particular community. Strategic elites are groups of individuals who hold scarce and valued resources in a community.[3] In the context of ante-bellum society, there were at least three appropriate strategic elites: the traditional elite; the commercial elite; and the positional elite. The wealthiest members of society, ranked from the manuscript tax records, formed the traditional elite.[4] Those who persisted as officers or directors of banks and insurance companies between 1827 and 1836 formed the commercial elite.[5] This group controlled liquid capital at a time when finance played an increasingly important role in a modernizing economy. The legislative and executive public officeholders on the local, state, and federal levels constituted the positional elite.[6] These three strategic elites, the traditional, the commercial, and the positional, serve to measure the distribution of community power.

The way power is distributed in a community can be used as an index of its stage of modernization. A community characterized by social and economic homogeneity and led by an oligarchy—a cohesive elite—can be defined as traditional; a community based on social and economic heterogeneity, and led by a polyarchy—a diverse elite—can be defined as modern. An oligarchy is highly unified by ties of wealth, close social interconnections, and tradition. Tradition should strongly influence elite recruitment where families who monopolize wealth and prestige are active and dominating. In an oligarchy there should be considerable overlap between the decisional elite and the various strategic elites. A polyarchy is at the opposite end of the modernization scale. The greater complexity of a modernizing community creates increased demand for specialized leadership and hence a need for a socially diverse elite. Tradition should not restrict entry into a polyarchy. Those who aspire to membership should be able to use resources other than wealth and family connections to advantage. Some leaders in a polyarchy might resemble an oligarchy, but in a more complex modern environment they would be but one of several groups sharing power. No single group could monopolize or perpetuate its power by claims of deference and tradition in a polyarchy. Change rather than continuity should be one of its characteristics.

These abstractions and definitions are essential for the systematic study of the distribution of power in order to avoid the ambiguity of such terms as politics and political leadership found in more traditional studies. Without coping with such primary concepts as power and modernization, or adopting systematic and comparative research procedures, community historians often fail to transcend a particularist emphasis when they should be striving to explain the process underlying change itself.

Analysis of Representative Communities

The significance of this study depends on the representativeness of the communities and the decisional situations being examined. On the surface, ante-bellum Maryland society appears to be relatively simple and undifferentiated, especially when viewed from the modern urban-industrial experience, but this apparent contrast distorts reality. The pressures of modernization were affecting Maryland in significant and various ways. The state was not a uniform socioeconomic unit, characterized by ethnic homogeneity and a moribund slave economy; it was a patchwork of areas accommodating or resisting change. An intensive analysis of representative communities illustrates this diversity.

The state may be divided into four fairly distinct regions based on economic and population characteristics: Southern Maryland, the Eastern Shore, Western Maryland, and the city of Baltimore.[7] The southern counties of the Western Shore contained the largest concentration of slaves and produced almost all of the state's tobacco crop during this era. As its population declined slowly but steadily during this period, it maintained the same social and cultural characteristics that it had had in the previous century. Many of the Eastern Shore counties also had a similarly homogeneous population that endured a gradual numerical decline in the ante-bellum years. Rather than specializing in one crop, however, farmers utilized slaves and an ever-growing free black population to produce diversified agricultural crops, especially cereals, in this area. The upper Western Shore was populated by a more ethnically diverse group than any other rural area of the state. Drawing from earlier German migrations from Pennsylvania, this area differed socially and culturally from the Eastern Shore or Southern Maryland. It was also more agriculturally diversified, and slavery was less prevalent than in the other rural regions.

As an urban enclave in a predominately rural state, Baltimore City was the most atypical area in Maryland. It was a source of great wealth, social and cultural diversity, and it became a haven for an increasing number of the state's free black population in the decades prior to the Civil War. It prospered as a mercantile city, rather than developing as an industrial city, and its increasing size and wealth made it uniquely influential in state affairs. Given evolving political and social egalitarianism, such growth constituted a threat to the continued dominance of the less populous rural counties in the state government.

In view of the comparative and comprehensive objectives of this study, the choice of sample communities is critical. Such a selection should not be random. It should separate prospective communities into similar groupings and then study several comparative units. Considering the above-mentioned regions and the primary data available, this analysis will focus on community decision making in three areas: Baltimore City, Talbot County, and Frederick County. The one region not represented, Southern Maryland, was omitted because of a paucity of official records and an absence of period newspapers. The units selected, however, epitomize dominant trends in the ante-bellum period and should exemplify the variety of the state as a whole. Talbot County, on the Eastern Shore, typified the small rural county with a diversified agricultural economy, tied closely to black freedmen and slaves as a labor force. Frederick County, on the Western Shore, was demographically, socially, and economically mixed. Baltimore City, as the richest and most populous area in the state, is an essential unit for any study of community power in this period.

Once sample communities have been picked, it is necessary to identify and isolate specific community decisions and decision makers. As mentioned earlier, the specific issues selected for intensive analysis were political nominations, internal improvements, and political reform.[8] These produced decisions that required the public allocation of resources that affected the whole community. Private decisions, such as a businessman's decision to build a plant in a community, were excluded from consideration because they were not binding on the whole community, nor did they involve public allocation of community resources. A systematic analysis of patronage was also undertaken to ascertain if a covert system of private influence coexisted with patterns of overt decision making.[9]

Among the most important community decisions in this period were political nominations. During Andrew Jackson's presidency the convention system was reintroduced and refined as the authoritative nomination vehicle for political recruitment. This system not only regulated intraparty rivalry, as well as interparty competition, but it also discouraged nonpartisan candidacy. Individuals who put themselves forward in nomination, ostensibly without party affiliation or as a protest against the undemocratic caucus nomination, fared poorly against party candidates as the second party system matured. Those who selected the candidates for public offices, as well as those who ran the party machinery, had great immediate and potential impact on the political system.[10]

During the late 1820s and throughout the following decade, the internal improvement issue fascinated Maryland residents. Cut-throat competition between the canal and the railroad interests reflected a fundamental rivalry between the Potomac region and that of Baltimore City. In 1836 the state finally resolved this long-term controversy. It underwrote a statewide internal improvements program unifying the rival canal and railroad projects. There were two levels of leadership in this decisional process: at public meetings and conventions called to influence the legislature to support the project; and through lobbyists who worked directly in Annapolis.[11]

The issue of political reform, also a long-standing controversy, reached its flash point at the meeting in 1836 of the Senatorial Electoral College. Here the nineteen Van Buren electors refused to attend and form a quorum unless the other electors agreed beforehand to elect a proreform Senate. The issue was hotly debated throughout the state, because any change would alter the distribution of power in state government. Small counties would lose power to larger counties if the basis of representation were changed from county to population, while rural counties in general feared the potential power of Baltimore City. In the past, reform legislation sometimes passed the lower house, but it was always rejected by a Senate drawn heavily from rural counties. There were many local public meetings and conventions on the regional and state levels during this period.

In order to determine the decisional elites, the men who actively concerned themselves with each of these issues were assigned scores for their leadership roles, and leaders were ranked comparatively. By looking at these community leadership roles over time, those who participated infrequently could be eliminated, and those who were active in community affairs were identified unambiguously. Members of the strategic elites were also identified by the means already described. After assembling a list of community leaders for each area, both for the decisional and strategic elites, basic biographical and economic data were gathered for each individual.[12]

The following three sections will probe community leadership patterns in the sample units. Talbot County, representing a traditional rural community, will come first. Baltimore City, epitomizing a diverse and rapidly modernizing environment, will follow. Frederick County, a rural area undergoing the pressures of modernization, will be the last unit examined. The remainder of this essay will elaborate this information.

Talbot County

The political community most representative of rural Maryland was Talbot County. Unaffected by the immigration of Germans, Irish, or native Americans who settled in Baltimore City and Western Maryland in the early nineteenth century, its population remained relatively homogeneous. Its economy prospered through the utilization of slaves and free blacks to produce a diversified agricultural crop. It is not surprising, therefore, to discover that an oligarchy dominated community leadership.

The decisional elite was both indigenous and wealthy.[13] All of the members of this elite for whom birthplace could be determined were born in Maryland, most within the county itself. There was no suggestion of ethnic variety, nor was there remarkable variation in occupational categories. Professionals and farmers of varying levels of affluence made up the elite. Their average age was forty-one, while 87 percent of them held property with a mean value of $5,945. Over three-fourths (77 percent) of them owned real property, averaging 706 acres, while slightly fewer (75 percent) owned an average of fourteen slaves.

Such statistics, however, only partially describe the principal actors. To appreciate how the oligarchy operated, one must look also at the strategic elites. By taking the fifty wealthiest persons from the county tax lists as the traditional elite, several patterns become apparent. To a far greater degree than in the urban environment of Baltimore City, the Talbot County traditional elite was active in politics. Over half of its members could be identified as political activists, while 42 percent of the decisional elite belonged to the traditional elite as well. The wealthy, furthermore, monopolized both political leadership and local officeholding. Not only did they dominate the best federal and state political positions, but also their sons were normally recruited as party nominees for other state and local elective offices.[14] Prominent families, holding political positions by virtue of their wealth and traditional prestige, ruled as a vital oligarchy in Talbot County during the Jacksonian era.

The commercial elite did not provide alternative opportunities for community leadership in Talbot County. There was only a single bank in Easton, the Eastern Shore branch of the Farmers' Bank, and beyond that only Colonel William Hughlett, whose wealth and position placed him firmly in the oligarchy, belonged to the Baltimore banking elite. As a result,

TABLE 14.1
Talbot County: Comparison of Elites

	Community Decisional Elite N = 31	Traditional Elite N = 50	Commercial Elite N = 16	Positional Elite N = 36
Average Age	41 (48%)*	47 (22%)	44 (25%)	40 (38%)
Slave Ownership	14 (74%)	36 (88%)	24 (69%)	14 (64%)
Average Acreage	706 (77%)	1,183 (100%)	848 (75%)	676 (70%)
Mean Value	$5,945 (87%)	$11,613 (100%)	$9,848 (81%)	$5,326 (83%)

*The percentages for tables 14.1–14.5 refer to individuals for whom an attribute was determined. Obviously, everyone had an age; the records, however, provided specific ages for only 48% of the decisional elite. Data for slaves, acreage, and value came from tax records. The difference between 100% and the percentage given represents those who fell below the legal minimum taxable holding or those without any property.

the rural commercial elite reinforced the dominance of the wealthy and traditional leaders rather than fragmenting men into competing elites.

A comparison between the various Talbot County elites is presented in table 14.1. While there appears to be real variation among these elites, it may be explained partially by the fact that sons of prominent families, men who had little property in their own name but great expectation of inheriting the family estate, deflated the figures for the decisional and positional elites. In general, community leaders in Talbot County were slaveowners with substantial wealth.

The competition between Colonel Edward Lloyd and Robert H. Goldsborough, which lasted from the Federalist through the Jacksonian eras, illustrates the characteristics and longevity of the local oligarchy.[15] Both had competed as adversaries and leaders during the first party system, just as each played an active role in the development of the second party system in the late 1820s. About the time of President Jackson's election, Colonel Lloyd retired from active political participation, but the Lloyd tradition of democratic community leadership continued through the activities of his three sons.[16] While his sons made only a slight imprint on the tax rolls, Colonel Lloyd was the wealthiest man in Talbot County with over 12,000 acres and 577 slaves in 1832. Robert H. Goldsborough, who had earlier opposed Colonel Lloyd as a Federalist and became the nucleus of the Talbot County anti-Jackson party, reached the pinnacle of his political career in the 1830s when he was elected to the United States Senate. Goldsborough, who ranked third on the counry tax rolls in 1832, with 2,382 acres and 64 slaves, also belonged to a prominent Eastern Shore family.

Following the same pattern, John Leeds Kerr, a member of an old and well-connected family, who also married advantageously, ranked seventh on the tax rolls at this time. He served in three congresses in this period, while he was also a member of the local commercial elite. His son John Bozman Kerr, a young attorney, was simultaneously beginning a promising political career by service in the state House of Delegates.

Richard Spencer, who unexpectedly unseated Congressman Kerr in the 1829 election, began his political career in the lower house of the state legislature in the early 1820s, but he gained his greatest notoriety as the editor of the Jackson press of Easton, *The Eastern Shore Whig and People's Advocate,* and as an active political leader. While Spencer thought of himself as in the mainstream of the explicit egalitarianism of the Jackson movement, his property holdings placed him among the top twenty-five individuals ranked according to wealth.[17] The examples of both Spencer and the Lloyd family illustrate the hazards of generalizing that planters as a class abjured one party and favored another.

Rural Talbot County was ruled by an oligarchy. In the pastoral isolation of the Eastern Shore, secluded from the social tensions associated with ethnic diversity or expanding commerce, families who had been in competition for political power since the Revolution continued to dominate the community during the Jacksonian era. Responding to external change, they adapted to the convention system. They also polarized under the standards of the competing political parties. Still, an oligarchy of wealth and status prevailed.

Baltimore City

A wealthy elite did not monopolize community leadership in Baltimore City. Drawn from the diversity of the community itself, including the remnants of an earlier oligarchy, several groups shared power in the city and thus formed a polyarchy. The existence of a polyarchy does not indicate a lack of order or system within the realm of community power; rather, it expresses the successful assimilation of diverse groups into the dynamic structure of power. A comparison of urban decision makers and strategic elites can clarify the essential differences between a polyarchy and an oligarchy.

The Baltimore City decisional elite, consisting of 110 individuals, represents a remarkably heterogeneous group.[18] Divided by occupation, 38 percent were merchants, 18 percent skilled laborers, 32 percent professionals, and 5 percent clerical. A further 4 percent listed only addresses in the city directory. In an era when the majority of urban dwellers fell below the legal minimum of property holding on the tax rolls, 79 percent of this elite owned some type of taxable property, and 25 percent owned slaves. The mean property assessment was $3,224, for a mean holding of seven city lots, and the mean age was forty-six years. All but one of the members of the decisional elite could be identified as a leader or activist in the competing political parties.

The city acted as a magnet to attract persons from other states and from the rural areas of Maryland itself. Of the sixty-eight individuals for whom birth place could be determined, 56 percent were born in Maryland, 34 percent were born in other states, and 10 percent were born abroad. Attorneys and editors frequently migrated to the city. If the opportunities of an urban area were so attractive and open, we should anticipate a mix between enduring families and new arrivals in the decisional elite. This mix occurs. Old, established families like the Howards, which included William G. Read who married Colonel John E. Howard's daughter, were mixed with immigrants who arrived at the end of the eighteenth century from abroad and from other states,[19] and both were diluted by more recent arrivals as the nineteenth century progressed.[20] While information for ethnicity and religion is fragmentary at best, it reinforces the trend of diversity and heterogeneity.[21] The elite making decisions in the urban community of Baltimore was not monolithic nor exclusive.

In order to ascertain the bounds of urban community decision making, this decisional elite must be compared to the three strategic elites. Comparisons based on age and wealth are presented in table 14.2. The data indicate some internal separation of elite clusters. Not surprisingly, the traditional elite ranks highest in all the variables and the commercial elite scores second. The decisional elite falls into the third place, followed by the positional elite. Such separation suggests variations in career goals among members of elites. If we assume that elite membership signifies the combination of a person's immediate place in society and his ambition to further his career opportunities, then this separation reflects differing patterns of political socialization for various social groups. In this urban system men with a minimum of property interacted with more substantial citizens in the positional and decisional elites. Through such interaction those less wealthy could be assimilated into the community power structure.

TABLE 14.2
Baltimore City: Comparison of Elites

	Community Decisional Elite N = 110	Traditional Elite N = 100	Commercial Elite N = 145	Positional Elite N = 160
Average Age	46 (85%)	54 (29%)	53 (35%)	42 (53%)
Slave Ownership	— (25%)	— (41%)	— (25%)	— (20%)
Lots Owned	6.9 (72%)	12.3 (100%)	8.1 (63%)	4.2 (65%)
Mean Value	$3,224 (79%)	$8,002 (100%)	$4,628 (66%)	$1,683 (67%)

TABLE 14.3
Baltimore Elites: Occupational Comparison (percentage)

Class	Community Decisional Elite N = 110	Traditional Elite N = 100	Commercial Elite N = 145	Positional Elite N = 160
Merchant	38	52	45	32
Skilled Worker	18	1	5	20
Professional	32	8	4	24
Clerical	5	6	27	5
City Address Only	4	16	5	8
Unknown	3	17	14	11

If this generalization is valid, then there ought to be variations within the occupational structure of the several community elites.[22] Table 14.3 presents this data. Not surprisingly in a commercial center, the merchants not only dominated the traditional and commercial elites but they also played an impressive role among the decisional and positional elites. On the other hand, skilled workers and professionals also assumed active leadership roles among the decisional and positional elites. This occupational heterogeneity among decision makers and officeholders reinforces the assertion that in Baltimore men with varying social background characteristics could assume responsible roles in community affairs.

Tracing members of Baltimore's decisional elite among strategic elites uncovers important patterns. Over one-fourth (29 percent) of the decisional elite did not belong to any strategic elite. Only 14 percent were also members of the traditional elite; 38 and 37 percent were affiliated with the commercial and positional elites, respectively. Congressmen Benjamin C. Howard and Isaac McKim, as well as John B. Morris and Colonel Beale Randall, were part of all three strategic elites. Nineteen persons (17 percent) in the decisional elite were included in at least two strategic elites.

There is an obvious pattern in this overlap. Besides common membership in the decisional elite, all nineteen who were members of at least three elite groups belonged to the commercial elite. Eight were also members of the traditional elite, and the remaining nine belonged to the positional elite. In a cosmopolitan commercial center, membership in the commercial elite was especially attractive to men who made decisions in and for the community.

There was a high interconnection between the traditional elite and the commercial elite. Only two members of the first were not members of the second. However, the strong association between landed wealth and liquid capital was not extended into the realm of political position holding. Few members of the traditional elite also held public office, but those few who did held the most important positions. Both of the city's long-term congressmen and two of the state senators were members of this group.[23] Such an overlap pinpoints the balance reached within the urban political system——there could be a sharing of offices at the lower elective level, and there could be shared responsibility in reaching party nominations, but the higher governmental positions, both elective and appointive, would be controlled primarily by the wealthy and the prominent.

This balancing among groups was reflected especially in the positional elite. As the foregoing tables suggest, men of varied backgrounds entered the community power structure through political service. Members of the first families, such as Benjamin Chew Howard, Charles Carroll Harper, or John Spear Nicholas, shared public office with men of far more modest social lineage. Jesse Hunt, a saddler by trade, or Joshua Vansant, a hatter, also served in the House of Delegates in Annapolis.

Several individual examples will illustrate the undercurrents of community leadership in Baltimore City. B. C. Howard, whose father was the wealthy Federalist leader Colonel John Eager Howard, was a congressman and a Jackson partisan. His brother was the state governor and an active anti-Jackson partisan during these same years. He was educated at Princeton College, practiced law in the city, and participated in the War of 1812. In a less complex system, he would obviously have been the nucleus of an oligarchy. In Baltimore, however, Howard epitomized an interesting process that pitched the remnants of an earlier oligarchy into a power struggle with other contenders supported by different bases of community strength.

The career of John Van Lear McMahon symbolizes the experiences of a group, many of them young professionals, who migrated to the city to further their careers. As a young attorney, favored with a college education and descended from an obscure but politically active Western Maryland family, he moved to Baltimore in 1826 after representing Allegany County in the state legislature for two terms. Once in Baltimore he served twice more in the House of Delegates before aspiring to the Jackson party nomination for Congress. He was thwarted in this goal by proponents of B. C. Howard, who won the nomination and the seat in 1829. As a result, McMahon gradually shifted political allegiances until, by 1832, he had become a mainstay of the anti-Jackson party. McMahon's legal and oratorical gifts made it easy for him to be assimilated into the power structure of the city.

Some rose through the ranks to become community decision makers. Jesse Hunt, for example, a saddler and harness maker by trade, did so without benefit of august family tradition or a remunerative profession. Born in Baltimore County, Hunt was active as a Jackson partisan starting in 1827; he served in the state legislature for three terms beginning in 1829. In 1832 he was elected mayor of the city. Although forced to resign that office after the bank riots of 1835, he was so entrenched in the ruling establishment that he was appointed city registrar after his resignation, a position that he held for the next decade. Complementing his public service, Hunt was also a director of the ill-fated Bank of Maryland. During his term as mayor, he was one of the leading spokesmen for internal improvements.

Some members of the Baltimore merchant community held major political positions, such as United States Senator Samuel Smith and Congressman Isaac McKim, while others, such as Jacob Albert, entered the decisional elite through nonpolitical community leadership. Albert, a native of Pennsylvania, was a prosperous hardware merchant. As president of the Commercial and Farmers Bank in the city, he belonged to the commercial elite, and since his property holdings placed him among the wealthiest citizens on the city's tax ledgers in 1834, he was also among the traditional elite. But Albert abstained from public association with either of the major political parties in this time of partisan excess. While many persons of varied backgrounds belonged to the decisional elite because of their political activities, Albert belonged because he had led community efforts to obtain various internal improvements.

The Baltimore decisional elite also included prominent newspaper editors. Hezekiah Niles, editor of the *Niles Weekly Register,* was a national journalist at the same time that he was an indefatigable party organizer for the anti-Jacksonians in the seventh ward of the city. Three other editors, Isaac Munroe of the *Patriot,* Samuel Barnes of the *Chronicle,* and Samuel Harker of the *Republican,* were frequent political organizers who also served in the city council. Not one was a native-born Baltimorean. Two, born outside the state, had migrated to the city in response to the demand for their professional services; the other two came from rural Maryland.

During the Jacksonian era the Baltimore ruling elite constituted a polyarchy, rather than an oligarchy as in Talbot County. The traditional and commercial elites shared power with leaders of new community groups and, very importantly, with leaders of hitherto inarticulate groups. The evolution of a stable two-party competition, with an emphasis on recurring organizational activities, opened community leadership to individuals who represented various underlying social and economic forces of the community. This pattern of wide distribution of political power, shared among several groups, was repeated in the various strategic elites.

Frederick County

Frederick County was unlike Talbot County because of its social and economic diversity. Rural and agricultural, it was also unlike Baltimore City. Contrasted to the compact oligarchy of Talbot, community leadership was accessible to various groups and represented a polyarchy. Compared to the polyarchy of the city, however, Frederick was much less stable and was atomized by leadership conflicts within ostensibly unified groups.

The decisional elite for the county consisted of seventy-two individuals.[24] Their mean age was forty-seven, and they owned a mean of 490 acres and six slaves. Efforts to discover birthplace produced inconclusive results, but judging from the number who held taxable property (86 percent), all were permanent members of the community. For lack of reliable occupational information even for Fredericktown, occupations are here subsumed under the two broad categories of farmer and professional (that is, editor, attorney, and doctor). Following a pattern midway between the Baltimore and Talbot experiences, older established families, such as the Duvals, the Schleys, or the McPhersons, were mixed with newer families, like the Taneys or the Wormans, to form this rural decisional elite.

Table 14.4 presents the attributes of the decisional and strategic elites. Like the Talbot County elites, Frederick County community leaders were predominately propertied and slaveowning. Unlike the Talbot experience, many of them owned lots in the various towns throughout the county. Thirty-four percent of the decisional elite was unassociated with any strategic elite. One quarter belonged to the traditional elite, and almost as many (22 percent) belonged to the commercial elite; 40 percent were among the positional elite. Only Moses Worman and Dr. William S. McPherson were members of all elites.

Much in the same pattern as Talbot County, the political elite constituted a large part of the final community decisional elite. Unlike Talbot County, however, the positional elite was not dominated by an oligarchy. Some members of long established families participated in politics, but they did not influence political nominations nor officeholding as they did in Talbot County or even in Baltimore City. Individuals such as Francis Thomas and William Cost Johnson, men without remarkable lineage, were sent to Congress, and men of notoriety and obscurity were elevated to state and local offices without any underlying pattern. Thomas Carlton, the mayor of Fredericktown, like Mayor Jesse Hunt of Baltimore City, represented the new politician drawn from the larger pool of society. Simultaneously, an old

TABLE 14.4
Frederick County: Comparison of Elites

	Community Decisional Elite N = 73		Traditional Elite N = 100		Commercial Elite N = 43		Positional Elite N = 72	
Average Age	47	(66%)	53	(64%)	51	(60%)	44	(53%)
Slave Ownership	6	(65%)	11	(79%)	6	(58%)	7	(64%)
Average Acreage	490	(58%)	730	(99%)	893	(49%)	390	(68%)
Lots Owned	2.1	(47%)	3.6	(26%)	2.1	(51%)	2.5	(37%)
Mean Value	$2,539	(86%)	$5,234	(100%)	$3,285	(79%)	$2,339	(85%)

and distinguished family such as the Schleys continued to wield power through officeholding at both the elective and appointive levels.

At the same time that there was apparently freer access into the political elite at all levels than in other rural areas, the members of traditionally powerful families were not totally displaced nor isolated from community leadership, although they mostly were not officeholders. Colonel John McPherson will stand as an example. He was the namesake and descendent of an earlier Federalist leader, and he inherited great family wealth and prestige. He was included in the decisional elite not as a positional leader but through his efforts as a party leader and as an organizer for reform. Some McPhersons held public office; others were nonpartisan and did not participate at all. This family, like others once prominent, no longer dominated all facets of community leadership, but it remained active. Nevertheless, over half (58 percent) of the traditional elite in Frederick County did not participate in any aspect of public political activity. The domination of wealthy families in Talbot County, or the continued presence of a single family, like the Howards in Baltimore City, was not evidenced in Frederick County.

If the structure of community power did not fit the patterns of oligarchy characteristic of rural Talbot County, it also was not necessarily analogous to the polyarchy of Baltimore City. Perhaps one reason behind a lack of clear definition between the competing elites was the unavailability of occupational identification for individuals in Frederick County. This lack may obscure the possibility that there was a cohesive merchant class. Another explanation for the absence of clear group definition in Frederick County could be the influence of Fredericktown on the structure of community power.

If members of the elites were organized according to their residences, the influence of Fredericktown and its environs is readily perceived. Fifty-seven percent of the decisional elite, 30 percent of the traditional elite, and 58 percent of the commercial elite resided in the city. But the positional elite, which by statute and custom was drawn from the various districts within the county, was more equitably distributed; only 16 percent came from Fredericktown. Although the dispersion of the positional elite and the concentration of the commercial elite might be anticipated, the concentration of the traditional and decisional elites in Fredericktown is remarkable. The city, acting as a magnet to professionals and the wealthy, apparently had an atomizing effect on the structure of community power.

Without the cohesive strength of urban economic associations, lacking the ethnic identification of a dynamic social group, and with old families apparently indifferent to exercising their traditional community leadership role, new associations emerged that were tied to institutions. Some members of important families still served the community by providing leaders, but obscure men such as Moses Worman or political leaders such as Francis Thomas were prominent in the decisional elite. They characterize these trends.

Moses Worman, who served on the county Levy Court and was a bank director, made his major contribution as an anti-Jackson party leader. He belonged to all four elites, and he was also associated with the Baltimore banking community. Without an old family name, Worman optimized the opportunities available to him in Fredericktown.

Francis Thomas, on the other hand, sought to monopolize the newly evolved political organization to wrest control away from members of the older establishment who were dominant at the early part of this era. First as a popular member of the House of Delegates, then as a congressman, he succeeded in identifying his cause with that of reform and democracy. Not only did he successfully challenge the leadership of Dr. William Tyler and John and Madison Nelson in the Frederick County Jackson party, but also his statewide popularity was such that he overcame the stigma of being a "revolutionary" in the 1836 senatorial electoral crisis and was elected the first popularly selected governor after the reform of 1837. Thomas, by controlling party institutions, helped to create one of the groups in a polyarchy.

The experience of Frederick County represents a middle path between the successful defense of an oligarchy in Talbot County and the example of an polyarchy in the city of Baltimore. Without the strong centralizing pressures that characterized the urban patterns in Baltimore, yet with sufficient pressure to undermine the rural oligarchical system, the Frederick example represents an atomized polyarchy, a polyarchy at an embryonic stage of development. Increasingly divorced from the first families, who might have perpetuated rural oligarchy, new groups formed around institutions such as political parties. Such institutions became one element in a system characterized by competition among groups.

The Jacksonian Era: An Alternative Explanation

A look at the distribution of power on the community level creates a perception of leadership that differs markedly from commonly accepted stereotypes for the Jackson period. While men of wealth may have led the anti-Jacksonian party, others like them were Jacksonian leaders, and both parties drew heavily from the remnants of the first party system. The explanation does not lie in a class argument, which calls for social groups in constant conflict and leaders who reflected a basic social cleavage. Similarly, the notion that the second party system was entirely new and elevated new community leaders is equally unsatisfactory. Modernization, however, suggests a plausible alternative.[25]

TABLE 14.5
Members of Decisional Elite in Other Elites (percentage)

	Traditional Elite	Positional Elite	Commercial Elite	None
Baltimore City	14	38	37	29
Talbot County	42	68	10	22
Frederick County	25	40	22	34

Note: Since members of the decisional elite sometimes belonged to several strategic elites, the percentages do not add to one hundred.

The concept of modernization is predicated on the assumption that underlying patterns of leadership are tied to the fundamental structure and development of the community itself. In an area with little social or economic diversity, one isolated from internal or external pressures for change, an oligarchy will dominate community decision making. Conversely, in an area with social and economic diversity, one undergoing constant change, different groups will compete for power, and the resulting elite will represent a polyarchy. The sample Maryland communities conform reasonably well to this model.

The distribution of the decisional elite in the strategic elites in table 14.5 demonstrates this pattern. Rural Talbot County relied heavily on its affluent and political officeholders to lead community decision making. Hidden in these statistics was the active role taken by the very wealthy to organize community activities and to place their sons in nomination for public offices. Frederick County community leadership relied less on its rich citizens and drew many leaders from the ranks of its positional elite. The contrast, however, was displayed vividly by the Baltimore City experience. Remarkably few decisional leaders belonged to the traditional elite, while almost an equal percentage were associated with the political and commercial elites.

Nevertheless, the concept of modernization and the working assumptions and procedures of systematically studying community decision making are at an embryonic stage of development. More work will be needed to refine and improve these concepts and research procedures. The result will be a more balanced appraisal of social interaction and change.

Appendix 1: Talbot County Decisional Elite

Key: * lawyer   ## editor   # merchant   *# skilled labor

Banning, Robert
Battee, John W.
Boyle, John
Bruff, Joseph

Denny, Spry
Dickinson, Dr. Samuel S.
Dickinson, Gen. Solomon
Dudley, George

Goldsborough, Robert H.
Graham, Alexander##
Hambleton, Edward N.
Hambleton, Samuel J.

Hughlett, Col. William
Kerr, John Bozman
Kerr, John Leeds*
Lloyd, Edward, Jr.
Lockerman, Theodore R.
Martin, Gov. Daniel
Martin, Nicholas

Martin, Thomas O.
Maynard, Foster
Millis, Levin
Mullikin, Edward##
Mullikin, Solomon
Nichols, Thomas C.*
Sherwood, George W.##

Spencer, Henry
Spencer, Richard*
Stevens, John
Tilghman, Dr. William H.
Townsend, William

Appendix 2: Baltimore City Decisional Elite

Key: * lawyer   ## editor   # merchant   *# skilled labor

Albert, Jacob#
Alcock, Dr. Edward J.
Bacon, James#
Barnes, Samuel##
Buchanan, James M.*
Campbell, Col. Bernard U.
Carroll, James, Jr.
Cohen, Benedict I.
Cole, William H.*
Crawford, William, Jr.#
Davies, Jacob G.*#
Delcher, John*#
Donaldson, John J.*
Dugan, Frederick J.*
Dunnington, William P.#
Etting, Solomon#
Evans, Hugh W.#
Fitch, Jonathan#
Freeman, William H.*
Frick, William*
Graves, Dr. John J.
Harker, Samuel##
Harwood, James#
Hawkins, James L.
Hayman, James R.
Heath, James P.
Heath, Upton S.*
Hillen, John#
Hoffman, Samuel#
Hollins, John Smith
Hook, Capt. Joseph#
House, Samuel#
Howard, Benjamin C.*
Howard, Charles*
Hubbard, William#
Hunt, Jesse*#
Johnson, Reverdy *

Jones, Joshua##
Karthaus, Charles W.#
Keerl, Samuel#
Kelso, Thomas
Kennedy, John P.*
Kettlewell, John#
Krebs, William*
Lauderman, Henry R.*#
Laurenson, Philip#
Law, James O.*#
Leakin, Gen. Shepard C.##
Leary, Peter*#
Lilly, Richard*#
McClellan, Samuel M.
McCulloch, James W.*
McDonald, Gen. William#
McKim, Isaac#
McKim, John, Jr.#
McKinnell, Henry#
Manning, Col. Samuel*
Marriott, Gen. William H.*
Mass, Samuel#
Mayer, Charles F.*
Medtart, Maj. Joshua*#
Meeteer, William#
Miller, Dr. James H.
Millington, John N.##
Miltenberger, Gen. Anthony#
Moale, Col. Samuel*
Moore, Col. Samuel*#
Morris, John B.
Munroe, Isaac##
Murphy, Dr. Thomas L.
Needles, Edward*#
Neilson, Robert##
Niles, Hezekiah##
Patterson, William#

Peters, Edward J.#
Piper, James
Purviance, Robert#
Randall, Col. Beale#
Read, William George*
Ready, Samuel*#
Rogers, Jacob*#
Roney, Capt. William#
Sanders, Benedict I.#
Sands, Samuel##
Slee, Israel
Smith, Gen. Samuel#
Southcomb, Carey*#
Stansbury, Dr. James B.
Stansbury, John E.
Stapleton, Joseph K.#
Steuart, Gen. George H.*
Stewart, David*
Stewart, John M.*
Stewart, Col. William R.
Storm, Peter
Taylor, Col. George*#
Tiernan, Luke#
Turner, Joshua#
Vansant, Joshua*#
Vickers, Joel#
Warner, Andrew E.*#
Waters, Stephen*#
Watkins, John Wesley*#
White, Joseph*#
Wight, William J.
Williams, Nathaniel F.*
Wilmer, John W.#
Winchester, George*
Young, McClintock*

Appendix 3: Frederick County Decisional Elite

Key: * lawyer   ## editor   # merchant   *# skilled labor

Annan, Robert *#
Baltzell, Dr. John
Bantz, Gideon #

Bartgis, Matthias E. ##
Beall, William Murdock *
Bowlus, George

Brengle, Francis
Brown, Peter H.##
Burckhart, Charles H.

Carlton, Mayor Thomas
Dangerfield, William H.
Dill, Joshua
Dixon, James *
Dorsey, Roderick
Dudderar, Capt. John
Duvall, Capt. Daniel
Eichelberger, Col. George M.
Ent, Capt. George W.
Fulton, Capt. Robert
Gaither, Stewart #
Hammond, Thomas
Holtz, Maj. Nicholas
Hook, Col. Thomas
Jones, Abraham
Johnson, Dr. Thomas W.
Johnson, William Cost*
Kemp, Capt. David
Kemp, Henry
Kinser, John
Lambert, Frederick
McElfresh, Dr. John H.

McKeehan, Dr. Samuel L.##
McKinstry, Evan
McPherson, Edward B.
McPherson, Col. John
McPherson, Dr. William S.
Mantz, Cyrus
Markell, Jacob
Matthias, Maj. Jacob
Morsell, William
Nelson, John *
Nelson, Madison
Niles, William Ogden ##
Nixdorff, Henry
Palmer, Joseph M.*
Poe, Neilson ##
Potts, Richard
Price, George*
Quynn, Caspar
Ramsburgh, Lewis
Richardson, Darius
Rigney, John
Roberts, William

Rose, William
Sappington, Thomas
Schley, William*
Sharpe, George W.##
Shipley, Thomas C.
Shriver, Isaac
Shriver, Jacob
Sifford, John
Simmons, Col. John H.
Taney, Joseph
Thomas, Francis*
Tyler, Dr. John
Tyler, Dr. William
Tyler, Dr. William Bradley
Walters, Somerset R.
Willis, Dr. William
Woodbridge, George##
Worman, Moses
Worthington, Gen.
  Thomas Contee*

NOTES

1. See the following material: Ronald Hoffman, *A Spirit of Dissension: Economics, Politics, and the Revolution in Maryland* (Baltimore, 1973); L. Marx Renzulli, *Maryland: The Federalist Years* (Rutherford, N.J., 1972); Mark M. Haller, "The Rise of the Jackson Party in Maryland, 1820–1829," *Journal of Southern History* 28 (1962):307–26; Robert E. Leipheimer, "Maryland Political Leadership, 1789–1860" (M.A. thesis, University of Maryland, 1967); W. Wayne Smith, "Jacksonian Democracy on the Chesapeake: Class, Kinship, and Politics," *Maryland Historical Magazine* 63 (1968):55–67; W. Wayne Smith, "The Whig Party of Maryland, 1826–1856" (Ph.D. diss., University of Maryland, 1967); William J. Evitts, *A Matter of Allegiances: Maryland from 1850–1861* (Baltimore, 1974); Jean H. Baker, *The Politics of Continuity: Maryland Political Parties from 1858–1870* (Baltimore, 1973); and Frank A. Cassell, *Merchant Congressman in the Young Republic: Samuel Smith of Maryland* (Madison, 1971).

2. For an overview see Nelson W. Polsby, *Community Power and Political Theory* (New Haven, 1963); Claire W. Gilbert, *Community Power Structure,* University of Florida Social Science Monograph Series, No. 45 (Gainesville, Fl., 1972); Willis D. Hawley and James H. Svara, *The Study of Community Power: A Bibliographic Review* (Santa Barbara, Calif., 1972); William A. Welsh, "Methodological Problems in the Study of Leadership in Latin America," *Latin American Research Review* 5 (1970):3–34; Robert A. Dahl, *Who Governs? Democracy and Power in an American City* (New Haven, 1961); and Floyd Hunter, *Community Power Structure: A Study of Decision Makers* (1953; New York, 1961).

3. For a suggestive analysis of the concept of strategic elites see Susanne Keller, *Beyond the Ruling Class: Strategic Elites in Modern Society* (New York, 1963).

4. The local tax records were used to identify the wealthiest members of each community and were the source for all economic information for members of the other elites. The Maryland Hall of Records has the Frederick County data, i.e., County Commissioners, Tax Assessment Books, 1835; and the Talbot County data, i.e., County Commissioners, Tax Assessment Books, 1832. For Baltimore City the Tax Ledgers for 1828 and 1834 are in the Historical Records Division, Baltimore City Court House. A list of the wealthiest members for each community is presented in Whitman H. Ridgway, "A Social Analysis of Maryland Community Elites, 1827–1836: A Study of the Distribution of Power in Baltimore City, Frederick County, and Talbot County" (Ph.D. diss., University of Pennsylvania, 1973), pp. 427–34, 458–61, 502–7; hereafter cited as "A Social Analysis."

5. A list of the commerical elites, drawn from newspaper reports of the annual elections for directors and officers, may be found in Ridgway, "A Social Analysis," pp. 435–47, 462, 508–9.

6. The political elite was identified from newspapers, legislative reports, and federal and state directories. In addition, The Minutes of the Governor and Council, 1826–36, ms., Hall of Records, Annapolis, Md., was an invaluable source to determine who served in local government. For a list of the political elites see Ridgway, "A Social Analysis," pp. 448–51, 463–64, 510–12.

7. For a detailed examination of the agricultural and population characteristics of the state derived from the 1830 and 1840 federal censuses, see Ridgway, "A Social Analysis," pp. 46–73, 361–71.

8. Because of the likelihood that these issues may not have been the most significant local concerns, I conducted a contemporary content analysis using the competing party presses in Baltimore City, Easton, and Fredericktown. The results confirmed the importance of these issue areas and failed to suggest viable alternatives.

9. Besides published sources and the private correspondence of state and national political figures, records in two repositories were especially valuable for the study of patronage. The Hall of Records, Annapolis, Md., contains the Executive Papers, 1828–36. There were several specific collections in the National Archives, Record Group 59, U.S. Department of State: namely, Letters of Application and Recommendation during the Administration of John Q. Adams, 1825–29 (M-531); Letters of Application and Recommendation during the Administration of Andrew Jackson, 1829–37 (M-639); Lists of Recommended Newspapers, 1833 (#150); and Miscellaneous Letters Received Regarding Publishers of the Laws (#149). For a more detailed analysis based on these records, see my article "McCulloch vs. the Jacksonians: Patronage and Politics in Maryland," *Maryland Historical Magazine* 70 (Winter 1975): 350–62.

10. For a complete list of newspaper sources consulted for these issues areas see Ridgway, "A Social Analysis," pp. 514–30.

11. In addition to the well-known published materials concerning internal improvements and the newspaper sources cited above, the Records of the Chesapeake and Ohio Canal Company, U.S. National Park Service, Department of the Interior, Record Group 48, National Archives, contains a wealth of informative correspondence.

12. There are several excellent sources of biographical information at the Maryland Historical Society in Baltimore. Beyond its excellent collection of published materials, the Dielman-Hayward File and the Wilkins File proved invaluable. The 1840 and 1850 federal manuscript censuses at the National Archives were also searched for each area studied. For the uses and abuses of linking behavior with social attributes see Lawrence Stone, "Prosopography," *Daedalus* 100 (1971):46–70; and Lewis J. Edinger and Donald D. Searing, "Social Background in Elite Analysis," *American Political Science Review* 61 (1967):428–45.

13. See appendix 1 for a complete list. Their social and economic attributes are specified in Ridgway, "A Social Analysis," pp. 551–54.

14. For example, Edward Lloyd, Jr., Samuel Hambleton, Jr., and John Bozman Kerr were successful candidates; Daniel and James Murray Lloyd were unsuccessful candidates for public office.

15. See Oswald Tilghman, *History of Talbot County, Maryland, 1661–1861*, 2 vols. (1915; Baltimore, 1967), vol. 1, pp. 184–209; Ridgway, "A Social Analysis," pp. 154–80.

16. Namely Edward, Jr., Daniel, and James Murray Lloyd.

17. Compare Richard Spencer's autobiography in the 30 Sept. 1834 edition of the Easton *Eastern Shore Whig and People's Advocate* and his relative position in the community in Ridgway, "A Social Analysis," pp. 459, 554.

18. See appendix 2 for a complete list. Individual social and economic attributes are listed in Ridgway, "A Social Analysis," pp. 537–48.

19. For instance, individuals like William Patterson, General Samuel Smith, and Luke Tiernan.

20. For example, Jacob Albert, James Bacon, Benjamin J. Cohen, Hugh W. Evans, and Charles F. Mayer.

21. See Ridgway, "A Social Analysis," pp. 308–13.

22. Occupation alone is not a completely satisfactory index of social position. The line between a skilled artisan and a small shopkeeper, for instance, is not as distinct as it should be.

There is a further problem as to the meaning of occupations without a clear understanding of the prevailing economic structure of the economy. For comments on these issues see Edward Pessen, *Riches, Class, and Power before the Civil War* (Lexington, Mass., 1973), pp. 46–71; Michael B. Katz, "Occupational Classification in History," *Journal of Interdisciplinary History* 3 (1972):63–88; and Clyde Griffin, "Occupational Mobility in Nineteenth-Century America: Problems and Possibilities," *Journal of Social History* 5 (1972):310–30.

23. B. C. Howard and Isaac McKim were congressmen, John B. Morris and George Winchester were state senators; Reverdy Johnson had been a state senator in the 1820s.

24. See appendix 3 for the complete list. Their individual social and economic characteristics are specified in Ridgway, "A Social Analysis," 559–65. Besides the valuable sources for economic and social data specified earlier in notes 4 and 12, students of Frederick County benefit from a remarkable source of vital statistics contained in Jacob Mehrling Holdcraft, *Names in Stone: 75,000 Cemetery Inscriptions from Frederick County, Maryland,* 2 vols. (Ann Arbor, 1966).

25. Modernization is not a well-defined concept. For a sample of the better literature see E. A. Wrigley, "The Process of Modernization and the Industrial Revolution in England," *Journal of Interdisciplinary History* 3 (1972):225–59; Samuel P. Huntington, *Political Order in Changing Societies* (New Haven, 1968); Robert A. Dahl, *Polyarchy* (New Haven, 1971); and Marion J. Levy, Jr., *Modernization and the Structure of Societies* (Princeton, 1966).

FIFTEEN

POLITICAL NATIVISM: THE MARYLAND KNOW-NOTHINGS AS A CASE STUDY

Jean Baker

To historians armed with a retrospective view of nineteenth-century America, the central concerns of the 1850s were those that related to the extension of slavery in the territories, the continuation of the Union, and the rights of the South. Such a Civil War synthesis reduces the Know-Nothing party to an ineffectual attempt to avoid the true issues of the day. Likened to a red herring, the Know-Nothing party was also accused of irrelevancy —for its reluctance to speak to the agonizing problems of the 1850s; bigotry—for its anti-Catholic and anti-immigrant prejudices; and, somewhat contradictorily, failure—for its inability to divert attention from the deep sectional division within the United States.[1] Horace Greeley's oft-quoted jest that the Know-Nothings were "as devoid of the elements of persistence as an anti-Cholera or anti-Potato Rot party" sums up historical analysis of the party's rapid decline in the late 1850s.[2]

Such an approach ignores the power and success of a political organization that captured seventy congressional seats in 1855 and that, in its first nationwide election a year later, received 22 percent of the presidential vote.[3] Throughout the 1850s, Know-Nothings from California to Massachusetts elected legislative delegates and governors, as well as municipal and county officials. Astonished opponents likened this rapid growth to "a mushroom . . . which seems to have sprung into existence like fungi after a summer's rain."[4] Certainly such a popular organization deserves analysis on its own ideological, partisan, and structural terms, and there is no better laboratory for the investigation of political nativism than Maryland, where the Know-Nothing party controlled the state for most of the decade.

Maryland's firm attachment to the American party began in the fall of 1854, when Cumberland, Frederick, and Baltimore elected Know-Nothing mayors. The following year the size and extent of the party's support increased, and nativists elected fifty-four of the seventy-four members of the House of Delegates, won eight of the state's eleven contested Senate seats,

Note: Jean Baker is associate professor of history, Goucher College.

and in statewide contests elected a lottery commissioner and comptroller. In 1856 Millard Fillmore carried the state with 55 percent of the vote, and, in recognition of this singular triumph (Mayland's were his only electoral votes), supporters from other states presented the Maryland Know-Nothings with a symbolic gift–a portrait of Fillmore.[5] In 1857 allegiance to the Americans continued, when Thomas H. Hicks, the dour Dorchester county farmer and politician, became governor of the state with 55 percent of the vote. Only in 1859 did Maryland's devotion weaken as a revived Democratic organization threatened the hegemony of the Know-Nothings in many counties, and a Reform party, led mainly by Democrats, challenged the Know-Nothings in their stronghold—Baltimore.[6] By 1860, the party in Maryland was dead, its followers incorporated into the Constitutional Unionism of John Bell, and its slogan swallowed by fervent nonpartisan pleas for Unionism.

Despite this rapid decline, the party controlled the state during most of the 1850s and, hence, served not as a temporary third party filling a political vacuum but rather as an essential part of a two-party arrangement. Certainly other states flirted with, and in some cases embraced, the Know-Nothings, only to return to the Republicans and Democrats. But the border state of Maryland made a special commitment to the politics of nativism, and because of the duration and the intensity of this allegiance, Maryland provides the best information for evaluating the party. It is here that its two important legacies are most obvious—the Know-Nothings' successful realignment of Maryland's voting behavior and their effort to centralize party functions.

For many Marylanders, the problems of controlling immigration, reforming naturalization procedures, and preventing Roman Catholics from holding office took precedence in the 1850s. Playing artfully on the strings of community prejudice, fiery Protestant ministers like Andrew B. Cross and Robert J. Breckinridge and intolerant secret societies like the Order of United American Mechanics convinced their fellow citizens of the dangers of unrestricted immigration and unproscribed Roman Catholicism. Circumstances served to reinforce such appeals as the numbers of foreign born in Maryland increased dramatically from 1840 to 1860, and the swarms of immigrants disembarking in Baltimore—4,065 in 1845, 12,018 in 1847, and 14,148 in 1852—gave notice that the state's foreign population would continue to grow. By 1850, one out of every eight white Marylanders and one out of every five Baltimoreans was foreign born; ten years later the figures had increased to three out of twenty white Marylanders and one out of every four Baltimoreans, while in the United States as a whole only 15 percent of the white population had been born abroad.[7] In the view of some nativists, it was the composition as much as the quantity of this immigration that should disturb Marylanders, for beer-drinking radical Germans, brogue-tongued Papists and "paupers, lunatics, and criminals"[8] could never make acceptable Americans.

In the early 1850s the introduction into the state legislature of a bill that proposed the division of funds among private and parochial schools; the visit to Baltimore of the Roman Catholic Papal Legate Monsignor Bedini, who was promptly burned in effigy; and permissive election practices that allowed unnaturalized immigrants to vote gave a certain urgency to the pleas of nativists to place "the government of America in the hands of true Americans."[9] Uncertain economic conditions after the bankruptcy and depression of the early 1840s only intensified the receptiveness of some Marylanders to these appeals. Laborers already competing with free Negroes and hired-out slaves now found themselves threatened by immigrants.[10]

In 1852 the collapse of Maryland's Whig party that followed Winfield Scott's defeat and the political reshuffling that attended the adoption of a new constitution gave nativist secret societies a political opportunity that they were not reluctant to take in a state accustomed to a two-party system. Unknown in 1853, the Know-Nothing party a year later scored a stunning success in Baltimore with the election of Samuel Hinks, a local flour merchant, to the position of mayor. The rest of the decade was an almost uninterrupted succession of Know-Nothing triumphs–the victory in Maryland of the party's candidate, Millard Fillmore, in the 1856 three-way presidential race; the control of the Maryland legislature for four years; the election of ten congressmen and one United States senator; and in 1857 the success of Thomas Hicks in the governor's race.

To historians, the most memorable aspect of political nativism has always been the party's intolerant appeals to restrict immigration and prevent Roman Catholics from holding office. While Maryland Know-Nothings made only vague attempts to define how they wished to accomplish these ends and once in power did little to effect them, the party clearly rejected the melting pot for its own brew of cultural homogeneity and Anglo-Saxon superiority. "We mean," proclaimed one party pamphlet, "that the Anglo-Saxon element shall have superior sway."[11] Know-Nothing speakers were even more explicit. According to one Fillmore elector in 1856, "the American party are no proscriptionists, but just so sure as the people give them the power, Americans, and none but Americans, should rule America."[12]

Behind such rhetoric lay the disturbing political reality that immigrants were often illegally naturalized before elections and then led off to vote Democratic. Fearful of the creation of bloc voting influenced by Roman Catholic clergy and immigrant organizations, Know-Nothings presented themselves to the public as a conservative reform party dedicated "to cleans[ing] the Augean stable of politics, prevent[ing] herds of reckless prostitutes from plundering our offices . . . and stop[ping] the mercenary character of the foreign vote and the facility with which it can be influenced by the flimsiest demagogism."[13] Know-Nothing appeals reflected, and in turn encouraged, disenchantment with a supposedly corrupt political system. In reacting to the fraudulence of nineteenth-century elections, Know-Nothings, like many other Americans before and since their time, engaged in the popular national pastime of scapegoating; they blamed others, in this case Catholics and immigrants, for their own failure to regulate parties and politics.

To Marylanders, long accustomed to permissive election law and practice, nativist appeals raised hopes that elections could be cleaned up, that a larger police force could control voting irregularities, and that registration laws could prevent the corruption of the past. In Baltimore, where only one policeman patrolled each ward and where citizens still had the right to carry concealed weapons and routinely did so, Know-Nothings promised "a political salvation from corruptions which have long been festering upon the body politic."[14]

In practice, however, Know-Nothings came to depend on coercion and force for their own large pluralities in Baltimore. Party members justified such familiar political customs as cooping,[15] striping ballots, and using weapons as necessary to offset the foreign vote. Yet throughout the 1850s, Know-Nothings continued to appeal for the support of reformers and conservatives, and it was not by chance that Thomas Swann, Baltimore's Know-Nothing mayor in 1857, increased both the number of policemen and the number of voting booths in the city. Nor was it coincidence when during the Civil War, former Know-Nothings argued for the institution of a statewide registration system.

Neglected in the continuing emphasis on the violence attending Know-Nothing elections is the party's focus on nationalism. The Mexican-American War, a successful demonstration of Manifest Destiny, had clearly stimulated patriotic feelings in Maryland, and nativism, the internal expression of what in foreign affairs stands as nationalism, developed in the intellectual climate of the late 1840s. As Frederick Anspach, a dedicated nativist, explained:

> In this land will the fate of humanity be determined. The scene is happily chosen for the final struggle—there is a fitness between the magnificence of this country and the vast and far-reaching issues which are here to be decided. Behold this land! Is it not great in all its features? Look at its natural greatness! What an area of territory![16]

Anna Ella Carroll, a rabid if nonvoting Know-Nothing, agreed: "America has a mission to teach the world in her language, her history, and her laws."[17]

Stripped of their verbiage and rhetorical hyperbole, such sentiments reflected a nationalism that was inherited from the past and that was not an instant creation of the 1850s designed to avoid the problems of sectionalism.

For Know-Nothings, the American republic stood threatened by the decadence and tyranny of Europe, not by the corruption and brutality of slaveholders or the fanaticism of abolitionists. Henry Winter Davis, a Baltimore congressman and the spiritual leader of the Maryland party, found nativism necessary to oppose "threats to the cause of free government in this western world" and "the meddling of European nations with American concerns which do not concern them."[18] According to Davis and many other Know-Nothings, Americans carried the flag of liberty and freedom for all mankind.

In both a quantitative and qualitative sense, "America" was the key word for Maryland Know-Nothings,[19] and it was this symbol that provided the link between what has become the despised nativism of the 1850s and the admired Unionism of the war years. Henry Winter Davis was only one of many Maryland politicians who moved without difficulty from Know-Nothingism to Unionism. During the war years Davis seldom varied his earlier campaign promises for a strengthened American republic, an undivided Union, and an uncorrupted Constitution.[20]

The success of such political appeals depended in part on the leaders who delivered them, and Know-Nothing leaders, like their Democratic counterparts and like most nineteenth-century political leaders, were members of the elite. Representing the highest social and economic, as well as educational, strata of Maryland society, these gentlemen of property and standing came from upper middle-class families, whose religious affiliations were Episcopalian, Methodist, Lutheran, or Presbyterian. A collective biography of sixty Know-Nothing leaders, which includes local officials on the state executive committee as well as elected representatives in Congress and the House of Delegates, reveals that Know-Nothing leaders were more likely to be in business and commerce than their Democratic opponents. Of forty nine Know-Nothings whose occupations were determined in the manuscript census, twenty-five were bankers, proprietors of shops, owners of dry goods stores, or manufacturers, whereas only fifteen of a sample of sixty Democrats held similar occupations. Conversely, Democratic leaders were more likely to be lawyers, farmers, and planters than their Know-Nothing counterparts.[21] Despite the pleas of both parties for the support of Maryland's workingmen, there were few skilled, much less unskilled, workers among the leadership of either party. Indeed James Askew's position as a mechanic and Know-Nothing state legislator was so exceptional as to be remarkable.[22]

Politically the Know-Nothing leadership included both former Whigs and Democrats in roughly equivalent numbers. While Samuel Hinks and Thomas Hicks had been Democrats, Baltimore Congressmen Henry W. Davis and J. Morrison Harris, and Baltimore Mayor Thomas Swann were former Whigs. Conversely, some former Whig leaders like James A. Pearce, the state's senior United States senator, and Reverdy Johnson, the city's most prominent lawyer and a cabinet officer during President Zachary Taylor's administration, joined the Democrats. This left younger, less experienced men, some trained in the lodges of the secret nativist orders, to direct Know-Nothing campaigns. Thus the median age of the Know-Nothing sample was thirty-seven, compared to forty-five for the Democrats. Throughout the period the turnover in Know-Nothing legislators was remarkable; in 1855, of the fifty-four delegates elected to the lower House, only four had served in the legislature before, compared to one-half of the Democrats, and only five would serve again, either in the House or Senate. Much the same was true in 1857 and again in 1859, as legislative recidivism for Know-Nothings remained considerably lower than that for the Democrats or, indeed, for other Maryland parties.[23] A surprisingly large number of Know-Nothing leaders were Masons, and, certainly, membership in a fraternal brotherhood that encouraged the sanctity of the Constitution and the separation of church and state complemented support of a political party with the same ideals. In Maryland the stream of American political history did not flow, as some have suggested, from Federalist and anti-Mason to Whig and Know-Nothing.[24] Moreover, a number of Know-Nothing leaders held membership in several organizations, such as the Improved Order of Red Men, Baltimore's fire companies, the Temperance Society, as well as the more nativist-inclined American Protestant Association.

Despite the casual, often-made assumption that Know-Nothingism was "whiggery in disguise" and that "most of the [Whig] rank and file went into the new organization,"[25] Maryland Know-Nothings gained their greatest support in the former Democratic enclave of Baltimore. In the counties, however, Know-Nothings ran strongest in areas where Whigs had been weakest. Conversely, the former Whig strongholds of Southern Maryland—St. Mary's, Charles, Calvert, and Prince George's counties—became centers of Democratic strength. By accepting too uncritically contemporary newspaper evidence, historians have misapprehended the extent of Maryland's reshuffling of partisan allegiances and consequent electoral realignment.

Such a reshuffling is clearly demonstrated by certain statistical measures indicating that in 1853 a dramatic readjustment of political allegiances began in the state. Continuing until 1856, this electoral shifting transformed state voting patterns. By 1857 stable electoral allegiances were again reestablished as evidenced in high correlations between Democratic votes in the latter years of the decade and a correspondingly low index of discontinuity (rd^2) in table 15.3. Even the cataclysm of civil war did not shake these patterns of voting, which were a legacy of Maryland's Know-Nothing years.

TABLE 15.1
Matrix of Cross Correlations Based on Percentage of Whig Vote in Maryland Elections, 1840–1856

	Presidential Vote in 1840	Presidential Vote in 1844	Presidential Vote in 1848	Presidential Vote in 1852	Presidential Vote in 1856[a]
(1840) 1		.93	.75	.84	−.46
(1844) 2			.78	.87	−.38
(1848) 3				.84	−.38
(1852) 4					−.46

[a] Based on Know-Nothing vote.

Correlations between Whig and Know-Nothing votes, on a percentage county by county basis, also support the argument for realignment. Thus the correlation between the average Whig vote in the 1840s and that for Know-Nothings in 1856 is consistently, but insignificantly, negative (−.423), while that of a smaller unit, wards in Baltimore city, is meaningless (+.102). To sustain the argument that Whigs supported Know-Nothings, high positive correlations would be expected; yet Maryland politics of the 1850s provides few such associations, and surprisingly, the only positive correlations are those between the Know-Nothing vote for president in 1856 and the Democratic vote for governor in 1847 and president in 1844 (+.561 and +.676, respectively).[26]

Perhaps the best measure of party association is that of an index of discontinuity whereby a regression line is mathematically fitted for the period 1834–76, and residuals are derived for each election in the series. As modified here from Walter Burnham's application in *Critical Elections and the Mainsprings of American Politics*, statewide elections are taken sequentially at two- to three-year intervals, with the plotting of five 0's followed by five 1's on the x axis and appropriate residuals from a regression line based on the Maryland Democratic party's percentage of the two-party vote. Ten elections are then evaluated at a time, with a clear transition between the first and last five. If a systematic change in residual values appears at any point, this will be revealed in a discontinuity coefficient that will tend to approximate unity; if random fluctuation or no change occurs the coefficient will tend to approximate zero. Thus the high index of discontinuity (rd^2) values in table 15.3 for midpoint years 1853 to 1855 are further evidence of a realignment in voting patterns, while the low figures in the late 1850s and even during the Civil War indicate that, once established, the realignment was maintained until after the war.[27]

Such statistical measures contradict the belief that the Know-Nothing party was simply a temporary resting place for Whigs whose own organization disappeared in 1852; such an argument requires that Democrats continue to support Democrats while Whigs become Know-Nothings. Instead, despite some nostalgic and persistent efforts to restore the Whig party, both of Maryland's political organizations were transformed during the 1850s.[28]

The social and economic backgrounds of the Know-Nothing voters are more difficult to ascertain. Certainly the party gained little support among either the foreign born or the Catholics. In Westminster, a town in Carroll county with a heavy first-and second-generation German population, townsmen voted Democratic throughout the 1850s, although the surrounding county consistently supported Know-Nothing candidates. In St. Mary's, the so-called birthplace of American Catholicism and a strongly Catholic county in the 1850s, Know-Nothings never received more than 20 percent of the total vote during the 1850s. Yet such findings only support the very obvious conclusion that neither Catholics nor foreign born voted for a party that urged their proscription. The foreign-born population that might have excepted from such a position—the English and Protestant Irish—did not live in Maryland in significant numbers.[29]

Generally, Know-Nothings gained more support from towns and villages than from rural districts. Presumably the former provided closer association with Catholics and the foreign born, and such contact facilitated the organization of secret nativist societies. Baltimore, with its loyal Know-Nothing constituency, was an example, but even in the smaller towns the American party vote usually was higher than that recorded in the farming districts. For example, in Frostburg, a town in Western Maryland, 56 percent of the electorate voted for Fillmore in 1856 compared to 40 percent in the surrounding rural election district and 46 percent in the county at large. In Talbot county 65 percent of the voters in the town of St. Michael's voted for Fillmore, while those in the nearby rural district of Chapel reversed this vote, supporting Buchanan by 74 percent. In the county at large only 43 percent of the vote went to the Americans. Much the same pattern prevailed in Southern Maryland, where Annapolis, the region's largest town, narrowly split its vote between Fillmore (49.4 percent) and Buchanan (50.6 percent), while in the surrounding rural district Fillmore's vote dropped to 25 percent.

Historians have suggested that native-born mechanics and working men became the strength of the Know-Nothing party, and certainly such working-class groups were the mainstay of the infamous political clubs, which bore the exotic names of Bloody Tubs, Rip Raps, and Plug Uglies. Yet an examination of the lists of voters kept by election judges in four heavily Know-Nothing Baltimore wards reveals that these wards included more proprietors and clerks than did those supporting the Democrats. On the other hand, skilled workers divided about equally between the two parties, while unskilled laborers, many undoubtedly foreign born or first-

TABLE 15.2
Matrix of Cross Correlations between Percentage of Democratic Vote in
Maryland Elections 1840–1857

		Presidential Vote in 1840	Presidential Vote in 1844	Gubernatorial Vote in 1847	Presidential Vote in 1848	Gubernatorial Vote in 1850	Presidential Vote in 1852	Gubernatorial Vote in 1853	State Comptroller Vote in 1855	Presidential Vote in 1856	Gubernatorial Vote in 1857
Presidential vote in 1840	1		.93	.80	.74	.84	.83	.75	-.20	-.46	-.44
Presidential vote in 1844	2			.79	.77	.89	.88	.80	-.10	-.37	-.37
Gubernatorial vote in 1847	3				.89	.81	.89	.81	-.15	-.42	-.45
Presidential vote in 1848	4					.84	.84	.80	-.12	-.37	-.47
Gubernatorial vote in 1850	5						.86	.78	-.15	-.40	-.44
Presidential vote in 1852	6							.94	-.18	-.46	-.49
Gubernatorial vote in 1853	7								-.22	-.27	-.32
State Comptroller vote in 1855	8									.66	.64
Presidential vote in 1856	9										.93

TABLE 15.3
Discontinuity Variables over Time, Maryland 1834–1876,
Based on Percentage of Democratic Vote

Period	Midpoint Year	rd	rd²	Period	Year	rd	rd²
1834–56	1845	−.20	.04	1848–68	1858	−.17	.03
1836–57	1846	−.28	.08	1850–70	1860	.17	.03
1838–59	1848	−.37	.14	1852–72	1862	.42	.18
1840–60	1850	−.58	.34	1856–74	1865	.73	.53
1844–62	1853	−.89	.79	1857–76	1866	.85	.72
1847–64	1855	−.81	.66				

generation Americans, voted Democratic. Baltimore's silk-stocking wards adjacent to Mount Vernon Square also voted Democratic, whereas some of the middle-class wards—the 3d, 5th, 7th, 16th, and 19th—were heavily Know-Nothing.[30] Thus it appears that the Know-Nothing party in Maryland was a coalition of Protestant middle-class town dwellers. Although the party recruited its leaders from the highest social and economic rungs of society, this group did not give overwhelming support to the party. Know-Nothing majorities came instead from artisans, skilled laborers and storekeepers—the middle Americans of the nineteenth century.

To its opponents, the Know-Nothing party was little more than an ephemeral creation of intolerant bigots and greedy politicians. Democrats, confusing the party with the secret societies from which it had sprung, insisted that Know-Nothingism was simply a collection of nativist lodges "never more formidable than a jack o'lantern covered by a flimsy sheet and topped with an illuminated pumpkin."[31] In an age of decentralized party structure, such critical observations obscured Know-Nothing attempts to control both membership and finances.

While previous state parties of both the Whigs and Democrats were accustomed to only the most fleeting and intangible relationships with any national organization, from the beginning of their political life the Maryland Know-Nothings were influenced by the American National Council, composed of delegates from state councils throughout the United States, and financed by dues from state organizations.[32] Designed to control membership, policy, and finances, in 1855 this council established a party platform that committed Know-Nothings "to the cultivation and development of a sentiment of profoundly intense American feeling, the maintenance of the Union, the radical revision of laws regulating immigration, and resistance to the aggressive policy and corrupting policies of the Roman Catholic church."[33] Furthermore, the council met twice a year and insisted that state delegates support its resolutions and, in turn, require their local membership to do so. Such attempts to control membership and to define party objectives between national elections had few parallels in the nineteenth century, and while the restrictive basis on which Know-Nothings chose to define membership was indefensible, this effort at centralization remains a rare effort in American politics to create a disciplined party apparatus responsive to national direction.[34]

In Maryland, as well as in other states, the American State Council, a committee composed of delegates elected from district councils, tried to regulate membership by requiring that followers swear allegiance to the party's ideals and promise support of Know-Nothing candidates. In the early years of the party, members had to swear that they would vote for the organization's nominees, a quite different practice from that employed in most American political parties, where membership was based on more casual attachments. Failure to vote for fellow Know-Nothings could lead to expulsion from the party, and nativist election judges enforced this regulation by observing whether party members actually cast the red-striped Know-Nothing ballots. Gradually, as the organization moved from its position as a secret society running occasional candidates to an important political party, Maryland Know-Nothings abandoned their efforts to bar native-born Roman Catholics from membership, and it was a Maryland delegate to the 1855 National Convention, William Alexander, who fought unsuccessfully to admit Catholics to the party.[35]

Improved party fortunes also made it impossible for the powerful Maryland State Council to control policy and nominations. Soon there were too many local councils, with little relation to political boundaries, to agree on ward and district candidates. After 1856 the Know-Nothings duplicated the nominating system employed by other parties as they discarded their tightly knit structures. Local councils representing election districts chose delegates to conventions, which in turn made nominations for state offices. The state convention and the executive committee chosen at the convention were separate from the American State Council; the latter had evolved from the organization of older nativist societies, while the executive committee served the purely political function of organizing campaigns and running the party between elections. Gradually as the Know-Nothings exchanged their early ease of movement for the difficult restraints of a major party, the State Council became less influential. Policy was directed toward winning elections and not proscribing immigrants and Catholics. By 1856 even the loyal Baltimore *Clipper* insisted that Know-Nothings in the state legislature repay their political debts by electing a former Whig to the United States Senate instead of giving the position to a fervent, if politically impotent, nativist.[36] Thus the fears of John Pendleton Kennedy, the Maryland novelist and former Whig cabinet officer, that the party was "disposed to be loyal in its appointments to those who have gone through the forms of initiation" proved unwarranted.[37]

In 1857, the Know-Nothing National Council, split like the Democrats on the issue of slavery in the territories, gave up its efforts at centralization and turned the party over to state organizations.[38] Lacking the support of any national organization, the Maryland Know-Nothings now faced the impossible task of continuing their party as a presidential election approached and as sectional divisions increasingly demanded loyalty to regional orthodoxies. Yet despite the absence of any realistic national prospects, the American party continued to control the state, winning the governorship in 1857 and the comptrollership in 1859. Only in 1860 did the demands of a presidential canvass and the power of a revived Democratic party force the Know-Nothings into the congenial home of Constitutional Unionism. Party members overwhelmingly supported the candidacy of the former Tennessee Know-Nothing, John Bell.[39] By 1861 most Know-Nothings had become Unionists, their pleas to preserve the American republic now incorporated into the patriotic sentiments of the Union party.

For too long the story of the Know-Nothing party in Maryland, as in other states, has been either a chapter in the coming of the Civil War or a footnote in what Richard Hofstadter has called "the paranoid style in American politics." In the border state of Maryland, nativism had deep and persistent roots that grew out of the nationalistic fervor of the 1840s and that were nurtured by the heavy immigration of the 1850s. In America's "Herrenvolk" democracy, where political equality was extended only to whte males. nativist positions were not consonant with the liberal tendencies of the United States and accordingly were condemned.[40] Yet Know-Nothing intolerance should not be viewed as exceptional in nineteenth-century American politics, but rather should be interpreted as stemming from the same racist exclusionism that led many Democrats to condemn free Negroes.

As many historians have noted, the Know-Nothings did little to implement their ideals and only half-heartedly attempted to investigate nunneries, tighten naturalization regulations, and ostracize Roman Catholics from officeholding. Such a lack of commitment has led to charges that while the party was a vehicle for ambitious young politicians it was also a temporary way station for status-conscious Americans. Again a double historical standard prevails, for few state or national parties have ever effected the promises of their campaigns, and few have had the abbreviated time period granted the Know-Nothings. Hence Maryland politics under the Know-Nothings continued to involve, as it had in times of Democratic and Whig control, such nonpartisan but pertinent issues as the prohibition of swine from "going at large" in Cecil county and the efficient use of the resources of the Chesapeake Bay. Lost in the emotional criticism of the Know-Nothings are two important legacies of political nativism: the realignment of Maryland's party allegiances and the attempt by nativists to centralize party functions. The irony is, of course, that these two ends were mutually exclusive, for in the process of reshuffling the state's voting behavior and political leadership, Know-Nothings could not maintain their tight, highly centralized party machinery, which came, more and more, to resemble that of America's mass political parties. The counterpoint to election victories and partisan realignment was a gradual abandonment of ideology and a disciplined organization. Winning politics required, for the Maryland Know-Nothings, losing their nativism.

NOTES

1. Because members frequently replied "I know nothing" to queries about their organization, the party was called, by friend and foe alike, the Know-Nothings, although its official name was the American party. The literature on the Know-Nothings is largely monographic, and there are a number of state studies written under the direction of Professor Richard J. Purcell at Catholic University. In most cases these studies describe the party's platform and policies in rather censorious terms. See for example Sister Mary McConville, *Political Nativism in the State of Maryland* (Washington, D.C., 1928); Sister Agnes McGann, *Nativism in Kentucky in 1860* (Washington, D.C., 1944); Sister Paul McGrath, *Political Nativism in Texas* (Washington, D.C., 1930); Carroll J. Noonan, *Nativism in Connecticut, 1829-1860* (Washington, D.C., 1938). More tolerant of the party's purposes are two fine studies that describe, but do not analyze, the origins, leaders, platforms, and decline of the party—Louis Scisco's *Political Nativism in New York State* (New York, 1901), and Laurence Schmeckebier's *History of the Know-Nothing Party in Maryland* (Baltimore, 1899). There are two important general studies relating to political nativism: W. Darrell Overdyke's *The Know-Nothing Party in the South* (Baton Rouge, La., 1950), and Ray Billington's *The Protestant Crusade 1800-1850* (New York; 1938). The most recent additions to the literature are Ira Leonard and Robert Parmet's *American Nativism* (New York, 1971) and Michael Holt's fine article "The Politics of Impatience: The Origins of Know Nothingism," *Journal of American History* 60 (1973):309-31, and the same author's "The Antimasonic and Know-Nothing Parties" in *History of United States Political Parties,* ed. Arthur Schlesinger, Jr. (New York, 1973), pp. 575-620.

2. Horace Greeley, *Whig Almanac for 1854* (New York, 1854), p. 10.

3. It is extremely difficult to determine the party allegiances of some congressmen. Overdyke counts 73 Know-Nothings in the 34th Congress, while Greeley finds 43 "Fillmore Americans" and Billington, 75; see Overdyke, *Know-Nothing Party in the South,* p. 162; Greeley, *Whig Almanac for 1857,* p. 17; and Billington, *Protestant Crusade,* pp. 387-88.

4. *Articles from the Maryland Republican* (Annapolis, n.d.), p. 5.

5. Baltimore *Clipper,* 3 Dec. 1857.

6. For the political derivation of these reformers, see Jean H. Baker, *The Politics of Continuity: Maryland Political Parties from 1858 to 1970* (Baltimore, 1973), pp. 27, 43 n; and William J. Evitts, *A Matter of Allegiances: Maryland from 1850-1861* (Baltimore, 1974), pp. 119-23; 128-33.

7. For an abstract of census data on Maryland, see Richard Edwards, *Statistical Gazetteer of the State of Maryland* (Baltimore, 1852); J. D. B. DeBow, *Statistical View of the United States* (New York, 1970); and Joseph C. G. Kennedy, *Preliminary Report on the Eighth Census, 1860* (Washington, D.C., 1862). The 1840 manuscript census does not include information on foreign birth, although general statistics based on the alien passengers arriving in the United States are available in U.S. Bureau of the Census, *Historical Statistics of the United States, Colonial Times to 1957* (Washington, D.C., 1960), p. 57. According to such statistics, which are not broken down by state, the annual number of immigrants arriving in the United States rose to 427,833 or by 400 percent in the decade 1844-54.

8. Anna Ella Carroll, *The Great American Battle* (New York, 1856), p. 344. For an extended criticism of the immigrants, see also Thomas Whitney, *A Defense of the American Policy* (New York, 1856).

9. *Baltimore American,* 10 June, 1854.

10. For a careful study of various aspects of the problem of Negro labor in Maryland, see Ray Della, "The Problems of Negro Labor in the 1850s," *Maryland Historical Magazine* 66 (1971):14–32.

11. William Ryder, ed., *Our Country or the American Parlor Keepsake* (Boston, 1854), p. 5.

12. Baltimore *Sun,* 3 Oct. 1856.

13. Cecil *Whig* (Elkton), 3 Nov. 1855.

14. Frederick Anspach, *The Sons of the Sires* (Philadelphia, 1855), p. 38.

15. Cooping, the political version of the shanghai, involved kidnapping citizens before an election, keeping them "cooped" in a cellar until election day, and marching them to the polls to vote for a certain candidate. Long associated with the Know-Nothings, in fact, cooping was first used in the 1840s by Democrats, and some Baltimoreans insist that Edgar Allan Poe's death in 1849 resulted from his enforced incarceration in a dank cellar before an election. For a vivid description of cooping and other practices, see "Testimony Taken before the Committee of the House of Delegates on Contested Elections, 1860," *Minority Report of the Committee on Elections,* Maryland Senate, 1860, document W. (n.p., n.d.).

16. Anspach, *Sons of the Sires,* pp. 109, 110.

17. Carroll, *Great American Battle,* p. iv. Such sentiments are examples of the exultant, prophetic, and utopian rhetoric so popular in nineteenth-century politics. For other examples, see Fred Somkin's provocative *Unquiet Eagle: Memory and Desire in the Idea of American Freedom, 1815–1860* (Ithaca, 1967).

18. Henry Winter Davis, *The War of Ormuzd and Ahriman in the Nineteenth Century* (Baltimore, 1852), p. 419; idem, *The Origin, Principles, and Purposes of the American Party* (n.p.; n.d.), p. 47.

19. A frequency count of several key Know-Nothing statements, including Davis's *Origin, Principles and Purposes of the American Party,* the Maryland American Convention platforms of 1857 and 1859, and J. Morrison Harris's address to his constituents, 1858, reveals that America is the most frequently used "content" word with 57 uses; Catholic is second (51), and constitution is third (20).

20. Davis, *Origin, Principles, and Purposes of the American Party,* passim; see also idem, *Speeches and Addresses* (New York, 1867), pp. 260–92, and Gerald Henig's new biography *Henry Winter Davis: Ante Bellum and Civil War Congressman from Maryland* (New York, 1973).

21. Of the 52 Democratic leaders located, 29 were farmers, doctors, lawyers, and planters, compared to 16 of 49 Know-Nothings. Newspaper editors and a variety of miscellaneous occupations completed the sample, although there are no significant differences between the two groups in these categories. While a difference in the number of preachers and ministers might be anticipated—Know-Nothings presumably including more Protestant ministers—I found none in my sample, although the Episcopalian minister Rev. J. N. McJilton served as an American party city councilman in Baltimore. In part, this reflects Maryland's constitutional prohibition against ministers serving in the legislature.

22. Baltimore *Clipper,* 25 Sept. 1855.

23. Usually about a third of a legislative class returned to the legislature within ten years.

24. Seventeen of the sample of Know-Nothing leaders were identified as Masons in the newspapers or in Edward Schultz, *A History of Freemasonry in Maryland,* 4 vols. (Baltimore, 1882–87), vol. 3, p. 469. Only six Democratic leaders were so identified; see also Baltimore *Clipper,* 17 Jan. 1855, 12 April, 1856. For a statement of this progression see Wilfred Binkley, *American Political Parties—Their Natural History* (New York, 1958), pp. 158–62, 194. The most startling example occurs in Svend Peterson, *A Statistical History of American Presidential Elections* (New York, 1963), which cites the Know-Nothing presidential vote in 1856 as that of the Whigs.

25. *Baltimore American,* 10 Oct. 1854; *Planter's Advocate (Upper Marlboro,)* 14 June 1854.

26. Correlations measure the relationship between variables on a scale of + 1.00 (a perfect direct relationship) to -1.00 (a perfect inverse relationship). Significant relationships are indicated when the coefficient is greater than plus or minus .50. The Pearson product moment formula used here to calculate coefficients of correlation is

$$\frac{N(\text{sum of } xy) - (\text{sum of } y)\,(\text{sum of } x)}{\sqrt{N(\text{sum of } x^2) - (\text{sum of } x)^2} \cdot \sqrt{N(\text{sum of } y^2) - (\text{sum of } y)^2}}$$

27. See Walter Dean Burnham, *Critical Elections and the Mainsprings of American Politics* (New York, 1970), pp. 11–33. Democratic figures are used, due to the change in name from Whigs to Know-Nothings to Union to Republican party. Indeed one of the persistent challenges in the evaluation of political nativism derives from the difficulty of obtaining longitudinal statistics.

28. Both parties appealed throughout the period for Whig support, arguing that it was their party that most consistently followed the principles of Whigs; see for example *Baltimore American,* 4 Aug. 1856. Indeed the editors of the *Baltimore American* consistently presented the argument for the restoration of the Whig party.

29. *Baltimore American,* 10 Oct. 1854. Coefficient of correlations between the foreign-born and American vote in Baltimore city in 1855, 1856, and 1857, on a ward-by-ward basis in state and federal elections, are consistently negative (-.753 in 1855, -.816 in 1856, and -.821 in 1857). See also Evitts, *A Matter of Allegiances;* Joseph C. G. Kennedy, *History and Statistics of the State of Maryland According to the Returns of the United States, 1850* (Washington, 1852), p. 28.

30. See Baltimore City Poll Books, City Hall, Baltimore, Md. Poll books were lists of voters collected by judges at the time of election, and in wards like the 18th where the Know-Nothing vote was high, voters were checked person by person against the Baltimore city registers to determine the occupational composition of ward voters. See also *Maryland Contested Election—Third Congressional District, 1858,* 35th Cong., misc. doc. no. 68, pp. 366–68; and the *Baltimore Register* (Baltimore, 1855, 1856, 1857).

31. *Baltimore American,* 9 July 1853.

32. Ralph J. Buxton Scrapbook, Buxton Papers, North Carolina State Archives, Raleigh, North Carolina.

33. Schmeckebier, *Know-Nothing Party in Maryland,* pp. 262–65; see also the *New York Times,* 8 March 1855.

34. In the twentieth century many political scientists have encouraged the development of more responsible, disciplined, and unified parties based on structural principles similar to those of the Know-Nothings; see "Toward a More Responsible Two-Party System," *American Political Science Review,* 44 (Sept. 1950), supplement.

35. Overdyke, *Know-Nothing Party in the South,* p. 129.

36. Baltimore *Clipper,* 22 Jan. 1856.

37. John Kennedy to A. Bryan, 3 Dec. 1855, Kennedy Papers, Peabody Library, Baltimore, Maryland.

38. *Baltimore American,* 3, 5 June, 1857; Overdyke, *Know-Nothing Party in the South,* pp. 167–69.

39. The coefficient of correlation on a county-by-county basis between the Know-Nothing vote in 1856 for president and the vote for Bell in 1860 is (+.857), and between the Know-Nothing vote for governor in 1857 and the Bell vote is (+.916).

40. For a description of this system whereby egalitarian ideals are restricted to certain citizens, in this case white males over 21, see Pierre L. Van den Berghe, *Race and Racism* (New York, 1967) and idem., *Caneville: The Structure of a South African Town* (Middletown, Conn., 1964).

BIBLIOGRAPHY OF THE WRITINGS
OF MORRIS LEON RADOFF

Compiled by Frank F. White, Jr.

A. *BOOKS, ARTICLES, MANUSCRIPTS*

1. Books

Buildings of the State of Maryland at Annapolis. Annapolis: Hall of Records Commission, 1954.

Calendar of Maryland State Papers, No. 2, The Bank Stock Papers. Annapolis: Hall of Records Commission, 1947.

The County Courthouses and Records of Maryland, Part One: The Courthouses. Annapolis: Hall of Records Commission, 1960.

Fifth [to Thirty-Fifth] Annual Report of the Archivist of the Hall of Records, State of Maryland, [for the Fiscal Years October 1, 1939 through June 30, 1970.]. N.p., n.d.

First to Fourth Annual Reports of the Archivist of the Hall of Records, State of Maryland, for the Fiscal Years October 1, 1935 through September 30, 1939. N.p., n.d.

Inventory of the County and Town Archives of Maryland, No. 11, Garrett County (Oakland). Mimeographed. Baltimore: The Maryland Historical Records Survey, June 1938.

Inventory of the County and Town Archives of Maryland, No. 21, Washington County (Hagerstown). Mimeographed. Baltimore: The Maryland Historical Records Survey, December 1937.

Inventory of the County Archives of Maryland, No. 1, Allegany County (Cumberland). Mimeographed. Baltimore: The Maryland Historical Records Survey, September 1937.

The Old Line State: A History of Maryland. 3 vols. Hopkinsville, Ky.: Historical Record Association, 1956.

The Old Line State: A History of Maryland, 2d ed., rev. Annapolis: Hall of Records Commission, 1971.

The State House at Annapolis. Annapolis: Hall of Records Commission, 1972.

2. Articles

"Captain Gordon of the Constellation," *Maryland Historical Magazine* 67 (1972):389–418.

"Charles Wallace as Undertaker of the State House," *Maryland Historical Magazine* 51 (1956):50–53.

"Colonial Records of Anne Arundel County," *Inventory of the County and Town Archives of Maryland, No. 2, Anne Arundel County (Annapolis)*, pp. 308–14. Mimeographed. The Maryland Historical Records Survey, December 1941.

"The Date of the Gentilhomme et Son Page," *Modern Language Notes* 51 (1936):30–32.

"Early Annapolis Records," *Inventory of the County and Town Archives of Maryland, No. 2, Anne Arundel County (Annapolis)*, pp. 315–17. Mimeographed. Baltimore: The Maryland Historical Records Survey, December 1941.

"Early Annapolis Records," *Maryland Historical Magazine* 35 (1940):74–78.

"An Elusive Manuscript—The Proceedings of the Maryland Convention of 1774," *The American Archivist* 30 (1967):59–65.

"Governmental Records in Time of War," *Bulletin No. 4, Maryland Committee for the Conservation of Cultural Resources.* Processed. N.p., n.d.

"A Guide to Practical Calendaring," *The American Archivist* 11 (1948):123–40, 203–22.

"The Hall of Records, Annapolis, Maryland," *Weston's Record* 18 [1943]:2–3.

"How to Transfer the Governor's Papers," *The American Archivist* 23 (1960): 185–89.

"Influence of the French Farce in *Henry V* and *The Merry Wives*," *Modern Language Notes* 48 (1933):7.

"Maryland," *National Historical Magazine* 76 (1942):704–7.

"The Maryland Hall of Records: In Which the Archivist and Records Administrator of the State of Maryland Recounts the Formation of an Archive," *Manuscripts* 20 (1968):16–19.

"The Maryland Records in the Revolutionary War," *The American Archivist* 37 (1974):277–85.

"Moral Science—Censorship among the Learned," *The American Mercury* 110 (1933):206–10.

"Notes on Baltimore County Land Records," *Maryland Historical Magazine* 33 (1938):183–86.

"A Possible Etymology for English Nincompoop," *Philological Quarterly* 10 (1931):312–13.

"Reports of State Archivists," *The American Archivist* 17 (1954):331–39.

"The Settlement." In *The Old Line State: A History of Maryland*, 3 vols., edited by Morris L. Radoff, vol. 1, pp. 1–10. Hopkinsville, Ky.: Historical Record Association, 1956. Reprinted by Hall of Records Commission, Annapolis, 1971.

"Tout Craché and Cher Comme Crême," *Modern Language Notes* 53 (1938):328–34.

"What Should Bind Us Together," *The American Archivist* 19 (1956):3–10.

3. Manuscripts

"The Characters in Farce and Comedy of the French Renaissance." Ph.D. dissertation, The Johns Hopkins University, 1933.

"The Libraries of Etienne Pasquier and Claude Fauchet." Master's thesis, University of North Carolina, 1927.

4. Forthcoming Publication

"Annapolis in the Revolution," in *The Role of the Chesapeake Bay in the Revolution.* Edited by Ernest M. Eller, Rear Admiral, U.S.N., Retired. Centreville, Md.: Tidewater Publishing Corp.

B. *CO-PUBLICATIONS*

"Claude Fauchet and His Library," with Urban T. Holmes. *Publications of the Modern Language Association of America* 44 (1929):229–42.

The County Courthouses and Records of Maryland, Part Two: The Records, with Gust Skordas and Phebe R. Jacobsen. Annapolis: Hall of Records Commission, 1963.

Maryland Manual, [1949–74], with John P. Hively (1949–55), Lois Green Clark (1956–60), and Frank F. White, Jr. (1961–74). Annapolis: Hall of Records Commission, 1949–74.

"Notes on the Burlador," with W. G. Salley, *Modern Language Notes* 45 (1935):239.

C. *TRANSLATIONS*

Belaunde, Victor Andres. *Bolivar and Political Thought of the Spanish American Revolution.* Baltimore: The Johns Hopkins Press, 1938.

D. *FOREWORDS, INTRODUCTIONS, AND PREFACES*

Foreword to *History of Maryland,* 3 vols., by J. Thomas Scharf, 1879. Reprint. Hatboro, Pa.: Tradition Press, 1965.

Foreword to *Index to the Wills of Maryland, Garrett County 1872–1960, Harford County 1774–1960,* edited by Joan Hume. Baltimore: Magna Carta Book Co., 1970.

Foreword to *Land Office and Prerogative Court Records of Colonial Maryland,* by Elisabeth Hartsook and Gust Skordas. Annapolis: Hall of Records Commission, 1946.

Foreword to *The Early Settlers of Maryland,* with an Introduction by Gust Skordas. Baltimore: Genealogical Publishing Co., 1968. Reprinted, 1974.

Introduction to *Catalogue of Archival Material, Hall of Records, State of Maryland.* Annapolis: Hall of Records Commission, 1942.

Introduction to *History of Maryland, Province and State,* by Matthew Page Andrews, 1929. Reprint. Hatboro, Pa.: Tradition Press, 1965.

Introduction to *Maryland Tax List, 1783, Baltimore County.* Philadelphia: Rhistoric Publications, 1970.

Preface to *Calendar of Maryland State Papers, No. 1: The Black Books,* edited by Elizabeth W. Meade, Emil Fossan, and Roger Thomas. Annapolis: Hall of Records Commission, 1943.

INDEX

Abigail (Negro), 181
Abraham (Negro), 181, 182, 188
"Act for ascertaining the Gage & Tare of tobacco Hhds," 4
"Act for the Incouragement of Learning . . . this Province," 87
Act of Religious Toleration, 70
Acton, Henry, 48, 58
Adams, John, 16, 18, 35, 36
Adams, John Q., 316
Adams, John W., & Co., 224
Adams, Joseph, 6, 7, 24
Addington, Henry, 19, 22, 26, 28, 37, 38
Addison, John, 79
Addison, Thomas, 81, 86
Addison family, 179, 184, 195
Adger, Black, 220
Administration accounts, 43, 47, 209
Administrators, 43, 47, 48
Africa Company, 6
African (in Africa), 172, 173 ff.; (in Maryland), 191–96
Afro-American: community life, 171–96; family life, 171–96; household types, 172, 174, 175, 178ff., life-cycle, 183–89; voting patterns, 257–63
Agents, colonial in England, 4
Agricultural inputs and outputs, Prince George's County, 1860–80, 233–34
Agricultural land use, Prince George's County, 1860–80, 228–47
Alexander (Negro), 183
Alexander, Robert, 38
Alexander, William, 328
Alien and Sedition Acts, 279, 281
Allen's Freshes, Charles County, 191
The American and Commercial Advertiser, 295, 296
The American and Daily Advertiser, 295
American National Council, 327
American party, 318–30
American Protestant Association, 323
American State Council, 328
Ammerman, David L., 56, 107, 109, 131, 168
Anastatia (Negro), 183
Anderson, William, 35
Andre (Negro), 181
Andrewe, Thomas, 61
Annapolis Quarter, 181

Anne Arundel County, 139; economy of, 141–49
Annual Reports of the Archivist of the Hall of Records, xiii
"Another Mechanic," pseud., 287
Anspach, Frederick, 321, 331
Apsley, Ann, 59
Apsley, Edward, 59
Apsley, William, 59
Arbitration commissioners, under Jay Treaty, 18ff.
Archives of Maryland, 34, 35, 57, 61, 83, 84, 86, 87, 98, 106, 108, 131, 150, 170, 196, 209
Arden, Richard Pepper, 11, 13, 14
Ark (ship), xii
Askew, James, 322
Assembly of Maryland: role of selection of colonial agents, 4–5; paper money acts of, 5–8; and Bank Stock controversy, 5–6, 10, 25; British confiscated property acts of, 8–10; acts concerning testamentary affairs and guardianship, 43ff.; House of Delegates, elections, 286 ff.
Associators, 75–76, 78
Astor, John Jacob, 217
Atlas of Early American History, 211
Atlas of Fifteen Miles Around Washington, 237, 239
Attorney-General (Crown), 11, 15

Bacon, James, 314, 316
Bacon, Thomas, ed., *The Laws of Maryland,* 57, 61, 62
Bailyn, Bernard, 66, 83, 106, 133
Baker, Jean, 315, 318–32
Baldwin, Jane, compiler, *The Maryland Calendar of Wills,* 91, 106, 107
Ball, Charles, 188
Baltimore American and Daily Advertiser, 282, 285, 287, 288, 331, 332
Baltimore American & Daily Commercial Advertiser, 225
Baltimore & Ohio Railroad Company, 223
Baltimore and Potomac Railroad, 241
Baltimore Branch, Second Bank of the U.S., 225, 226
Baltimore Brigade, 290
Baltimore City: trade, 213, 215, 219; political structure, 1795–1812, 277–96; leadership

patterns, 305–9, 314 ff.; Know-Nothing Party in, 318–70
Baltimore *Clipper*, 328, 330ff.
Baltimore County Court, 49
Baltimore *Chronicle*, 309
Baltimore *Federal Republican*, 289
Baltimore fire companies, political activities, 280, 284, 285
Baltimore mechanics, political activities, 286ff.
Baltimore militia, political activities, 283 ff., 290–91
Baltimore *Patriot*, 224, 225, 309
Baltimore *Republican*, 309
Baltimore *Sun*, 331
Baltimore-Washington markets, 229, 230, 243
Baltimore *Whig*, 292, 296
Baltzell, Dr. John, 314
Bank of Baltimore, 215
Bank of England. *See* Bank stock
Bank of Maryland, 215, 309
Bank of North America, 215
Bank of the United States, 217, 219; Baltimore Branch of, 217–20
Bank Stock: creation of, 4–5; value of, 7, 10–11, 13, 17, 25, 27, 29ff.; litigation over, 10–18, 23–29; diplomatic negotiations over, 18–23
Bank Stock Papers, 3–40
Bank Stock trustees: appointment of, 4 ff.; negotiations of, with Samuel Chase, 10ff. *See also* Bank Stock
Banking elites: Talbot County, 303–5; Baltimore City, 305–9; Frederick County, 309–12
Banks and banking, Baltimore, 214ff.
Banning, Robert, 313
Bantz, Gideon, 314
Banytine, John, 38
Barber, Luke, 72, 85
Barclay, David, 16, 17, 36
Barclay, David, & Co., 30
Barclay et al. v. *Russell et al.*, 17, 18, 20, 21, 25, 26, 28, 30, 31, 39
Baring, Francis, & Co., 32, 33, 39, 40
Barnes, Samuel, 309, 314
Bartgis, Matthias E., 314
Barton, William, 60
Bartram, Nicholas, 55
Bateman, John, 72, 85
Battee, John W., 313
Battle Creek Nanny (Negro), 194
Bayne, Jno. H., 229, 245
Beall, William Murdock, 314
Beanes, Millicent, 177
Bedini, Msgr., 320
Bell, John, 319, 329, 332

Bell, Richard, 226
Belton, William, 291
Bend, William B., 226
Bennet, John, 55
Bennett, Richard, 69, 170
Betsey (Negro), 183
Biays, Captain, 291
Bibliography of Writings of Morris Leon Radoff, compiled by Frank F. White, Jr., 333–35
Biggs, Seth, 79, 86, 87
Blackstock, Richard, & Co., 224, 225
Blackwell, Francis, 226
Blakiston, Nathaniel, 79
Blakiston, Nehemiah, 86
Blathwayt, William, 76
"Bloody Tubs," (political club), 323
Board of Control, for India, 21
Board of Trade, 86ff., 109
Bob (Negro), 181, 183
Bob of Fanny (Negro), 181
Bogue, Allan G., 271
Bohmer, David A., 251–75
Bond, Thomas, 224
Bonds: for performance of guardianship agreements, 42, 44, 46, 47; for payment of portions, 43; administration, 48, 53
Bowie, Gov. Robert, 34, 39, 40
Bowles, James, 81
Bowls, Justice John, 121
Bowlus, George, 314
Boyd, Anna, 226
Boyle, John, 313
Bradford, Justice John, 53, 61
Brand, Thomas, 219
Breams, Christopher, 120, 122
Breams, Richard, 120
Breams, William, 120
Breckinridge, Robert J., 319
Breen, T. H., 109, 133
Brengle, Francis, 314
Brent, Giles, 67, 84
Bridgett (Negro), 183
British government: and debt claims, 9, 19, 21–23; and Band stock controversy, 10, 18–25, 33–34; policies affect Baltimore City; politics, 279, 289–90
Brooke, Anne (Calvert), Mrs. Baker, 72, 74
Brooke, Baker, 68, 72, 74
Brooke, Robert, 70, 72, 84
Brooke, Thomas, 68, 76, 79, 81, 86, 87
Brown, Alex, & Sons, 224ff.
Brown, Peter H., 314
Brown, Thomas, 59
Browne, David, 76
Browne, Gary L., 212–27
Bruff, Joseph, 313

Bryantown, 191
Buchan, Lord. *See* Erskine, David Steuart
Buchanan, Gilbert, 13
Buchanan, Rev. Gilbert, 38
Buchanan, James A., 217, 218, 219
Buchanan, James M., 283, 314, 325
Buchanan, John, 7, 13, 15, 17, 24, 37, 38, 39
Buckeystown District, 275
Buildings of the State of Maryland at Annapolis, xvi
Burckhart, Charles H., 314
Burgess, William, 75
Burr, Aaron, 289, 290
Butler, James, 61

Caesar (Negro), 182
Cage, John, 123
Caleb (Negro), 183
Calendar of Maryland State Papers, No. 1, No. 2, xv, 24
Calhoun, James, 290
Calvert, Benedict Leonard, 87
Calvert, Cecilius, 65, 67, 69, 74, 208
Calvert, Charles, 69, 71ff., 79, 80, 82
Calvert, Charles B., 242
Calvert, Frederick, 6th Lord Baltimore, 197, 198
Calvert, Leonard, 67, 69, 85
Calvert, Philip, 42, 43, 48, 49, 57, 68, 69, 72, 73
Calvert, William, 72, 85
Calvert County, 139; economy of, 141–49
Calvert Papers No. 1, No. 2, 85, 87, 208
Campbell, Col. Bernard U., 314
Campbell & McIlvain, 227
Capron, Horace, 242
Carlton, Thomas, 310, 315
Carmarthen, Marquess of, 11, 12
Carpenter, Harry, 182, 189, 194, 195
Carr, Lois Green, xvi, 41–62, 83, 85, 107, 108, 110, 130–33, 167, 272, 273
Carroll, Anna Ella, 321, 331
Carroll, Charles, 186
Carroll, Charles, of Annapolis, 193, 195, 209
Carroll, Charles, of Carrollton, 179
Carroll, Daniel, 193
Carroll, Daniel, of Duddington, 193
Carroll, James, Jr., 314
Carroll, Robert, 230
Carroll family, 184
Carruthers, James, 225, 226
Carter, Landon, 182, 188, 189
Carvile, Robert, 74, 75, 85
Cassell, Frank A., 277–96, 315
Caucuses, party, 288
Ceasar (Negro), 195
Cecil, Joshua, 58

Cecil County Court, 49
Cecil Monthly Meeting, 274
Cecil *Whig,* 331
Cecilia (Negro), 182, 189
Chancery Court, 3, 13, 15, 16ff., 23ff., 28, 29
Chandler, Job, 70, 84
Chapel District, Talbot County, 325
Charity (Negro), 181, 182
Charles (Negro), 181
Charles County, 130; orphans, 59, 60, 61; servants, 90; marriages, 93; mortality, 106; characteristics of servants immigrating to, 111–15; servants careers, 115–30; economy of, 141–49; Zachiah Manor in, 199 ff.
Chase, Samuel, 10ff., 25, 26, 28, 31, 33, 35ff., 282
Chase v. *Russell, et al.,* 36
Chastellux, Marquis de, 210
Chesapeake (U.S. warship), 289ff.
Chesapeake and Ohio Canal Co., 316
Chesapeake Bay Economy, 1670–1720, 134, 52
Chester, Donald, 224
Chester Parish, 274
Chester River, 153
Cheves, Langdon, 219, 225, 226
City Bank 215, 219
Civil War, social and economic impact of, 229
Clagett, Thomas, Jr., 245
Claiborne, William, 69
Clap, Benjamin, 224, 226
Clara (Negro), 182
Clark, Charles, 188
Clark, Charles B., editor, *The Eastern Shore of Maryland and Virginia,* 272
Clark, Thomas, 188
Clarke, Robert, 71, 72, 85
"Claude Fauchet and His Library," by Morris L. Radoff, xxi
Clem (Negro), 182
Clemens, Paul, G. E., 153–70, 272
Clerk, James, 11, 16
Cohen, Benedict I., 314, 316
Cole, William H., 314
Commercial and Farmers Bank, 215, 309
Commercial elites: Talbot County, 303–5; Baltimore City, 305–9; Frederick County, 309–12
Commissary General, 48, 49
Community power distribution, 297–317
Confiscation of British property, 8–10, 13, 15
Constitution of 1864, 230
Constitutional Union Party, 319
Contee, John, 79, 86
Contee, Mary Townley, Mrs. John, 86
Cook, Margaret, 194
Cooke, William, 224

Cooper Joe (Negro), 181, 182, 186, 189
Copley, Lionel, 76, 77
Corbin, Richard, 188
Cornwallis, Thomas, 67, 84
Council, Maryland, 65–87
Councillors: qualifications of, 65–80; composition of 67ff., 76, 78, 80–81; tenure of, 68, 81; religion of, 69ff., 76
County court orphan jurisdiction, 43–45, 54
The County Courthouses and Records of Maryland, xvi
Coursey, Henry, 49, 68, 72, 73, 85
Coursey, Jean, 47
Coursey, Thomas, 47
Courts, Anne, 49
Courts, John, 60, 76, 86
Cox, James, 224
Crane, R., 224
Crane, Thomas, 188
Craven, Wesley Frank, 57, 83, 84, 89, 90, 96, 106, 108, 109, 130, 150
Crawford, William, Jr., 314
Credit: and purchase of servants, 119; and economic opportunity, 157, 162; and purchase of slaves, 163; and Baltimore trade, 214, 220–23; in post Civil-War South, 229, 233, 236
Creditors, Prerogative Court, protection of, 42, 49–50
Crop liens, 233
Cross, Andrew B., 319
Cruikshank, Robert, 5, 6
Cullen, John, 225
Culpeper, Lord, 106
Currency: paper, 2, 7, 8, 24; specie based, 221–22
Curtin, Philip, 99

Dairy farming, Prince George's County, 1860–80, 242
Dangerfield, William H., 315
D'Arcy, John, 225
Darnall, Henry, 188
Darnall, Robert, 209
Darnall family, 176, 177
Davies, Jacob G., 314
Davis, Henry Winter, 322, 331
Dayler, Elinor, 121
Debt claims, pre-Revolutionary, 19
Decisional elites: defined, 298–99; Talbot County, 303-5, 313-4; Baltimore City, 305-9, 314; Frederick County, 309–12, 314-15
De Drusina, James, 11
De Drusina, Ritter, and Clerk, 11
Delcher, John, 314
Delone, Mary, 59

Democratic Greens, 284
Democratic Party, 322, 323, 325ff.
Dennis (Negro), 182, 186, 195
Denny, Spry, 313
Dentler, Robert A., 275
Deputy commissary 47, 50, 58, 61, 193
Dick (Negro), 181, 183
Dickey, Robert, 225, 226
Dickinson, Gen. Solomon, 313
Digges, William, 75, 176, 177
Dill, Joshua, 315
Dinah (Negro), 181, 182, 195
Dixon, James, 315
Donaldson, John J., 314
Donnell, John, 220
"Doohoregan," 180, 182, 183, 193, 194
Dorcas (Negro), 182
Dorsey, Roderick, 315
Douglass, Richard H., 215, 224, 225
Douglass, William, 214, 224, 225
Dove (ship), xii
Dudderar, Capt. John, 315
Dudley, George, 313
Dugan, Frederick J., 314
Dulany, Daniel, 16, 25, 30, 38, 209, 211
Dulany, Daniel, the Elder, 272
Dulany, Daniel, the Younger, 272
Dulany, Walter, 16
Dundas, Henry, 21, 37
Dunlap's Maryland Gazette, 187
Dunlop & Orgain, 226
Dunnington, William P. 314
Duvall, Capt. Daniel, 315
Duvall, Gabriel, 282
Duvall, Mareen, 49

East India Company, 5
Eastern Shore of Maryland, economy, 153–155
Eastern Shore Whig and People's Advocate, 305, 316
Economic diversification, 141–43, 147–48, 153–54, 167, 234–35
Economic returns, for tenant farmers, 156, 206–7
Eddis, William, 203ff.
Edith (Negro), 182
Education of orphans, 52, 53
Eichelberger, Col. George M., 315
Eldon, Lord. *See* Scott, Sir John
Elections, by year: 1798, 281–82; 1800, 281–82; 1801, 286; 1804, 286; 1805, 287; 1808, 292; 1809, 293; 1810, 293; 1834–76, 324, 327; 1840–56, 324, 326; 1855, 318, 323; 1856, 319; 1857, 319, 323, 329; 1859, 319, 323, 329; 1860, 319, 329
Electoral behavior, 1796–1802, 251–75

Elisha (Negro), 182, 186, 195
Elites: in 17th-century Maryland, 65–87; in Talbot County, 164–66, 303–05, 313–14; in Frederick County and Baltimore City, 305–14
Elizabeth (Negro), 182
Ellicott, Andrew, 286
Eltonhead, William, 84
Emelia (Negro), 182
Emigration: from England, 90, 92, 109, 139, 140, 162; from Maryland, 92–93, 151; from Virginia, 93
Emmitsburgh Presbyterian Church, 275
English Crown, appointments to Maryland Council, 76–80
Ennalls, Thomas, 79
Ent, Capt. George W., 315
Episcopalians, 262–63, 274–75
Erskine, David Steuart, Lord Buchan, 12
Erskine, Thomas, 12
Erving, George W., 32, 39
Ethnicity, and voting patterns, 255–57, 260–61, 264–70, 271, 279, 285, 319–22, 325–26
Etting, Solomon, 314
Evans, Hugh W., 314, 316
Evans, William, 73, 85
Ewer, John, 13ff., 20, 24, 37
Ewer, Walter, 13ff., 20, 24, 36, 37
Ewers v. *Russell*, 36
Executors, 41

Fanny (Negro), 180ff., 189
Fanny's Quarter, 182
Faneuil brothers, 149
Farm crops valuation, 141, 206–7, 240
Farm mortgages, Prince George's County, 1860–80, 232
Farm size: in Talbot County, 1689–1733, 156, 164; on proprietary manors, 200; in Prince George's County, 1860–80, 158, 231, 232
Farmers' and Merchants' Bank, 215
Farmers' Bank, 33, 303
Fauchet, Claude, ix, xi
Federal Gazette and Baltimore Daily Advertiser, 224, 225, 295
Federal Intelligencer and Baltimore Daily Advertiser, 295
Federalist Party, 253–70, 278–94
Fendall, Josias, 71, 72, 89
Fendall's Rebellion, 67
Fertility rates, 92, 101, 102
Field, Capt., 194
Fillmore, Millard, 319, 320, 325
Fitch, Jonathan, 314
Fitzherbert, Edward, 73, 84
Flanigan, William H., 271

Folly Quarter, 194
Foodstuff production, Prince George's County, 1860–80, 236
Forrest, Uriah, 18, 36
France, in Baltimore politics, 279, 283, 289
Frances (Negro), 182
Franch, Mrs., 211
Franklin, Benjamin, 8, 9, 35
Franklin Bank, 215
Franklin Fire Co., 285
Frederick County: Monocacy Manor in, 199ff.; voting behavior in, 253–70; early history of, 255; population profile, 1790s, 256–63; leadership patterns in, 309–12, 314–15
Fredericktown, leadership patterns, 309–12
Fredericktown Evangelical Reformed Church, 275–76
Freedman: occupation, 118; careers, Charles County, 1658–1705, 118–28. See also Servants
Freeman, William H., 314
French & Co., 9
French & Hobson, 9
French, V. & P., & Nephew, 9
Frick, William, 314
Frisby, James, 76, 86
Frost's Quarter, 189, 194
Frostburg, 325
Fulton, Capt. Robert, 315

Gaither, Stewart, 315
Gallatin, Albert, 32, 39
Gambra, Richard, 48, 58
General Guide to the Holdings of the Maryland Hall of Records, xii
George I, of England, 4
George III, of England, 9
Georgetown, 190
Gerard, Thomas, 67, 72, 84
German Republican Society, 285
Germans, 199, 205, 206, 210–11, 319; voting patterns of, 255, 264–67, 273–74
Gibson, Justice Miles, 49
Gihon, William, & Son, 224ff.
Gilmor, Robert, & Sons, 33
Goldsborough, Robert H., 304, 313
Gordon, George, 177
Graham, Alexander, 313
Grain production, Prince George's County, 1860–80, 235, 236, 242. See also Wheat production
Grand Committee of Twenty, 76
Graves, Dr. John J., 314
Great Choptank River, 153
Green, Duff, 218
Greene, Thomas, 67, 84

Greenfield, Thomas, 79, 86
Grenville, Lord, 18ff., 25, 37
Grosse, Nicholas, 120
Grove, Silvanus, 10ff., 17, 35, 39
Grundy, Felix, 223
Guardianship, 42–56
"A Guide to Practical Calendaring," xv
Gurney, Richard, 17, 36
Guy (Negro), 189

Hagar (Negro), 186
Hall of Records, xii–xvi
Hall of Records Commission, xiv
Hambleton, Edward N., 313
Hambleton, Samuel, Jr., 316
Hambleton, Samuel J., 313
Hamilton, Alexander, 279, 295
Hammond, George, 21, 23, 29, 37ff.
Hammond, John, 79
Hammond, Thomas, 315
Hanbury, Capel, 6, 7, 16
Hanbury, John, 6, 8, 13, 16, 17, 20, 24, 25, 34, 36
Hanbury, Osgood, 6, 7, 10, 13, 16, 17, 30, 31
Hanbury, Osgood, & Co., 16, 18, 30
Hanbury, Sampson, 31, 37, 38
The Hanbury Family, 335
Handicrafts; 52, 141, 142
Hanson, Alexander Contee, 289, 291, 292, 296
Hanson, Randall, 123
Harbard, Francis, 177, 188
Harbard, Peter, 177, 188
Harbard, Susan, 177
Hardie, William, 193
Hardy, Justice Henry, 121
Harford, Henry, 9, 17, 20, 24, 26ff., 30, 33, 36, 38, 209
Harker, Samuel, 309, 314
Harper, Charles Carroll, 308
Harper, Robert Goodloe, 286, 287, 289ff.
Harris, J. Morrison, 322, 331
Harris, P. M. G., 56, 60, 107, 108, 132, 133, 272
Harrowby, Earl of, 19, 29, 39
Harry (Negro), 171, 182, 183, 190
Harwood, James, 314
Hatch, John, 72, 84, 123
Hatton, Thomas, 69, 70
Hawkesbury, Lord, 19, 23, 25ff., 37ff.
Hawkins, James L., 314
Hawkins, John, 53
Hawley, Jerome, 67, 84
Hayman, James R., 314
Headrights, 89, 90, 108, 131
Heads of Families at the First Census . . . 1790, Maryland, 194

Heath, James P., 314
Heath, Upton S., 314
Hibernian Society, 285
Hicks, Thomas H., 319, 320, 322
"Hier Dier Lloyd," Talbot County, 158
Higgenbotham, Ralph, 219
Higgins, James, 230, 233, 236, 245, 246
Hill, Clement, 85, 229
Hillary (Negro), 183
Hillen, John, 314
Hinks, Samuel, 320, 322
Historical Records Survey, xi, xiii
Historical Statistics of the United States, 105, 134, 137, 138, 150, 151, 209, 330
Hoffman, Samuel, 314
Hoffman, Bond & Co., 226
Holland, William 79
Hollingsworth, Samuel, 224, 225, 291
Hollins, John, 283
Hollins, John Smith, 314
Hollis, William, 41, 47, 49
Holte, William, 157
Holtz, Maj. Nicholas, 315
Hook, Capt. Joseph, 314
Hook, Col. Thomas, 315
Hopkins, G. M., *Atlas*, 237, 239
Hoskins, Lawrence, 121, 122
House, Samuel, 314
Household formation: in Talbot County, 155–57; among slaves, 183–84
Housing: in Talbot County, 164–65; on proprietary manors, 202ff.
Howard, Benjamin C., 307, 308, 314, 317
Howard, Charles, 314
Howard, John Eager, 281, 292, 306, 308
Hubbard, William, 314
Hughlett, Col. William, 303, 314
Hunt, Jesse, 308, 310, 314
Hunt, William, 5, 6, 34
Hurt, Nicholas, 60
Husey (Negro), 183
Hussey, Thomas, 122
Hutchinson, Bury, 11ff.
Hutchinson, William, 86
Hyde, Althea, 34
Hyde, Herbert, 34
Hyde, Jane, 34
Hyde, John, 4, 34
Hyde, Capt. John, 4, 5
Hyde, Samuel, 4, 5, 6, 34

Illegitimacy, 97, 108
Immigrants: characteristics of, 96, 102–3, 111–15, 131; in Baltimore politics, 279, 285; and Know-Nothings, 319–22, 325–26
Immigration, statistics, 90, 91, 96, 102, 111, 128–29, 131, 319

Improved Order of Red Men, 323
Indentures of servants, 112–15, 129, 131
Ingle's Rebellion, 69, 85
Inheritance, 43–45, 48–50, 52, 53, 56
Intestacy, 43, 45
Inventories of estates, 43, 49, 50; how taken, 44, 209; marriage information from, 95, 108; servant and slave populations in, 128–29, 139–45, 147; composition of assets in, 147–48, 200–1; mean wealth in, by county, 148; biases in, 151, 209; distribution of wealth, in Talbot County, 166; of proprietary tenants, 200–1
Irvine, Baptiste, 292, 293

Jack (Negro), 182, 183, 186, 188
Jackson, Andrew, 297–317
Jacob (Negro), 182, 189
Jacob, Mordecai, 177
Jacob, Ruth (Tyler), Mrs. Mordecai, 177
Jacob's Quarter, 194
Jacobsen, Phebe, xvi
James (Negro), 194
James, Mayara, 180
Jay, John, 18ff.
Jay Treaty, 279, 280
Jefferson, Thomas, 22, 28, 32, 37, 277–96
Jem (Negro), 181, 191
Jenine (Negro), 183
Jenkins, David, 55
Jenkins, Francis, 79
Jenkins, John, 171
Jessop, William, 281
Jian, (Negro), 182
Joe (Negro), 181, 182, 184, 189, 194, 195
Johnny (Negro), 194
Johnson, Edward, 109
Johnson, Joshua, 8, 35
Johnson, Reverdy, 245, 314, 317, 323
Johnson, Thomas, 8
Johnson, Dr. Thomas W., 315
Johnson, William Cost, 310, 315
Joice, Ann, 176, 177, 188
Jonathan (Negro), 182
Jones, Abraham, 315
Jones, David, 188
Jones, Howard Mumford, 14
Jones, Joshua, 314
Jones, William 217ff.
Jordan, David W., 65–87, 108, 109, 110
Joseph, William, 74, 85
Judith (Negro), 194
Juliett (Negro), 183
Juries, orphans' court, 44, 54

Karthaus, Charles W., 314
Kate (Negro), 181ff., 189ff., 195

Keen, Richard, 60
Keerl, Samuel, 314
Kelso, Thomas, 314
Kemp, Capt. David, 315
Kemp, Henry, 315
Kennedy, John P., 314, 328, 332
Kent County, 48, 139; orphans, 59, 60, 61; economy of, 141–49; immigration into, 163; voting behavior in, 253–70; early history of, 254–55; population profile, 256–63
Kent Island, 71, 90
Kenyon, Lloyd, 11
Kerr, John Bozman, 305, 314, 316
Kerr, John Leeds, 304, 314
Kettlewell, John, 314
Keziah (Negro), 182
King, Rufus, 3, 19ff., 23ff., 33, 34, 37ff., 295
Kinser, John, 315
Kinship networks: of whites, 41–42, 44; of slaves, 172–73, 179ff.
Know-Nothing National Council, 328, 329
Know-Nothing Party, 318–332
Krebs, William, 314
Kulikoff, Allan, 100, 171–196

Labor supply, 136ff., 140, 141, 143, 158–60, 206
Lambert, Frederick, 315
Lancaster Road, 210
Land, Aubrey C., ix–xvi, 83, 167, 210, 211, 272
Land Office, 56, 106, 224
Land prices: Talbot County, 1683–1733, 158; Prince George's County, 1860–80, 243, 244
Land rents: Talbot County, 156; on proprietary manors, 198, 207
Landowners; inventoried in Prince George's County, 1696–1709, 59; among Charles County ex-servants, 1658–1705, 123–26; in Talbot County, 1689–1733, 157–58, 165, 67; in late colonial period, 197, 208
La Reintrie, John L., 220
Lauderman, Henry R., 314
Laurenson, Philip, 314
Law, James O., 314
Lawrence, Sir Thomas, 76, 78, 86
Lawrence, Thomas, Jr., 78
Laws of Maryland, (Kilty), 35, 36, 37, 39, 40, 295
The Laws of Maryland, (Thomas Bacon), 57, 61, 62
Lazarsfeld, Paul F., 271
Leakin, Gen. Sheppard C., 314
Leary, Peter, 314

Leases: in Talbot County, 1689–1733, 156–67; proprietary manor, 198, 200, 201
Lee, John, 11
Lee, Philip, 81
Lee, Richard, 7
Lee, Thomas Sim, 8, 9, 35, 36
Leopard (British frigate), 289
Lewger, John, 67, 84
Lewis, John, 55
Liberty Fire Company, 285
Libertytown District, 275
"The Libraries of Eitenne Pasquier and Claude Fauchet," by Morris L. Radoff, ix, xi
Life expectancy. *See* Mortality
Lilly, Richard, 314
Lincoln, Abraham, 229, 245
Lindsay, James, 123
Livestock production, Prince George's County, 1860–80, 243
Lloyd, Edward, 72, 73, 79, 80, 82, 84, 158, 209
Lloyd, Col. Edward, 304
Lloyd, Edward, Jr., 314, 316
Lloyd, James, 81
Lloyd, John, 12, 16, 17, 30, 31, 36
Lloyd, Philemon, 80, 161
Lockerman, Theodore R., 314
Loften, John, 59
London Assurance Co., 7, 34
Long Caln Forge, 9
Lord Chancellor (Great Britain), 4, 13–15, 21
Lords of Trade, 75, 82
Loughborough, Lord. *See* Wedderburn, Alexander
Lovejoy, John, 178
Lovejoy, Samuel, 178
Lubbar, Jack, 182
Luckett, Elizabeth (Hussey), Mrs. Samuel, 123
Luckett, Samuel, 122
Lucy (Negro), 181
Lucy (Iron Works), 181
Lutherans, 262–63, 274–75
Lynes, James, 121, 122
Lynes, Philip, 79, 86, 121, 126
Lyon, John, 15, 20
Lyon, William, 15, 25, 38
Lyon, and Collyer, 26, 38, 39

McCauley, Donald 228–47
McClellan, Samuel M., 314
McCulloch, James W., 314
McCulloch vs. *Maryland*, 217
McCulloh, James William, 217ff.
Macdonald, Sir Archibald, 18

McDonald, Gen. William, 314
McElderry, Thomas, 290
McElfresh, Dr. John H., 315
McHenry, James, 280, 281, 291, 295
McKeehan, R. Samuel L., 315
McKim, Alexander, 309
McKim, Isaac, 307, 309, 314, 317
McKim, John, Jr., 314
McKinnell, Henry, 314
McKinstry, Evan, 315
McMahon, John Van Lear, 308
McPherson, Edward B., 315
McPherson, Col. John, 311, 315
McPherson, Dr. William S., 310, 315

Maddocks, John, 12, 13
Madge (Negro), 183
Madison, James, 24, 27, 38, 39
Magdalene (Negro), 183
Magruder, Alexander, 55, 177
Magruder, Hezekiah, 177, 178
Main, Gloria L., 134-52
Manning, Col. Samuel, 314
Manors, proprietary, 197, 198, 203ff.
Mansfield, James, 8, 11, 12
Mantz, Cyrus, 315
Manuel, (Negro), 188
Marine Bank, 215
Mark (Negro), 181
Markell, Jacob, 315
Market gardening and orchard produce, Prince George's County, 1860–80, 240ff.
Marriage: and composition of 17th-century Council, 74, 79; and mortality pattern, 93–94, 95; age at, 95, 100, 101, 107ff.; in Talbot County, 161–62, 167; among slaves, 187–88
Marriott, Gen. William H., 314
Martenet's Map of Prince George's County, Maryland, 239
Martin, Gov. Daniel, 314
Martin, Luther, 289, 290
Martin, Nicholas, 314
Martin, Thomas O., 314
Maryland Agricultural College, 230
Maryland claim to Bank Stock, 3–10, 30, 32–34
Maryland Gazette, 187, 193, 195, 196
Maryland Journal, 187, 196
Maryland Republican, 330
Maryland State Council, 328
Mass, Samuel, 314
Matthias, Maj. Jacob, 315
Mayara James Quarter, 194
Mayer, Charles F., 224, 314, 316

Maynard, Foster, 314
Mechanical Fire Company, 285, 295
Mechanical Society, 280, 281
Mechanics' Bank, 215, 287
Mechanics of Baltimore, 286, 287, 325
Medtart, Major Joshua, 314
Meeteer, William, 314
Menard, Russell R., 56, 60, 83, 84, 85, 88–110, 130–33, 142, 150, 151, 167, 168, 192ff., 209, 272
Mercer, John F., 27, 28, 38, 39
Merchants: as Bank Stock trustees, 4–6; and British debt claims, 6, 21, 22; as principals in Bank Stock litigation, 7–18; on 17th-century Council, 72, 73, 79; and Council appointments, 1692, 76; and servant trade, 102–3, 107, 158–59; regional specialization of, 142–43, 147–48; and slave trade, 148–49; in Talbot County, 1689–1733, 164–66; Baltimore, 213–15, 219–23, 278
Methodists, 262–63, 274–75
Middlesex County, Va., 94
Milk production, Prince George's County, 1860–80, 241
Miller, Dr. James H., 314
Miller, Michael, 59
Millington, John N., 314
Millis, Levin, 314
Miltenberger, Gen. Anthony, 314
Mitchell, Frances, 181ff.
Mitchell, William, 70, 84
Moale, Col. Samuel, 314
Modernization, 299, 312–13, 317
Moll (Negro), 183
Molleson, William, 7, 12, 20, 22, 37
Monica (Negro), 182
Monocacy Manor, 198ff., 204, 206ff., 211
Monocacy River, 199, 204
Monroe, James, 19, 27, 28, 30ff., 38ff.
Moore, Col. Samuel, 314
Morbidity rates, 95, 97, 99, 103
Morning Chronicle & Baltimore Advertiser, 224
Morris, Jenkin, 59
Morris, John B., 307, 314, 317
Morsell, William, 315
Mortality: and orphans' courts, 41–42, 56; and political leadership, 68; measures, 92ff.; studies, 93–94; effect on reproductive increase, 99–100, 101, 103; of slaves, 116, 132
Moses' Quarter, 189, 194
Mulatto Ned (Negro), 188
Mullikin, Edward, 314
Mullikin, Solomon, 314
Munroe, Isaac, 309, 314

Murdock, William, 31, 38, 39
Murphy, Dr. Thomas L., 314

Nacy (Negro), 194
Nan (Negro), 177
Nanjemy Parish, Charles County, 61
Nanny (Negro), 181, 183
Nanny of Kate (Negro), 181, 183
National Science Foundation, 56, 107, 108, 132
Native-born: appearance on Council, 79–83; population statistics, 98–99, 103, 106, 108; social effects of, in Talbot County, 1689–1733, 162–63
Nativism. *See* Know-Nothing Party
Neale, James, 68, 71, 84
Needles, Edward, 314
Neilson, Robert, 314
Nelson, John, 312, 315
Nelson, Madison, 312, 315
New England demography, 102–4, 109
Nicholas, John Spear, 308
Nichols, Thomas C., 314
Nicholson, Francis, 52, 55, 77, 78, 80, 82, 86, 116, 151
Nicholson, Joseph Hopper, 31ff., 39, 40
Niles, Hezekiah, 226, 309, 314
Niles, William Ogden, 315
Niles' Weekly Register, 224ff., 309
Nixdorff, Henry, 315
Nominations, political party, 288, 289, 293, 328
North Lord Frederick, 2nd Earl of Guilford, 11
Notes on the State of Virginia, Thomas Jefferson, 210
Notley, Thomas, 73, 85
Nottingham Iron Works, 7, 9, 13
Nutt, John, 22

Occupations, and political alignments, 282, 317, 322
O'Donnell, John, 284
Ogle, Gov. Benjamin, 37
Old Grace, (Negro), 183
Oligarchy, 299, 303–5, 311, 312
Oliver, John, 225
Oliver, Robert, 225, 280, 295
Opportunity: for Charles County servants, 1658–1705, 118–28, 133; in Talbot County, 1689–1733, 155–67
Orchards, on proprietary manors, 203
Order of United American Mechanics, 319
Orphans, minors, 43–62; defined, 44
Orphans' Courts: Virginia, 41–42, 56; Maryland, 41–62; England, 42, 57

Oswald, Richard, 11
Outbuildings, manor, 202ff.

Paca, William, 35, 36
Page (Negro), 190
Palmer, Joseph M., 315
Panic of 1819, 212–27
Papenfuse, Edward C., xvi
Paper money emission, 5, 7, 8, 24
Parker, Gabriel, 188
Pasquier, Etienne, 273, 275
Patience (Negro), 182
Patterson, William, 283, 314, 316
Pearce, James, A. 323
Pechin, William, 288
Pennsylvania, 133
Perceval, Spencer, 26, 28, 39
Perkins, Thomas H., 225
Perry, Micajah, 76
Peter (Negro), 181, 194
Peters, Edward J., 314
Phil (Negro), 194
Pickering, Timothy, 37
Pinckney, Thomas, 19, 20
Pinkney, William, 19, 20, 27ff., 33, 34, 36, 38, 39
Pinner, Richard, 120
Piper, James, 314
Piscataway, 190
Pitt, William, 11, 13, 14, 18, 19, 21, 29
"Plug Uglies" (political club), 325
Poe, Edgar Allan, 331
Poe, Neilson, 315
Political elites: Talbot County, 303–5; Baltimore City, 305–9; Frederick County, 309–12
Political socialization, 263–67
Poll books, 253
Polyarchy, 299, 305, 309, 311, 312
Polygyny, 173
Popple, William, 105
Popular Island, Annapolis Quarter, 193, 194
Population: statistics, 88–89, 97–98, 134, 135, 319; reproductive increase of, 89, 97–105; redistribution of, 141, 147, 149–50, 163, 170; Talbot County, 1689–1733, 163–64; on proprietary manors, 199–200; Kent and Frederick counties, 1790s, 256–63; Baltimore City, 1790–1810, 278, 282
Port Tobacco, Charles County, 191
Positional elites: defined, 298; Talbot County, 304–5; Baltimore City, 305–9; Frederick County, 309–12
Potomac Company, 33
Potts, James, 224, 225
Potts, Richard, 315
Prerogative Court, Maryland, 42, 46–48

Presbyterians, 262–63, 275
Price, George, 315
Price, Jacob M., 3–40, 167
Price, John, 69ff., 84, 85
Prince George's County Agricultural Society, 229
Prince George's County: orphans in, 48, 50, 52, 58ff., 62; servant careers, 132, 133; slavery in, 171–92; agriculture in, 1860–80, 228–47
Pringle, Mark, 290
Priscilla (Negro), 181
Probate court. *See* Prerogative Court
Productivity of labor, 136–37, 206–7
Proprietary tenants, Maryland, 197–211
Protestants: as guardians, 43; on 17th-century Council, 69–70, 72–76; voting patterns of, 261–70
Provincial Court, 43, 55
Provisioning war fleets, 149
Prudence (Negro), 183
Pulcheria (Negro), 182
Purviance, Robert, 314

Quakers, 6, 7, 10; as guardians, 55; voting patterns of, 1790s, 261–63
Quarry, Robert, 81, 82, 87
Quarter sessions (English), 45, 46, 57
Queen Anne's County, 155, 163, 164, 169, 170
Queen Anne's War, 149, 157, 158
Quynn, Caspar, 315

Rachael (Negro), 171, 177
Radoff, Morris Leon, ix–xvi, 3, 34, 333–35
Ramsburgh, Lewis, 315
Randall, Col. Beale, 307, 314
Randolph, Edward, 19, 36, 77, 81, 86, 88, 104
Randolph, John, of Roanoke, 287
Read, William G., 306, 314
Ready, Samuel, 314
Redhead, William, & Co., 224, 225
Religion: and guardianship, 43; and appointments to the 17th-century council, 69–70, 72–76; and voting patterns, 256, 257, 261–63, 274–76
Remarriage, 96–97, 169
Replacement rates, 91–92, 98
Republican Company, 284
Republican Fire Company, 285
Republican Party, 253–71, 278–94
Republican Society, 285
Revolution of 1689, 75–76, 80
Rice, Howard C., Jr., 210
Richardson, Darius, 315
Ridgely, Charles, of Hampton, 291–92
Ridgway, Whitman H., 297–317
Rigney, John, 315

Riggs Quarter 181, 182, 189, 194
"Rip Raps" (political club), 325
Roberts, William, 315
Robertson, James A., xii
Rogers, Jacob, 314
Roman Catholics: as guardians, 43; on 17th-century Council, 69, 72–76; voting patterns of, 1790s, 262–63; and the Know-Nothings, 319ff., 325, 327ff.
Roney, Capt. William, 314
Rose, George, 9
Rose, William, 315
Roundall, Samuel, 177, 178
Rousby, Christopher, 75
Royal Exchange Assurance, 6
Russell, Ann, Mrs. James, 7, 8, 17, 20, 21, 35, 37, 39
Russell, James, 7ff., 16, 22, 24, 26, 27, 35, 36, 39
Russell, James, & Co., 9
Russell v. *Bank*, 35
Rutman, Anita, 56, 94, 100, 104, 107, 108, 110
Rutman, Darrett B., 56, 94, 100, 104, 107, 108, 110

St. Andrews Society, 285
St. George Society, 285
St. Mary's City Commission, 56, 83, 104, 106ff., 132, 133, 194, 272
St. Mary's County, 106, 325
St. Mary's County Court, 49
St. Michaels, Talbot County, 325
St. Paul's Parish, 274
Sall (Negro), 181, 182
Sam (Negro), 189, 191
Sam's Quarter, 194
Sanders, Benedict I., 314
Sands, Samuel, 314
Sans Cullottes (club), 284
Sappington, Thomas, 315
Sarah (Negro), 188
Schley, William, 315
Scott, Sir John, Lord Eldon, 9, 20, 21, 23ff., 28, 37ff.
Scott, Winfield, 320
Secret societies, 323, 325
Servants, 90; orphan, 43, 46, 50, 51, 52; age at marriage of, 97; recruitment of, 102, 103, 107, 113, 139–40; characteristics of, in Charles County, 1658–1705, 111–15; mortality, 17th-century, 115–17, 129–30; changes in status of, 118–19; owners of, 118–19; numbers of, in Charles County, 1658–1705, 128–29; supply of, to Chesapeake, 139–41; supply of, in Talbot County, 1689–1733, 158–60; prices, 160;

numbers of, in Talbot County, 1689–1733, 161, 169. *See also* Freedmen
Sewall, Henry, 72, 74–85
Sex ratios: among whites, 91ff., 99ff., 109, 161; among slaves, 174–75, 191
Seymour, John, 79, 86, 87
Sharecroppers: Talbot County, 1689–1733, 155, 166, 167; in South, 1860–80, 231, 233
Sharpe, George W., 315
Sherwood, George C., 314
Shipley, Thomas C., 315
Shriver, Isaac, 315
Shriver, Jacob, 315
Sifford, John, 315
Simmons, Col. John H. 315
Sixth Regiment, 284
Skordas, Gust, xvi, 56, 106, 131
Slave statistics, 93, 116, 128–29, 139, 161, 168–69
Slaves: supply of, 135ff., 159–60; distribution of, 143; and concentration of wealth, 144–47; prices, 160; population of, in Talbot County, 163–65, 168–69; runaway, 171, 172, 187, 190, 191; childhood of, 174, 180, 181, 184; family life of, 171–96; household types of, 172, 174, 175, 178ff.; kinship networks of, 172–73, 179ff.; sales and bequests of, 176ff.; old age of, 180, 181, 188; work of, 181, 184, 185; of proprietary tenants, 200ff.; effects of emancipation of, 229–31; wealth in, Kent and Frederick counties, 257–58, 273; and Know-Nothing Party, 329
Slave quarters, 179ff.
Slee, Israel, 314
Slye, Robert, 72, 84
Smith, Dennis A. 218
Smith, James Morton, 83, 130
Smith, Richard, 79
Smith, Robert, 283
Smith, Samuel, 217, 218, 280ff., 290, 291, 296, 309, 314, 316
Snowden's Iron Works, 188
Socage tenure, guardianship, 45, 48, 49, 53
Social hierarchy: opportunity for Charles County servants in, 1658–1705, 118–28; development of, in Talbot County, 1689–1733, 155–67
Society of American Archivists, xv
Soil associations, Prince George's County, 238ff.
Somerset County, 139; orphans, 60; marriages, 93–95; fertility, 101–2; life expectancy, 107; servant careers in, 132; economy of, 141, 49
Sophia (Negro), 182, 183, 189, 195
South River, 190

Southcomb, Carey, 314
Spencer, Henry, 314
Spencer, John Canfield, 219
Spencer, Richard, 305, 314, 316
Stamp, George, 178
Standard of living: in Talbot County, 164–66;
  on proprietary manors, 200–3
Stanley, John, 13, 14
Stanley, William, 59, 60
Stansbury, Dr. James B., 314
Stansbury, John E., 314
Stapleton, Joseph K., 314
The State House at Annapolis, xvi
Sten's Quarter, 194
Stephen, John, 286
Sterett, James, 219
Sterret, Samuel, 290
Steuart, George H., 314
Steuart, Robert, 287, 288, 293
Stevens, William, 74, 75
Steward, Stephen, & Son, 9
Stewart, David, 224, 314
Stewart, John M., 314
Stewart, Col. William R., 314
Stiverson, Gregory A., 197–211
Stokes, Donald E., 275
Stone, William, 69, 70, 94
Storm, Peter, 314
Strategic elites: defined, 299; Talbot County,
  303–5; Baltimore City, 305–9; Frederick
  County, 309–12
Stricker, John, 290, 291
Sue (Negro), 189, 191
Sukey's Quarter, 194
Swan, John, 284, 291
Swann, Thomas, 321, 322
Sydnor, Charles, 81, 87, 275

Talbot, George, 75, 85
Talbot, William, 72, 73, 84
Talbot County: servants, 90; economy of,
  141–149; settlement of, 153; eco-
  nomic opportunity in, 155–67; leadership
  patterns in, 303–5, 313–14
Talent, Lord, 12
Tammany Society, 285
Taney, Joseph, 315
Taneytown District, 275
Tasker, Benjamin, 81, 208
Tasker, Thomas, 79
Tate, Thad W., 56, 107, 109, 131, 168
Taxables: Chesapeake Bay area, 135ff., 142;
  Talbot County, 165
Taylor, Col. George, 314
Taylor, Lemuel, 218
Taylor, Thomas, 73, 75, 84

Taylor, Zachary, 323
Temperance Society, 323
Tenant farmers: Talbot County, 1689–1733,
  155ff., 165ff.; on proprietary manors,
  197–208, 311; in post-Civil War South,
  231–33
Thickpenny, Thomas, 59
39th Regiment, 291
Thomas, Francis, 310, 312, 315
Thomas, Hugh, 120
Thomas, Major James, 224
Thorpe, Thomas, 55
Thurlow, Lord, 13, 14, 18
Tiernan, Luke, 314, 316
Tilghman, Richard, 81
Tilghman, Dr. William H., 314
Tobacco: exports, 135ff.; prices, 138–41, 153,
  158, 159, 198; planting and cultivation,
  200, 204
Tobacco economy: and opportunity for freed-
  men, 98–99, 123, 126–27; and timing of
  immigration, 102, 103, 158, 159; and intro-
  duction of slavery, 134–50; in Talbot
  County, 1689-1733, 153–54, 162-163
Tobacco production, 134ff., 141; cost of, 154;
  labor requirements of, 206–7; in Prince
  George's County, 1860–80, 239ff.
Tomlinson, John, 6
Tony (Negro), 181
Townsend, William, 314
Trade: tobacco, 3–10, 102, 103, 134–50, 158,
  159, 153–54, 162–63; servant, 102–3,
  111–15, 140, 143, 159, 162; slave, 135,
  140–41, 143, 150, 159–60; Baltimore, 213,
  215, 219
Traditional elites: Talbot County, 303–5; Bal-
  timore City, 305–9; Frederick County,
  309–12
Train, James, 59
Transportation networks, Prince George's
  County, 1860–80, 236-37
Treasurer of the Western Shore, 9, 33
Treaty of Paris (1783), 9–10
Trueman, Thomas, 68, 74, 75
Turner, Frederick Jackson, xi
Turner, Joshua, 314
Turner, Thomas, 245
27th Regiment, 291
Tyer, James, 121
Tyler, Dr. John, 315
Tyler, Robert, Sr., 177
Tyler, Robert, III, 177
Tyler, Dr. William, 312, 315
Tyler, Dr. William Bradley, 315

Union Bank of Maryland, 215, 219
Union Fire Co., 295

Unionism, 329
U.S. Bureau of the Census: *Historical Statistics of the United States*, 134, 137, 138, 150, 151, 209, 330; abstracts and reports, 231, 232, 234, 244, 245, 246
United States Congress: election to, 288; *Debates and Proceedings*, 288
U.S. Department of Agriculture, *Soil Survey of Prince George's County, Maryland*, 238, 246
U.S. Freedmen's Bureau, 230
United States Government: and British debt claims, 9, 21–23; and Bank Stock negotiations, 10, 18–25, 33–34
"Unpublished Provincial Records," 86
Upper Marlboro, Prince George's County, 240, 241
Usher, Thomas, 55
Utie, Nathaniel, 68, 71, 72

Van Buren, Martin, 302
Van Heck, Sarah, 49
Vansant, Joshua, 308, 314
Vaughan, Robert, 69, 71, 85
Vickers, Joel, 314
Virginia: orphans' Courts, 41–42; 17th-century political leadership, 66; life expectancy, 94, 107; sex ratios, 96; age at first marriage, 100, 101; native-born, 102; reproductive increase, 102; opportunity for freedmen in, 133; population, 134, 135, 137; tobacco per taxable, 137
Viva-voce voting, 253
Von Thunen land-use patterns, 246, 247
Voter alignments, 263–67

Wakefield, Jacob, 224
Wakefield, John, 224
Wall, Mr., 171
Wallace, James, 8
Walsh, Lorena S., 56, 84, 100, 107, 108, 111–33, 169
Walters, Somerset R., 315
Ward, Matthew Tilghman, 81
Wardrop, James, 179, 195
Wardrop family, 184
Warner, Andrew E., 314
Warner, Thomas, 59
Warren, Justice Humphrey, 121
Warren, John, 60
Washington, George, 211, 280
Washington Benevolent Society of Baltimore 291, 292
Washington Branch Railroad, 236
Waters, Stephen, 314
Wathen, John, 120, 122

"Wathen's Adventure," Charles County, 120
Watkins, John Wesley, 314
Watt (Negro), 181
Watts, William, 41, 48, 49, 55
Wealth: as qualification for council 70–73, 78–79; of freedmen in Charles County, 1658–1705, 133; growing concentration of, before 1720, 144 ff.; distribution of, in Talbot County, 1689–1733, 163–66; in Kent and Frederick counties, 1790s, 257–58; of Know-Nothing voters, 322
Wedderburn, Alexander, Lord Loughborough, 18, 20, 21, 25, 26, 37
Wells, John, 47, 48
Westminister, 325
Wharton, Dr. Jesse, 73, 85
Wheat production, 141, 142, 207–8, 256
Wheeler, Clement, 171
Wheeler, James, 122
Whig Almanac, 318, 330
Whig Party, 320, 322ff.
White, Frank F., Jr., 333–35
White, Jerome, 73, 84
White, John, 219, 220, 225, 226
White, Joseph, 26, 29, 30, 38, 39, 314
White Marsh Furnace, 9
Wicomico River, 199
Wight, John, 60–61
Wight, William J., 314
Wilkinson, Lancelot, 121
Wilkinson, Margaret Moulton, Mrs. Lancelot, 121
Will (Negro), 181, 183, 191
Willet, Edward, 58
William and Mary, 75
Williams, Amos A., 218
Williams, Cumberland Dugan, 218
Williams, George, 218
Williams, Nathaniel, 218
Williams, Nathaniel F., 314
Williams, William 53
Willis, Dr. William, 315
Wills, 41, 42, 47ff., 91
Willson, Josiah, 60
Wilmer, John W., 314
Wilmot, J., 37
Wilson, Woodrow, xi
Winchester, George, 314, 317
Winchester, James, 281, 295
Wintour, Robert, 67
Wolcott, Oliver, 295
Wolstenholme, Daniel, 7
Women: as guardians, 44, 47, 49, 57; mortality of, 93–95; shortage of, 95–97, 99, 101; productivity of, 150. *See also* Marriage
Wood, John, 188
Woodbridge, George, 315

Woolman, John, 196
Worman, Moses, 310, 312, 315
Worthington, Gen. Thomas Contee, 315
Wyld, John, 224, 225

Young, McClintock, 314

Zachiah Manor, 198ff., 204, 210, 211
Zachiah Swamp, 199

The Johns Hopkins University Press

This book was composed in Times Roman text and display type by Jones Composition Company from a design by Susan Bishop. It was printed on 50-lb. Publishers Eggshell Wove paper and bound in Bayside vellum cloth by The Maple Press Company.

Library of Congress Cataloging in Publication Data

Conference on Maryland History, 1st, Annapolis, 1974.
    Law, society, and politics in early Maryland: Proceedings of the First Conference on Maryland History, June 14–15, 1974.

    (Studies in Maryland history and culture)
    "Bibliography of the writings of Morris Leon Radoff, compiled by Frank F. White, Jr." : pp. 333–335
    Includes index.
    I. Maryland—Politics and government—Colonial period, ca. 1600–1775—Congresses. 2. Maryland—Economic conditions—Congresses. 3. Law—Maryland—History and criticism——Congresses. 4. Radoff, Morris Leon, 1905–   I. Land, Aubrey C. II. Carr, Lois Green. III. Papenfuse, Edward C. IV. Radoff, Morris Leon, 1905–   V. Title. VI. Series.

F184.C7 1974   309.1'752'02   76–47374
ISBN 0-8018-1872-9